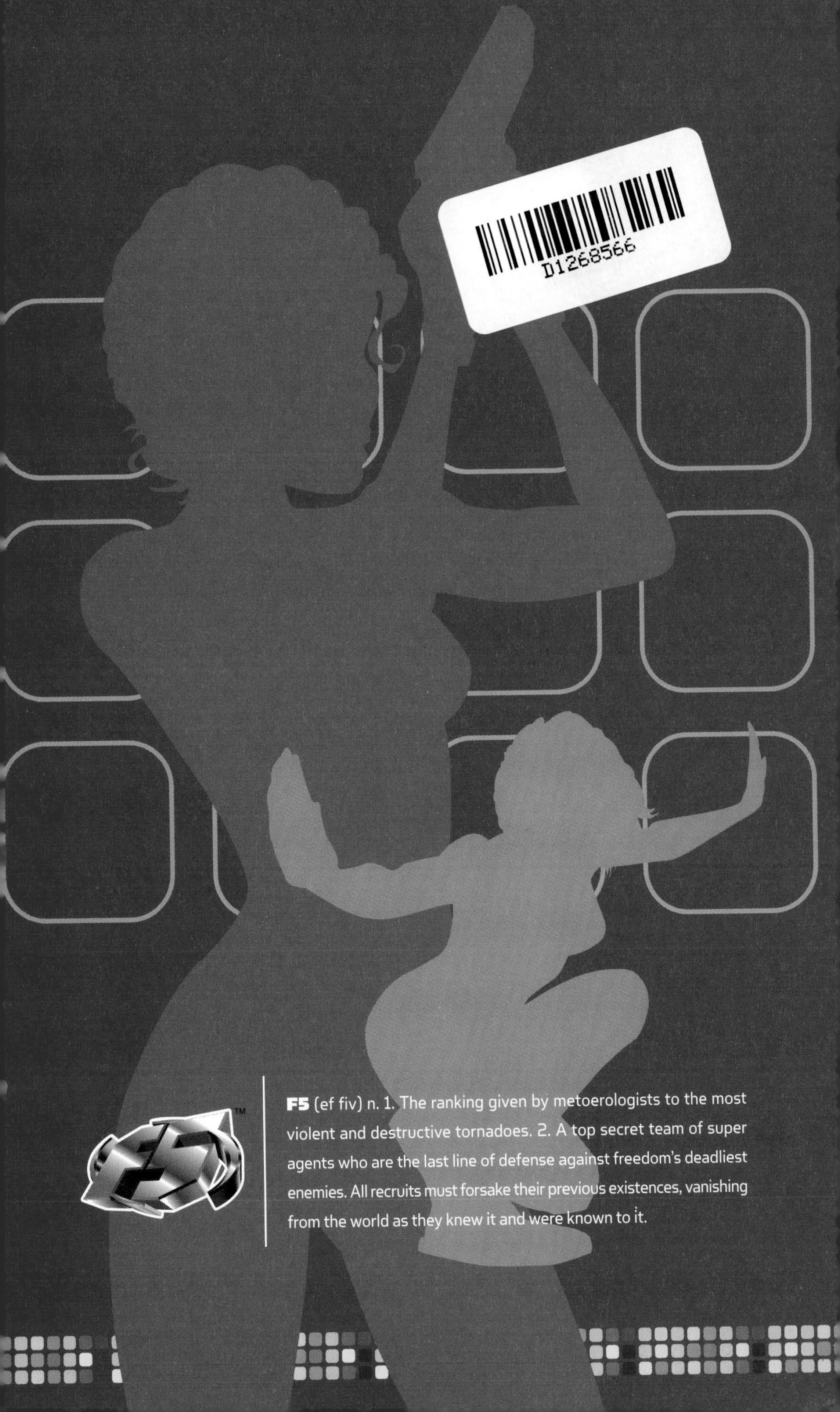

F5 (ef fiv) n. 1. The ranking given by metoerologists to the most violent and destructive tornadoes. 2. A top secret team of super agents who are the last line of defense against freedom's deadliest enemies. All recruits must forsake their previous existences, vanishing from the world as they knew it and were known to it.

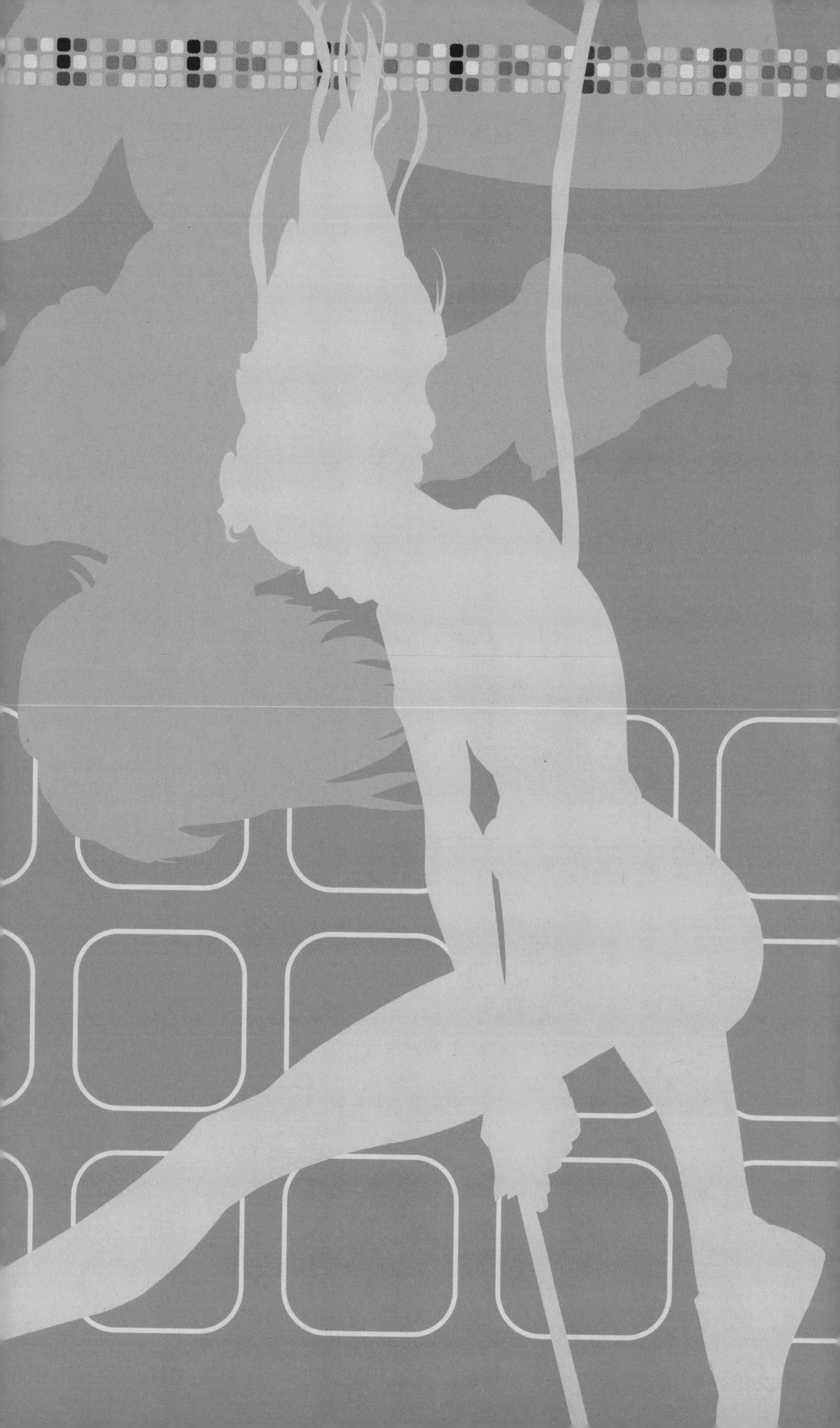

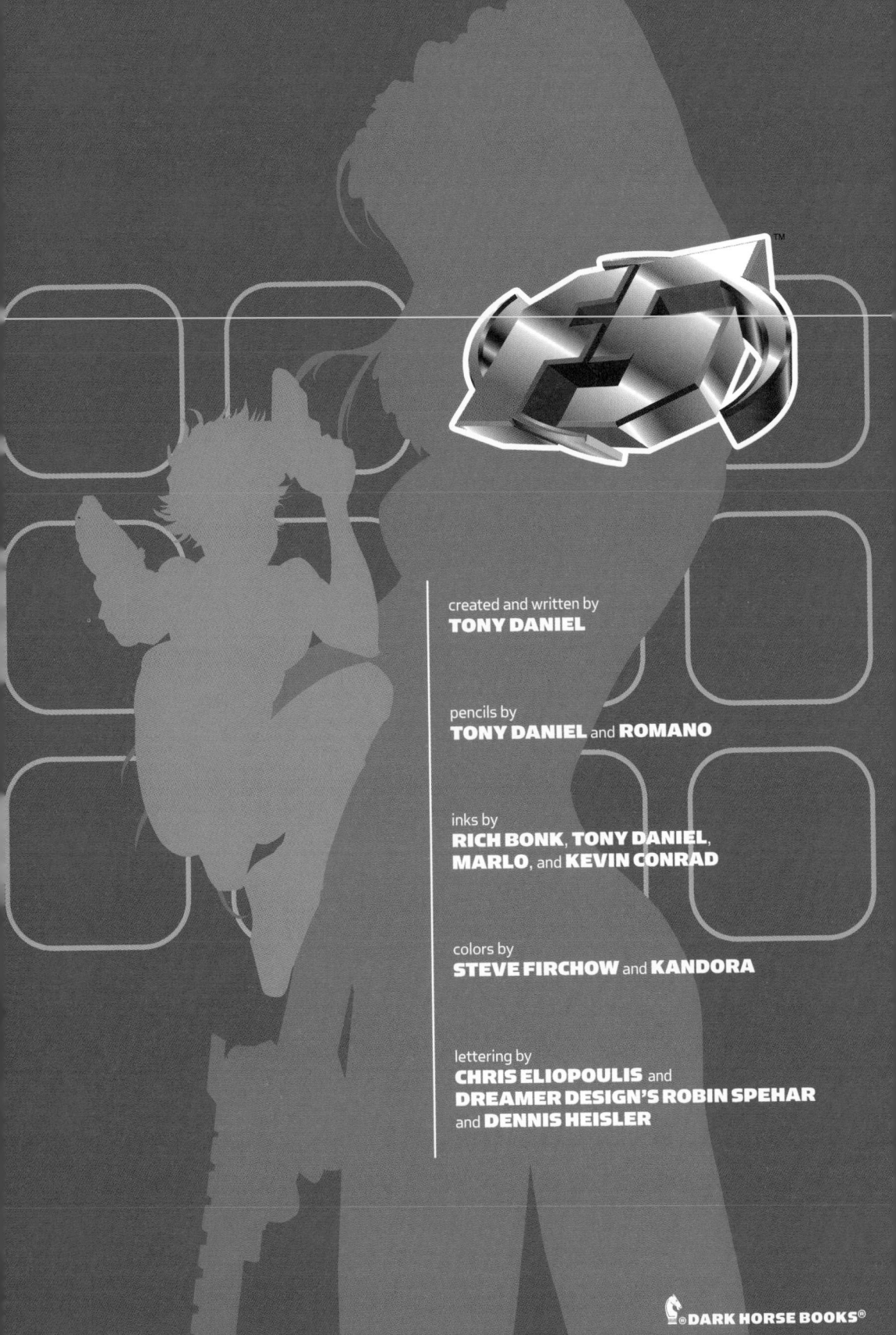

created and written by
TONY DANIEL

pencils by
TONY DANIEL and **ROMANO**

inks by
RICH BONK, **TONY DANIEL**,
MARLO, and **KEVIN CONRAD**

colors by
STEVE FIRCHOW and **KANDORA**

lettering by
CHRIS ELIOPOULIS and
DREAMER DESIGN'S ROBIN SPEHAR
and **DENNIS HEISLER**

® DARK HORSE BOOKS®

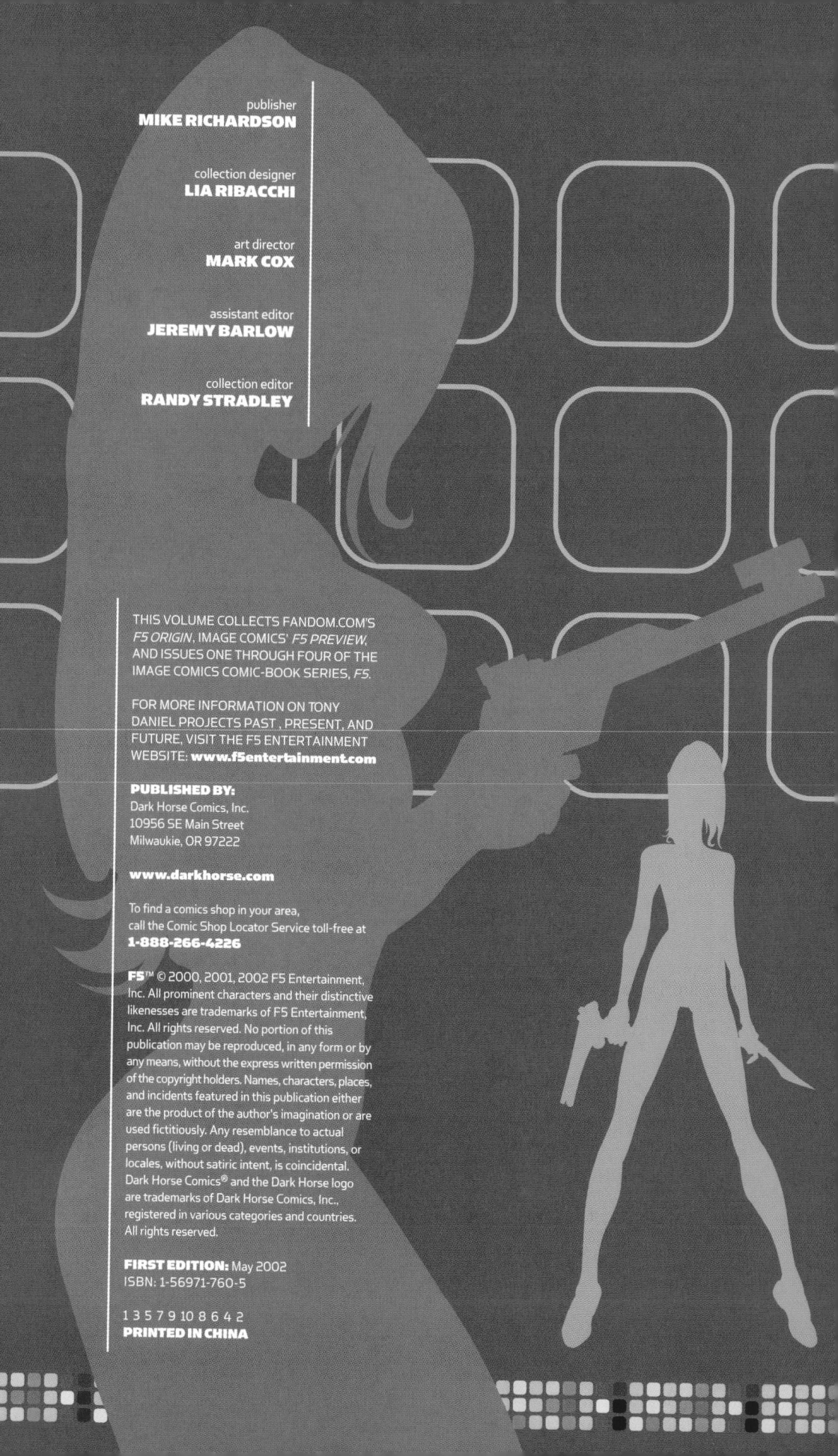

publisher
MIKE RICHARDSON

collection designer
LIA RIBACCHI

art director
MARK COX

assistant editor
JEREMY BARLOW

collection editor
RANDY STRADLEY

THIS VOLUME COLLECTS FANDOM.COM'S
F5 ORIGIN, IMAGE COMICS' *F5 PREVIEW*,
AND ISSUES ONE THROUGH FOUR OF THE
IMAGE COMICS COMIC-BOOK SERIES, *F5*.

FOR MORE INFORMATION ON TONY
DANIEL PROJECTS PAST , PRESENT, AND
FUTURE, VISIT THE F5 ENTERTAINMENT
WEBSITE: **www.f5entertainment.com**

PUBLISHED BY:
Dark Horse Comics, Inc.
10956 SE Main Street
Milwaukie, OR 97222

www.darkhorse.com

To find a comics shop in your area,
call the Comic Shop Locator Service toll-free at
1-888-266-4226

FIRST EDITION: May 2002
ISBN: 1-56971-760-5

1 3 5 7 9 10 8 6 4 2
PRINTED IN CHINA

chapter one

OIL AND WATER

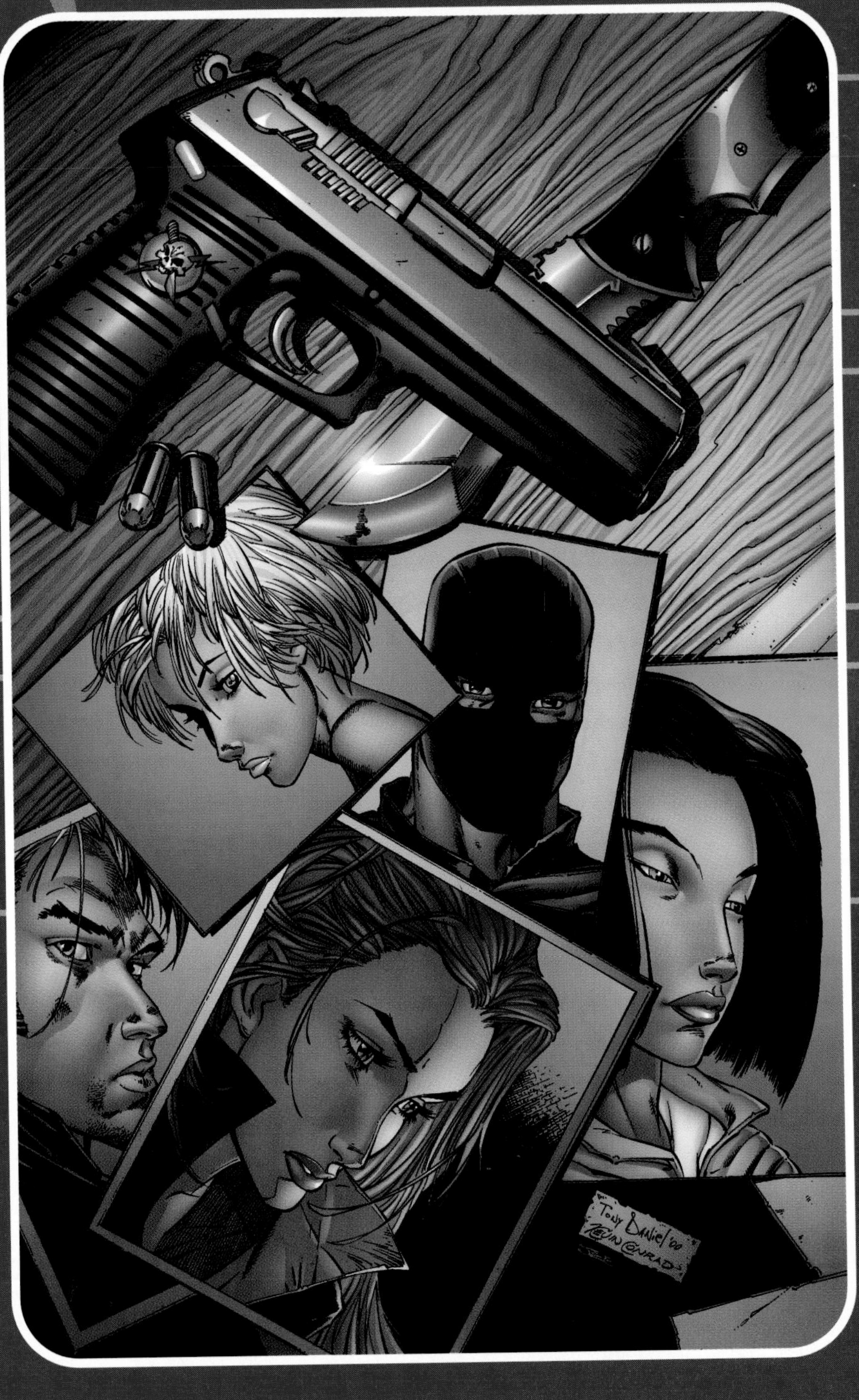
Tony Daniel '00
Kevin Conrad

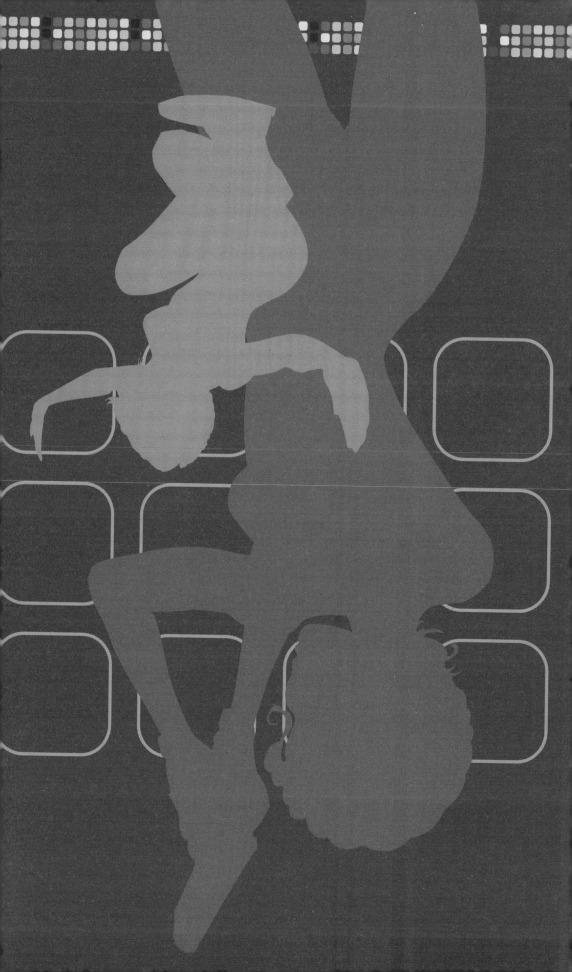

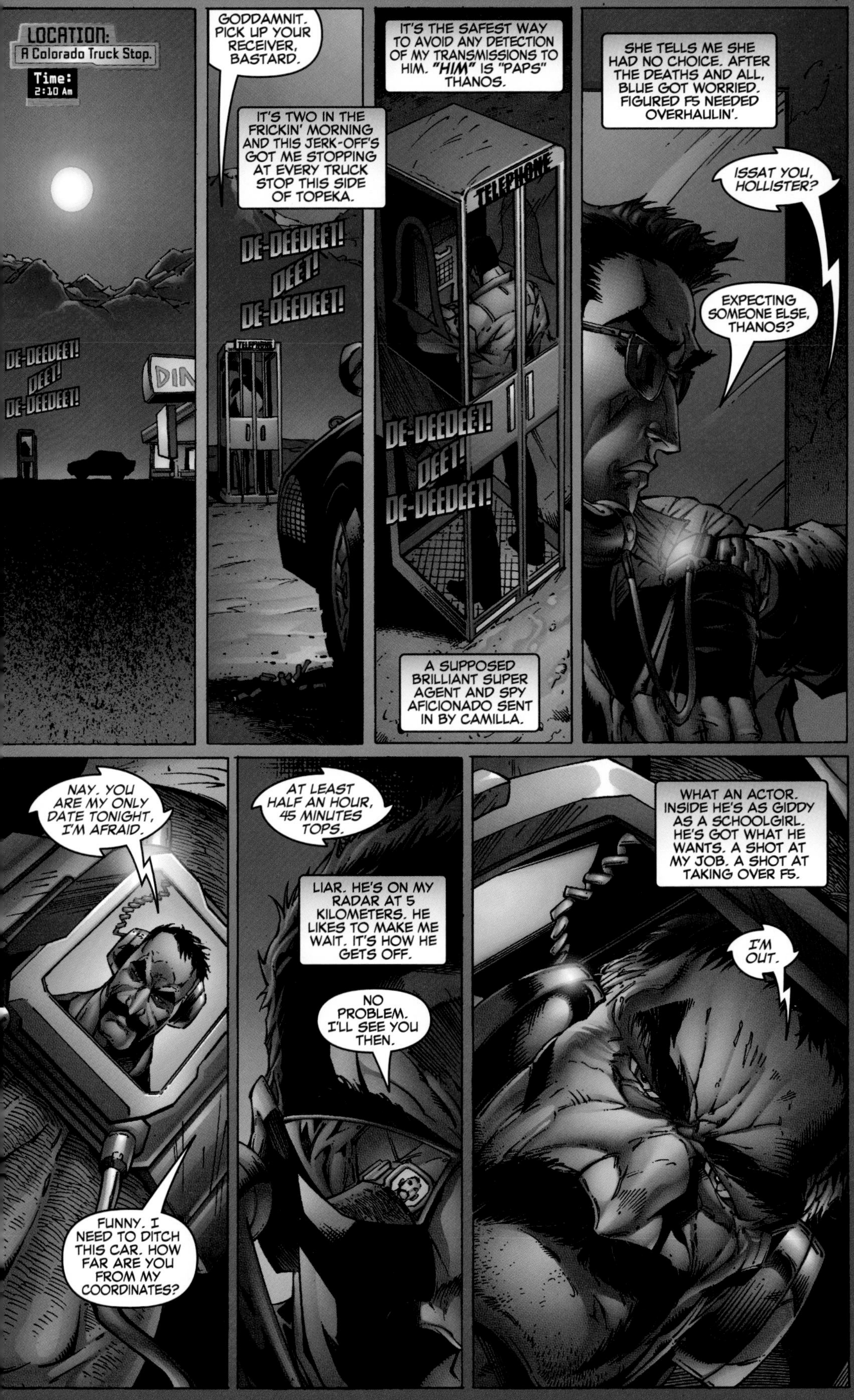
LOCATION:
A Colorado Truck Stop.
Time:
2:10 Am
DE-DEEDEET! DEET! DE-DEEDEET!
GODDAMNIT. PICK UP YOUR RECEIVER, BASTARD.
IT'S TWO IN THE FRICKIN' MORNING AND THIS JERK-OFF'S GOT ME STOPPING AT EVERY TRUCK STOP THIS SIDE OF TOPEKA.
DE-DEEDEET! DEET! DE-DEEDEET!
IT'S THE SAFEST WAY TO AVOID ANY DETECTION OF MY TRANSMISSIONS TO HIM. "HIM" IS "PAPS" THANOS.
TELEPHONE
DE-DEEDEET! DEET! DE-DEEDEET!
A SUPPOSED BRILLIANT SUPER AGENT AND SPY AFICIONADO SENT IN BY CAMILLA.
SHE TELLS ME SHE HAD NO CHOICE. AFTER THE DEATHS AND ALL, BLUE GOT WORRIED. FIGURED F5 NEEDED OVERHAULIN'.
ISSAT YOU, HOLLISTER?
EXPECTING SOMEONE ELSE, THANOS?
NAY. YOU ARE MY ONLY DATE TONIGHT, I'M AFRAID.
FUNNY. I NEED TO DITCH THIS CAR. HOW FAR ARE YOU FROM MY COORDINATES?
AT LEAST HALF AN HOUR, 45 MINUTES TOPS.
LIAR. HE'S ON MY RADAR AT 5 KILOMETERS. HE LIKES TO MAKE ME WAIT. IT'S HOW HE GETS OFF.
NO PROBLEM. I'LL SEE YOU THEN.
WHAT AN ACTOR. INSIDE HE'S AS GIDDY AS A SCHOOLGIRL. HE'S GOT WHAT HE WANTS. A SHOT AT MY JOB. A SHOT AT TAKING OVER F5.
I'M OUT.

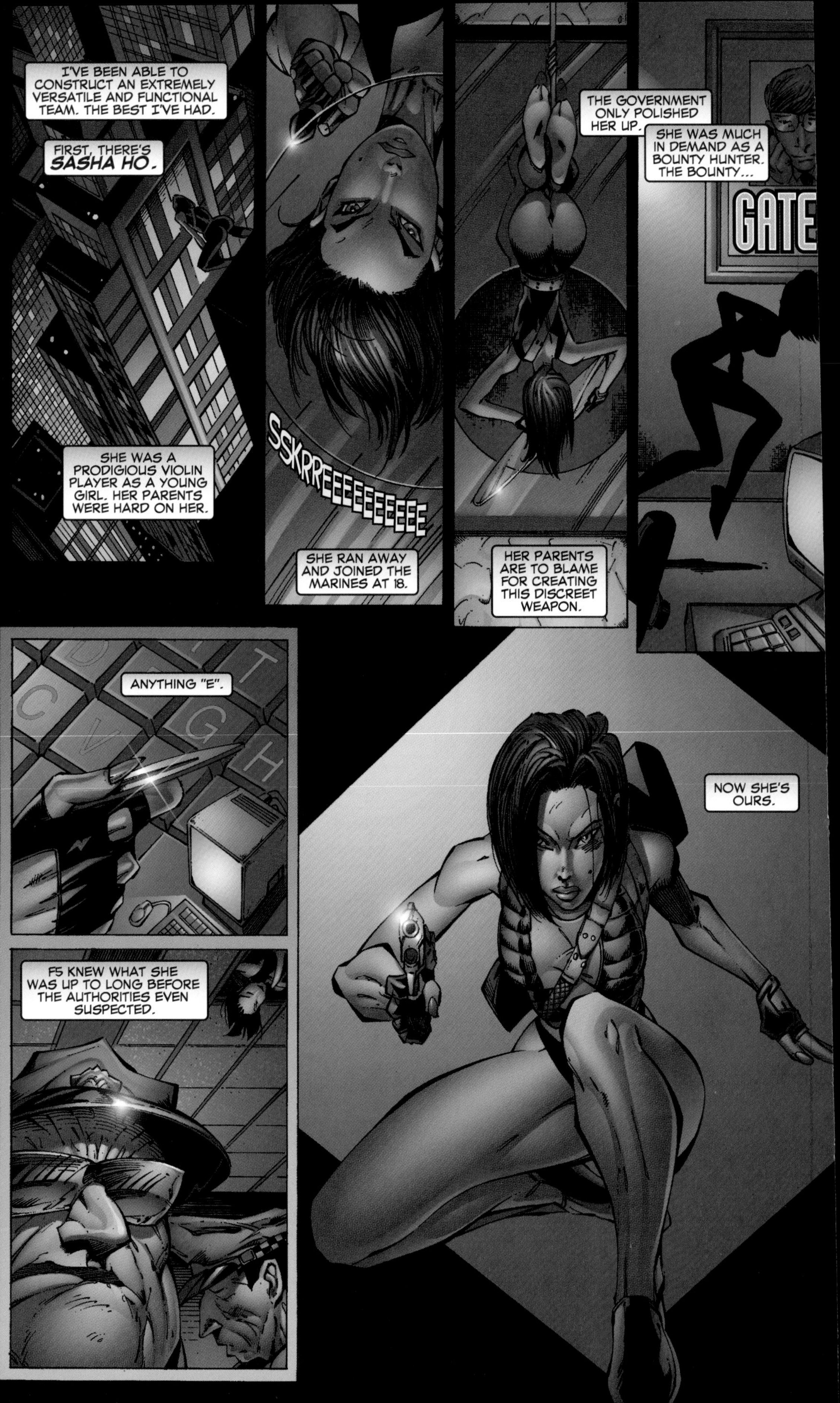
I'VE BEEN ABLE TO CONSTRUCT AN EXTREMELY VERSATILE AND FUNCTIONAL TEAM. THE BEST I'VE HAD.
FIRST, THERE'S *SASHA HO*.
SHE WAS A PRODIGIOUS VIOLIN PLAYER AS A YOUNG GIRL. HER PARENTS WERE HARD ON HER.
SSKRREEEEEEEEEE
SHE RAN AWAY AND JOINED THE MARINES AT 18.
THE GOVERNMENT ONLY POLISHED HER UP.
HER PARENTS ARE TO BLAME FOR CREATING THIS DISCREET WEAPON.
SHE WAS MUCH IN DEMAND AS A BOUNTY HUNTER. THE BOUNTY...
GATE
ANYTHING "E".
F5 KNEW WHAT SHE WAS UP TO LONG BEFORE THE AUTHORITIES EVEN SUSPECTED.
NOW SHE'S OURS.

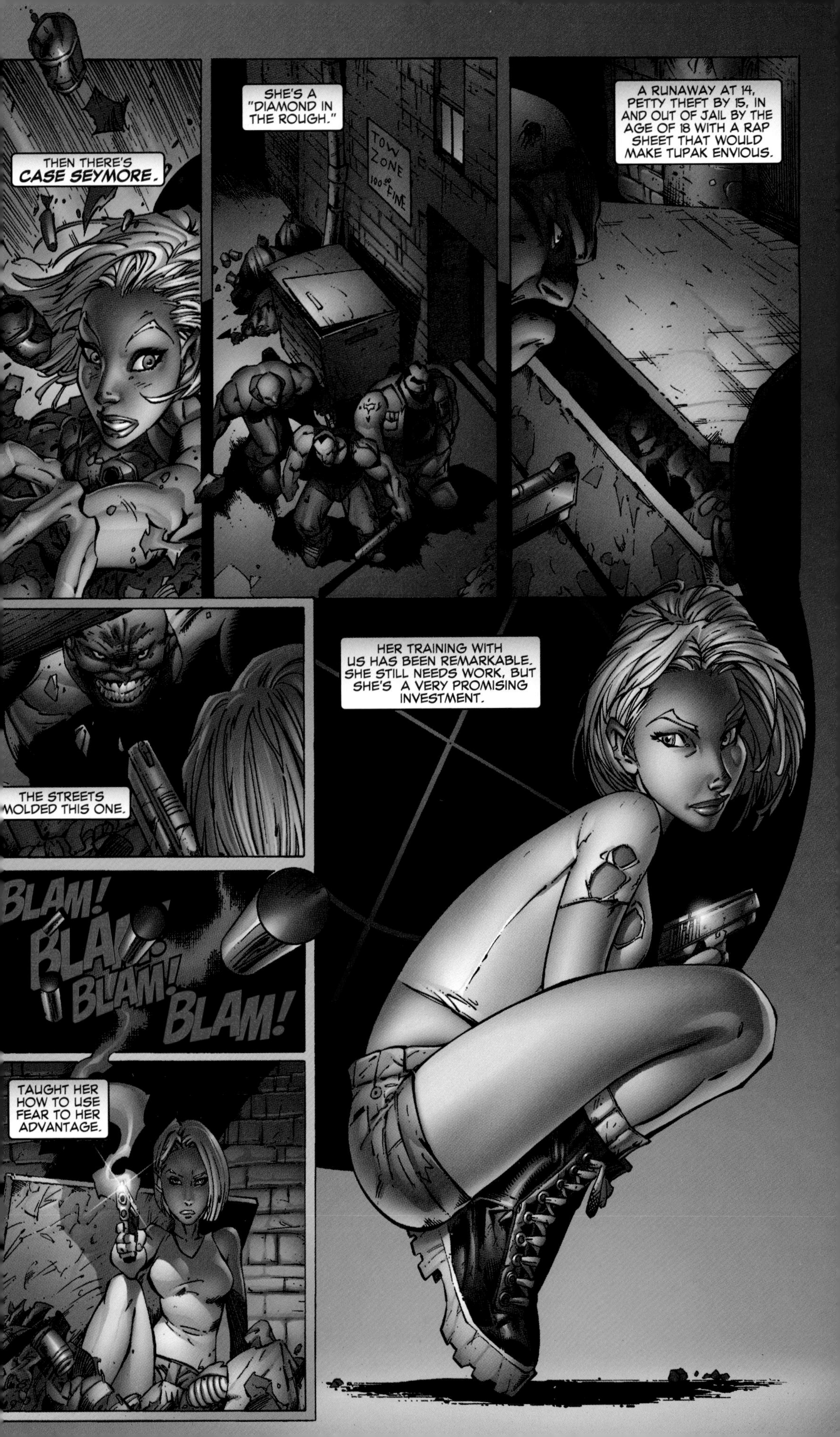
THEN THERE'S CASE SEYMORE.
SHE'S A "DIAMOND IN THE ROUGH."
TOW ZONE 100.00 FINE
A RUNAWAY AT 14, PETTY THEFT BY 15, IN AND OUT OF JAIL BY THE AGE OF 18 WITH A RAP SHEET THAT WOULD MAKE TUPAK ENVIOUS.
HER TRAINING WITH US HAS BEEN REMARKABLE. SHE STILL NEEDS WORK, BUT SHE'S A VERY PROMISING INVESTMENT.
THE STREETS MOLDED THIS ONE.
BLAM!
BLAM!
BLAM!
TAUGHT HER HOW TO USE FEAR TO HER ADVANTAGE.

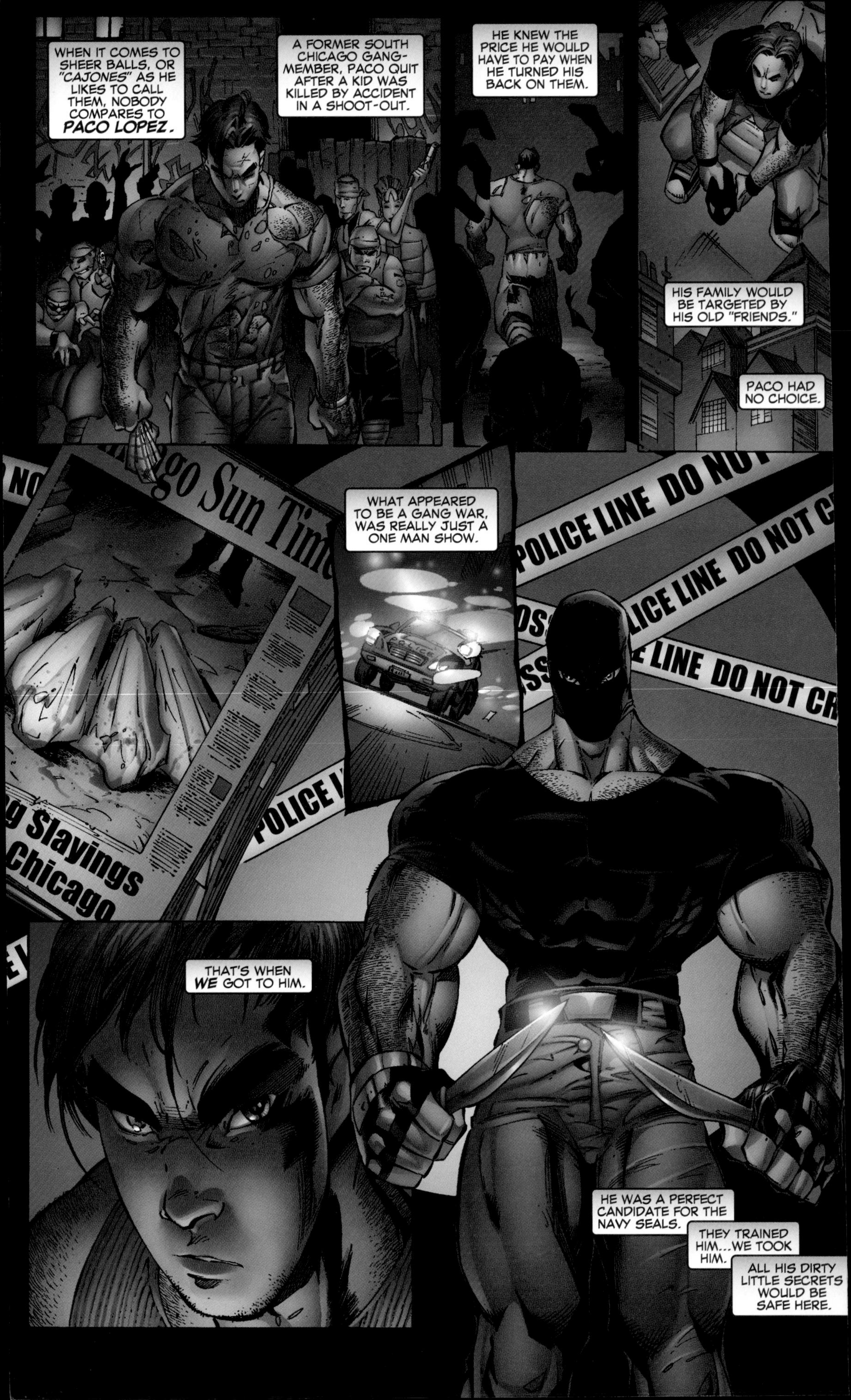
WHEN IT COMES TO SHEER BALLS, OR "CAJONES" AS HE LIKES TO CALL THEM, NOBODY COMPARES TO **PACO LOPEZ**.
A FORMER SOUTH CHICAGO GANG-MEMBER, PACO QUIT AFTER A KID WAS KILLED BY ACCIDENT IN A SHOOT-OUT.
HE KNEW THE PRICE HE WOULD HAVE TO PAY WHEN HE TURNED HIS BACK ON THEM.
HIS FAMILY WOULD BE TARGETED BY HIS OLD "FRIENDS."
PACO HAD NO CHOICE.
WHAT APPEARED TO BE A GANG WAR, WAS REALLY JUST A ONE MAN SHOW.
Slayings
Chicago
POLICE LINE DO NOT CROSS
THAT'S WHEN *WE* GOT TO HIM.
HE WAS A PERFECT CANDIDATE FOR THE NAVY SEALS.
THEY TRAINED HIM...WE TOOK HIM.
ALL HIS DIRTY LITTLE SECRETS WOULD BE SAFE HERE.

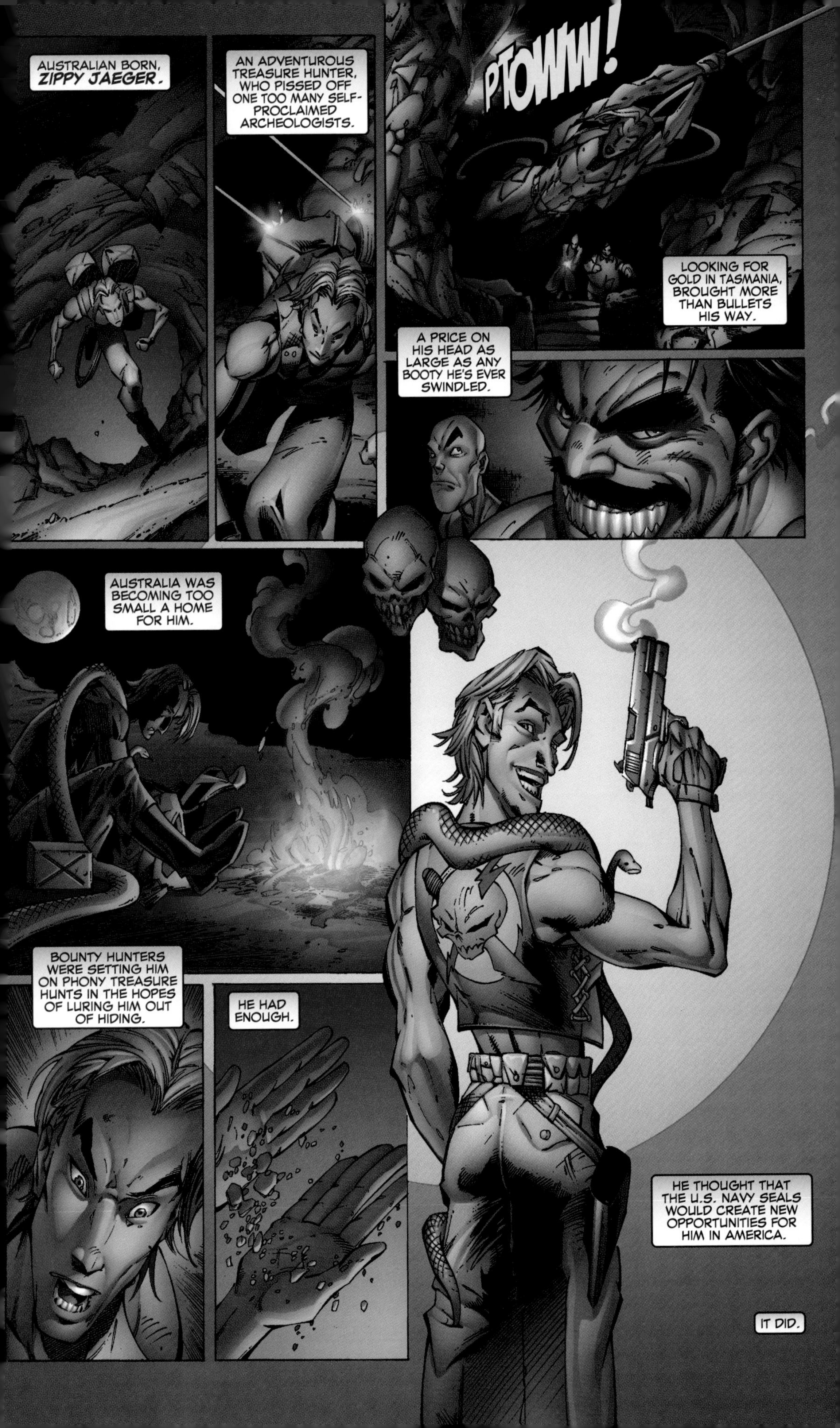
AUSTRALIAN BORN, ZIPPY JAEGER.
AN ADVENTUROUS TREASURE HUNTER, WHO PISSED OFF ONE TOO MANY SELF-PROCLAIMED ARCHEOLOGISTS.
PTOWW!
LOOKING FOR GOLD IN TASMANIA, BROUGHT MORE THAN BULLETS HIS WAY.
A PRICE ON HIS HEAD AS LARGE AS ANY BOOTY HE'S EVER SWINDLED.
AUSTRALIA WAS BECOMING TOO SMALL A HOME FOR HIM.
BOUNTY HUNTERS WERE SETTING HIM ON PHONY TREASURE HUNTS IN THE HOPES OF LURING HIM OUT OF HIDING.
HE HAD ENOUGH.
HE THOUGHT THAT THE U.S. NAVY SEALS WOULD CREATE NEW OPPORTUNITIES FOR HIM IN AMERICA.
IT DID.

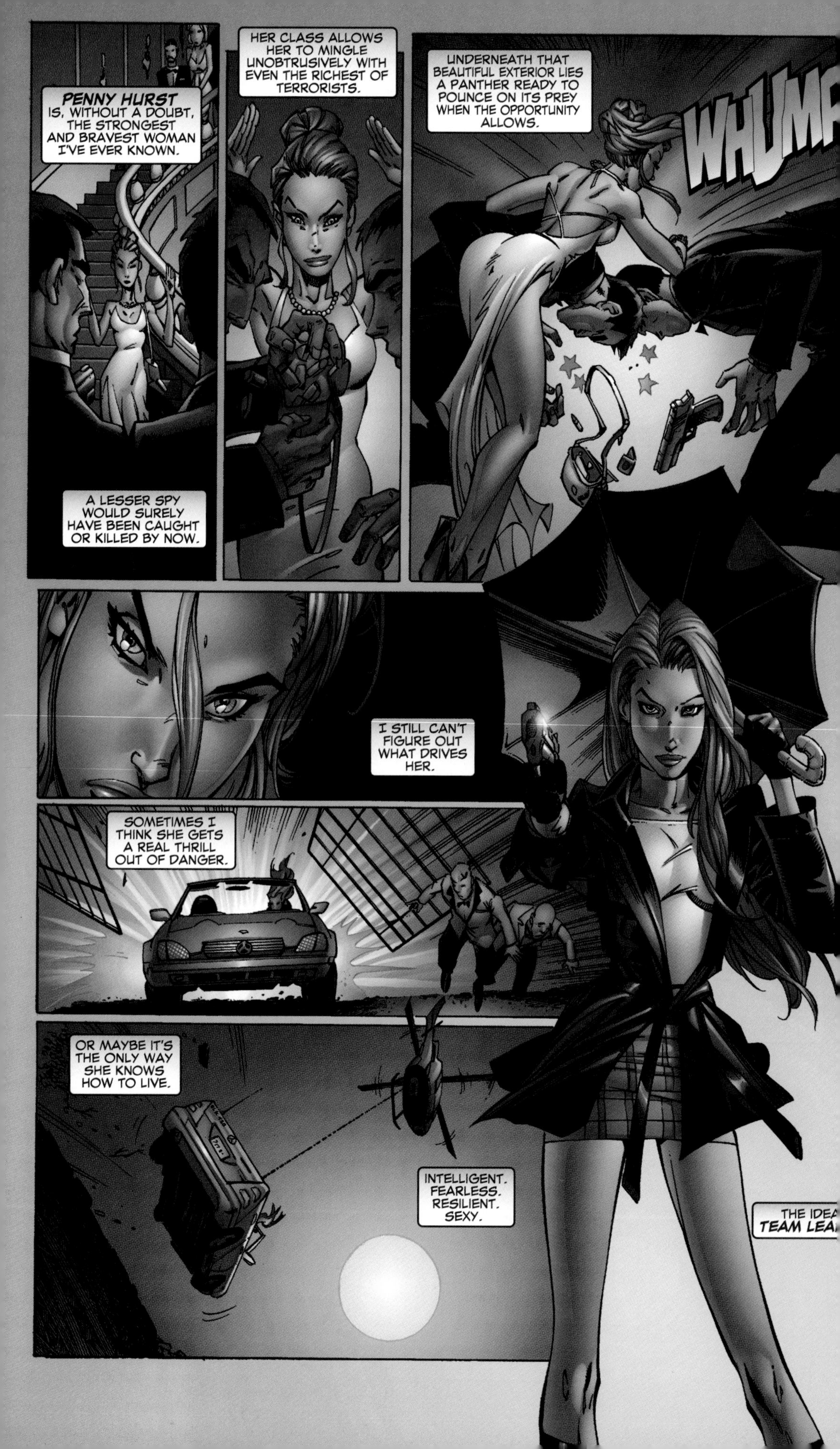
PENNY HURST IS, WITHOUT A DOUBT, THE STRONGEST AND BRAVEST WOMAN I'VE EVER KNOWN.
A LESSER SPY WOULD SURELY HAVE BEEN CAUGHT OR KILLED BY NOW.
HER CLASS ALLOWS HER TO MINGLE UNOBTRUSIVELY WITH EVEN THE RICHEST OF TERRORISTS.
UNDERNEATH THAT BEAUTIFUL EXTERIOR LIES A PANTHER READY TO POUNCE ON ITS PREY WHEN THE OPPORTUNITY ALLOWS.
I STILL CAN'T FIGURE OUT WHAT DRIVES HER.
SOMETIMES I THINK SHE GETS A REAL THRILL OUT OF DANGER.
OR MAYBE IT'S THE ONLY WAY SHE KNOWS HOW TO LIVE.
INTELLIGENT. FEARLESS. RESILIENT. SEXY.

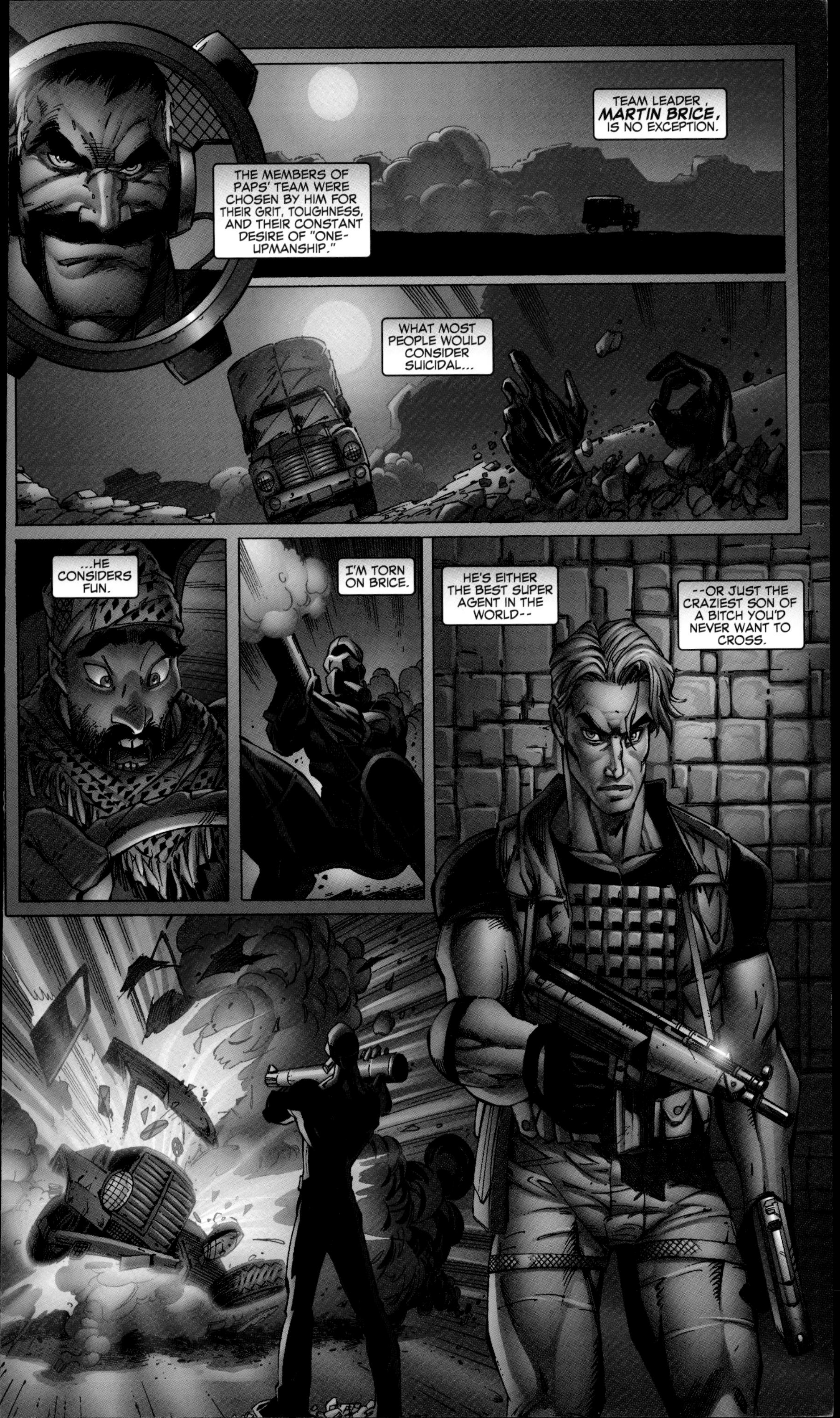
THE MEMBERS OF PAPS' TEAM WERE CHOSEN BY HIM FOR THEIR GRIT, TOUGHNESS, AND THEIR CONSTANT DESIRE OF "ONE-UPMANSHIP."
TEAM LEADER, MARTIN BRICE, IS NO EXCEPTION.
WHAT MOST PEOPLE WOULD CONSIDER SUICIDAL...
...HE CONSIDERS FUN.
I'M TORN ON BRICE.
HE'S EITHER THE BEST SUPER AGENT IN THE WORLD--
--OR JUST THE CRAZIEST SON OF A BITCH YOU'D NEVER WANT TO CROSS.

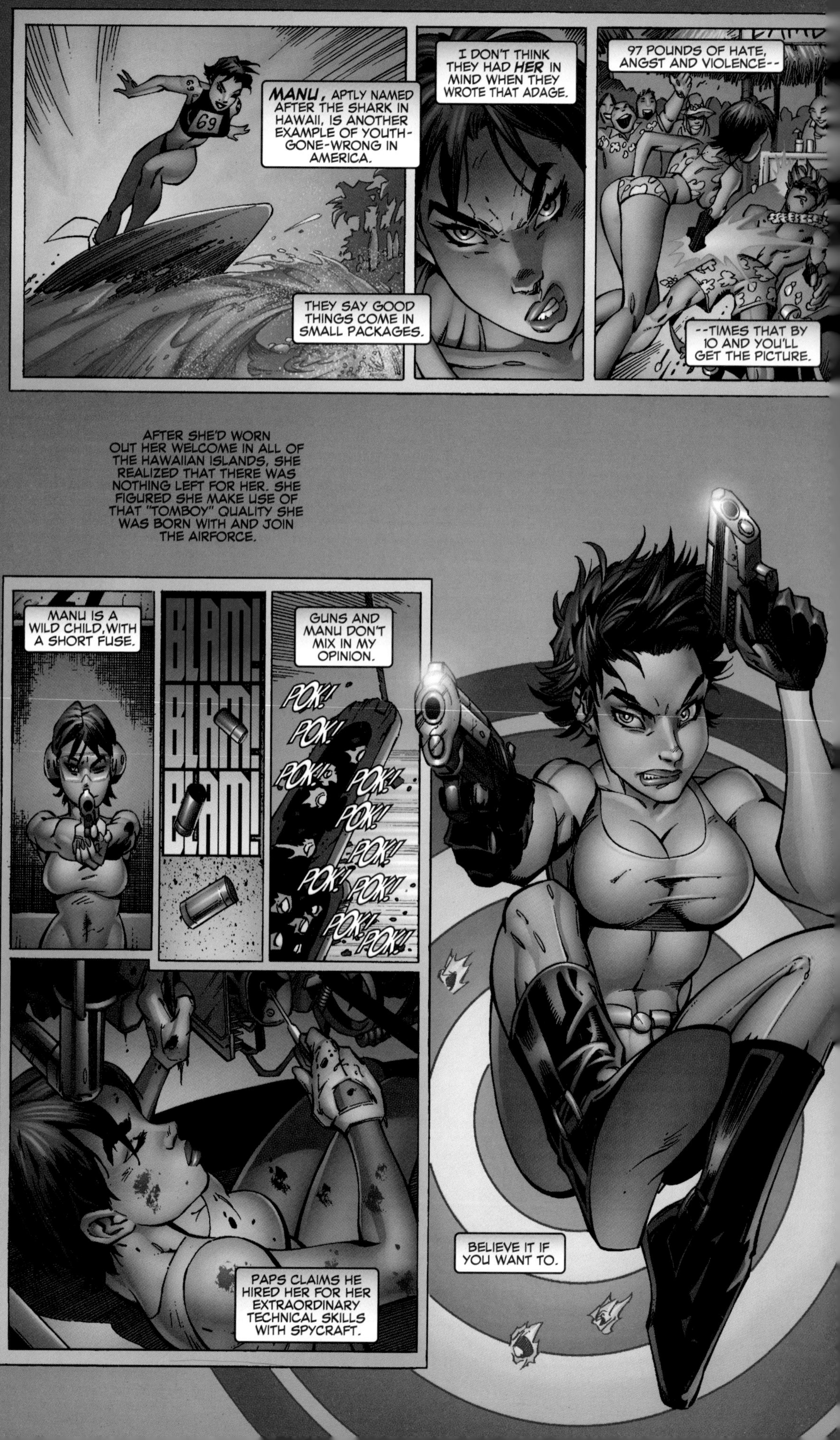
MANU, APTLY NAMED AFTER THE SHARK IN HAWAII, IS ANOTHER EXAMPLE OF YOUTH-GONE-WRONG IN AMERICA.
69
THEY SAY GOOD THINGS COME IN SMALL PACKAGES.
I DON'T THINK THEY HAD HER IN MIND WHEN THEY WROTE THAT ADAGE.
97 POUNDS OF HATE, ANGST AND VIOLENCE--
--TIMES THAT BY 10 AND YOU'LL GET THE PICTURE.
AFTER SHE'D WORN OUT HER WELCOME IN ALL OF THE HAWAIIAN ISLANDS, SHE REALIZED THAT THERE WAS NOTHING LEFT FOR HER. SHE FIGURED SHE MAKE USE OF THAT "TOMBOY" QUALITY SHE WAS BORN WITH AND JOIN THE AIRFORCE.
MANU IS A WILD CHILD, WITH A SHORT FUSE.
BLAM! BLAM! BLAM!
GUNS AND MANU DON'T MIX IN MY OPINION.
POK! POK! POK! POK! POK! POK! POK! POK! POK! POK!
PAPS CLAIMS HE HIRED HER FOR HER EXTRAORDINARY TECHNICAL SKILLS WITH SPYCRAFT.
BELIEVE IT IF YOU WANT TO.

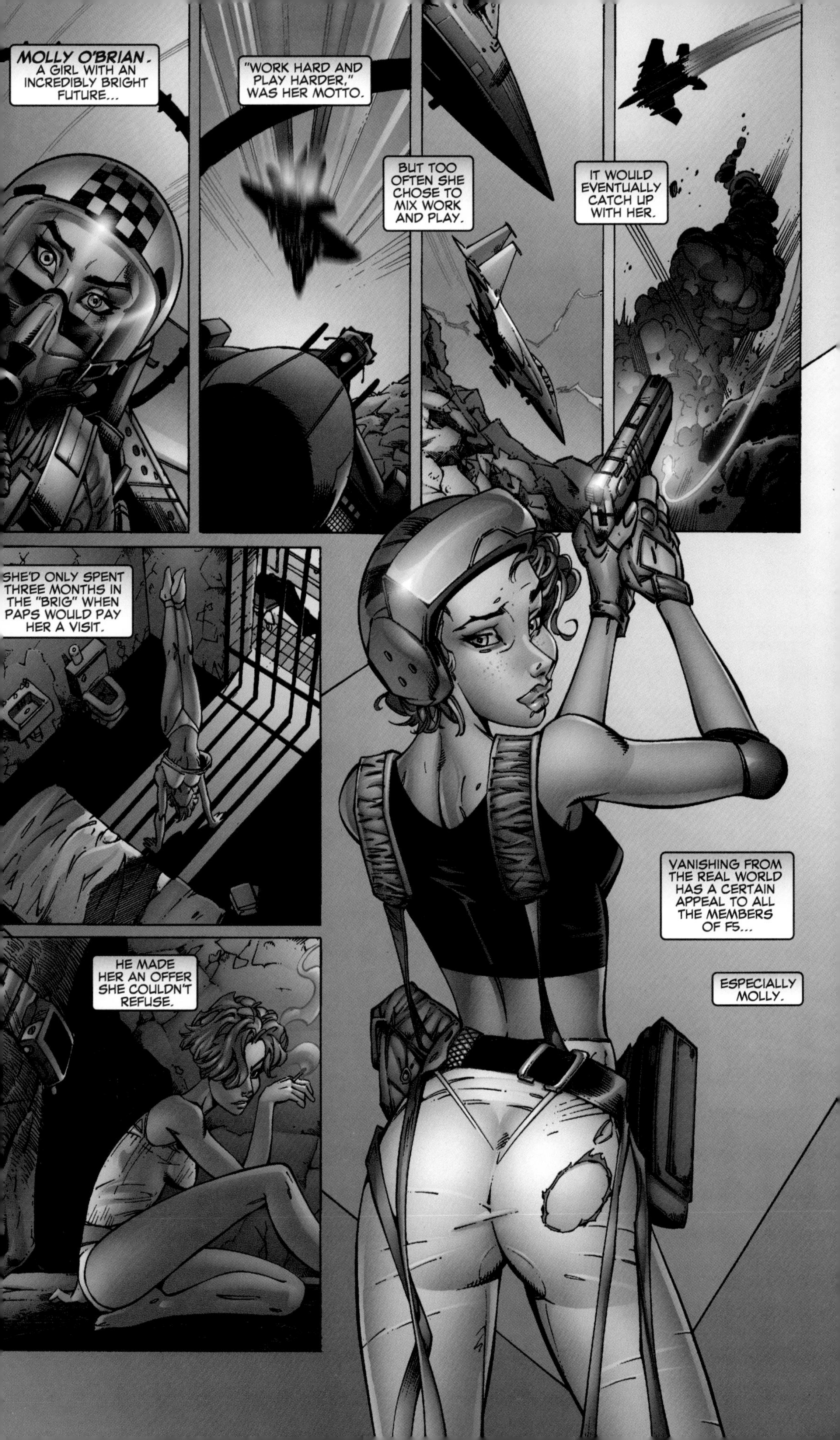
MOLLY O'BRIAN. A GIRL WITH AN INCREDIBLY BRIGHT FUTURE...
"WORK HARD AND PLAY HARDER," WAS HER MOTTO.
BUT TOO OFTEN SHE CHOSE TO MIX WORK AND PLAY.
IT WOULD EVENTUALLY CATCH UP WITH HER.
SHE'D ONLY SPENT THREE MONTHS IN THE "BRIG" WHEN PAPS WOULD PAY HER A VISIT.
HE MADE HER AN OFFER SHE COULDN'T REFUSE.
VANISHING FROM THE REAL WORLD HAS A CERTAIN APPEAL TO ALL THE MEMBERS OF F5...
ESPECIALLY MOLLY.

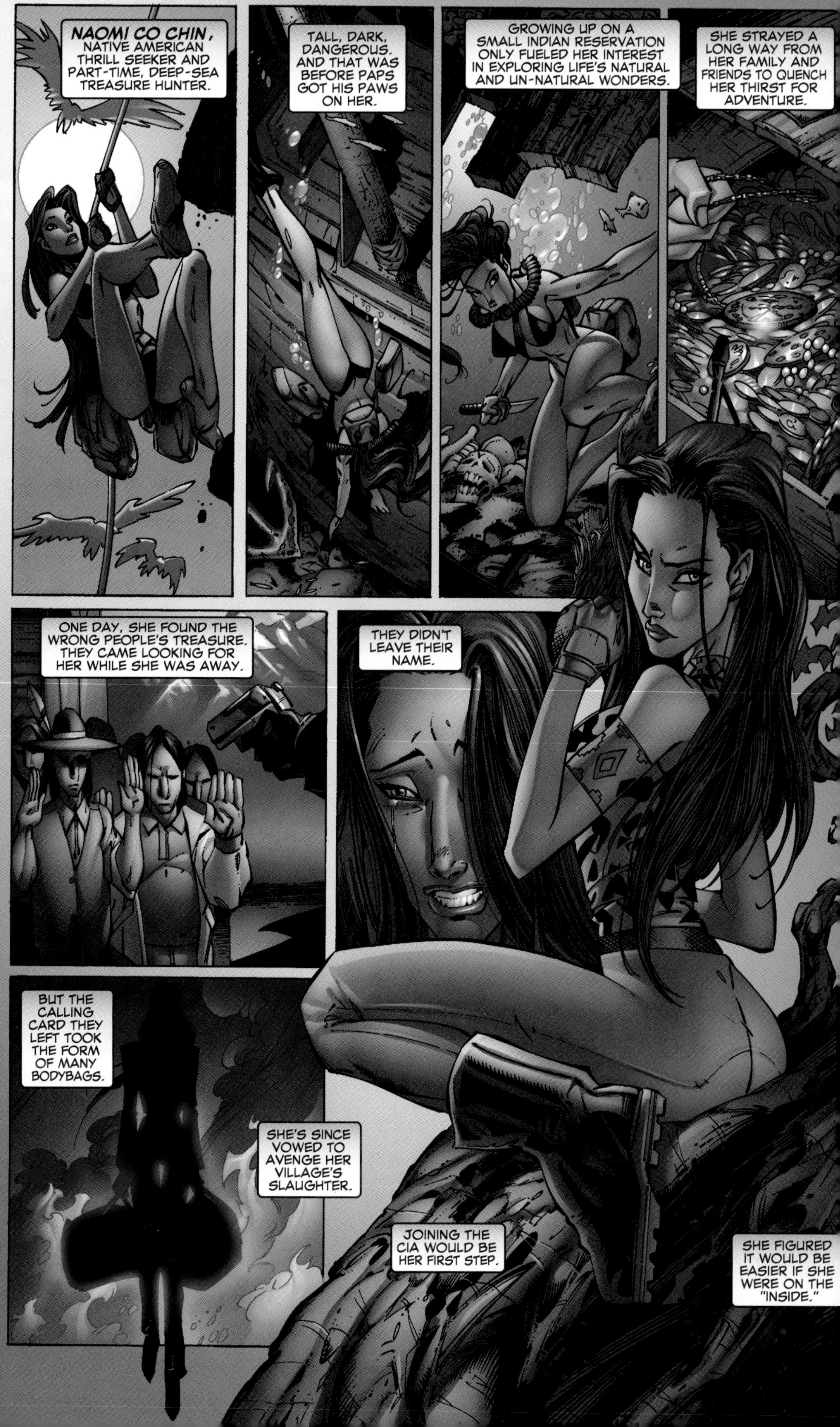
NAOMI CO CHIN, NATIVE AMERICAN THRILL SEEKER AND PART-TIME, DEEP-SEA TREASURE HUNTER.
TALL, DARK, DANGEROUS. AND THAT WAS BEFORE PAPS GOT HIS PAWS ON HER.
GROWING UP ON A SMALL INDIAN RESERVATION ONLY FUELED HER INTEREST IN EXPLORING LIFE'S NATURAL AND UN-NATURAL WONDERS.
SHE STRAYED A LONG WAY FROM HER FAMILY AND FRIENDS TO QUENCH HER THIRST FOR ADVENTURE.
ONE DAY, SHE FOUND THE WRONG PEOPLE'S TREASURE. THEY CAME LOOKING FOR HER WHILE SHE WAS AWAY.
THEY DIDN'T LEAVE THEIR NAME.
BUT THE CALLING CARD THEY LEFT TOOK THE FORM OF MANY BODYBAGS.
SHE'S SINCE VOWED TO AVENGE HER VILLAGE'S SLAUGHTER.
JOINING THE CIA WOULD BE HER FIRST STEP.
SHE FIGURED IT WOULD BE EASIER IF SHE WERE ON THE "INSIDE."

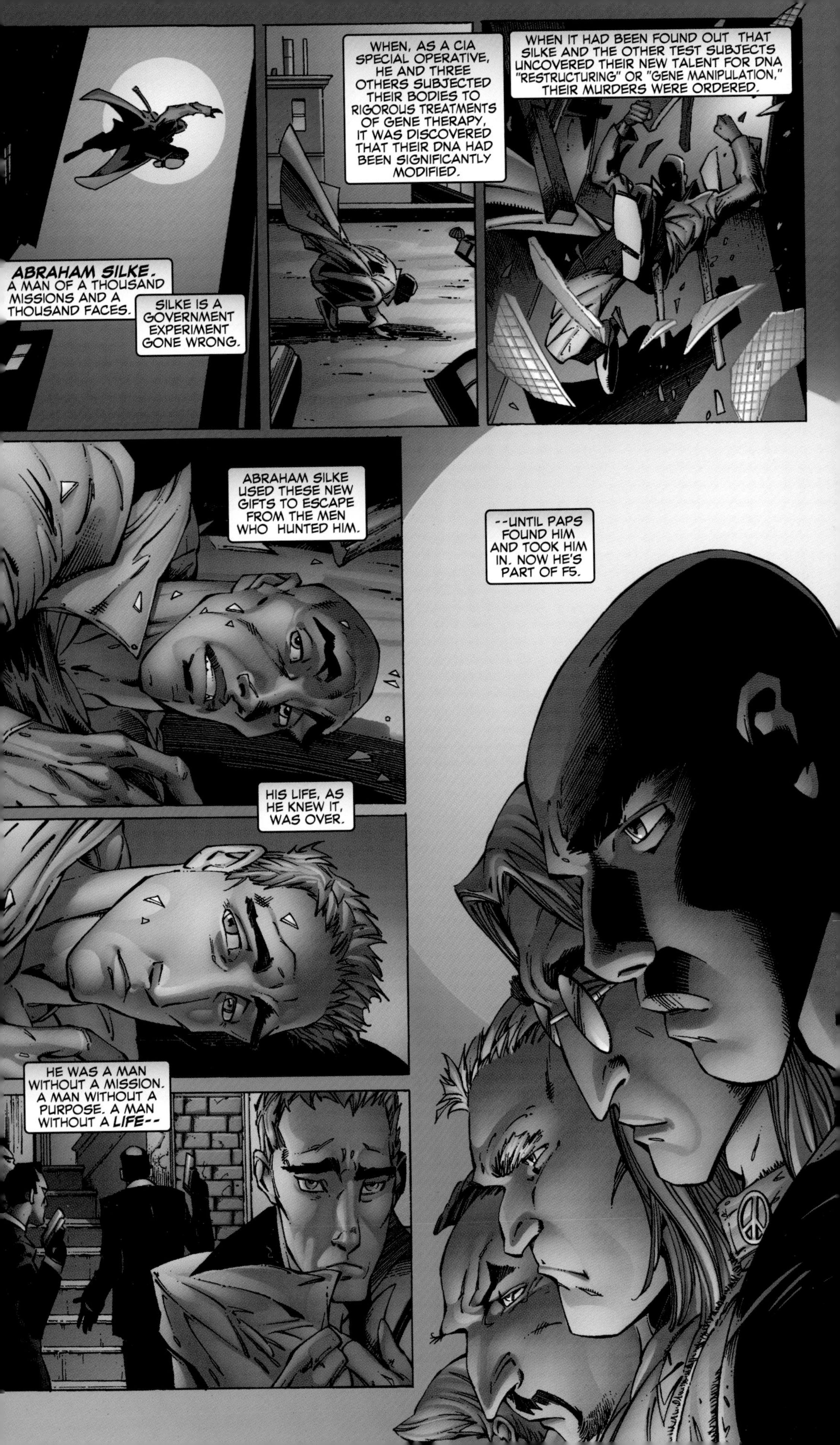
ABRAHAM SILKE. A MAN OF A THOUSAND MISSIONS AND A THOUSAND FACES.
SILKE IS A GOVERNMENT EXPERIMENT GONE WRONG.
WHEN, AS A CIA SPECIAL OPERATIVE, HE AND THREE OTHERS SUBJECTED THEIR BODIES TO RIGOROUS TREATMENTS OF GENE THERAPY, IT WAS DISCOVERED THAT THEIR DNA HAD BEEN SIGNIFICANTLY MODIFIED.
WHEN IT HAD BEEN FOUND OUT THAT SILKE AND THE OTHER TEST SUBJECTS UNCOVERED THEIR NEW TALENT FOR DNA "RESTRUCTURING" OR "GENE MANIPULATION," THEIR MURDERS WERE ORDERED.
ABRAHAM SILKE USED THESE NEW GIFTS TO ESCAPE FROM THE MEN WHO HUNTED HIM.
HIS LIFE, AS HE KNEW IT, WAS OVER.
HE WAS A MAN WITHOUT A MISSION. A MAN WITHOUT A PURPOSE. A MAN WITHOUT A LIFE--
--UNTIL PAPS FOUND HIM AND TOOK HIM IN. NOW HE'S PART OF F5.

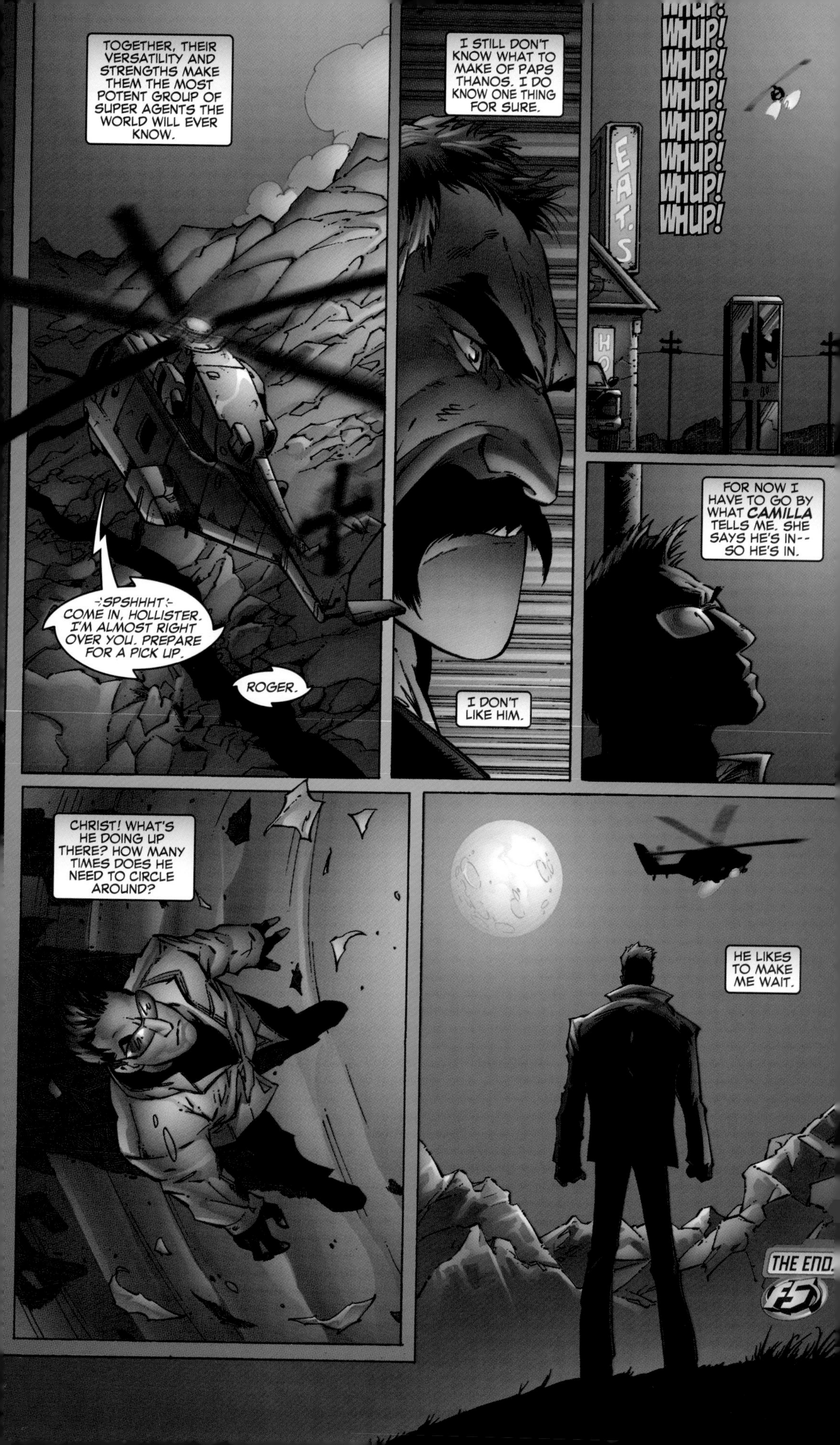
TOGETHER, THEIR VERSATILITY AND STRENGTHS MAKE THEM THE MOST POTENT GROUP OF SUPER AGENTS THE WORLD WILL EVER KNOW.
-SPSHHHT- COME IN, HOLLISTER. I'M ALMOST RIGHT OVER YOU. PREPARE FOR A PICK UP.
ROGER.
I STILL DON'T KNOW WHAT TO MAKE OF PAPS THANOS. I DO KNOW ONE THING FOR SURE.
I DON'T LIKE HIM.
WHUP! WHUP! WHUP! WHUP! WHUP! WHUP! WHUP!
EATS
FOR NOW I HAVE TO GO BY WHAT CAMILLA TELLS ME. SHE SAYS HE'S IN-- SO HE'S IN.
CHRIST! WHAT'S HE DOING UP THERE? HOW MANY TIMES DOES HE NEED TO CIRCLE AROUND?
HE LIKES TO MAKE ME WAIT.
THE END.

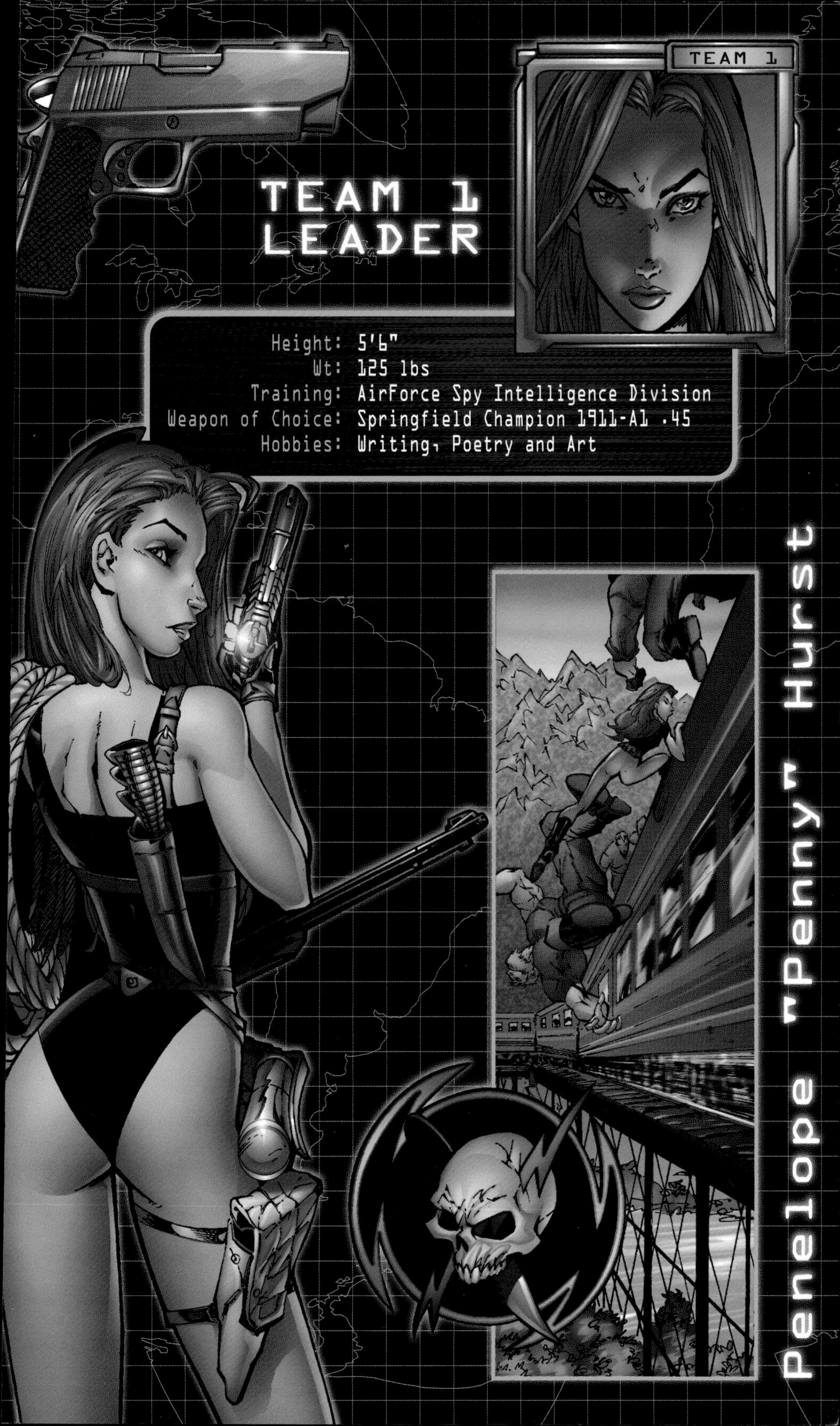
TEAM 1
TEAM 1 LEADER
Height: 5'6"
Wt: 125 lbs
Training: AirForce Spy Intelligence Division
Weapon of Choice: Springfield Champion 1911-A1 .45
Hobbies: Writing, Poetry and Art
Penelope "Penny" Hurst

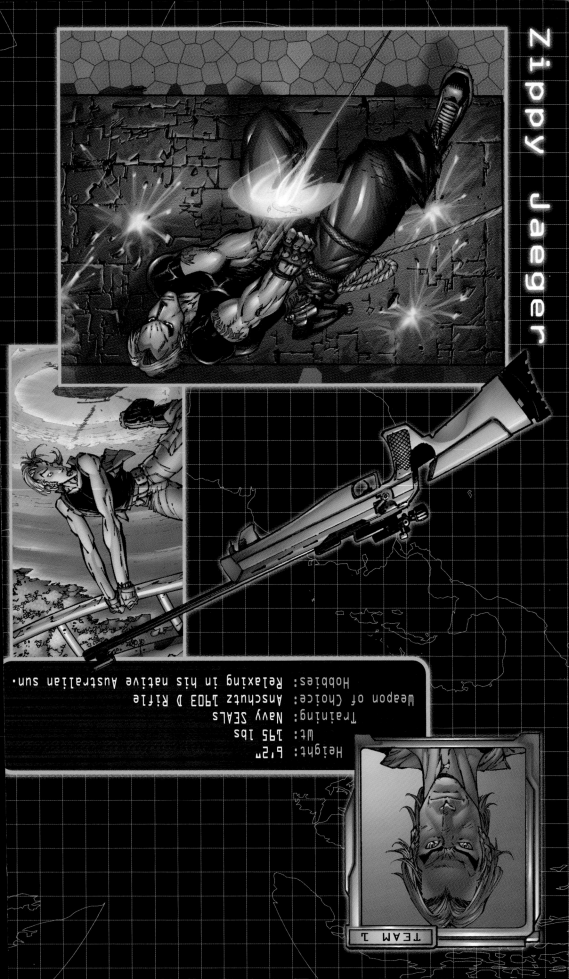

Zippy Jaeger

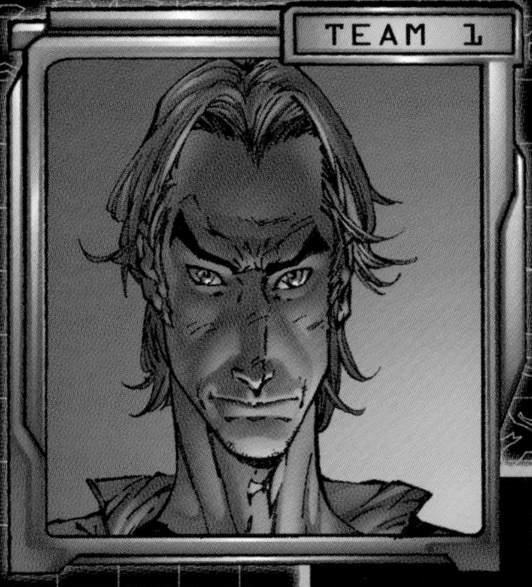
TEAM 1

Height: 6'2"
Wt: 195 lbs
Training: Navy SEALs
Weapon of Choice: Anschutz 1903 D Rifle
Hobbies: Relaxing in his native Australian sun.

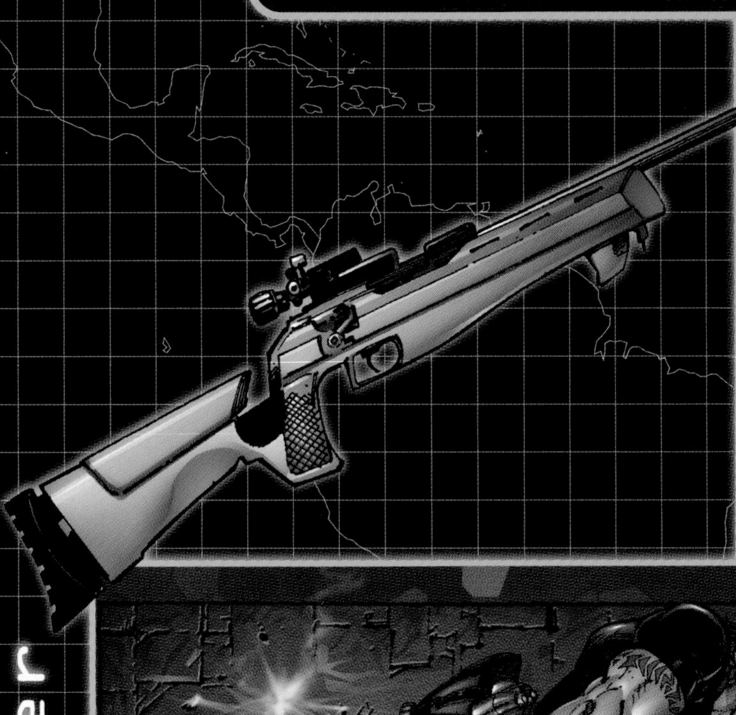

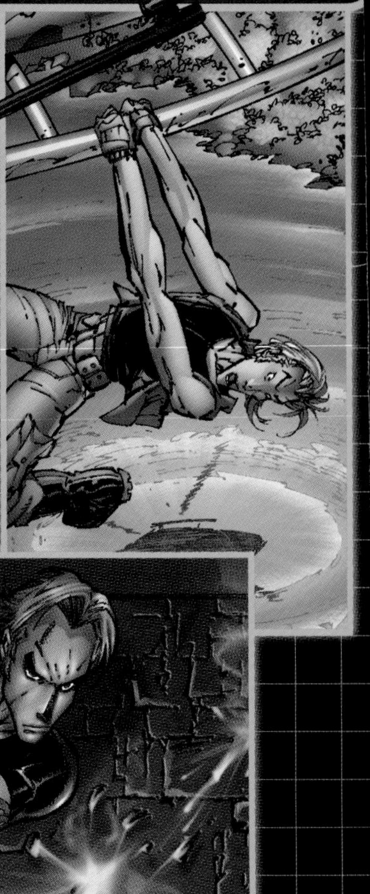

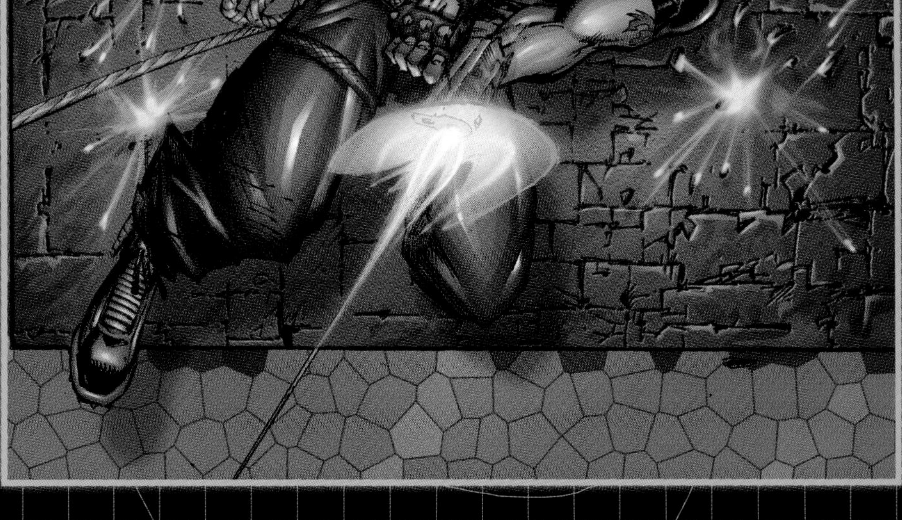

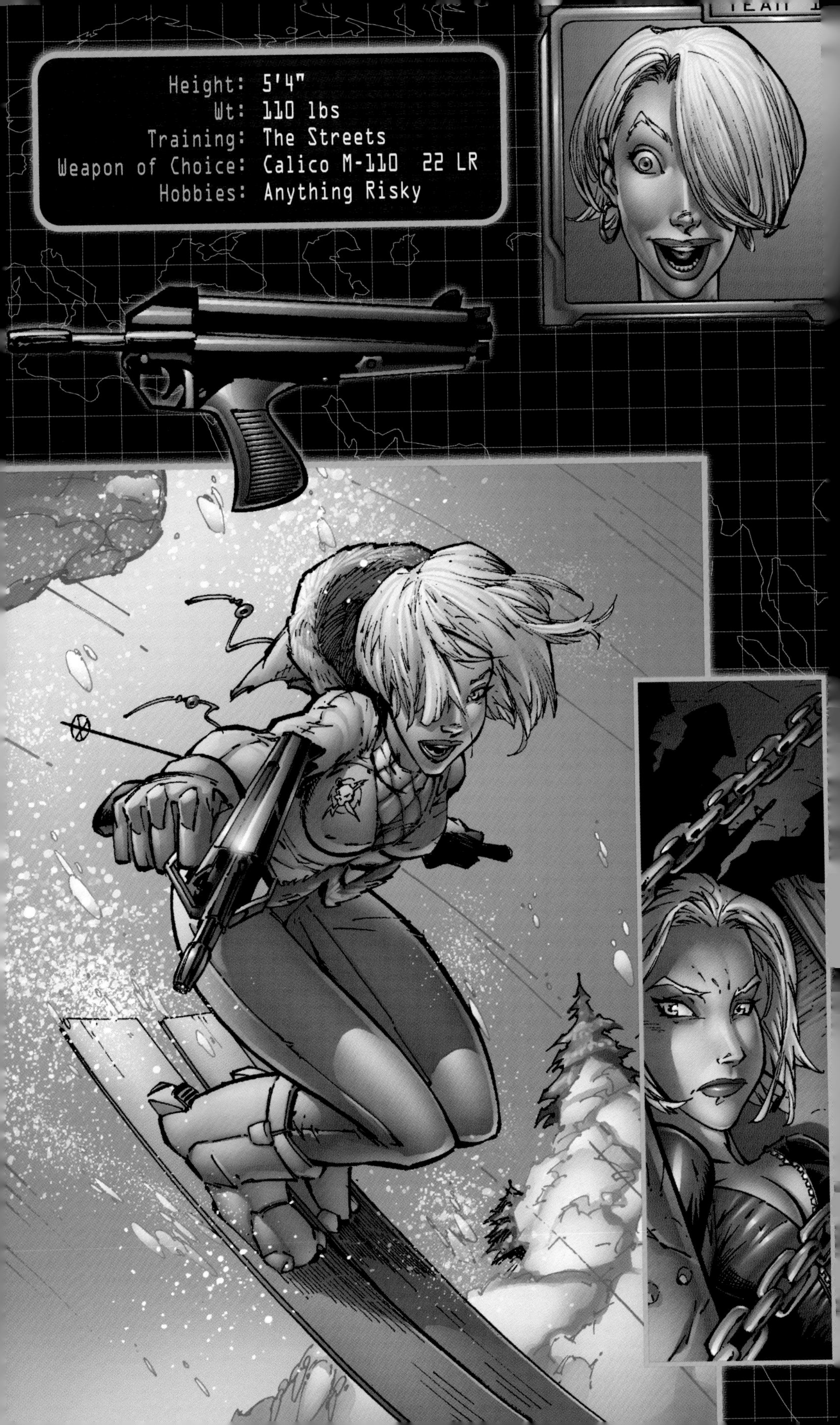
Height: 5'4"
Wt: 110 lbs
Training: The Streets
Weapon of Choice: Calico M-110 22 LR
Hobbies: Anything Risky

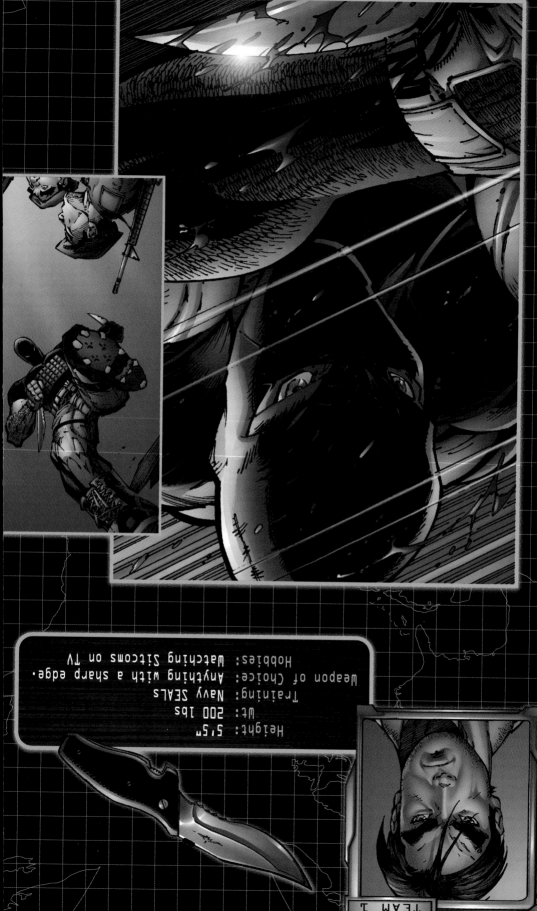

Height: 5'5"
Wt: 200 lbs
Training: Navy SEALS
Weapon of Choice: Anything with a sharp edge.
Hobbies: Watching Sitcoms on TV

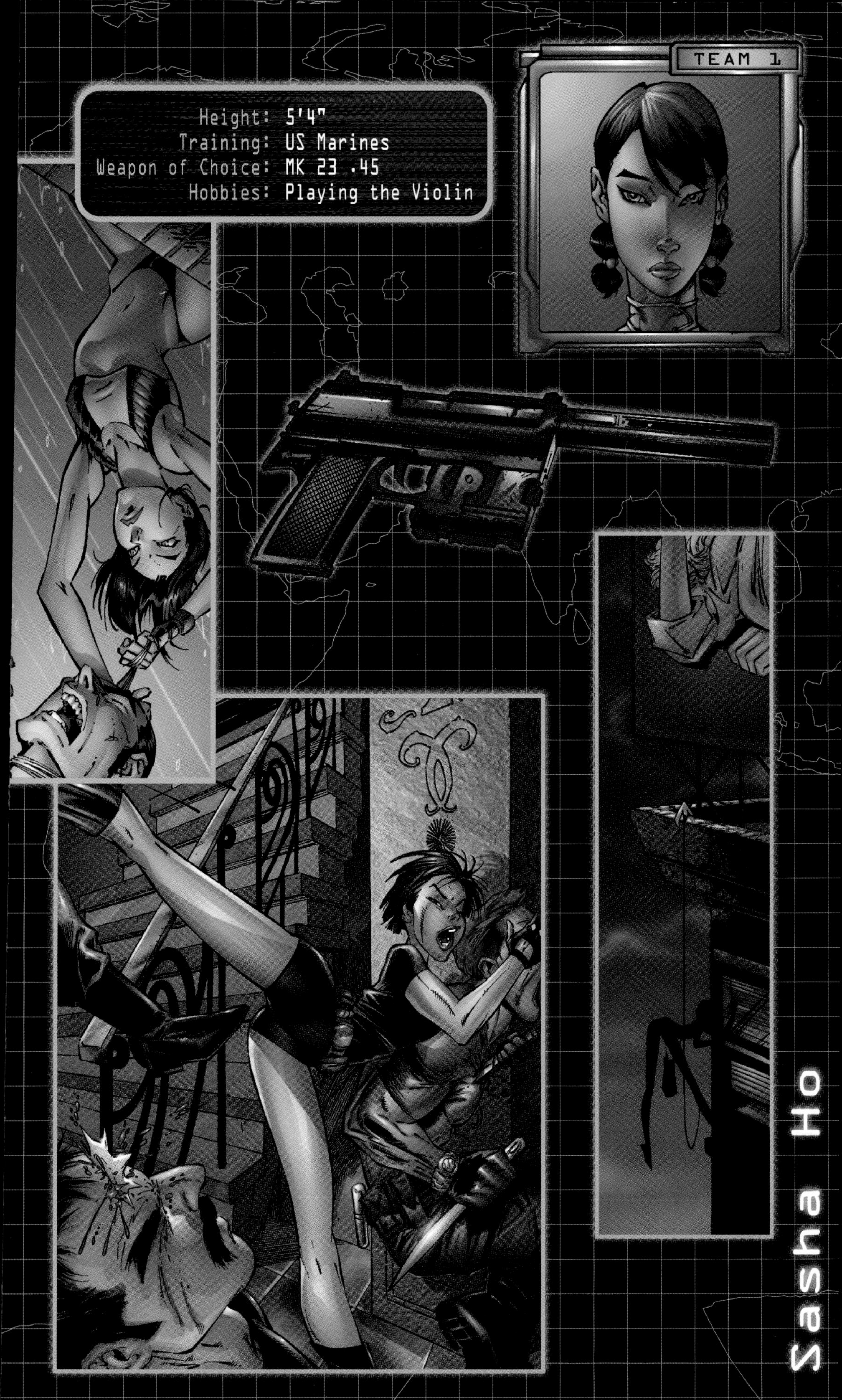
TEAM 1
Height: 5'4"
Training: US Marines
Weapon of Choice: MK 23 .45
Hobbies: Playing the Violin
Sasha Ho

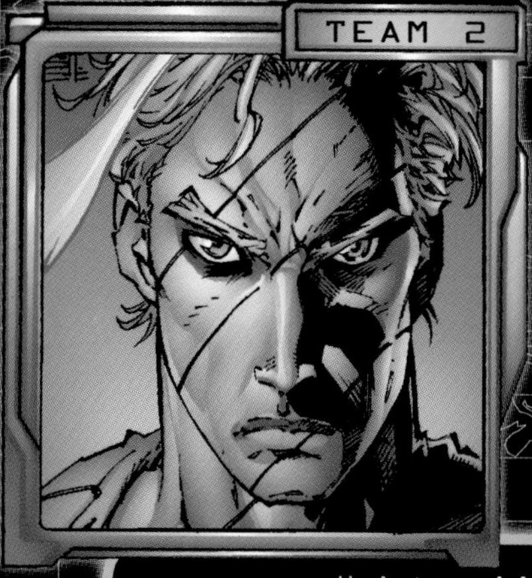
TEAM 2

TEAM 2 LEADER

Height: 6'1"
Wt: 210 lbs
Training: CIA Counter-Terrorism Division
Weapon of Choice: Ruger Stainless Government Target Slab Side 22 LR
Hobbies: Eating Cajun Cuisine

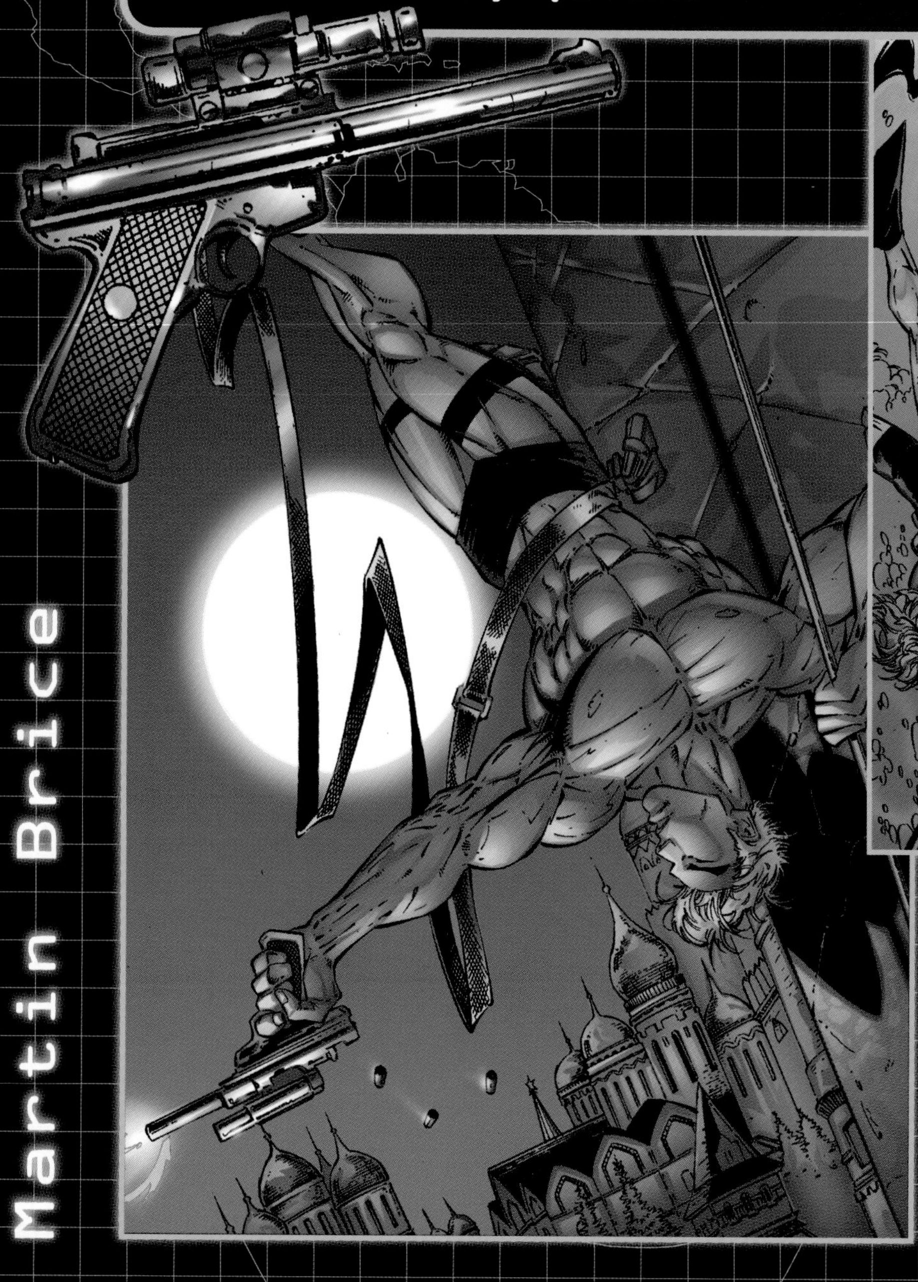

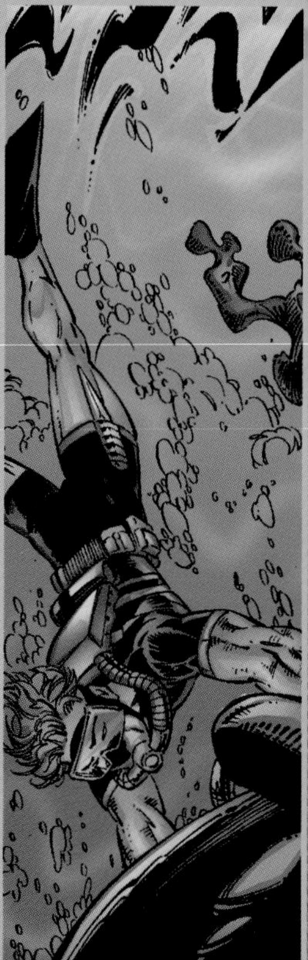

Martin Brice

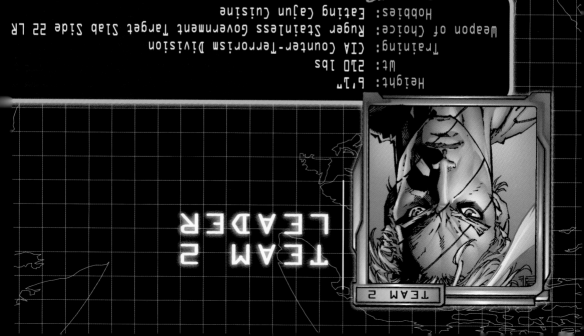

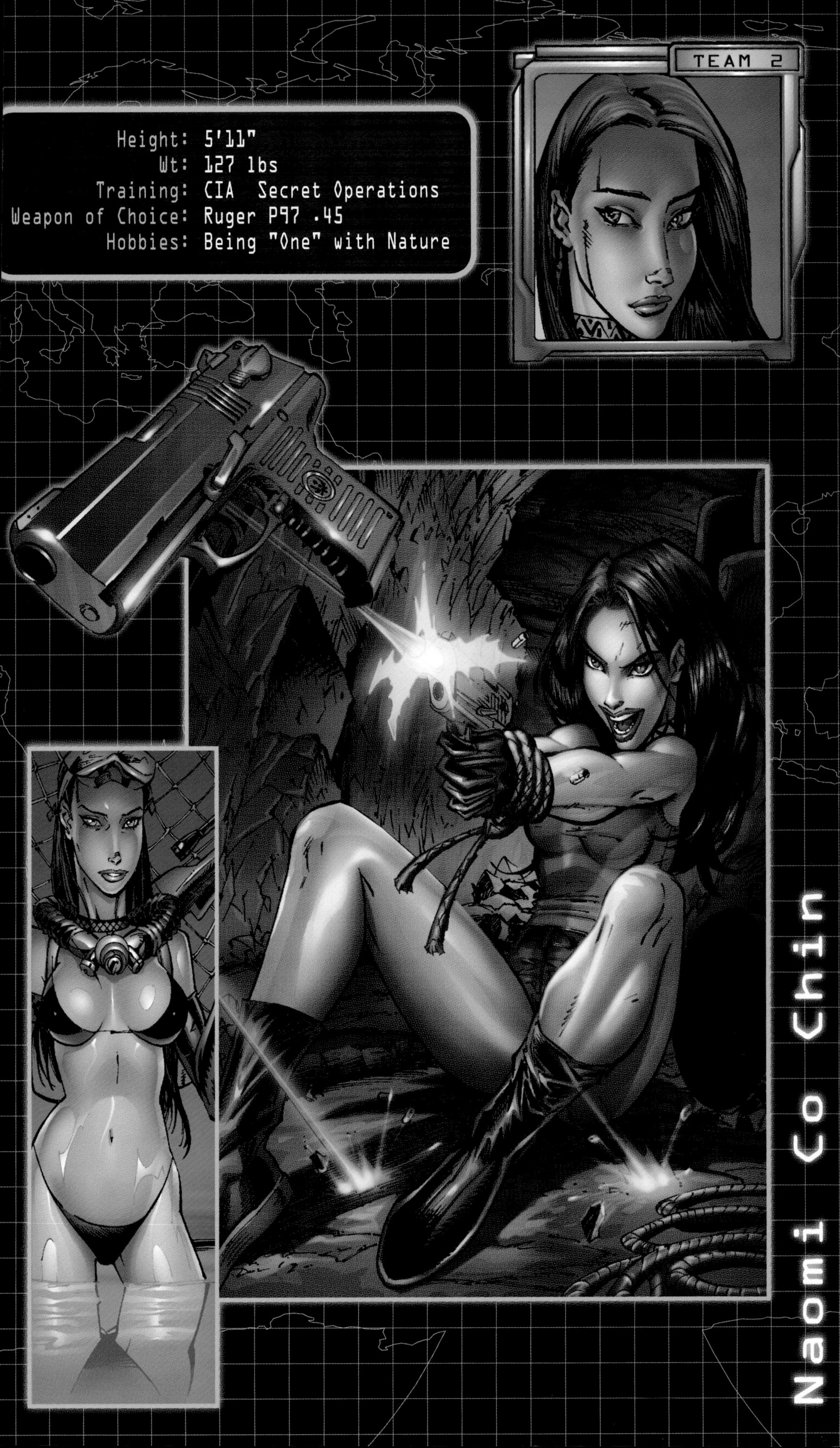
TEAM 2
Height: 5'11"
Wt: 127 lbs
Training: CIA Secret Operations
Weapon of Choice: Ruger P97 .45
Hobbies: Being "One" with Nature
Naomi Co Chin

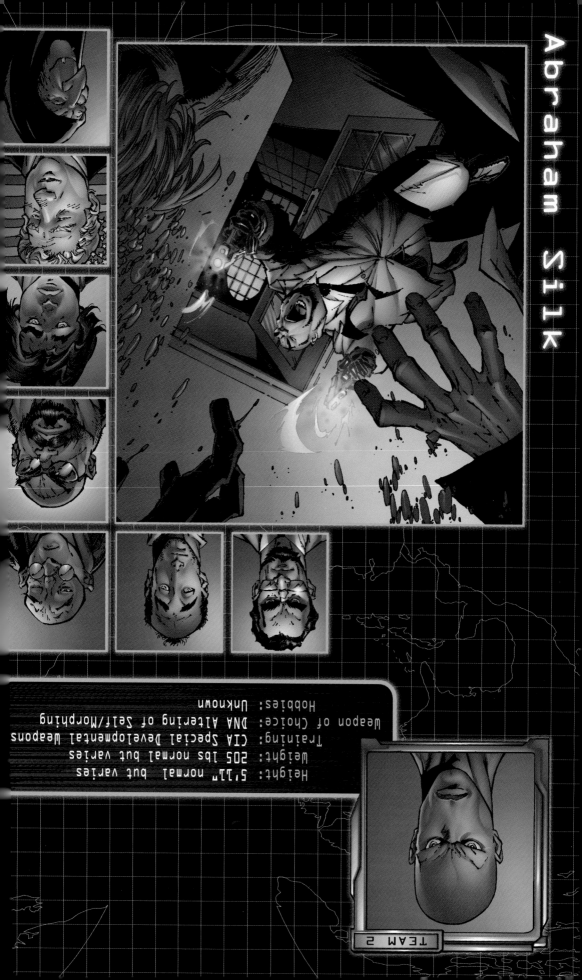

Abraham Silk

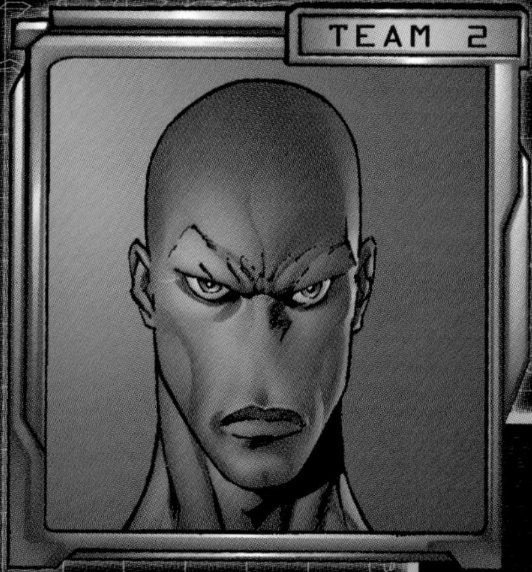
TEAM 2

Height: 5'11" normal but varies
Weight: 205 lbs normal but varies
Training: CIA Special Developmental Weapons
Weapon of Choice: DNA Altering of Self/Morphing
Hobbies: Unknown

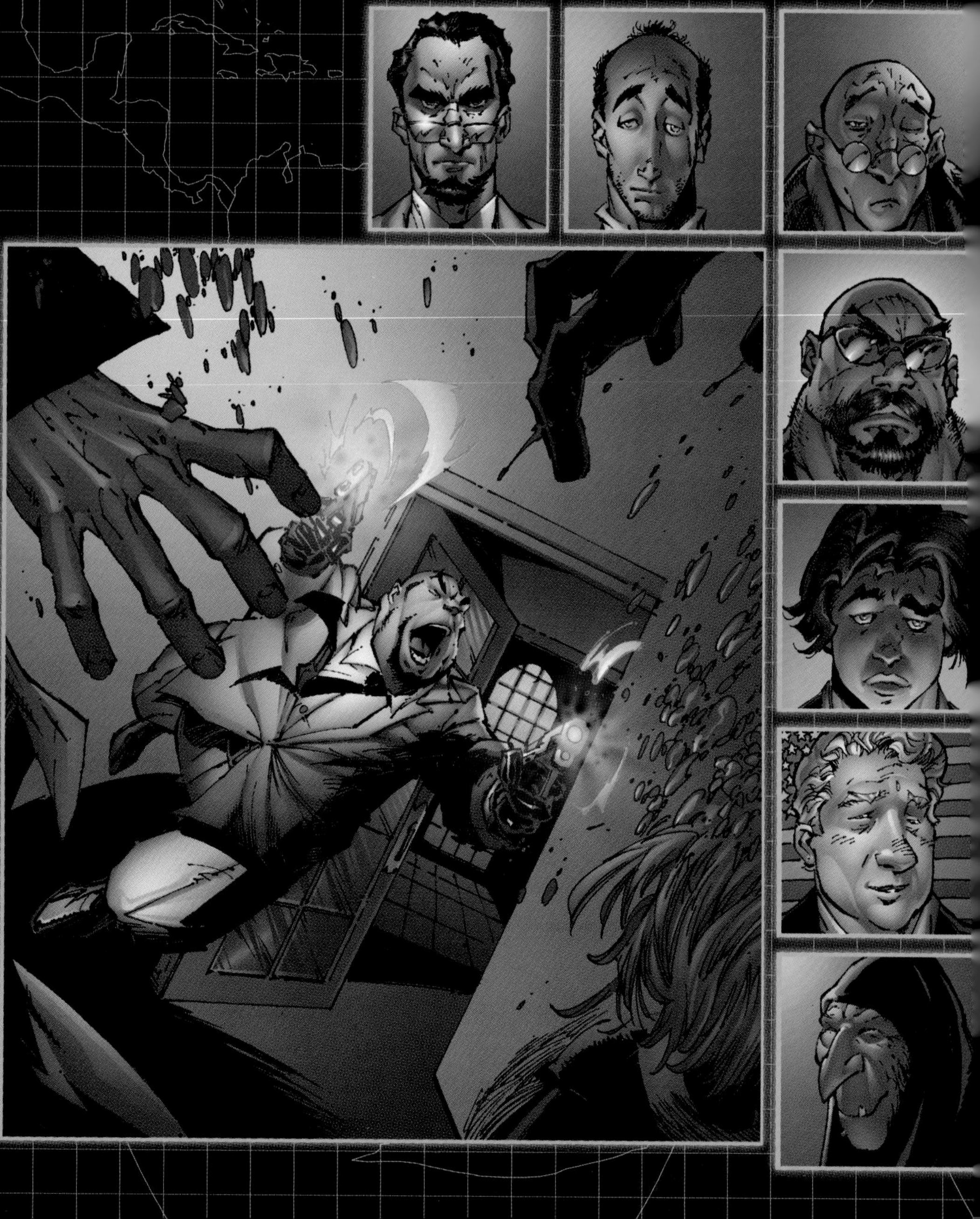

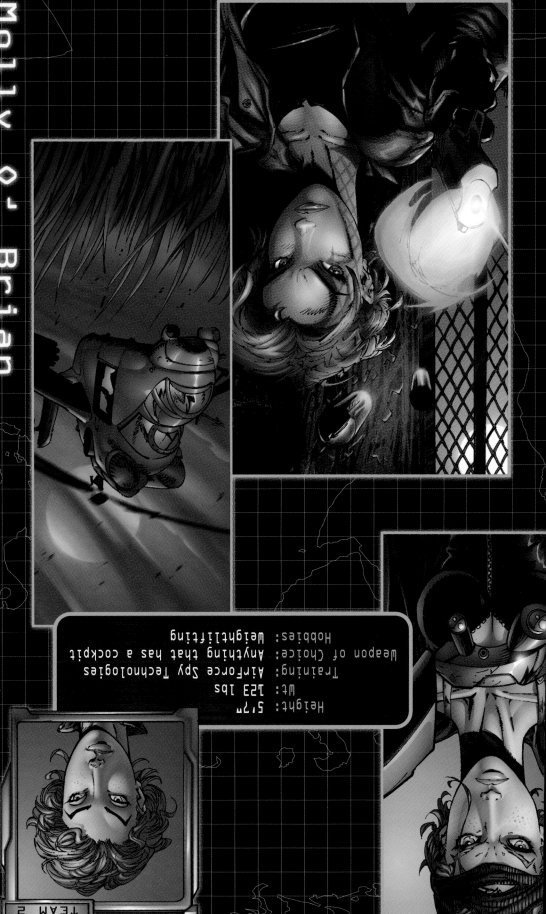

Molly & Brian

Height: 5'7"
Wt: 123 lbs
Training: Airforce Spy Technologies
Weapon of Choice: Anything that has a cockpit
Hobbies: Weightlifting

TEAM 2

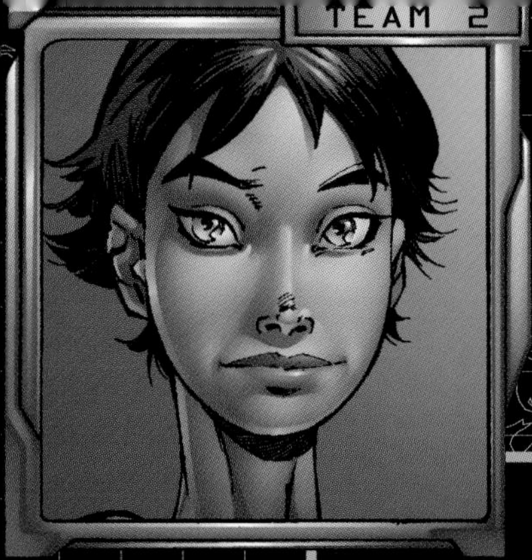
TEAM 2

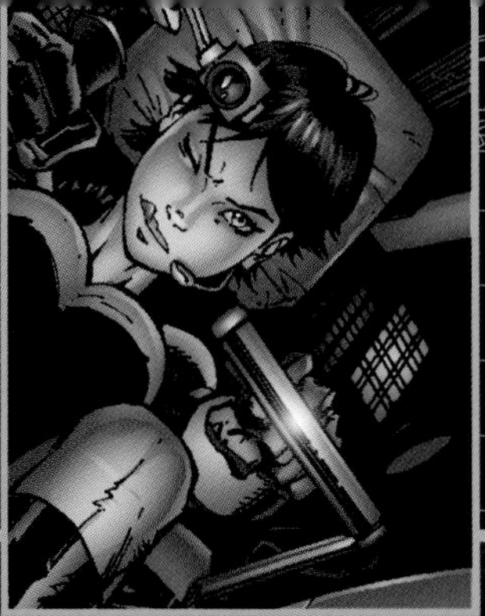

Height: 5'1"
Wt: 97 lbs
Training: AirForce Surviellance and Technical
Special Equipment: Any tool
Hobbies: Surfing in Hawaii

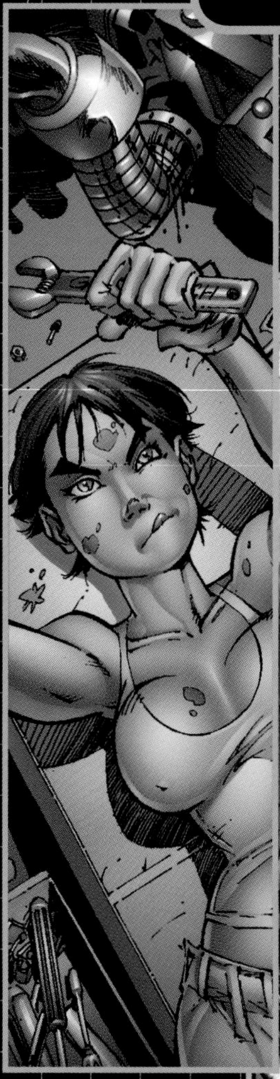

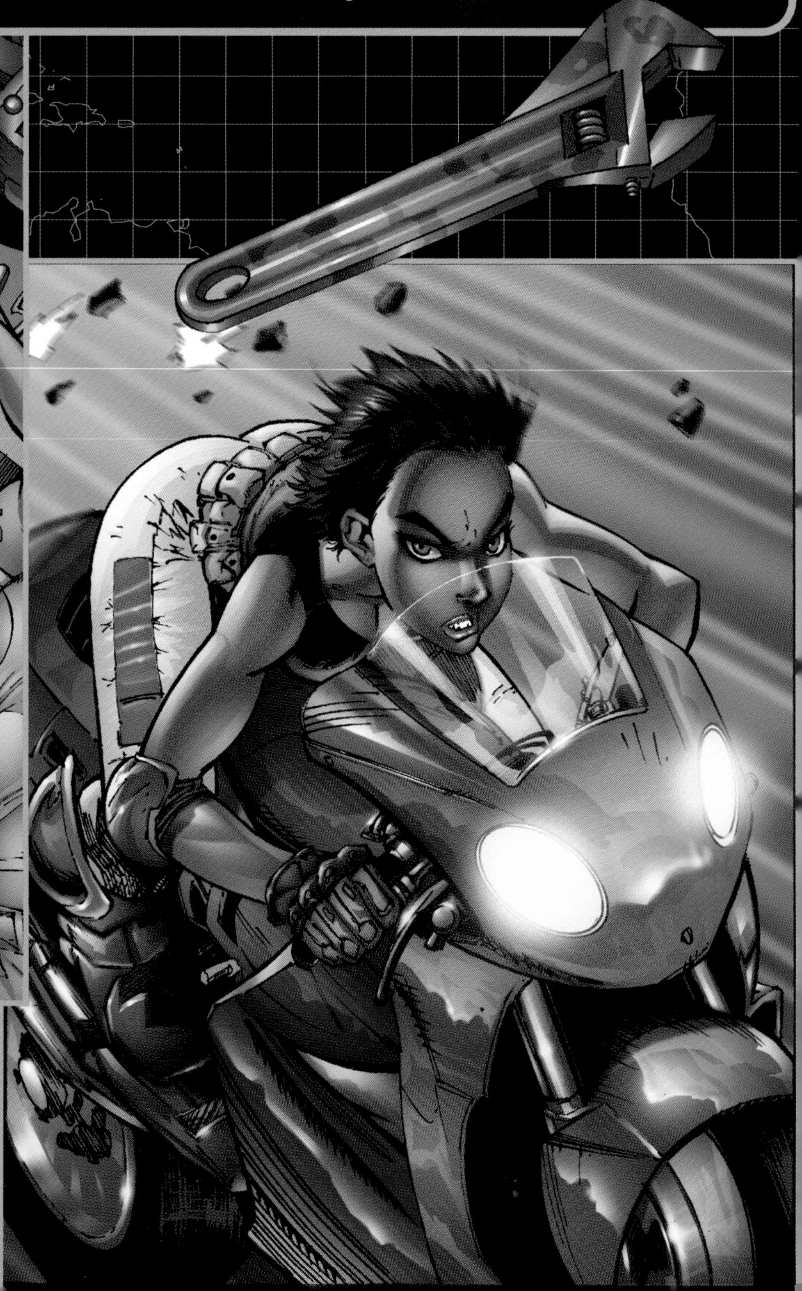

chapter two

FIRE AND ICE

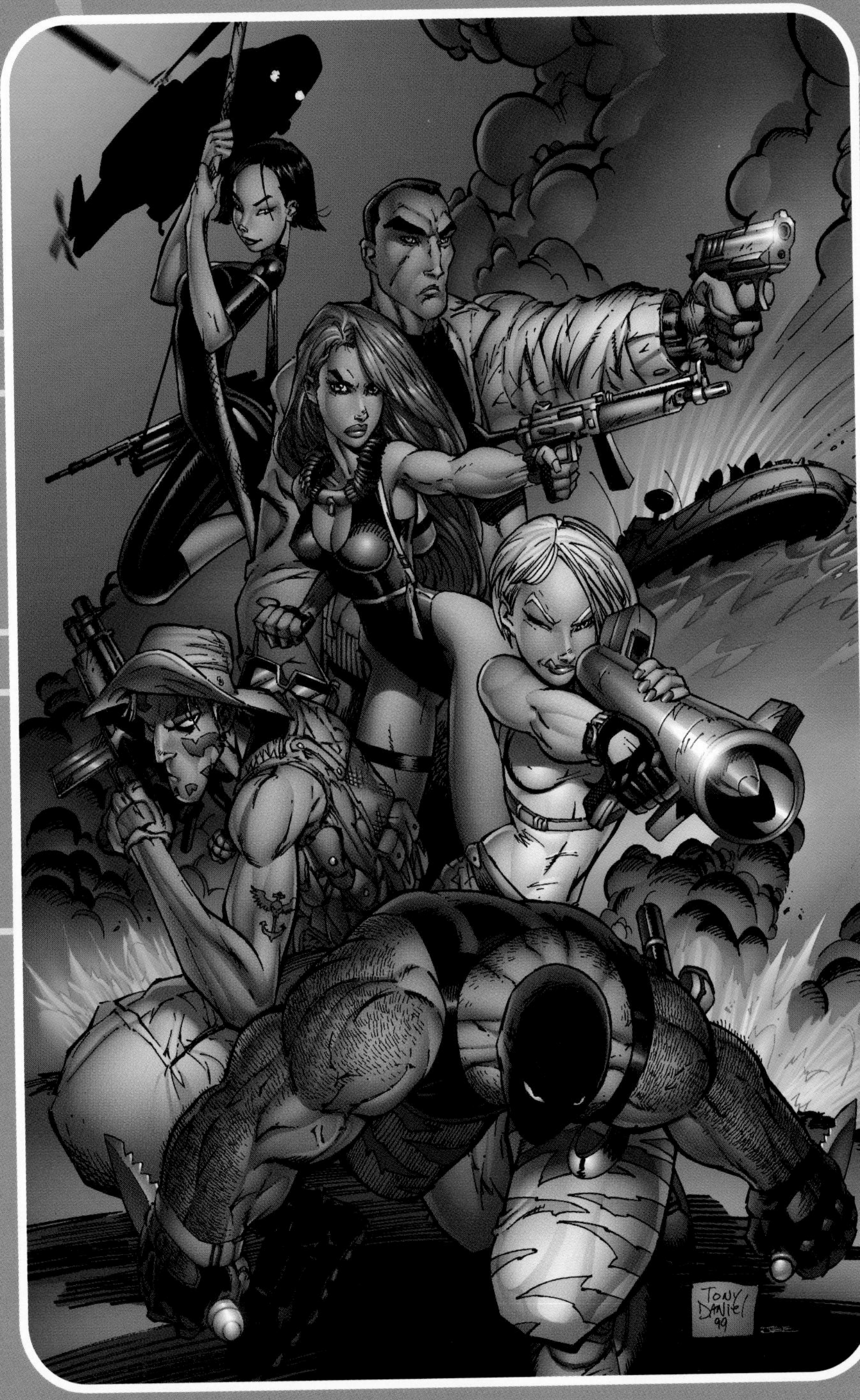
TONY DANIEL 99

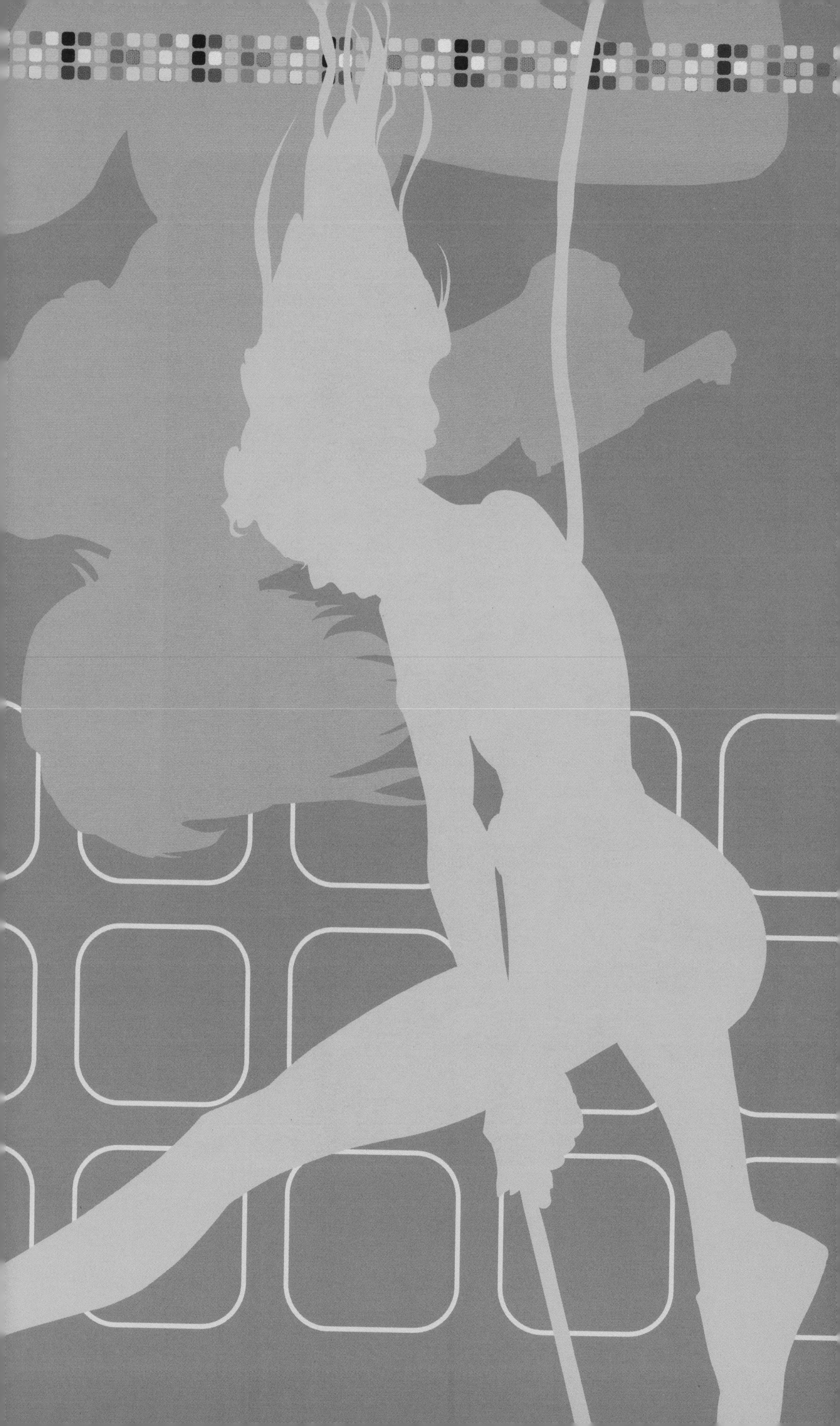

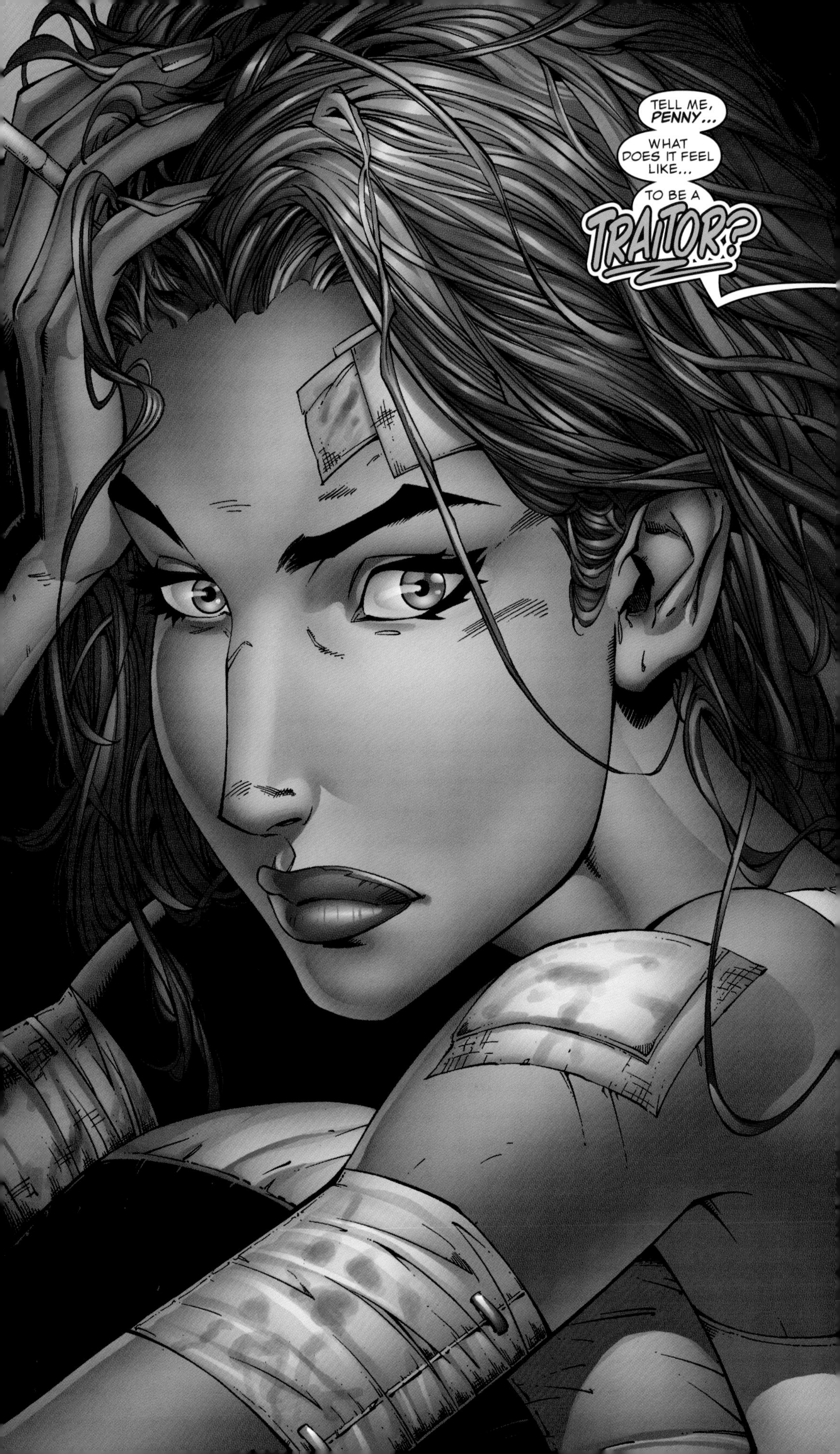
TELL ME, PENNY...
WHAT DOES IT FEEL LIKE...
TO BE A TRAITOR?

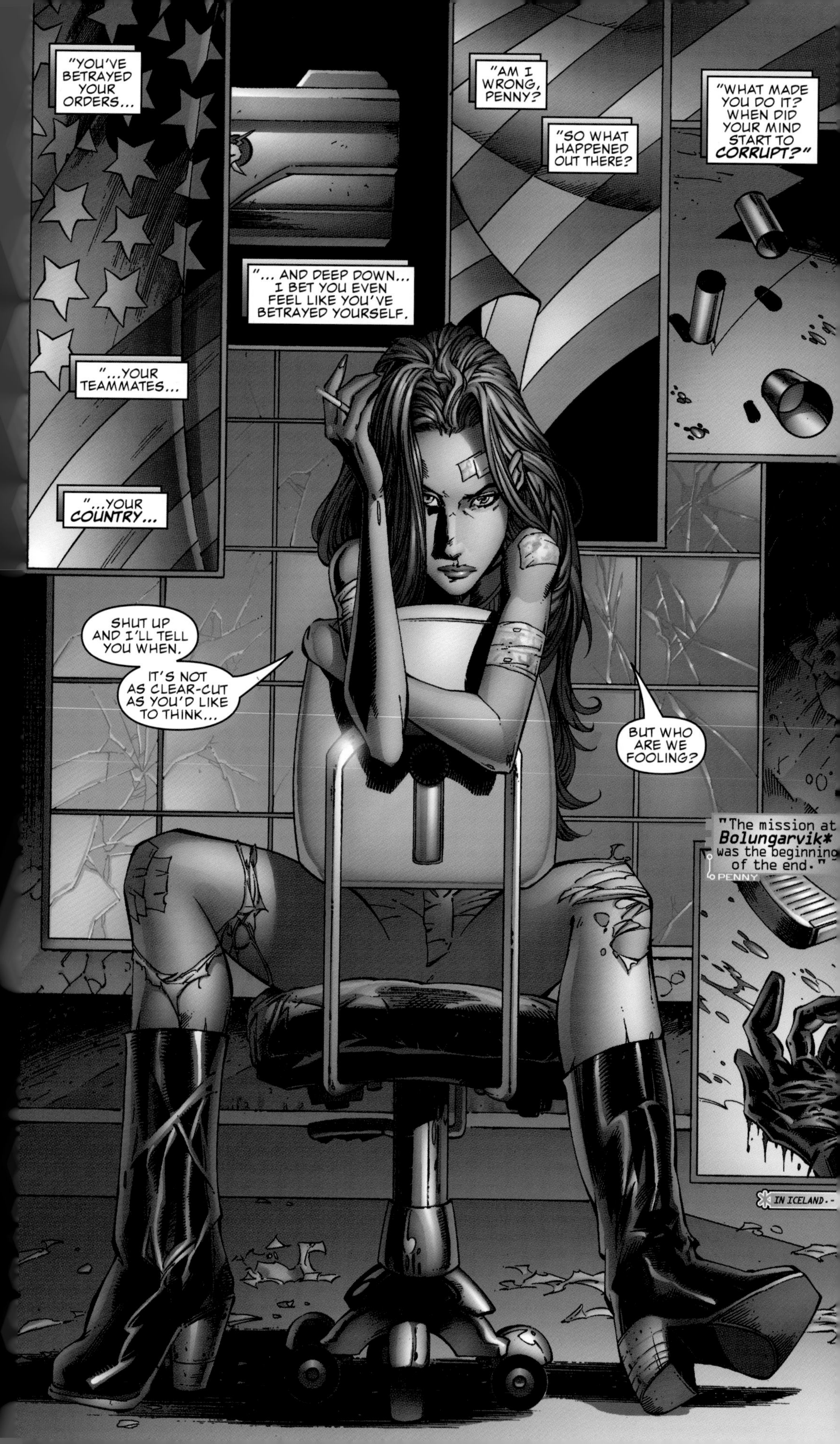
"YOU'VE BETRAYED YOUR ORDERS...
"...YOUR TEAMMATES...
"...YOUR COUNTRY...
"AM I WRONG, PENNY?
"SO WHAT HAPPENED OUT THERE?
"... AND DEEP DOWN... I BET YOU EVEN FEEL LIKE YOU'VE BETRAYED YOURSELF.
"WHAT MADE YOU DO IT? WHEN DID YOUR MIND START TO CORRUPT?"
SHUT UP AND I'LL TELL YOU WHEN.
IT'S NOT AS CLEAR-CUT AS YOU'D LIKE TO THINK...
BUT WHO ARE WE FOOLING?
"The mission at Bolungarvik* was the beginning of the end."
PENNY
* IN ICELAND.-

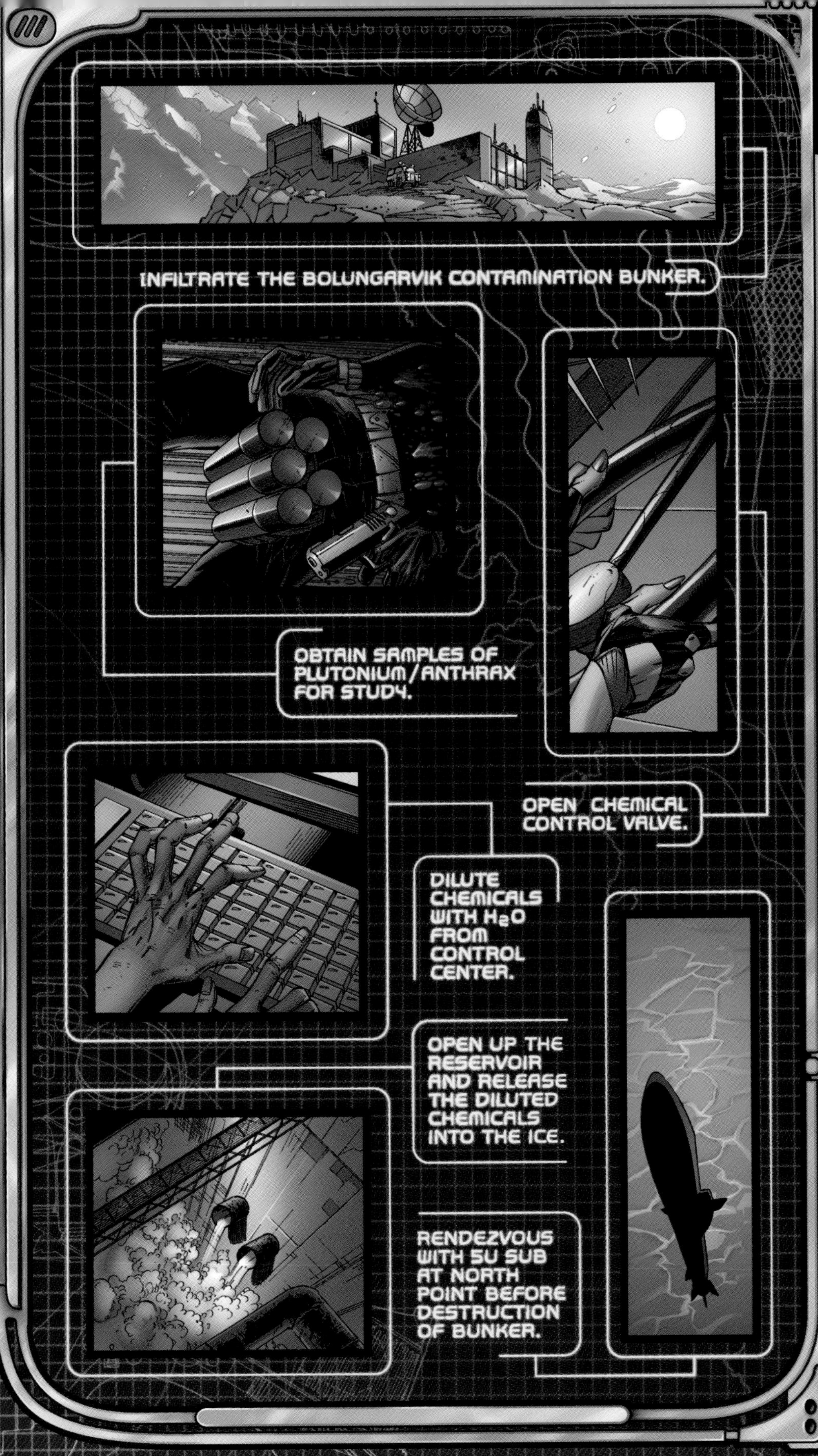
INFILTRATE THE BOLUNGARVIK CONTAMINATION BUNKER.
OBTAIN SAMPLES OF PLUTONIUM/ANTHRAX FOR STUDY.
OPEN CHEMICAL CONTROL VALVE.
DILUTE CHEMICALS WITH H2O FROM CONTROL CENTER.
OPEN UP THE RESERVOIR AND RELEASE THE DILUTED CHEMICALS INTO THE ICE.
RENDEZVOUS WITH SU SUB AT NORTH POINT BEFORE DESTRUCTION OF BUNKER.

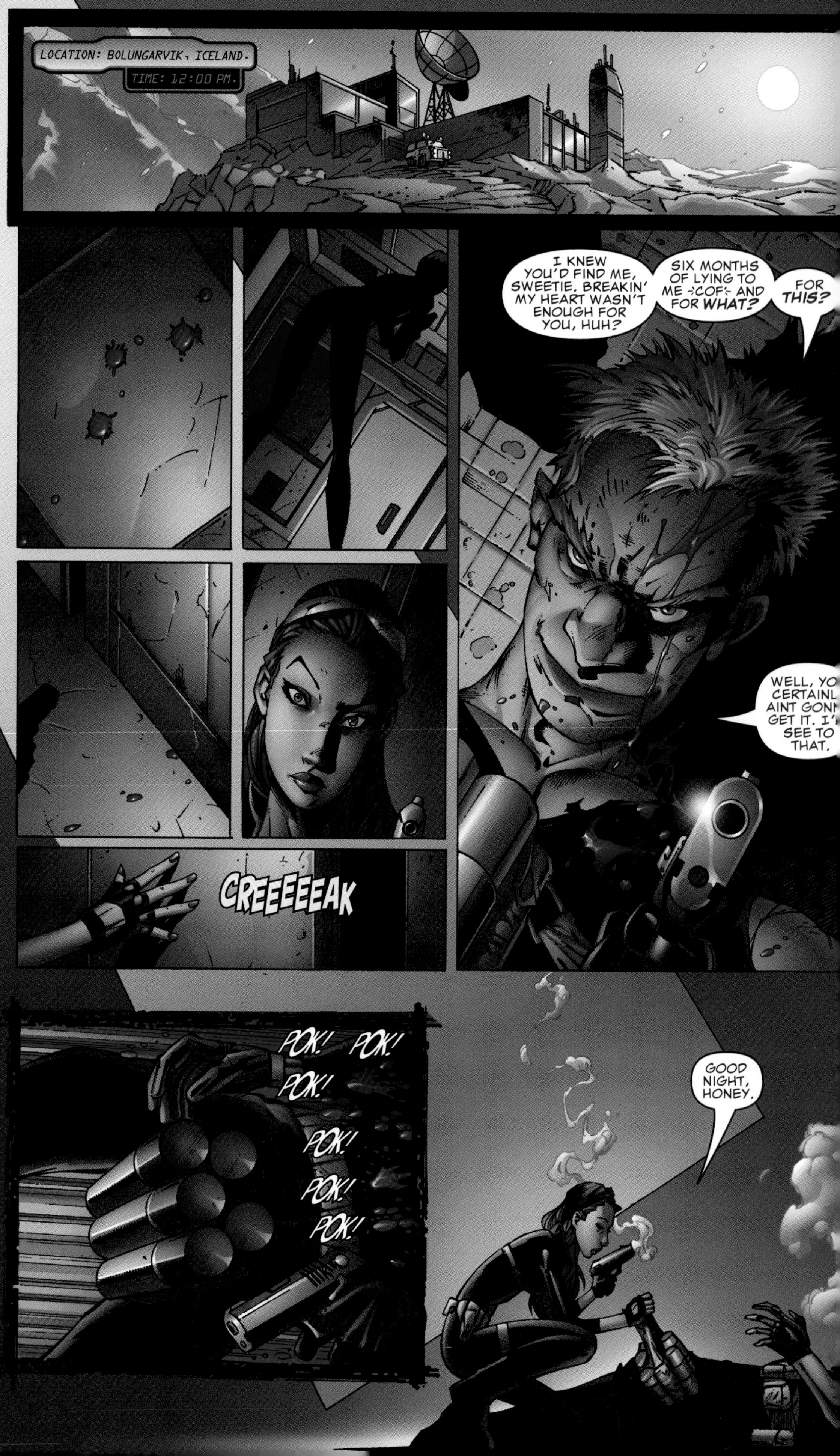

LOCATION: BOLUNGARVIK, ICELAND.
TIME: 12:00 PM.
I KNEW YOU'D FIND ME, SWEETIE. BREAKIN' MY HEART WASN'T ENOUGH FOR YOU, HUH?
SIX MONTHS OF LYING TO ME -COF- AND FOR WHAT?
FOR THIS?
WELL, YO CERTAINL AINT GONN GET IT. I' SEE TO THAT.
CREEEEEAK
POK! POK!
POK!
POK!
POK!
POK!
GOOD NIGHT, HONEY.

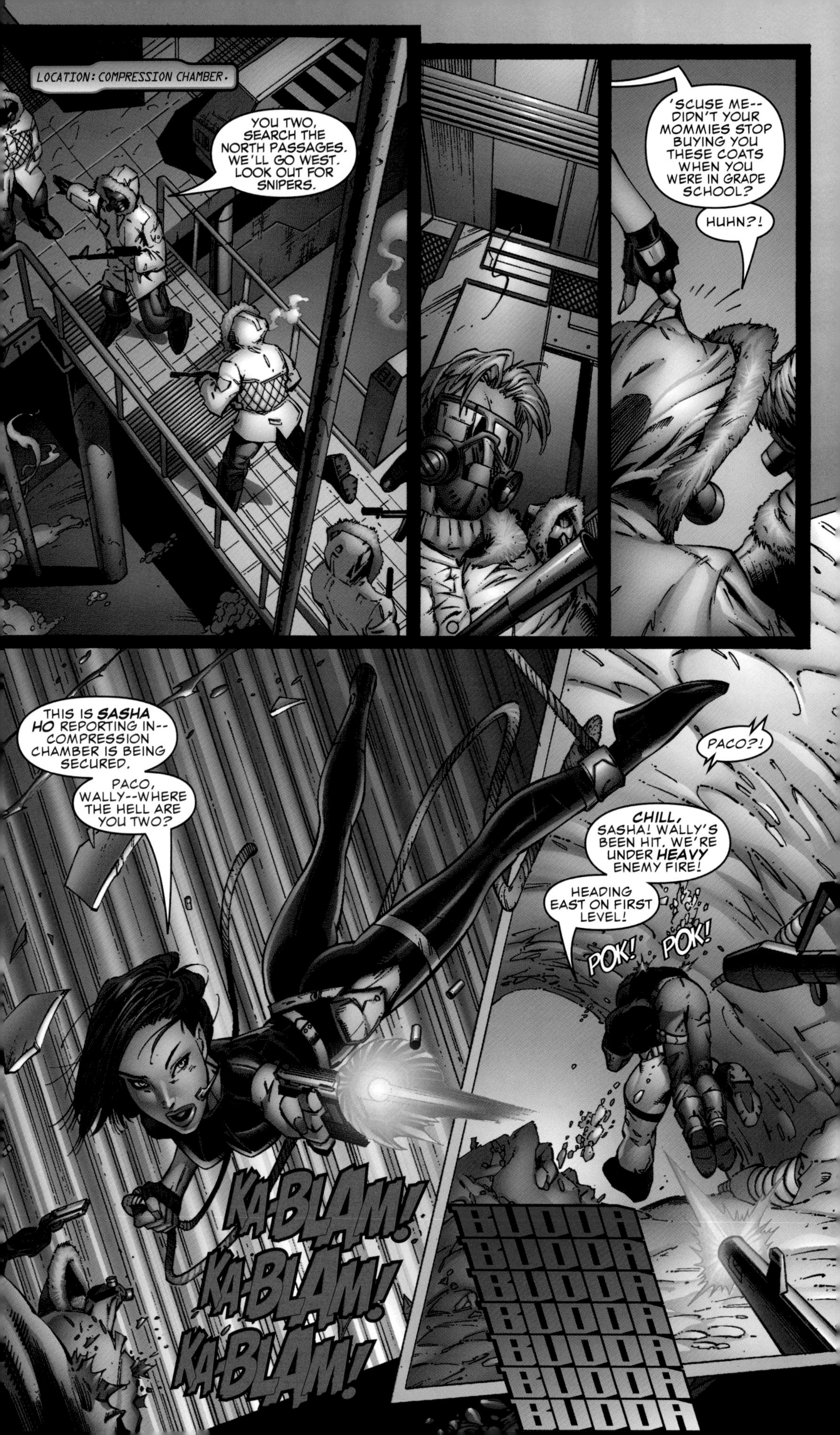
LOCATION: COMPRESSION CHAMBER.
YOU TWO, SEARCH THE NORTH PASSAGES. WE'LL GO WEST. LOOK OUT FOR SNIPERS.
'SCUSE ME-- DIDN'T YOUR MOMMIES STOP BUYING YOU THESE COATS WHEN YOU WERE IN GRADE SCHOOL?
HUHN?!
THIS IS SASHA HO REPORTING IN-- COMPRESSION CHAMBER IS BEING SECURED.
PACO, WALLY--WHERE THE HELL ARE YOU TWO?
PACO?!
CHILL, SASHA! WALLY'S BEEN HIT, WE'RE UNDER HEAVY ENEMY FIRE!
HEADING EAST ON FIRST LEVEL!
POK! POK!
KA-BLAM! KA-BLAM! KA-BLAM!
BUDDA BUDDA BUDDA BUDDA BUDDA BUDDA BUDDA

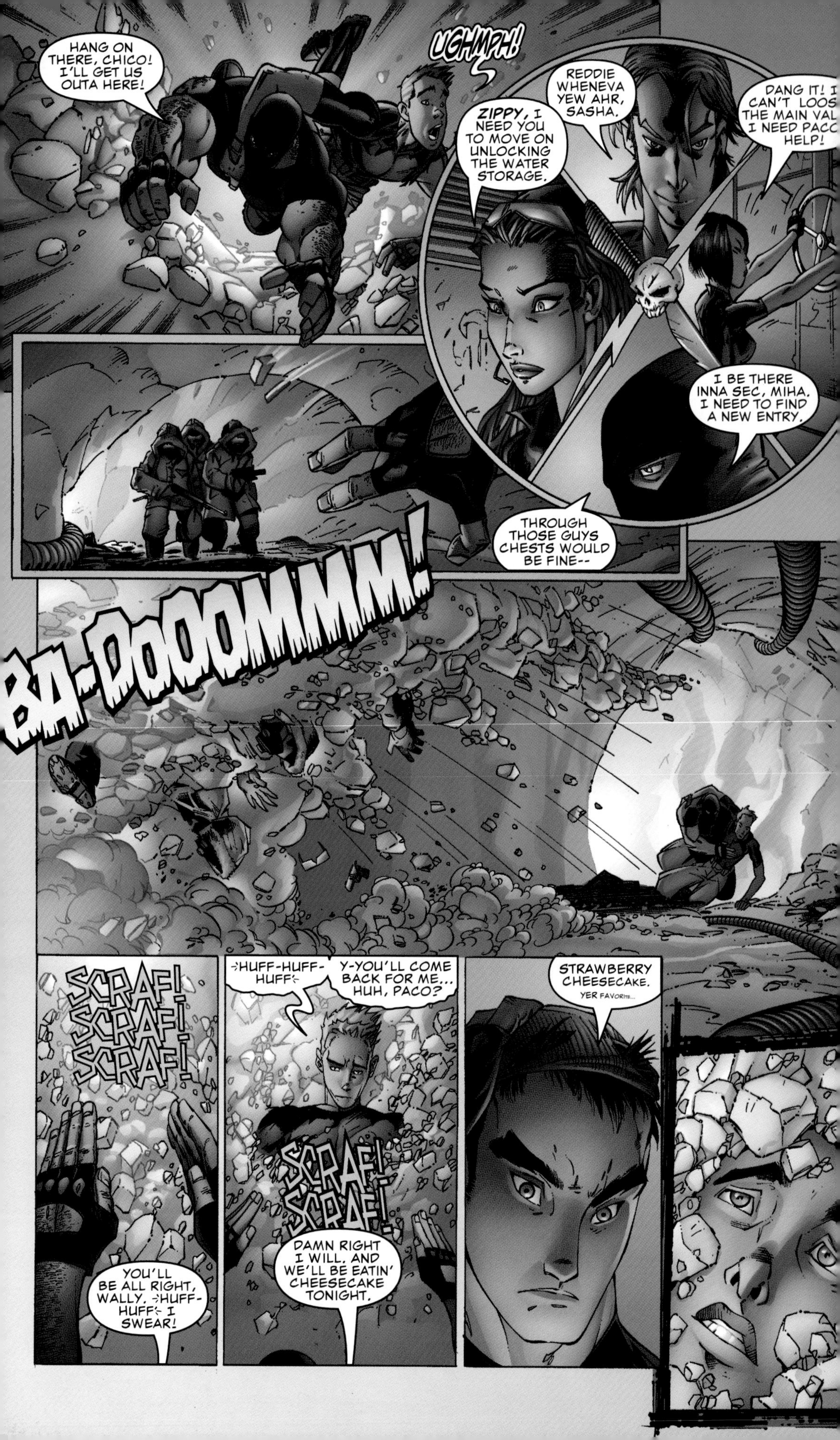
HANG ON THERE, CHICO! I'LL GET US OUTA HERE!
UGHMPH!
ZIPPY, I NEED YOU TO MOVE ON UNLOCKING THE WATER STORAGE.
REDDIE WHENEVA YEW AHR, SASHA.
DANG IT! I CAN'T LOOS THE MAIN VAL I NEED PACO HELP!
I BE THERE INNA SEC, MIHA. I NEED TO FIND A NEW ENTRY.
THROUGH THOSE GUYS CHESTS WOULD BE FINE--
BA-DOOOMMM!
SCRAF! SCRAF! SCRAF!
YOU'LL BE ALL RIGHT, WALLY. ⇒HUFF-HUFF⇐ I SWEAR!
⇒HUFF-HUFF-HUFF⇐
Y-YOU'LL COME BACK FOR ME... HUH, PACO?
SCRAF! SCRAF!
DAMN RIGHT I WILL. AND WE'LL BE EATIN' CHEESECAKE TONIGHT.
STRAWBERRY CHEESECAKE.
YER FAVORITE...

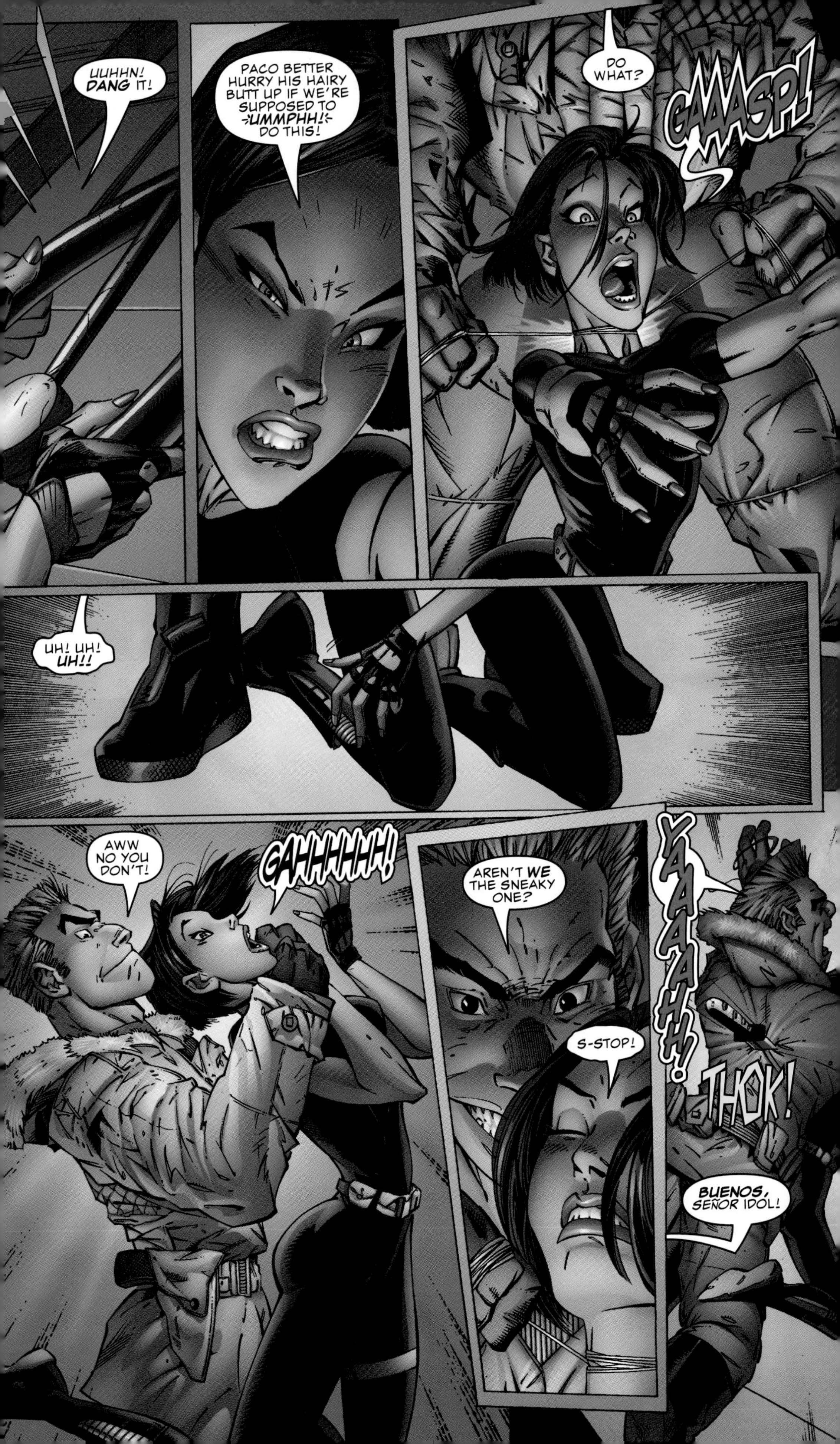
UUHHN! DANG IT!
PACO BETTER HURRY HIS HAIRY BUTT UP IF WE'RE SUPPOSED TO -UMMPHH!- DO THIS!
DO WHAT?
GAAASP!
UH! UH! UH!!
AWW NO YOU DON'T!
GAHHHHH!
AREN'T WE THE SNEAKY ONE?
S-STOP!
YAAAAHH!
THOK!
BUENOS, SEÑOR IDOL!

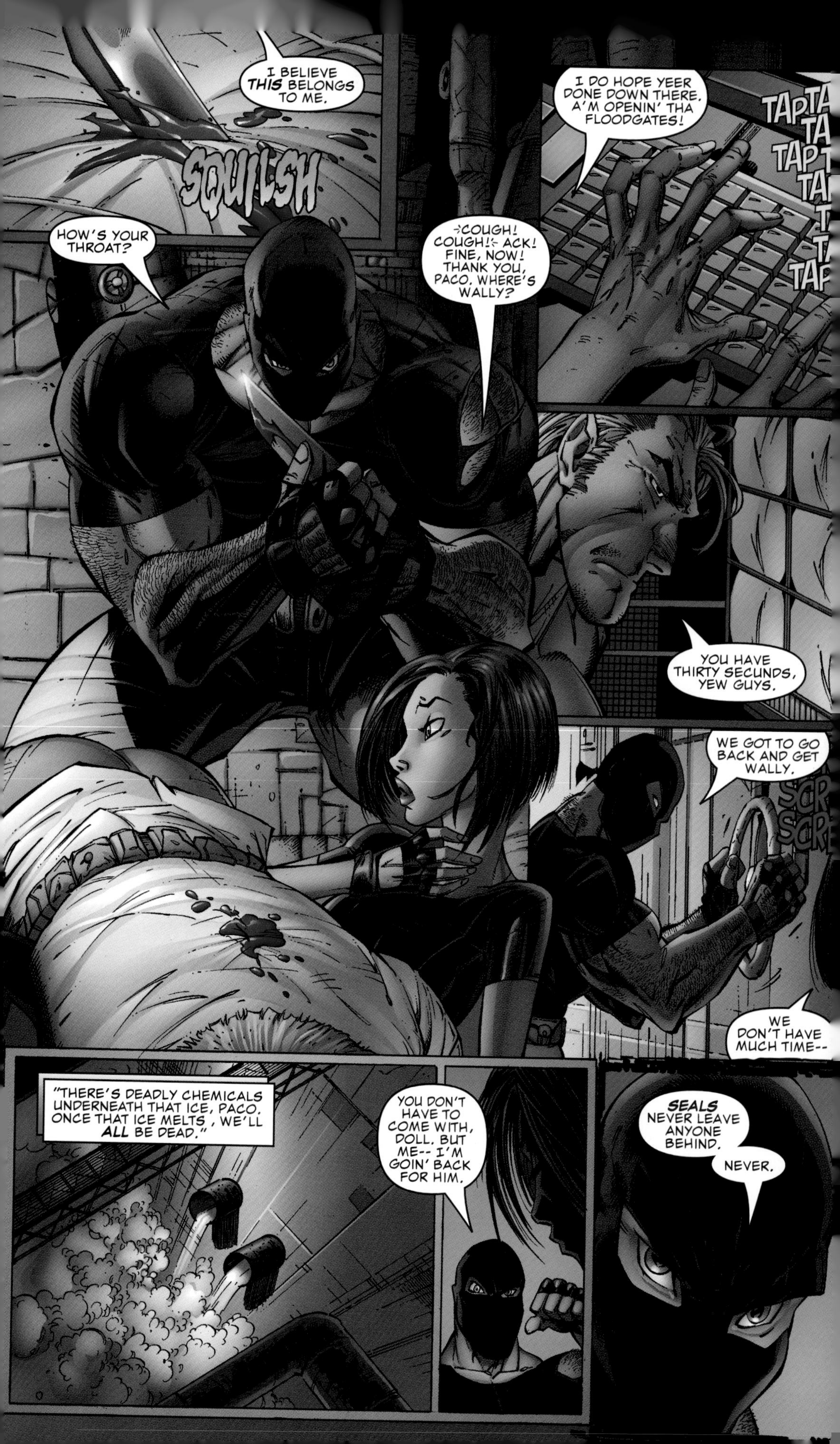
I BELIEVE **THIS** BELONGS TO ME.
SQUILSH
HOW'S YOUR THROAT?
I DO HOPE YEER DONE DOWN THERE. A'M OPENIN' THA FLOODGATES!
TAPTA TA TAP T TA T T TAP
-:-COUGH! COUGH!-:- ACK! FINE, NOW! THANK YOU, PACO. WHERE'S WALLY?
YOU HAVE THIRTY SECUNDS, YEW GUYS.
WE GOT TO GO BACK AND GET WALLY.
SCR SCR
WE DON'T HAVE MUCH TIME--
"THERE'S DEADLY CHEMICALS UNDERNEATH THAT ICE, PACO. ONCE THAT ICE MELTS, WE'LL **ALL** BE DEAD."
YOU DON'T HAVE TO COME WITH, DOLL. BUT ME-- I'M GOIN' BACK FOR HIM.
SEALS NEVER LEAVE ANYONE BEHIND.
NEVER.

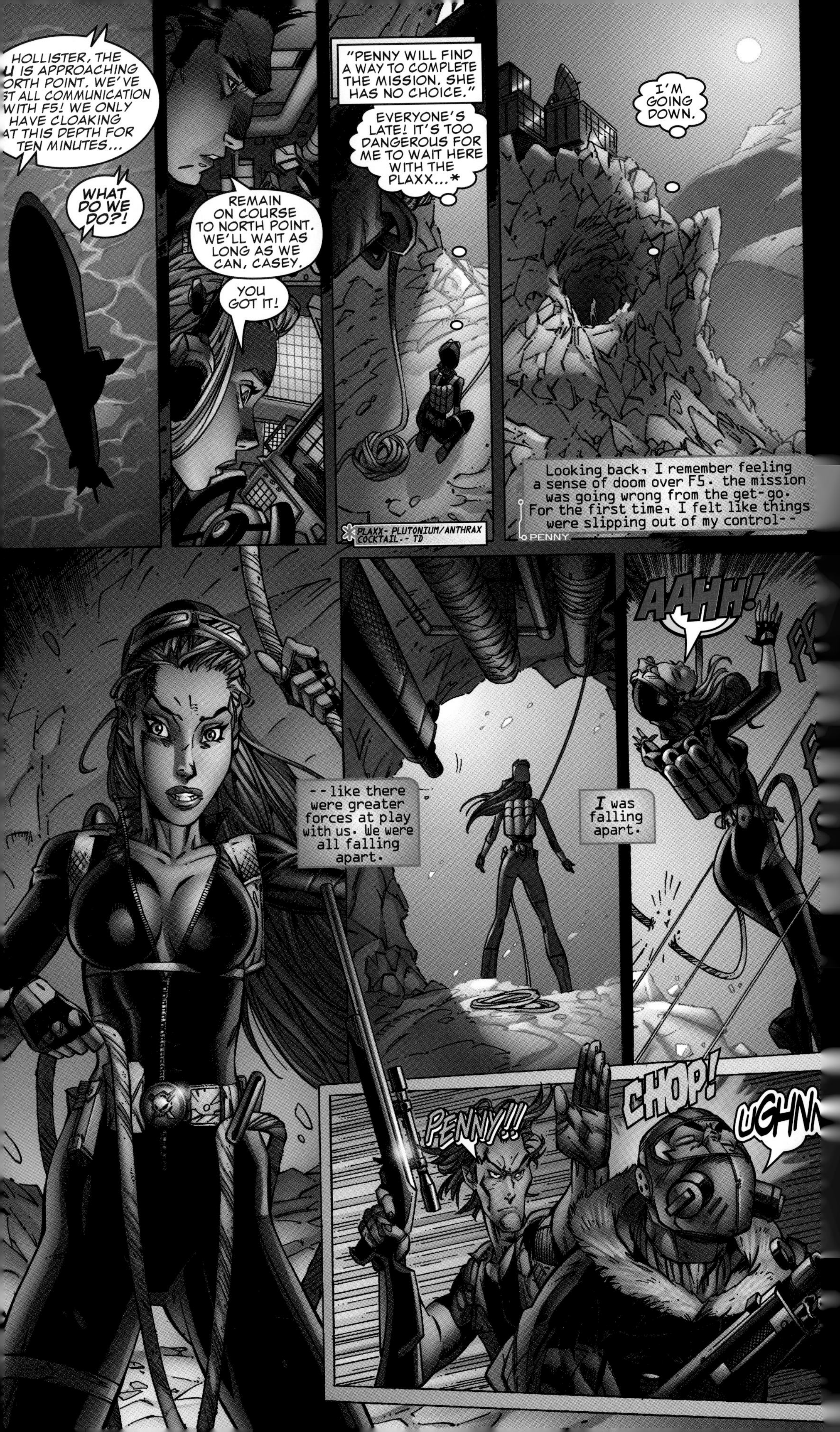
HOLLISTER, THE
U IS APPROACHING
ORTH POINT. WE'VE
ST ALL COMMUNICATION
WITH F5! WE ONLY
HAVE CLOAKING
AT THIS DEPTH FOR
TEN MINUTES...
WHAT DO WE DO?!
REMAIN ON COURSE TO NORTH POINT. WE'LL WAIT AS LONG AS WE CAN, CASEY.
YOU GOT IT!
"PENNY WILL FIND A WAY TO COMPLETE THE MISSION. SHE HAS NO CHOICE."
EVERYONE'S LATE! IT'S TOO DANGEROUS FOR ME TO WAIT HERE WITH THE PLAXX...*
*PLAXX- PLUTONIUM/ANTHRAX COCKTAIL.- TD
I'M GOING DOWN.
Looking back, I remember feeling a sense of doom over F5. the mission was going wrong from the get-go. For the first time, I felt like things were slipping out of my control--
PENNY
--like there were greater forces at play with us. We were all falling apart.
I was falling apart.
AAHH!
PENNY!!
CHOP!
UGHN

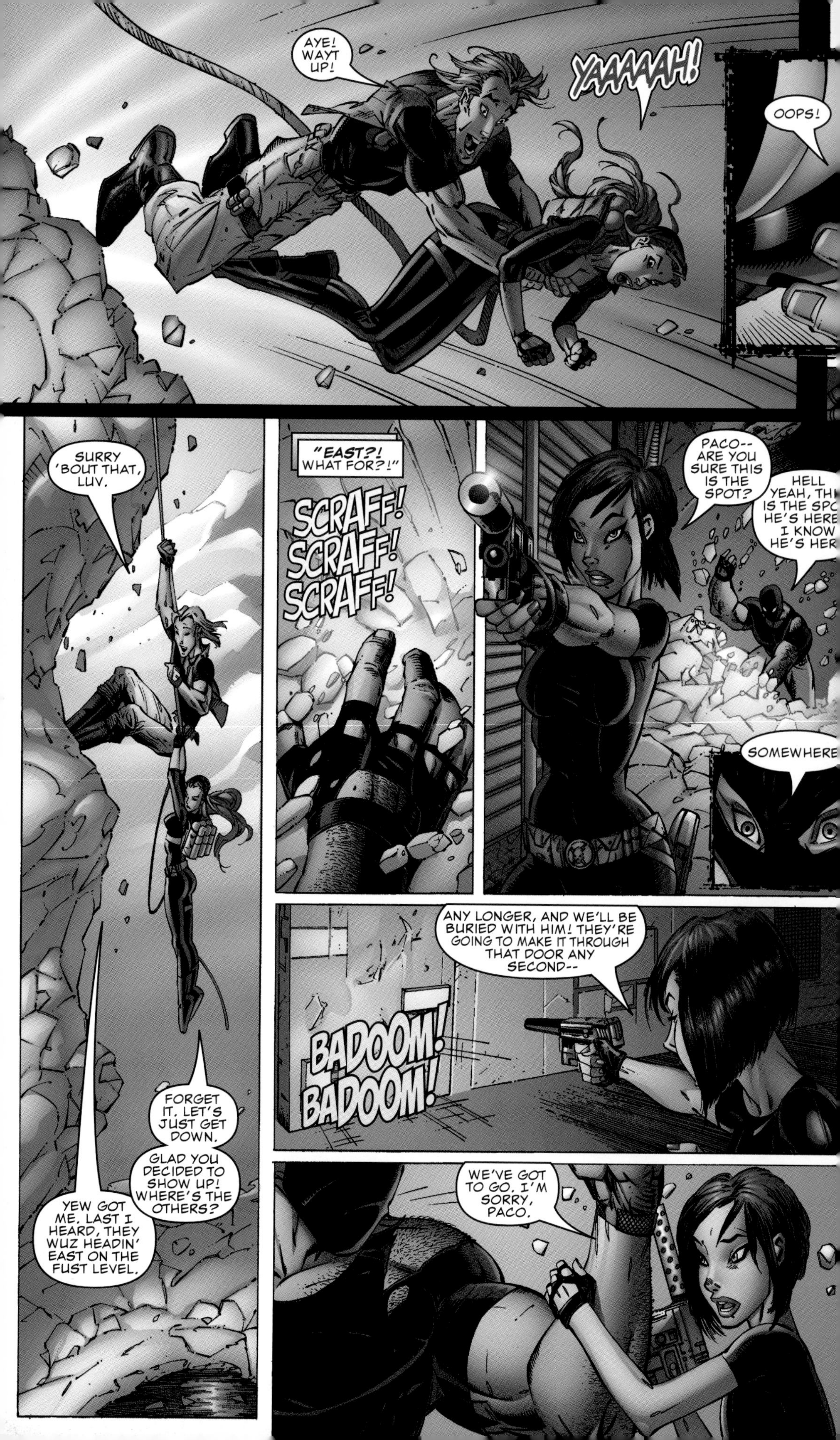
AYE! WAYT UP!
YAAAAAH!
OOPS!
SURRY 'BOUT THAT, LUV.
"EAST?! WHAT FOR?!"
SCRAFF! SCRAFF! SCRAFF!
PACO-- ARE YOU SURE THIS IS THE SPOT?
HELL YEAH, THI IS THE SPO HE'S HERE I KNOW HE'S HER
SOMEWHERE
FORGET IT. LET'S JUST GET DOWN.
GLAD YOU DECIDED TO SHOW UP! WHERE'S THE OTHERS?
YEW GOT ME. LAST I HEARD, THEY WUZ HEADIN' EAST ON THE FUST LEVEL.
ANY LONGER, AND WE'LL BE BURIED WITH HIM! THEY'RE GOING TO MAKE IT THROUGH THAT DOOR ANY SECOND--
BADOOM! BADOOM!
WE'VE GOT TO GO. I'M SORRY, PACO.

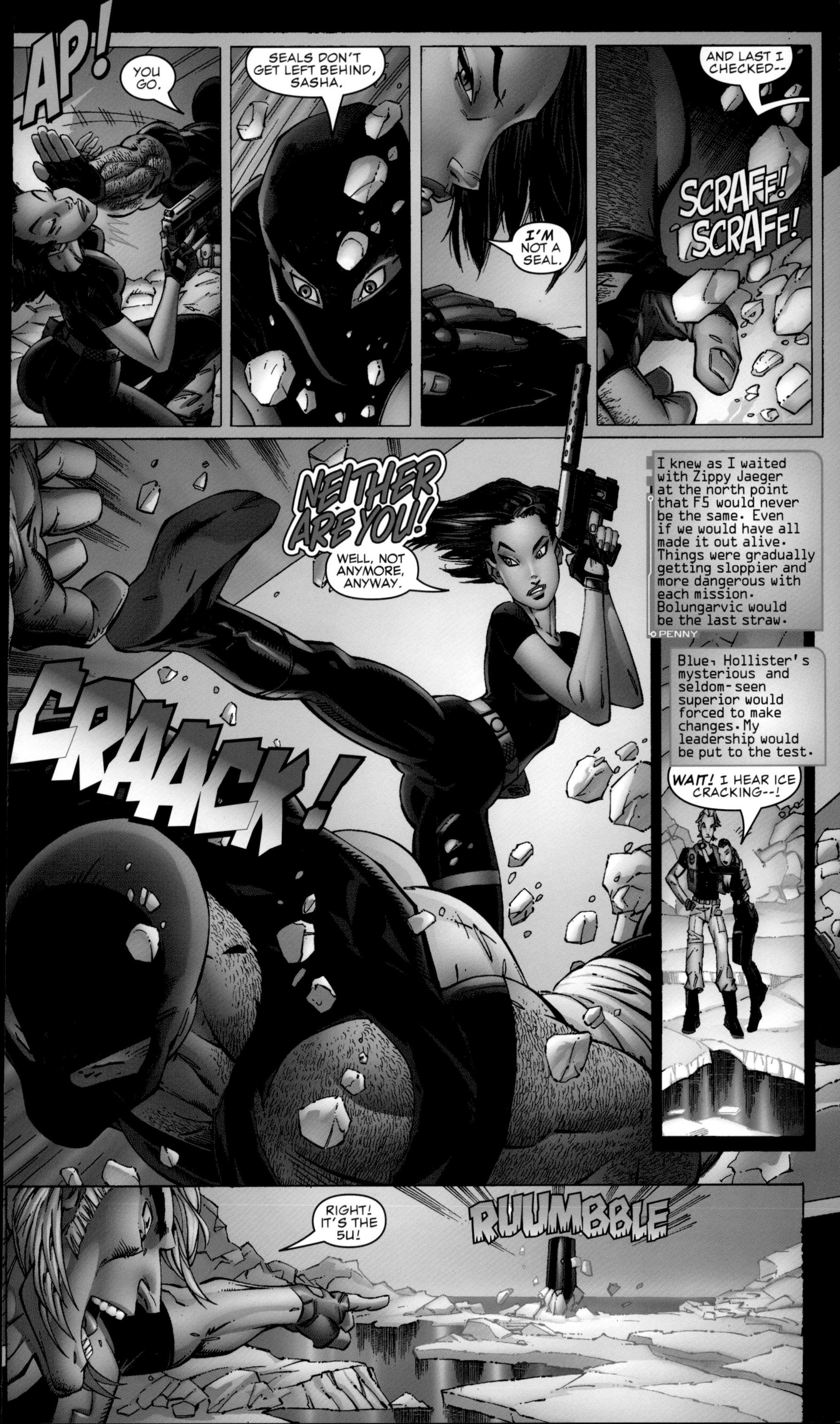

-AP!
YOU GO.
SEALS DON'T GET LEFT BEHIND, SASHA.
I'M NOT A SEAL.
AND LAST I CHECKED--
SCRAFF! SCRAFF!
NEITHER ARE YOU!
WELL, NOT ANYMORE, ANYWAY.
I knew as I waited with Zippy Jaeger at the north point that F5 would never be the same. Even if we would have all made it out alive. Things were gradually getting sloppier and more dangerous with each mission. Bolungarvic would be the last straw.
PENNY
Blue, Hollister's mysterious and seldom-seen superior would forced to make changes. My leadership would be put to the test.
CRAACK!
WAIT! I HEAR ICE CRACKING--!
RIGHT! IT'S THE 5U!
RUUMBBLE

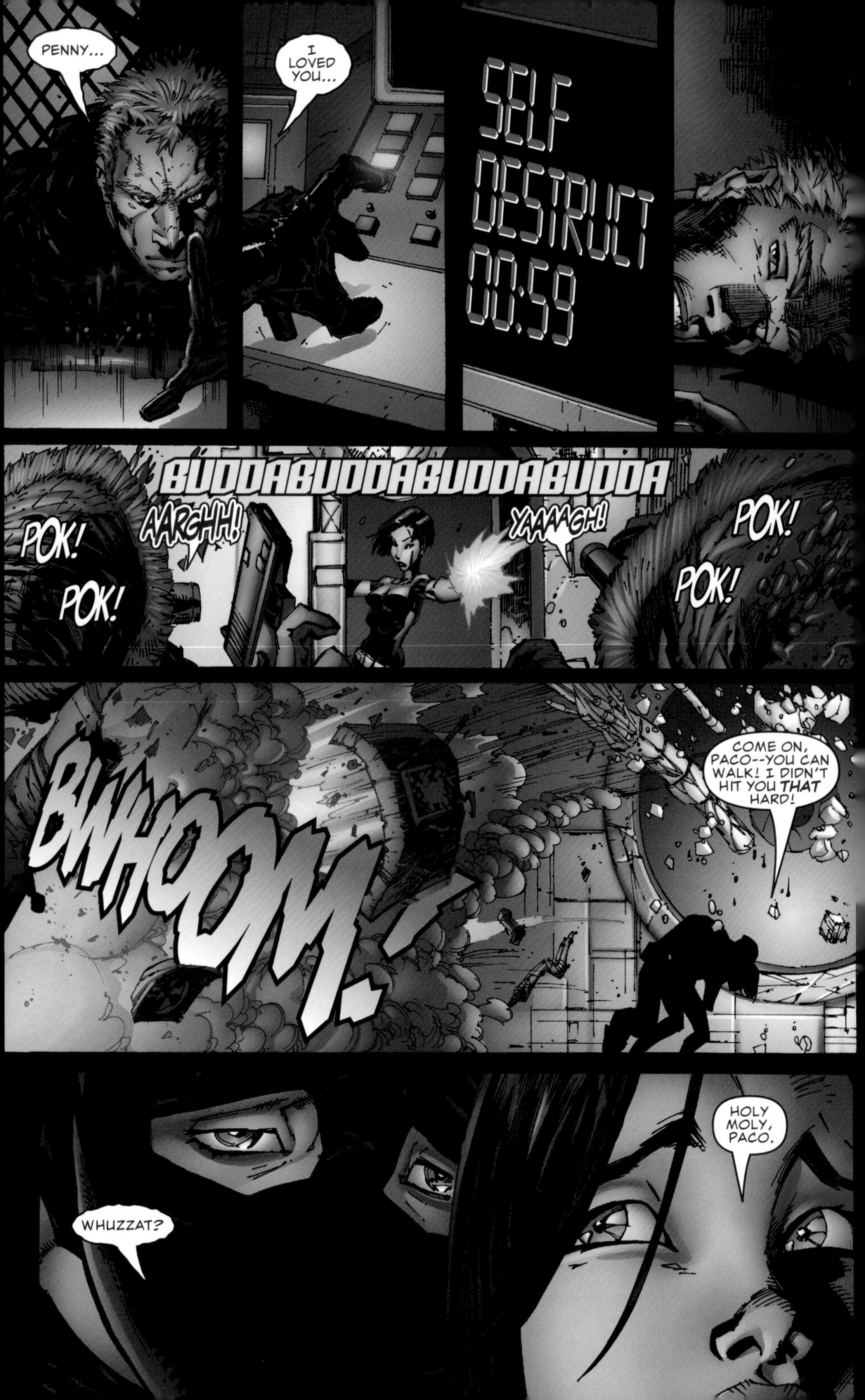
PENNY...
I LOVED YOU...
SELF DESTRUCT 00:59
BUDDABUDDABUDDABUDDA
POK!
POK!
AARGHH!
YAAAAGH!
POK!
POK!
BWHOOM!
COME ON, PACO--YOU CAN WALK! I DIDN'T HIT YOU **THAT** HARD!
HOLY MOLY, PACO.
WHUZZAT?

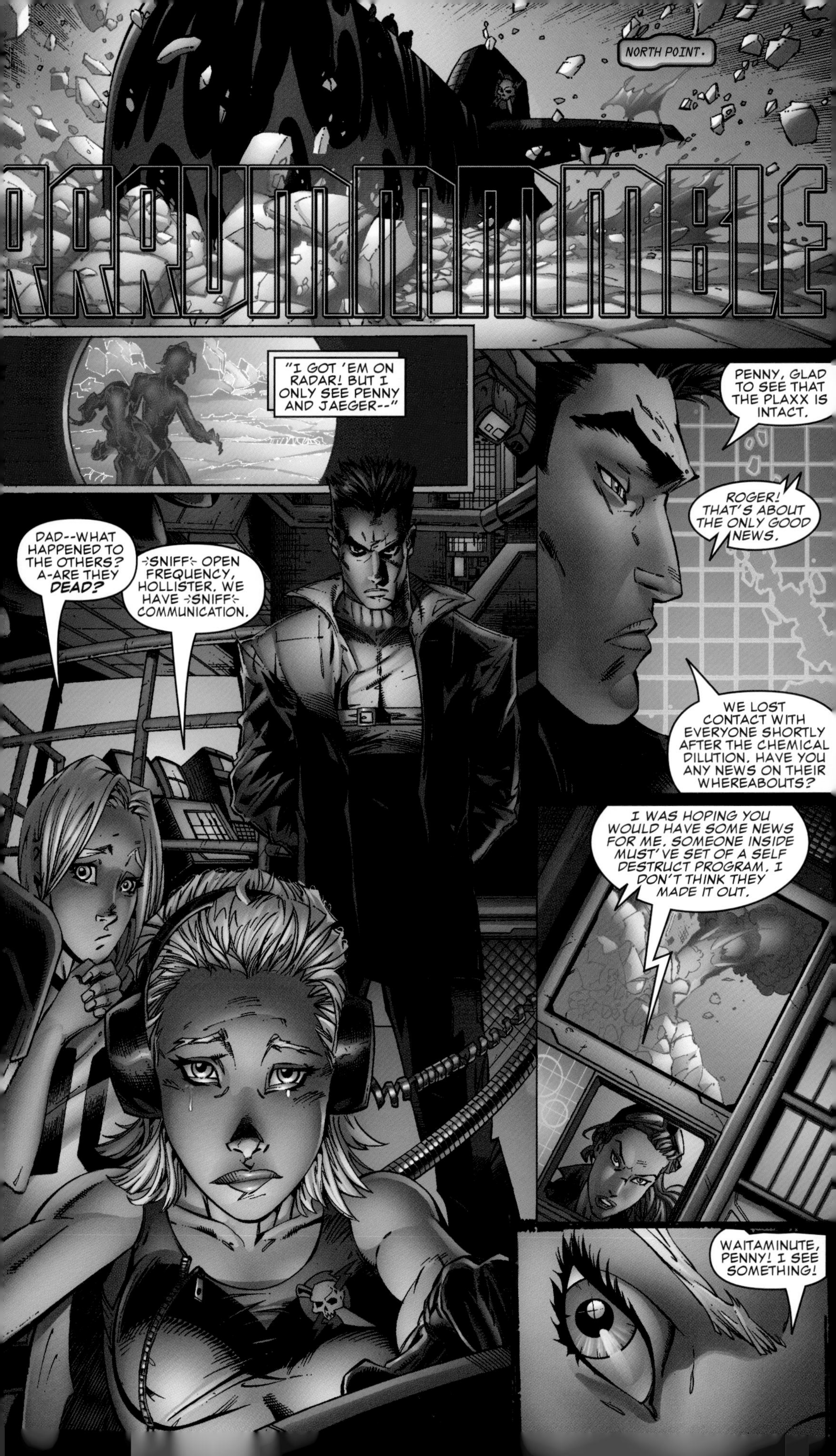
NORTH POINT.
RRRUMMMMBLE
"I GOT 'EM ON RADAR! BUT I ONLY SEE PENNY AND JAEGER--"
PENNY, GLAD TO SEE THAT THE PLAXX IS INTACT.
ROGER! THAT'S ABOUT THE ONLY GOOD NEWS.
DAD--WHAT HAPPENED TO THE OTHERS? A-ARE THEY DEAD?
-SNIFF- OPEN FREQUENCY, HOLLISTER. WE HAVE -SNIFF- COMMUNICATION.
WE LOST CONTACT WITH EVERYONE SHORTLY AFTER THE CHEMICAL DILUTION. HAVE YOU ANY NEWS ON THEIR WHEREABOUTS?
I WAS HOPING YOU WOULD HAVE SOME NEWS FOR ME. SOMEONE INSIDE MUST'VE SET OF A SELF DESTRUCT PROGRAM. I DON'T THINK THEY MADE IT OUT.
WAITAMINUTE, PENNY! I SEE SOMETHING!

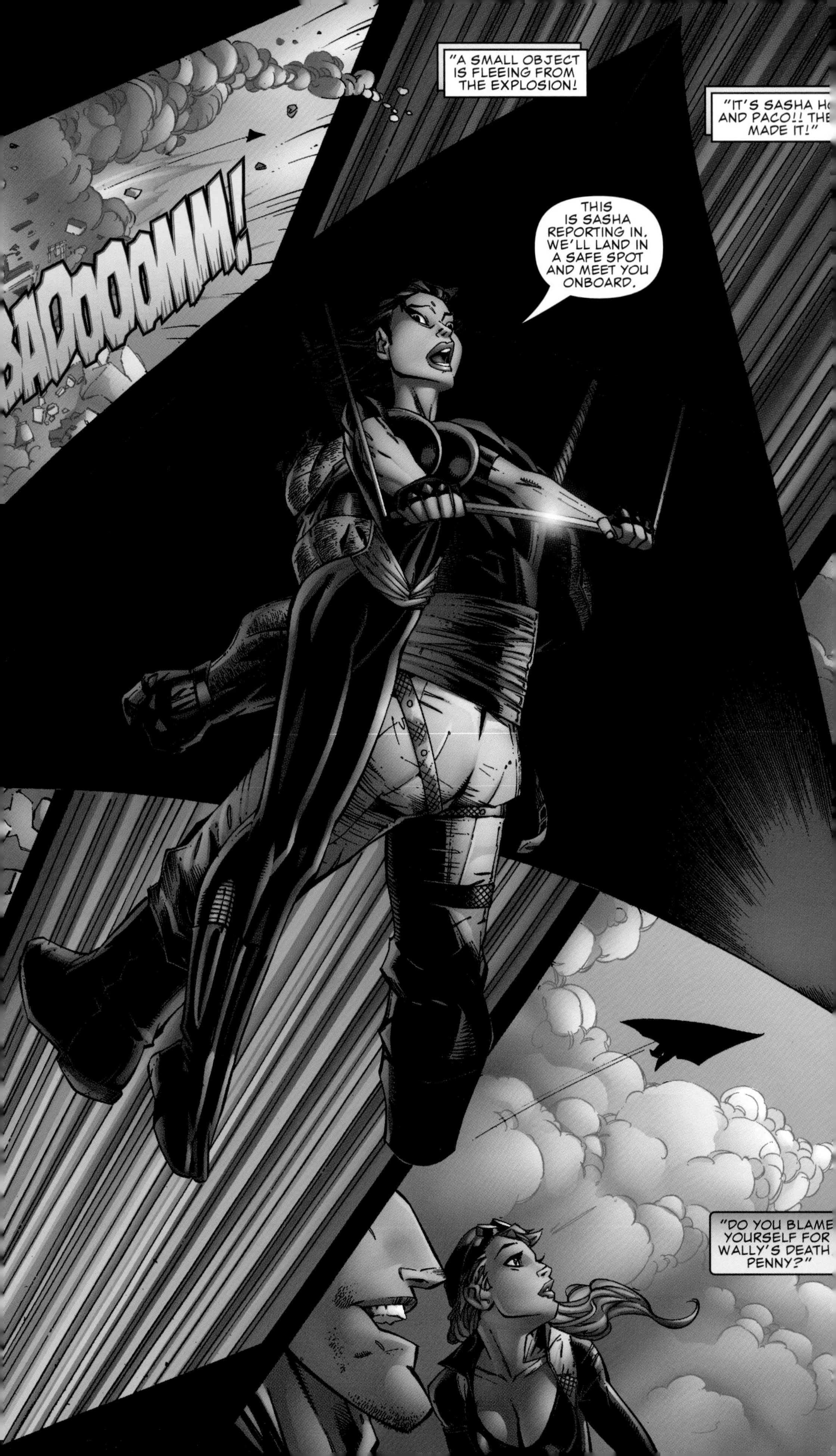
"A SMALL OBJECT IS FLEEING FROM THE EXPLOSION!
ADOOOMM!
"IT'S SASHA H AND PACO!! THE MADE IT!"
THIS IS SASHA REPORTING IN. WE'LL LAND IN A SAFE SPOT AND MEET YOU ONBOARD.
"DO YOU BLAME YOURSELF FOR WALLY'S DEATH PENNY?"

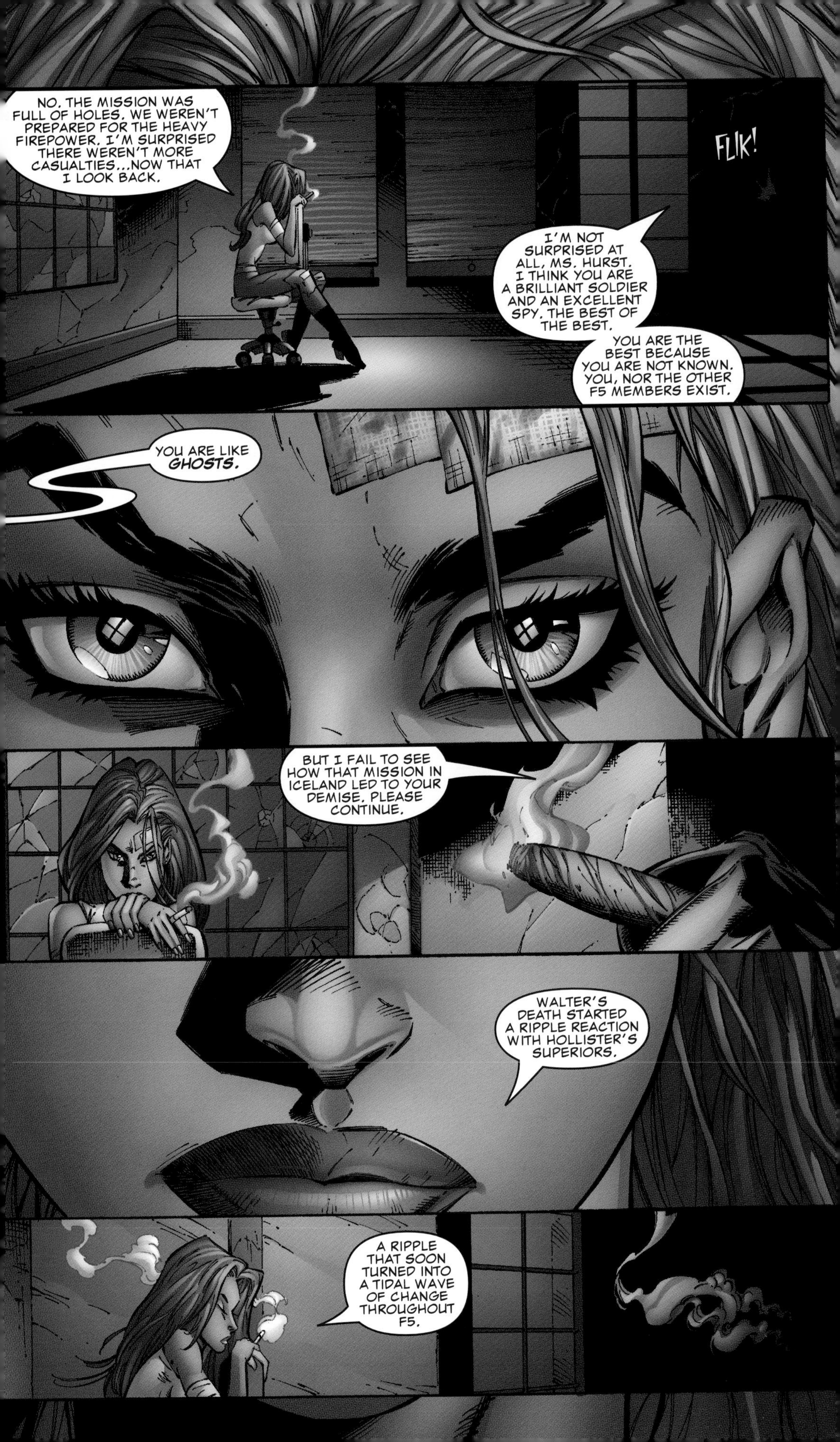
NO. THE MISSION WAS FULL OF HOLES. WE WEREN'T PREPARED FOR THE HEAVY FIREPOWER. I'M SURPRISED THERE WEREN'T MORE CASUALTIES...NOW THAT I LOOK BACK.
FLIK!
I'M NOT SURPRISED AT ALL, MS. HURST. I THINK YOU ARE A BRILLIANT SOLDIER AND AN EXCELLENT SPY. THE BEST OF THE BEST.
YOU ARE THE BEST BECAUSE YOU ARE NOT KNOWN. YOU, NOR THE OTHER F5 MEMBERS EXIST.
YOU ARE LIKE **GHOSTS**.
BUT I FAIL TO SEE HOW THAT MISSION IN ICELAND LED TO YOUR DEMISE. PLEASE CONTINUE.
WALTER'S DEATH STARTED A RIPPLE REACTION WITH HOLLISTER'S SUPERIORS.
A RIPPLE THAT SOON TURNED INTO A TIDAL WAVE OF CHANGE THROUGHOUT F5.

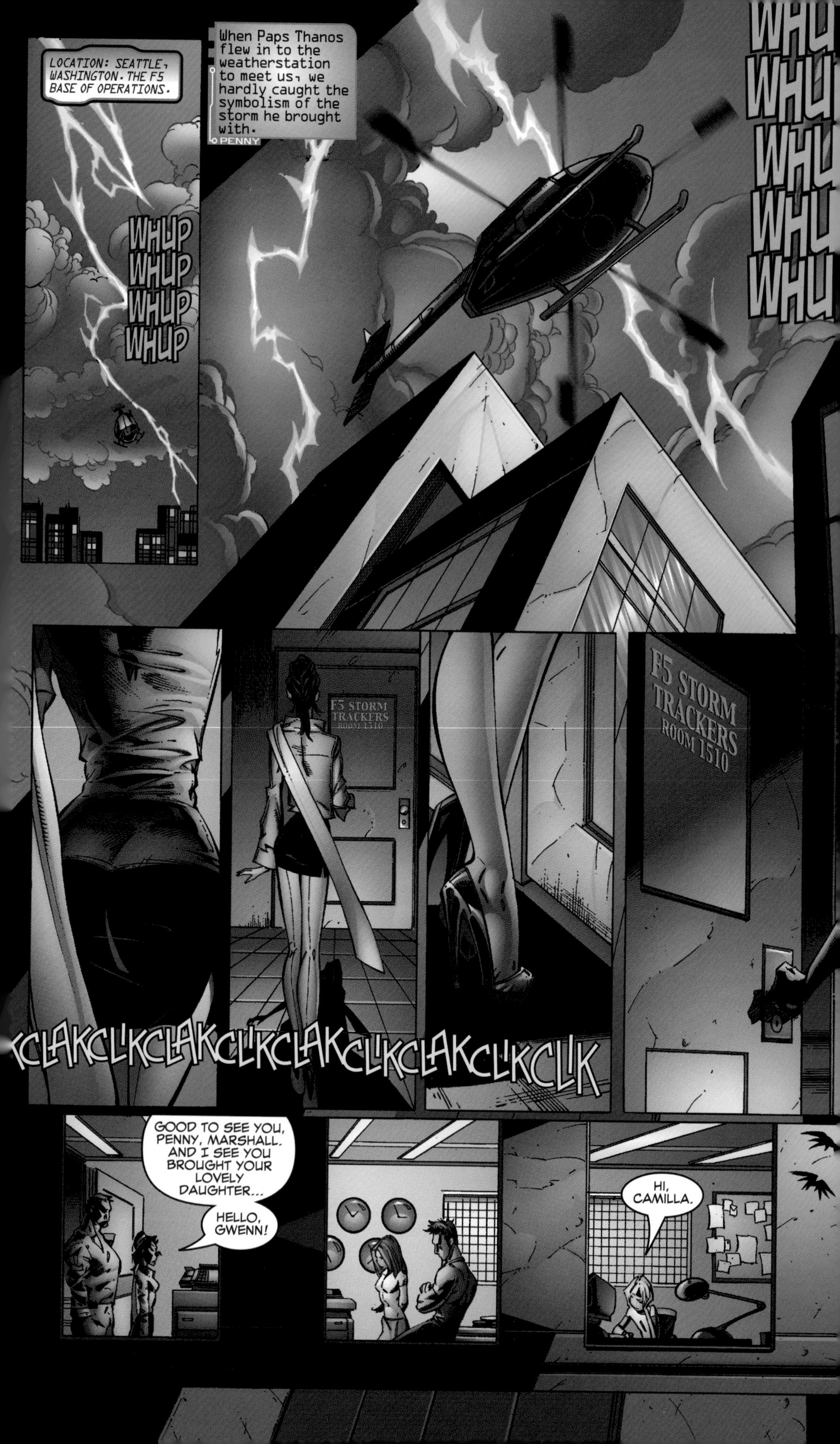
LOCATION: SEATTLE, WASHINGTON. THE F5 BASE OF OPERATIONS.
When Paps Thanos flew in to the weatherstation to meet us, we hardly caught the symbolism of the storm he brought with.
PENNY
WHUP WHUP WHUP WHUP
WHU WHU WHU WHU WHU
F5 STORM TRACKERS ROOM 1510
F5 STORM TRACKERS ROOM 1510
CLAKCLIKCLAKCLIKCLAKCLIKCLAKCLIKCLAKCLIKCLIK
GOOD TO SEE YOU, PENNY, MARSHALL. AND I SEE YOU BROUGHT YOUR LOVELY DAUGHTER...
HELLO, GWENN!
HI, CAMILLA.

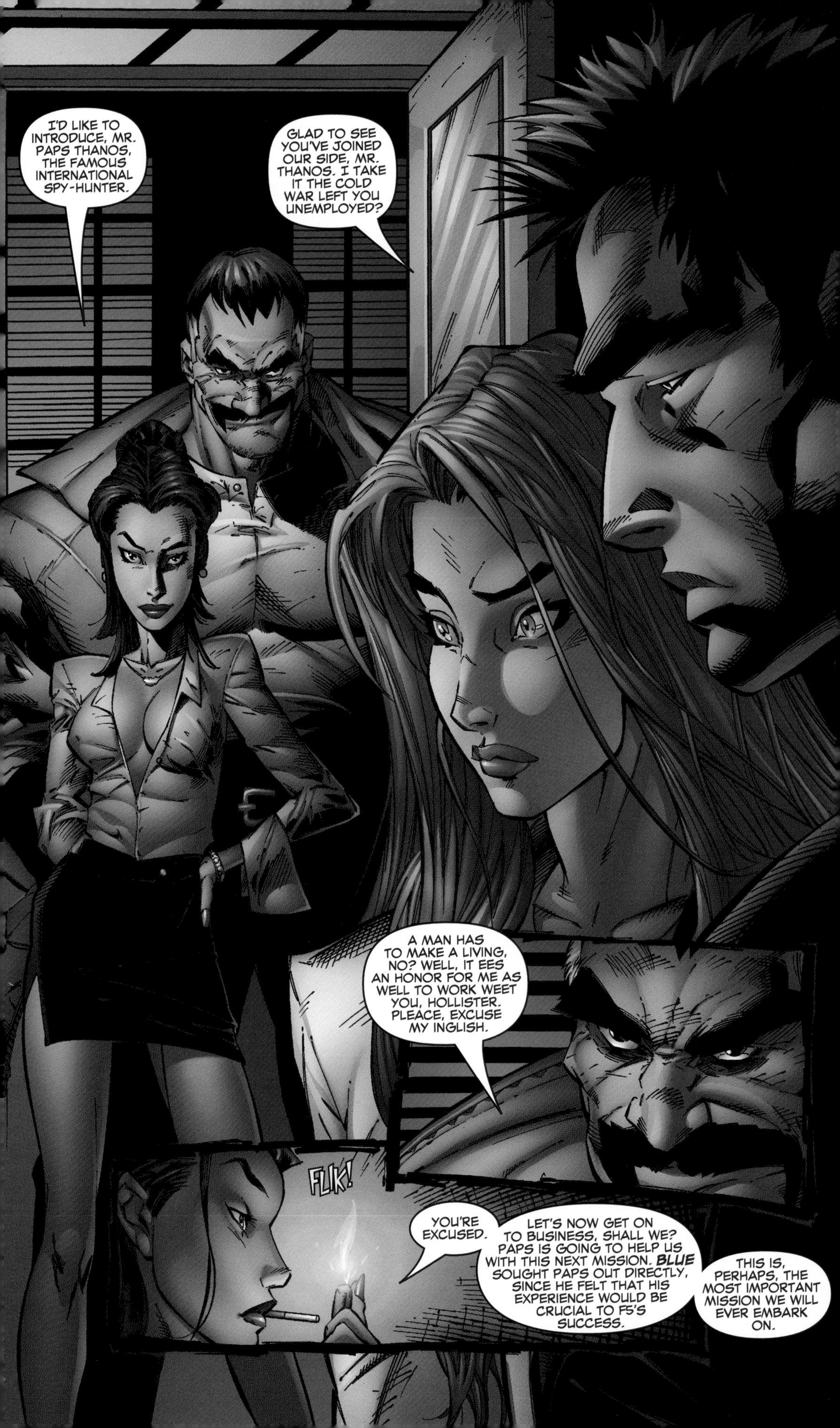
I'D LIKE TO INTRODUCE, MR. PAPS THANOS, THE FAMOUS INTERNATIONAL SPY-HUNTER.
GLAD TO SEE YOU'VE JOINED OUR SIDE, MR. THANOS. I TAKE IT THE COLD WAR LEFT YOU UNEMPLOYED?
A MAN HAS TO MAKE A LIVING, NO? WELL, IT EES AN HONOR FOR ME AS WELL TO WORK WEET YOU, HOLLISTER. PLEACE, EXCUSE MY INGLISH.
FLIK!
YOU'RE EXCUSED.
LET'S NOW GET ON TO BUSINESS, SHALL WE? PAPS IS GOING TO HELP US WITH THIS NEXT MISSION. BLUE SOUGHT PAPS OUT DIRECTLY, SINCE HE FELT THAT HIS EXPERIENCE WOULD BE CRUCIAL TO F5'S SUCCESS.
THIS IS, PERHAPS, THE MOST IMPORTANT MISSION WE WILL EVER EMBARK ON.

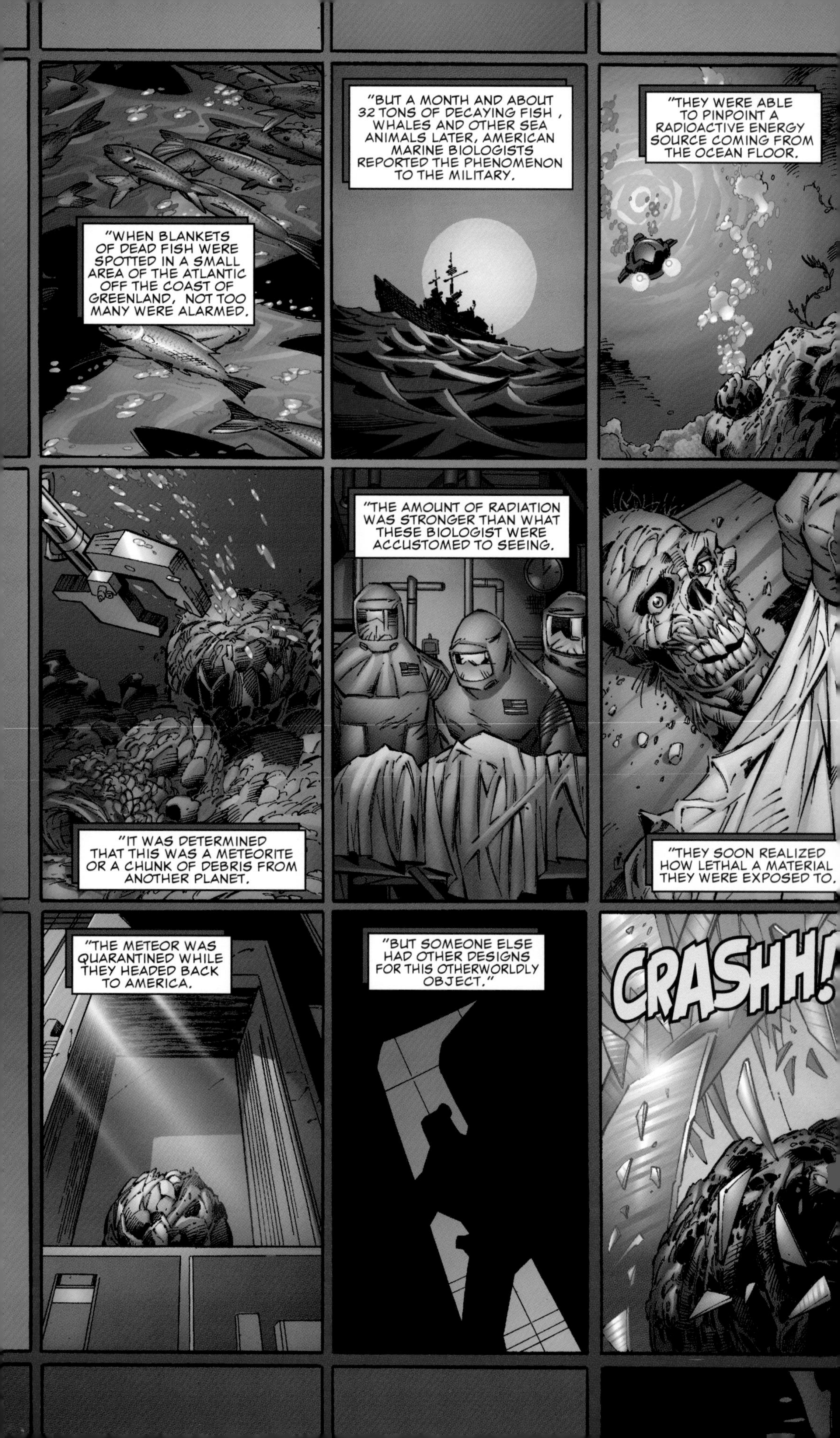
"WHEN BLANKETS OF DEAD FISH WERE SPOTTED IN A SMALL AREA OF THE ATLANTIC OFF THE COAST OF GREENLAND, NOT TOO MANY WERE ALARMED.
"BUT A MONTH AND ABOUT 32 TONS OF DECAYING FISH , WHALES AND OTHER SEA ANIMALS LATER, AMERICAN MARINE BIOLOGISTS REPORTED THE PHENOMENON TO THE MILITARY.
"THEY WERE ABLE TO PINPOINT A RADIOACTIVE ENERGY SOURCE COMING FROM THE OCEAN FLOOR.
"IT WAS DETERMINED THAT THIS WAS A METEORITE OR A CHUNK OF DEBRIS FROM ANOTHER PLANET.
"THE AMOUNT OF RADIATION WAS STRONGER THAN WHAT THESE BIOLOGIST WERE ACCUSTOMED TO SEEING.
"THEY SOON REALIZED HOW LETHAL A MATERIAL THEY WERE EXPOSED TO.
"THE METEOR WAS QUARANTINED WHILE THEY HEADED BACK TO AMERICA.
"BUT SOMEONE ELSE HAD OTHER DESIGNS FOR THIS OTHERWORLDLY OBJECT."
CRASHH!

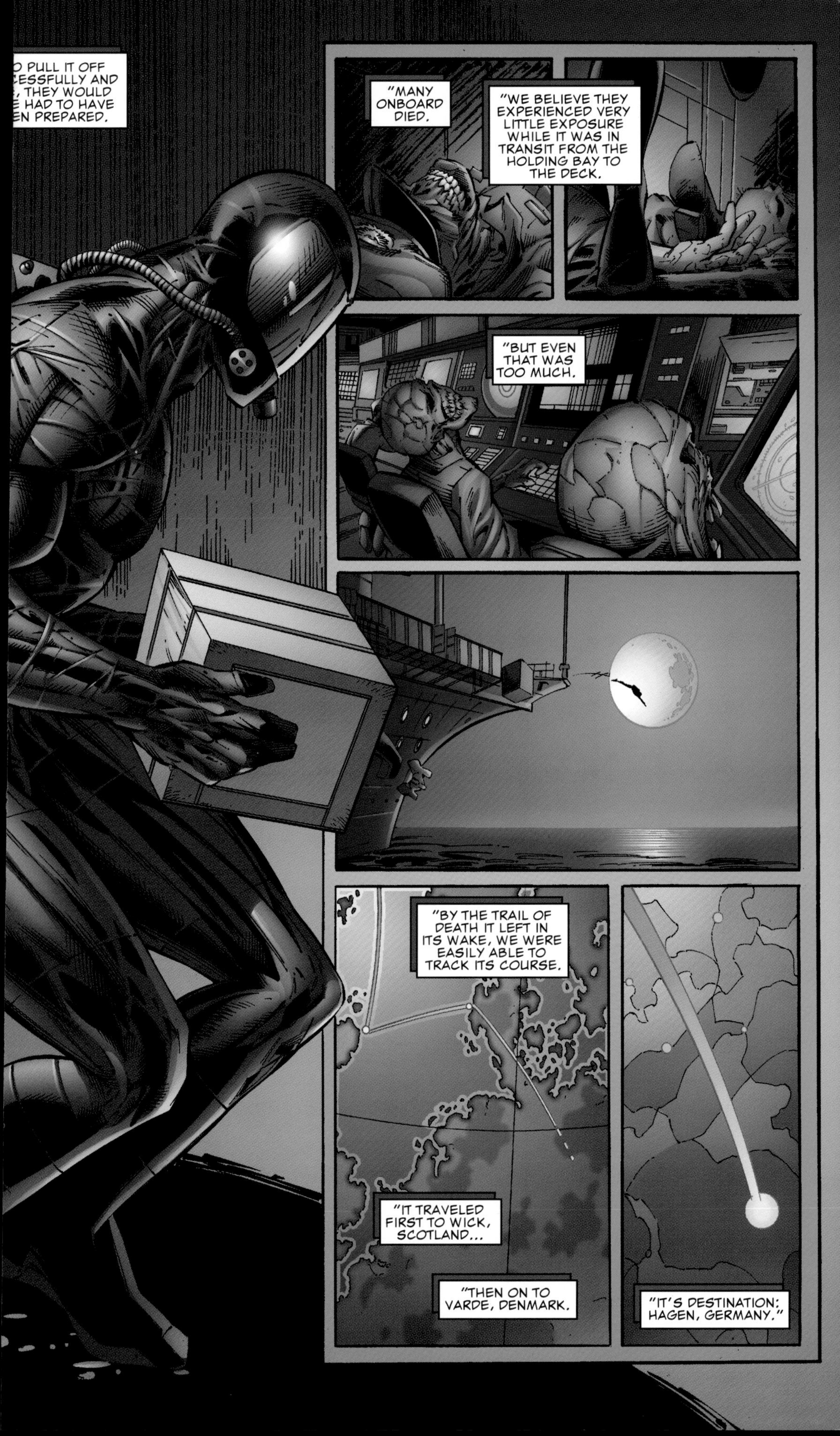
O PULL IT OFF
CESSFULLY AND
, THEY WOULD
E HAD TO HAVE
EN PREPARED.
"MANY ONBOARD DIED.
"WE BELIEVE THEY EXPERIENCED VERY LITTLE EXPOSURE WHILE IT WAS IN TRANSIT FROM THE HOLDING BAY TO THE DECK.
"BUT EVEN THAT WAS TOO MUCH.
"BY THE TRAIL OF DEATH IT LEFT IN ITS WAKE, WE WERE EASILY ABLE TO TRACK ITS COURSE.
"IT TRAVELED FIRST TO WICK, SCOTLAND...
"THEN ON TO VARDE, DENMARK.
"IT'S DESTINATION: HAGEN, GERMANY."

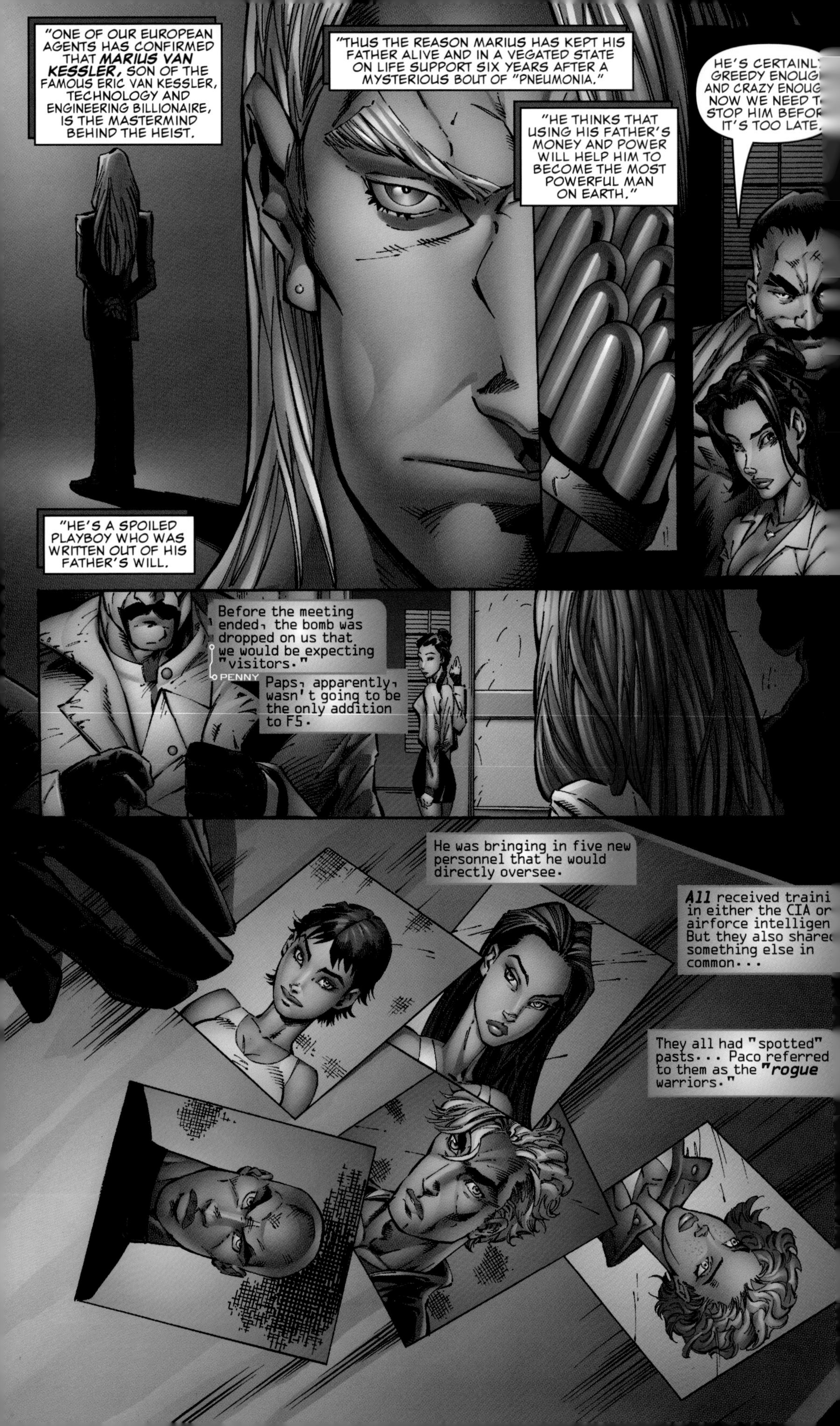
"ONE OF OUR EUROPEAN AGENTS HAS CONFIRMED THAT **MARIUS VAN KESSLER,** SON OF THE FAMOUS ERIC VAN KESSLER, TECHNOLOGY AND ENGINEERING BILLIONAIRE, IS THE MASTERMIND BEHIND THE HEIST.
"HE'S A SPOILED PLAYBOY WHO WAS WRITTEN OUT OF HIS FATHER'S WILL.
"THUS THE REASON MARIUS HAS KEPT HIS FATHER ALIVE AND IN A VEGATED STATE ON LIFE SUPPORT SIX YEARS AFTER A MYSTERIOUS BOUT OF "PNEUMONIA."
"HE THINKS THAT USING HIS FATHER'S MONEY AND POWER WILL HELP HIM TO BECOME THE MOST POWERFUL MAN ON EARTH."
HE'S CERTAINL GREEDY ENOUG AND CRAZY ENOUG NOW WE NEED T STOP HIM BEFOR IT'S TOO LATE.
Before the meeting ended, the bomb was dropped on us that we would be expecting "visitors."
PENNY
Paps, apparently, wasn't going to be the only addition to F5.
He was bringing in five new personnel that he would directly oversee.
All received traini in either the CIA or airforce intelligen But they also share something else in common...
They all had "spotted" pasts... Paco referred to them as the "***rogue*** warriors."

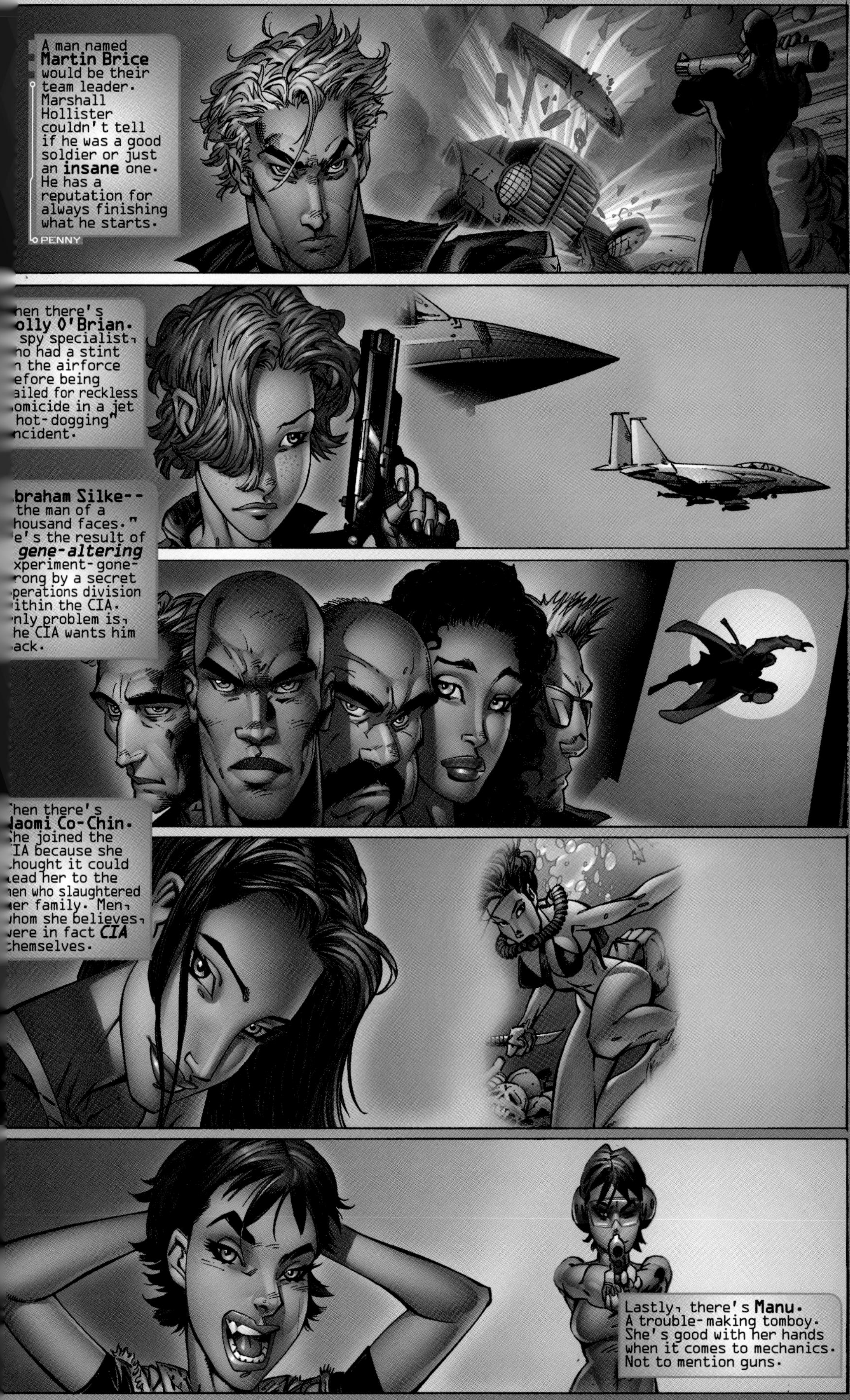

A man named Martin Brice would be their team leader. Marshall Hollister couldn't tell if he was a good soldier or just an insane one. He has a reputation for always finishing what he starts.
PENNY
hen there's olly O'Brian. spy specialist, ho had a stint n the airforce efore being ailed for reckless omicide in a jet "hot-dogging" ncident.
braham Silke-- the man of a housand faces." e's the result of gene-altering xperiment-gone-rong by a secret perations division ithin the CIA. nly problem is, he CIA wants him ack.
hen there's aomi Co-Chin. he joined the IA because she hought it could ead her to the en who slaughtered er family. Men, hom she believes, ere in fact CIA hemselves.
Lastly, there's Manu. A trouble-making tomboy. She's good with her hands when it comes to mechanics. Not to mention guns.

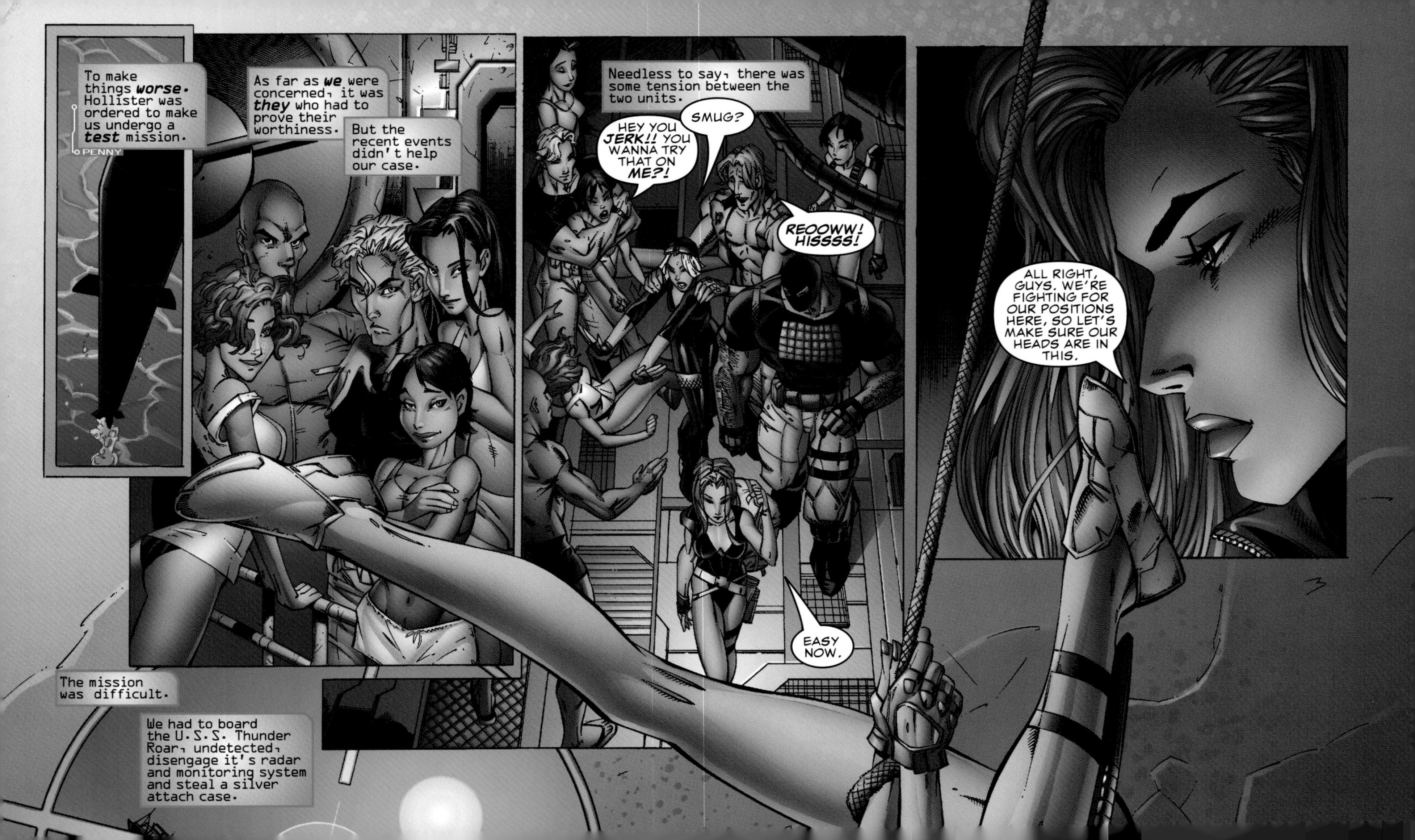
To make things **worse.** Hollister was ordered to make us undergo a **test** mission.
PENNY
As far as **we** were concerned, it was **they** who had to prove their worthiness.
But the recent events didn't help our case.
Needless to say, there was some tension between the two units.
HEY YOU **JERK!!** YOU WANNA TRY THAT ON **ME?!**
SMUG?
REOOWW! HISSSS!
EASY NOW.
ALL RIGHT, GUYS. WE'RE FIGHTING FOR OUR POSITIONS HERE, SO LET'S MAKE SURE OUR HEADS ARE IN THIS.
The mission was difficult.
We had to board the U.S.S. Thunder Roar, undetected, disengage it's radar and monitoring system and steal a silver attach case.

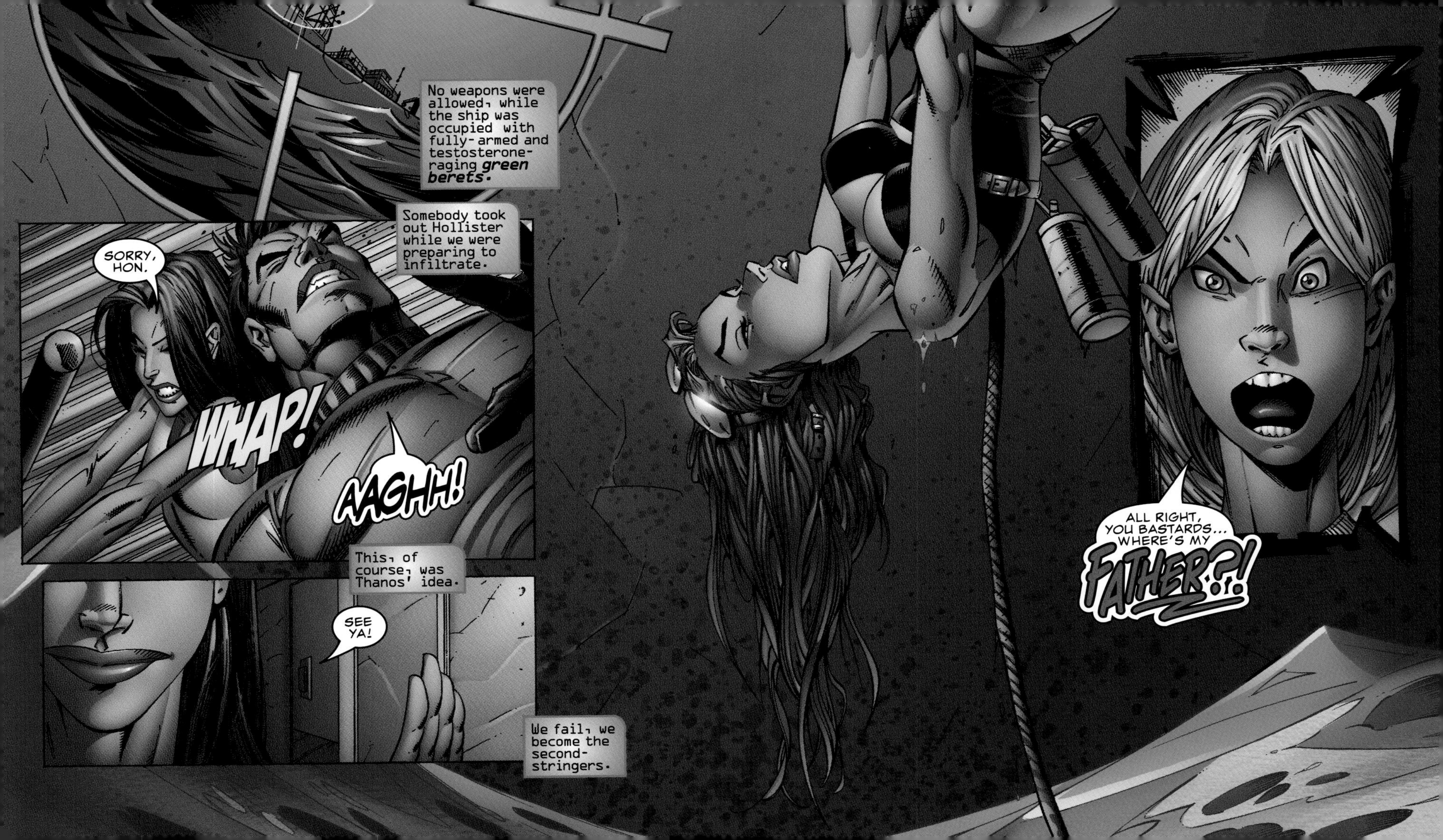
No weapons were allowed, while the ship was occupied with fully-armed and testosterone-raging *green berets.*
Somebody took out Hollister while we were preparing to infiltrate.
SORRY, HON.
WHAP!
AAGHH!
This, of course, was Thanos' idea.
SEE YA!
We fail, we become the second-stringers.
ALL RIGHT, YOU BASTARDS... WHERE'S MY
FATHER?!

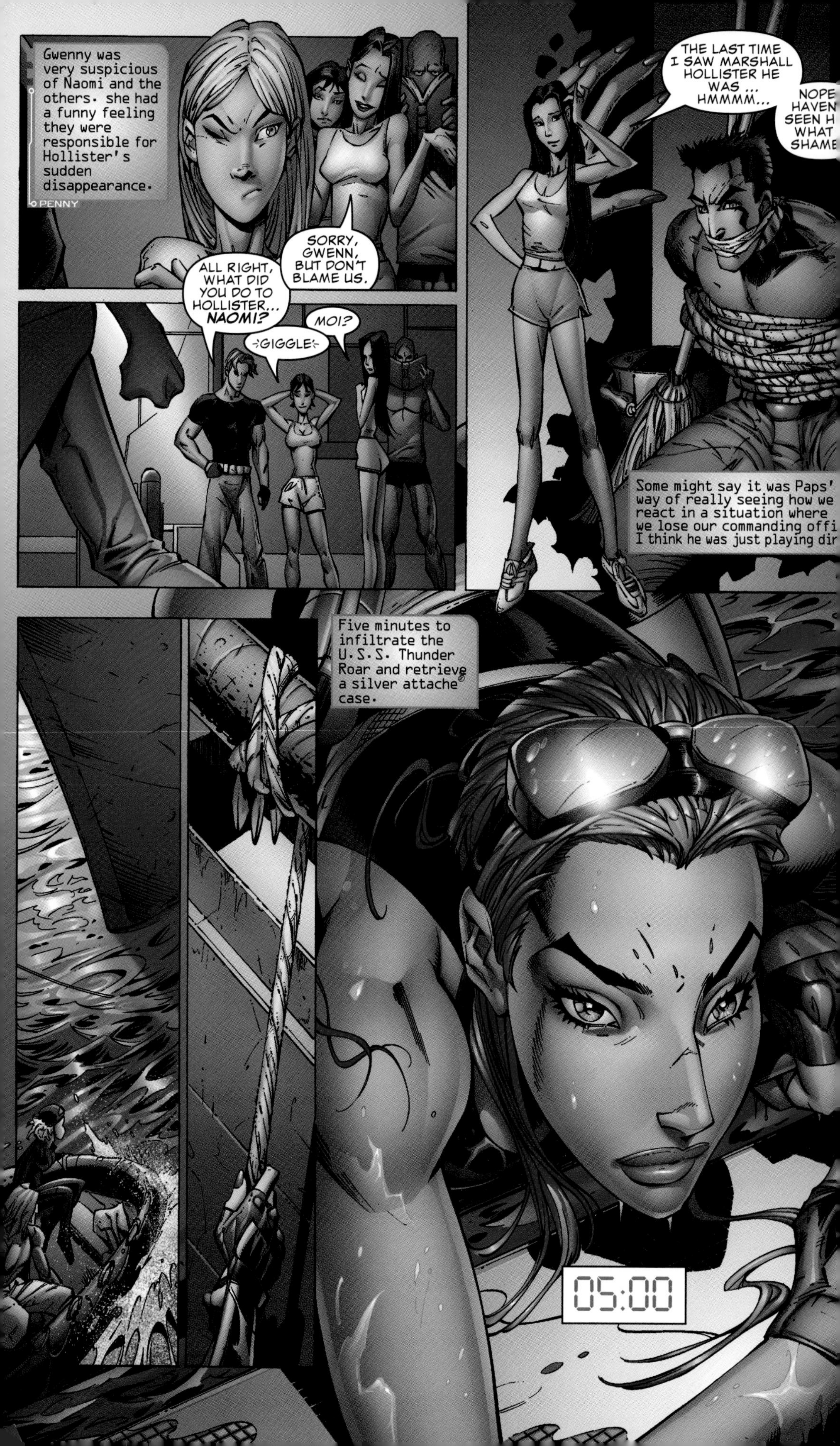
Gwenny was very suspicious of Naomi and the others. she had a funny feeling they were responsible for Hollister's sudden disappearance.
PENNY
SORRY, GWENN, BUT DON'T BLAME US.
ALL RIGHT, WHAT DID YOU DO TO HOLLISTER... NAOMI?
MOI?
-GIGGLE-
THE LAST TIME I SAW MARSHALL HOLLISTER HE WAS ... HMMMM...
NOPE HAVEN SEEN H WHAT SHAME
Some might say it was Paps' way of really seeing how we react in a situation where we lose our commanding offi I think he was just playing dir
Five minutes to infiltrate the U.S.S. Thunder Roar and retrieve a silver attache case.
05:00

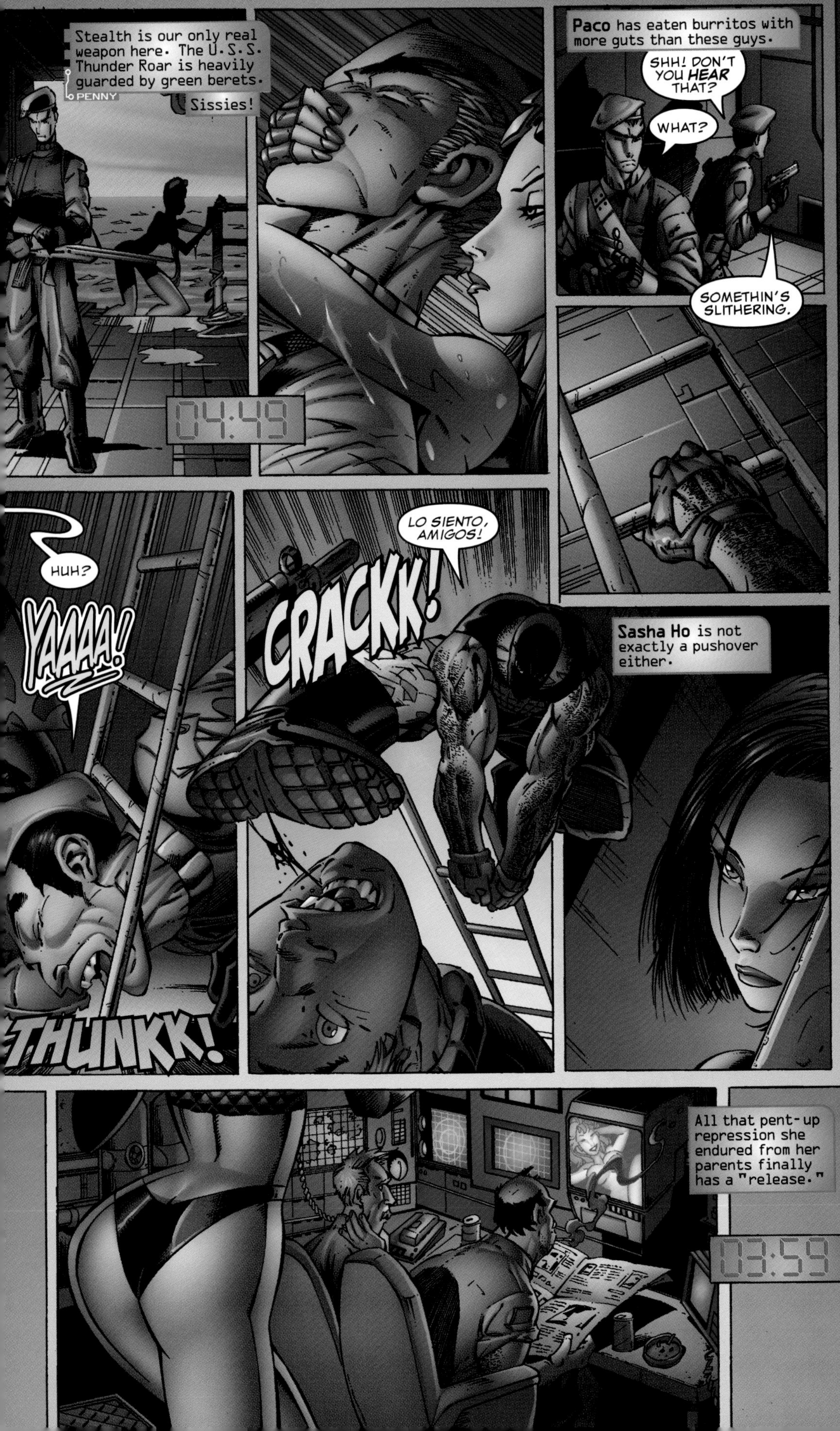
Stealth is our only real weapon here. The U.S.S. Thunder Roar is heavily guarded by green berets.
PENNY
Sissies!
04:49
Paco has eaten burritos with more guts than these guys.
SHH! DON'T YOU HEAR THAT?
WHAT?
SOMETHIN'S SLITHERING.
HUH?
YAAAA!
LO SIENTO, AMIGOS!
CRACKK!
THUNKK!
Sasha Ho is not exactly a pushover either.
All that pent-up repression she endured from her parents finally has a "release."
03:59

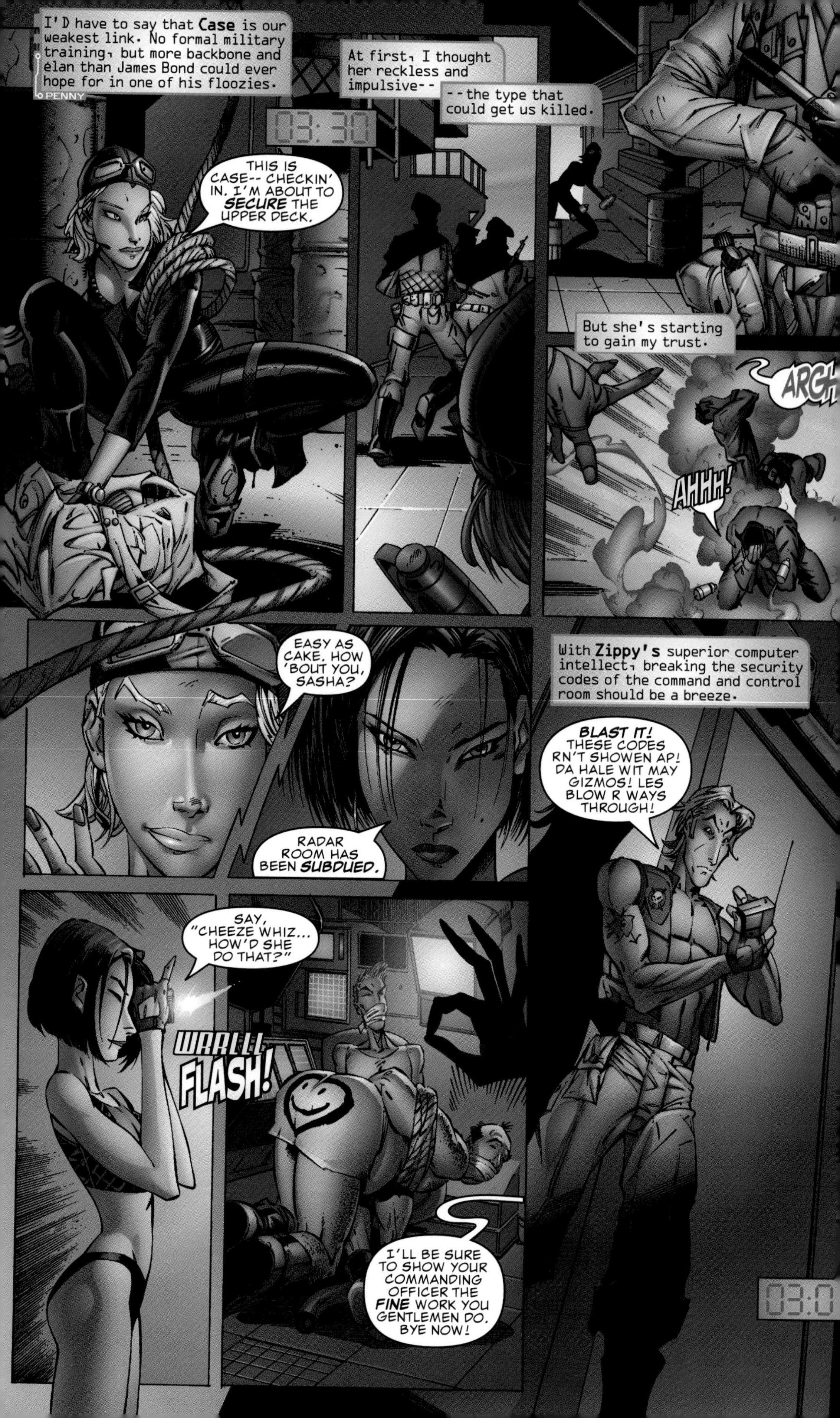
I'D have to say that Case is our weakest link. No formal military training, but more backbone and élan than James Bond could ever hope for in one of his floozies.
PENNY
At first, I thought her reckless and impulsive--
--the type that could get us killed.
03:30
THIS IS CASE-- CHECKIN' IN. I'M ABOUT TO SECURE THE UPPER DECK.
But she's starting to gain my trust.
ARGH
AHHH!
EASY AS CAKE. HOW 'BOUT YOU, SASHA?
RADAR ROOM HAS BEEN SUBDUED.
With Zippy's superior computer intellect, breaking the security codes of the command and control room should be a breeze.
BLAST IT! THESE CODES RN'T SHOWEN AP! DA HALE WIT MAY GIZMOS! LES BLOW R WAYS THROUGH!
SAY, "CHEEZE WHIZ... HOW'D SHE DO THAT?"
WRRLLL FLASH!
I'LL BE SURE TO SHOW YOUR COMMANDING OFFICER THE FINE WORK YOU GENTLEMEN DO. BYE NOW!

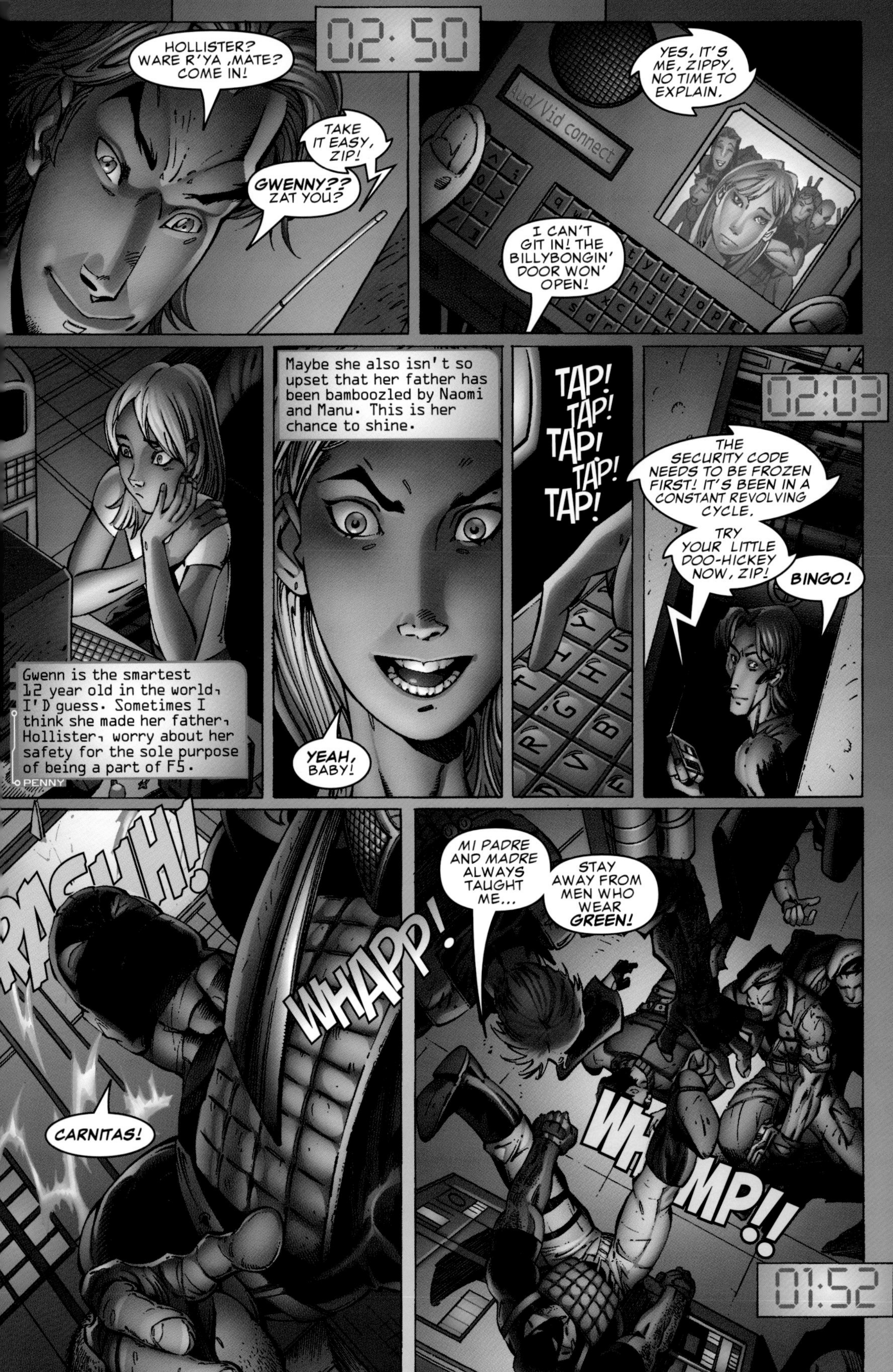
02:50
HOLLISTER? WARE R'YA ,MATE? COME IN!
TAKE IT EASY, ZIP!
GWENNY?? ZAT YOU?
YES, IT'S ME, ZIPPY, NO TIME TO EXPLAIN.
Aud/Vid connect
I CAN'T GIT IN! THE BILLYBONGIN' DOOR WON' OPEN!
Gwenn is the smartest 12 year old in the world, I'D guess. Sometimes I think she made her father, Hollister, worry about her safety for the sole purpose of being a part of F5.
PENNY
Maybe she also isn't so upset that her father has been bamboozled by Naomi and Manu. This is her chance to shine.
YEAH, BABY!
TAP! TAP! TAP! TAP! TAP!
02:03
THE SECURITY CODE NEEDS TO BE FROZEN FIRST! IT'S BEEN IN A CONSTANT REVOLVING CYCLE.
TRY YOUR LITTLE DOO-HICKEY NOW, ZIP!
BINGO!
WHAPP!
CARNITAS!
MI PADRE AND MADRE ALWAYS TAUGHT ME...
STAY AWAY FROM MEN WHO WEAR GREEN!
MP!!
01:52

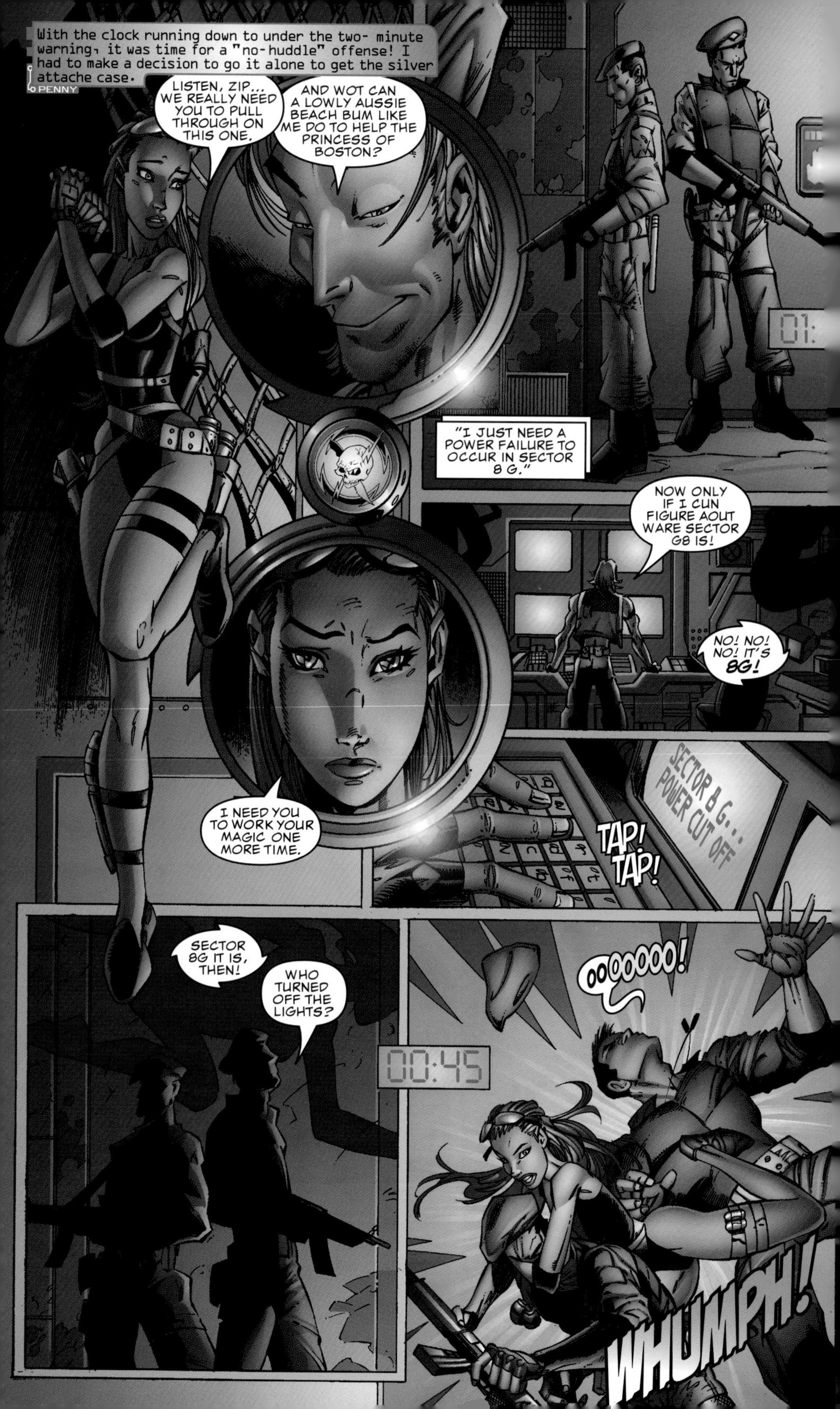
With the clock running down to under the two- minute warning, it was time for a "no-huddle" offense! I had to make a decision to go it alone to get the silver attache case.
PENNY
LISTEN, ZIP... WE REALLY NEED YOU TO PULL THROUGH ON THIS ONE.
AND WOT CAN A LOWLY AUSSIE BEACH BUM LIKE ME DO TO HELP THE PRINCESS OF BOSTON?
01:
"I JUST NEED A POWER FAILURE TO OCCUR IN SECTOR 8 G."
NOW ONLY IF I CUN FIGURE AOUT WARE SECTOR G8 IS!
NO! NO! NO! IT'S 8G!
I NEED YOU TO WORK YOUR MAGIC ONE MORE TIME.
SECTOR 8 G... POWER CUT OFF
TAP! TAP!
SECTOR 8G IT IS, THEN!
WHO TURNED OFF THE LIGHTS?
00:45
OOOOOOO!
WHUMPH!

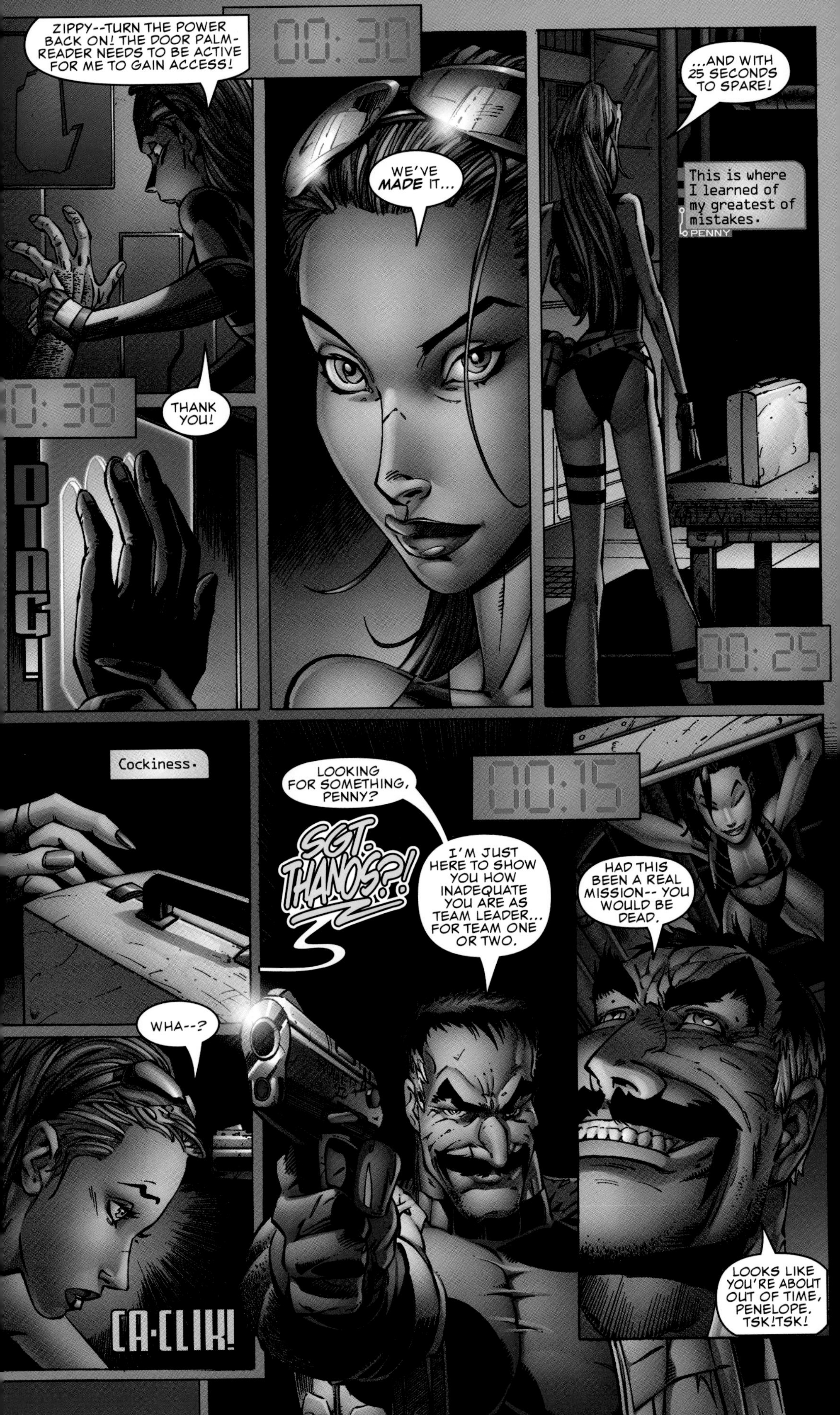
ZIPPY--TURN THE POWER BACK ON! THE DOOR PALM-READER NEEDS TO BE ACTIVE FOR ME TO GAIN ACCESS!
00:30
THANK YOU!
00:38
DING
WE'VE MADE IT...
...AND WITH 25 SECONDS TO SPARE!
This is where I learned of my greatest of mistakes.
PENNY
00:25
Cockiness.
WHA--?
CA-CLIK!
LOOKING FOR SOMETHING, PENNY?
SGT. THANOS?!
I'M JUST HERE TO SHOW YOU HOW INADEQUATE YOU ARE AS TEAM LEADER... FOR TEAM ONE OR TWO.
00:15
HAD THIS BEEN A REAL MISSION-- YOU WOULD BE DEAD.
LOOKS LIKE YOU'RE ABOUT OUT OF TIME, PENELOPE. TSK!TSK!

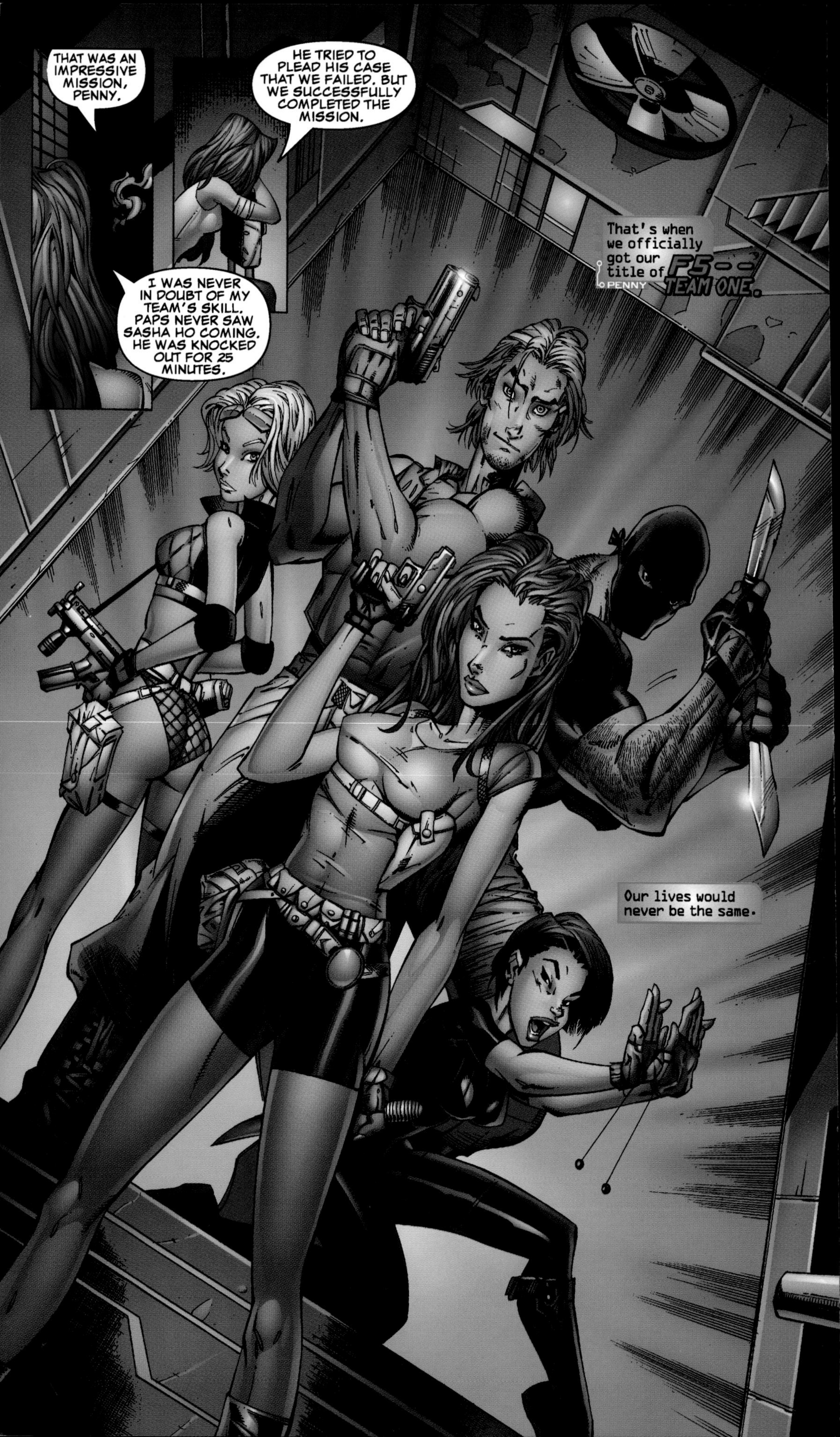
THAT WAS AN IMPRESSIVE MISSION, PENNY.
HE TRIED TO PLEAD HIS CASE THAT WE FAILED, BUT WE SUCCESSFULLY COMPLETED THE MISSION.
I WAS NEVER IN DOUBT OF MY TEAM'S SKILL. PAPS NEVER SAW SASHA HO COMING. HE WAS KNOCKED OUT FOR 25 MINUTES.
That's when we officially got our title of F5 -- TEAM ONE.
PENNY
Our lives would never be the same.

chapter three

HITS AND MISSES

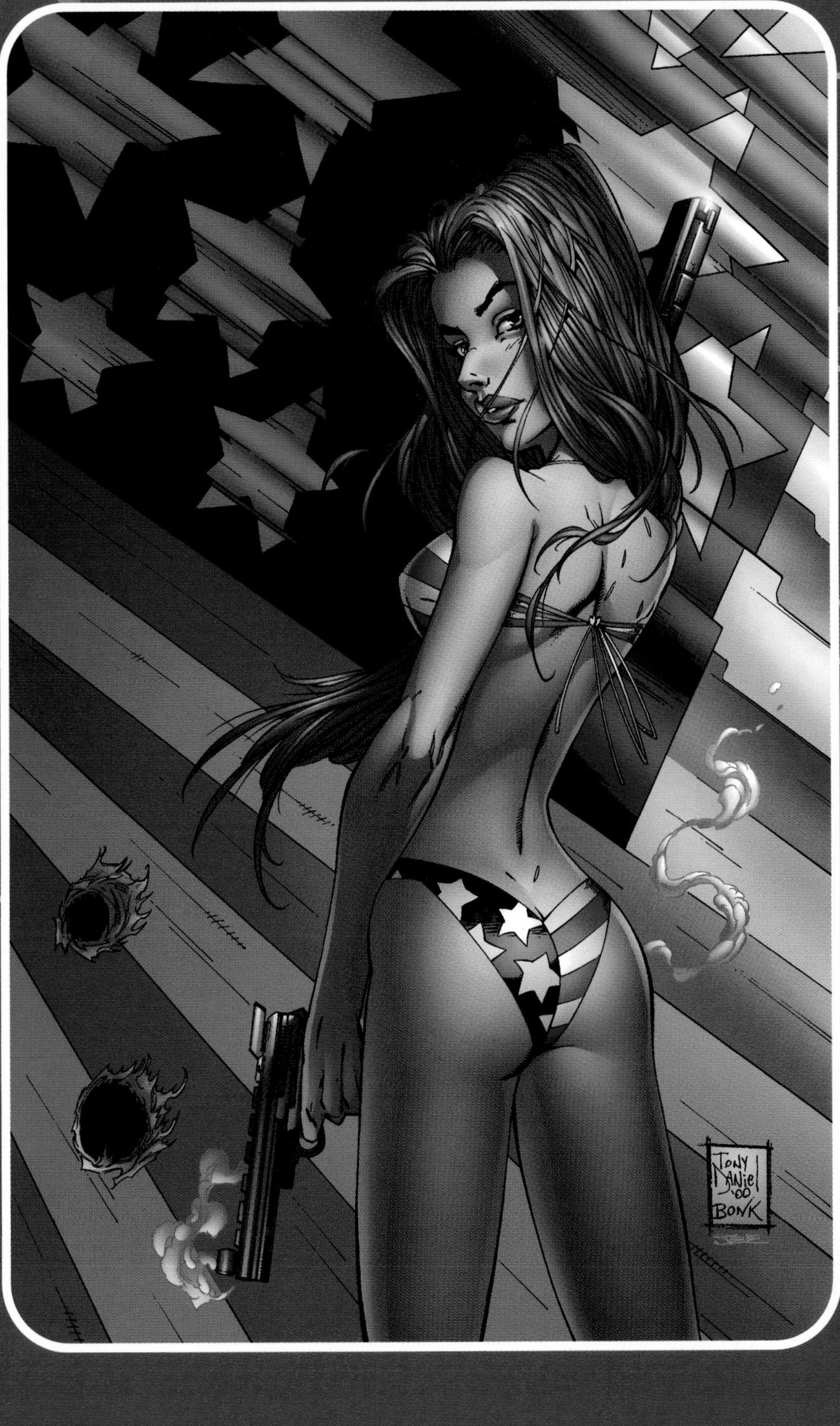
TONY DANIEL '00
BONK

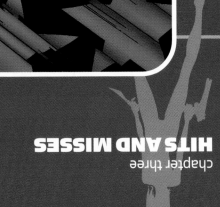

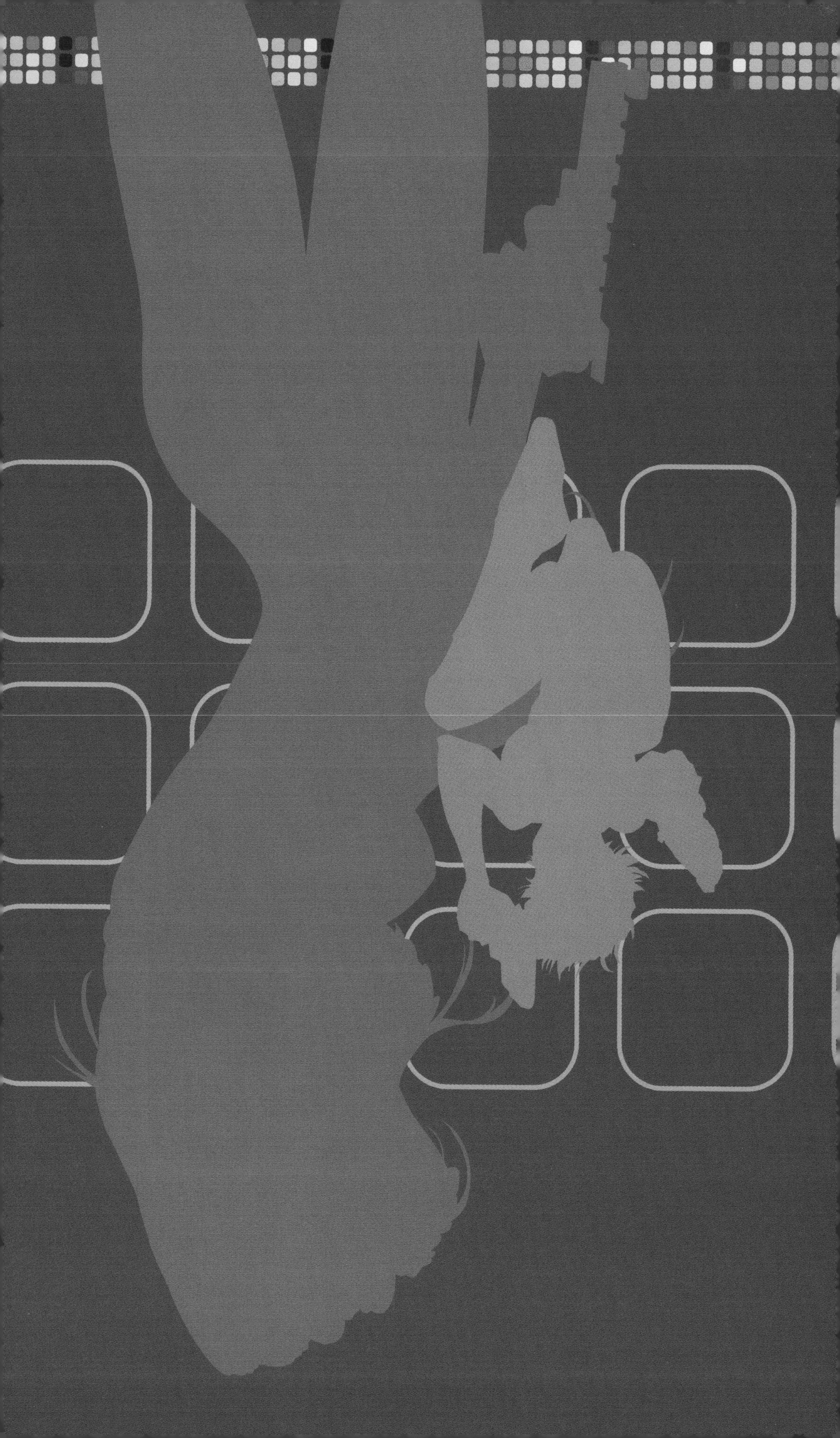

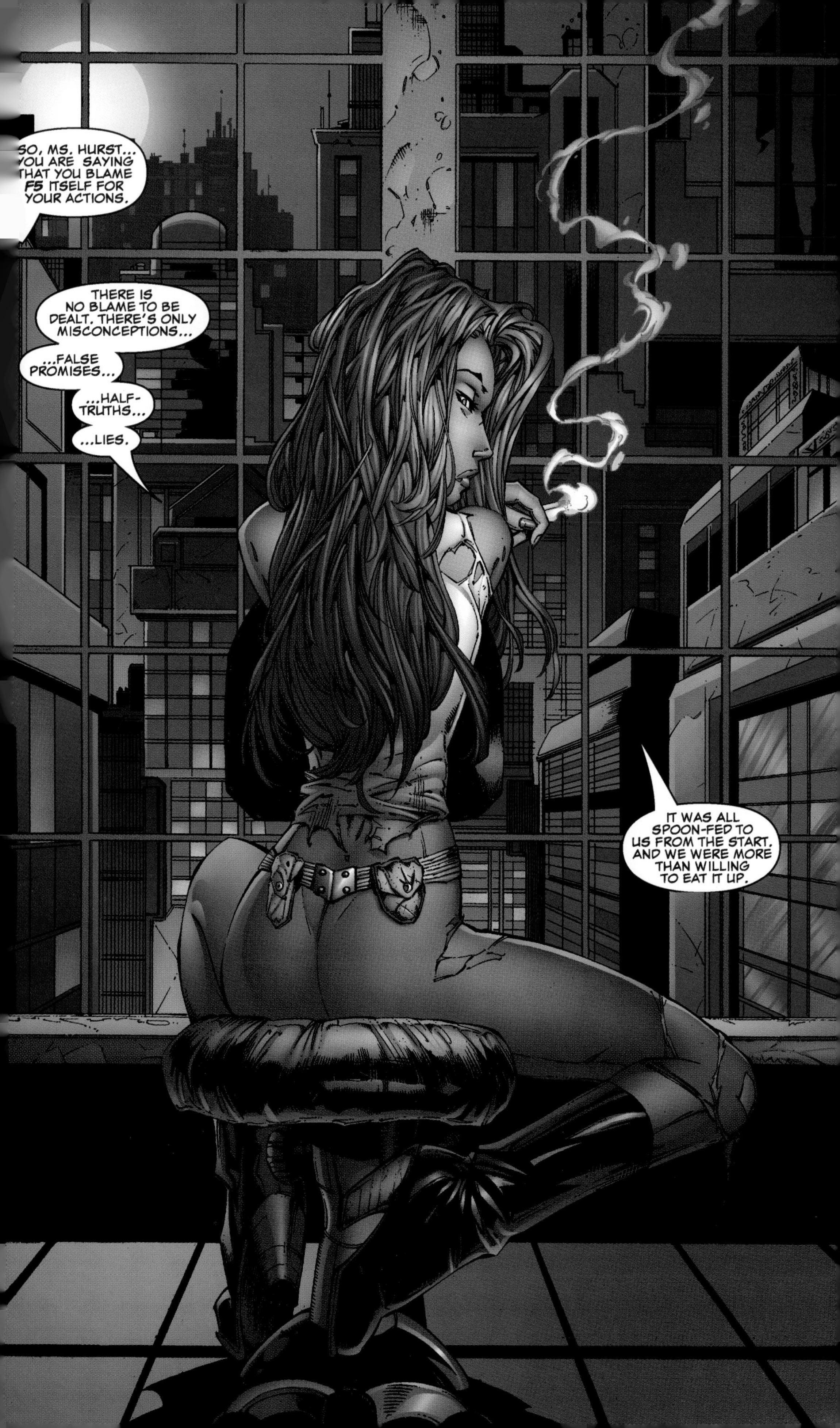
SO, MS. HURST... YOU ARE SAYING THAT YOU BLAME F5 ITSELF FOR YOUR ACTIONS.
THERE IS NO BLAME TO BE DEALT. THERE'S ONLY MISCONCEPTIONS...
...FALSE PROMISES...
...HALF-TRUTHS...
...LIES.
IT WAS ALL SPOON-FED TO US FROM THE START, AND WE WERE MORE THAN WILLING TO EAT IT UP.

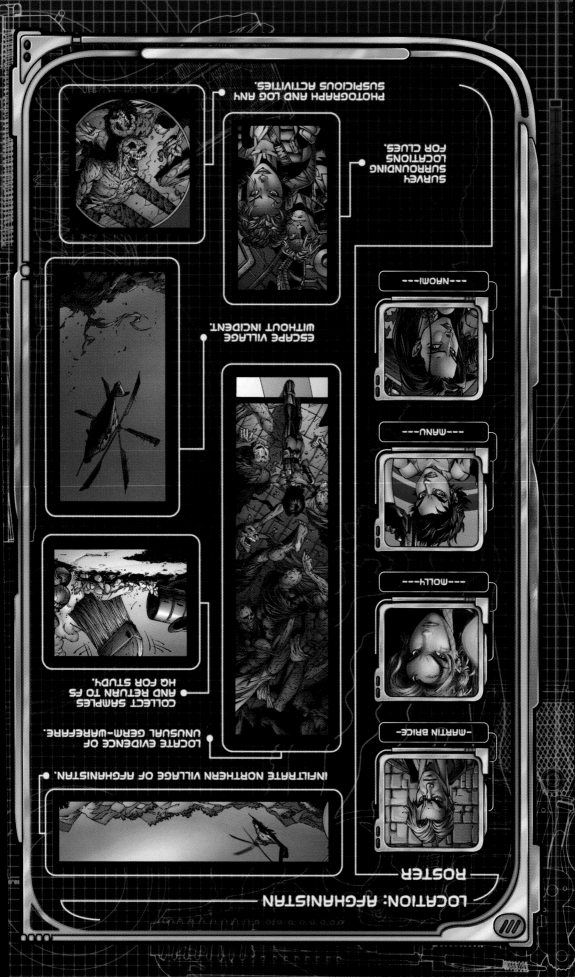

PHOTOGRAPH AND LOG ANY
SUSPICIOUS ACTIVITIES.

SURVEY
SURROUNDING
LOCATIONS
FOR CLUES.

ESCAPE VILLAGE
WITHOUT INCIDENT.

COLLECT SAMPLES
AND RETURN TO FS
HQ FOR STUDY.

LOCATE EVIDENCE OF
UNUSUAL GERM-WARFARE.

INFILTRATE NORTHERN VILLAGE OF AFGHANISTAN.

---NAOMI---

---MANU---

---MOLLY---

-MARTIN BRICE-

ROSTER

LOCATION: AFGHANISTAN

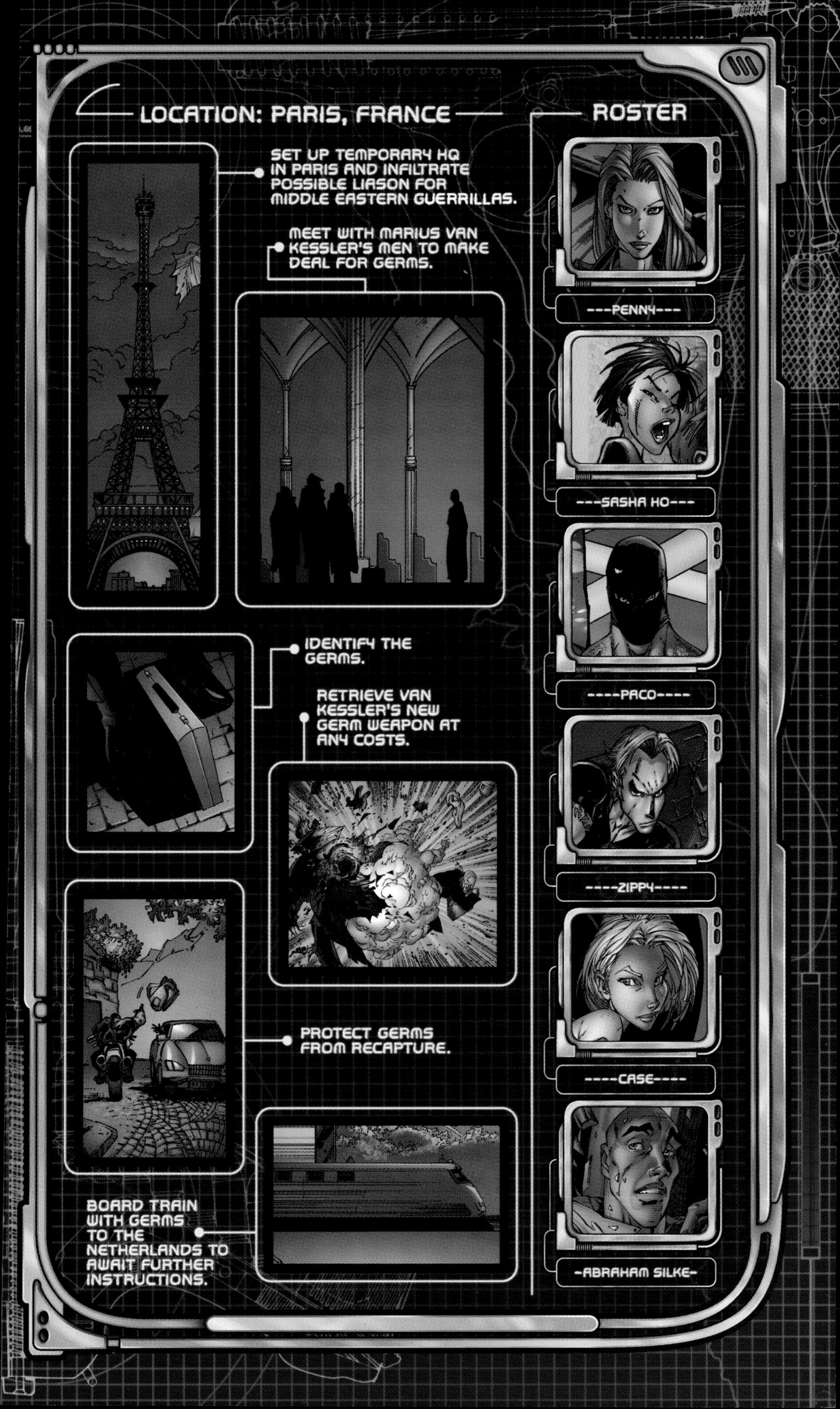
LOCATION: PARIS, FRANCE
ROSTER
SET UP TEMPORARY HQ IN PARIS AND INFILTRATE POSSIBLE LIASON FOR MIDDLE EASTERN GUERRILLAS.
MEET WITH MARIUS VAN KESSLER'S MEN TO MAKE DEAL FOR GERMS.
IDENTIFY THE GERMS.
RETRIEVE VAN KESSLER'S NEW GERM WEAPON AT ANY COSTS.
PROTECT GERMS FROM RECAPTURE.
BOARD TRAIN WITH GERMS TO THE NETHERLANDS TO AWAIT FURTHER INSTRUCTIONS.
---PENNY---
---SASHA HO---
----PACO----
----ZIPPY----
----CASE----
-ABRAHAM SILKE-

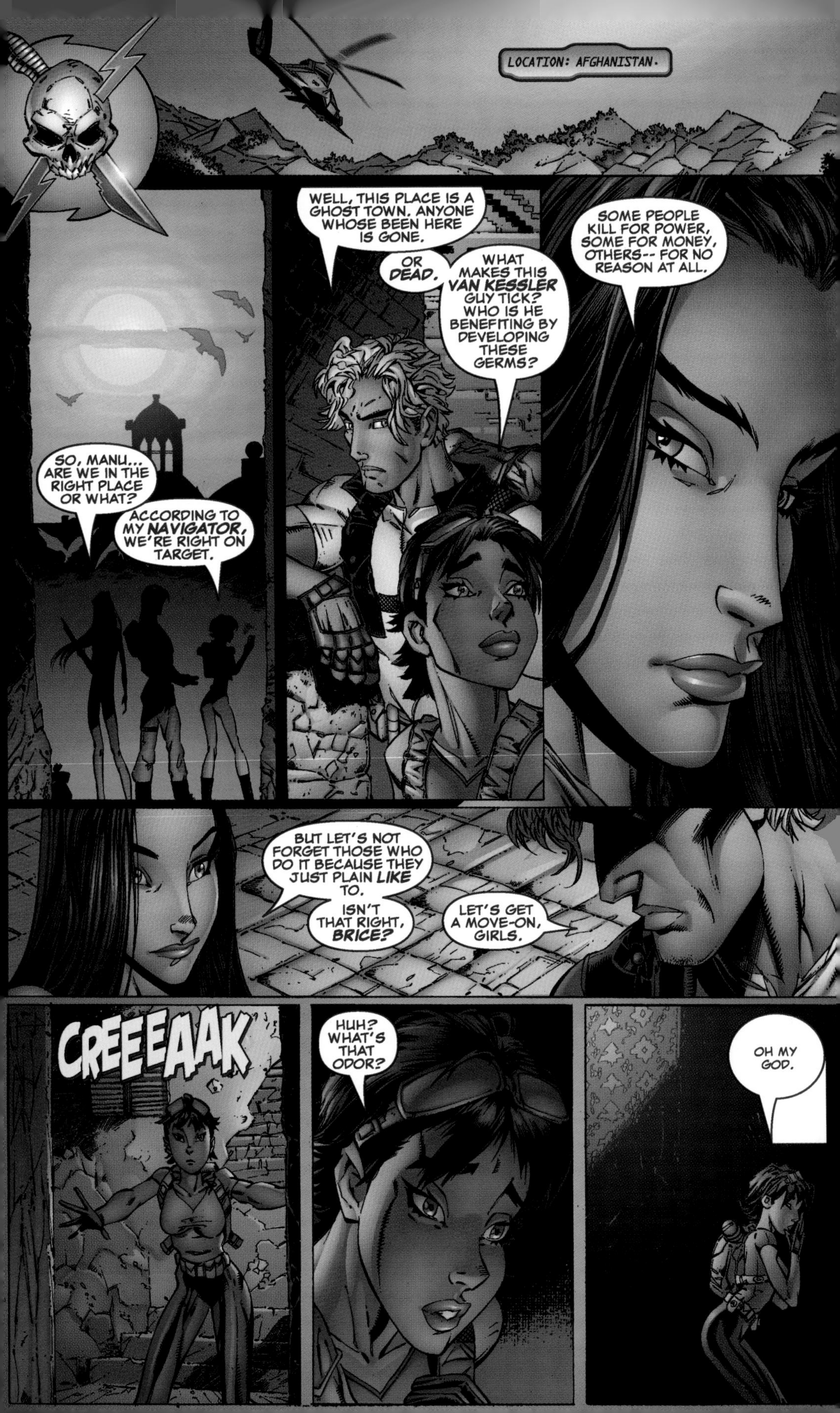
LOCATION: AFGHANISTAN.
SO, MANU... ARE WE IN THE RIGHT PLACE OR WHAT?
ACCORDING TO MY NAVIGATOR, WE'RE RIGHT ON TARGET.
WELL, THIS PLACE IS A GHOST TOWN. ANYONE WHOSE BEEN HERE IS GONE.
OR DEAD.
WHAT MAKES THIS VAN KESSLER GUY TICK? WHO IS HE BENEFITING BY DEVELOPING THESE GERMS?
SOME PEOPLE KILL FOR POWER, SOME FOR MONEY, OTHERS-- FOR NO REASON AT ALL.
BUT LET'S NOT FORGET THOSE WHO DO IT BECAUSE THEY JUST PLAIN LIKE TO.
ISN'T THAT RIGHT, BRICE?
LET'S GET A MOVE-ON, GIRLS.
CREEEAAK
HUH? WHAT'S THAT ODOR?
OH MY GOD.

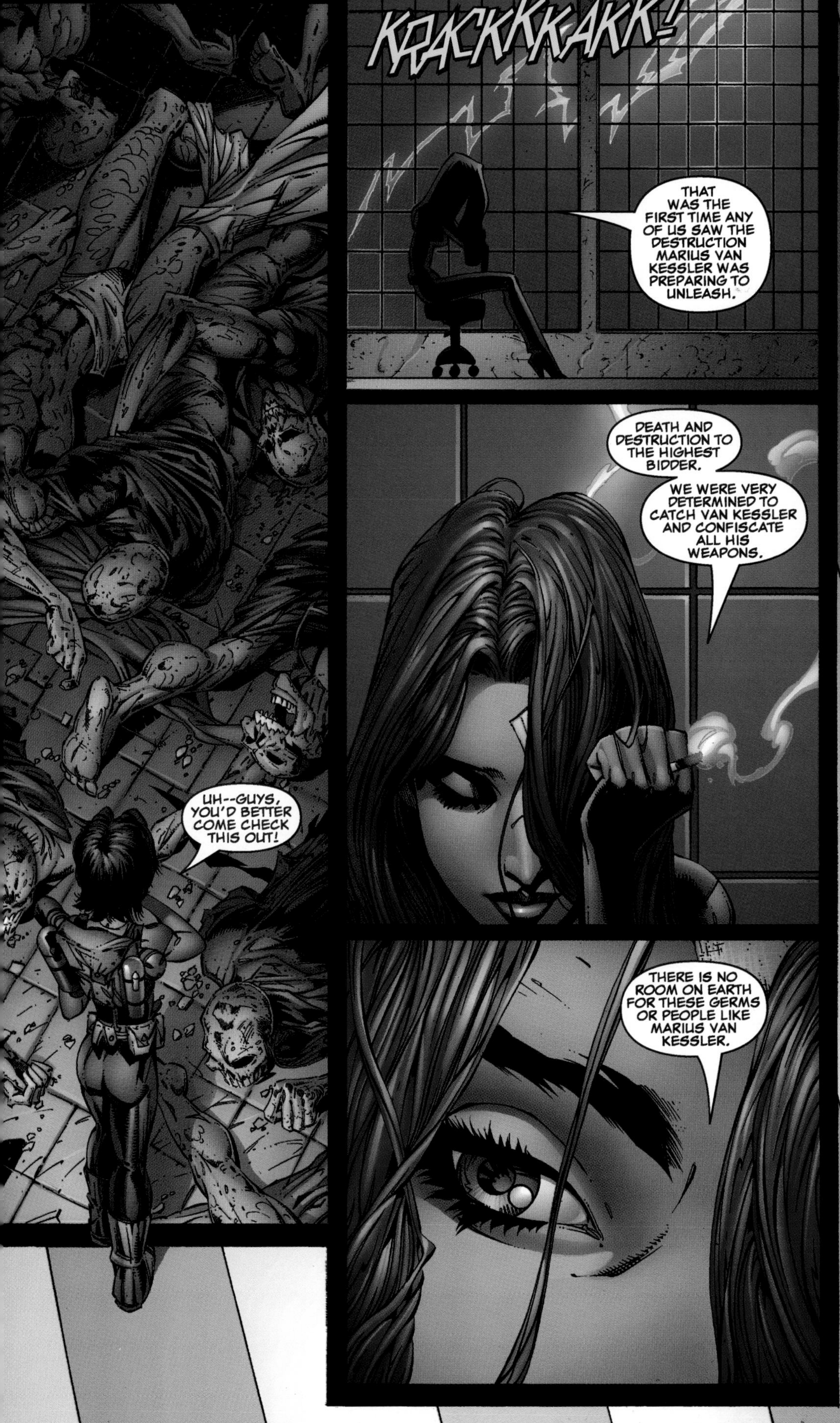
KRACKKKAKK!
THAT WAS THE FIRST TIME ANY OF US SAW THE DESTRUCTION MARIUS VAN KESSLER WAS PREPARING TO UNLEASH.
DEATH AND DESTRUCTION TO THE HIGHEST BIDDER.
WE WERE VERY DETERMINED TO CATCH VAN KESSLER AND CONFISCATE ALL HIS WEAPONS.
THERE IS NO ROOM ON EARTH FOR THESE GERMS OR PEOPLE LIKE MARIUS VAN KESSLER.
UH--GUYS, YOU'D BETTER COME CHECK THIS OUT!

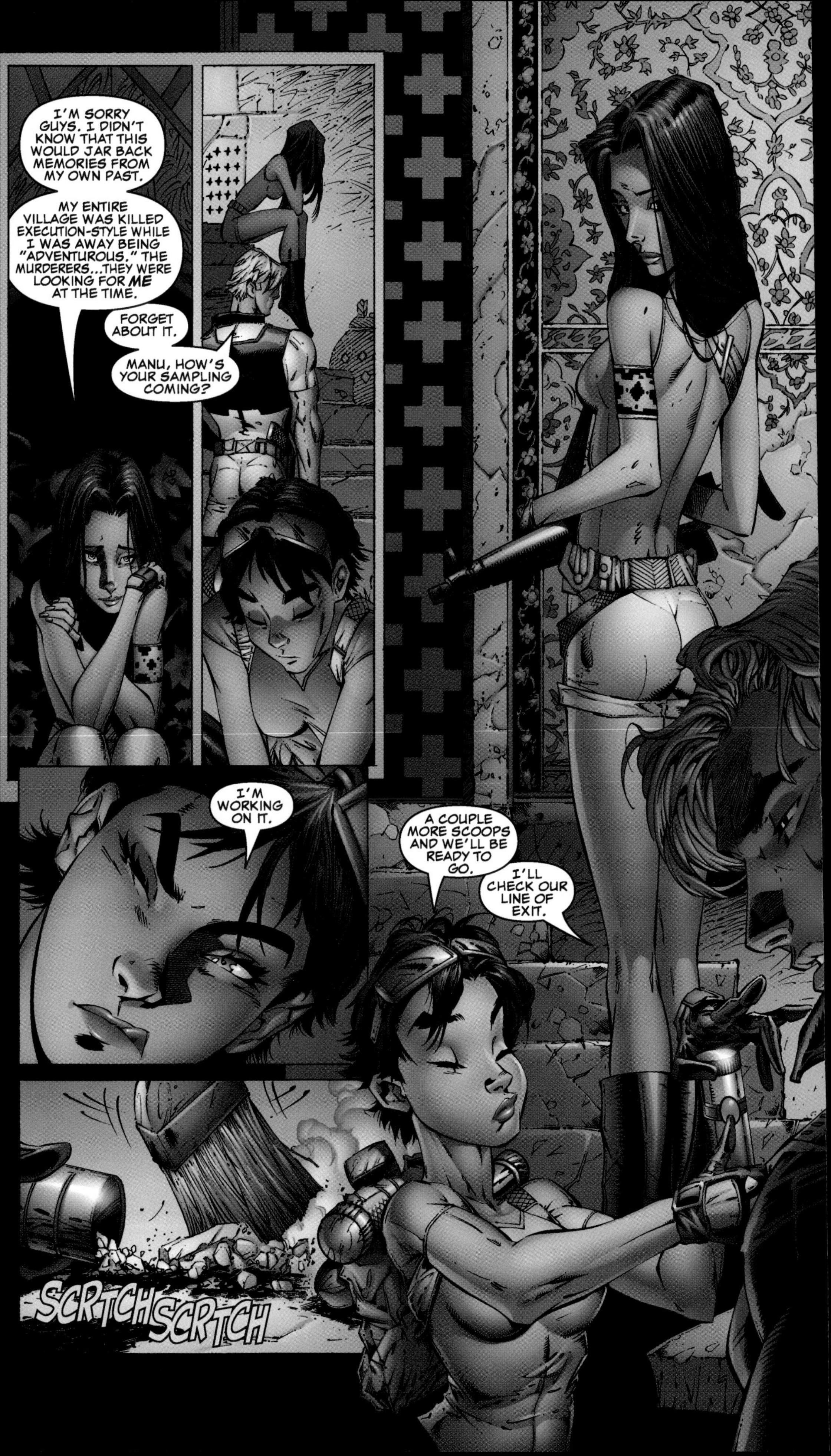
I'M SORRY GUYS. I DIDN'T KNOW THAT THIS WOULD JAR BACK MEMORIES FROM MY OWN PAST.
MY ENTIRE VILLAGE WAS KILLED EXECUTION-STYLE WHILE I WAS AWAY BEING "ADVENTUROUS." THE MURDERERS...THEY WERE LOOKING FOR *ME* AT THE TIME.
FORGET ABOUT IT.
MANU, HOW'S YOUR SAMPLING COMING?
I'M WORKING ON IT.
A COUPLE MORE SCOOPS AND WE'LL BE READY TO GO.
I'LL CHECK OUR LINE OF EXIT.
SCRTCHSCRTCH

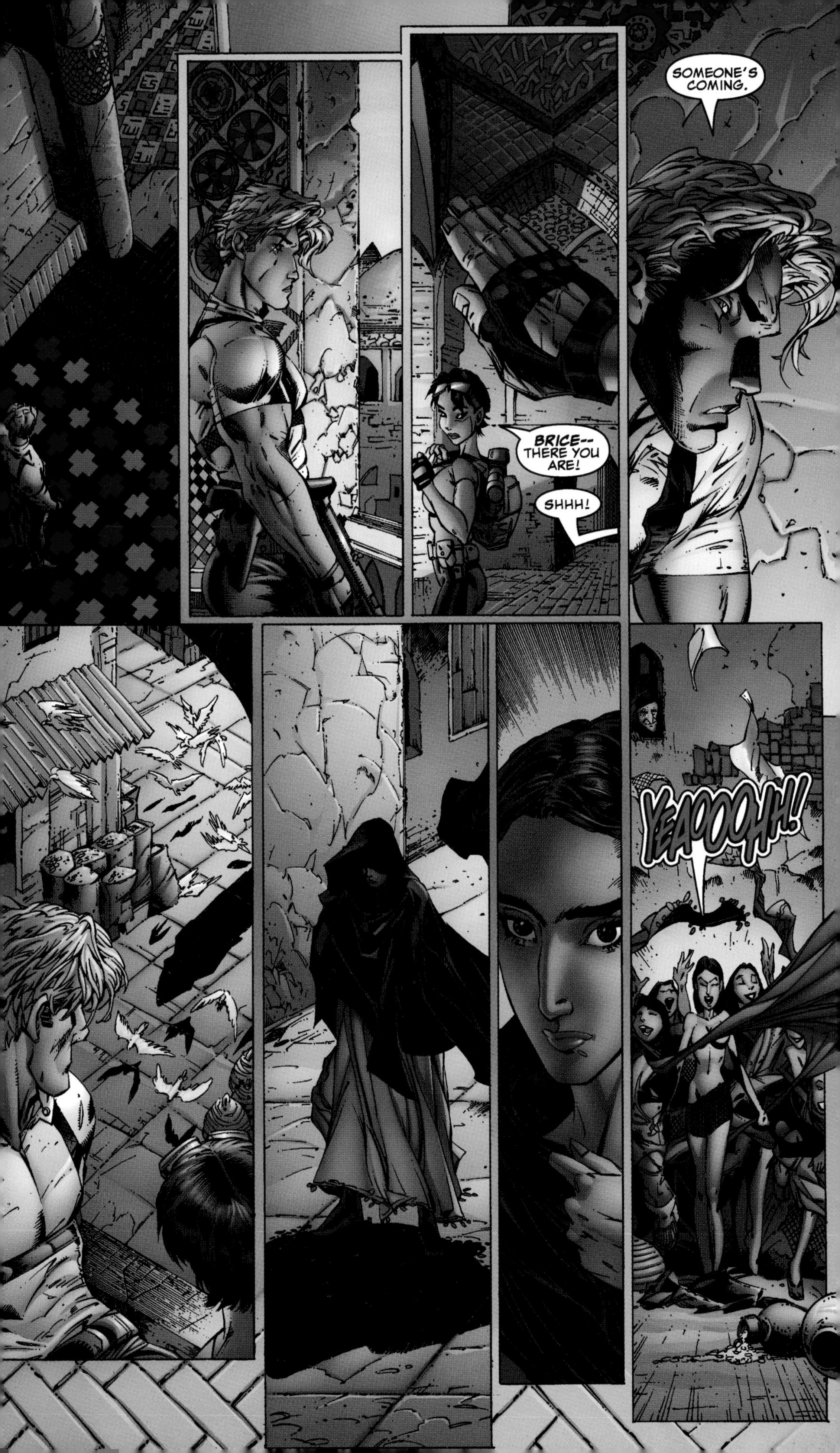
SOMEONE'S COMING.
BRICE-- THERE YOU ARE!
SHHH!
YEAOOOHH!

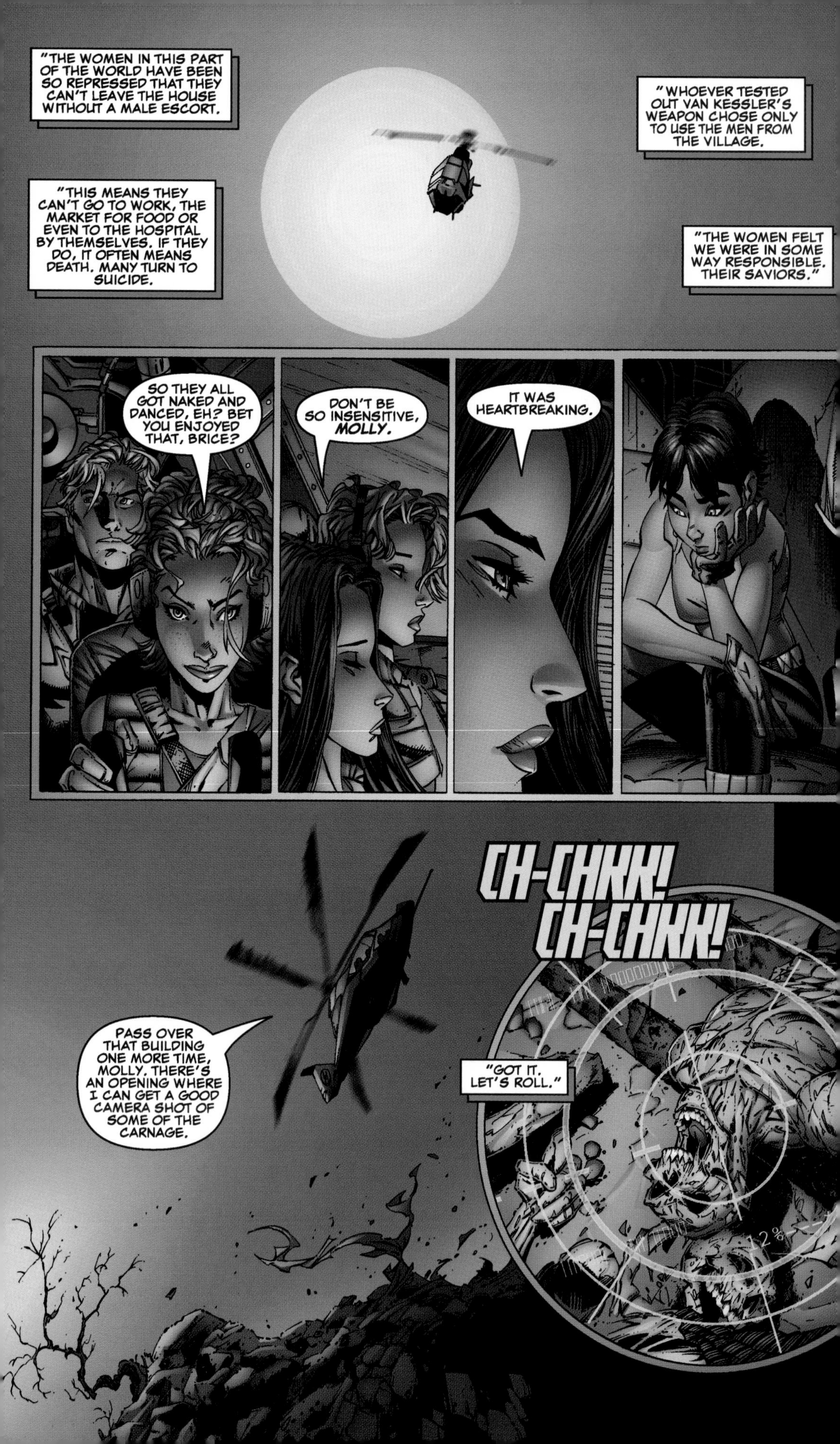
"THE WOMEN IN THIS PART OF THE WORLD HAVE BEEN SO REPRESSED THAT THEY CAN'T LEAVE THE HOUSE WITHOUT A MALE ESCORT.
"THIS MEANS THEY CAN'T GO TO WORK, THE MARKET FOR FOOD OR EVEN TO THE HOSPITAL BY THEMSELVES. IF THEY DO, IT OFTEN MEANS DEATH. MANY TURN TO SUICIDE.
"WHOEVER TESTED OUT VAN KESSLER'S WEAPON CHOSE ONLY TO USE THE MEN FROM THE VILLAGE.
"THE WOMEN FELT WE WERE IN SOME WAY RESPONSIBLE. THEIR SAVIORS."
SO THEY ALL GOT NAKED AND DANCED, EH? BET YOU ENJOYED THAT, BRICE?
DON'T BE SO INSENSITIVE, MOLLY.
IT WAS HEARTBREAKING.
PASS OVER THAT BUILDING ONE MORE TIME, MOLLY. THERE'S AN OPENING WHERE I CAN GET A GOOD CAMERA SHOT OF SOME OF THE CARNAGE.
CH-CHKK! CH-CHKK!
"GOT IT. LET'S ROLL."

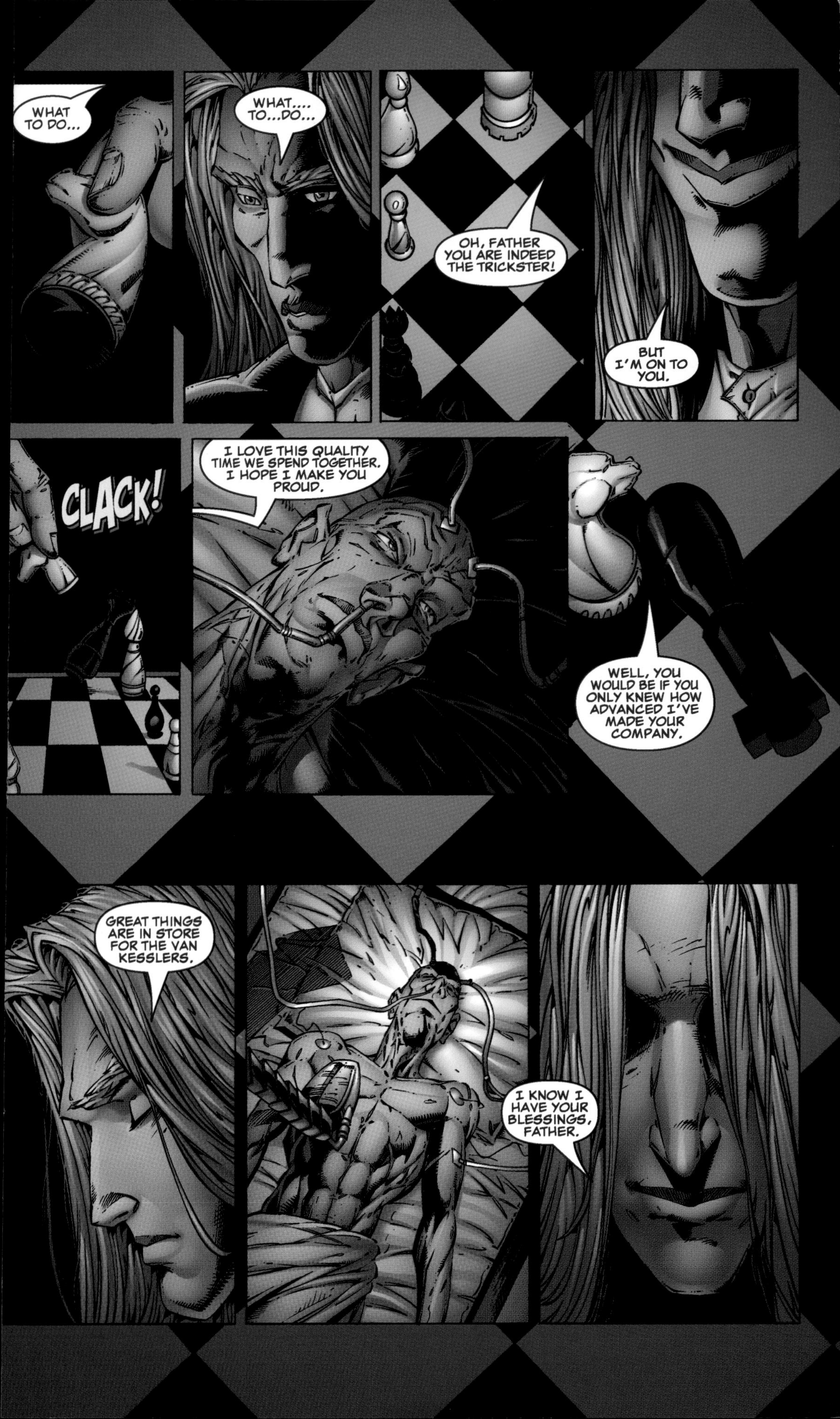
WHAT TO DO...
WHAT.... TO...DO...
OH, FATHER YOU ARE INDEED THE TRICKSTER!
BUT I'M ON TO YOU.
CLACK!
I LOVE THIS QUALITY TIME WE SPEND TOGETHER. I HOPE I MAKE YOU PROUD.
WELL, YOU WOULD BE IF YOU ONLY KNEW HOW ADVANCED I'VE MADE YOUR COMPANY.
GREAT THINGS ARE IN STORE FOR THE VAN KESSLERS.
I KNOW I HAVE YOUR BLESSINGS, FATHER.

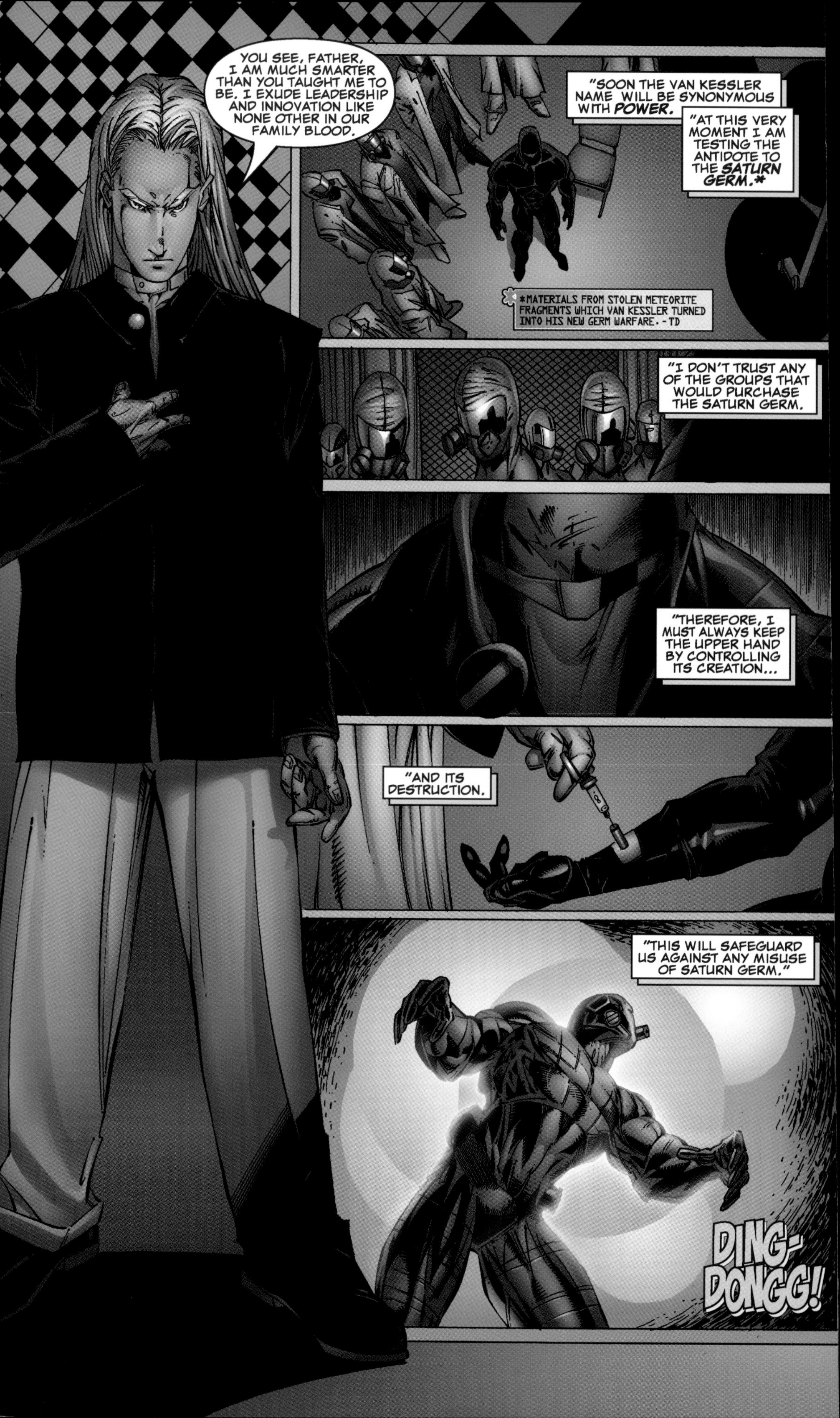
YOU SEE, FATHER, I AM MUCH SMARTER THAN YOU TAUGHT ME TO BE. I EXUDE LEADERSHIP AND INNOVATION LIKE NONE OTHER IN OUR FAMILY BLOOD.
"SOON THE VAN KESSLER NAME WILL BE SYNONYMOUS WITH **POWER.**
"AT THIS VERY MOMENT I AM TESTING THE ANTIDOTE TO THE ***SATURN GERM.****
*MATERIALS FROM STOLEN METEORITE FRAGMENTS WHICH VAN KESSLER TURNED INTO HIS NEW GERM WARFARE. -TD
"I DON'T TRUST ANY OF THE GROUPS THAT WOULD PURCHASE THE SATURN GERM.
"THEREFORE, I MUST ALWAYS KEEP THE UPPER HAND BY CONTROLLING ITS CREATION...
"AND ITS DESTRUCTION.
"THIS WILL SAFEGUARD US AGAINST ANY MISUSE OF SATURN GERM."
DING-DONGG!

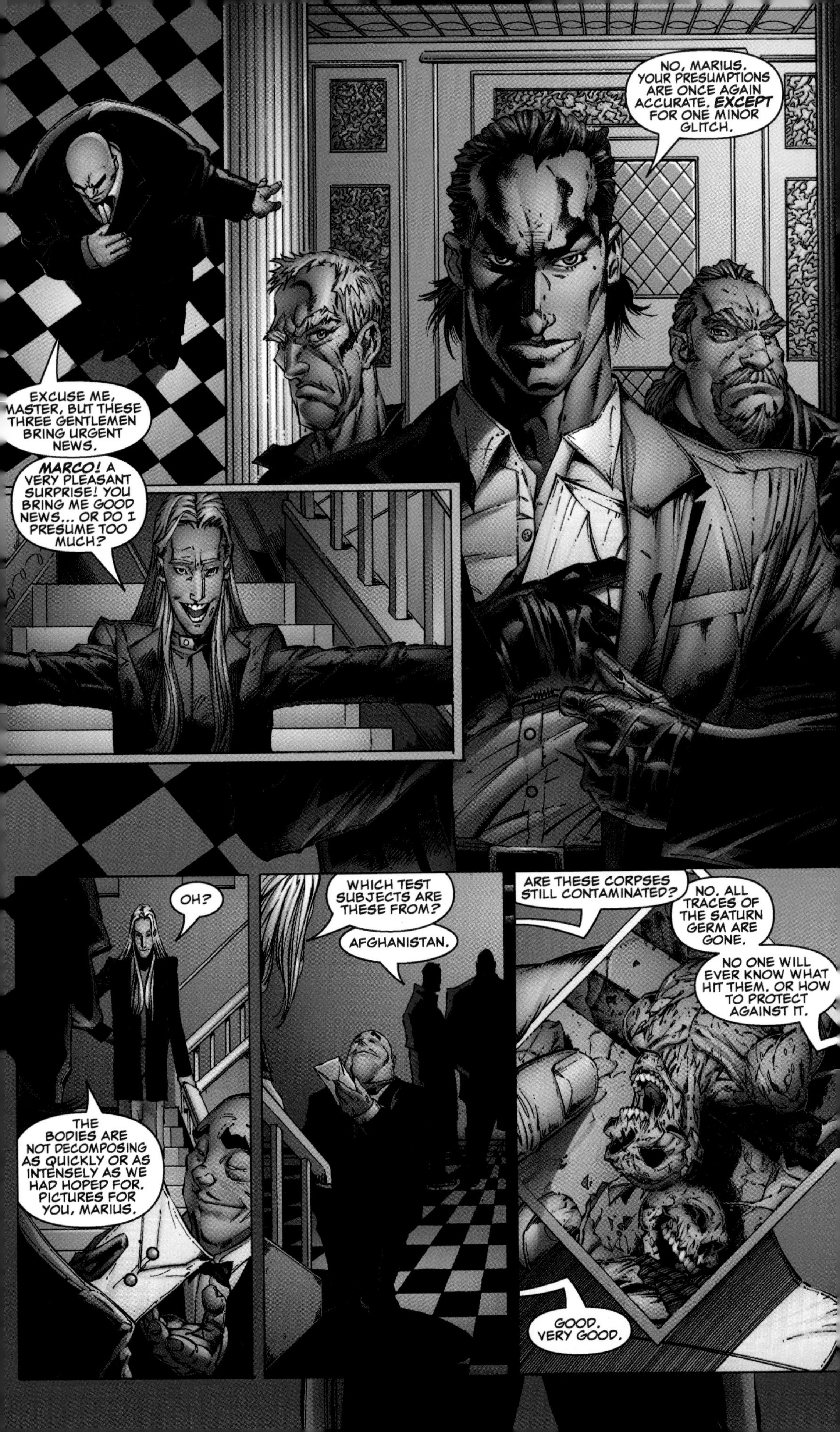
EXCUSE ME, MASTER, BUT THESE THREE GENTLEMEN BRING URGENT NEWS.
MARCO! A VERY PLEASANT SURPRISE! YOU BRING ME GOOD NEWS... OR DO I PRESUME TOO MUCH?
NO, MARIUS. YOUR PRESUMPTIONS ARE ONCE AGAIN ACCURATE. EXCEPT FOR ONE MINOR GLITCH.
OH?
THE BODIES ARE NOT DECOMPOSING AS QUICKLY OR AS INTENSELY AS WE HAD HOPED FOR. PICTURES FOR YOU, MARIUS.
WHICH TEST SUBJECTS ARE THESE FROM?
AFGHANISTAN.
ARE THESE CORPSES STILL CONTAMINATED?
NO. ALL TRACES OF THE SATURN GERM ARE GONE.
NO ONE WILL EVER KNOW WHAT HIT THEM. OR HOW TO PROTECT AGAINST IT.
GOOD. VERY GOOD.

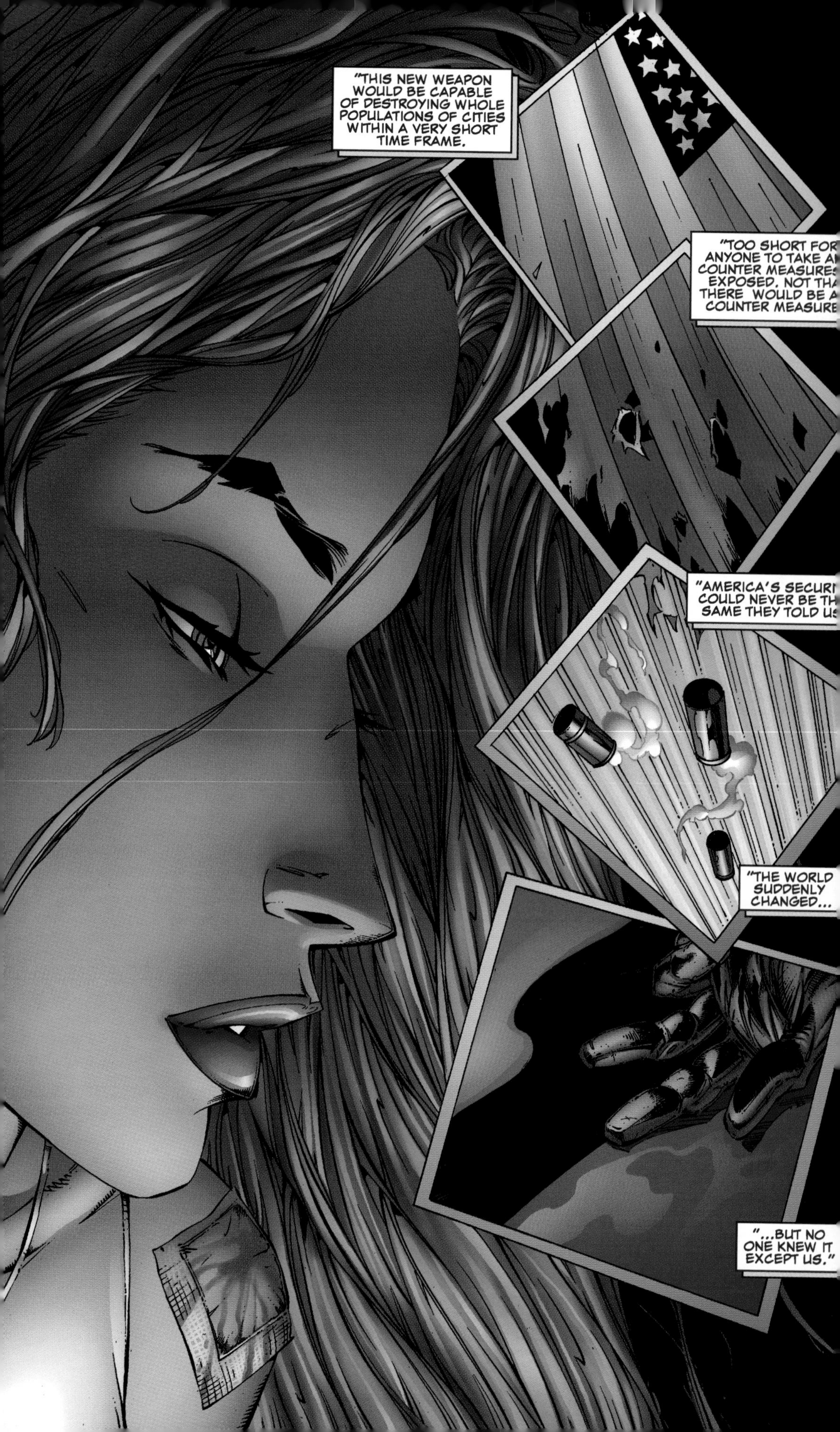
"THIS NEW WEAPON WOULD BE CAPABLE OF DESTROYING WHOLE POPULATIONS OF CITIES WITHIN A VERY SHORT TIME FRAME.
"TOO SHORT FOR ANYONE TO TAKE A COUNTER MEASURES EXPOSED. NOT THA THERE WOULD BE A COUNTER MEASURE
"AMERICA'S SECURI COULD NEVER BE TH SAME THEY TOLD US
"THE WORLD SUDDENLY CHANGED...
"...BUT NO ONE KNEW IT EXCEPT US."

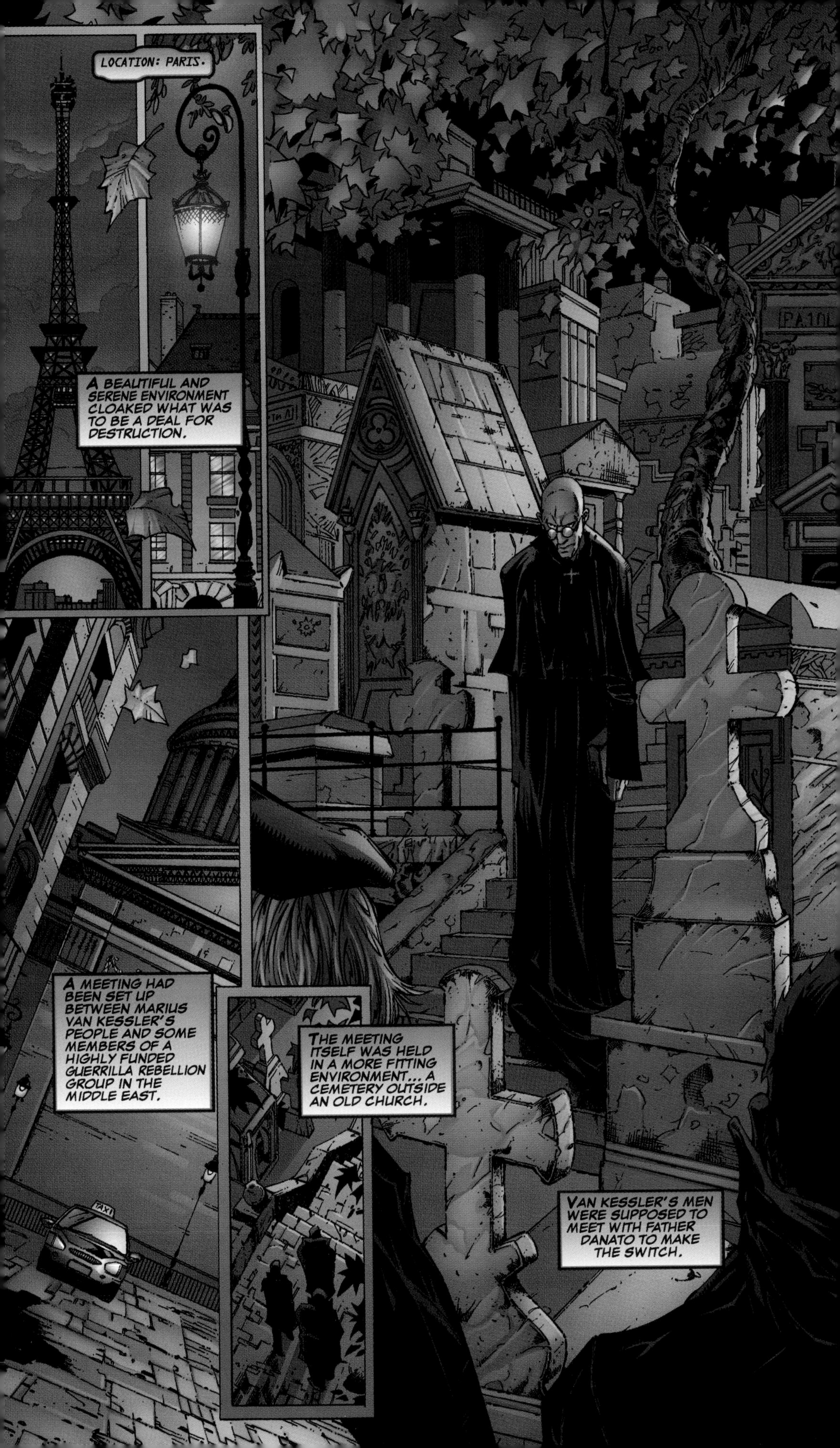
LOCATION: PARIS.
A BEAUTIFUL AND SERENE ENVIRONMENT CLOAKED WHAT WAS TO BE A DEAL FOR DESTRUCTION.
A MEETING HAD BEEN SET UP BETWEEN MARIUS VAN KESSLER'S PEOPLE AND SOME MEMBERS OF A HIGHLY FUNDED GUERRILLA REBELLION GROUP IN THE MIDDLE EAST.
THE MEETING ITSELF WAS HELD IN A MORE FITTING ENVIRONMENT... A CEMETERY OUTSIDE AN OLD CHURCH.
VAN KESSLER'S MEN WERE SUPPOSED TO MEET WITH FATHER DANATO TO MAKE THE SWITCH.

"HE SPOTTED OUR ERROR."

"ONE MAN IN PARTICULAR WAS VERY SHARP."

"THE FATHER NOTICES A BREEZE OF PARANOIA FILL THE ROOM AFTER HE DISCLOSES THAT HE HAS THE MONEY."

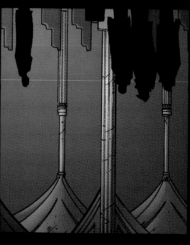
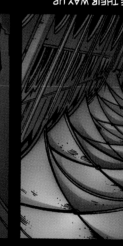

"ALL FOR WHAT WAS CONTAINED IN A MEDIUM-SIZED SUITCASE."

"THE FATHER, REPRESENTING THE MIDDLE EASTERN REBEL GUERRILLAS, WAS READY FOR THE DEAL, EIGHTY MILLION DOLLARS."

"THEY MADE THEIR WAY UP THE BACK STAIRS AND INTO THE CHURCH ITSELF, LED BY FATHER DANATO."

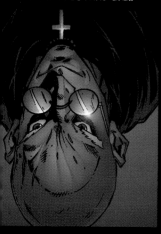

"THE ONLY PROBLEM WAS WITH THE PRIEST, BUT I'LL GET TO HIM IN A SECOND."

"THE EARLY MOMENTS OF THE MEETING WENT AS PLANNED. THEY ARRIVED AT THE CORRECT COORDINATES, BROUGHT THE SATURN GERMS, AND ONLY THREE MEN TO PROTECT IT."

"OUR EARLY SURVEILLANCE PAID OFF NICELY. WE PLANNED TO INTERCEPT THE DEADLY GERMS AND TAKE INTO CUSTODY VAN KESSLER'S HENCHMEN."

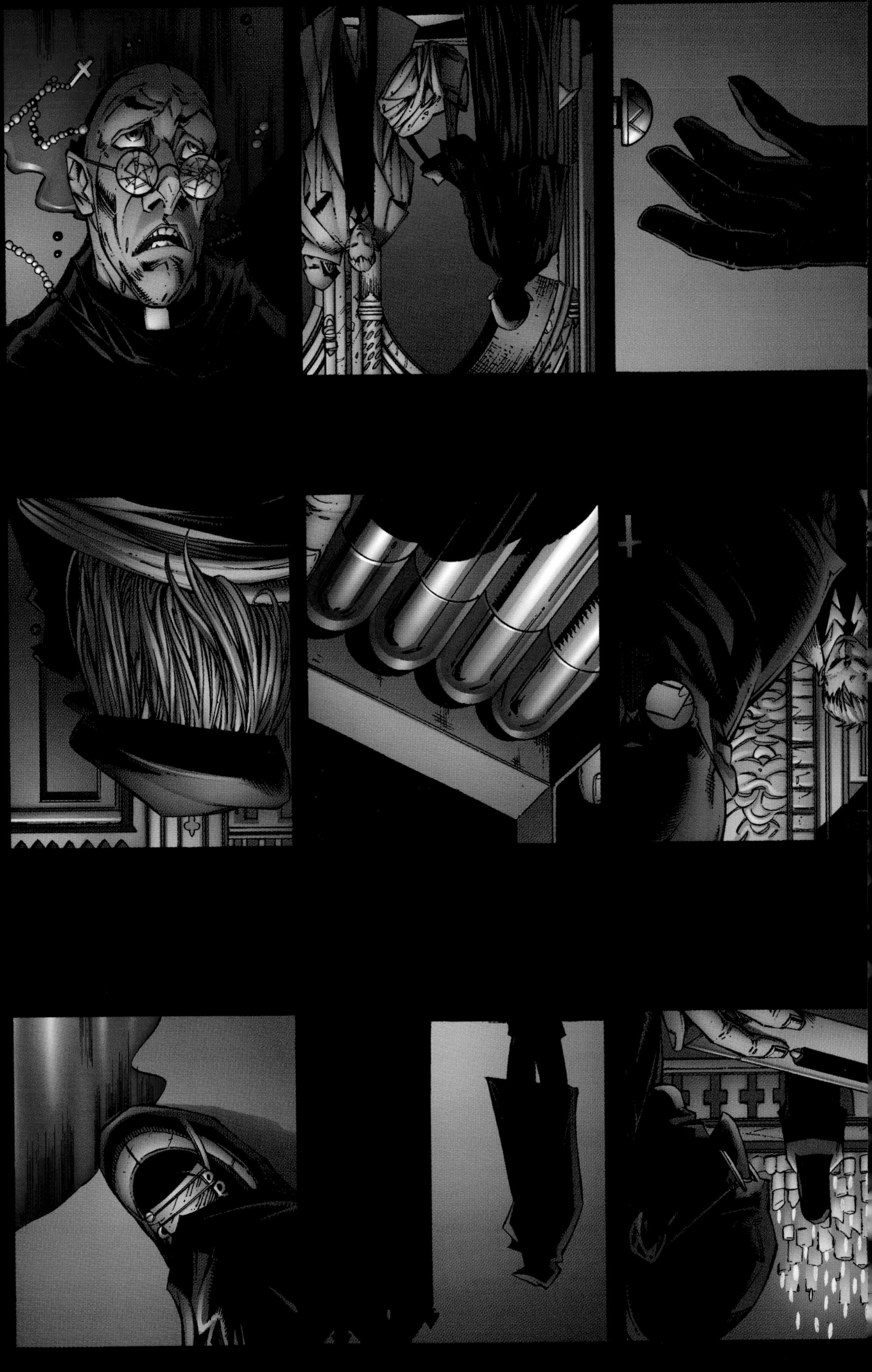

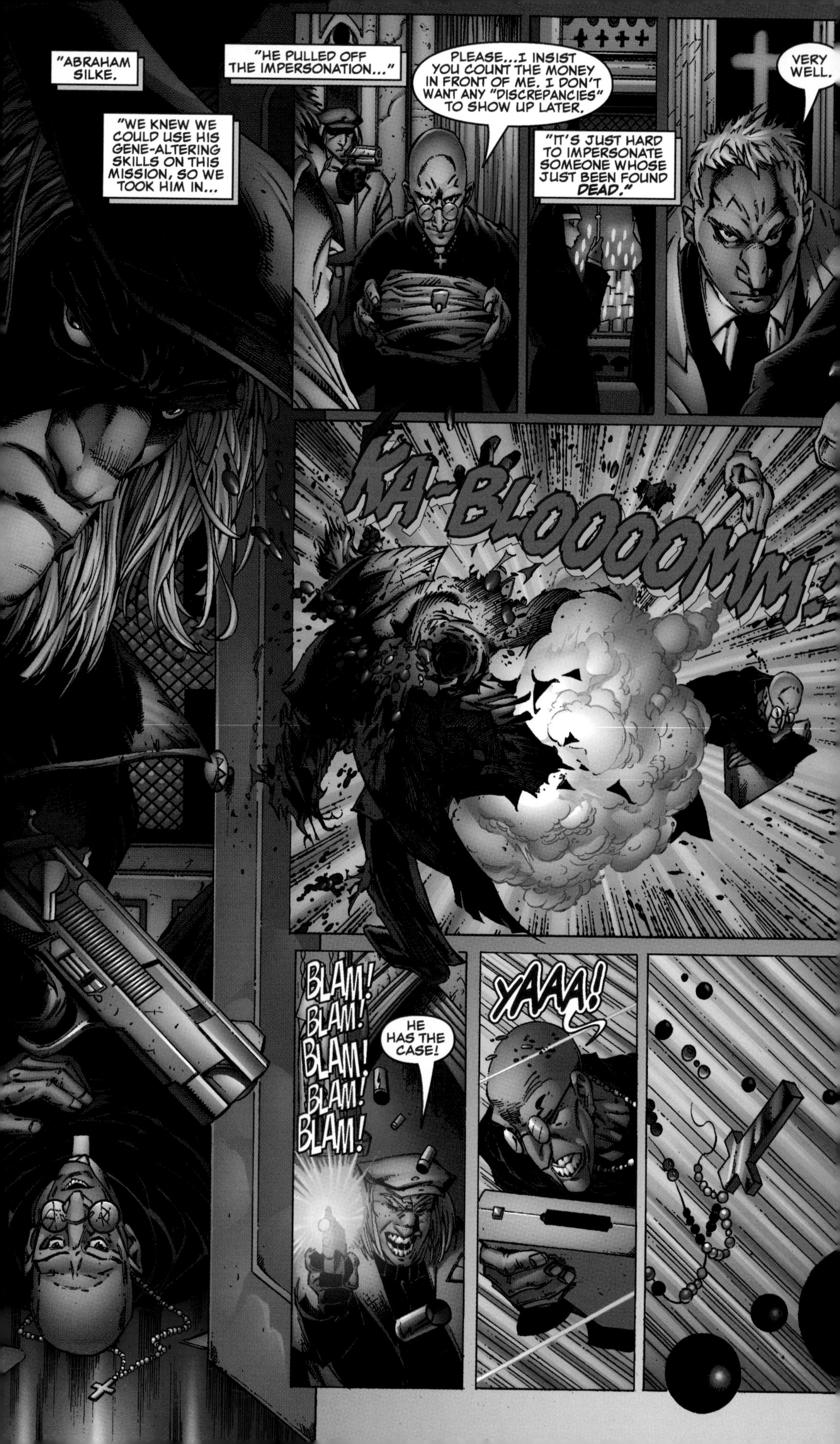
"ABRAHAM SILKE.
"WE KNEW WE COULD USE HIS GENE-ALTERING SKILLS ON THIS MISSION, SO WE TOOK HIM IN...
"HE PULLED OFF THE IMPERSONATION..."
PLEASE...I INSIST YOU COUNT THE MONEY IN FRONT OF ME. I DON'T WANT ANY "DISCREPANCIES" TO SHOW UP LATER.
"IT'S JUST HARD TO IMPERSONATE SOMEONE WHOSE JUST BEEN FOUND DEAD."
VERY WELL.
KA-BLOOOOOMM!
BLAM! BLAM! BLAM! BLAM! BLAM!
HE HAS THE CASE!
YAAA!

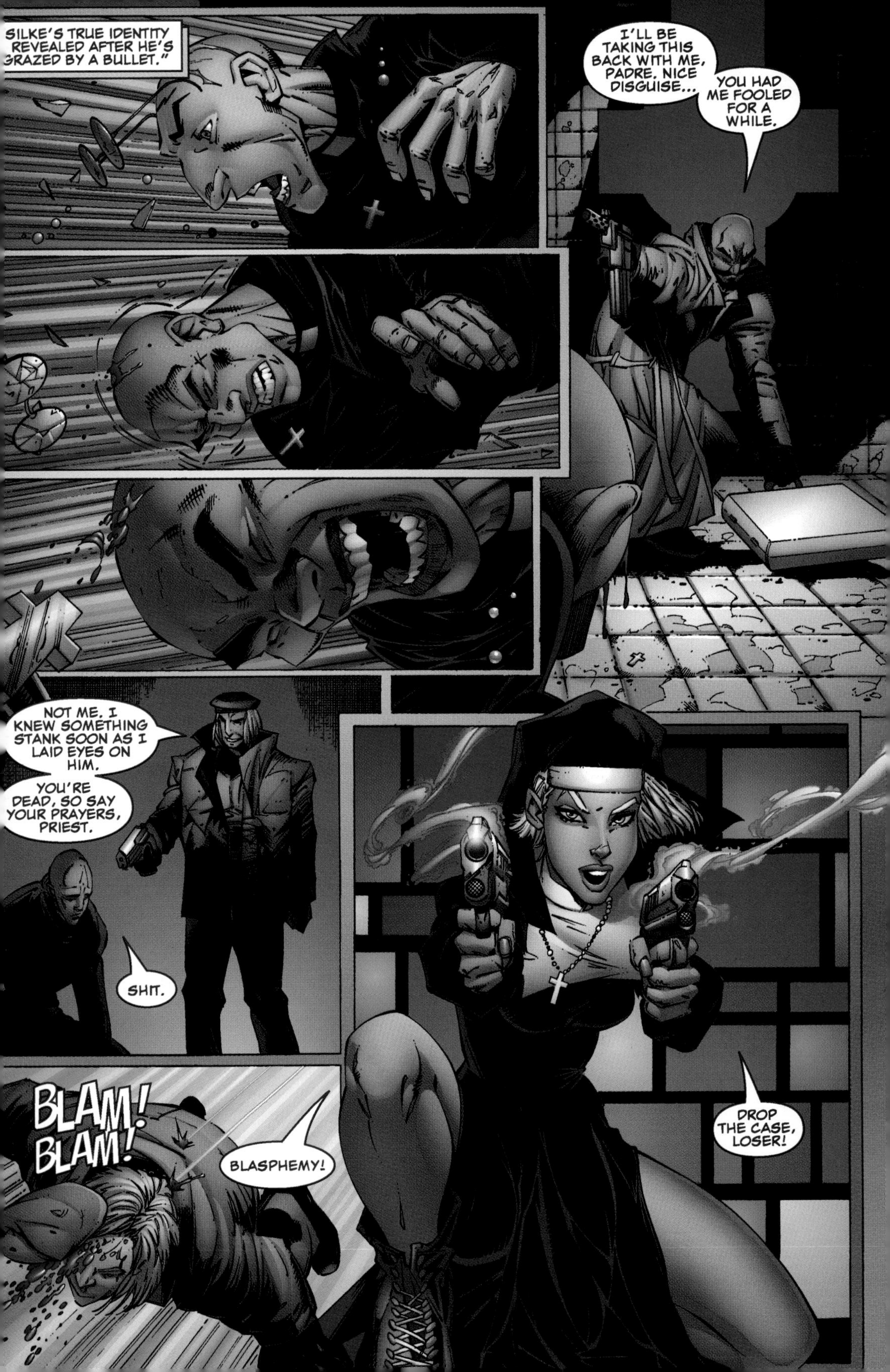

SILKE'S TRUE IDENTITY REVEALED AFTER HE'S GRAZED BY A BULLET."
I'LL BE TAKING THIS BACK WITH ME, PADRE. NICE DISGUISE...
YOU HAD ME FOOLED FOR A WHILE.
NOT ME. I KNEW SOMETHING STANK SOON AS I LAID EYES ON HIM.
YOU'RE DEAD, SO SAY YOUR PRAYERS, PRIEST.
SHIT.
DROP THE CASE, LOSER!
BLAM! BLAM!
BLASPHEMY!

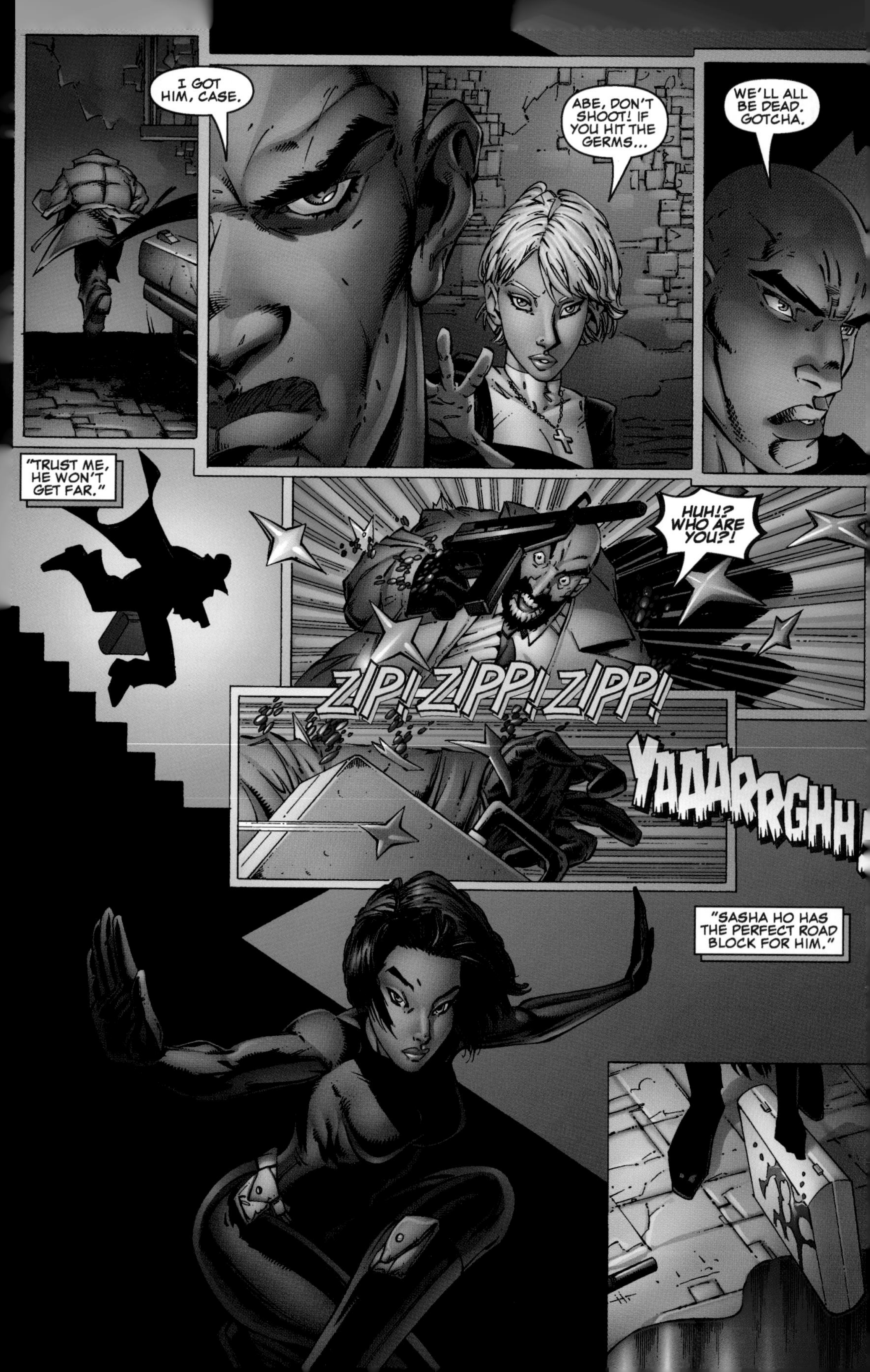
I GOT HIM, CASE.
ABE, DON'T SHOOT! IF YOU HIT THE GERMS...
WE'LL ALL BE DEAD. GOTCHA.
"TRUST ME, HE WON'T GET FAR."
HUH!? WHO ARE YOU?!
ZIP! ZIPP! ZIPP!
YAAARRGHH
"SASHA HO HAS THE PERFECT ROAD BLOCK FOR HIM."

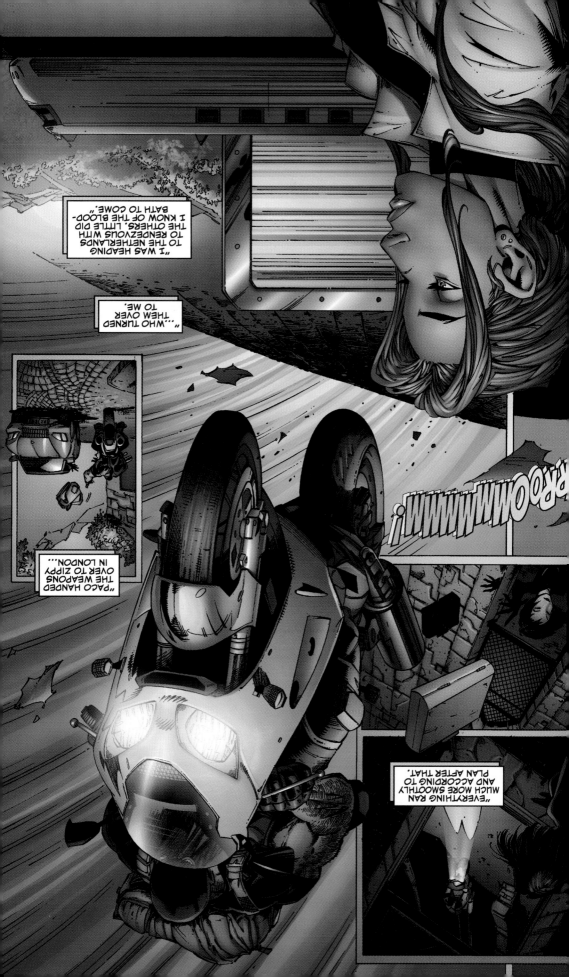

"I WAS HEADING TO THE NETHERLANDS TO RENDEZVOUS WITH THE OTHERS. LITTLE DID I KNOW OF THE BLOOD-BATH TO COME."

"'...WHO TURNED THEM OVER TO ME.'"

"PACO HANDED THE WEAPONS OVER TO ZIPPY IN LONDON..."

¡WWWWWWROOOM!

"EVERYTHING RAN MUCH MORE SMOOTHLY AND ACCORDING TO PLAN AFTER THAT."

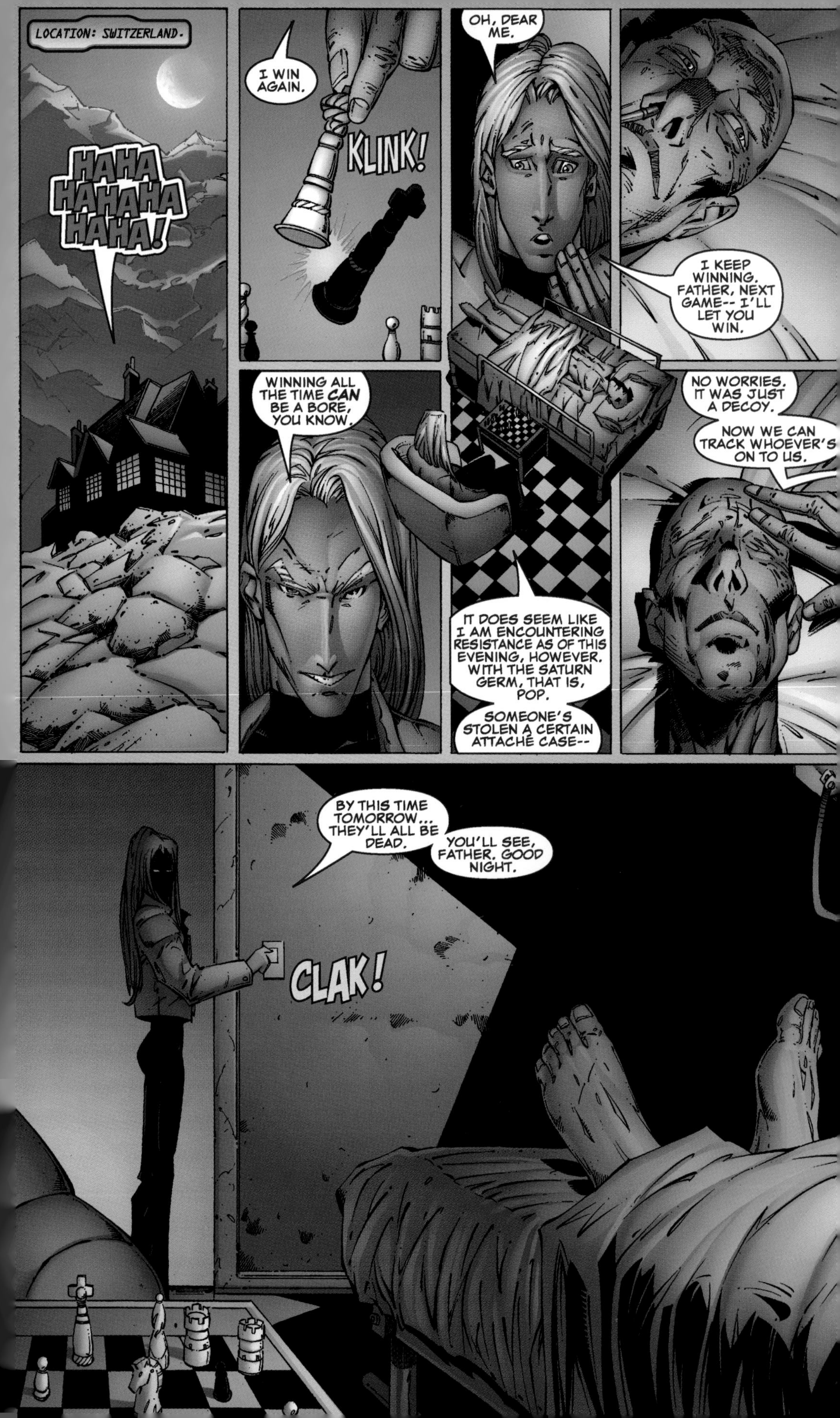
LOCATION: SWITZERLAND.
HAHA HAHAHA HAHA!
I WIN AGAIN.
KLINK!
OH, DEAR ME.
I KEEP WINNING. FATHER, NEXT GAME-- I'LL LET YOU WIN.
WINNING ALL THE TIME CAN BE A BORE, YOU KNOW.
IT DOES SEEM LIKE I AM ENCOUNTERING RESISTANCE AS OF THIS EVENING, HOWEVER. WITH THE SATURN GERM, THAT IS, POP.
SOMEONE'S STOLEN A CERTAIN ATTACHÉ CASE--
NO WORRIES. IT WAS JUST A DECOY.
NOW WE CAN TRACK WHOEVER'S ON TO US.
BY THIS TIME TOMORROW... THEY'LL ALL BE DEAD.
YOU'LL SEE, FATHER. GOOD NIGHT.
CLAK!

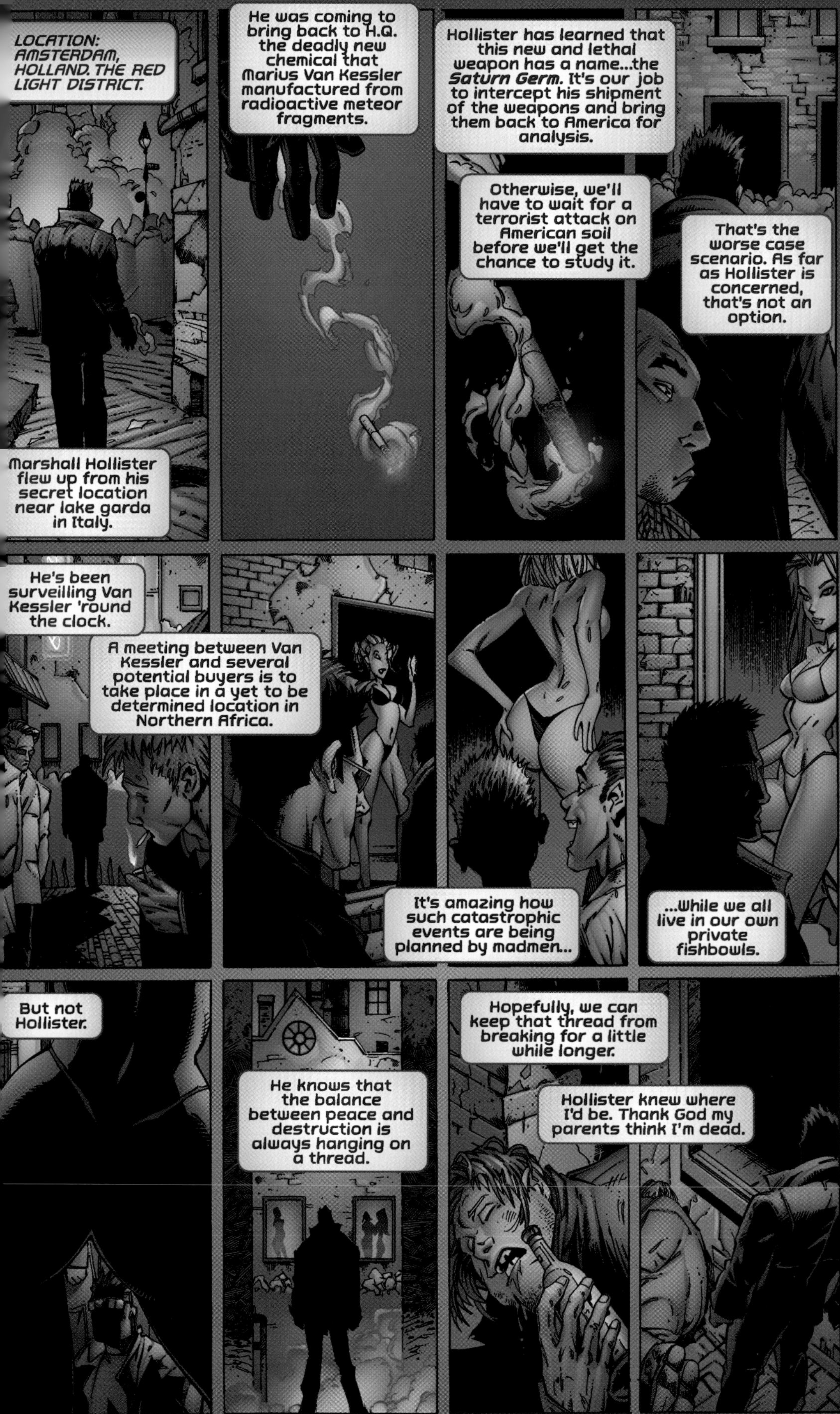

LOCATION: AMSTERDAM, HOLLAND. THE RED LIGHT DISTRICT.
Marshall Hollister flew up from his secret location near lake garda in Italy.
He was coming to bring back to H.Q. the deadly new chemical that Marius Van Kessler manufactured from radioactive meteor fragments.
Hollister has learned that this new and lethal weapon has a name...the *Saturn Germ*. It's our job to intercept his shipment of the weapons and bring them back to America for analysis.
Otherwise, we'll have to wait for a terrorist attack on American soil before we'll get the chance to study it.
That's the worse case scenario. As far as Hollister is concerned, that's not an option.
He's been surveilling Van Kessler 'round the clock.
A meeting between Van Kessler and several potential buyers is to take place in a yet to be determined location in Northern Africa.
It's amazing how such catastrophic events are being planned by madmen...
...while we all live in our own private fishbowls.
But not Hollister.
He knows that the balance between peace and destruction is always hanging on a thread.
Hopefully, we can keep that thread from breaking for a little while longer.
Hollister knew where I'd be. Thank God my parents think I'm dead.

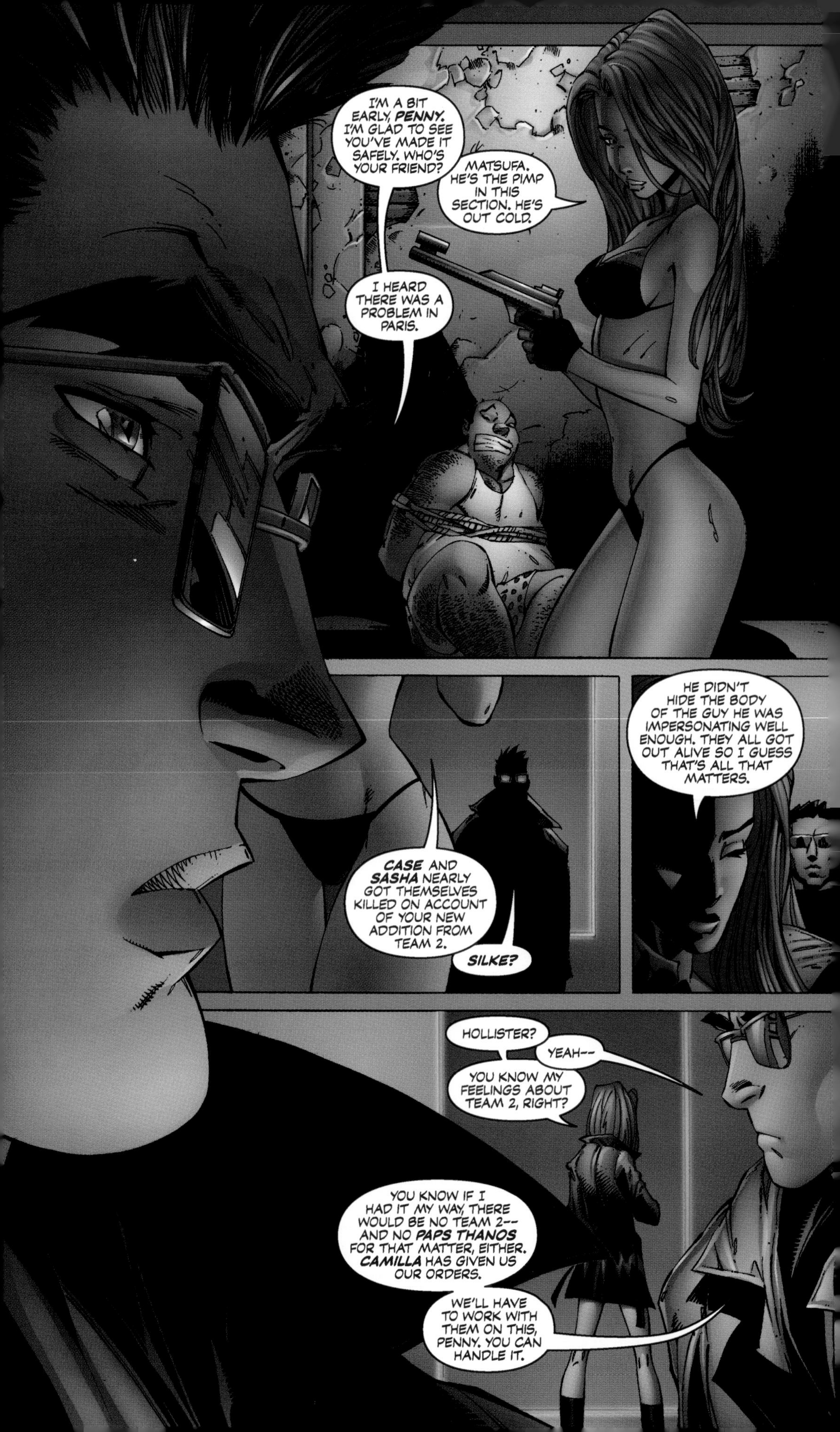
I'M A BIT EARLY, **PENNY.** I'M GLAD TO SEE YOU'VE MADE IT SAFELY. WHO'S YOUR FRIEND?
MATSUFA. HE'S THE PIMP IN THIS SECTION. HE'S OUT COLD.
I HEARD THERE WAS A PROBLEM IN PARIS.
HE DIDN'T HIDE THE BODY OF THE GUY HE WAS IMPERSONATING WELL ENOUGH. THEY ALL GOT OUT ALIVE SO I GUESS THAT'S ALL THAT MATTERS.
CASE AND **SASHA** NEARLY GOT THEMSELVES KILLED ON ACCOUNT OF YOUR NEW ADDITION FROM TEAM 2.
SILKE?
HOLLISTER?
YEAH--
YOU KNOW MY FEELINGS ABOUT TEAM 2, RIGHT?
YOU KNOW IF I HAD IT MY WAY, THERE WOULD BE NO TEAM 2-- AND NO **PAPS THANOS** FOR THAT MATTER, EITHER. **CAMILLA** HAS GIVEN US OUR ORDERS.
WE'LL HAVE TO WORK WITH THEM ON THIS, PENNY. YOU CAN HANDLE IT.

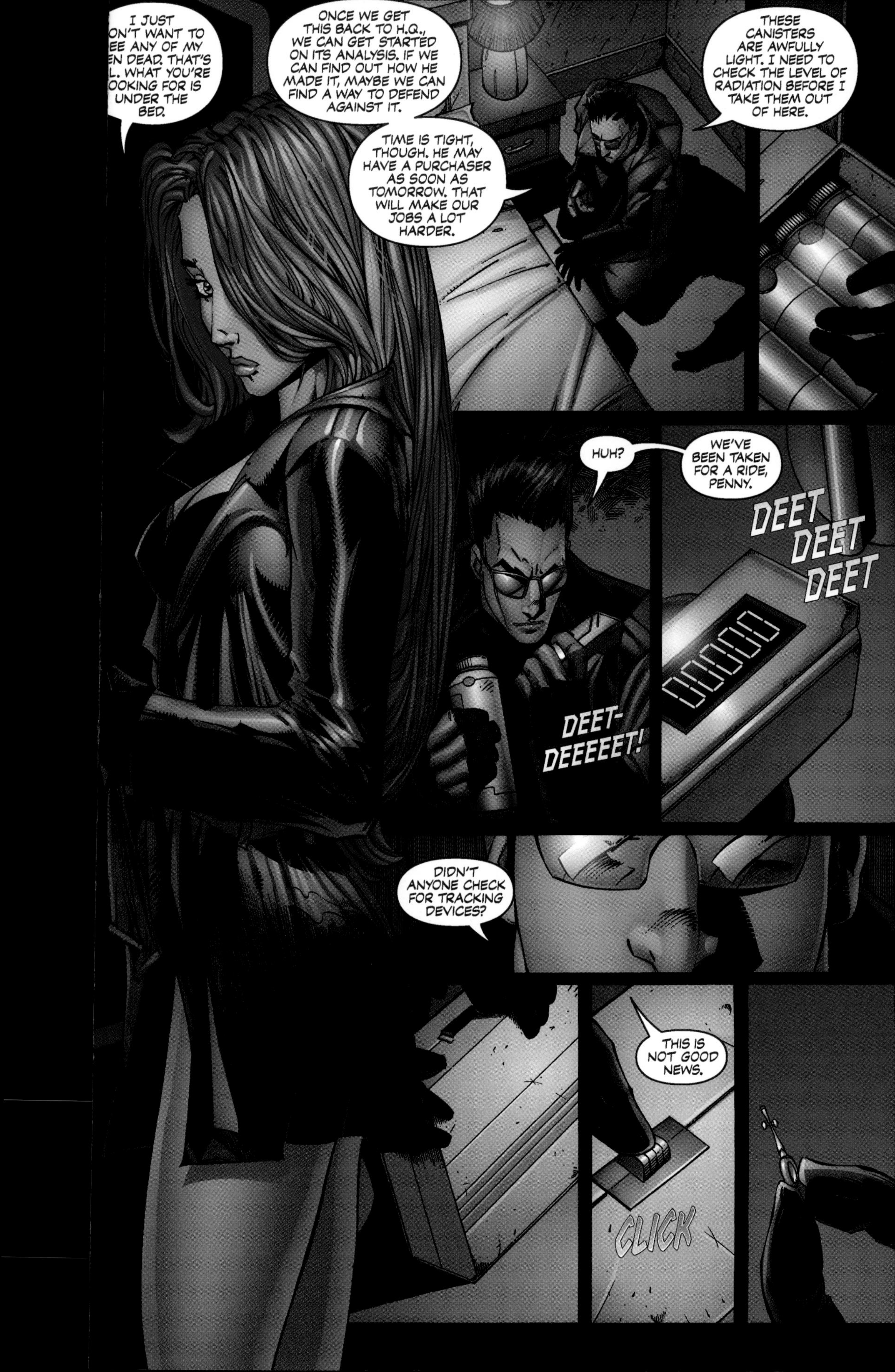
I JUST ON'T WANT TO EE ANY OF MY EN DEAD. THAT'S L. WHAT YOU'RE OOKING FOR IS UNDER THE BED.
ONCE WE GET THIS BACK TO H.Q., WE CAN GET STARTED ON ITS ANALYSIS. IF WE CAN FIND OUT HOW HE MADE IT, MAYBE WE CAN FIND A WAY TO DEFEND AGAINST IT.
TIME IS TIGHT, THOUGH. HE MAY HAVE A PURCHASER AS SOON AS TOMORROW. THAT WILL MAKE OUR JOBS A LOT HARDER.
THESE CANISTERS ARE AWFULLY LIGHT. I NEED TO CHECK THE LEVEL OF RADIATION BEFORE I TAKE THEM OUT OF HERE.
HUH?
WE'VE BEEN TAKEN FOR A RIDE, PENNY.
DEET DEET DEET
DEET-DEEEEET!
DIDN'T ANYONE CHECK FOR TRACKING DEVICES?
THIS IS NOT GOOD NEWS.
CLICK

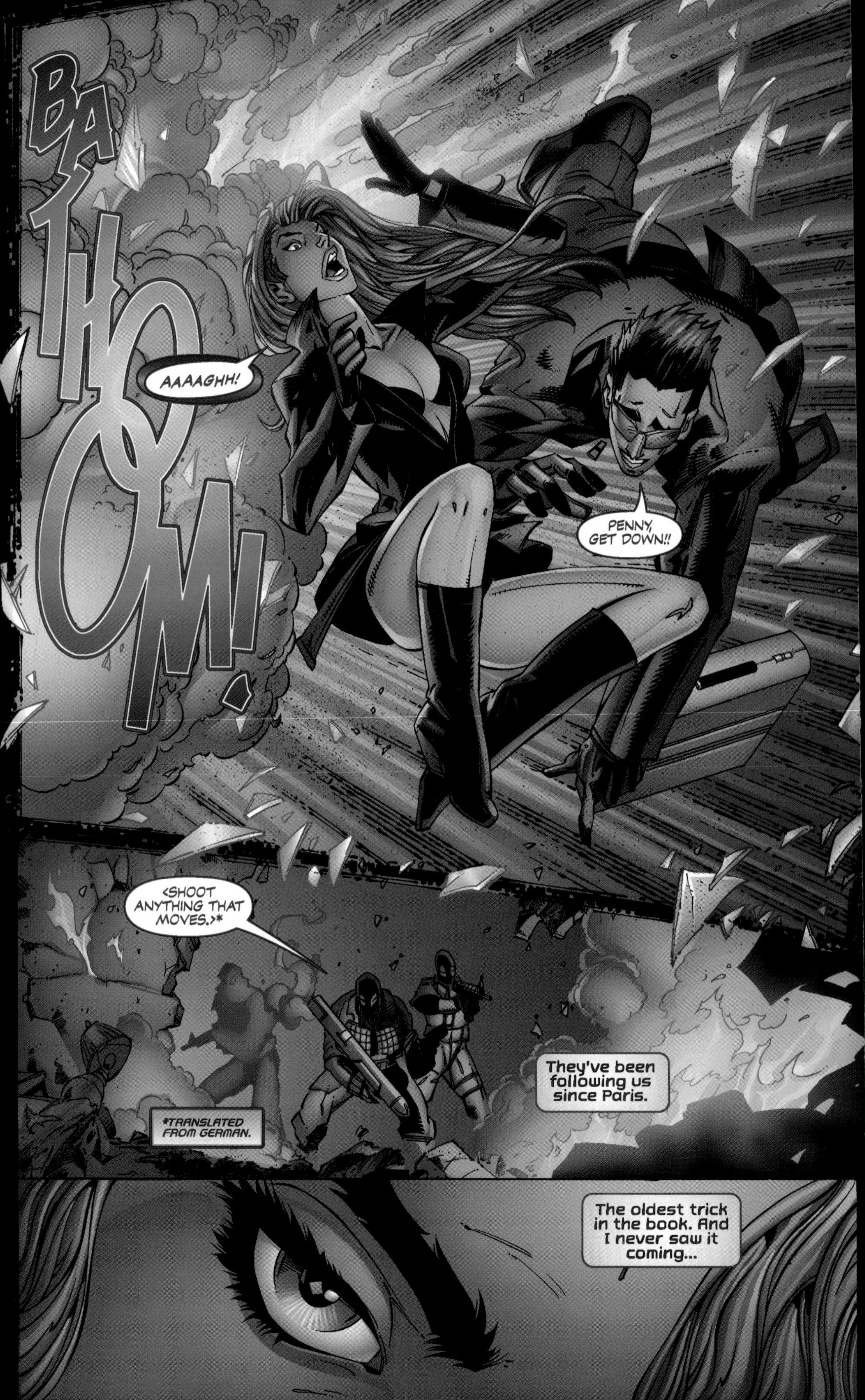
BATHOOM!
AAAAGHH!
PENNY, GET DOWN!!
<SHOOT ANYTHING THAT MOVES.>*
They've been following us since Paris.
*TRANSLATED FROM GERMAN.
The oldest trick in the book. And I never saw it coming...

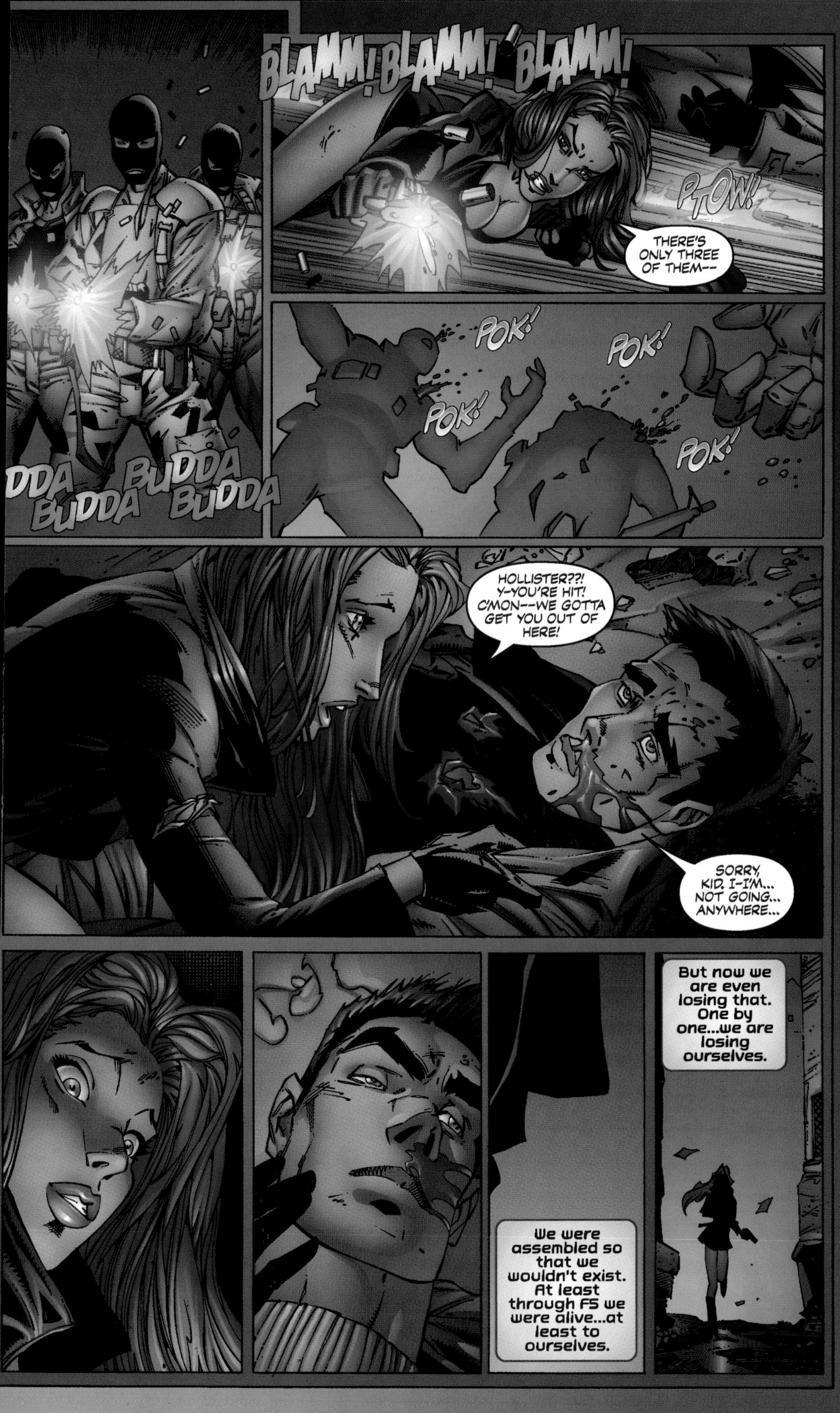
BLAMM! BLAMM! BLAMM!
PTOW!
THERE'S ONLY THREE OF THEM--
BUDDA BUDDA BUDDA BUDDA
POK! POK! POK! POK!
HOLLISTER??! Y-YOU'RE HIT! C'MON--WE GOTTA GET YOU OUT OF HERE!
SORRY, KID. I-I'M... NOT GOING... ANYWHERE...
We were assembled so that we wouldn't exist. At least through F5 we were alive...at least to ourselves.
But now we are even losing that. One by one...we are losing ourselves.

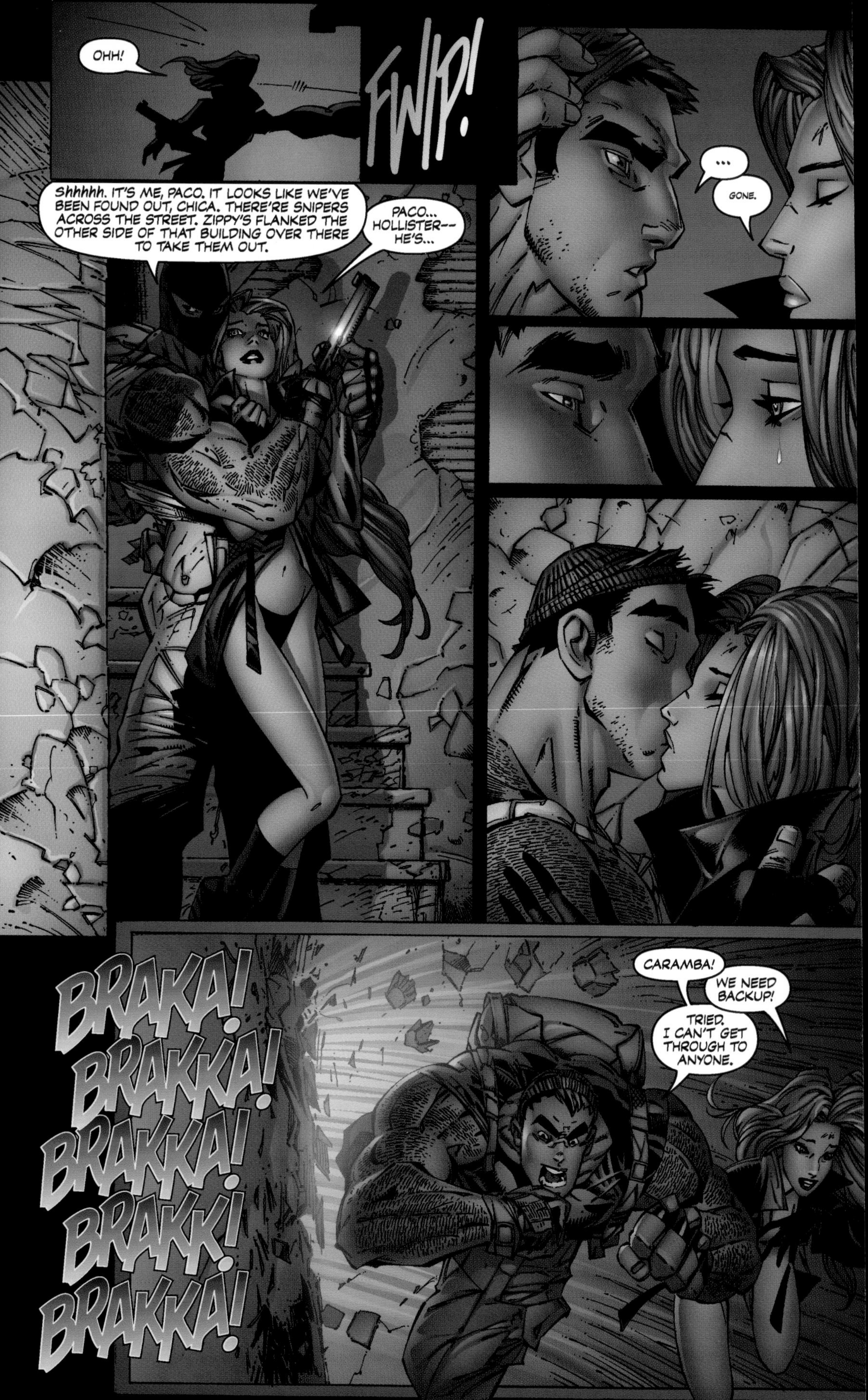
OHH!
FWIP!
Shhhhh. IT'S ME, PACO. IT LOOKS LIKE WE'VE BEEN FOUND OUT, CHICA. THERE'RE SNIPERS ACROSS THE STREET. ZIPPY'S FLANKED THE OTHER SIDE OF THAT BUILDING OVER THERE TO TAKE THEM OUT.
PACO... HOLLISTER-- HE'S...
...
GONE.
BRAKA! BRAKKA! BRAKKA! BRAKK! BRAKKA!
CARAMBA!
WE NEED BACKUP!
TRIED. I CAN'T GET THROUGH TO ANYONE.

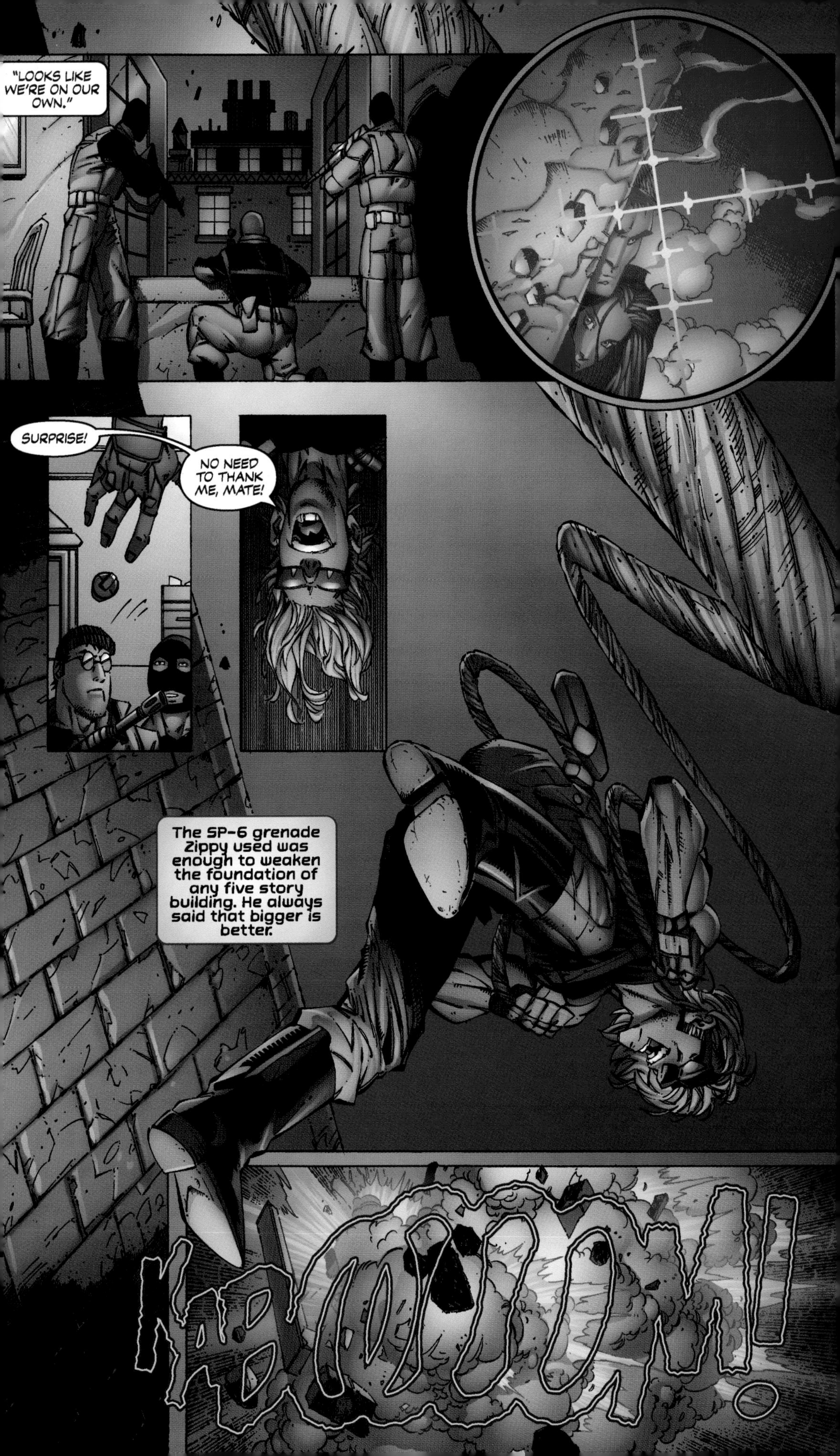
"LOOKS LIKE WE'RE ON OUR OWN."
SURPRISE!
NO NEED TO THANK ME, MATE!
The SP-6 grenade Zippy used was enough to weaken the foundation of any five story building. He always said that bigger is better.
KABOOOOM!

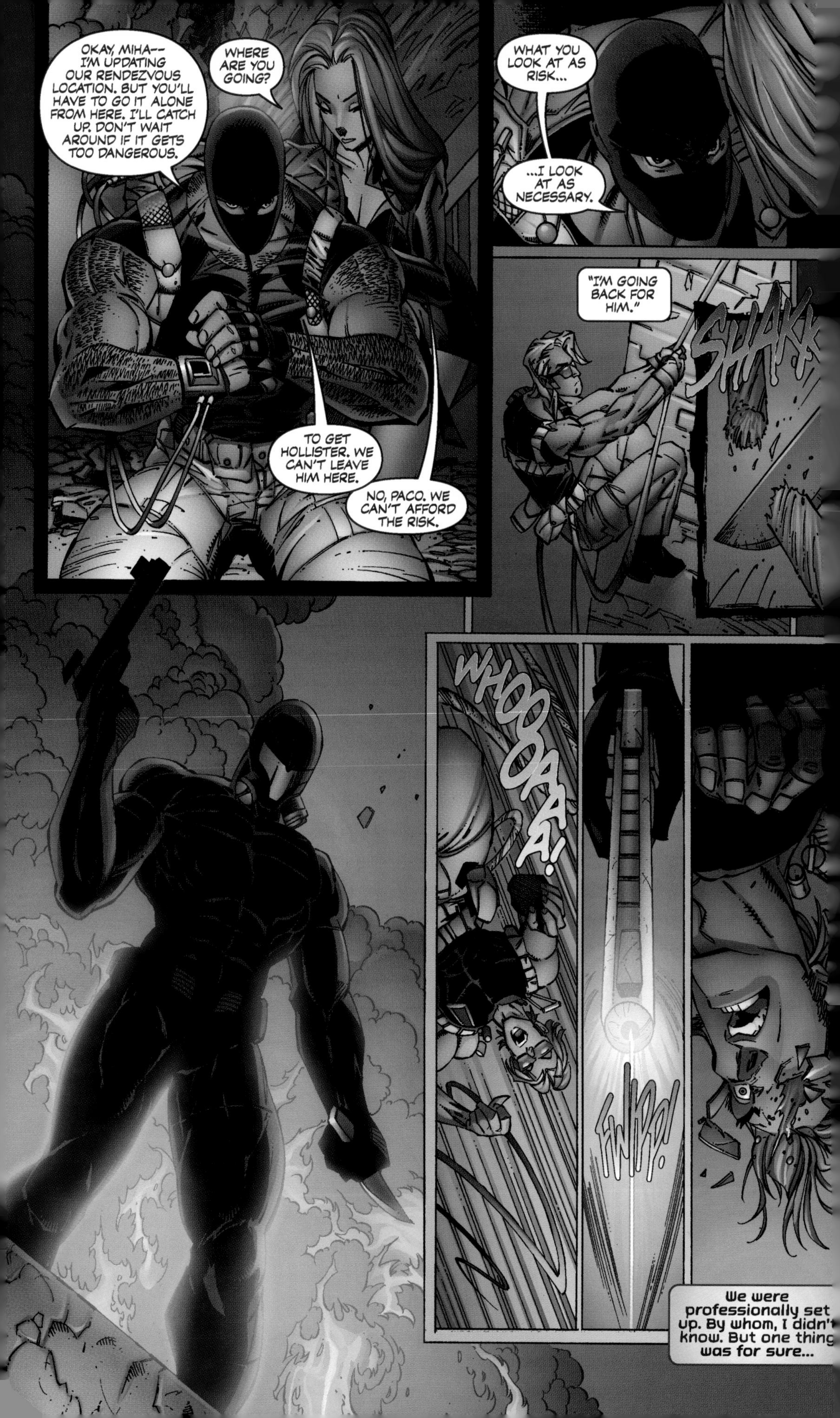
OKAY, MIHA-- I'M UPDATING OUR RENDEZVOUS LOCATION. BUT YOU'LL HAVE TO GO IT ALONE FROM HERE. I'LL CATCH UP. DON'T WAIT AROUND IF IT GETS TOO DANGEROUS.
WHERE ARE YOU GOING?
TO GET HOLLISTER. WE CAN'T LEAVE HIM HERE.
NO, PACO. WE CAN'T AFFORD THE RISK.
WHAT YOU LOOK AT AS RISK...
...I LOOK AT AS NECESSARY.
"I'M GOING BACK FOR HIM."
SHAKK
WHOOOAAA!
FWIPP!
We were professionally set up. By whom, I didn't know. But one thing was for sure...

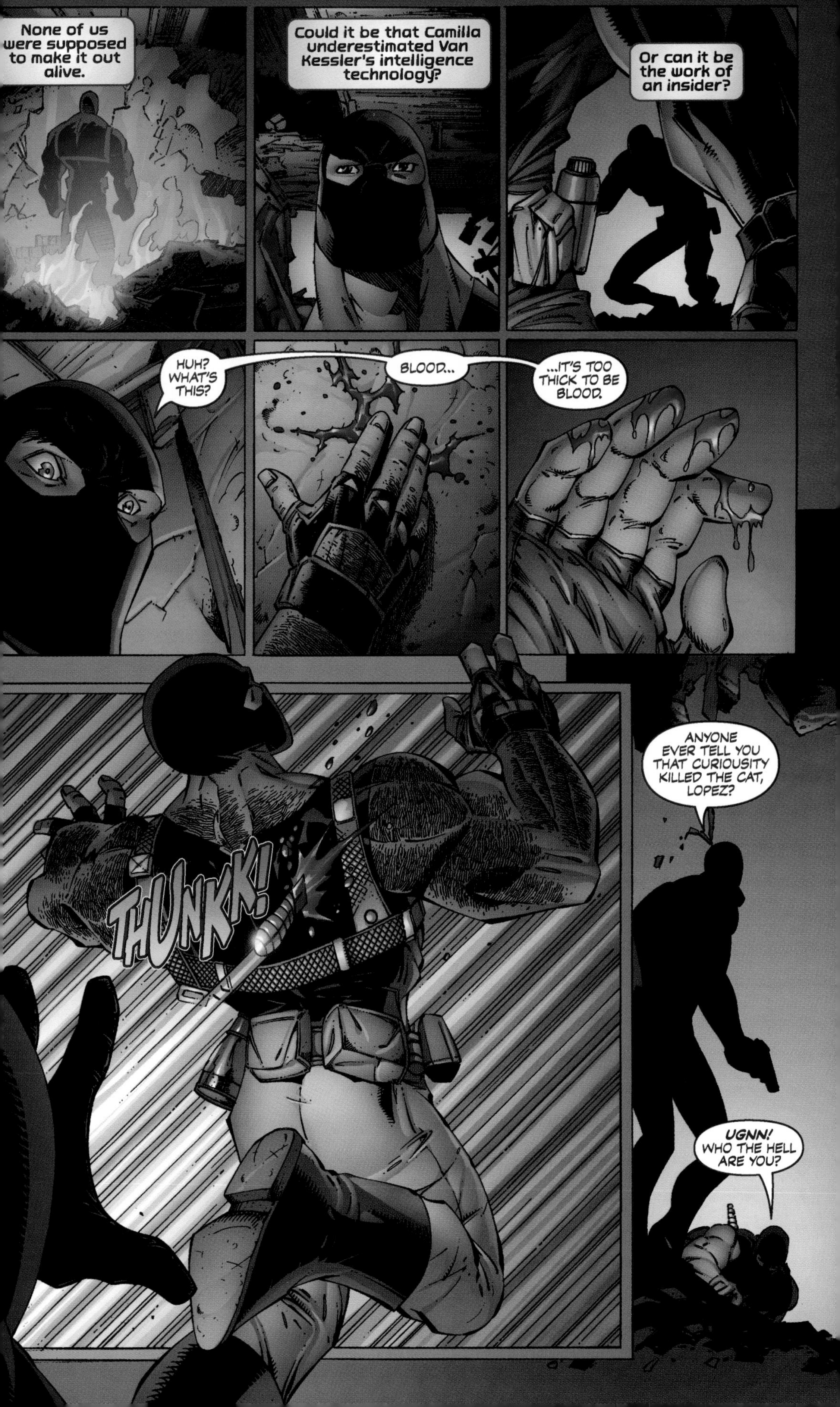
None of us were supposed to make it out alive.
Could it be that Camilla underestimated Van Kessler's intelligence technology?
Or can it be the work of an insider?
HUH? WHAT'S THIS?
BLOOD...
...IT'S TOO THICK TO BE BLOOD.
THUNKK!
ANYONE EVER TELL YOU THAT CURIOUSITY KILLED THE CAT, LOPEZ?
UGNN! WHO THE HELL ARE YOU?

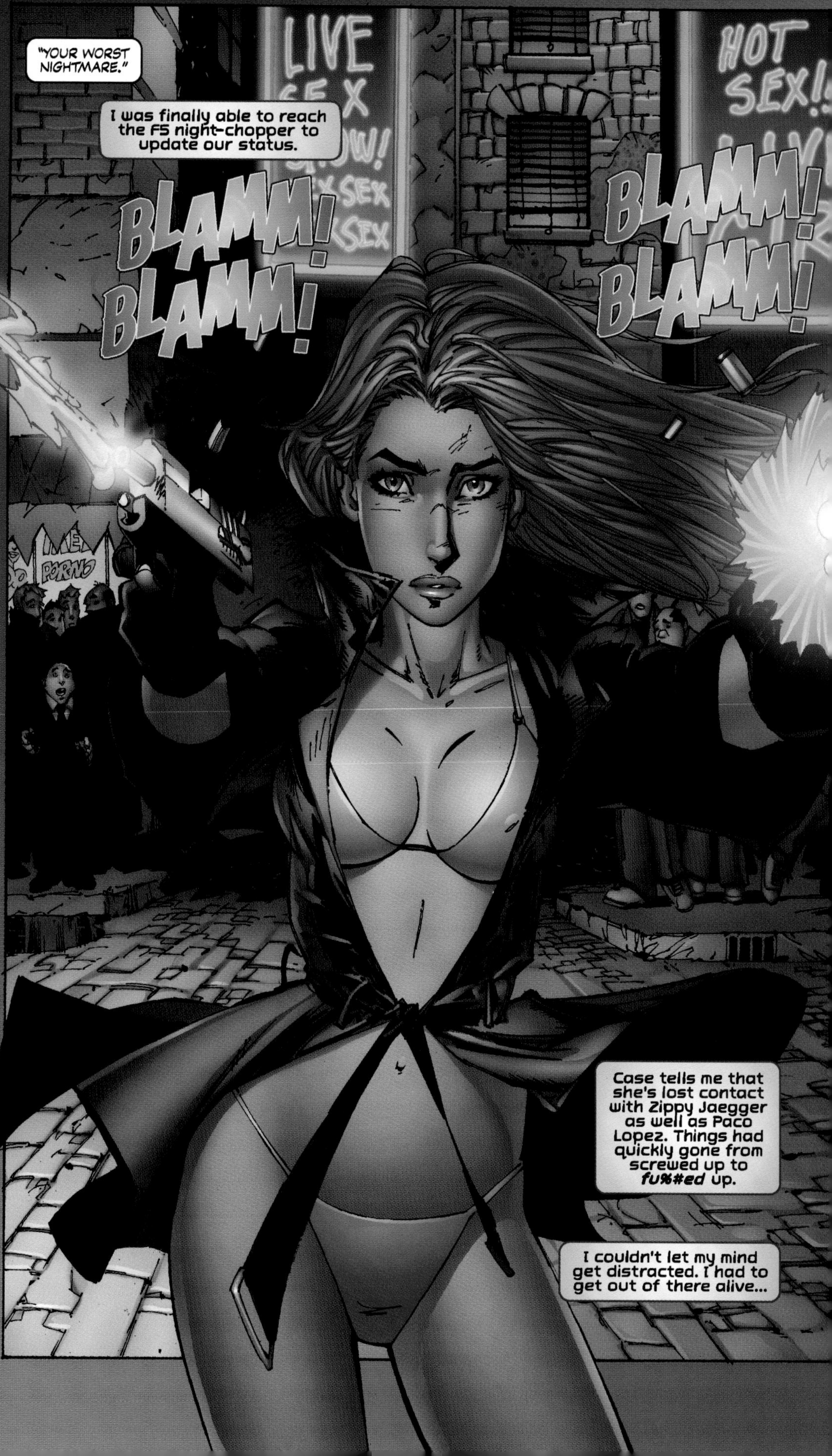
"YOUR WORST NIGHTMARE."
I was finally able to reach the F5 night-chopper to update our status.
LIVE
SEX
BLAMM! BLAMM!
HOT SEX!
BLAMM! BLAMM!
PORNO
Case tells me that she's lost contact with Zippy Jaegger as well as Paco Lopez. Things had quickly gone from screwed up to fu%#ed up.
I couldn't let my mind get distracted. I had to get out of there alive...

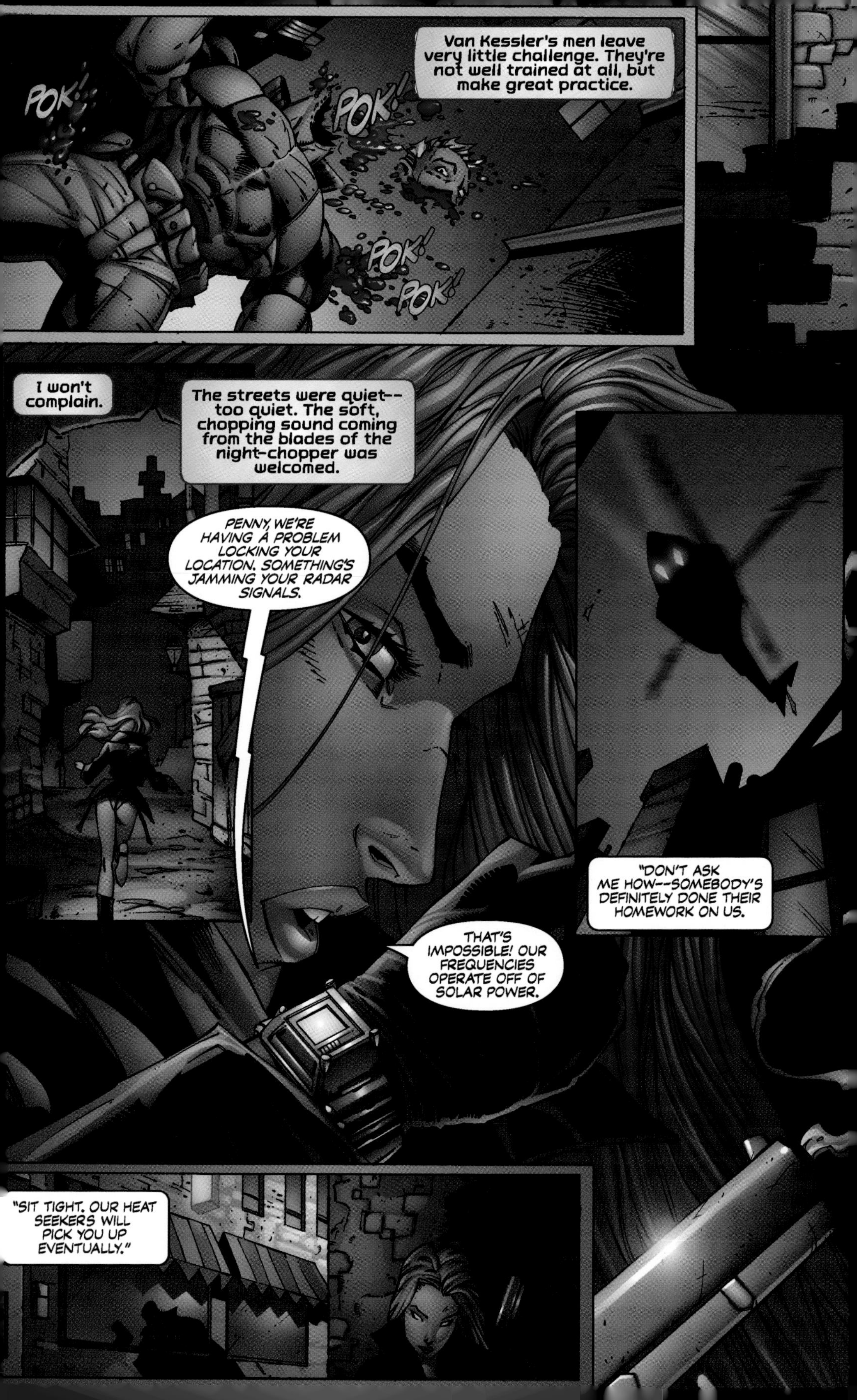
Van Kessler's men leave very little challenge. They're not well trained at all, but make great practice.
POK!
POK!
POK!
POK!
I won't complain.
The streets were quiet--too quiet. The soft, chopping sound coming from the blades of the night-chopper was welcomed.
PENNY, WE'RE HAVING A PROBLEM LOCKING YOUR LOCATION. SOMETHING'S JAMMING YOUR RADAR SIGNALS.
"DON'T ASK ME HOW--SOMEBODY'S DEFINITELY DONE THEIR HOMEWORK ON US.
THAT'S IMPOSSIBLE! OUR FREQUENCIES OPERATE OFF OF SOLAR POWER.
"SIT TIGHT. OUR HEAT SEEKERS WILL PICK YOU UP EVENTUALLY."

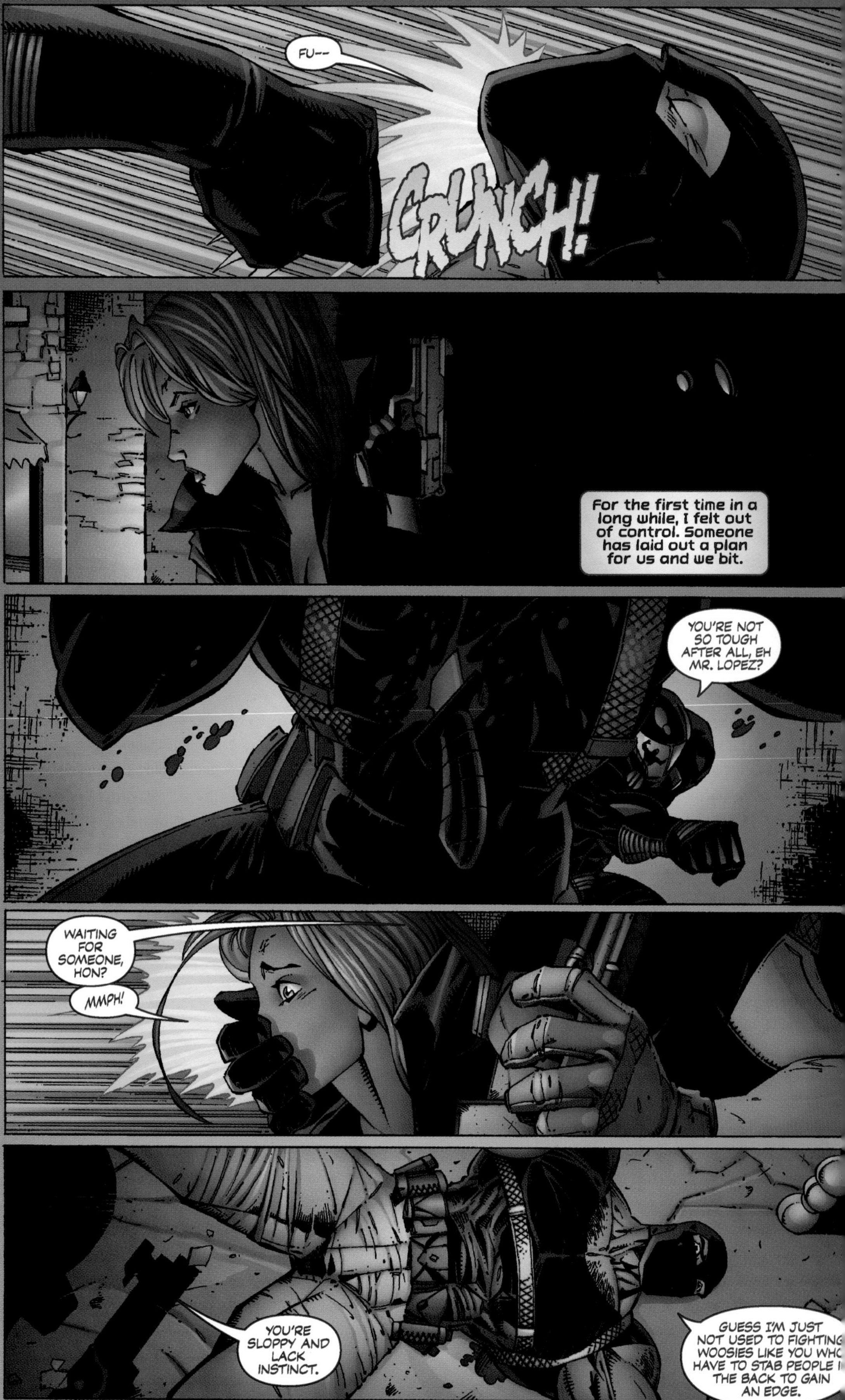
FU--
CRUNCH!
For the first time in a long while, I felt out of control. Someone has laid out a plan for us and we bit.
YOU'RE NOT SO TOUGH AFTER ALL, EH MR. LOPEZ?
WAITING FOR SOMEONE, HON?
MMPH!
YOU'RE SLOPPY AND LACK INSTINCT.
GUESS I'M JUST NOT USED TO FIGHTING WOOSIES LIKE YOU WHO HAVE TO STAB PEOPLE IN THE BACK TO GAIN AN EDGE.

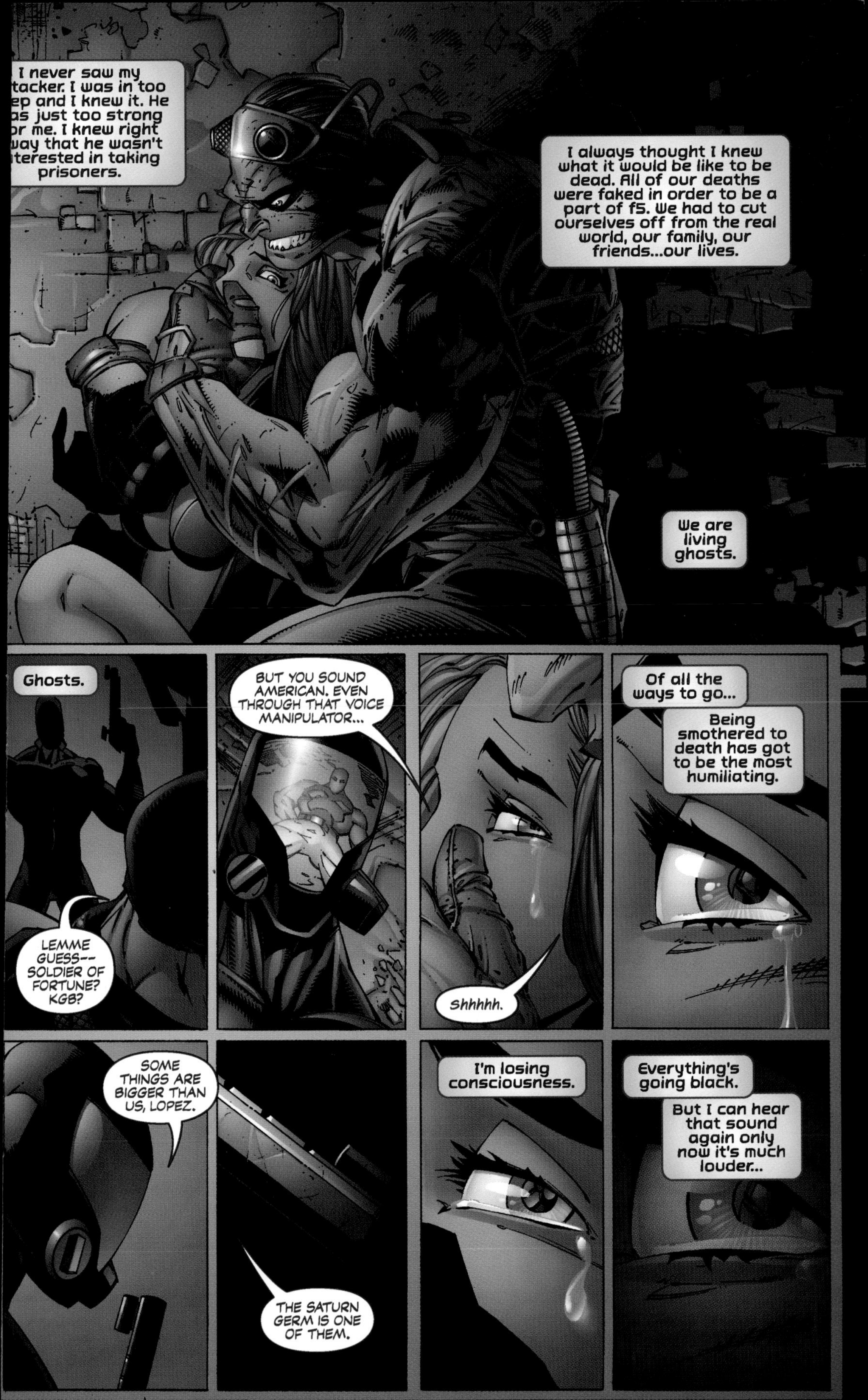
I never saw my tacker. I was in too ep and I knew it. He as just too strong or me. I knew right way that he wasn't terested in taking prisoners.
I always thought I knew what it would be like to be dead. All of our deaths were faked in order to be a part of f5. We had to cut ourselves off from the real world, our family, our friends...our lives.
We are living ghosts.
Ghosts.
LEMME GUESS-- SOLDIER OF FORTUNE? KGB?
BUT YOU SOUND AMERICAN. EVEN THROUGH THAT VOICE MANIPULATOR...
Shhhhh.
Of all the ways to go...
Being smothered to death has got to be the most humiliating.
SOME THINGS ARE BIGGER THAN US, LOPEZ.
THE SATURN GERM IS ONE OF THEM.
I'm losing consciousness.
Everything's going black.
But I can hear that sound again only now it's much louder...

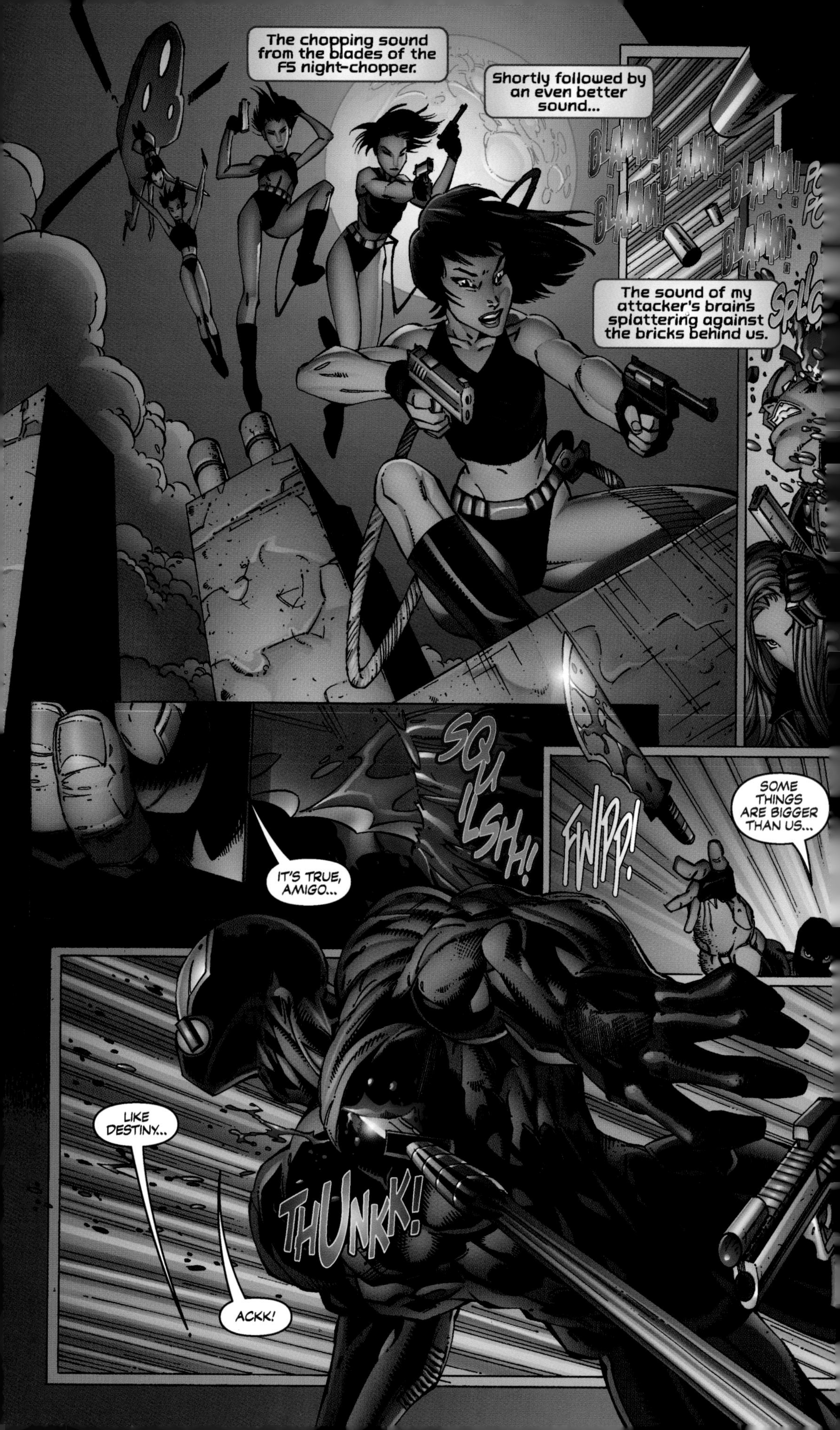
The chopping sound from the blades of the F5 night-chopper.
Shortly followed by an even better sound...
BLAMM! BLAMM! BLAMM! BLAMM! BLAMM!
The sound of my attacker's brains splattering against the bricks behind us.
SQUILSHH!
FWIPP!
SOME THINGS ARE BIGGER THAN US...
IT'S TRUE, AMIGO...
LIKE DESTINY...
THUNKK!
ACKK!

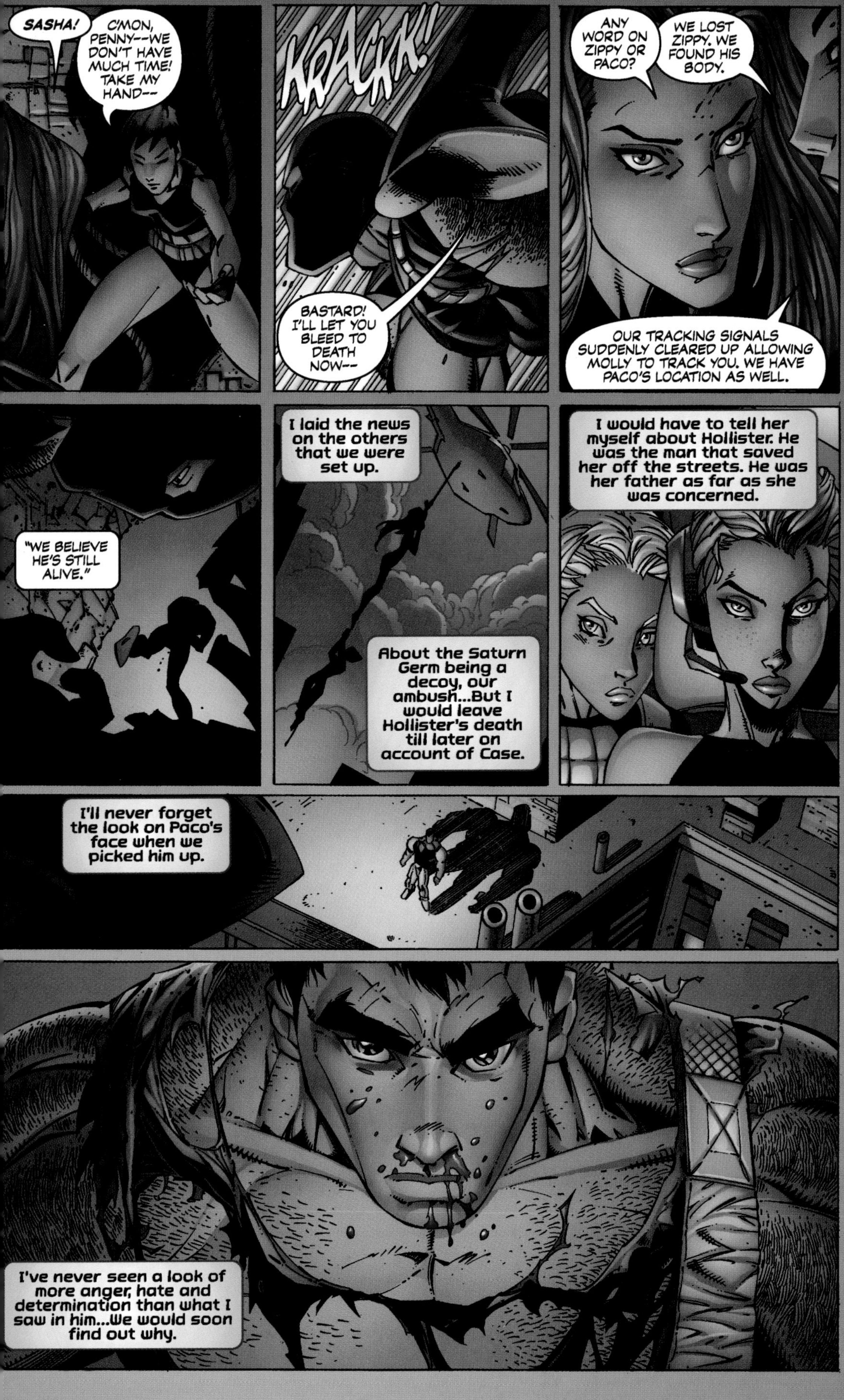
SASHA!
C'MON, PENNY--WE DON'T HAVE MUCH TIME! TAKE MY HAND--
KRACKK!
BASTARD! I'LL LET YOU BLEED TO DEATH NOW--
ANY WORD ON ZIPPY OR PACO?
WE LOST ZIPPY. WE FOUND HIS BODY.
OUR TRACKING SIGNALS SUDDENLY CLEARED UP ALLOWING MOLLY TO TRACK YOU. WE HAVE PACO'S LOCATION AS WELL.
"WE BELIEVE HE'S STILL ALIVE."
I laid the news on the others that we were set up.
About the Saturn Germ being a decoy, our ambush...But I would leave Hollister's death till later on account of Case.
I would have to tell her myself about Hollister. He was the man that saved her off the streets. He was her father as far as she was concerned.
I'll never forget the look on Paco's face when we picked him up.
I've never seen a look of more anger, hate and determination than what I saw in him...We would soon find out why.

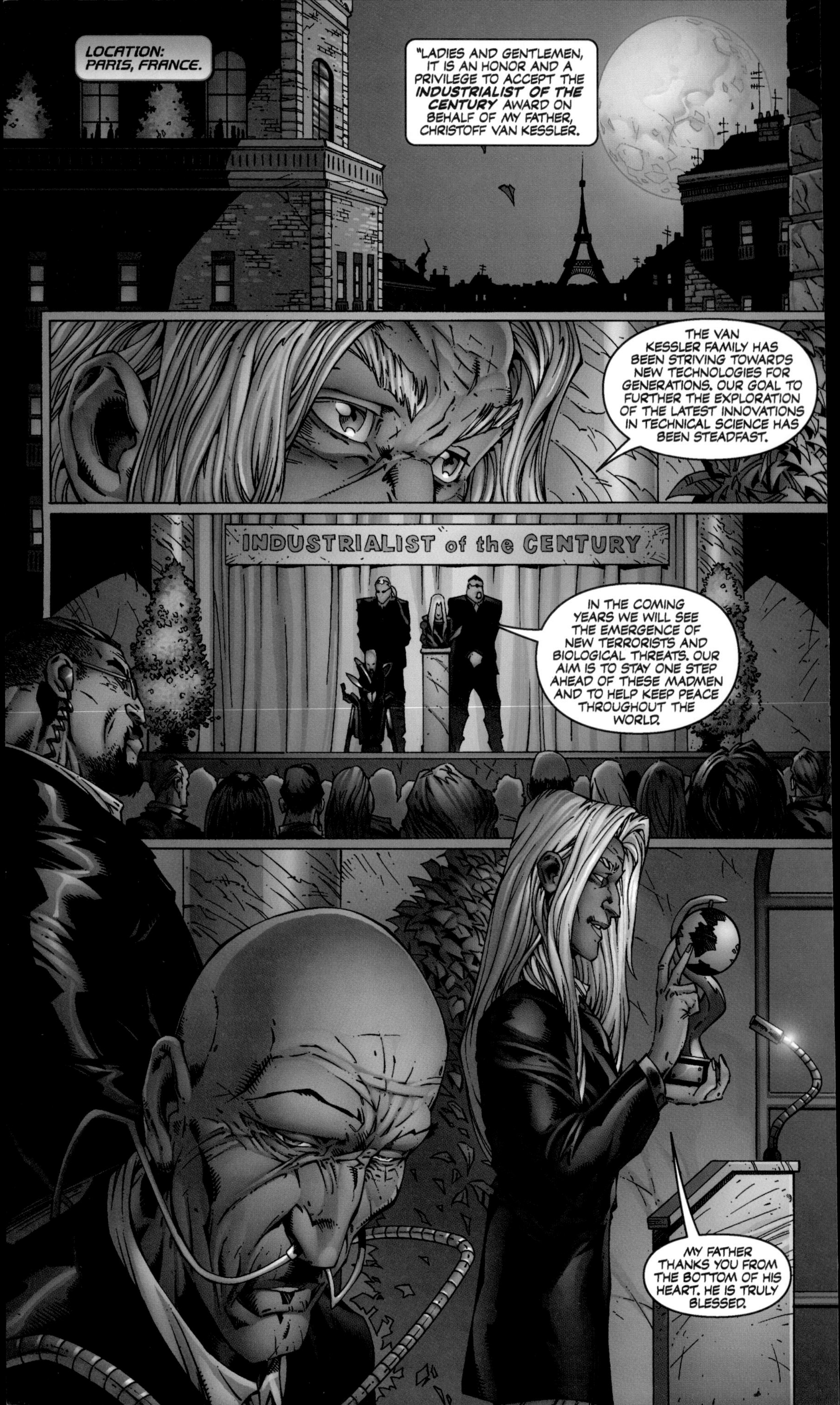
LOCATION: PARIS, FRANCE.
"LADIES AND GENTLEMEN, IT IS AN HONOR AND A PRIVILEGE TO ACCEPT THE ***INDUSTRIALIST OF THE CENTURY*** AWARD ON BEHALF OF MY FATHER, CHRISTOFF VAN KESSLER.
THE VAN KESSLER FAMILY HAS BEEN STRIVING TOWARDS NEW TECHNOLOGIES FOR GENERATIONS. OUR GOAL TO FURTHER THE EXPLORATION OF THE LATEST INNOVATIONS IN TECHNICAL SCIENCE HAS BEEN STEADFAST.
INDUSTRIALIST of the CENTURY
IN THE COMING YEARS WE WILL SEE THE EMERGENCE OF NEW TERRORISTS AND BIOLOGICAL THREATS. OUR AIM IS TO STAY ONE STEP AHEAD OF THESE MADMEN AND TO HELP KEEP PEACE THROUGHOUT THE WORLD.
MY FATHER THANKS YOU FROM THE BOTTOM OF HIS HEART. HE IS TRULY BLESSED.

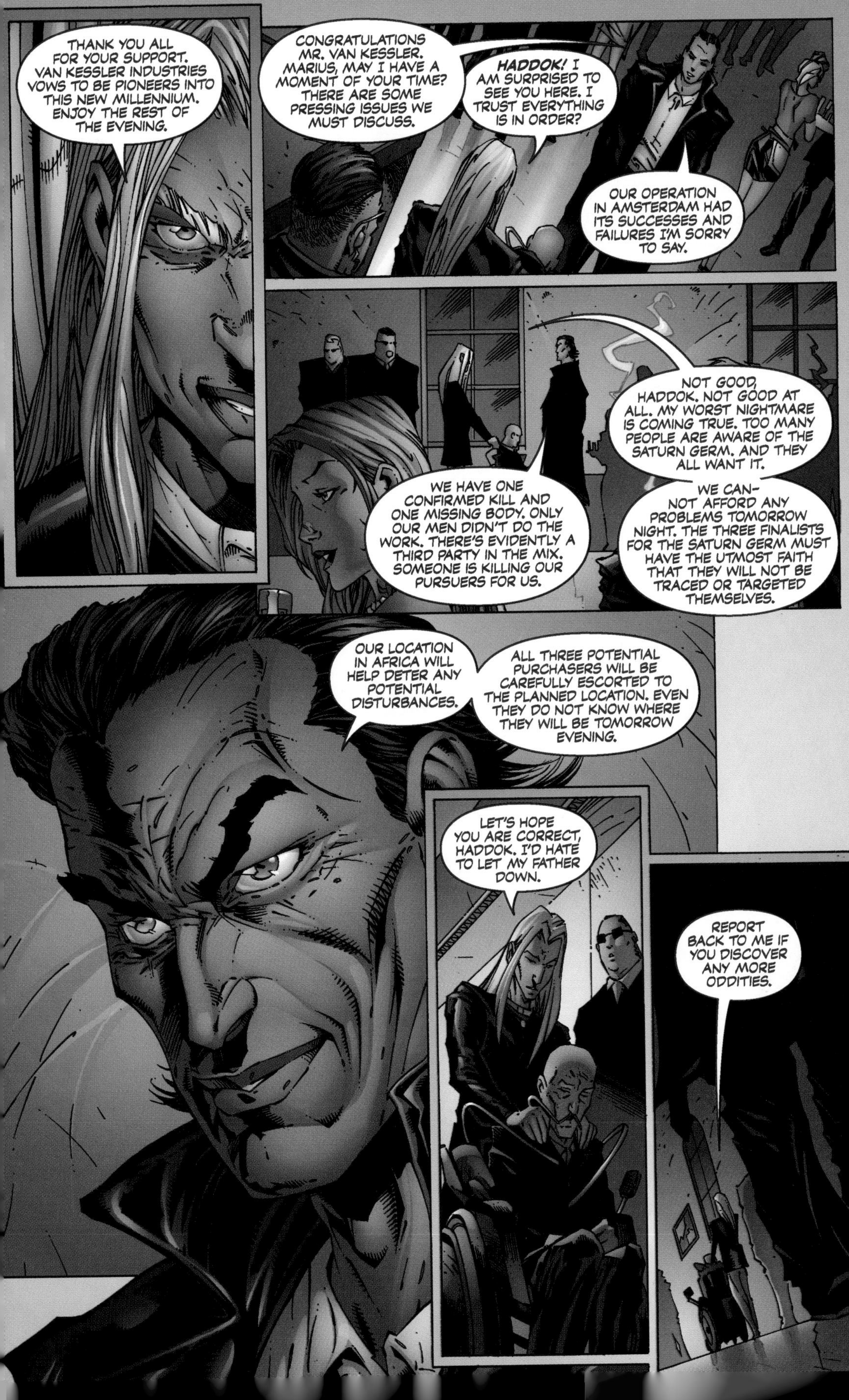
THANK YOU ALL FOR YOUR SUPPORT. VAN KESSLER INDUSTRIES VOWS TO BE PIONEERS INTO THIS NEW MILLENNIUM. ENJOY THE REST OF THE EVENING.
CONGRATULATIONS MR. VAN KESSLER. MARIUS, MAY I HAVE A MOMENT OF YOUR TIME? THERE ARE SOME PRESSING ISSUES WE MUST DISCUSS.
HADDOK! I AM SURPRISED TO SEE YOU HERE. I TRUST EVERYTHING IS IN ORDER?
OUR OPERATION IN AMSTERDAM HAD ITS SUCCESSES AND FAILURES I'M SORRY TO SAY.
WE HAVE ONE CONFIRMED KILL AND ONE MISSING BODY. ONLY OUR MEN DIDN'T DO THE WORK. THERE'S EVIDENTLY A THIRD PARTY IN THE MIX. SOMEONE IS KILLING OUR PURSUERS FOR US.
NOT GOOD, HADDOK. NOT GOOD AT ALL. MY WORST NIGHTMARE IS COMING TRUE. TOO MANY PEOPLE ARE AWARE OF THE SATURN GERM. AND THEY ALL WANT IT.
WE CAN-NOT AFFORD ANY PROBLEMS TOMORROW NIGHT. THE THREE FINALISTS FOR THE SATURN GERM MUST HAVE THE UTMOST FAITH THAT THEY WILL NOT BE TRACED OR TARGETED THEMSELVES.
OUR LOCATION IN AFRICA WILL HELP DETER ANY POTENTIAL DISTURBANCES.
ALL THREE POTENTIAL PURCHASERS WILL BE CAREFULLY ESCORTED TO THE PLANNED LOCATION. EVEN THEY DO NOT KNOW WHERE THEY WILL BE TOMORROW EVENING.
LET'S HOPE YOU ARE CORRECT, HADDOK. I'D HATE TO LET MY FATHER DOWN.
REPORT BACK TO ME IF YOU DISCOVER ANY MORE ODDITIES.

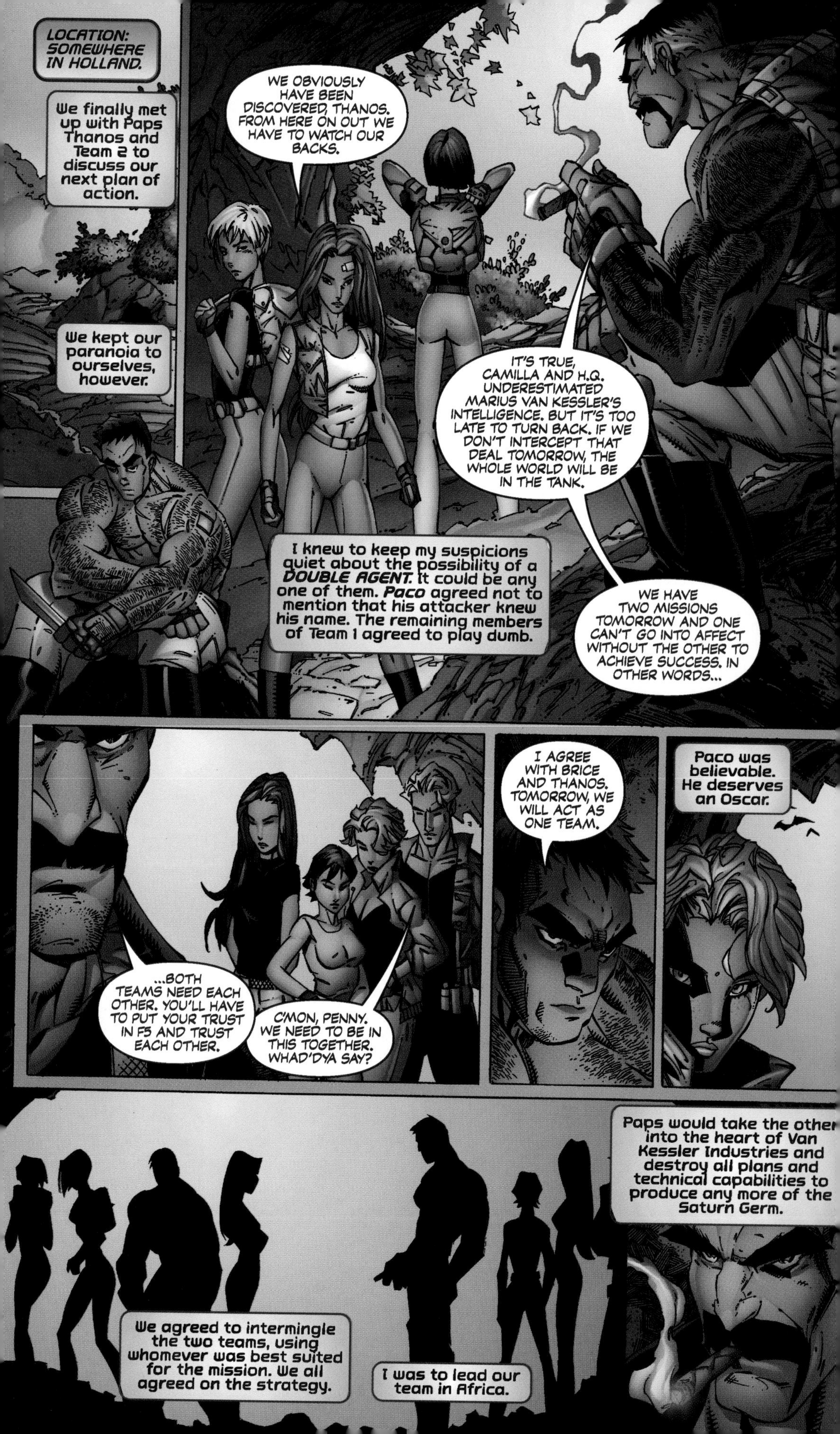

LOCATION: SOMEWHERE IN HOLLAND.
We finally met up with Paps Thanos and Team 2 to discuss our next plan of action.
WE OBVIOUSLY HAVE BEEN DISCOVERED, THANOS. FROM HERE ON OUT WE HAVE TO WATCH OUR BACKS.
We kept our paranoia to ourselves, however.
IT'S TRUE, CAMILLA AND H.Q. UNDERESTIMATED MARIUS VAN KESSLER'S INTELLIGENCE. BUT IT'S TOO LATE TO TURN BACK. IF WE DON'T INTERCEPT THAT DEAL TOMORROW, THE WHOLE WORLD WILL BE IN THE TANK.
I knew to keep my suspicions quiet about the possibility of a DOUBLE AGENT. It could be any one of them. Paco agreed not to mention that his attacker knew his name. The remaining members of Team 1 agreed to play dumb.
WE HAVE TWO MISSIONS TOMORROW AND ONE CAN'T GO INTO AFFECT WITHOUT THE OTHER TO ACHIEVE SUCCESS. IN OTHER WORDS...
...BOTH TEAMS NEED EACH OTHER. YOU'LL HAVE TO PUT YOUR TRUST IN F5 AND TRUST EACH OTHER.
C'MON, PENNY. WE NEED TO BE IN THIS TOGETHER. WHAD'DYA SAY?
I AGREE WITH BRICE AND THANOS. TOMORROW, WE WILL ACT AS ONE TEAM.
Paco was believable. He deserves an Oscar.
Paps would take the other into the heart of Van Kessler Industries and destroy all plans and technical capabilities to produce any more of the Saturn Germ.
We agreed to intermingle the two teams, using whomever was best suited for the mission. We all agreed on the strategy.
I was to lead our team in Africa.

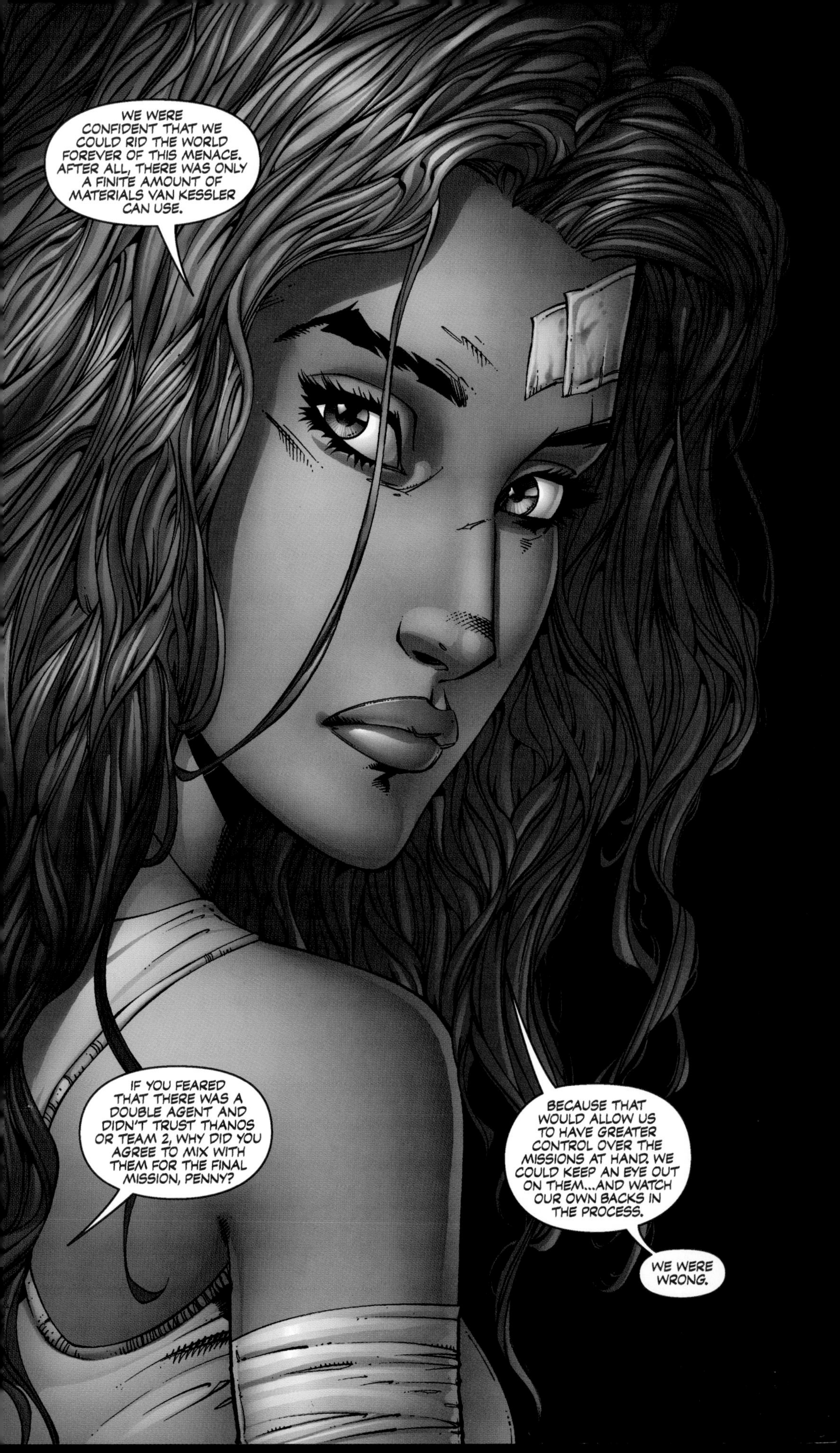
WE WERE CONFIDENT THAT WE COULD RID THE WORLD FOREVER OF THIS MENACE. AFTER ALL, THERE WAS ONLY A FINITE AMOUNT OF MATERIALS VAN KESSLER CAN USE.
IF YOU FEARED THAT THERE WAS A DOUBLE AGENT AND DIDN'T TRUST THANOS OR TEAM 2, WHY DID YOU AGREE TO MIX WITH THEM FOR THE FINAL MISSION, PENNY?
BECAUSE THAT WOULD ALLOW US TO HAVE GREATER CONTROL OVER THE MISSIONS AT HAND. WE COULD KEEP AN EYE OUT ON THEM...AND WATCH OUR OWN BACKS IN THE PROCESS.
WE WERE WRONG.

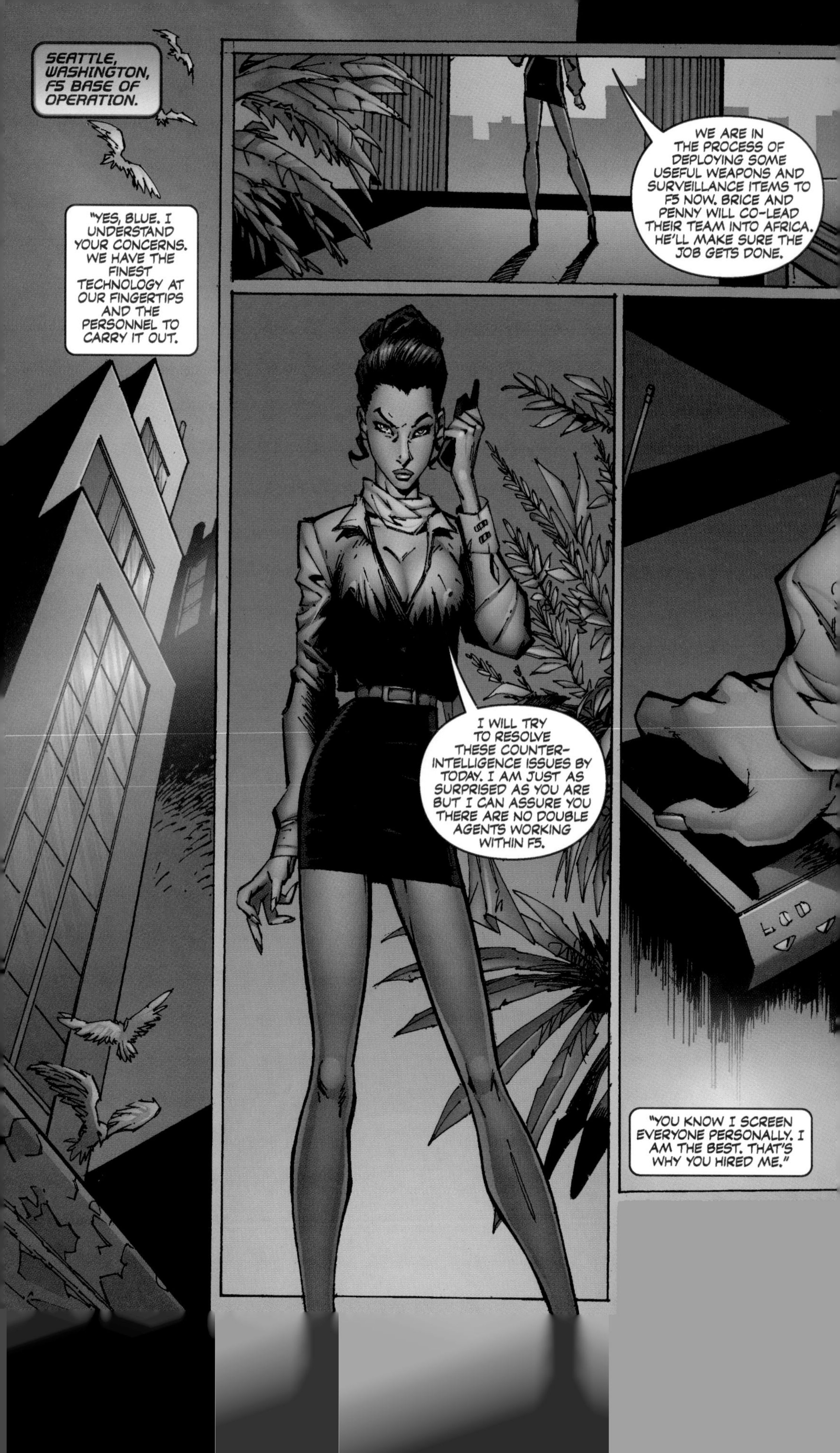
SEATTLE, WASHINGTON, F5 BASE OF OPERATION.
"YES, BLUE. I UNDERSTAND YOUR CONCERNS. WE HAVE THE FINEST TECHNOLOGY AT OUR FINGERTIPS AND THE PERSONNEL TO CARRY IT OUT.
WE ARE IN THE PROCESS OF DEPLOYING SOME USEFUL WEAPONS AND SURVEILLANCE ITEMS TO F5 NOW. BRICE AND PENNY WILL CO-LEAD THEIR TEAM INTO AFRICA. HE'LL MAKE SURE THE JOB GETS DONE.
I WILL TRY TO RESOLVE THESE COUNTER-INTELLIGENCE ISSUES BY TODAY. I AM JUST AS SURPRISED AS YOU ARE BUT I CAN ASSURE YOU THERE ARE NO DOUBLE AGENTS WORKING WITHIN F5.
"YOU KNOW I SCREEN EVERYONE PERSONALLY. I AM THE BEST. THAT'S WHY YOU HIRED ME."

chapter four

ENEMIES AND ALLIES

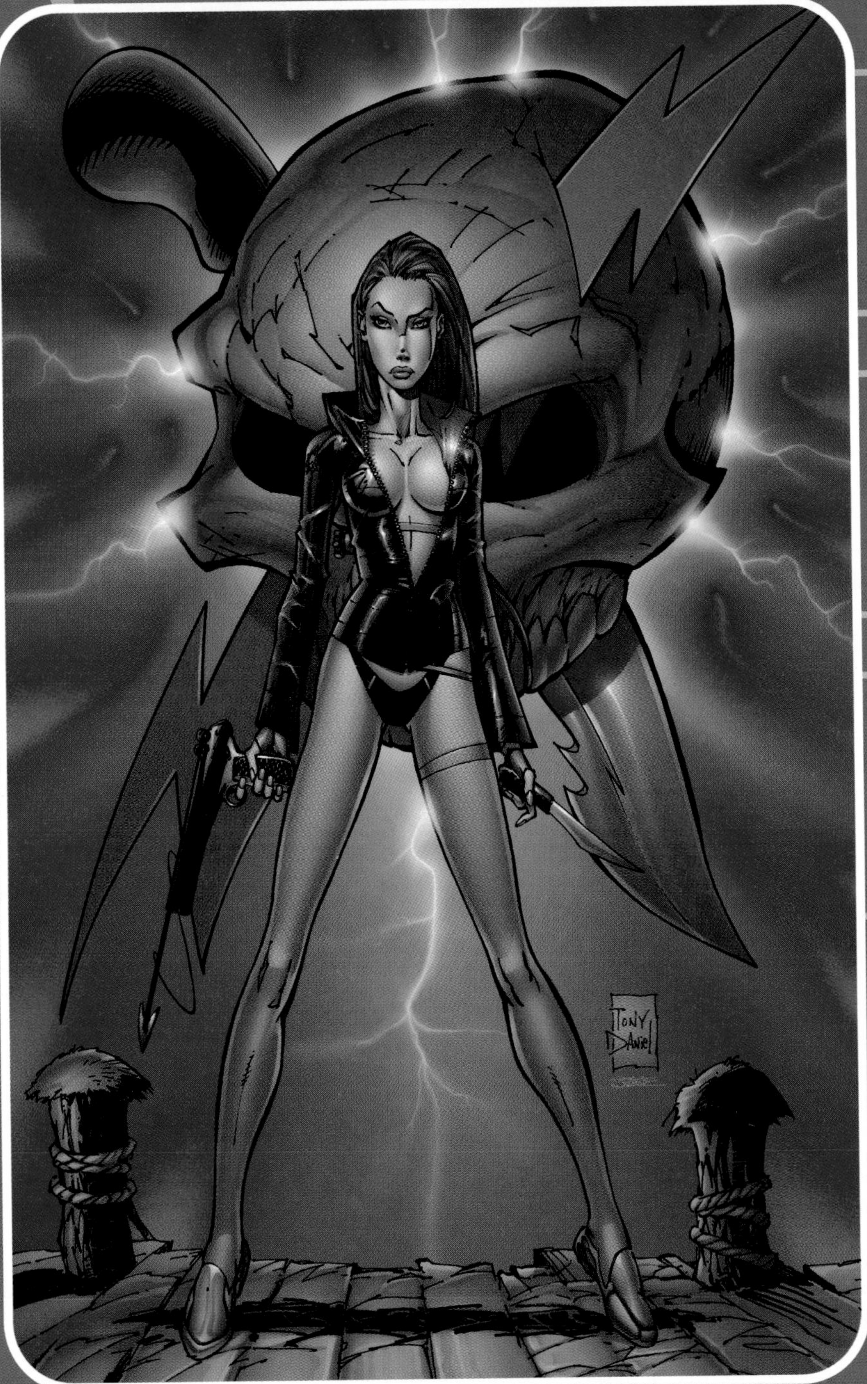

TONY DANIEL

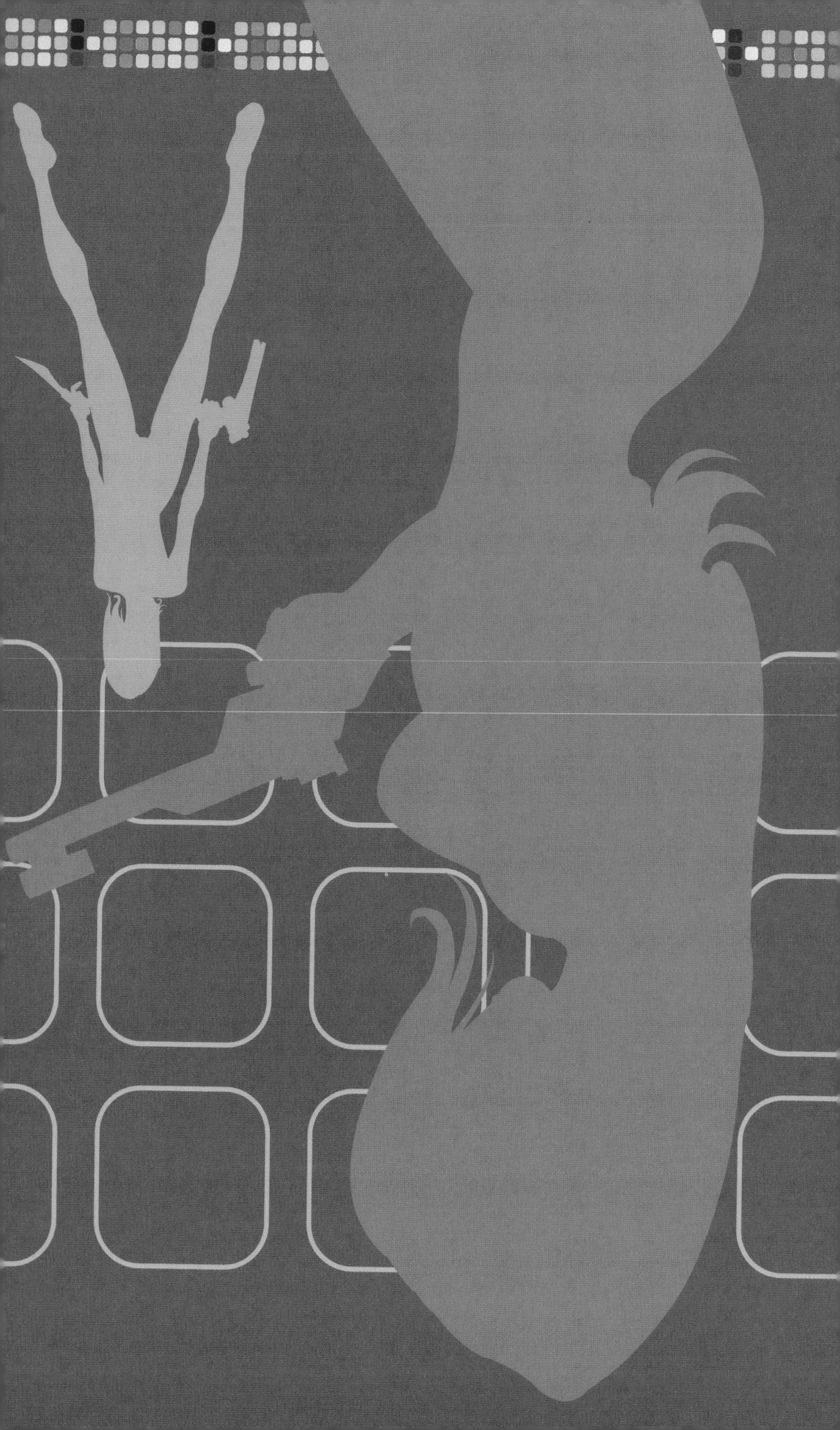

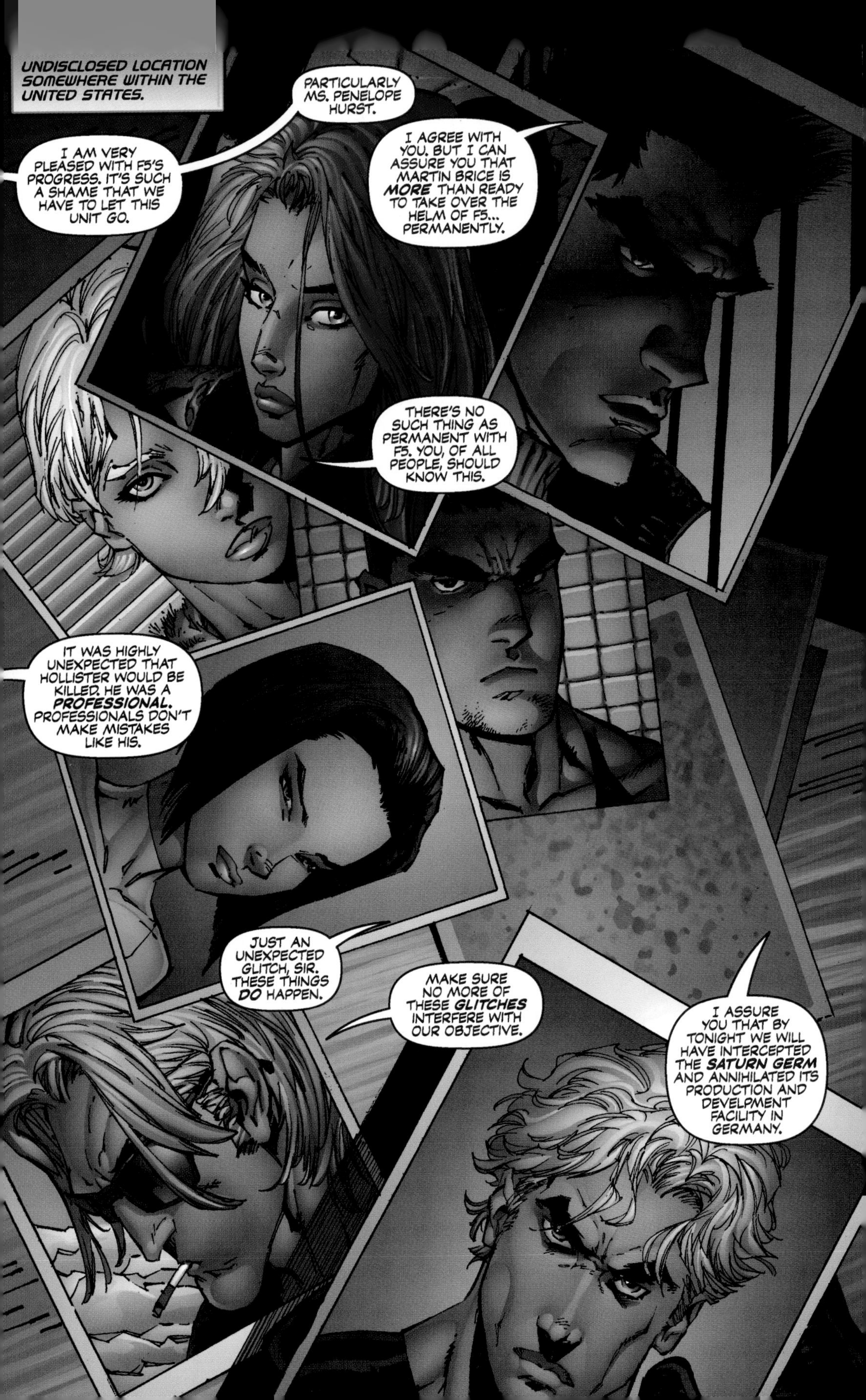

UNDISCLOSED LOCATION SOMEWHERE WITHIN THE UNITED STATES.
I AM VERY PLEASED WITH F5'S PROGRESS. IT'S SUCH A SHAME THAT WE HAVE TO LET THIS UNIT GO.
PARTICULARLY MS. PENELOPE HURST.
I AGREE WITH YOU. BUT I CAN ASSURE YOU THAT MARTIN BRICE IS ***MORE*** THAN READY TO TAKE OVER THE HELM OF F5... PERMANENTLY.
THERE'S NO SUCH THING AS PERMANENT WITH F5. YOU, OF ALL PEOPLE, SHOULD KNOW THIS.
IT WAS HIGHLY UNEXPECTED THAT HOLLISTER WOULD BE KILLED. HE WAS A ***PROFESSIONAL.*** PROFESSIONALS DON'T MAKE MISTAKES LIKE HIS.
JUST AN UNEXPECTED GLITCH, SIR. THESE THINGS ***DO*** HAPPEN.
MAKE SURE NO MORE OF THESE ***GLITCHES*** INTERFERE WITH OUR OBJECTIVE.
I ASSURE YOU THAT BY TONIGHT WE WILL HAVE INTERCEPTED THE ***SATURN GERM*** AND ANNIHILATED ITS PRODUCTION AND DEVELPMENT FACILITY IN GERMANY.

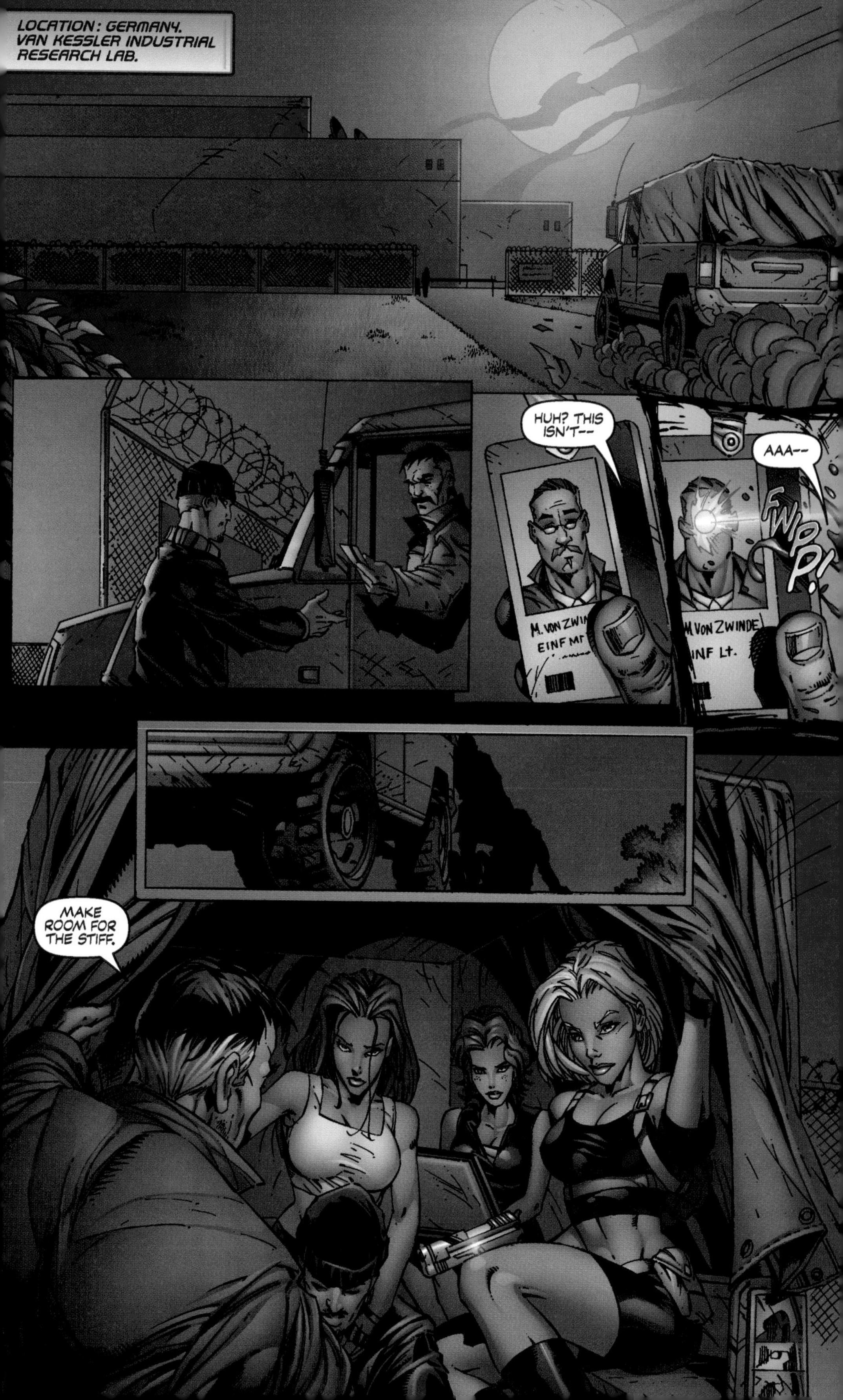
LOCATION: GERMANY.
VAN KESSLER INDUSTRIAL
RESEARCH LAB.
HUH? THIS ISN'T--
M. VON ZWINDE
EINF Lt.
AAA--
FWIPP!
MAKE ROOM FOR THE STIFF.

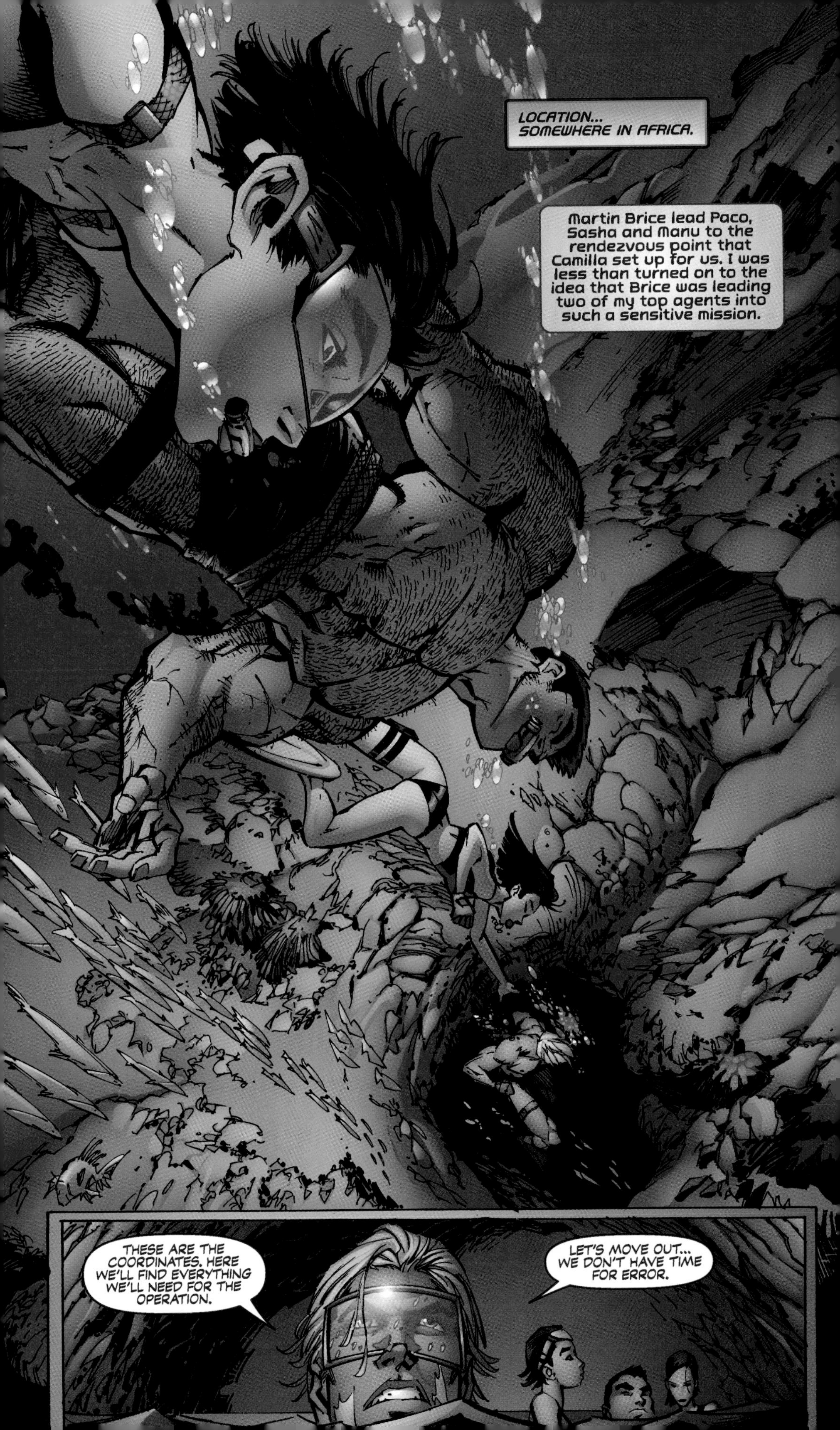
LOCATION... SOMEWHERE IN AFRICA.
Martin Brice lead Paco, Sasha and Manu to the rendezvous point that Camilla set up for us. I was less than turned on to the idea that Brice was leading two of my top agents into such a sensitive mission.
THESE ARE THE COORDINATES. HERE WE'LL FIND EVERYTHING WE'LL NEED FOR THE OPERATION.
LET'S MOVE OUT... WE DON'T HAVE TIME FOR ERROR.

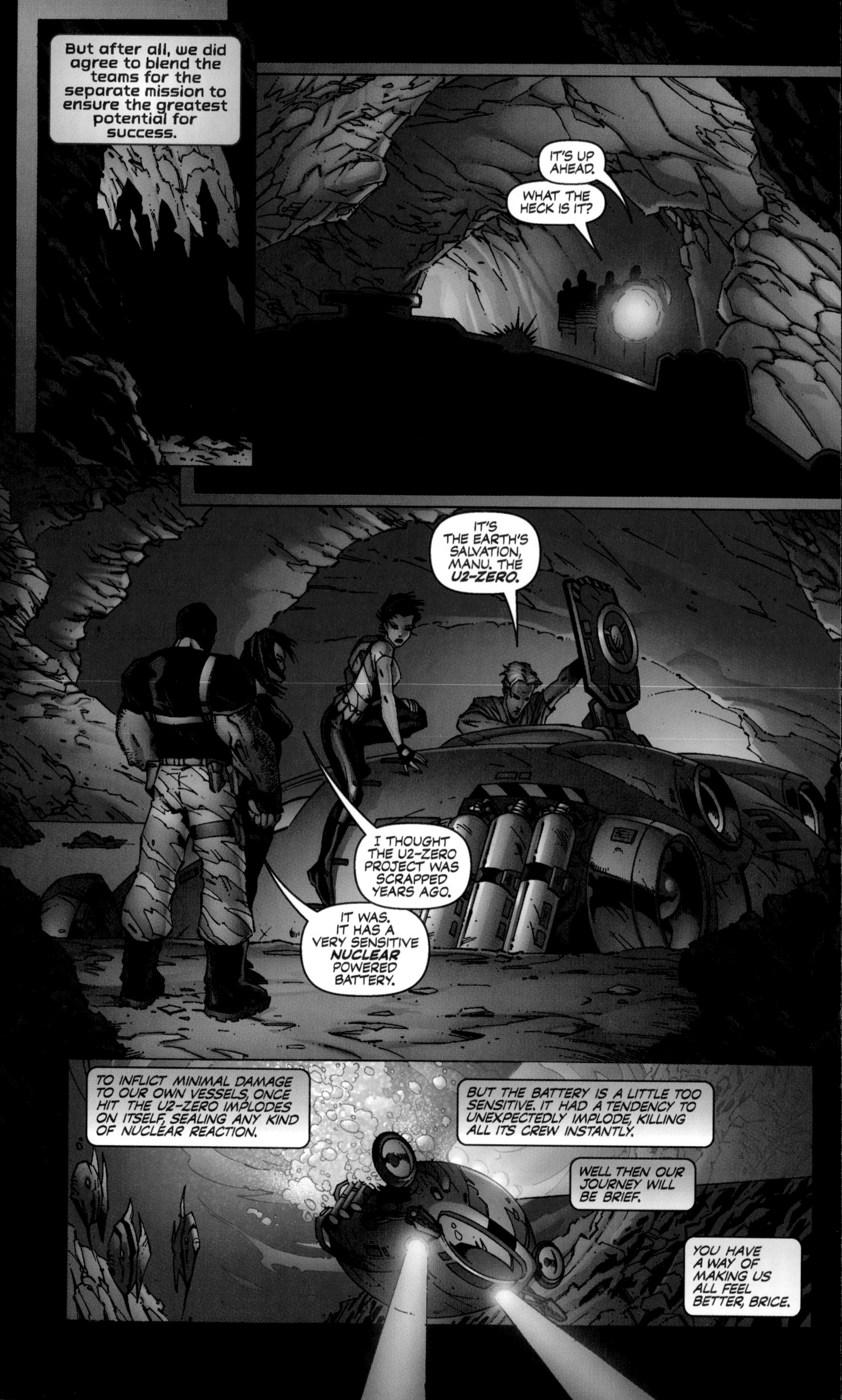

But after all, we did agree to blend the teams for the separate mission to ensure the greatest potential for success.
IT'S UP AHEAD.
WHAT THE HECK IS IT?
IT'S THE EARTH'S SALVATION, MANU. THE U2-ZERO.
I THOUGHT THE U2-ZERO PROJECT WAS SCRAPPED YEARS AGO.
IT WAS. IT HAS A VERY SENSITIVE NUCLEAR POWERED BATTERY.
TO INFLICT MINIMAL DAMAGE TO OUR OWN VESSELS, ONCE HIT THE U2-ZERO IMPLODES ON ITSELF, SEALING ANY KIND OF NUCLEAR REACTION.
BUT THE BATTERY IS A LITTLE TOO SENSITIVE. IT HAD A TENDENCY TO UNEXPECTEDLY IMPLODE, KILLING ALL ITS CREW INSTANTLY.
WELL THEN OUR JOURNEY WILL BE BRIEF.
YOU HAVE A WAY OF MAKING US ALL FEEL BETTER, BRICE.

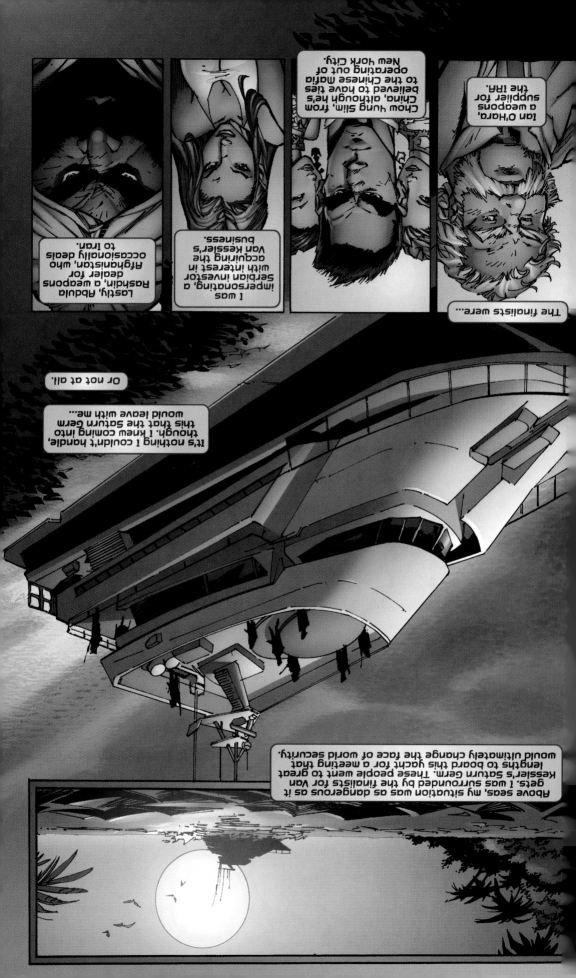

The finalists were...

Ian O'Hara, a weapons supplier for the IRA.

Chow Yung Slim, from China, although he's believed to have ties to the Chinese Mafia operating out of New York City.

I was impersonating, a Serbian investor with interest in acquiring the Van Kessler's business.

Lastly, Abdula Rashdin, a weapons dealer for Afghanistan, who occasionally deals to Iran.

It's nothing I couldn't handle, though. I knew coming into this that the Saturn Germ would leave with me....

Or not at all.

Above seas, my situation was as dangerous as it gets. I was surrounded by the finalists for Van Kessler's Saturn Germ. These people went to great lengths to board this yacht for a meeting that would ultimately change the face of world security.

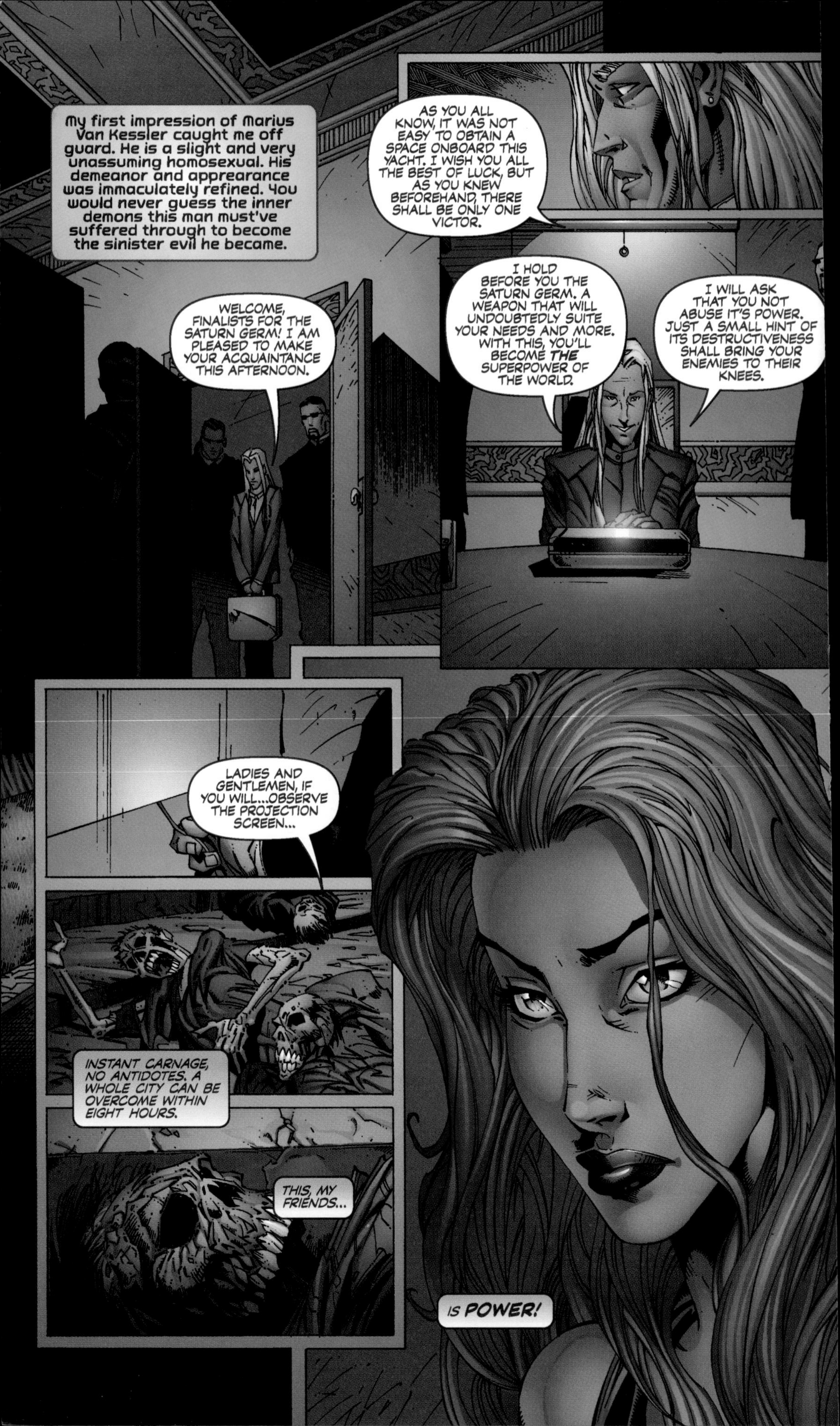
My first impression of Marius Van Kessler caught me off guard. He is a slight and very unassuming homosexual. His demeanor and appearance was immaculately refined. You would never guess the inner demons this man must've suffered through to become the sinister evil he became.
WELCOME, FINALISTS FOR THE SATURN GERM! I AM PLEASED TO MAKE YOUR ACQUAINTANCE THIS AFTERNOON.
AS YOU ALL KNOW, IT WAS NOT EASY TO OBTAIN A SPACE ONBOARD THIS YACHT. I WISH YOU ALL THE BEST OF LUCK, BUT AS YOU KNEW BEFOREHAND, THERE SHALL BE ONLY ONE VICTOR.
I HOLD BEFORE YOU THE SATURN GERM. A WEAPON THAT WILL UNDOUBTEDLY SUITE YOUR NEEDS AND MORE. WITH THIS, YOU'LL BECOME *THE* SUPERPOWER OF THE WORLD.
I WILL ASK THAT YOU NOT ABUSE IT'S POWER. JUST A SMALL HINT OF ITS DESTRUCTIVENESS SHALL BRING YOUR ENEMIES TO THEIR KNEES.
LADIES AND GENTLEMEN, IF YOU WILL...OBSERVE THE PROJECTION SCREEN...
INSTANT CARNAGE, NO ANTIDOTES. A WHOLE CITY CAN BE OVERCOME WITHIN EIGHT HOURS.
THIS, MY FRIENDS...
IS **POWER!**

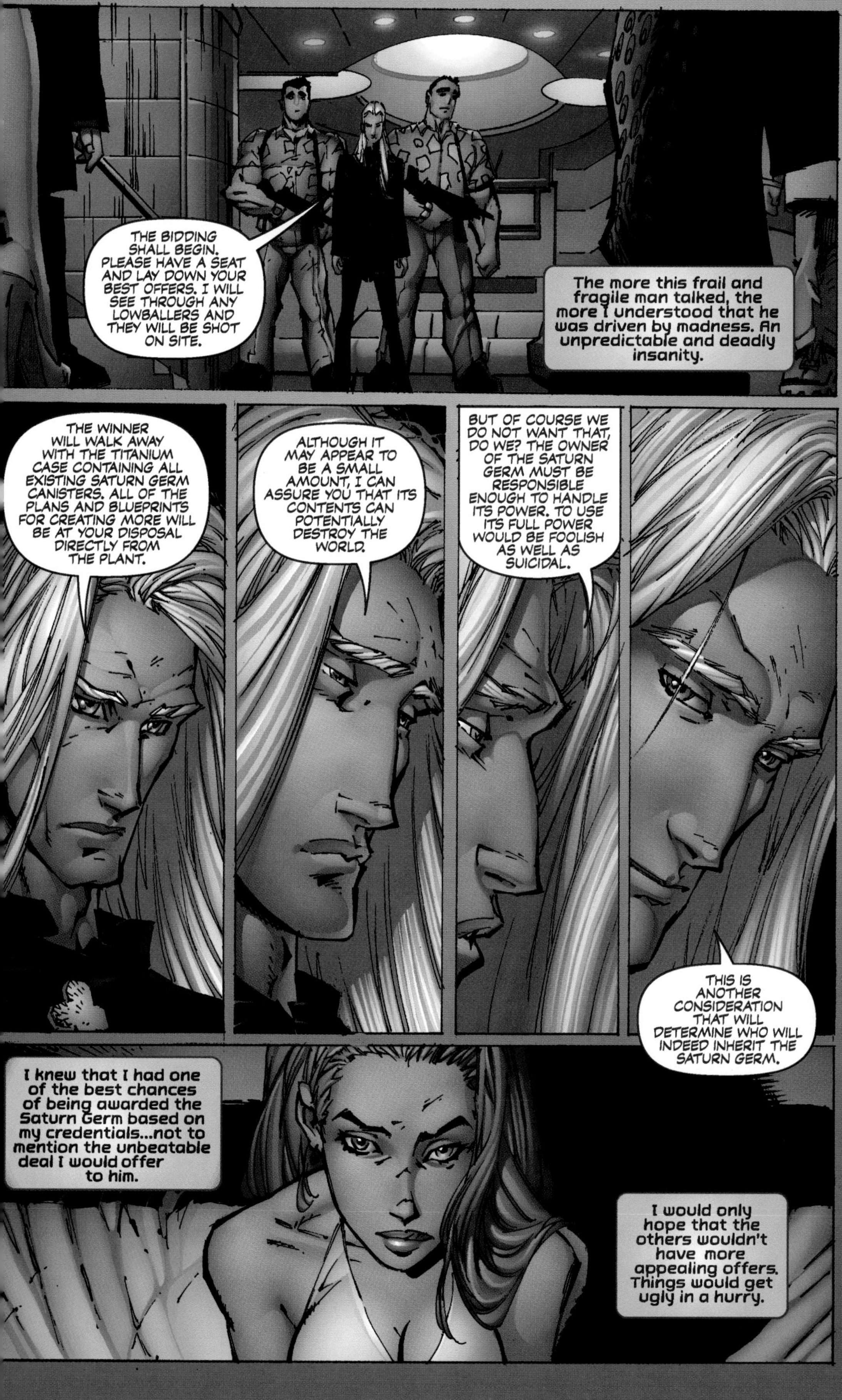
THE BIDDING SHALL BEGIN. PLEASE HAVE A SEAT AND LAY DOWN YOUR BEST OFFERS. I WILL SEE THROUGH ANY LOWBALLERS AND THEY WILL BE SHOT ON SITE.
The more this frail and fragile man talked, the more I understood that he was driven by madness. An unpredictable and deadly insanity.
THE WINNER WILL WALK AWAY WITH THE TITANIUM CASE CONTAINING ALL EXISTING SATURN GERM CANISTERS. ALL OF THE PLANS AND BLUEPRINTS FOR CREATING MORE WILL BE AT YOUR DISPOSAL DIRECTLY FROM THE PLANT.
ALTHOUGH IT MAY APPEAR TO BE A SMALL AMOUNT, I CAN ASSURE YOU THAT ITS CONTENTS CAN POTENTIALLY DESTROY THE WORLD.
BUT OF COURSE WE DO NOT WANT THAT, DO WE? THE OWNER OF THE SATURN GERM MUST BE RESPONSIBLE ENOUGH TO HANDLE ITS POWER. TO USE ITS FULL POWER WOULD BE FOOLISH AS WELL AS SUICIDAL.
THIS IS ANOTHER CONSIDERATION THAT WILL DETERMINE WHO WILL INDEED INHERIT THE SATURN GERM.
I knew that I had one of the best chances of being awarded the Saturn Germ based on my credentials...not to mention the unbeatable deal I would offer to him.
I would only hope that the others wouldn't have more appealing offers. Things would get ugly in a hurry.

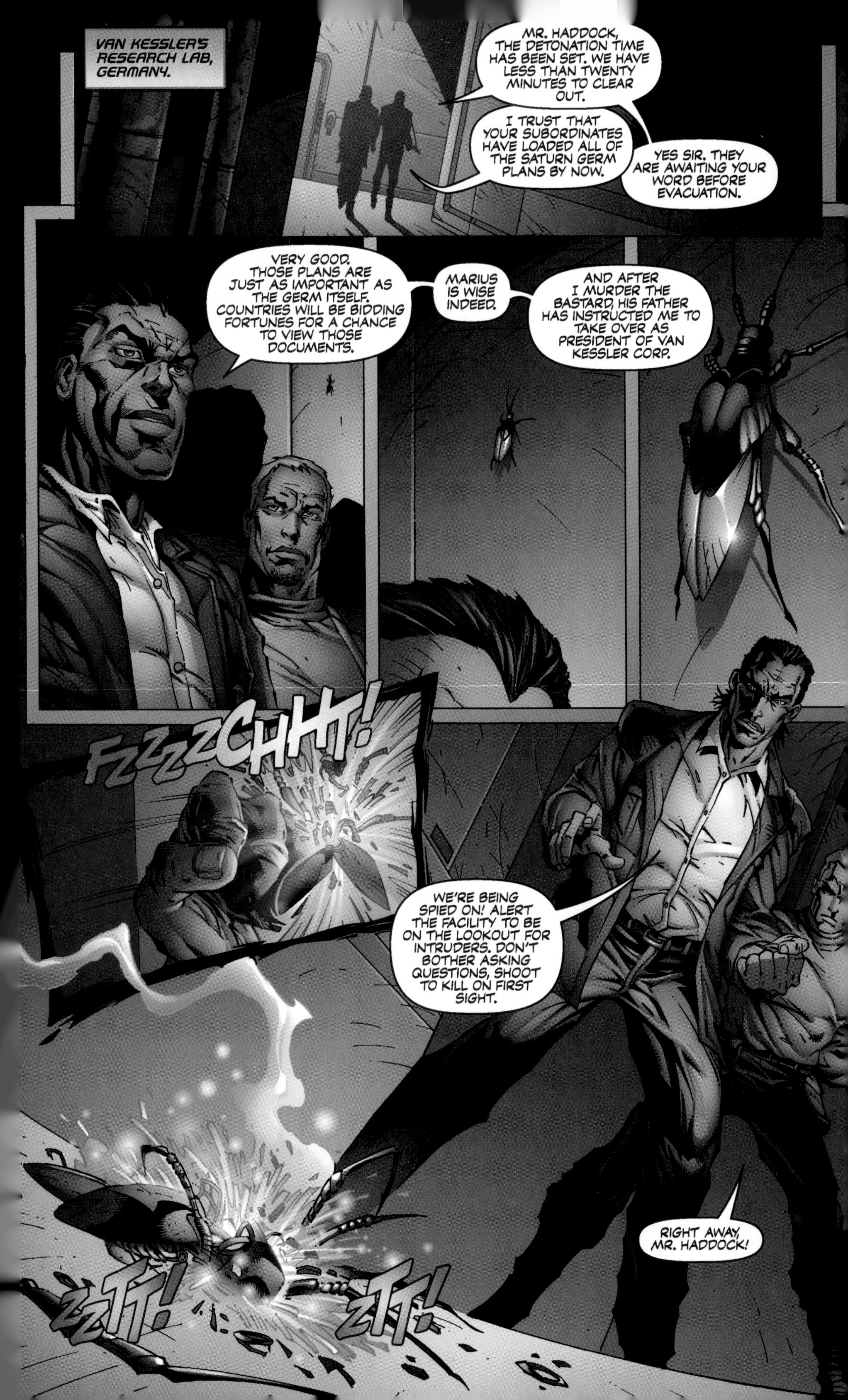
VAN KESSLER'S RESEARCH LAB, GERMANY.
MR. HADDOCK, THE DETONATION TIME HAS BEEN SET. WE HAVE LESS THAN TWENTY MINUTES TO CLEAR OUT.
I TRUST THAT YOUR SUBORDINATES HAVE LOADED ALL OF THE SATURN GERM PLANS BY NOW.
YES SIR. THEY ARE AWAITING YOUR WORD BEFORE EVACUATION.
VERY GOOD. THOSE PLANS ARE JUST AS IMPORTANT AS THE GERM ITSELF. COUNTRIES WILL BE BIDDING FORTUNES FOR A CHANCE TO VIEW THOSE DOCUMENTS.
MARIUS IS WISE INDEED.
AND AFTER I MURDER THE BASTARD, HIS FATHER HAS INSTRUCTED ME TO TAKE OVER AS PRESIDENT OF VAN KESSLER CORP.
FZZZZCHHT!
WE'RE BEING SPIED ON! ALERT THE FACILITY TO BE ON THE LOOKOUT FOR INTRUDERS. DON'T BOTHER ASKING QUESTIONS, SHOOT TO KILL ON FIRST SIGHT.
ZZTT!
ZTT!
RIGHT AWAY, MR. HADDOCK!

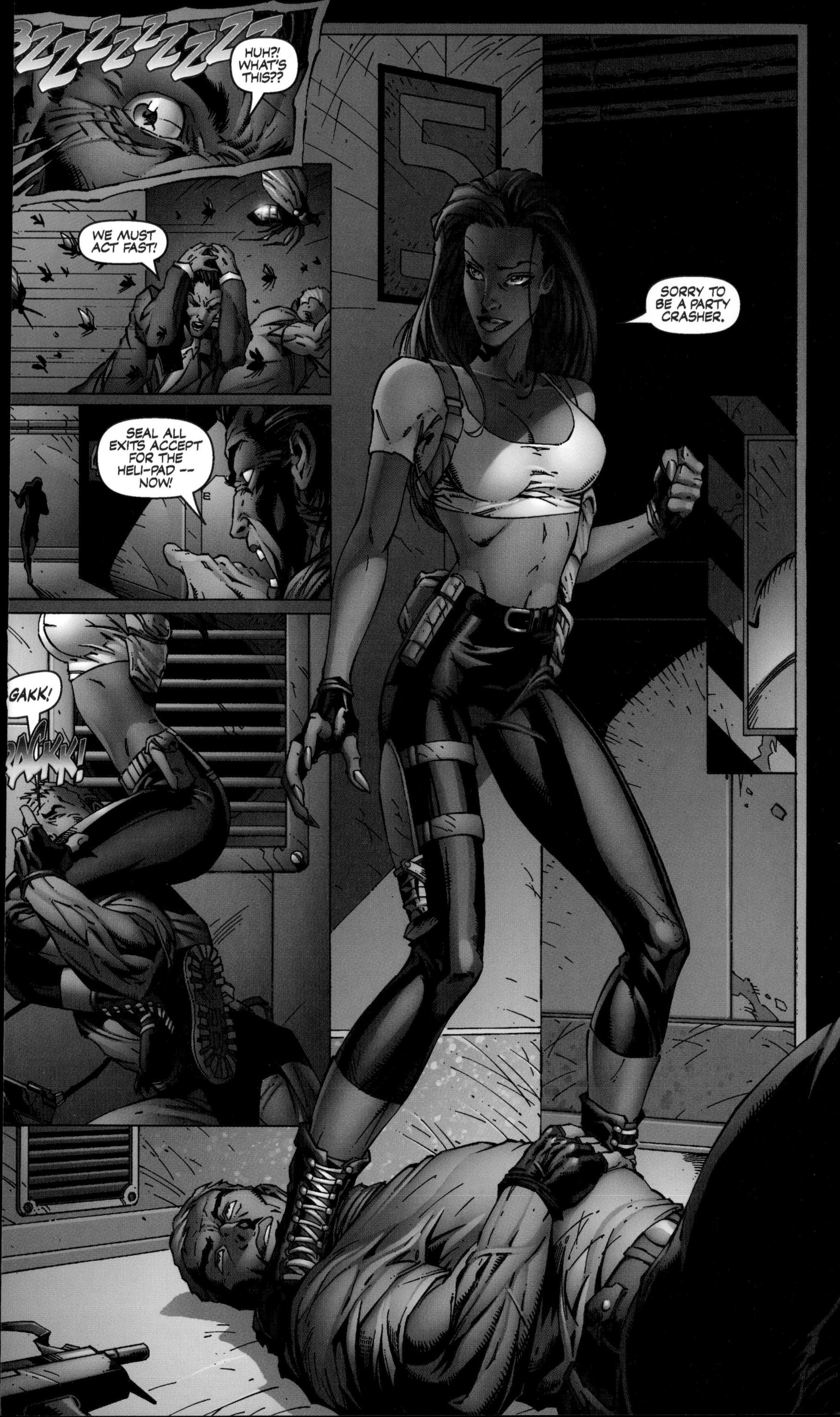
HUH?! WHAT'S THIS??
WE MUST ACT FAST!
SEAL ALL EXITS ACCEPT FOR THE HELI-PAD -- NOW!
GAKK!
SORRY TO BE A PARTY CRASHER.

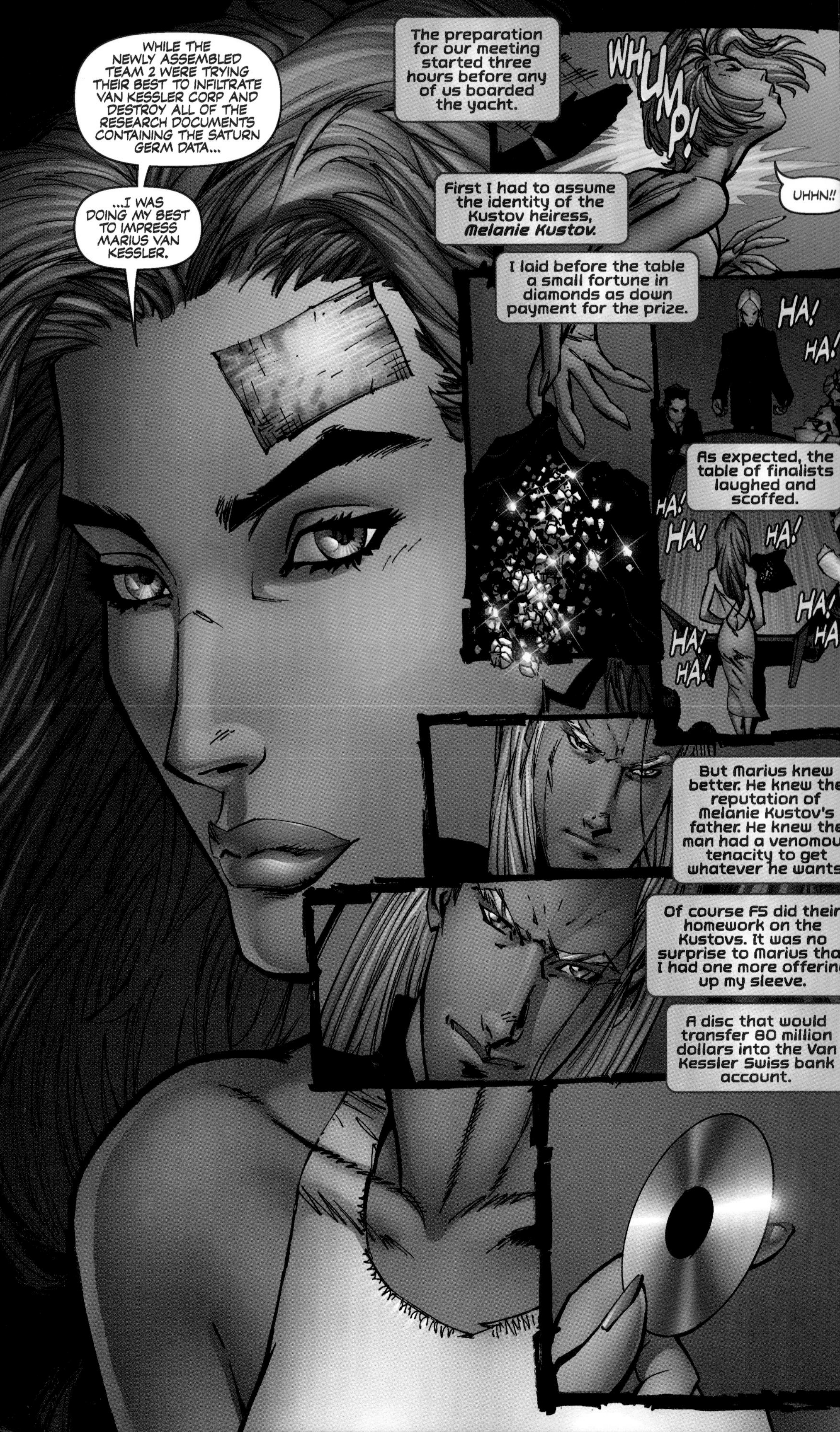
WHILE THE NEWLY ASSEMBLED TEAM 2 WERE TRYING THEIR BEST TO INFILTRATE VAN KESSLER CORP AND DESTROY ALL OF THE RESEARCH DOCUMENTS CONTAINING THE SATURN GERM DATA...
...I WAS DOING MY BEST TO IMPRESS MARIUS VAN KESSLER.
The preparation for our meeting started three hours before any of us boarded the yacht.
WHUMP!
UHHN!!
First I had to assume the identity of the Kustov heiress, *Melanie Kustov*.
I laid before the table a small fortune in diamonds as down payment for the prize.
HA! HA!
As expected, the table of finalists laughed and scoffed.
HA! HA! HA! HA! HA! HA! HA!
But Marius knew better. He knew the reputation of Melanie Kustov's father. He knew the man had a venomous tenacity to get whatever he wants.
Of course F5 did their homework on the Kustovs. It was no surprise to Marius that I had one more offering up my sleeve.
A disc that would transfer 80 million dollars into the Van Kessler Swiss bank account.

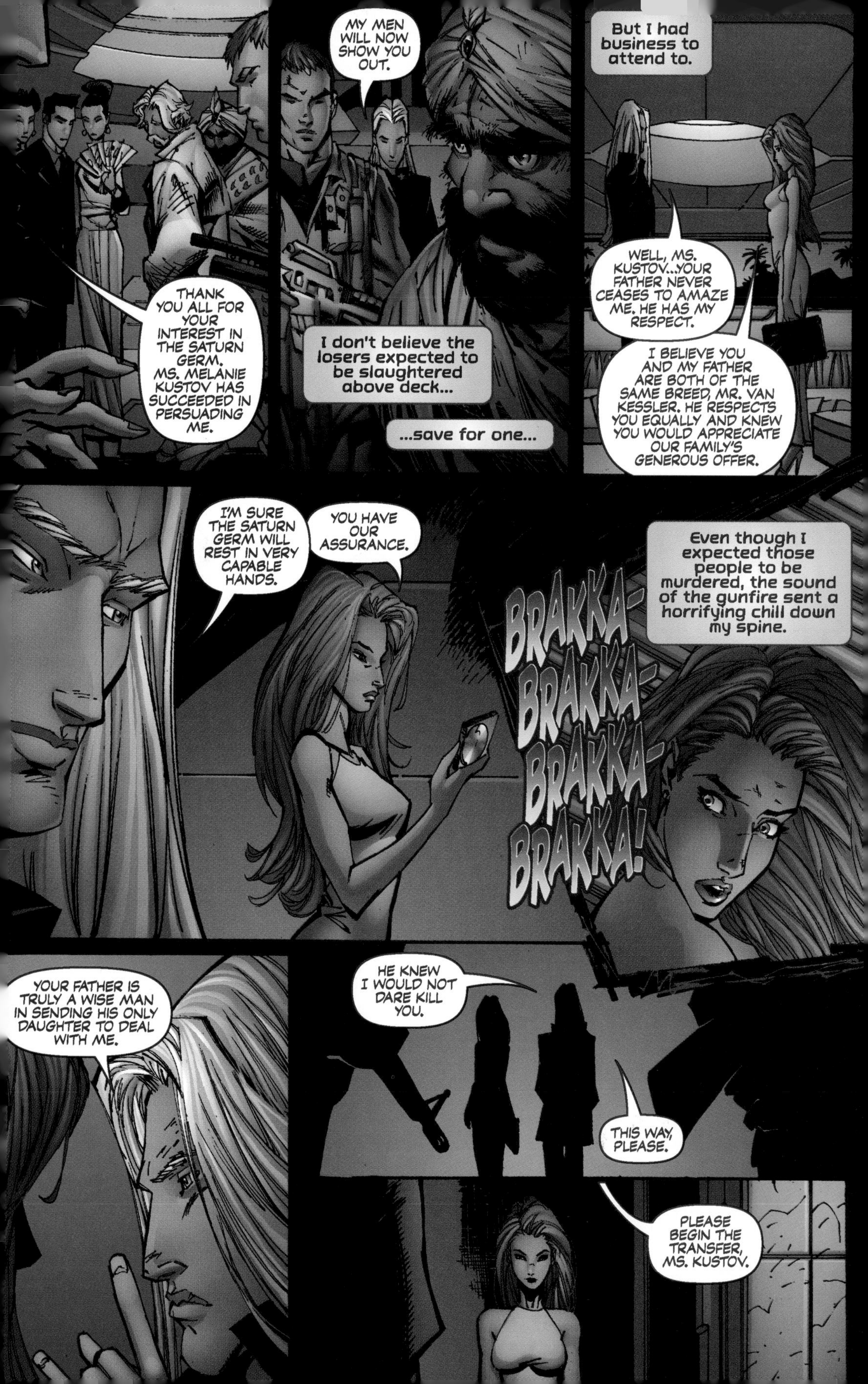

THANK YOU ALL FOR YOUR INTEREST IN THE SATURN GERM. MS. MELANIE KUSTOV HAS SUCCEEDED IN PERSUADING ME.
MY MEN WILL NOW SHOW YOU OUT.
I don't believe the losers expected to be slaughtered above deck...
...save for one...
But I had business to attend to.
WELL, MS. KUSTOV...YOUR FATHER NEVER CEASES TO AMAZE ME. HE HAS MY RESPECT.
I BELIEVE YOU AND MY FATHER ARE BOTH OF THE SAME BREED, MR. VAN KESSLER. HE RESPECTS YOU EQUALLY AND KNEW YOU WOULD APPRECIATE OUR FAMILY'S GENEROUS OFFER.
I'M SURE THE SATURN GERM WILL REST IN VERY CAPABLE HANDS.
YOU HAVE OUR ASSURANCE.
Even though I expected those people to be murdered, the sound of the gunfire sent a horrifying chill down my spine.
BRAKKA-BRAKKA-BRAKKA-BRAKKA!
YOUR FATHER IS TRULY A WISE MAN IN SENDING HIS ONLY DAUGHTER TO DEAL WITH ME.
HE KNEW I WOULD NOT DARE KILL YOU.
THIS WAY, PLEASE.
PLEASE BEGIN THE TRANSFER, MS. KUSTOV.

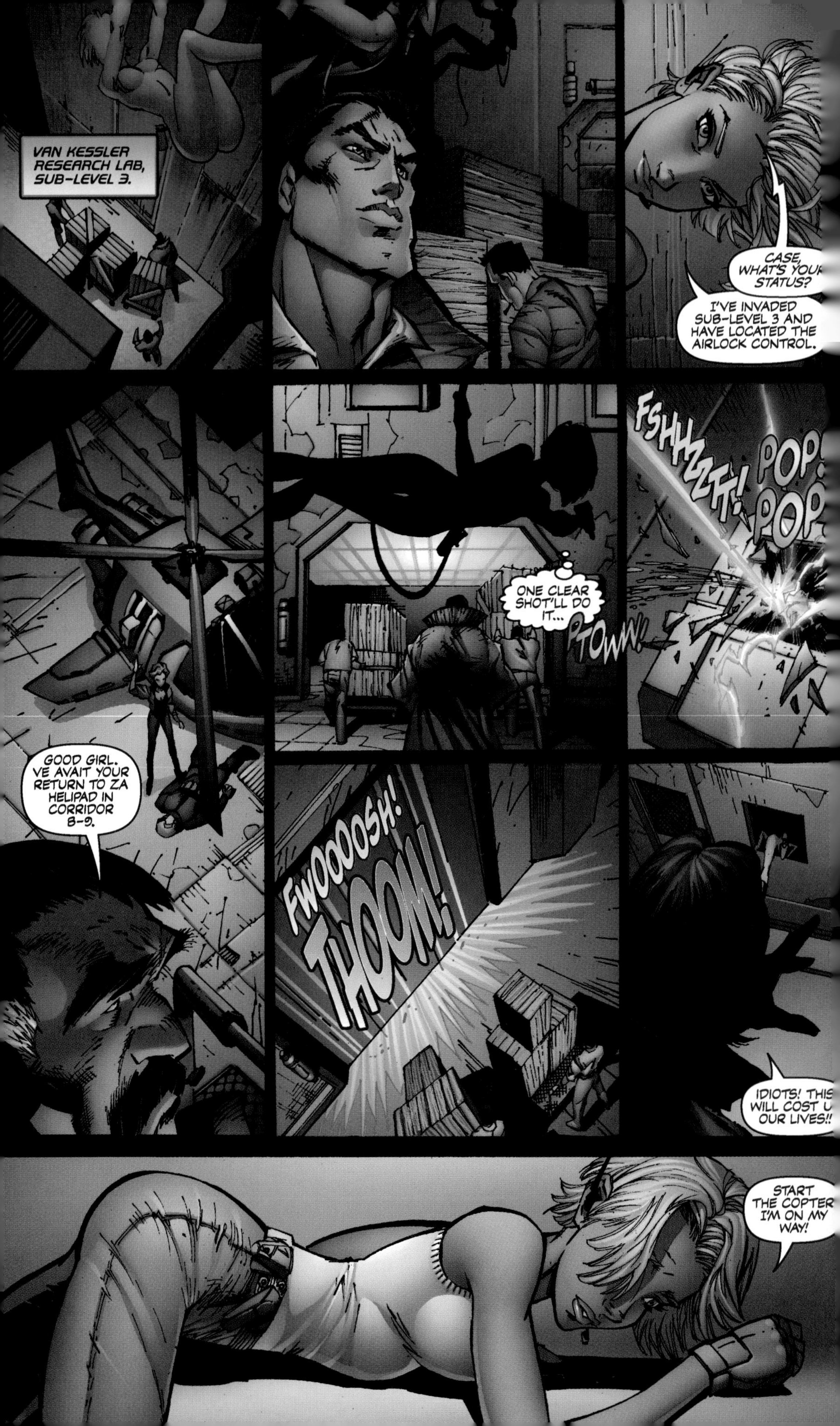
VAN KESSLER RESEARCH LAB, SUB-LEVEL 3.
CASE, WHAT'S YOUR STATUS?
I'VE INVADED SUB-LEVEL 3 AND HAVE LOCATED THE AIRLOCK CONTROL.
GOOD GIRL. VE AVAIT YOUR RETURN TO ZA HELIPAD IN CORRIDOR 8-9.
ONE CLEAR SHOT'LL DO IT...
PTOWW!
FSHHZZT! POP! POP!
FWOOOOSH! THOOM!
IDIOTS! THIS WILL COST U OUR LIVES!!
START THE COPTER I'M ON MY WAY!

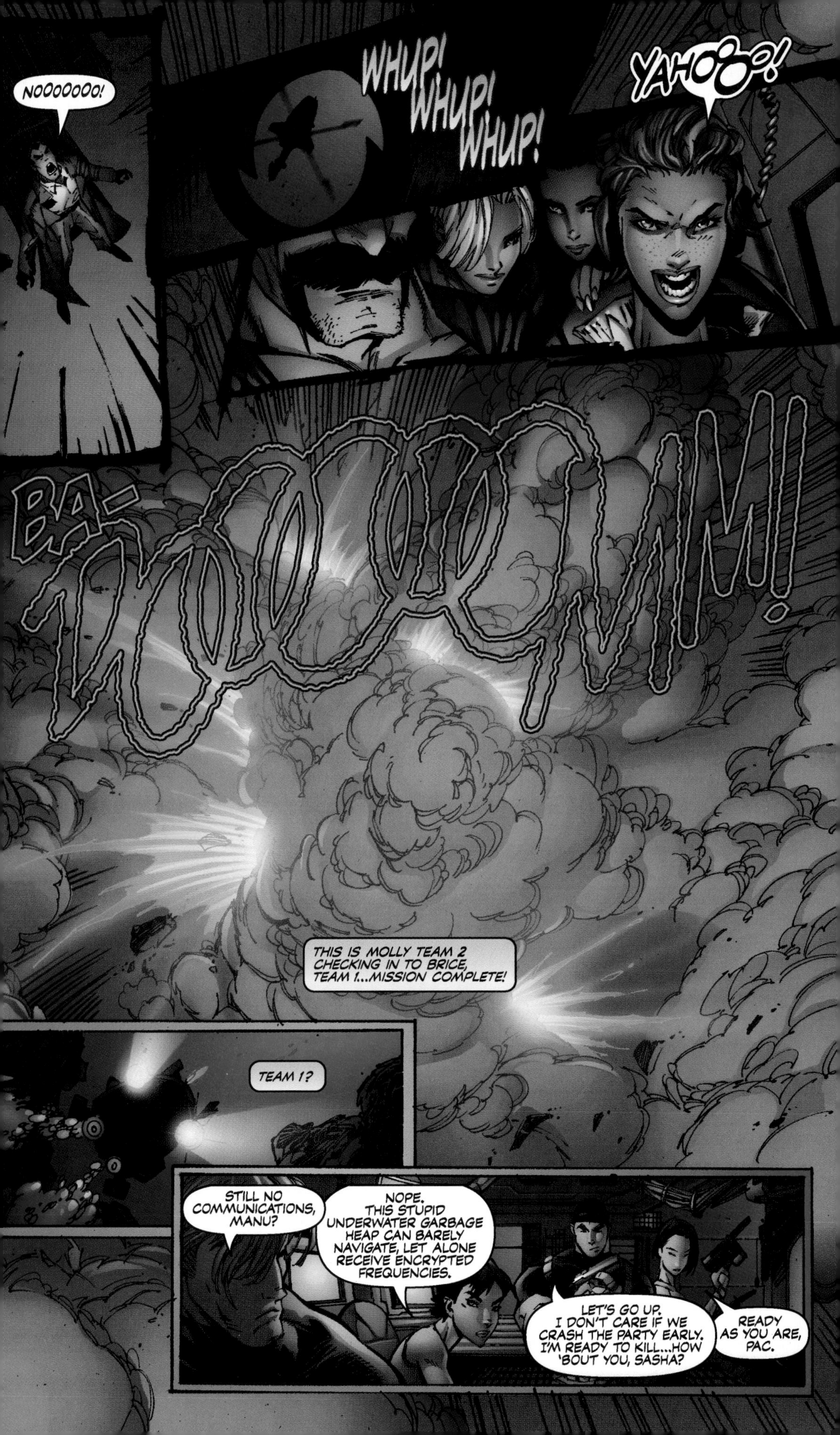
NOOOOOOO!
WHUP! WHUP! WHUP!
YAHOOOO!
BA-WOOOOOOM!
THIS IS MOLLY TEAM 2 CHECKING IN TO BRICE, TEAM 1...MISSION COMPLETE!
TEAM 1?
STILL NO COMMUNICATIONS, MANU?
NOPE. THIS STUPID UNDERWATER GARBAGE HEAP CAN BARELY NAVIGATE, LET ALONE RECEIVE ENCRYPTED FREQUENCIES.
LET'S GO UP. I DON'T CARE IF WE CRASH THE PARTY EARLY. I'M READY TO KILL...HOW 'BOUT YOU, SASHA?
READY AS YOU ARE, PAC.

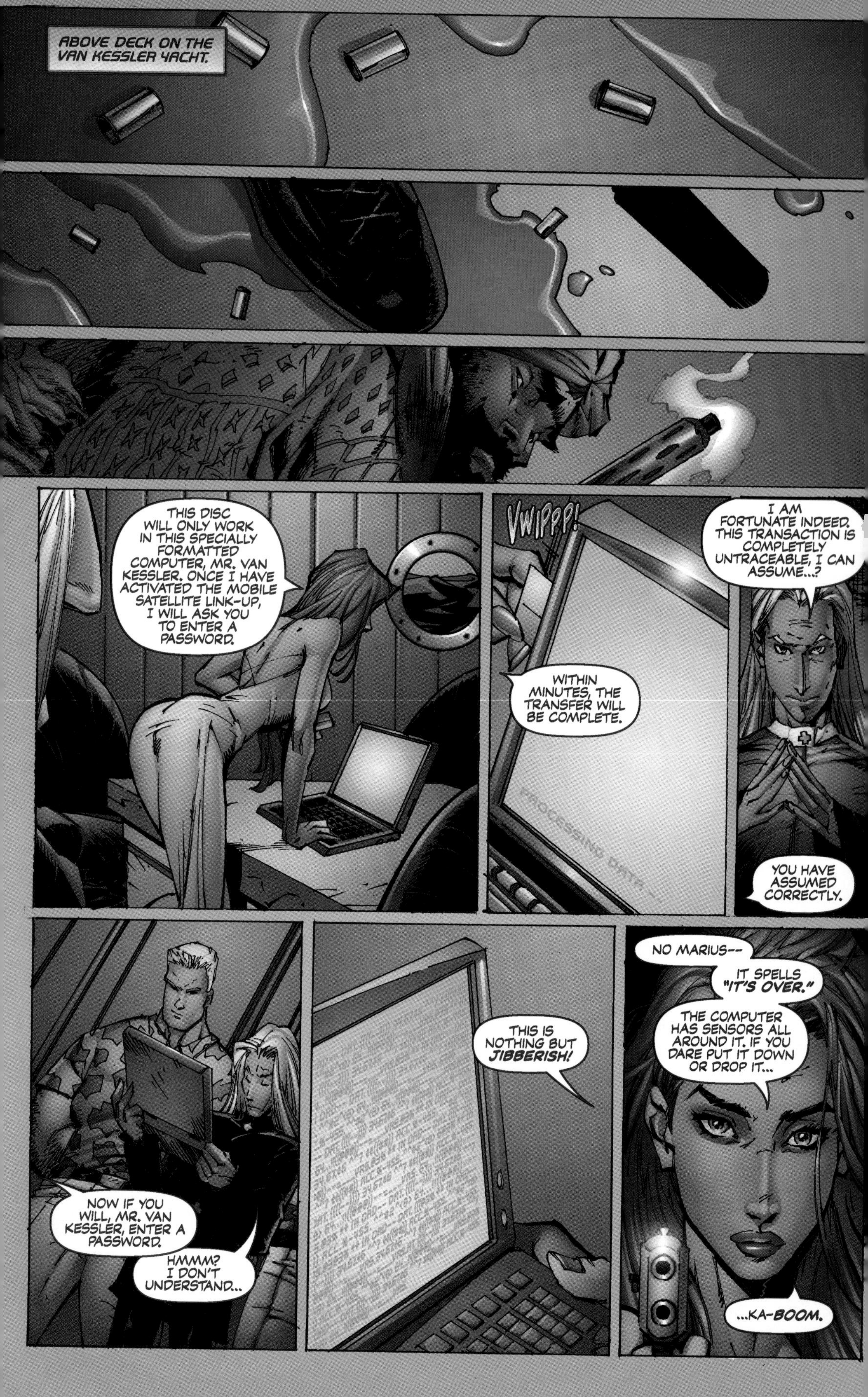
ABOVE DECK ON THE VAN KESSLER YACHT.
THIS DISC WILL ONLY WORK IN THIS SPECIALLY FORMATTED COMPUTER, MR. VAN KESSLER. ONCE I HAVE ACTIVATED THE MOBILE SATELLITE LINK-UP, I WILL ASK YOU TO ENTER A PASSWORD.
VWIPPP!
WITHIN MINUTES, THE TRANSFER WILL BE COMPLETE.
PROCESSING DATA --
I AM FORTUNATE INDEED. THIS TRANSACTION IS COMPLETELY UNTRACEABLE, I CAN ASSUME...?
YOU HAVE ASSUMED CORRECTLY.
NOW IF YOU WILL, MR. VAN KESSLER, ENTER A PASSWORD.
HMMM? I DON'T UNDERSTAND...
THIS IS NOTHING BUT ***JIBBERISH!***
NO MARIUS--
IT SPELLS ***"IT'S OVER."***
THE COMPUTER HAS SENSORS ALL AROUND IT. IF YOU DARE PUT IT DOWN OR DROP IT...
...KA-***BOOM.***

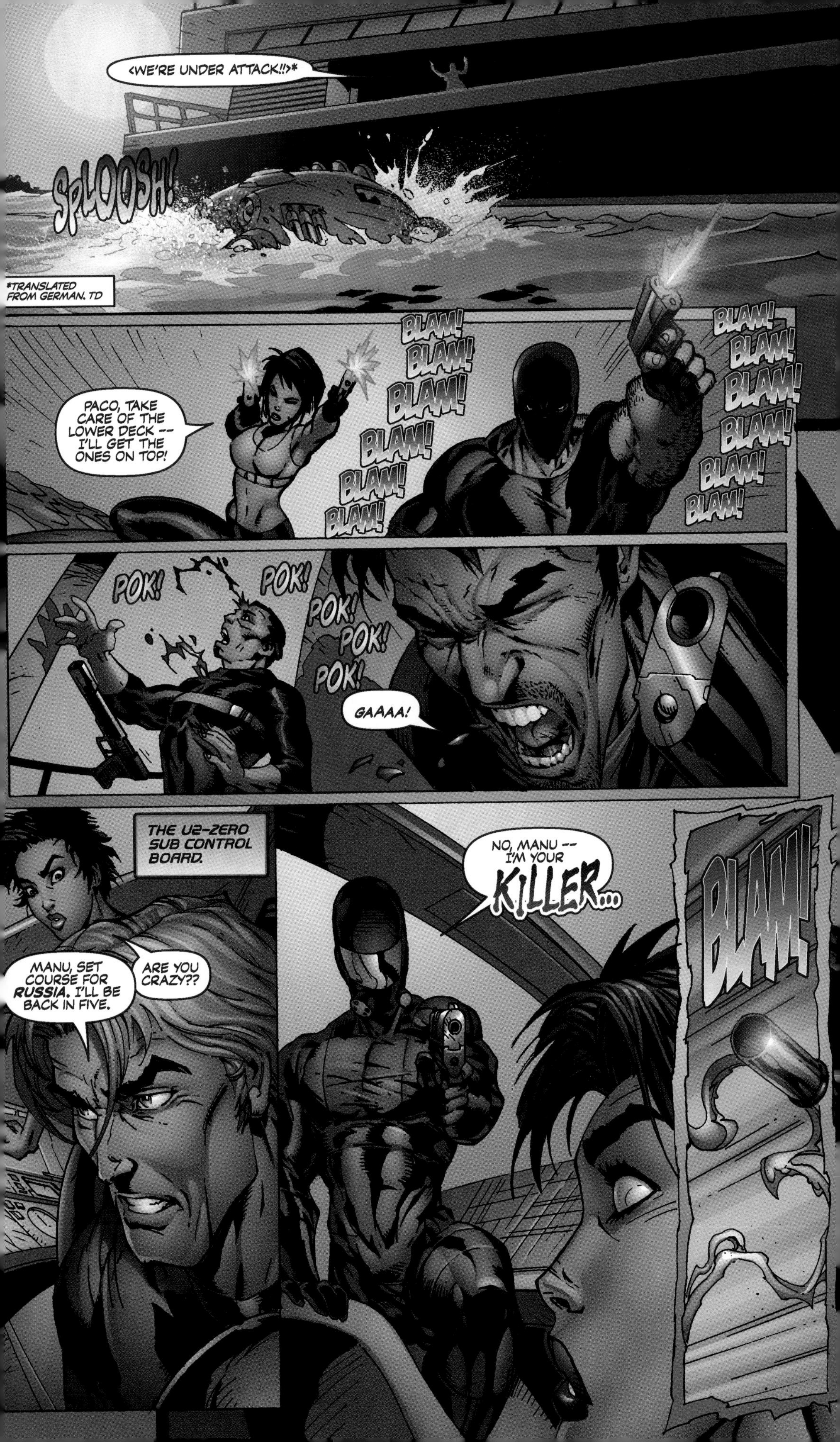
<WE'RE UNDER ATTACK!!>*
SPLOOSH!
*TRANSLATED FROM GERMAN. TD
PACO, TAKE CARE OF THE LOWER DECK -- I'LL GET THE ONES ON TOP!
BLAM! BLAM! BLAM! BLAM! BLAM! BLAM!
BLAM! BLAM! BLAM! BLAM! BLAM! BLAM!
POK! POK! POK! POK! POK!
GAAAA!
THE U2-ZERO SUB CONTROL BOARD.
MANU, SET COURSE FOR RUSSIA. I'LL BE BACK IN FIVE.
ARE YOU CRAZY??
NO, MANU -- I'M YOUR KILLER...
BLAM!

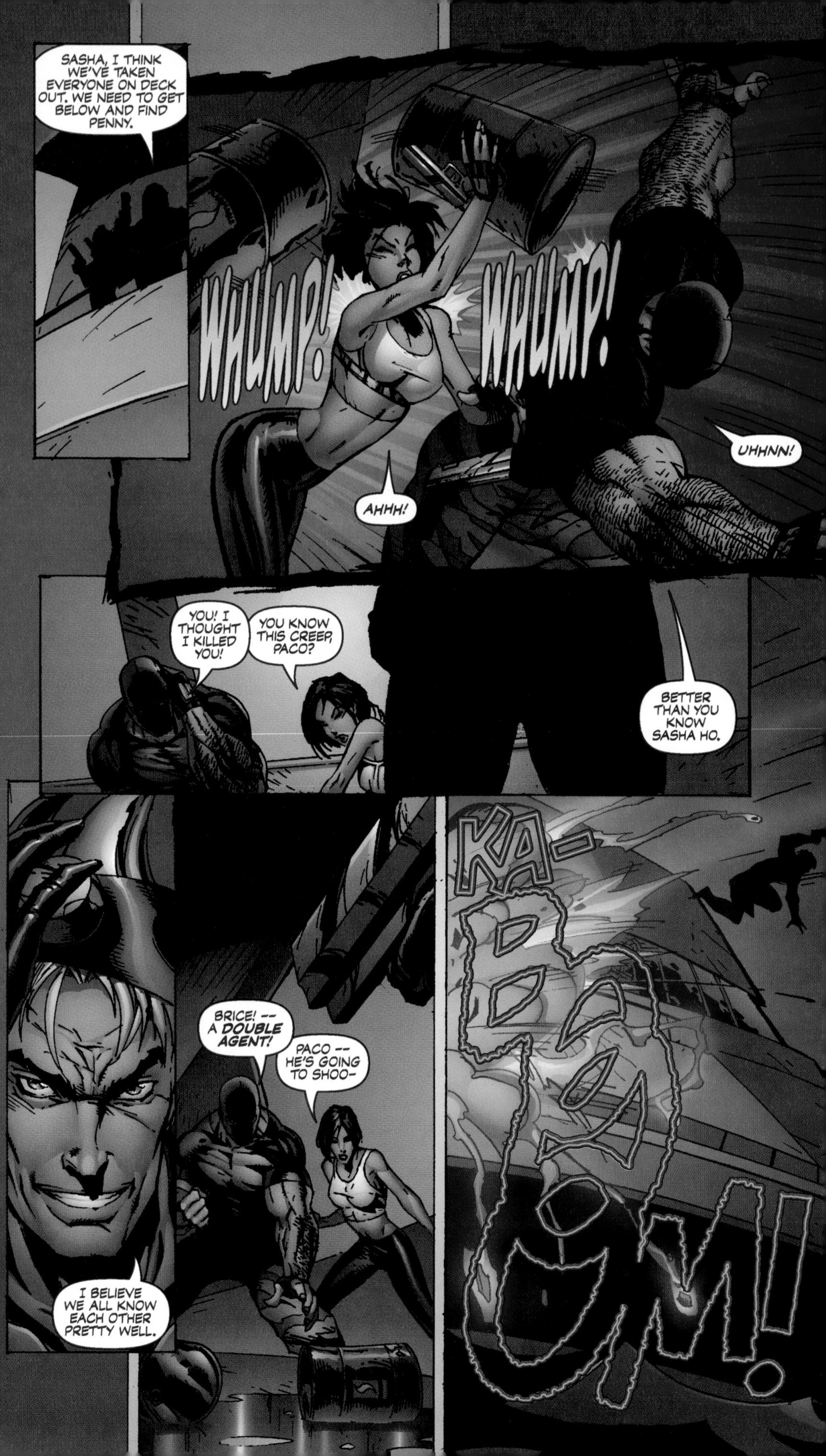
SASHA, I THINK WE'VE TAKEN EVERYONE ON DECK OUT. WE NEED TO GET BELOW AND FIND PENNY.
WHUMP!
WHUMP!
AHHH!
UHHNN!
YOU! I THOUGHT I KILLED YOU!
YOU KNOW THIS CREEP, PACO?
BETTER THAN YOU KNOW SASHA HO.
I BELIEVE WE ALL KNOW EACH OTHER PRETTY WELL.
BRICE! -- A DOUBLE AGENT!
PACO -- HE'S GOING TO SHOO-
KA-BOOM!

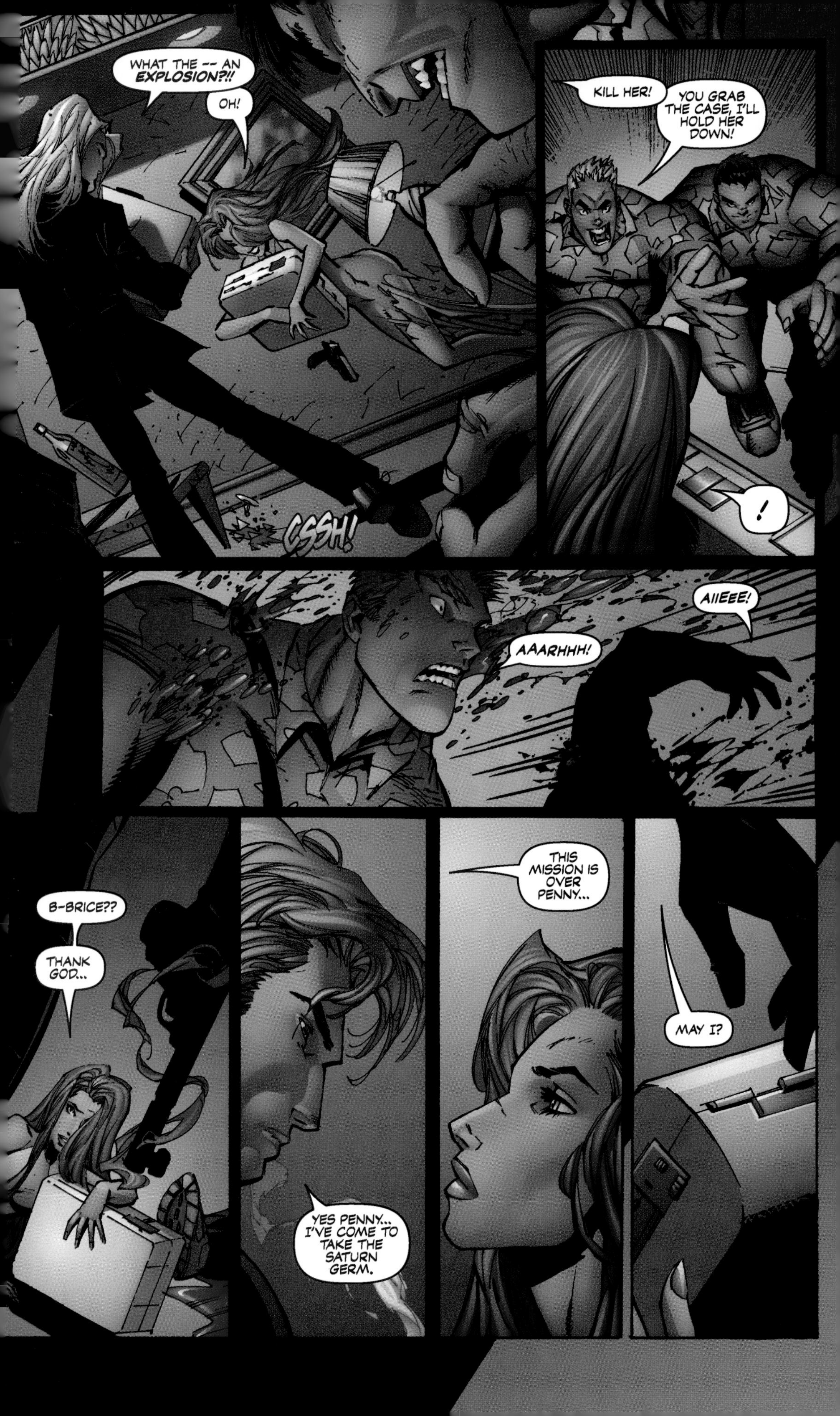
WHAT THE -- AN EXPLOSION?!!
OH!
CSSH!
KILL HER!
YOU GRAB THE CASE, I'LL HOLD HER DOWN!
!
AIIEEE!
AAARHHH!
B-BRICE??
THANK GOD...
YES PENNY... I'VE COME TO TAKE THE SATURN GERM.
THIS MISSION IS OVER PENNY...
MAY I?

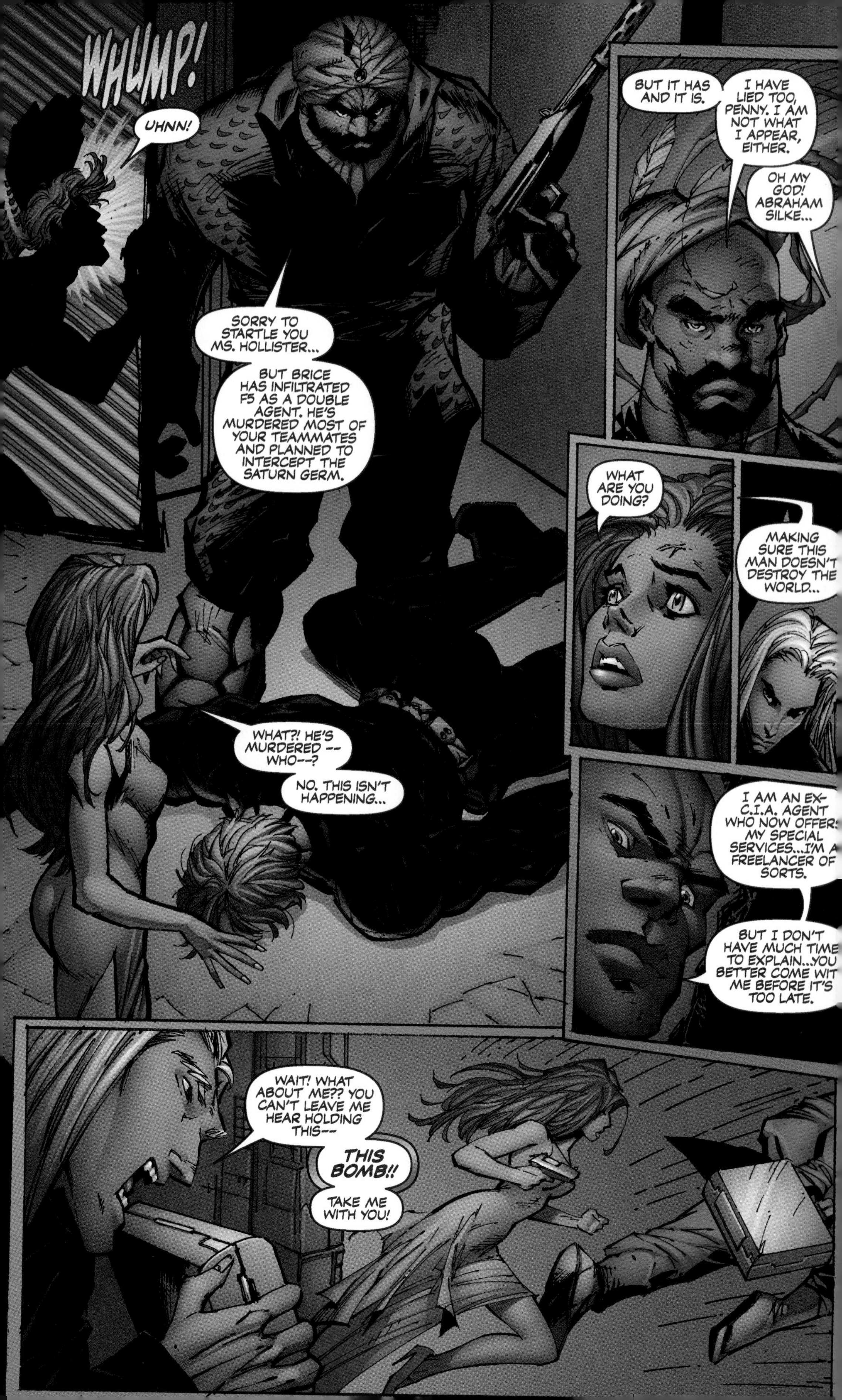
WHUMP!
UHNN!
SORRY TO STARTLE YOU MS. HOLLISTER...
BUT BRICE HAS INFILTRATED F5 AS A DOUBLE AGENT. HE'S MURDERED MOST OF YOUR TEAMMATES AND PLANNED TO INTERCEPT THE SATURN GERM.
BUT IT HAS AND IT IS.
I HAVE LIED TOO, PENNY. I AM NOT WHAT I APPEAR, EITHER.
OH MY GOD! ABRAHAM SILKE...
WHAT ARE YOU DOING?
MAKING SURE THIS MAN DOESN'T DESTROY THE WORLD...
WHAT?! HE'S MURDERED -- WHO--?
NO. THIS ISN'T HAPPENING...
I AM AN EX-C.I.A. AGENT WHO NOW OFFERS MY SPECIAL SERVICES...I'M A FREELANCER OF SORTS.
BUT I DON'T HAVE MUCH TIME TO EXPLAIN...YOU BETTER COME WIT ME BEFORE IT'S TOO LATE.
WAIT! WHAT ABOUT ME?? YOU CAN'T LEAVE ME HEAR HOLDING THIS--
THIS BOMB!!
TAKE ME WITH YOU!

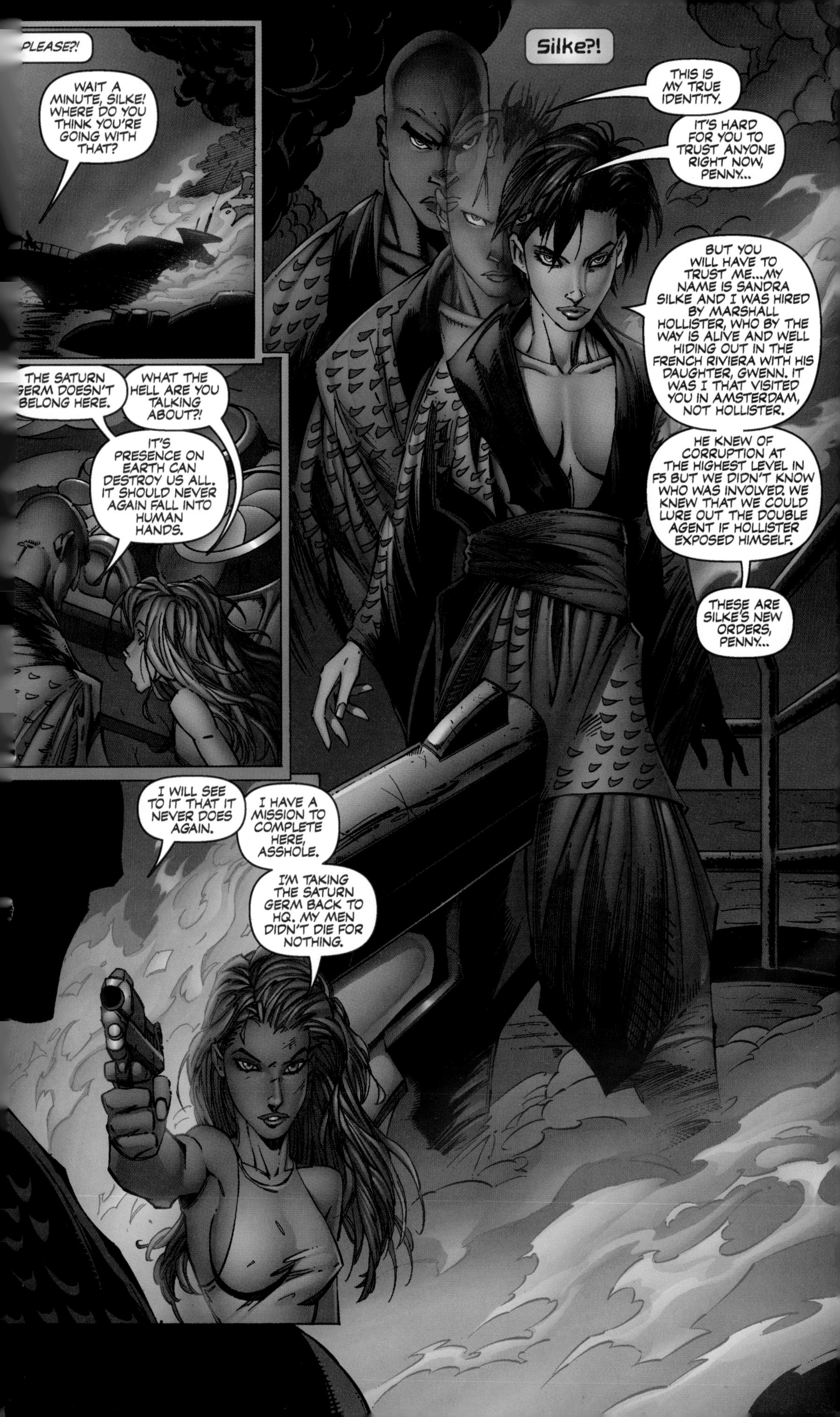
PLEASE?!
WAIT A MINUTE, SILKE! WHERE DO YOU THINK YOU'RE GOING WITH THAT?
THE SATURN GERM DOESN'T BELONG HERE.
WHAT THE HELL ARE YOU TALKING ABOUT?!
IT'S PRESENCE ON EARTH CAN DESTROY US ALL. IT SHOULD NEVER AGAIN FALL INTO HUMAN HANDS.
Silke?!
THIS IS MY TRUE IDENTITY.
IT'S HARD FOR YOU TO TRUST ANYONE RIGHT NOW, PENNY...
BUT YOU WILL HAVE TO TRUST ME...MY NAME IS SANDRA SILKE AND I WAS HIRED BY MARSHALL HOLLISTER, WHO BY THE WAY IS ALIVE AND WELL HIDING OUT IN THE FRENCH RIVIERA WITH HIS DAUGHTER, GWENN. IT WAS I THAT VISITED YOU IN AMSTERDAM, NOT HOLLISTER.
HE KNEW OF CORRUPTION AT THE HIGHEST LEVEL IN F5 BUT WE DIDN'T KNOW WHO WAS INVOLVED. WE KNEW THAT WE COULD LURE OUT THE DOUBLE AGENT IF HOLLISTER EXPOSED HIMSELF.
THESE ARE SILKE'S NEW ORDERS, PENNY...
I WILL SEE TO IT THAT IT NEVER DOES AGAIN.
I HAVE A MISSION TO COMPLETE HERE, ASSHOLE.
I'M TAKING THE SATURN GERM BACK TO HQ. MY MEN DIDN'T DIE FOR NOTHING.

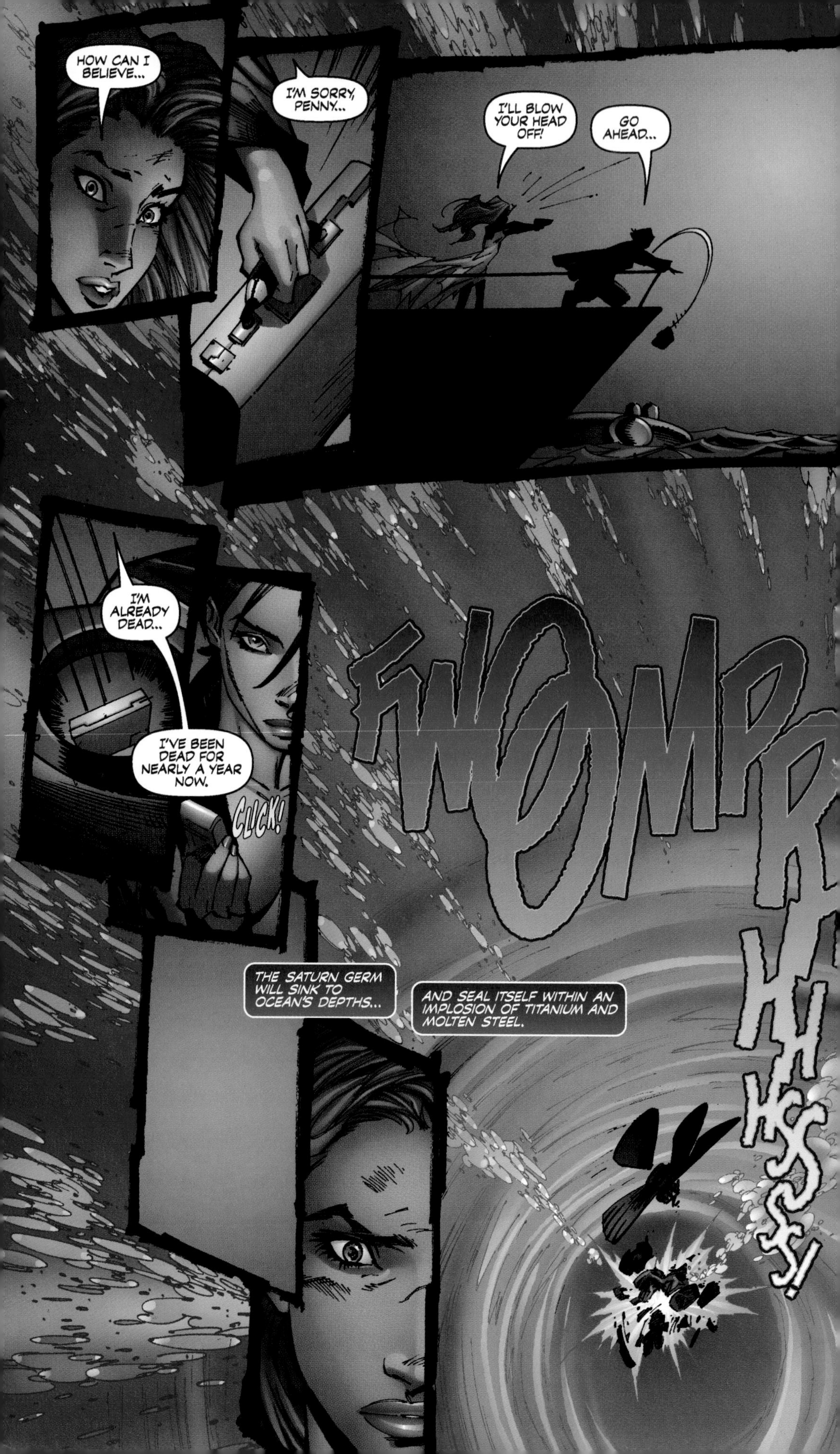
HOW CAN I BELIEVE...
I'M SORRY, PENNY...
I'LL BLOW YOUR HEAD OFF!
GO AHEAD...
I'M ALREADY DEAD...
I'VE BEEN DEAD FOR NEARLY A YEAR NOW.
CLICK!
FWOMPR
THE SATURN GERM WILL SINK TO OCEAN'S DEPTHS...
AND SEAL ITSELF WITHIN AN IMPLOSION OF TITANIUM AND MOLTEN STEEL.
HHSSS!

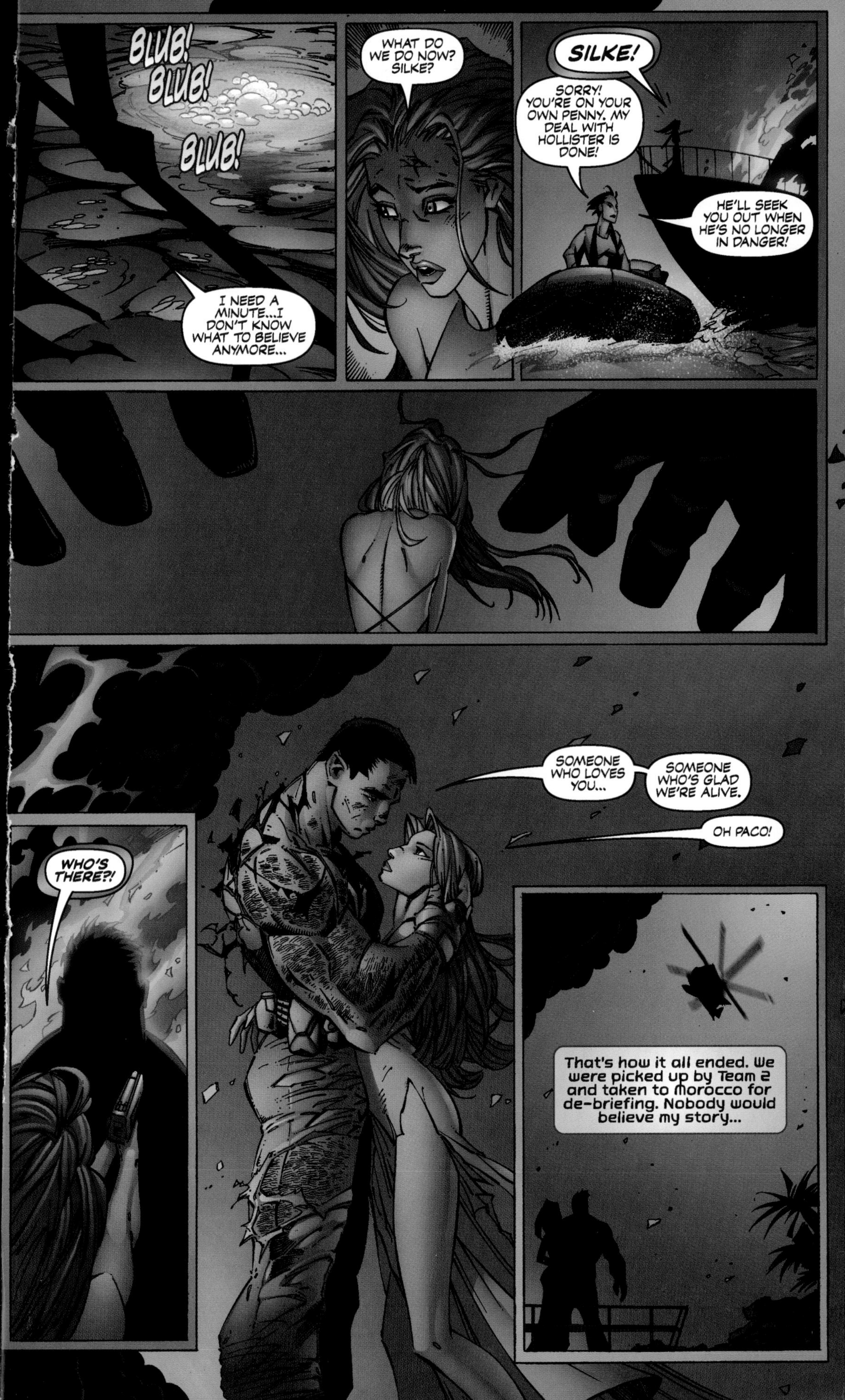
BLUB! BLUB! BLUB!
I NEED A MINUTE...I DON'T KNOW WHAT TO BELIEVE ANYMORE...
WHAT DO WE DO NOW? SILKE?
SILKE!
SORRY! YOU'RE ON YOUR OWN PENNY. MY DEAL WITH HOLLISTER IS DONE!
HE'LL SEEK YOU OUT WHEN HE'S NO LONGER IN DANGER!
WHO'S THERE?!
SOMEONE WHO LOVES YOU...
SOMEONE WHO'S GLAD WE'RE ALIVE.
OH PACO!
That's how it all ended. We were picked up by Team 2 and taken to Morocco for de-briefing. Nobody would believe my story...

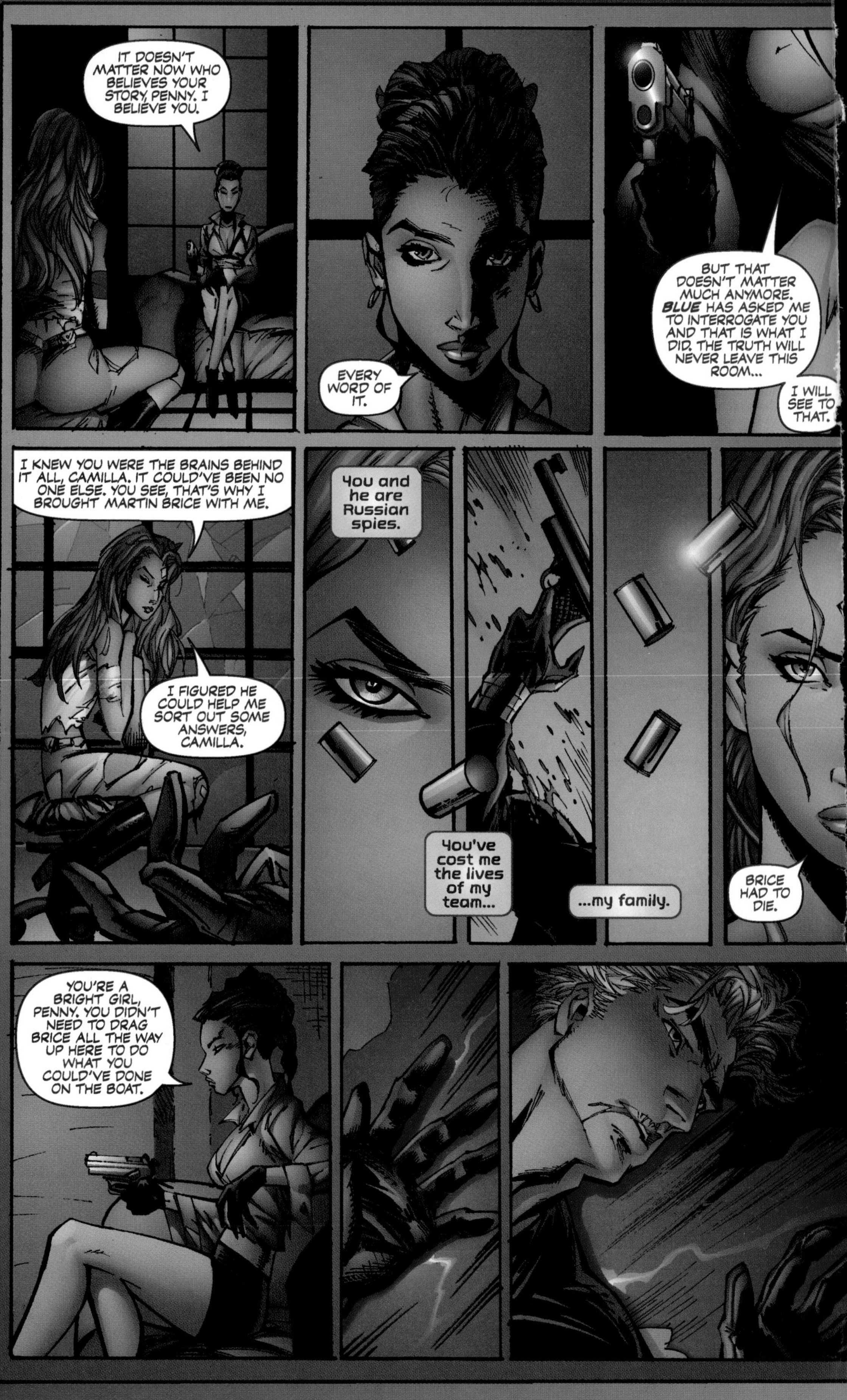
IT DOESN'T MATTER NOW WHO BELIEVES YOUR STORY, PENNY. I BELIEVE YOU.
EVERY WORD OF IT.
BUT THAT DOESN'T MATTER MUCH ANYMORE. **BLUE** HAS ASKED ME TO INTERROGATE YOU AND THAT IS WHAT I DID. THE TRUTH WILL NEVER LEAVE THIS ROOM...
I WILL SEE TO THAT.
I KNEW YOU WERE THE BRAINS BEHIND IT ALL, CAMILLA. IT COULD'VE BEEN NO ONE ELSE. YOU SEE, THAT'S WHY I BROUGHT MARTIN BRICE WITH ME.
I FIGURED HE COULD HELP ME SORT OUT SOME ANSWERS, CAMILLA.
You and he are Russian spies.
You've cost me the lives of my team...
...my family.
BRICE HAD TO DIE.
YOU'RE A BRIGHT GIRL, PENNY. YOU DIDN'T NEED TO DRAG BRICE ALL THE WAY UP HERE TO DO WHAT YOU COULD'VE DONE ON THE BOAT.

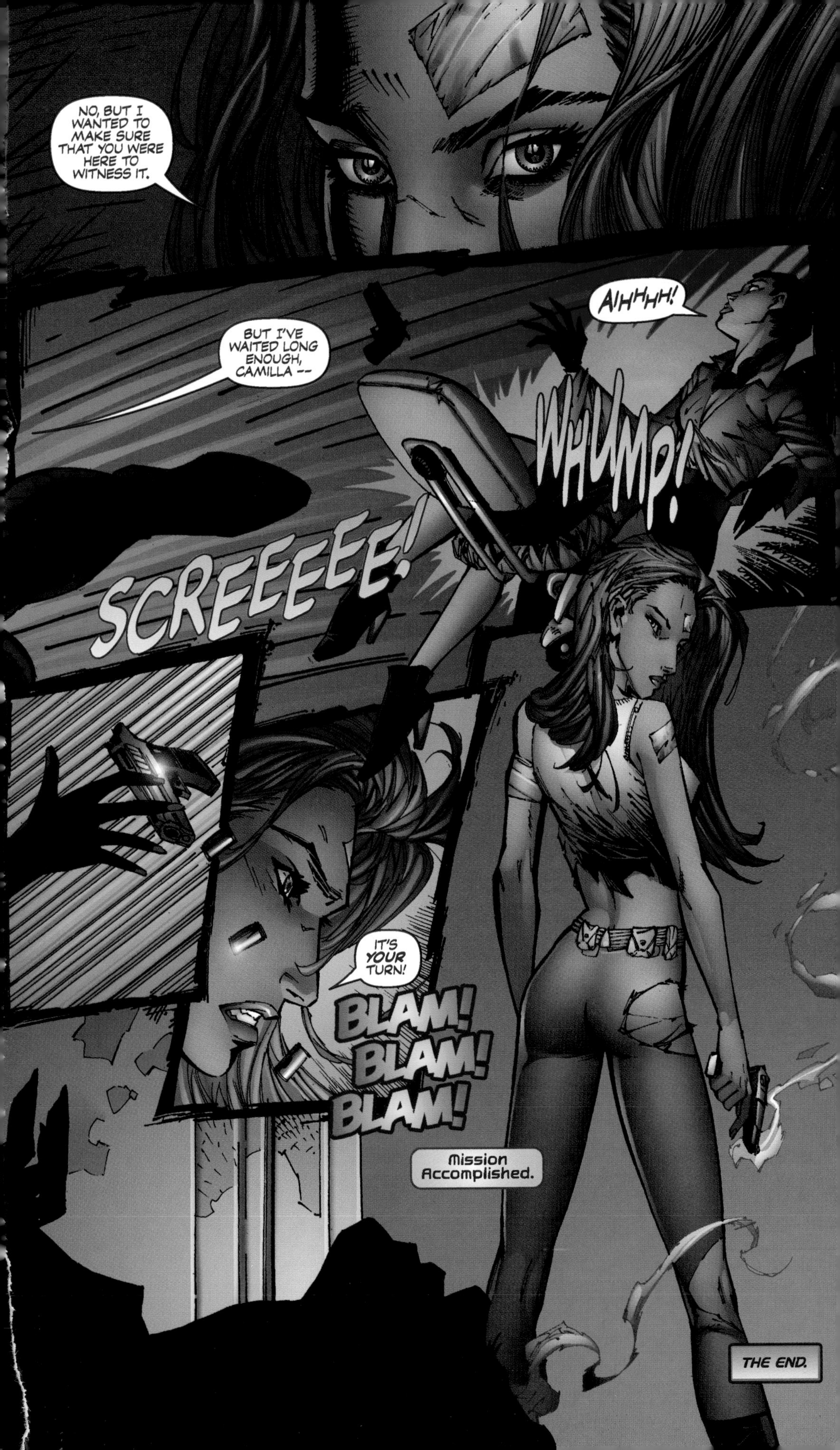
NO, BUT I WANTED TO MAKE SURE THAT YOU WERE HERE TO WITNESS IT.
BUT I'VE WAITED LONG ENOUGH, CAMILLA --
AIHHHH!
WHUMP!
SCREEEEEE!
IT'S YOUR TURN!
BLAM! BLAM! BLAM!
Mission Accomplished.
THE END.

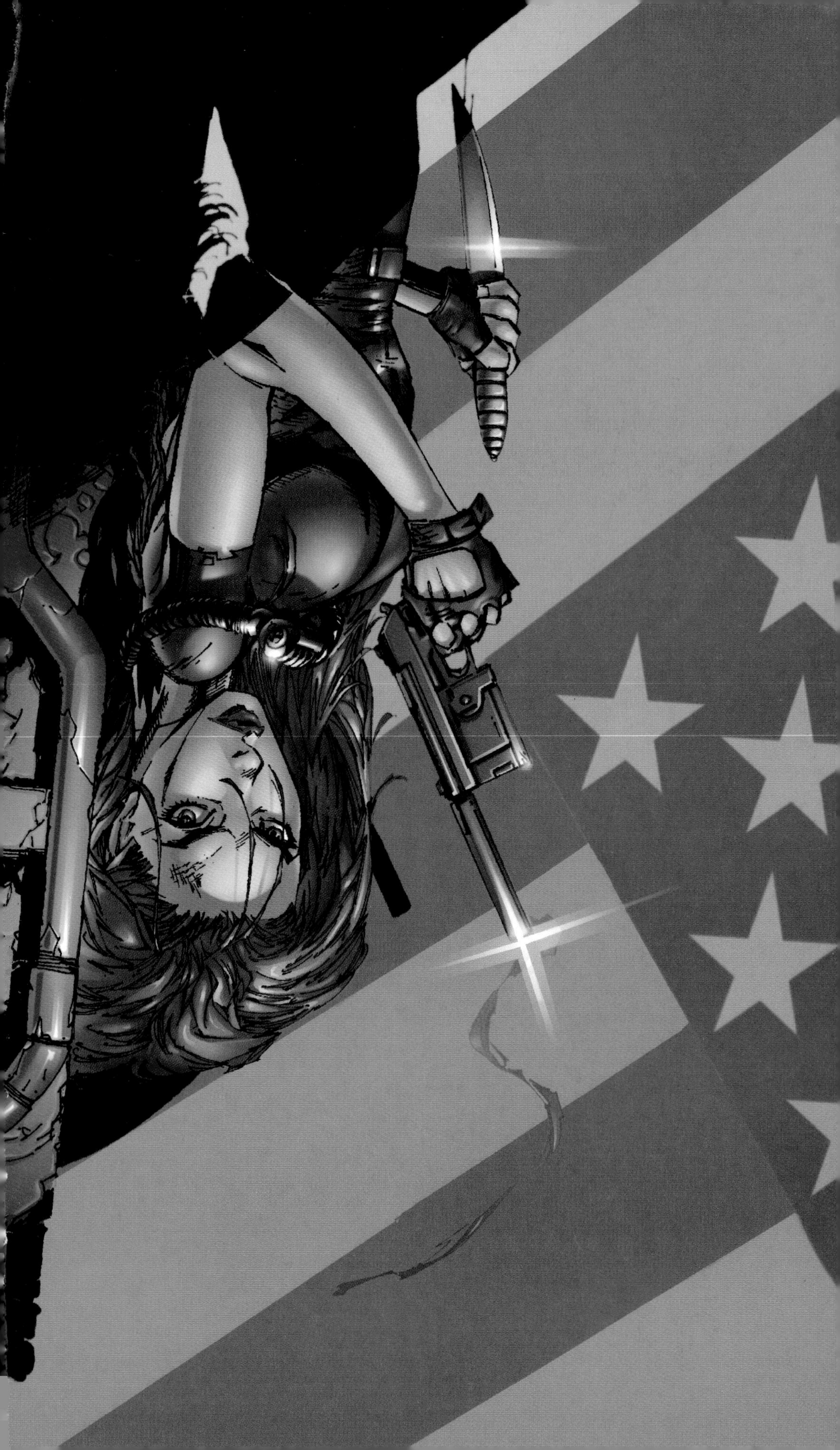

Red Menace

Written by
DANNY BILSON, PAUL DeMEO
and ADAM BRODY

Pencilled by
JERRY ORDWAY

Inked by
AL VEY

Colored by
JONNY RENCH
with CARRIE STRACHAN and WILDSTORM FX

Lettered by
ROB LEIGH

Collected Edition cover and Original series covers by JERRY ORDWAY
Variant Cover #1 by DARWYN COOKE
Variant Cover #2 by MIKE KALUTA and JONNY RENCH

Red Menace

EAGLE TESTIFIES BEFORE HUAC

COMMIE SYMPATHIZER?

McCARTHY: "YES."

RED MENACE, published by WildStorm Productions. 888 Prospect St. #240, La Jolla, CA 92037. Compilation and sketches copyright © 2007 Pet Fly Production, Inc., Flyworks Productions, Inc., Second Row Productions, Inc. and DC Comics. All Rights Reserved. Originally published in single magazine form as RED MENACE #1-6 © 2007 Pet Fly Production, Inc., Flyworks Productions, Inc., Second Row Productions, Inc. and DC Comics.

RED MENACE, all characters, the distinctive likenesses thereof and all related elements are trademarks of Pet Fly Production, Inc., Flyworks Productions, Inc., Second Row Productions, Inc. WildStorm and logo are trademarks of DC Comics. The stories, characters, and incidents mentioned in this magazine are entirely fictional. Printed on recyclable paper. WildStorm does not read or accept unsolicited submissions of ideas, stories or artwork. Printed in Canada.

DC Comics, a Warner Bros. Entertainment Company.

ISBN: 1-4012-1383-9   ISBN-13: 978-1-4012-1383-1

"THE FACT THAT YOU'VE COME HERE TODAY, OF YOUR OWN FREE WILL, SHOULD STAND AS AN EXAMPLE TO THOSE OF YOUR...*'FRATERNITY'* WHO'VE *REFUSED* TO COOPERATE."

Los Angeles Examiner

OCTOBER 1, 1953

EAGLE TO UNMASK FOR HUAC

COMMITTEE CALLS SPECIAL LOS ANGELES SESSION

.9 A·M· FINAL

THE EAGLE TODAY AT

McCarthy Roy Cohn

"I'M SURE THE GOOD PEOPLE OF LOS ANGELES ARE *GRATEFUL* THAT YOU'VE MADE THEIR STREETS SAFE. BUT THE PEOPLE NEED TO KNOW WHERE *LOYALTIES* LIE. THESE DANGEROUS TIMES CAN ILL AFFORD *SECRET IDENTITIES,* NO MATTER HOW WELL INTENDED."

"I JUST WANT TO HELP MY CITY, SENATOR. I DON'T NEED A *MASK* TO DO THAT."

UNITED STATES COURTHOUSE

SEND 'EM BACK TO MOSCOW!

TAIL GUNNER JOE McCARTHY IS OUR HERO!

GOD BLESS AMERICA AND JOE MCCAR

UNITE COUR

"SIR, ARE YOU *NOW* OR HAVE YOU EVER *BEEN* A MEMBER OF THE *COMMUNIST PARTY?*"

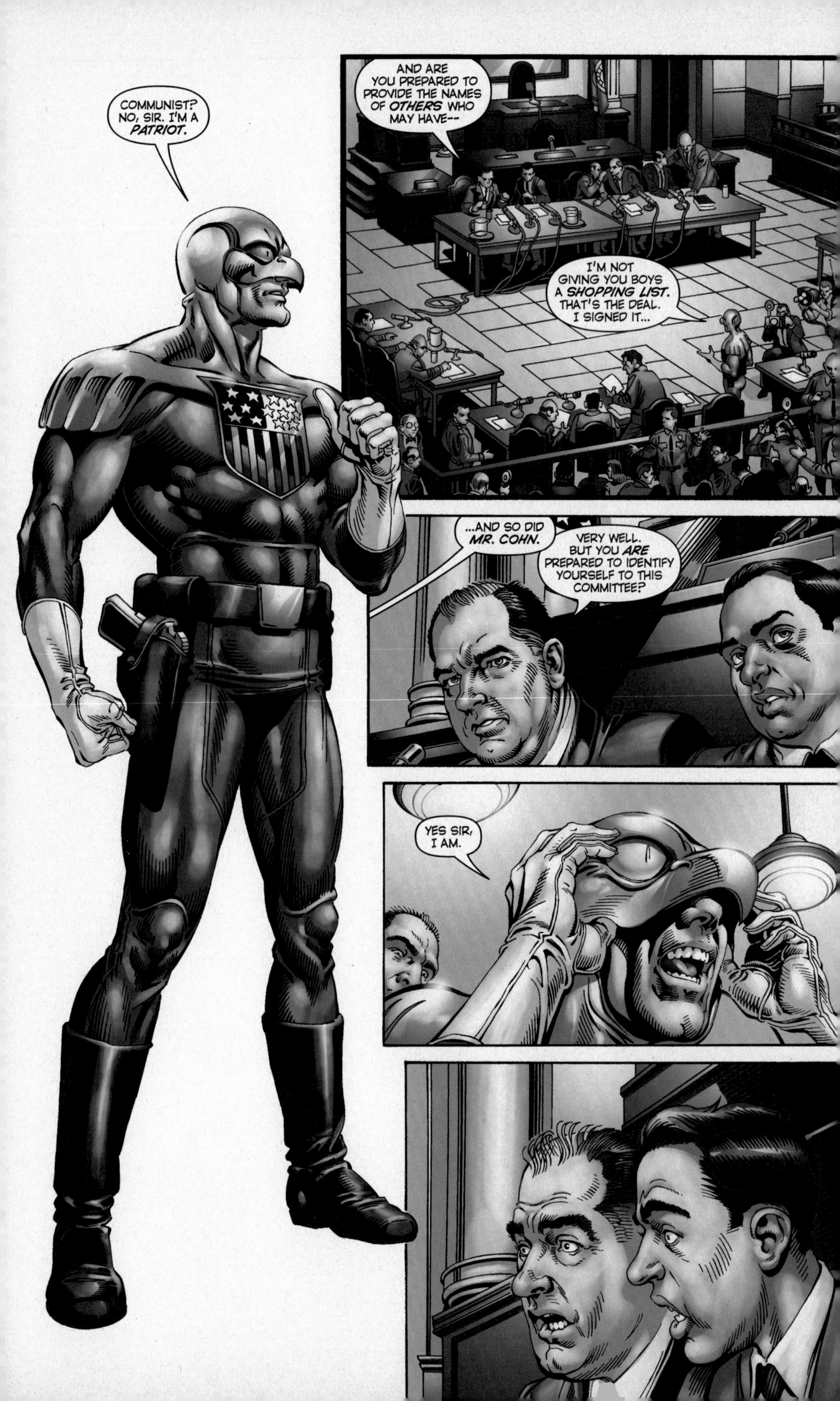
COMMUNIST? NO, SIR. I'M A *PATRIOT*.
AND ARE YOU PREPARED TO PROVIDE THE NAMES OF *OTHERS* WHO MAY HAVE--
I'M NOT GIVING YOU BOYS A *SHOPPING LIST*. THAT'S THE DEAL. I SIGNED IT...
...AND SO DID *MR. COHN*.
VERY WELL. BUT YOU *ARE* PREPARED TO IDENTIFY YOURSELF TO THIS COMMITTEE?
YES SIR, I AM.

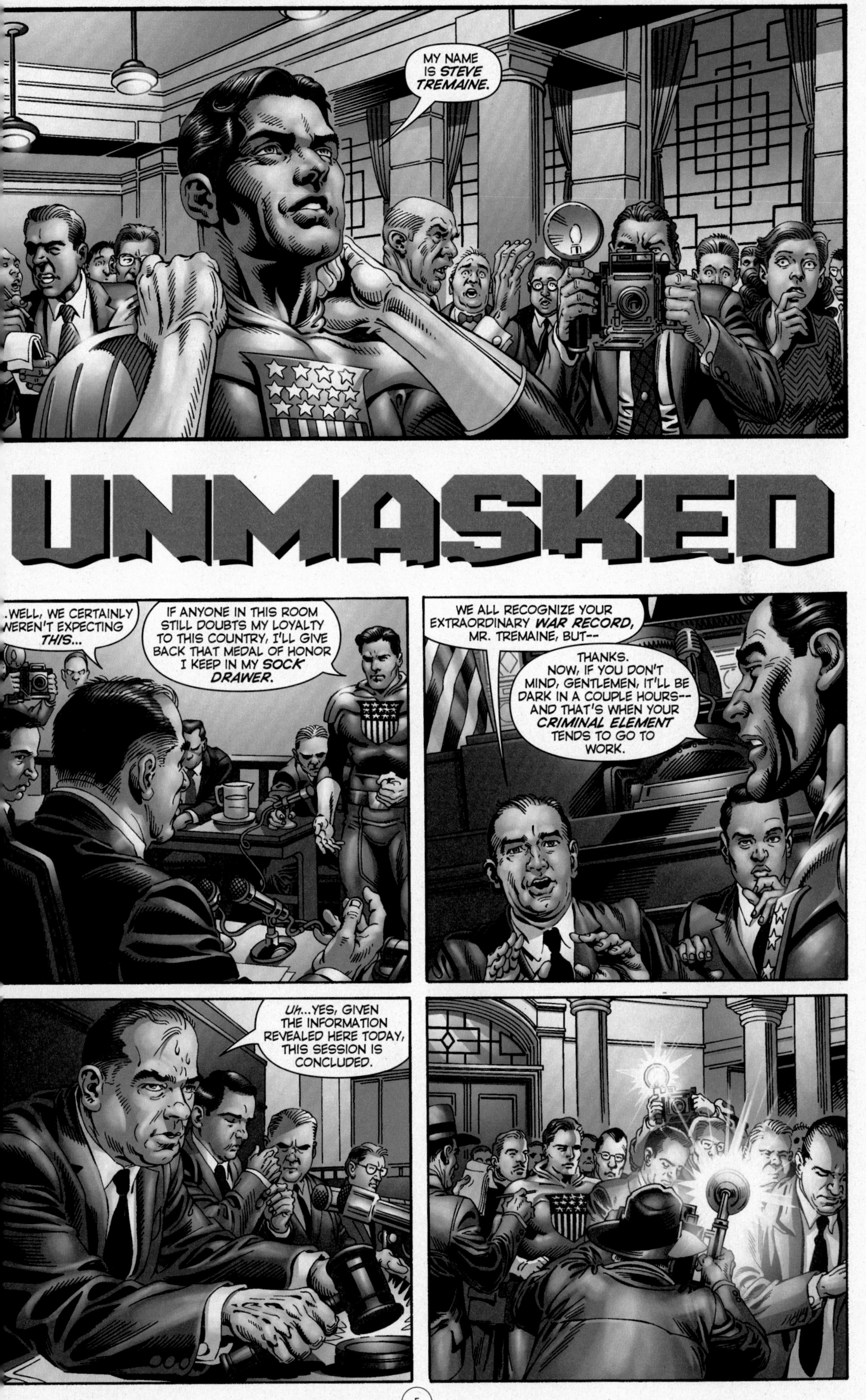
MY NAME IS STEVE TREMAINE.
UNMASKED
...WELL, WE CERTAINLY WEREN'T EXPECTING THIS...
IF ANYONE IN THIS ROOM STILL DOUBTS MY LOYALTY TO THIS COUNTRY, I'LL GIVE BACK THAT MEDAL OF HONOR I KEEP IN MY SOCK DRAWER.
WE ALL RECOGNIZE YOUR EXTRAORDINARY WAR RECORD, MR. TREMAINE, BUT--
THANKS. NOW, IF YOU DON'T MIND, GENTLEMEN, IT'LL BE DARK IN A COUPLE HOURS-- AND THAT'S WHEN YOUR CRIMINAL ELEMENT TENDS TO GO TO WORK.
Uh...YES, GIVEN THE INFORMATION REVEALED HERE TODAY, THIS SESSION IS CONCLUDED.

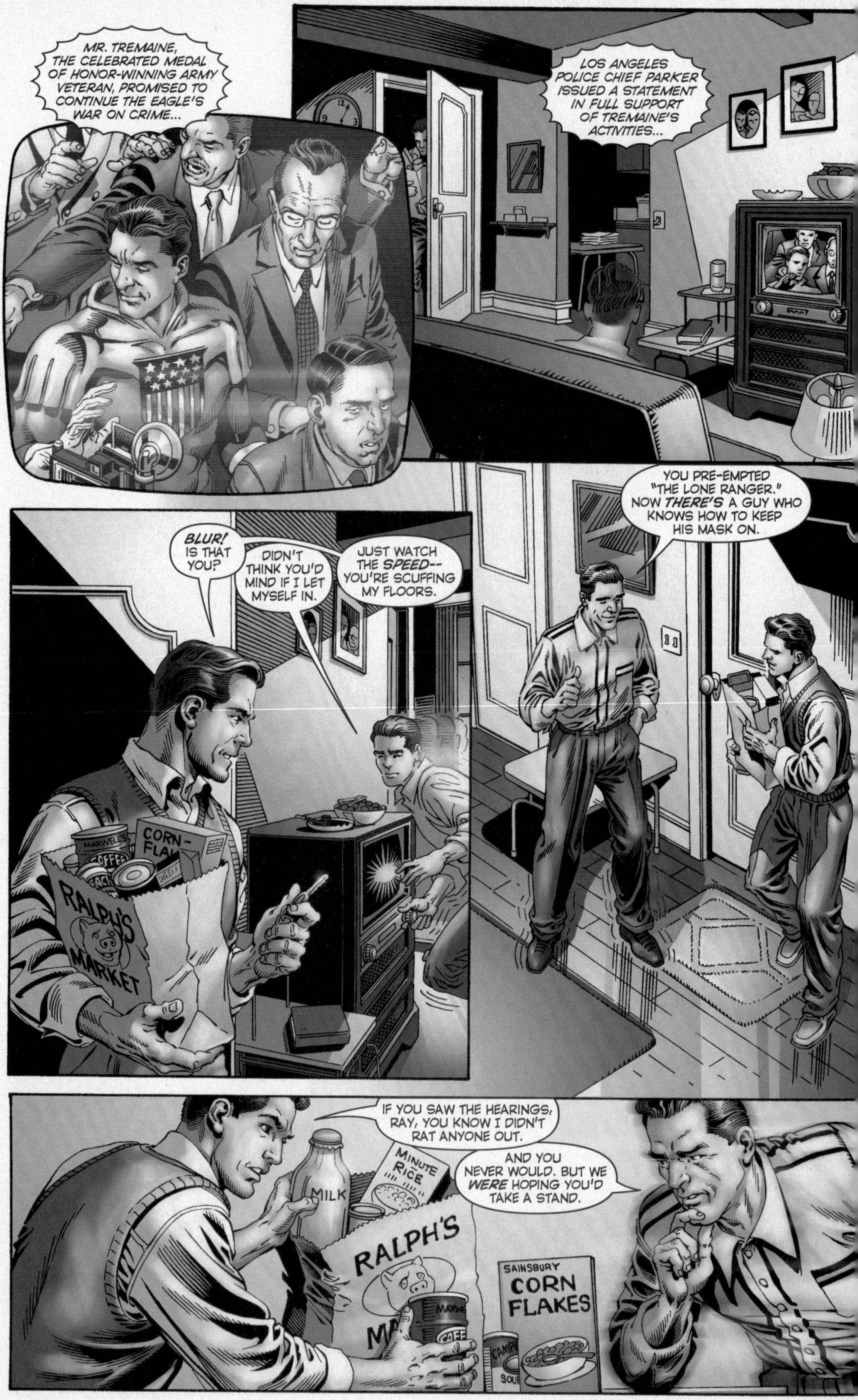

MR. TREMAINE, THE CELEBRATED MEDAL OF HONOR-WINNING ARMY VETERAN, PROMISED TO CONTINUE THE EAGLE'S WAR ON CRIME...
LOS ANGELES POLICE CHIEF PARKER ISSUED A STATEMENT IN FULL SUPPORT OF TREMAINE'S ACTIVITIES...
BLUR! IS THAT YOU?
DIDN'T THINK YOU'D MIND IF I LET MYSELF IN.
JUST WATCH THE SPEED-- YOU'RE SCUFFING MY FLOORS.
CORN FLA
RALPH'S MARKET
YOU PRE-EMPTED "THE LONE RANGER." NOW THERE'S A GUY WHO KNOWS HOW TO KEEP HIS MASK ON.
IF YOU SAW THE HEARINGS, RAY, YOU KNOW I DIDN'T RAT ANYONE OUT.
AND YOU NEVER WOULD. BUT WE WERE HOPING YOU'D TAKE A STAND.
MILK
MINUTE RICE
RALPH'S
SAINSBURY CORN FLAKES

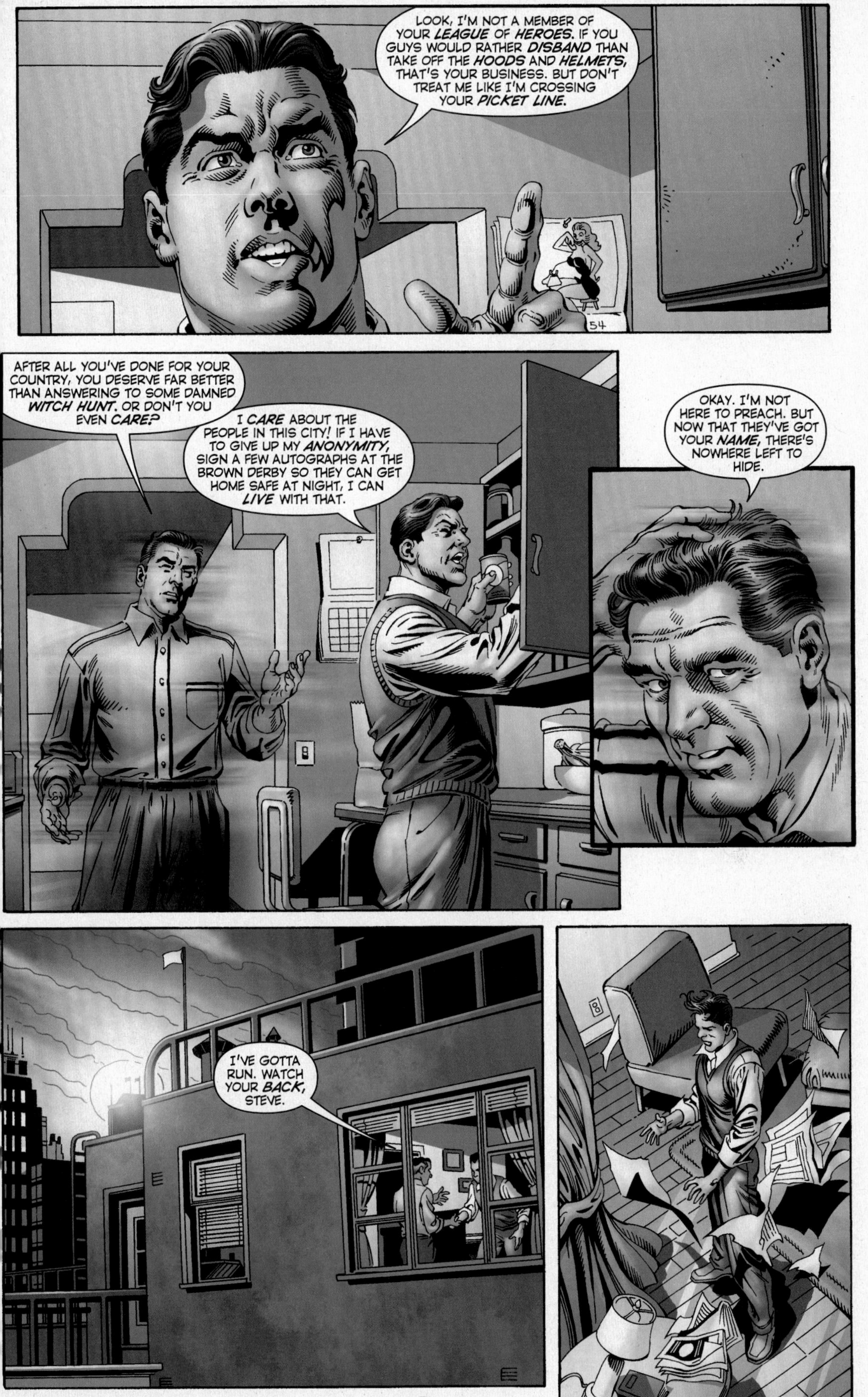
LOOK, I'M NOT A MEMBER OF YOUR LEAGUE OF HEROES. IF YOU GUYS WOULD RATHER DISBAND THAN TAKE OFF THE HOODS AND HELMETS, THAT'S YOUR BUSINESS. BUT DON'T TREAT ME LIKE I'M CROSSING YOUR PICKET LINE.
54
AFTER ALL YOU'VE DONE FOR YOUR COUNTRY, YOU DESERVE FAR BETTER THAN ANSWERING TO SOME DAMNED WITCH HUNT. OR DON'T YOU EVEN CARE?
I CARE ABOUT THE PEOPLE IN THIS CITY! IF I HAVE TO GIVE UP MY ANONYMITY, SIGN A FEW AUTOGRAPHS AT THE BROWN DERBY SO THEY CAN GET HOME SAFE AT NIGHT, I CAN LIVE WITH THAT.
OKAY. I'M NOT HERE TO PREACH. BUT NOW THAT THEY'VE GOT YOUR NAME, THERE'S NOWHERE LEFT TO HIDE.
I'VE GOTTA RUN. WATCH YOUR BACK, STEVE.

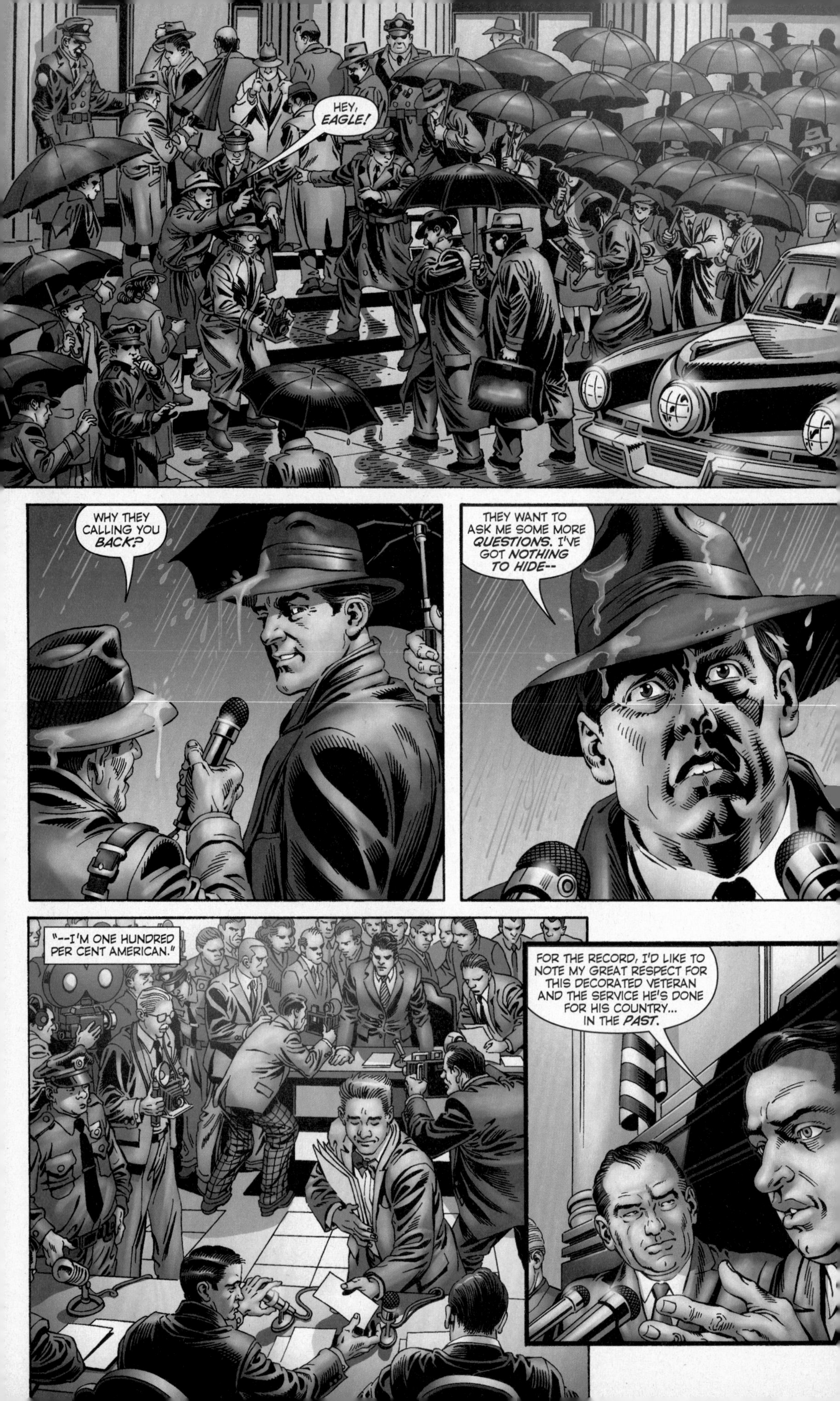
HEY, EAGLE!
WHY THEY CALLING YOU BACK?
THEY WANT TO ASK ME SOME MORE QUESTIONS. I'VE GOT NOTHING TO HIDE--
"--I'M ONE HUNDRED PER CENT AMERICAN."
FOR THE RECORD, I'D LIKE TO NOTE MY GREAT RESPECT FOR THIS DECORATED VETERAN AND THE SERVICE HE'S DONE FOR HIS COUNTRY... IN THE PAST.

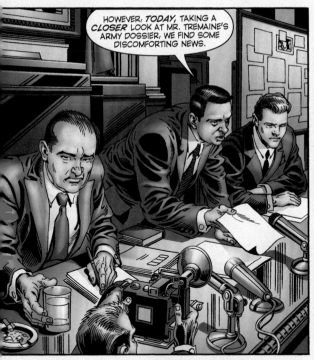

HOWEVER, *TODAY*, TAKING A *CLOSER* LOOK AT MR. TREMAINE'S ARMY DOSSIER, WE FIND SOME DISCOMFORTING NEWS.

WHAT THE HELL IS HE TALKING ABOUT?

MR. TREMAINE. IN THE WINTER OF '44, YOU LED A COMMANDO MISSION BEHIND GERMAN LINES, DEEP INTO THE *SOVIET UNION*, CORRECT?

I RAN LOTS OF MISSIONS, THAT WAS MY *JOB*.

DO YOU RECALL BEFRIENDING A RED ARMY COLONEL BY THE NAME OF *IVAN PETROVICH?*

OF COURSE. THE RUSSIANS WERE OUR *ALLIES* BACK THEN. WHAT ARE YOU GETTING AT?

IVAN PETROVICH IS *THE BEAR*, MR. TREMAINE--A *HERO* TO THE COMMUNISTS AND A *DANGEROUS ENEMY* OF FREEDOM.

The BEAR aka Ivan Petrovich 1944

TELEGRAM: LOS ANGELES

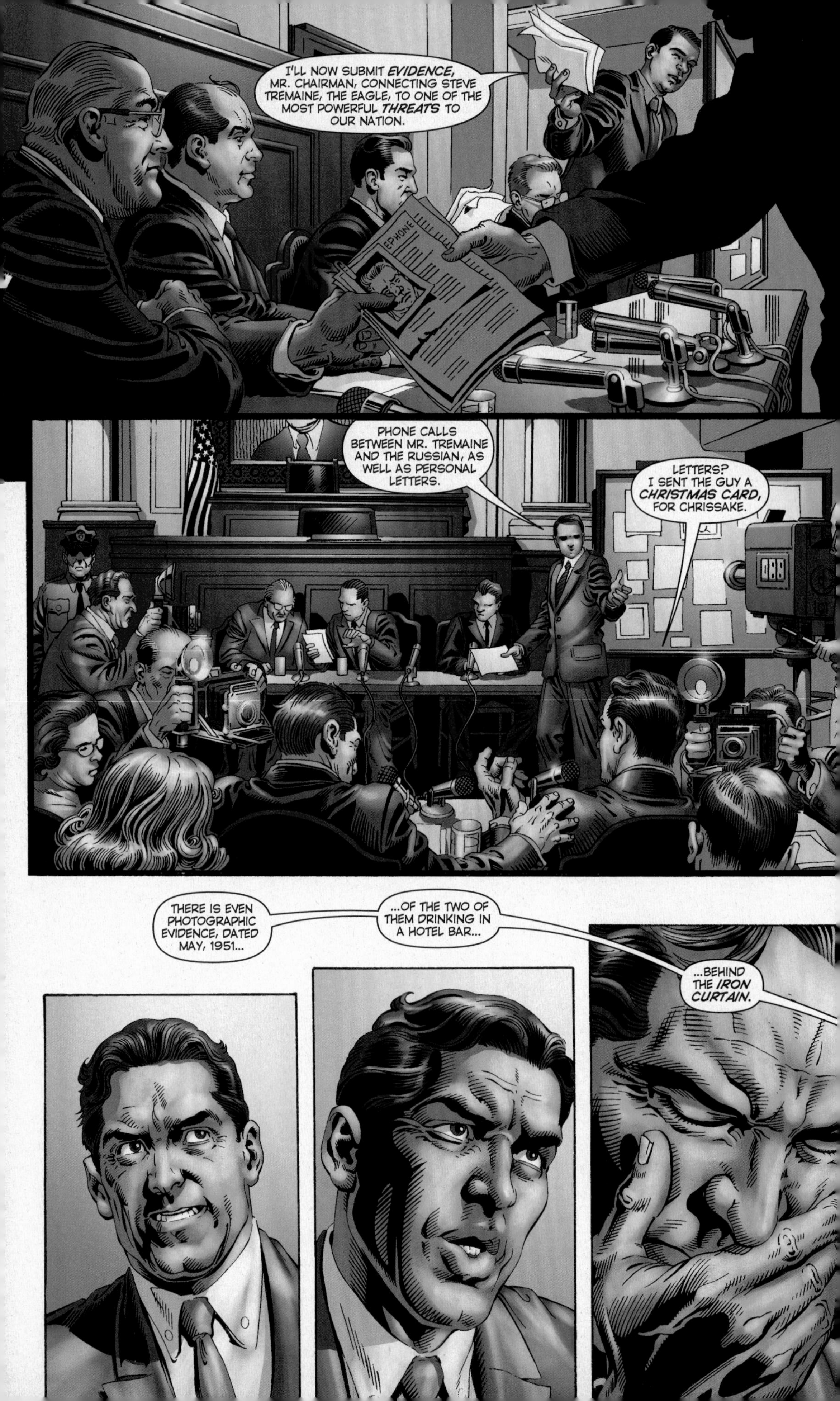
I'LL NOW SUBMIT EVIDENCE, MR. CHAIRMAN, CONNECTING STEVE TREMAINE, THE EAGLE, TO ONE OF THE MOST POWERFUL THREATS TO OUR NATION.
PHONE CALLS BETWEEN MR. TREMAINE AND THE RUSSIAN, AS WELL AS PERSONAL LETTERS.
LETTERS? I SENT THE GUY A CHRISTMAS CARD, FOR CHRISSAKE.
THERE IS EVEN PHOTOGRAPHIC EVIDENCE, DATED MAY, 1951...
...OF THE TWO OF THEM DRINKING IN A HOTEL BAR...
...BEHIND THE IRON CURTAIN.

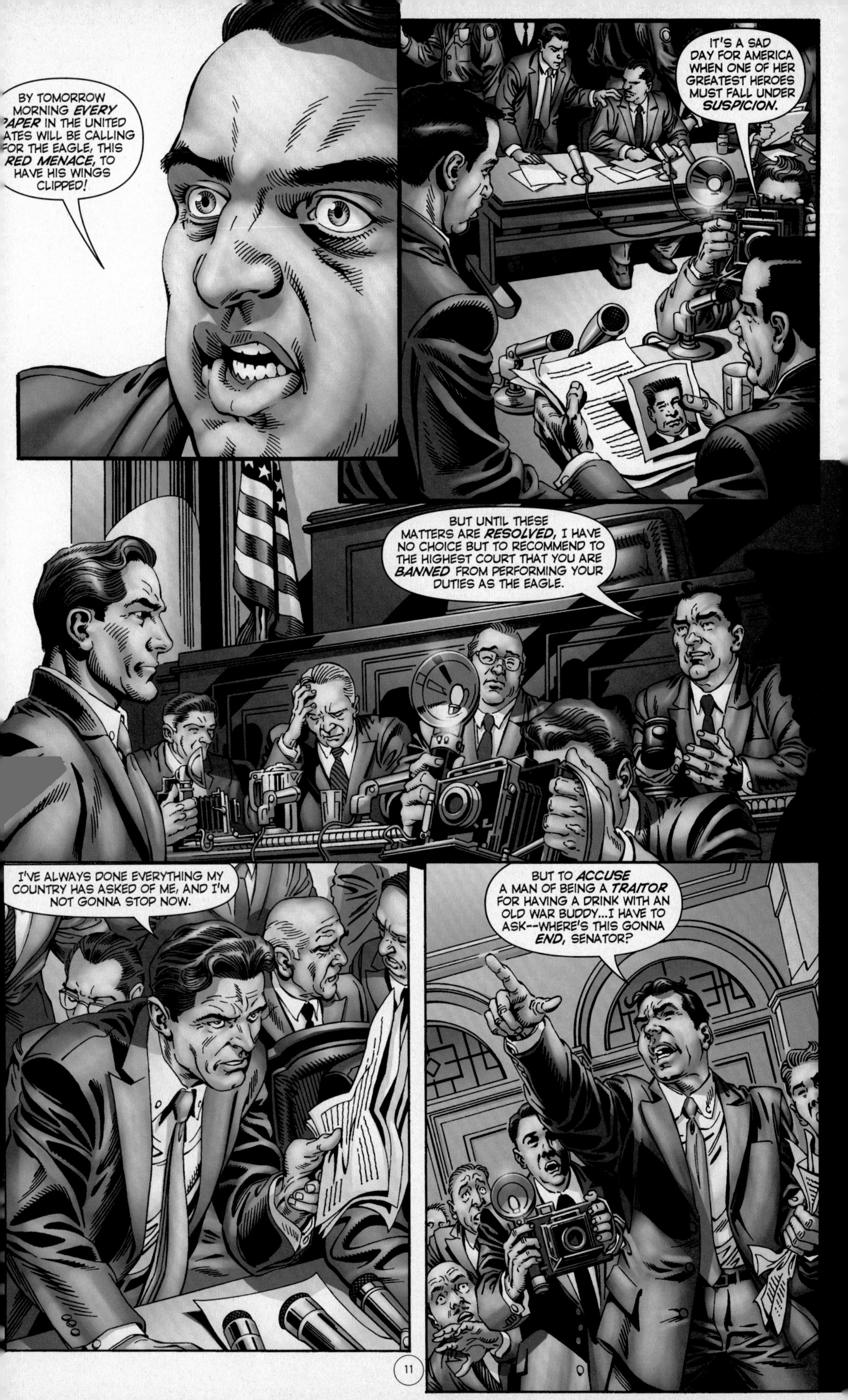

BY TOMORROW MORNING EVERY PAPER IN THE UNITED STATES WILL BE CALLING FOR THE EAGLE, THIS RED MENACE, TO HAVE HIS WINGS CLIPPED!
IT'S A SAD DAY FOR AMERICA WHEN ONE OF HER GREATEST HEROES MUST FALL UNDER SUSPICION.
BUT UNTIL THESE MATTERS ARE RESOLVED, I HAVE NO CHOICE BUT TO RECOMMEND TO THE HIGHEST COURT THAT YOU ARE BANNED FROM PERFORMING YOUR DUTIES AS THE EAGLE.
I'VE ALWAYS DONE EVERYTHING MY COUNTRY HAS ASKED OF ME, AND I'M NOT GONNA STOP NOW.
BUT TO ACCUSE A MAN OF BEING A TRAITOR FOR HAVING A DRINK WITH AN OLD WAR BUDDY...I HAVE TO ASK--WHERE'S THIS GONNA END, SENATOR?

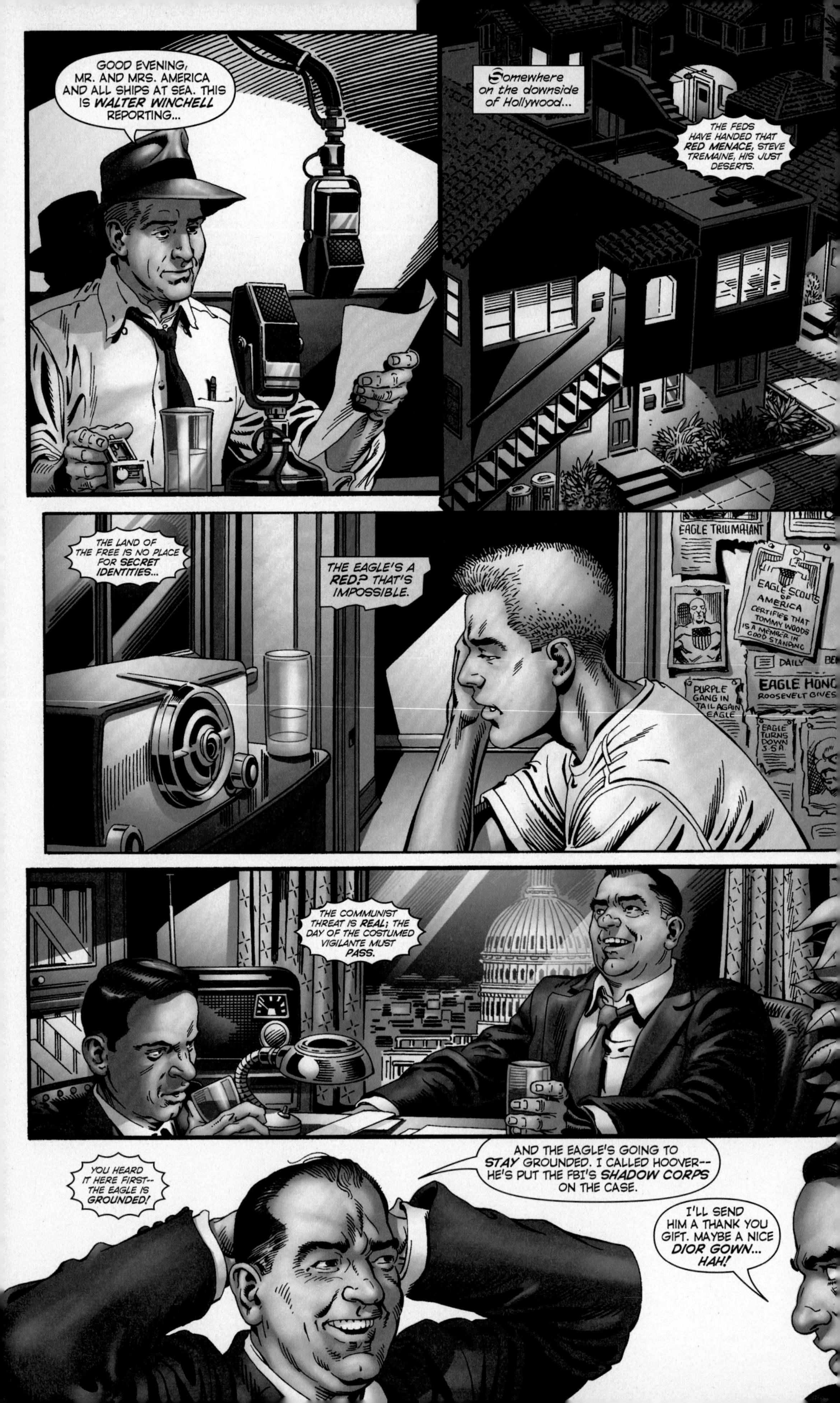

GOOD EVENING, MR. AND MRS. AMERICA AND ALL SHIPS AT SEA. THIS IS WALTER WINCHELL REPORTING...
Somewhere on the downside of Hollywood...
THE FEDS HAVE HANDED THAT RED MENACE, STEVE TREMAINE, HIS JUST DESERTS.
THE LAND OF THE FREE IS NO PLACE FOR SECRET IDENTITIES...
THE EAGLE'S A RED? THAT'S IMPOSSIBLE.
EAGLE TRIUMPHANT
EAGLE SCOUTS OF AMERICA CERTIFIES THAT TOMMY WOODS IS A MEMBER IN GOOD STANDING
PURPLE GANG IN TAIL AGAIN EAGLE
DAILY
EAGLE HONO
ROOSEVELT GIVES
EAGLE TURNS DOWN JSA
THE COMMUNIST THREAT IS REAL; THE DAY OF THE COSTUMED VIGILANTE MUST PASS.
YOU HEARD IT HERE FIRST-- THE EAGLE IS GROUNDED!
AND THE EAGLE'S GOING TO STAY GROUNDED. I CALLED HOOVER-- HE'S PUT THE FBI'S SHADOW CORPS ON THE CASE.
I'LL SEND HIM A THANK YOU GIFT. MAYBE A NICE DIOR GOWN... HAH!

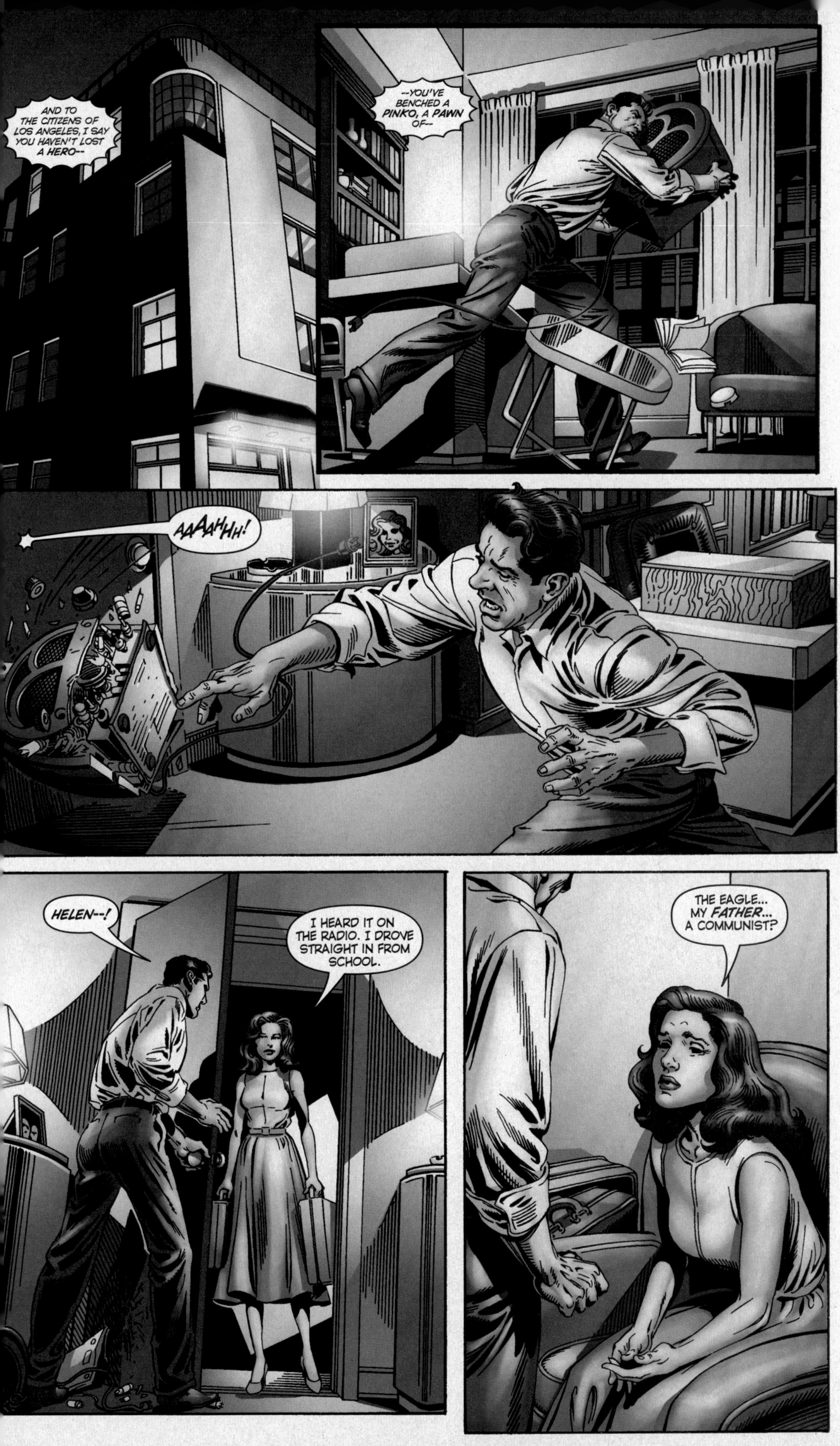
AND TO THE CITIZENS OF LOS ANGELES, I SAY YOU HAVEN'T LOST A HERO--
--YOU'VE BENCHED A PINKO, A PAWN OF--
AAAAHHH!
HELEN--!
I HEARD IT ON THE RADIO. I DROVE STRAIGHT IN FROM SCHOOL.
THE EAGLE... MY FATHER... A COMMUNIST?

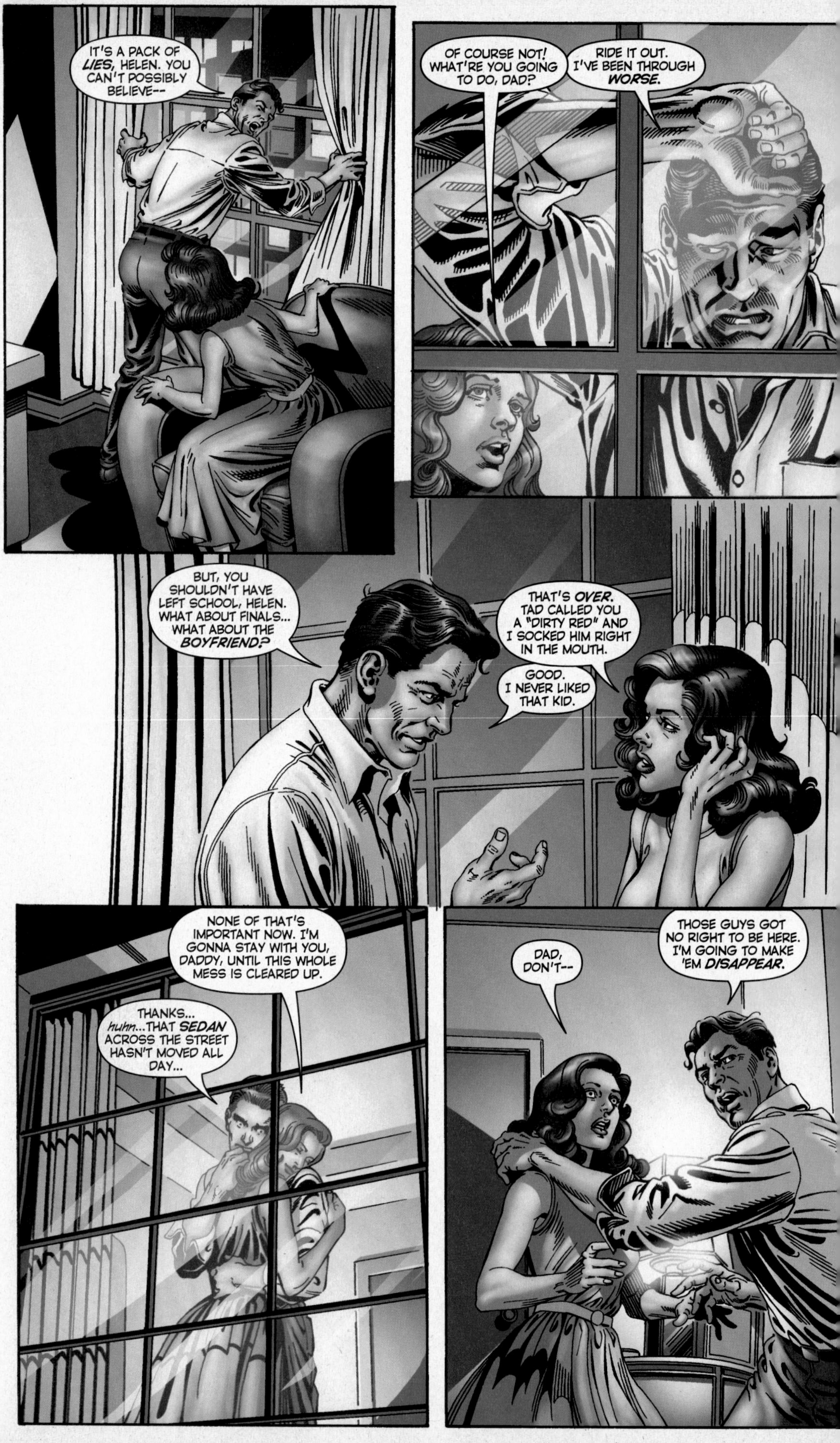
IT'S A PACK OF LIES, HELEN. YOU CAN'T POSSIBLY BELIEVE--
OF COURSE NOT! WHAT'RE YOU GOING TO DO, DAD?
RIDE IT OUT. I'VE BEEN THROUGH WORSE.
BUT, YOU SHOULDN'T HAVE LEFT SCHOOL, HELEN. WHAT ABOUT FINALS... WHAT ABOUT THE BOYFRIEND?
THAT'S OVER. TAD CALLED YOU A "DIRTY RED" AND I SOCKED HIM RIGHT IN THE MOUTH.
GOOD. I NEVER LIKED THAT KID.
NONE OF THAT'S IMPORTANT NOW. I'M GONNA STAY WITH YOU, DADDY, UNTIL THIS WHOLE MESS IS CLEARED UP.
THANKS... huhn...THAT SEDAN ACROSS THE STREET HASN'T MOVED ALL DAY...
DAD, DON'T--
THOSE GUYS GOT NO RIGHT TO BE HERE. I'M GOING TO MAKE 'EM DISAPPEAR.

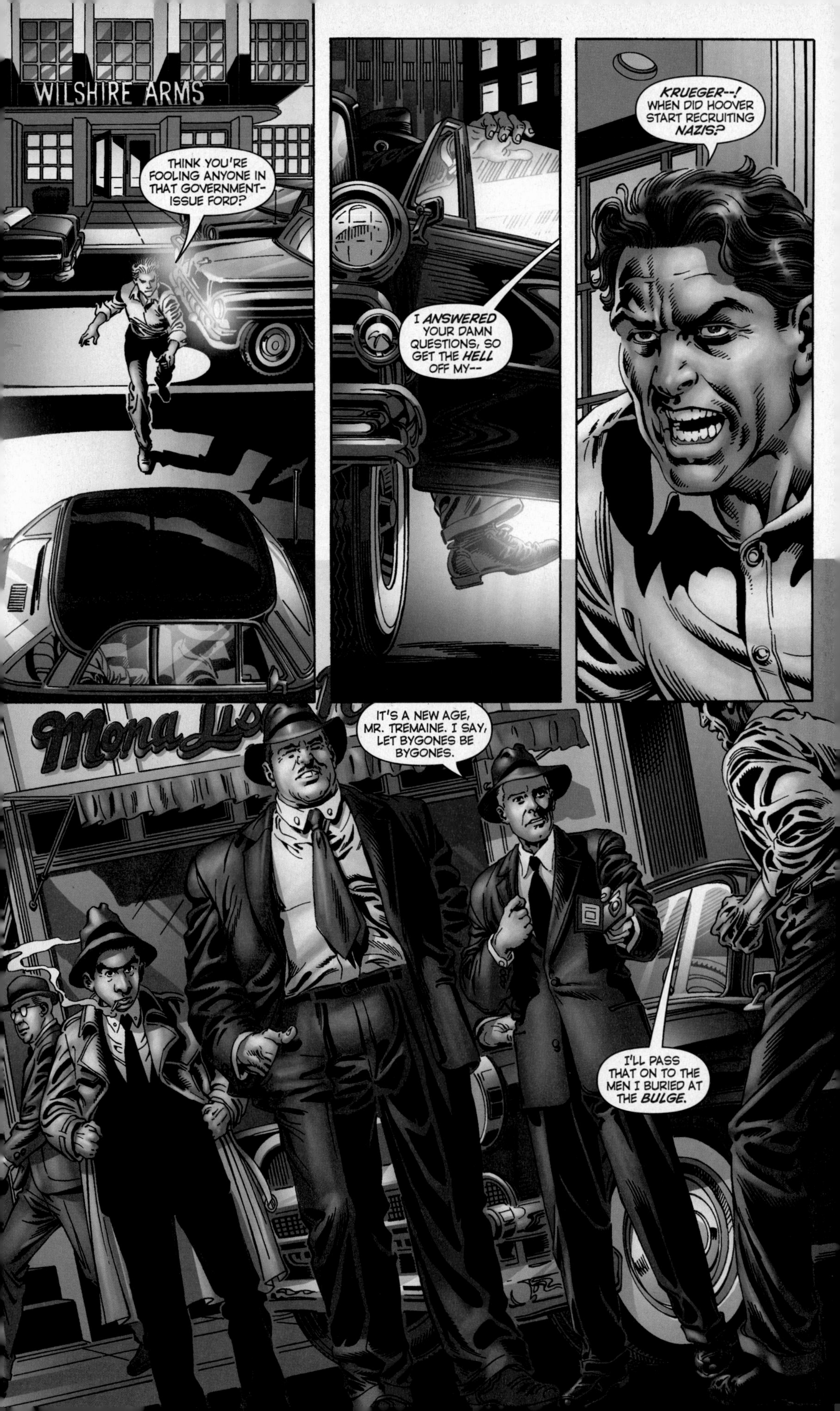
WILSHIRE ARMS
THINK YOU'RE FOOLING ANYONE IN THAT GOVERNMENT-ISSUE FORD?
I *ANSWERED* YOUR DAMN QUESTIONS, SO GET THE *HELL* OFF MY--
KRUEGER--! WHEN DID HOOVER START RECRUITING *NAZIS?*
IT'S A NEW AGE, MR. TREMAINE. I SAY, LET BYGONES BE BYGONES.
I'LL PASS THAT ON TO THE MEN I BURIED AT THE *BULGE*.

PLEASE. I'M A PROUD AMERICAN CITIZEN NOW. I FOUGHT THE GODLESS COMMUNISTS IN THE WAR, AND I CONTINUE THAT DUTY FOR YOUR FBI.

MR. MINTER'S PARTICULAR *SKILLS* ARE QUITE USEFUL.

THE MOLE'S A G-MAN, TOO? GUESS THEY DITCHED THE *HEIGHT* REQUIREMENT.

YEAH, I'M FAMILIAR WITH HIS "SKILLS." I PUT THE BEADY-EYED BASTARD IN *SING SING* MYSELF.

I *REMEMBER*.

CAN'T SAY I KNOW THE SON OF KONG HERE.

YOU DON'T *WANNA* KNOW ME SLICK. I'D JUST AS SOON BOUNCE YOU LIKE A RUBBER BALL.

NO NEED FOR *THREATS*, LAMONT. WE'RE ONLY HERE TO *OBSERVE*.

BUT ANY *HOSTILITY* ON THE PART OF MR. TREMAINE WILL JUST MAKE THINGS UNPLEASANT FOR HIM... AND HIS LOVELY *DAUGHTER*.

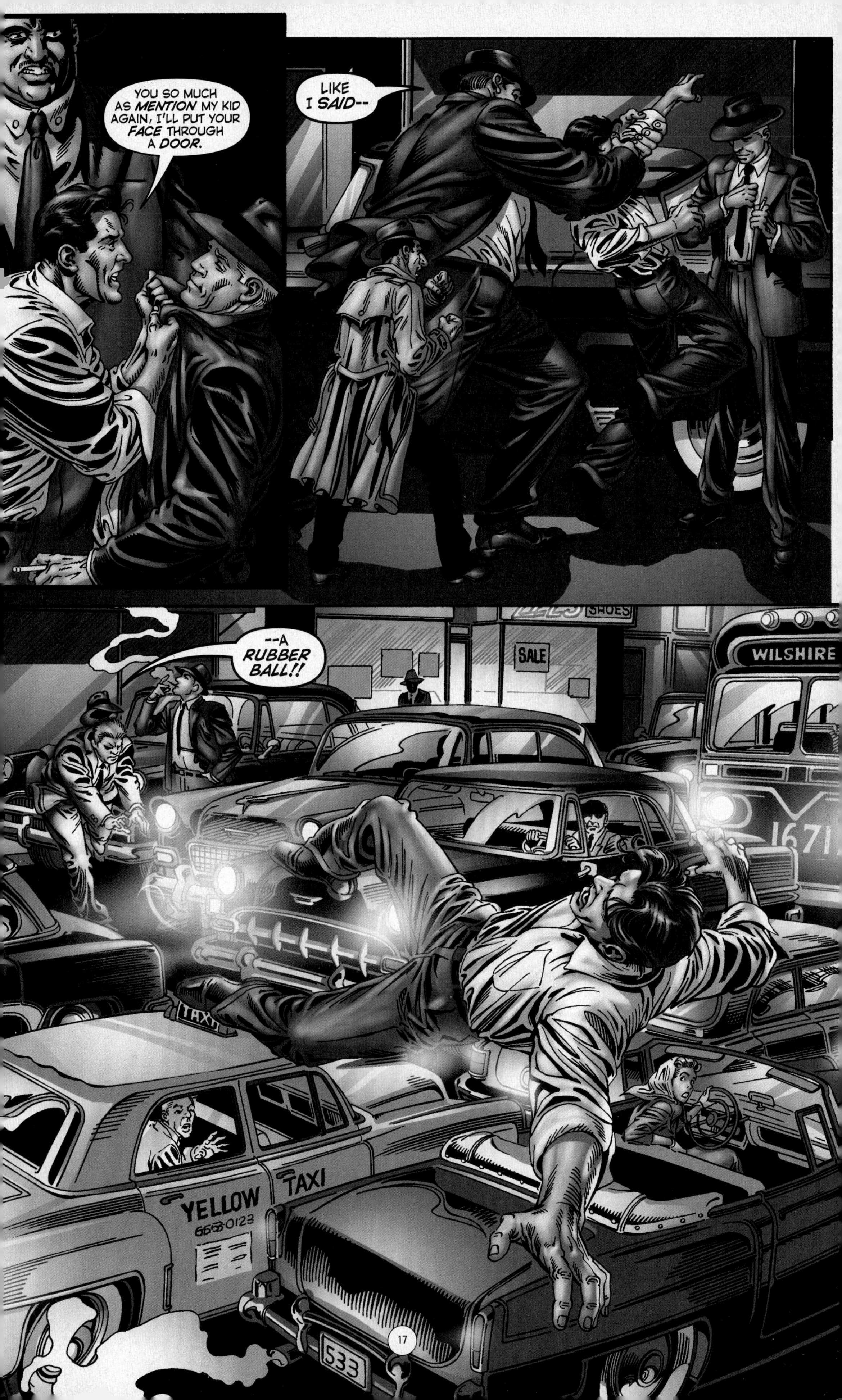

YOU SO MUCH AS MENTION MY KID AGAIN, I'LL PUT YOUR FACE THROUGH A DOOR.
LIKE I SAID--
--A RUBBER BALL!!
SHOES
SALE
WILSHIRE
1671
TAXI
YELLOW TAXI
666-0123
533

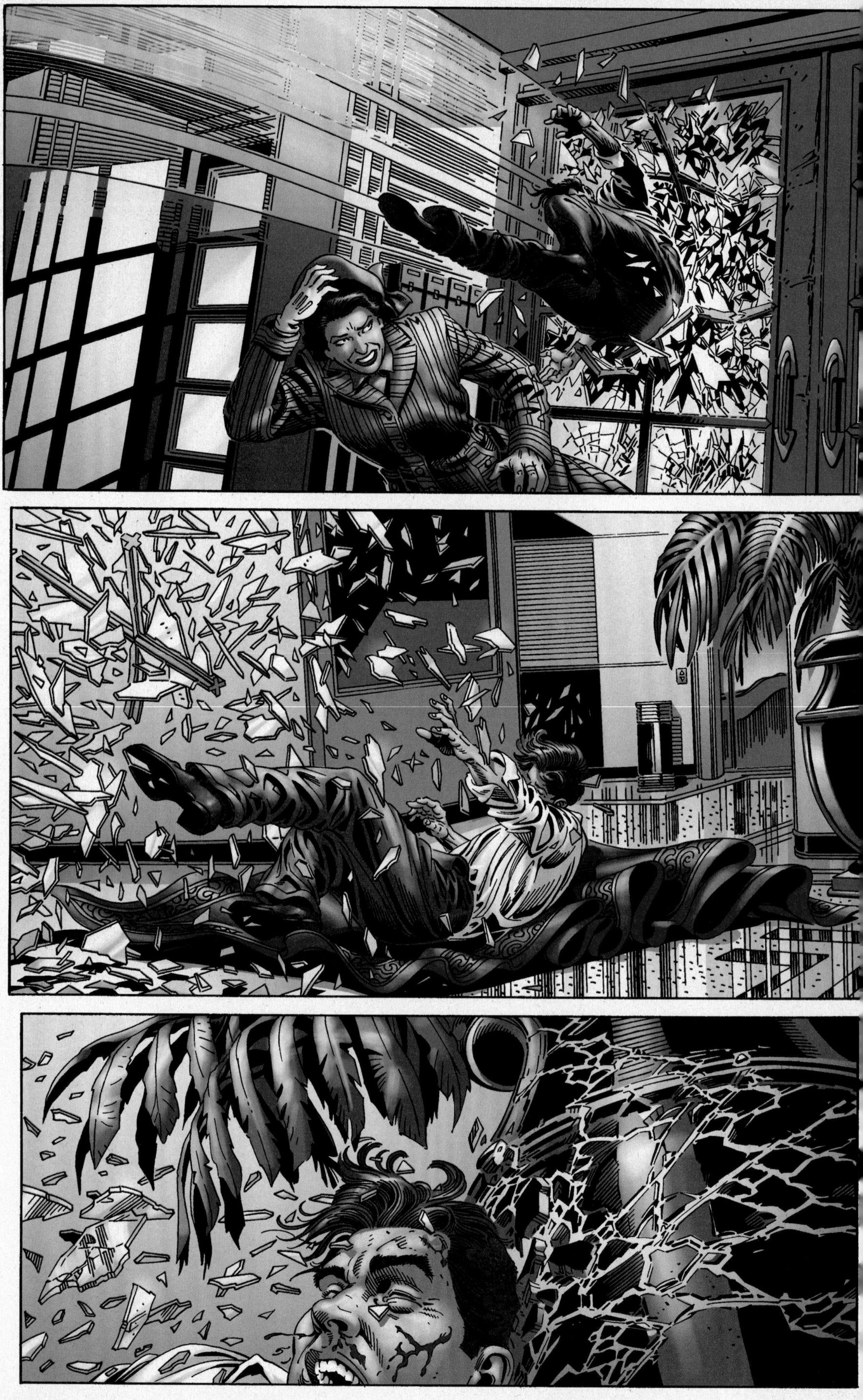

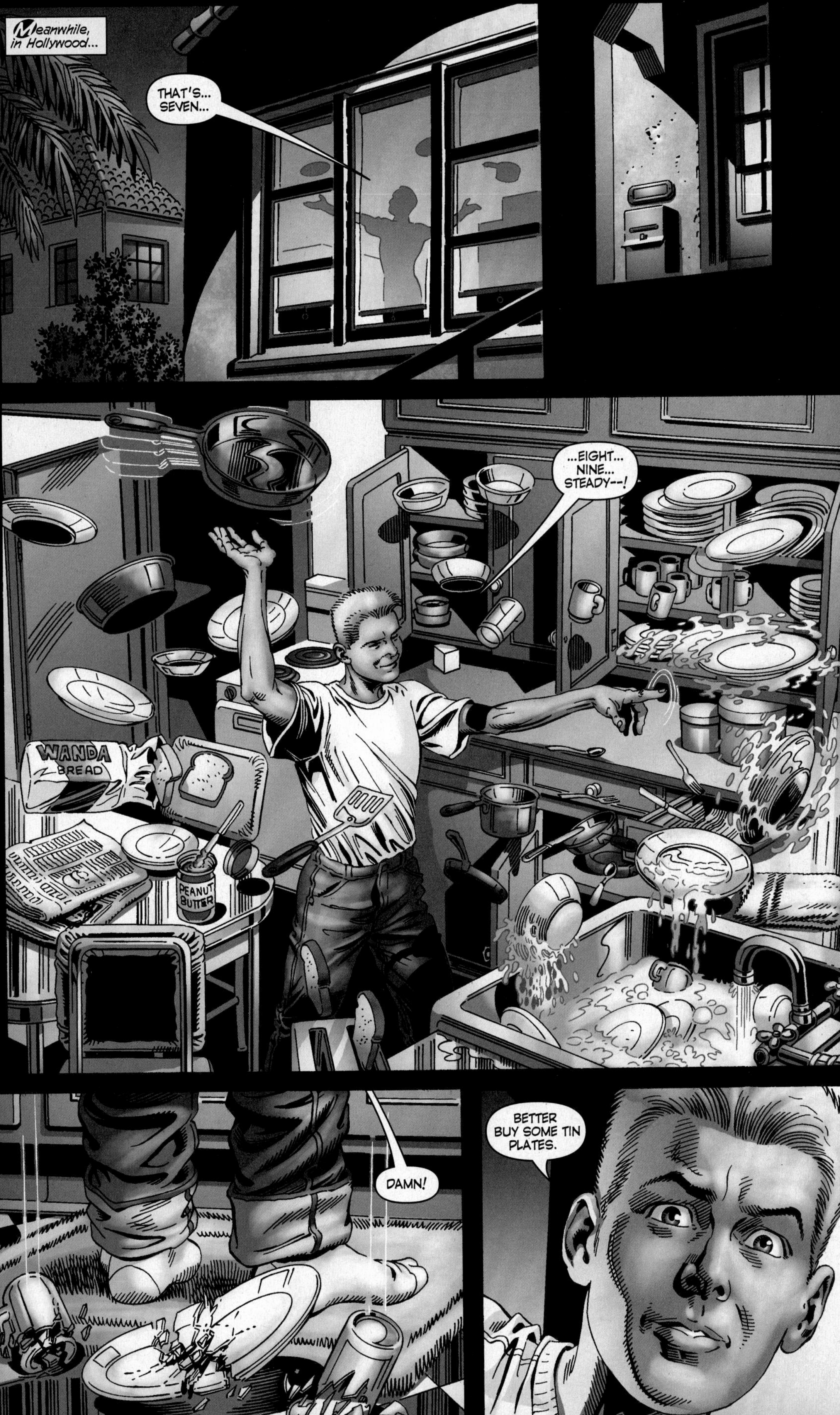
Meanwhile, in Hollywood...
THAT'S... SEVEN...
...EIGHT... NINE... STEADY--!
WANDA BREAD
PEANUT BUTTER
DAMN!
BETTER BUY SOME TIN PLATES.

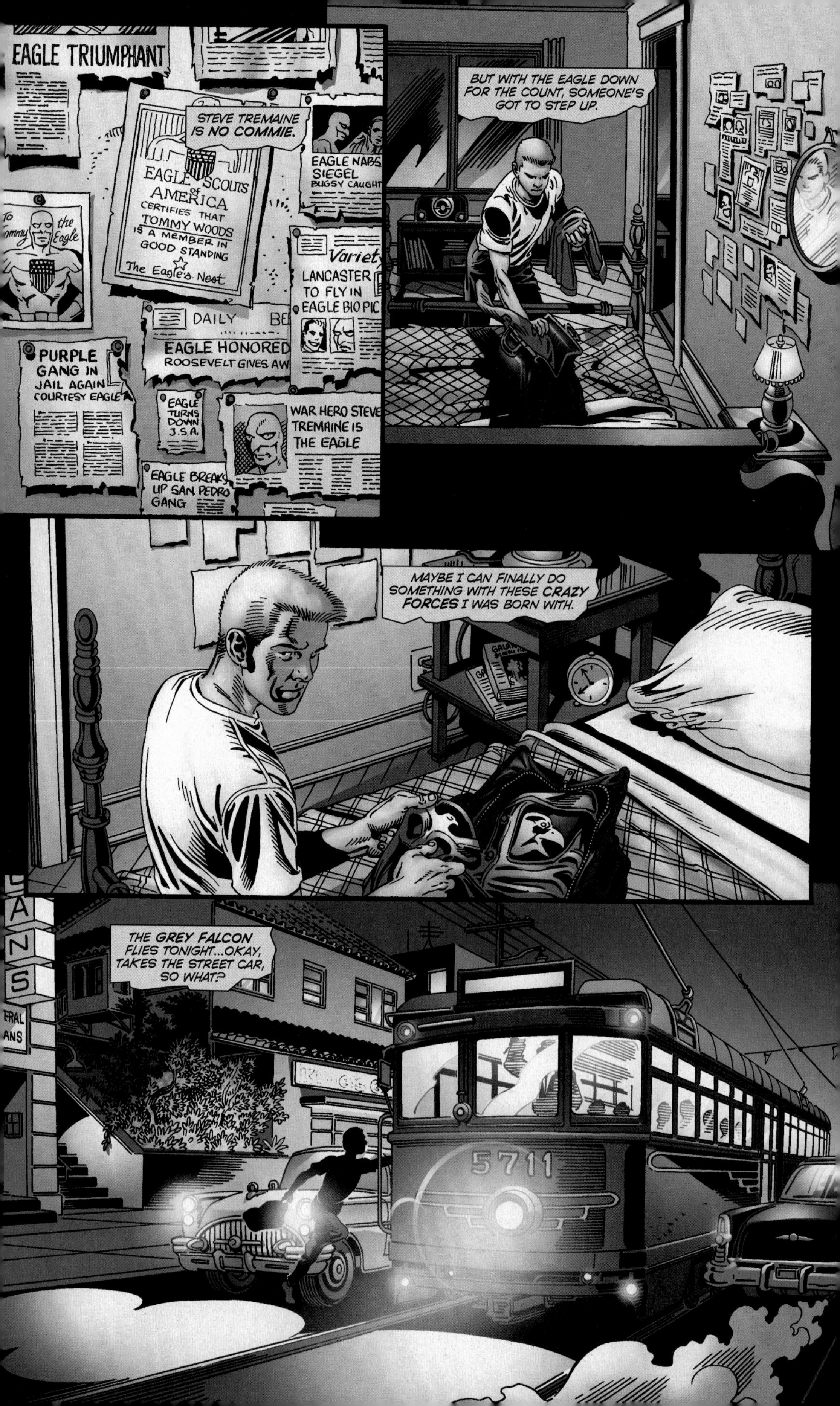

EAGLE TRIUMPHANT
STEVE TREMAINE IS NO COMMIE.
EAGLE SCOUTS of AMERICA CERTIFIES THAT TOMMY WOODS IS A MEMBER IN GOOD STANDING
The Eagle's Nest
EAGLE NABS SIEGEL BUGSY CAUGHT
Variety
LANCASTER TO FLY IN EAGLE BIO PIC
DAILY
EAGLE HONORED
ROOSEVELT GIVES AW
PURPLE GANG IN JAIL AGAIN COURTESY EAGLE
EAGLE TURNS DOWN J.S.A.
WAR HERO STEVE TREMAINE IS THE EAGLE
EAGLE BREAKS UP SAN PEDRO GANG
BUT WITH THE EAGLE DOWN FOR THE COUNT, SOMEONE'S GOT TO STEP UP.
MAYBE I CAN FINALLY DO SOMETHING WITH THESE CRAZY FORCES I WAS BORN WITH.
THE GREY FALCON FLIES TONIGHT...OKAY, TAKES THE STREET CAR, SO WHAT?
5711

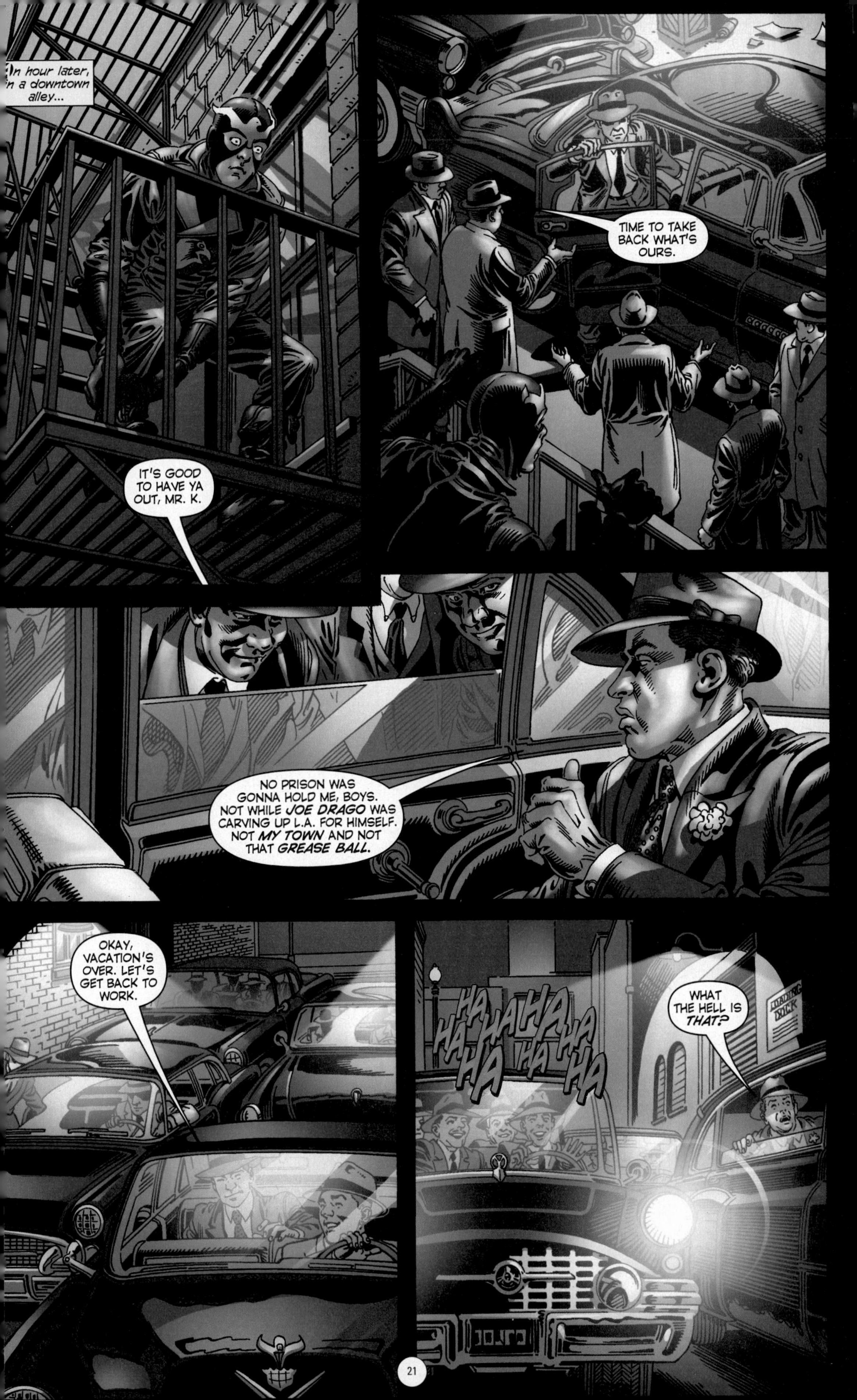
An hour later, in a downtown alley...
IT'S GOOD TO HAVE YA OUT, MR. K.
TIME TO TAKE BACK WHAT'S OURS.
NO PRISON WAS GONNA HOLD ME, BOYS. NOT WHILE JOE DRAGO WAS CARVING UP L.A. FOR HIMSELF. NOT MY TOWN AND NOT THAT GREASE BALL.
OKAY, VACATION'S OVER. LET'S GET BACK TO WORK.
HA HA HA HA HA HA HA HA HA HA HA
WHAT THE HELL IS THAT?

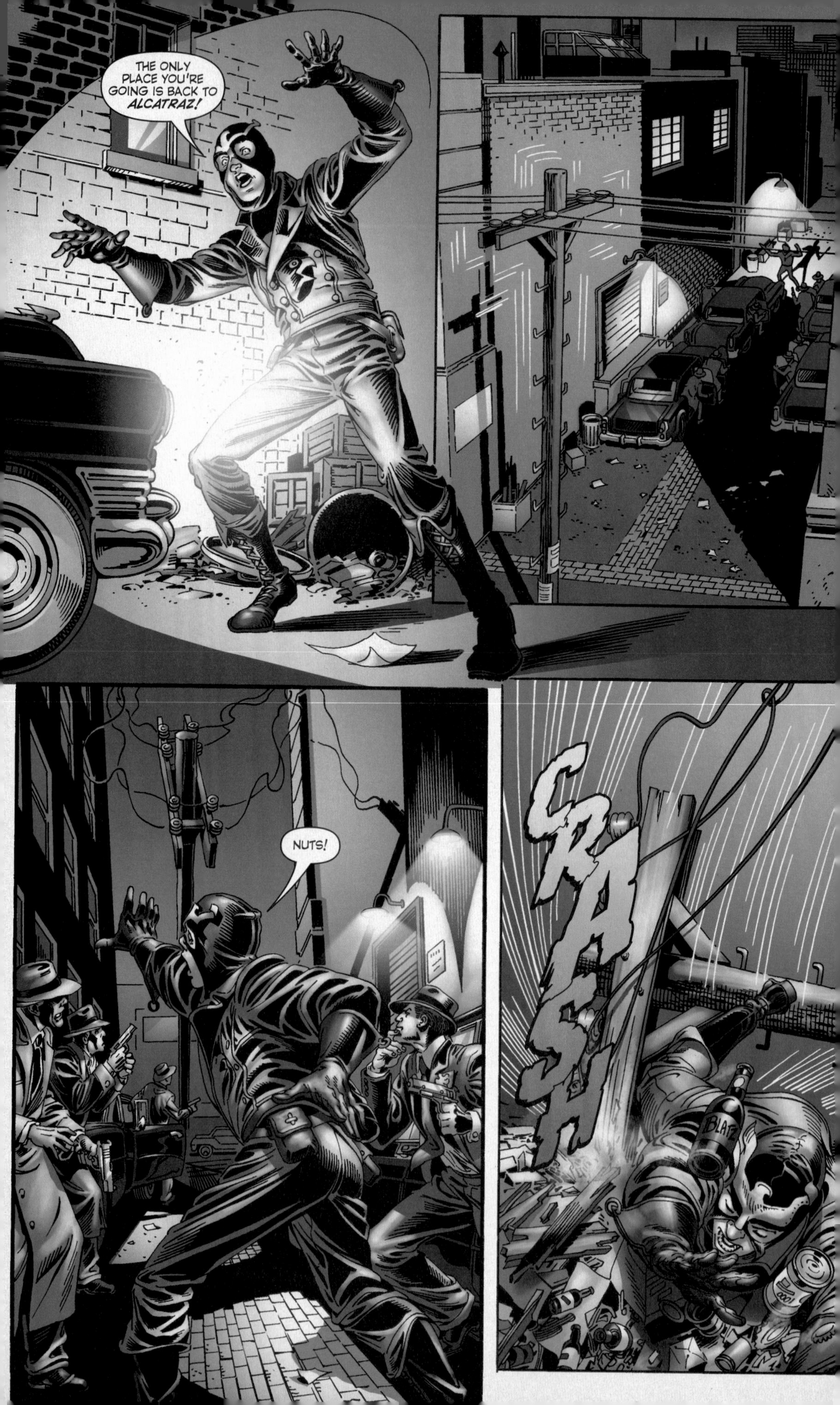
THE ONLY PLACE YOU'RE GOING IS BACK TO ALCATRAZ!
NUTS!
CRASH
BLATZ

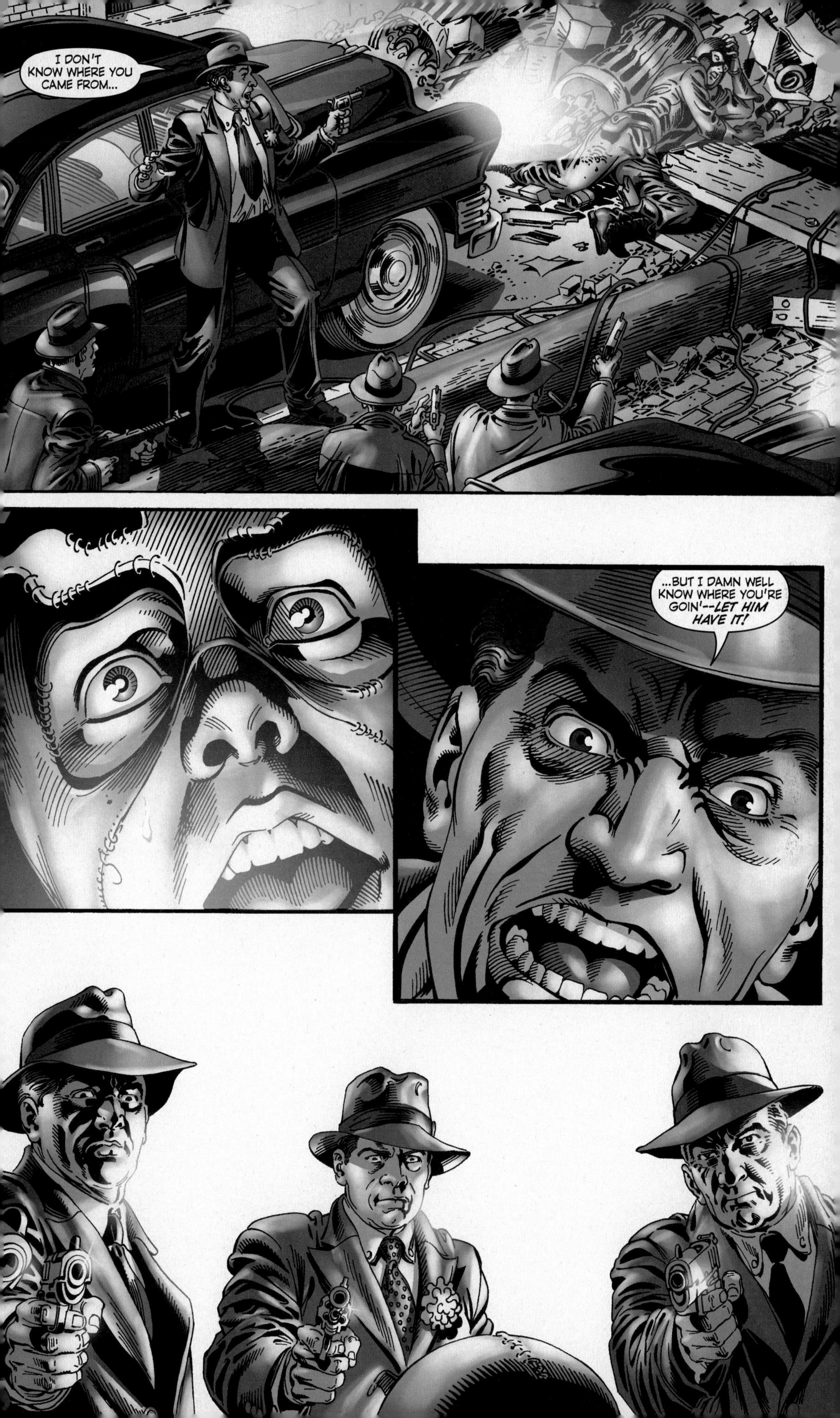
I DON'T KNOW WHERE YOU CAME FROM...
...BUT I DAMN WELL KNOW WHERE YOU'RE GOIN'--LET HIM HAVE IT!

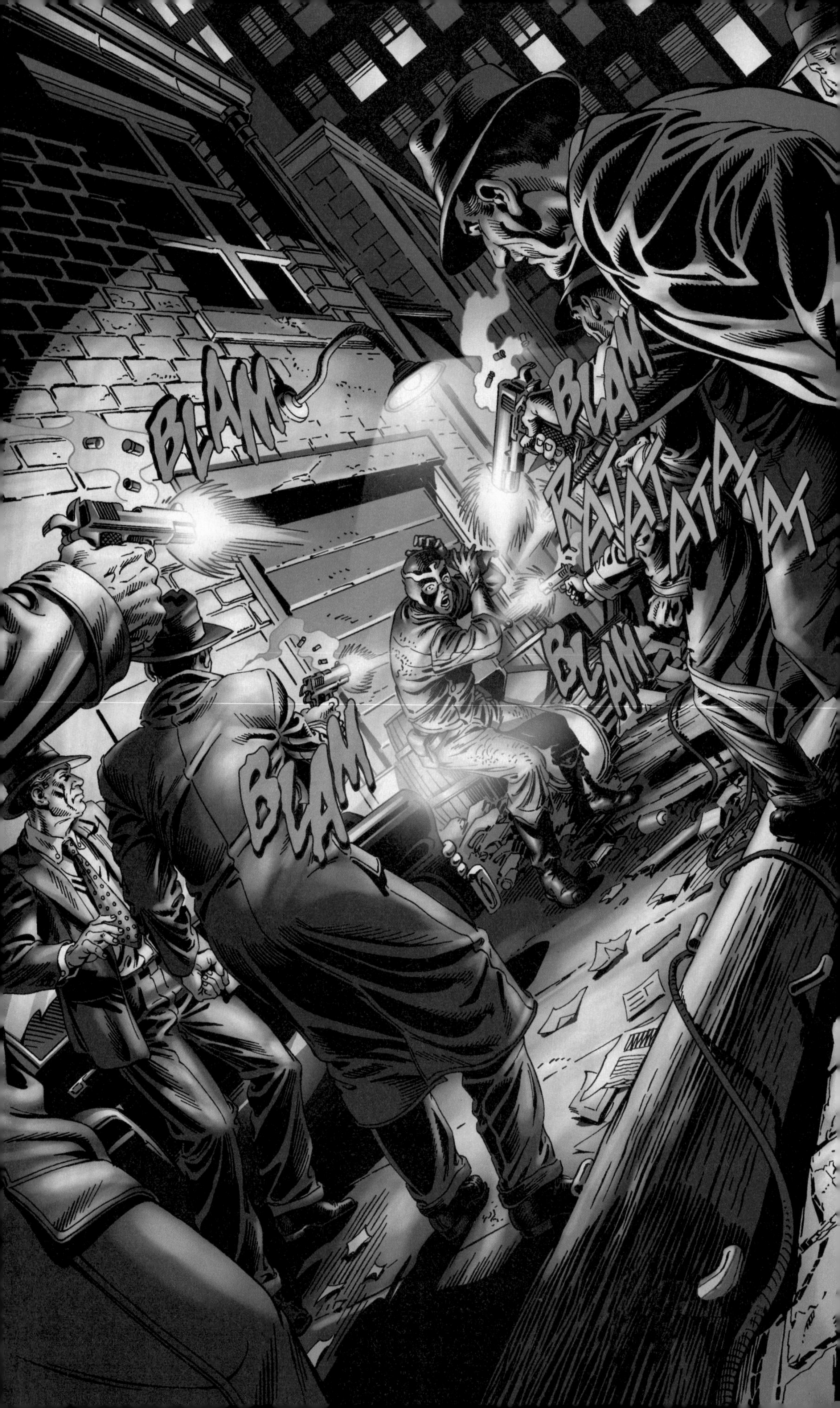
BLAM
BLAM
RATATATATAT
BLAM
BLAM

HAPTER 2

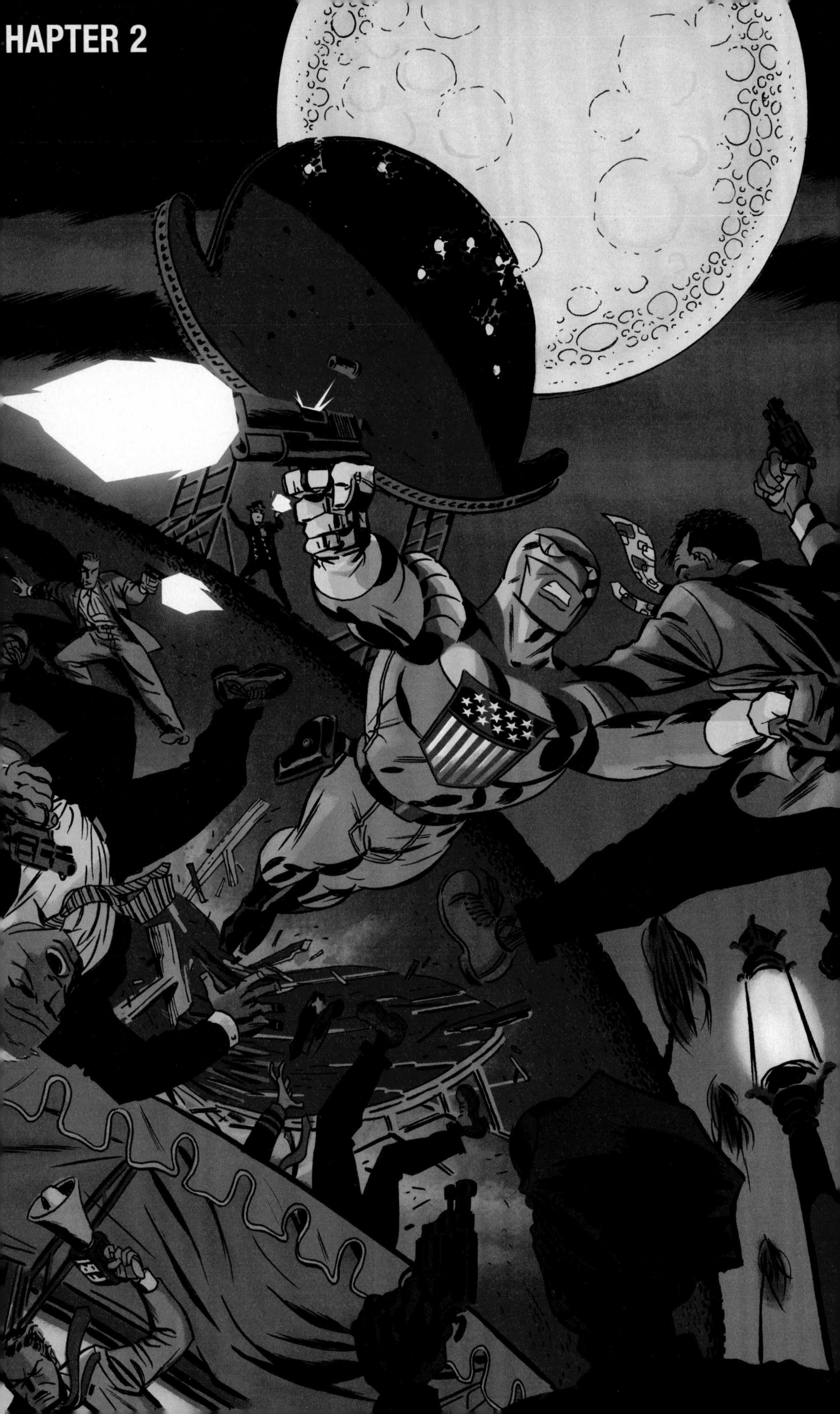
FBI

Red Menace

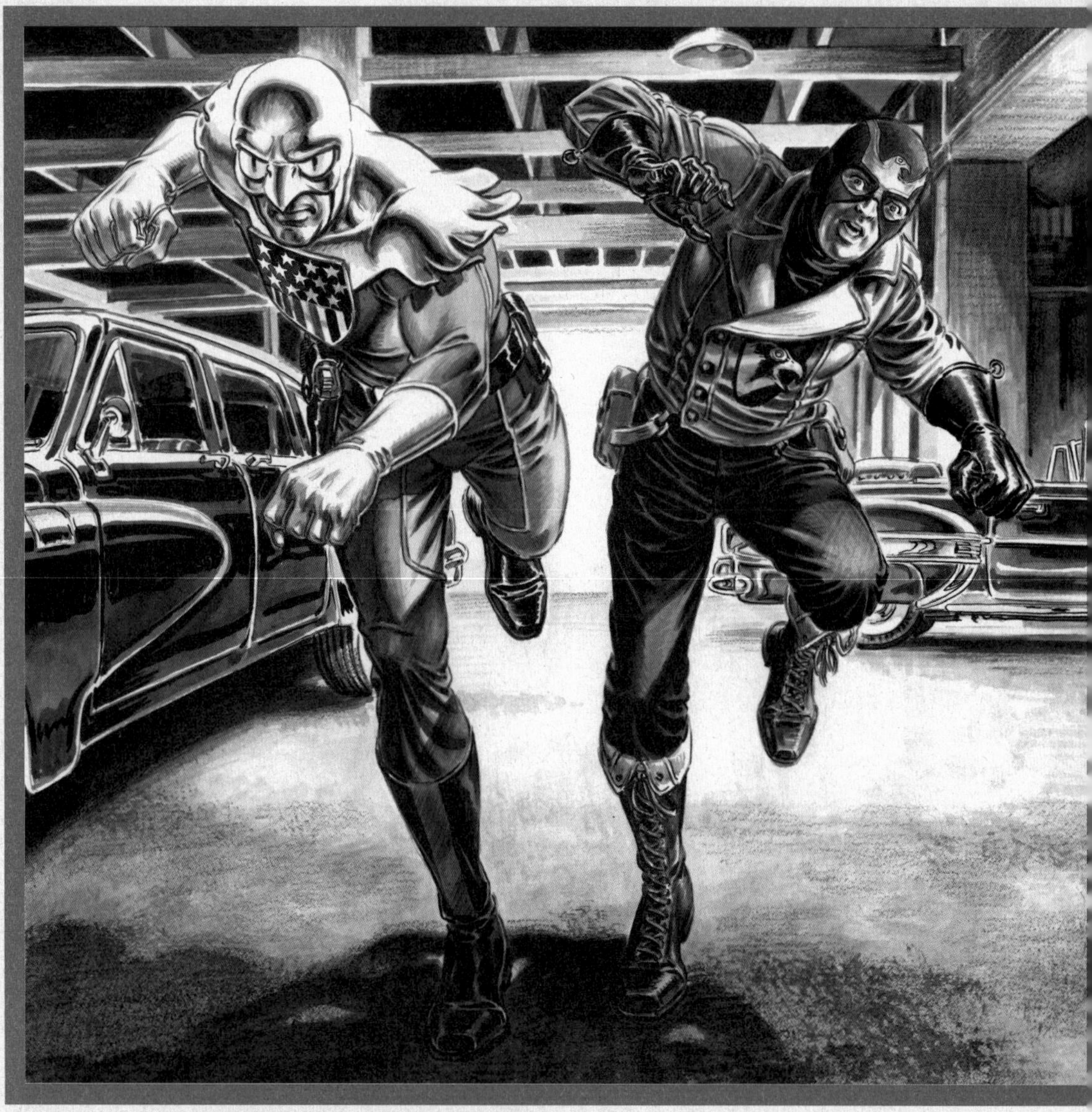

NEW BIRDMAN IN TOWN -- SIDEKICK OR RIVAL?

Restaurant, Hollywood. Steve is stood up by a studio boss who was supposed to meet him to sign a contract for "The Eagle" movie bio. The star who was to play Steve in the movie comes by and offers his condolences. He knows Steve's getting a bum rap

Tommy "Grey Falcon" Woods goes on patrol. With the Eagle out of commission, Tommy tries to "pick up the slack". However, he patrols from behind the wheel of a liquor store delivery van rather than a sleek, silenced motorcycle. Tommy finds himself in the middle of a rolling shootout down Santa Monica Blvd. between Coleman's and Drago's goons,

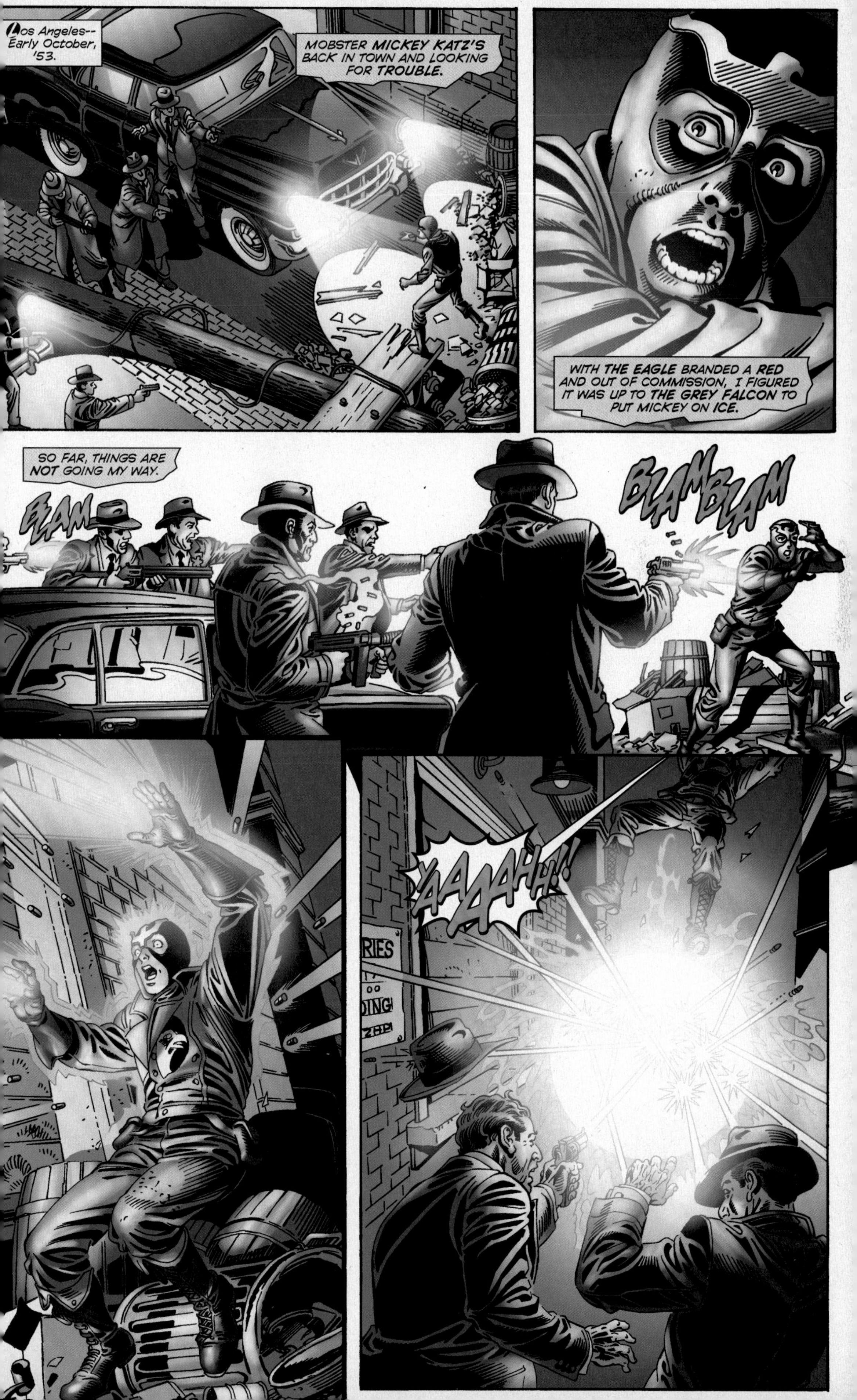

Los Angeles-- Early October, '53.
MOBSTER MICKEY KATZ'S BACK IN TOWN AND LOOKING FOR TROUBLE.
WITH THE EAGLE BRANDED A RED AND OUT OF COMMISSION, I FIGURED IT WAS UP TO THE GREY FALCON TO PUT MICKEY ON ICE.
SO FAR, THINGS ARE NOT GOING MY WAY.
BLAM
BLAM BLAM
YAAAAHH!!

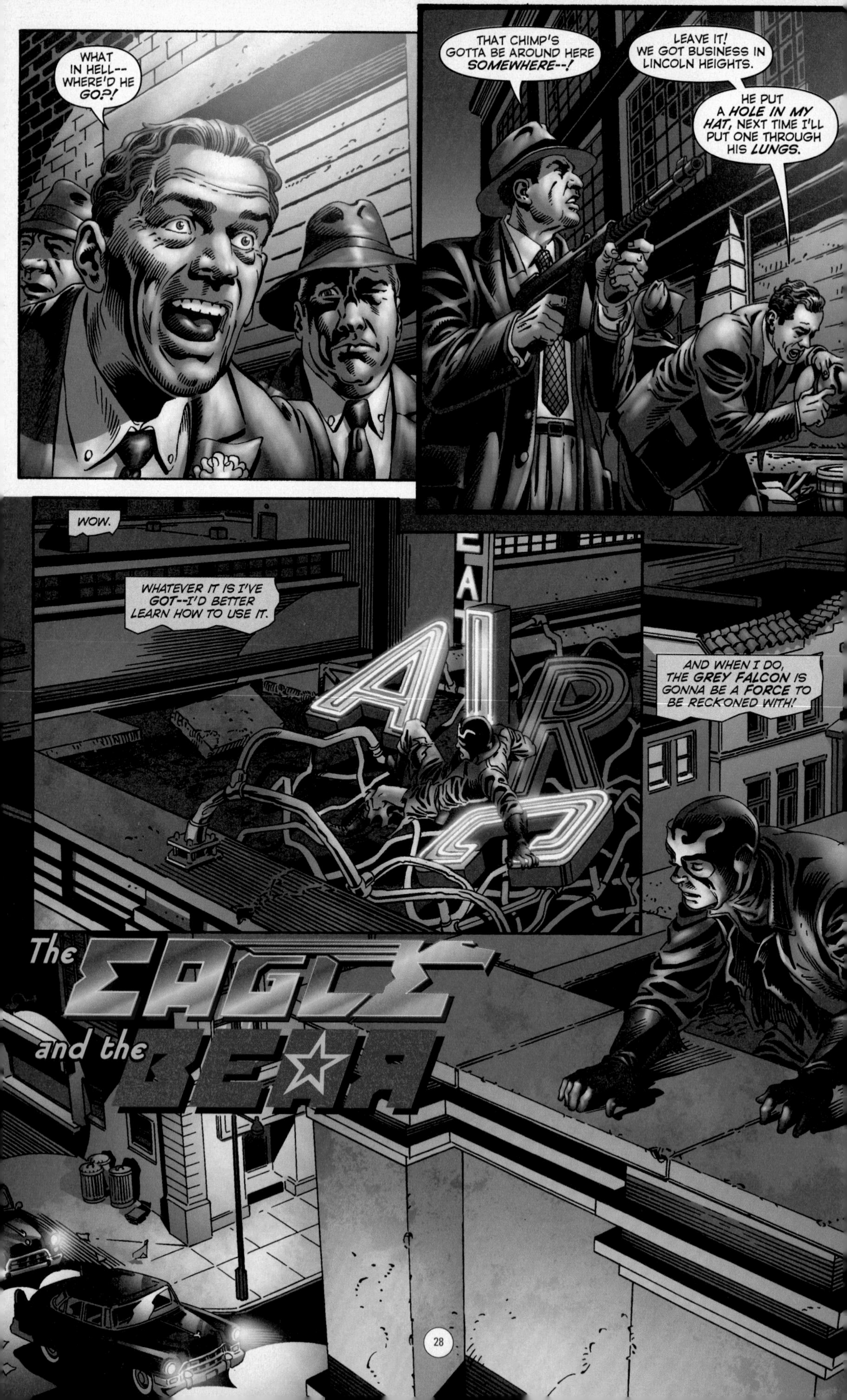
WHAT IN HELL-- WHERE'D HE GO?!
THAT CHIMP'S GOTTA BE AROUND HERE SOMEWHERE--!
LEAVE IT! WE GOT BUSINESS IN LINCOLN HEIGHTS.
HE PUT A HOLE IN MY HAT, NEXT TIME I'LL PUT ONE THROUGH HIS LUNGS.
WOW.
WHATEVER IT IS I'VE GOT--I'D BETTER LEARN HOW TO USE IT.
AND WHEN I DO, THE GREY FALCON IS GONNA BE A FORCE TO BE RECKONED WITH!
The EAGLE and the BEAR

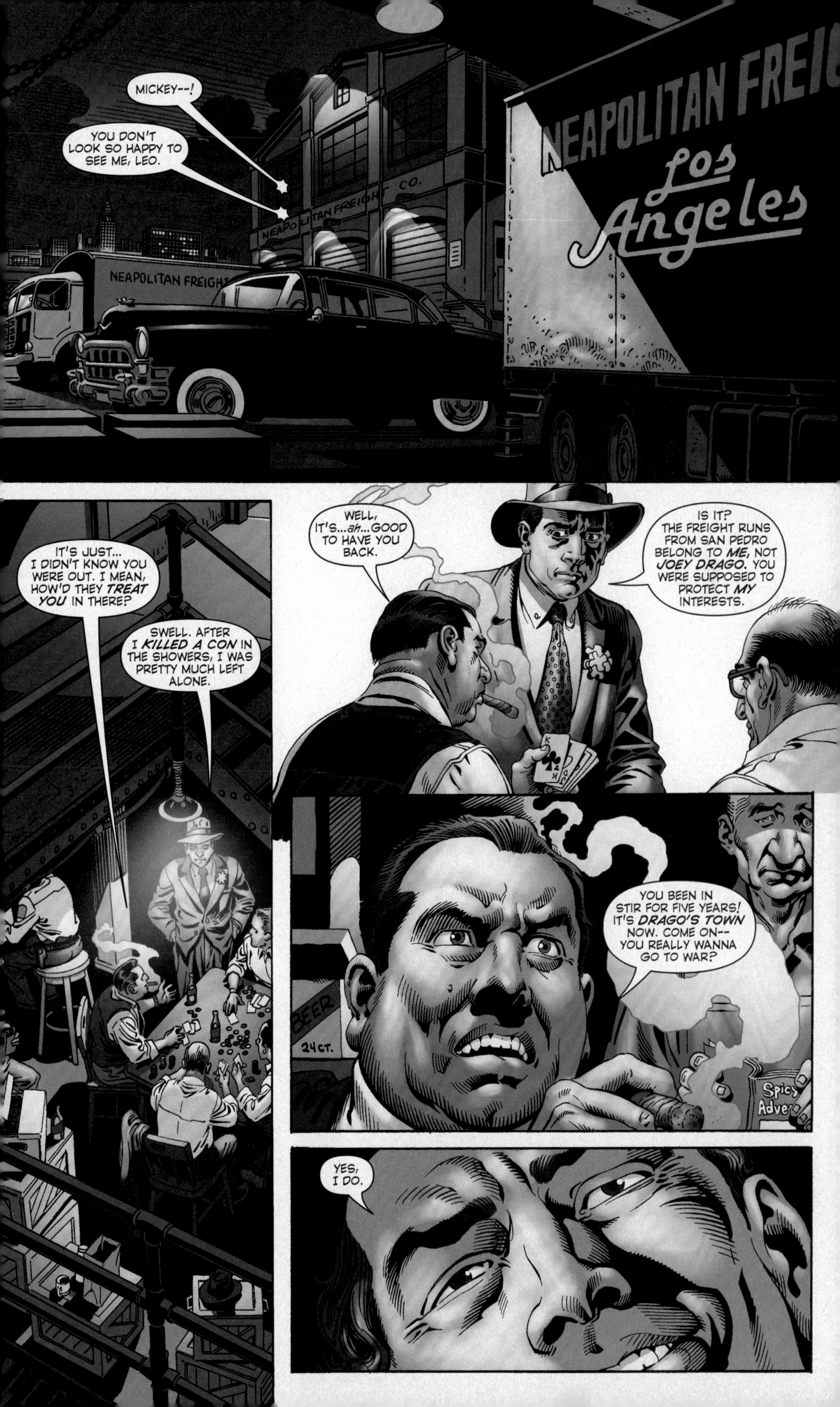
MICKEY--!
YOU DON'T LOOK SO HAPPY TO SEE ME, LEO.
NEAPOLITAN FREIG
Los Angeles
NEAPOLITAN FREIGHT CO.
NEAPOLITAN FREIGH
IT'S JUST... I DIDN'T KNOW YOU WERE OUT. I MEAN, HOW'D THEY TREAT YOU IN THERE?
SWELL. AFTER I KILLED A CON IN THE SHOWERS, I WAS PRETTY MUCH LEFT ALONE.
WELL, IT'S...ah...GOOD TO HAVE YOU BACK.
IS IT? THE FREIGHT RUNS FROM SAN PEDRO BELONG TO ME, NOT JOEY DRAGO. YOU WERE SUPPOSED TO PROTECT MY INTERESTS.
YOU BEEN IN STIR FOR FIVE YEARS! IT'S DRAGO'S TOWN NOW. COME ON-- YOU REALLY WANNA GO TO WAR?
BEER
24 CT.
YES, I DO.

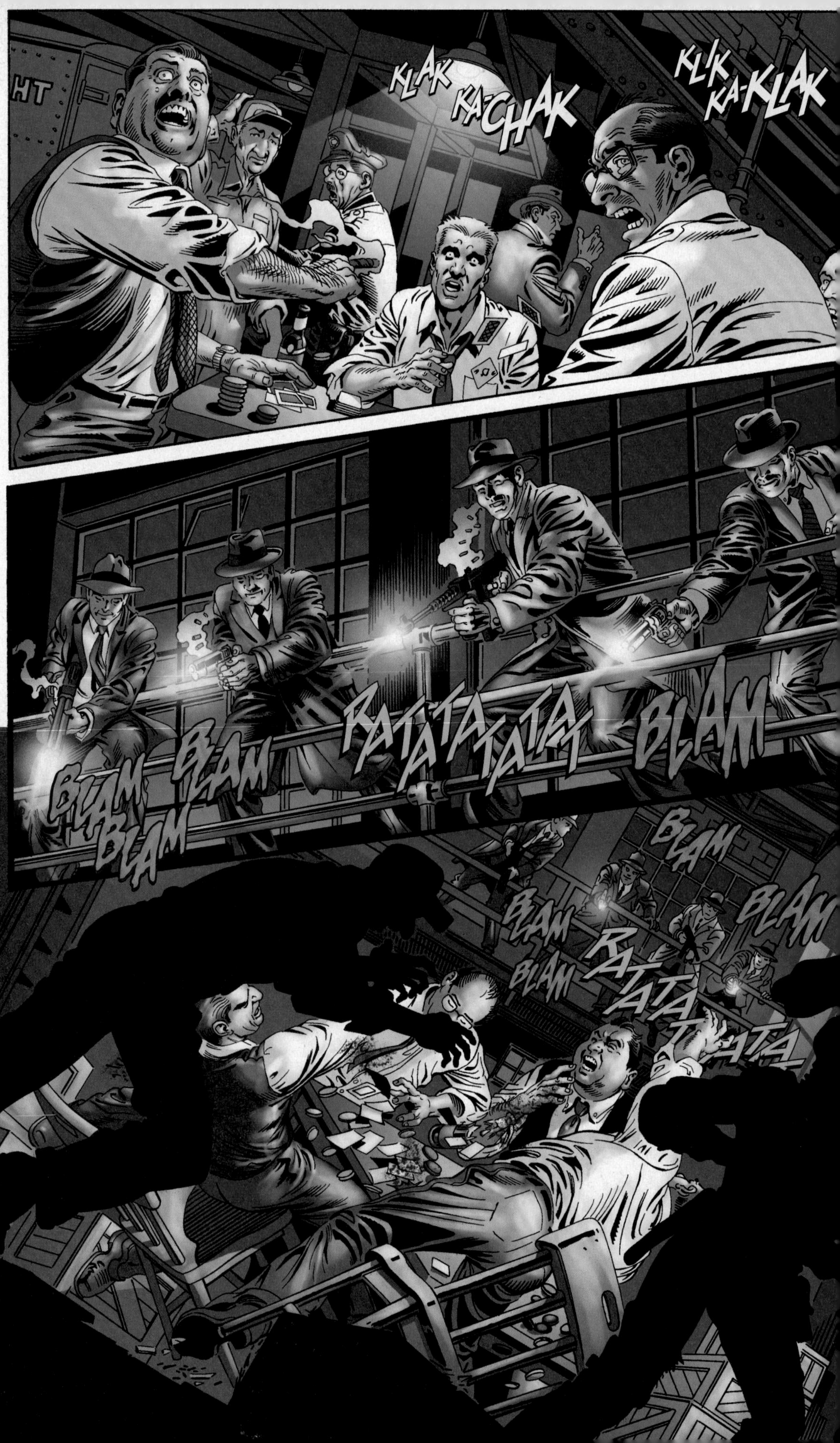
KLAK KA-CHAK
KLIK KA-KLAK
BLAM BLAM
BLAM BLAM
RATATATATAK
BLAM
BLAM
BLAM BLAM
BLAM
RATATATATA
BLAM

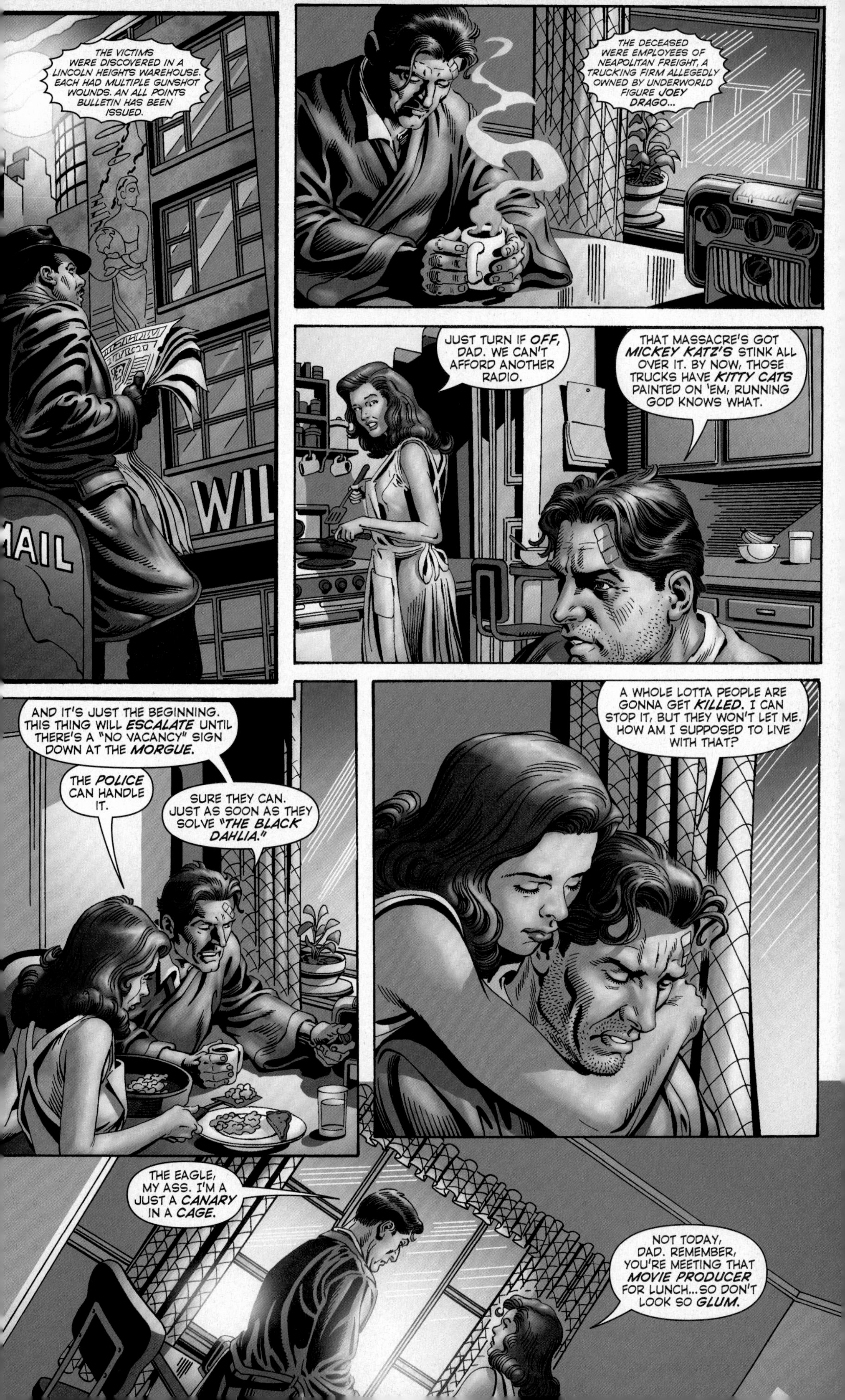
THE VICTIMS WERE DISCOVERED IN A LINCOLN HEIGHTS WAREHOUSE. EACH HAD MULTIPLE GUNSHOT WOUNDS. AN ALL POINTS BULLETIN HAS BEEN ISSUED.
WIL
MAIL
THE DECEASED WERE EMPLOYEES OF NEAPOLITAN FREIGHT, A TRUCKING FIRM ALLEGEDLY OWNED BY UNDERWORLD FIGURE JOEY DRAGO...
JUST TURN IF OFF, DAD. WE CAN'T AFFORD ANOTHER RADIO.
THAT MASSACRE'S GOT MICKEY KATZ'S STINK ALL OVER IT. BY NOW, THOSE TRUCKS HAVE KITTY CATS PAINTED ON 'EM, RUNNING GOD KNOWS WHAT.
AND IT'S JUST THE BEGINNING. THIS THING WILL ESCALATE UNTIL THERE'S A "NO VACANCY" SIGN DOWN AT THE MORGUE.
THE POLICE CAN HANDLE IT.
SURE THEY CAN. JUST AS SOON AS THEY SOLVE "THE BLACK DAHLIA."
A WHOLE LOTTA PEOPLE ARE GONNA GET KILLED. I CAN STOP IT, BUT THEY WON'T LET ME. HOW AM I SUPPOSED TO LIVE WITH THAT?
THE EAGLE, MY ASS. I'M A JUST A CANARY IN A CAGE.
NOT TODAY, DAD. REMEMBER, YOU'RE MEETING THAT MOVIE PRODUCER FOR LUNCH...SO DON'T LOOK SO GLUM.

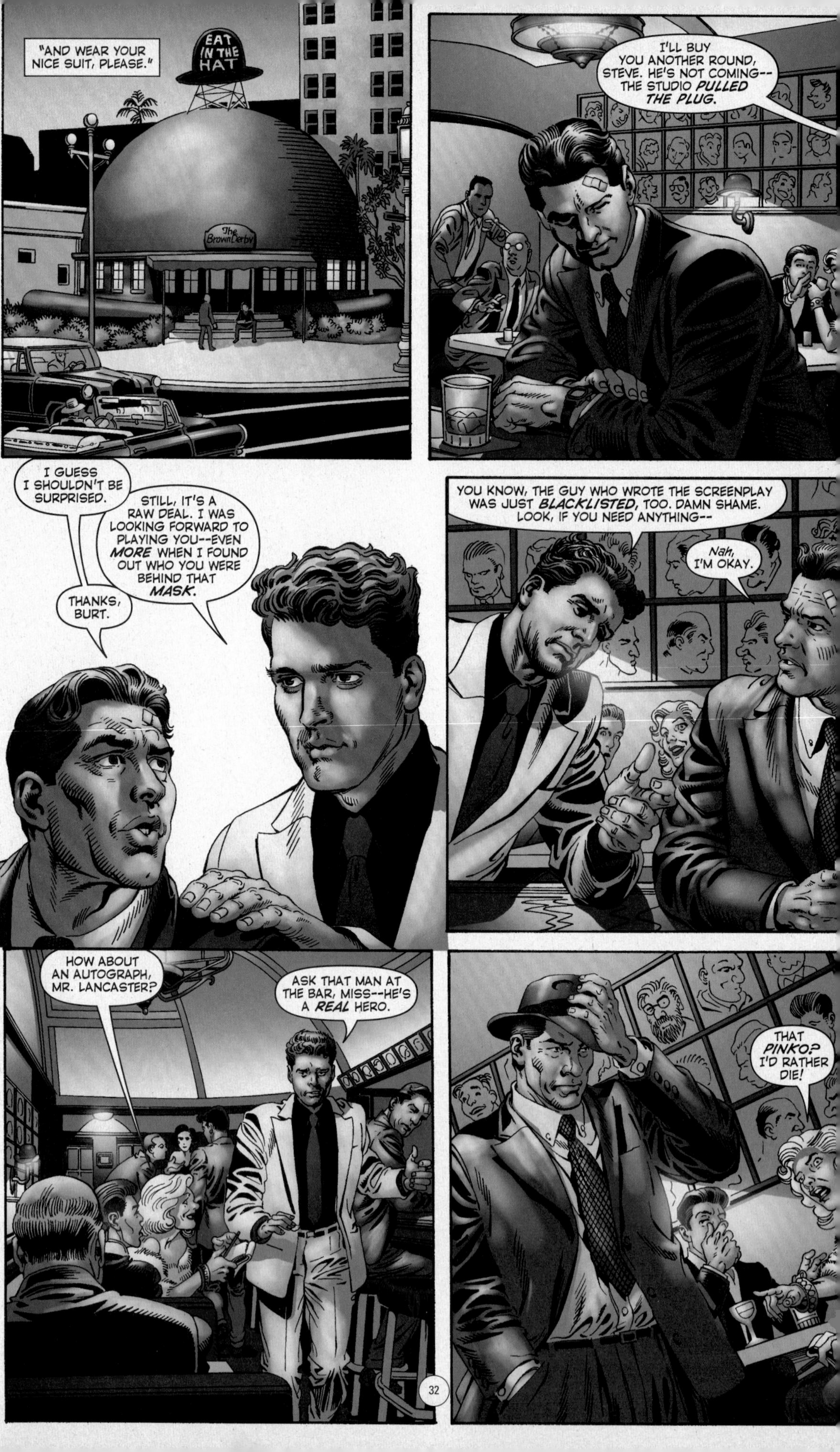

"AND WEAR YOUR NICE SUIT, PLEASE."
EAT IN THE HAT
The Brown Derby
I'LL BUY YOU ANOTHER ROUND, STEVE. HE'S NOT COMING-- THE STUDIO PULLED THE PLUG.
I GUESS I SHOULDN'T BE SURPRISED.
STILL, IT'S A RAW DEAL. I WAS LOOKING FORWARD TO PLAYING YOU--EVEN MORE WHEN I FOUND OUT WHO YOU WERE BEHIND THAT MASK.
THANKS, BURT.
YOU KNOW, THE GUY WHO WROTE THE SCREENPLAY WAS JUST BLACKLISTED, TOO. DAMN SHAME. LOOK, IF YOU NEED ANYTHING--
Nah, I'M OKAY.
HOW ABOUT AN AUTOGRAPH, MR. LANCASTER?
ASK THAT MAN AT THE BAR, MISS--HE'S A REAL HERO.
THAT PINKO? I'D RATHER DIE!

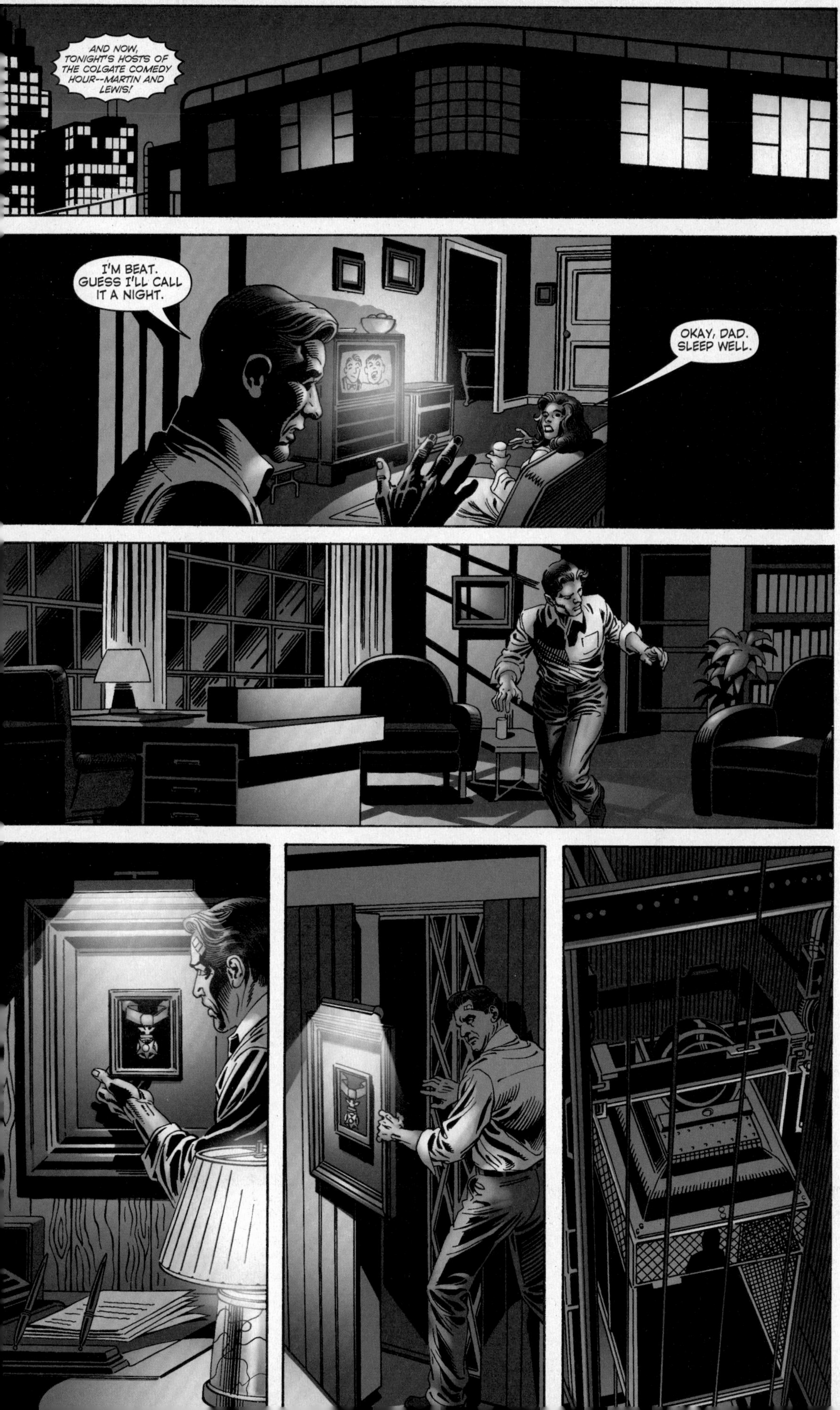
AND NOW, TONIGHT'S HOSTS OF THE COLGATE COMEDY HOUR--MARTIN AND LEWIS!
I'M BEAT. GUESS I'LL CALL IT A NIGHT.
OKAY, DAD. SLEEP WELL.

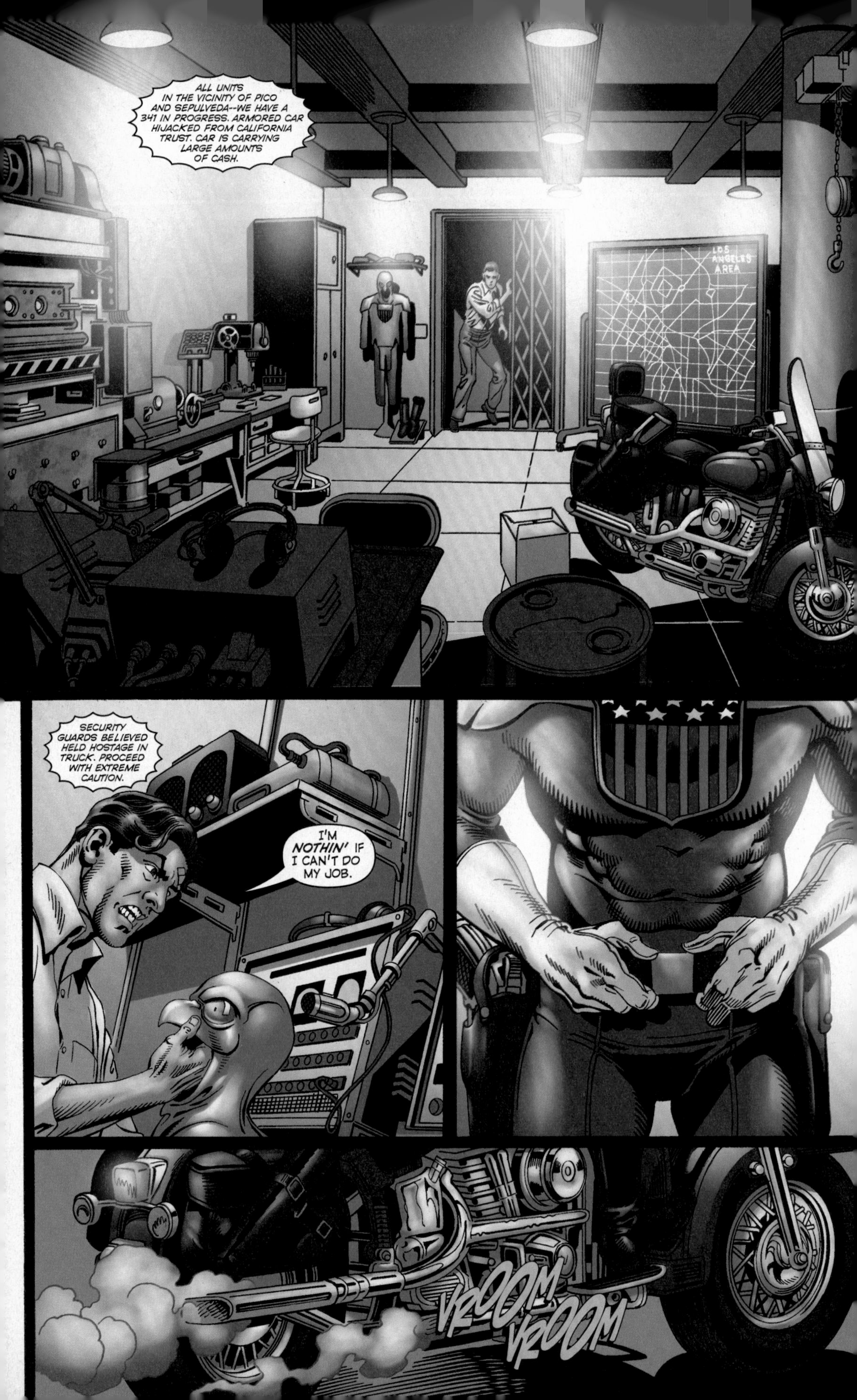
ALL UNITS IN THE VICINITY OF PICO AND SEPULVEDA--WE HAVE A 341 IN PROGRESS. ARMORED CAR HIJACKED FROM CALIFORNIA TRUST. CAR IS CARRYING LARGE AMOUNTS OF CASH.
LOS ANGELES AREA
SECURITY GUARDS BELIEVED HELD HOSTAGE IN TRUCK. PROCEED WITH EXTREME CAUTION.
I'M *NOTHIN'* IF I CAN'T DO MY JOB.
VROOM
VROOM

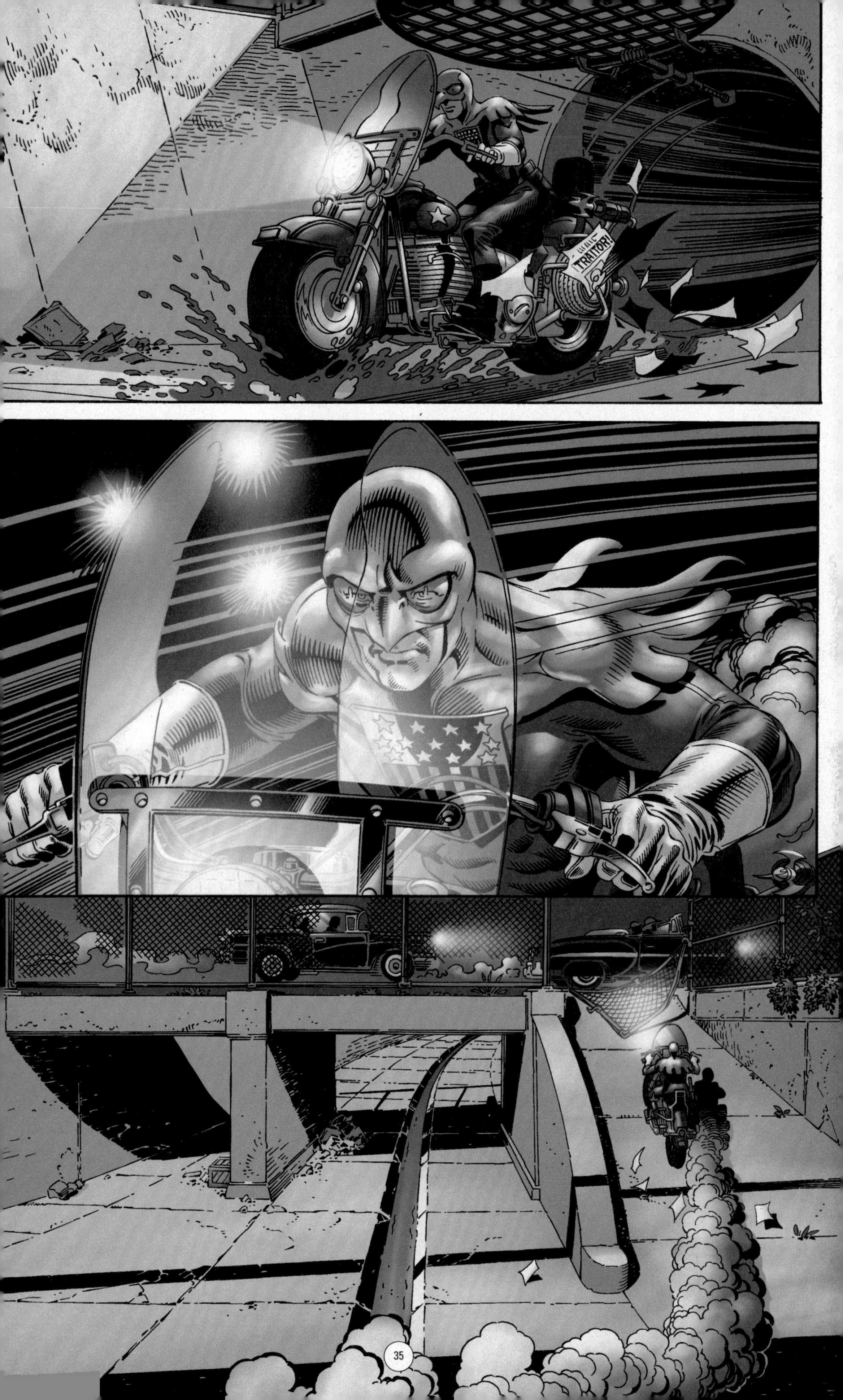
TRAITOR!

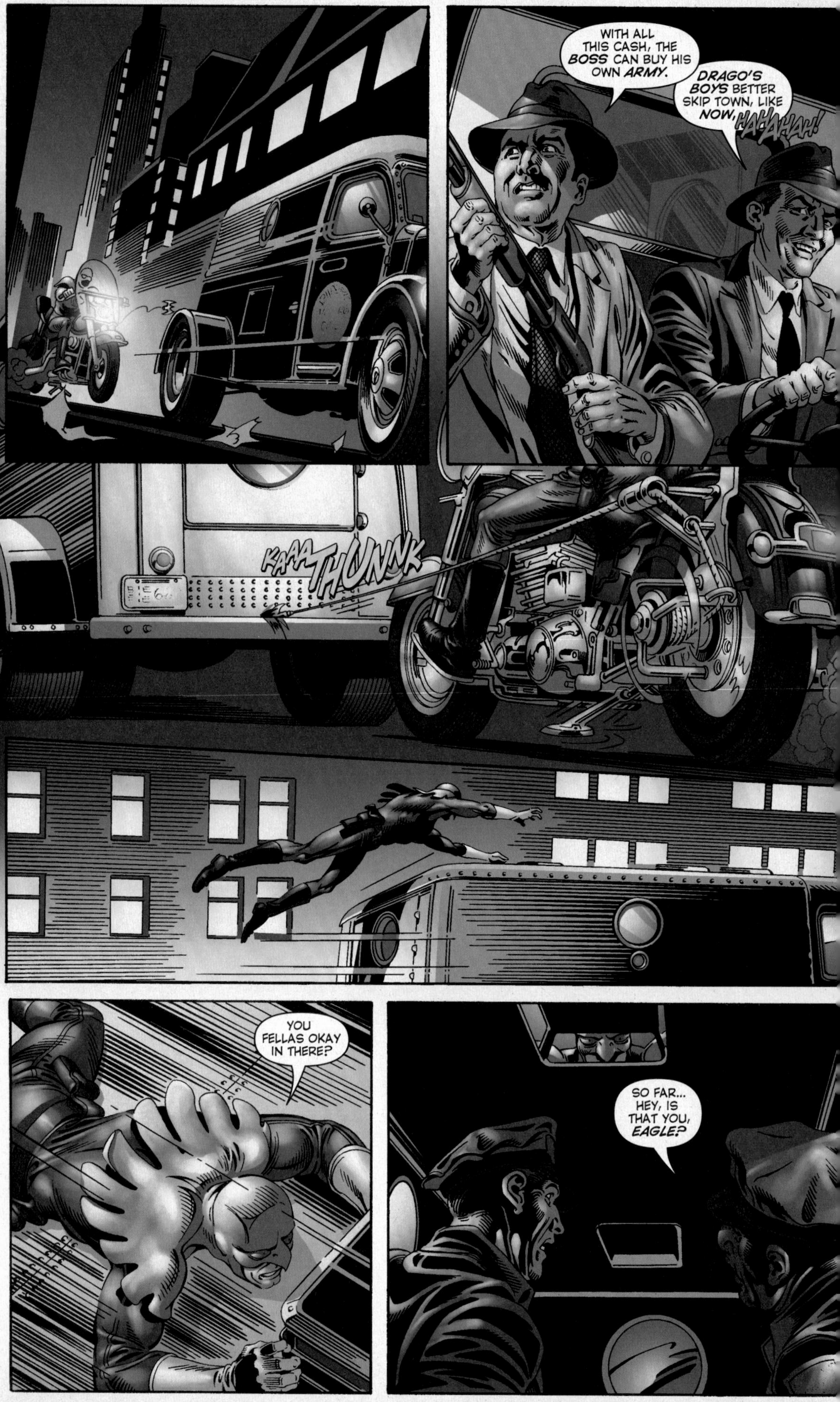
WITH ALL THIS CASH, THE BOSS CAN BUY HIS OWN ARMY.
DRAGO'S BOYS BETTER SKIP TOWN, LIKE NOW, HAHAHAH!
KAAA THUNNK
YOU FELLAS OKAY IN THERE?
SO FAR... HEY, IS THAT YOU, EAGLE?

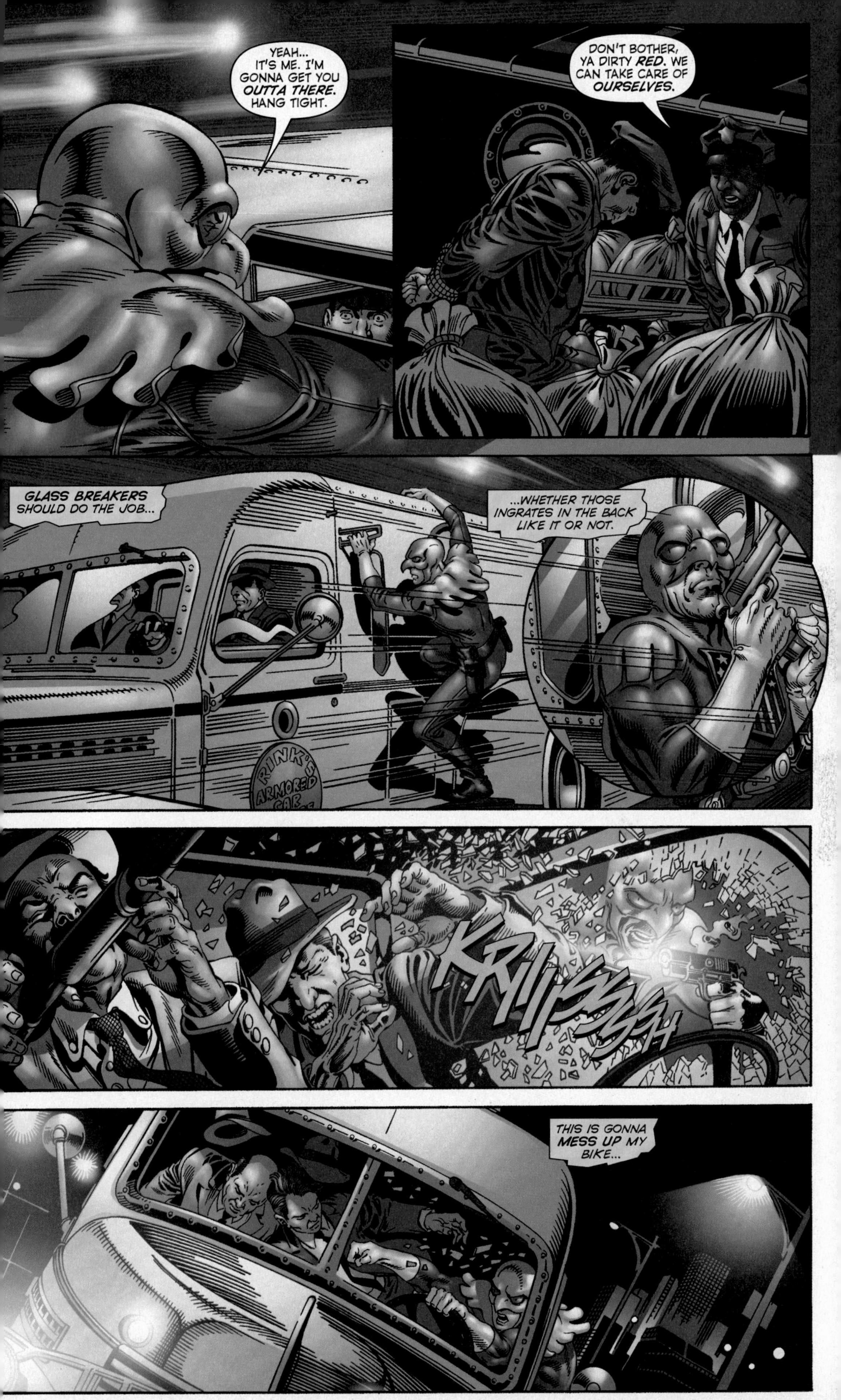
YEAH... IT'S ME. I'M GONNA GET YOU OUTTA THERE. HANG TIGHT.
DON'T BOTHER, YA DIRTY RED. WE CAN TAKE CARE OF OURSELVES.
GLASS BREAKERS SHOULD DO THE JOB...
...WHETHER THOSE INGRATES IN THE BACK LIKE IT OR NOT.
RINK'S ARMORED CAR
KRIIISSSHH
THIS IS GONNA MESS UP MY BIKE...

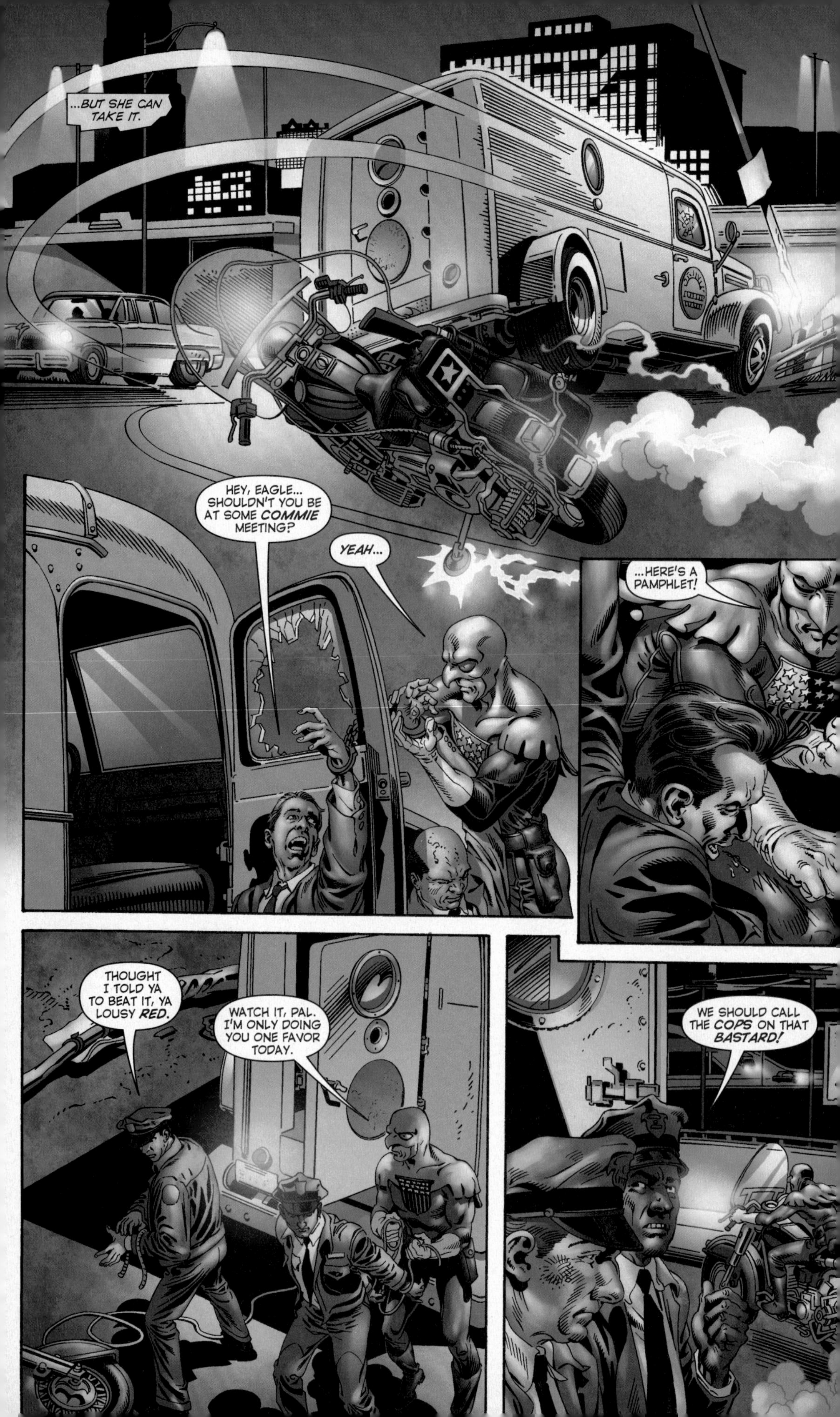
...BUT SHE CAN TAKE IT.
HEY, EAGLE... SHOULDN'T YOU BE AT SOME COMMIE MEETING?
YEAH...
...HERE'S A PAMPHLET!
THOUGHT I TOLD YA TO BEAT IT, YA LOUSY RED.
WATCH IT, PAL. I'M ONLY DOING YOU ONE FAVOR TODAY.
WE SHOULD CALL THE COPS ON THAT BASTARD!

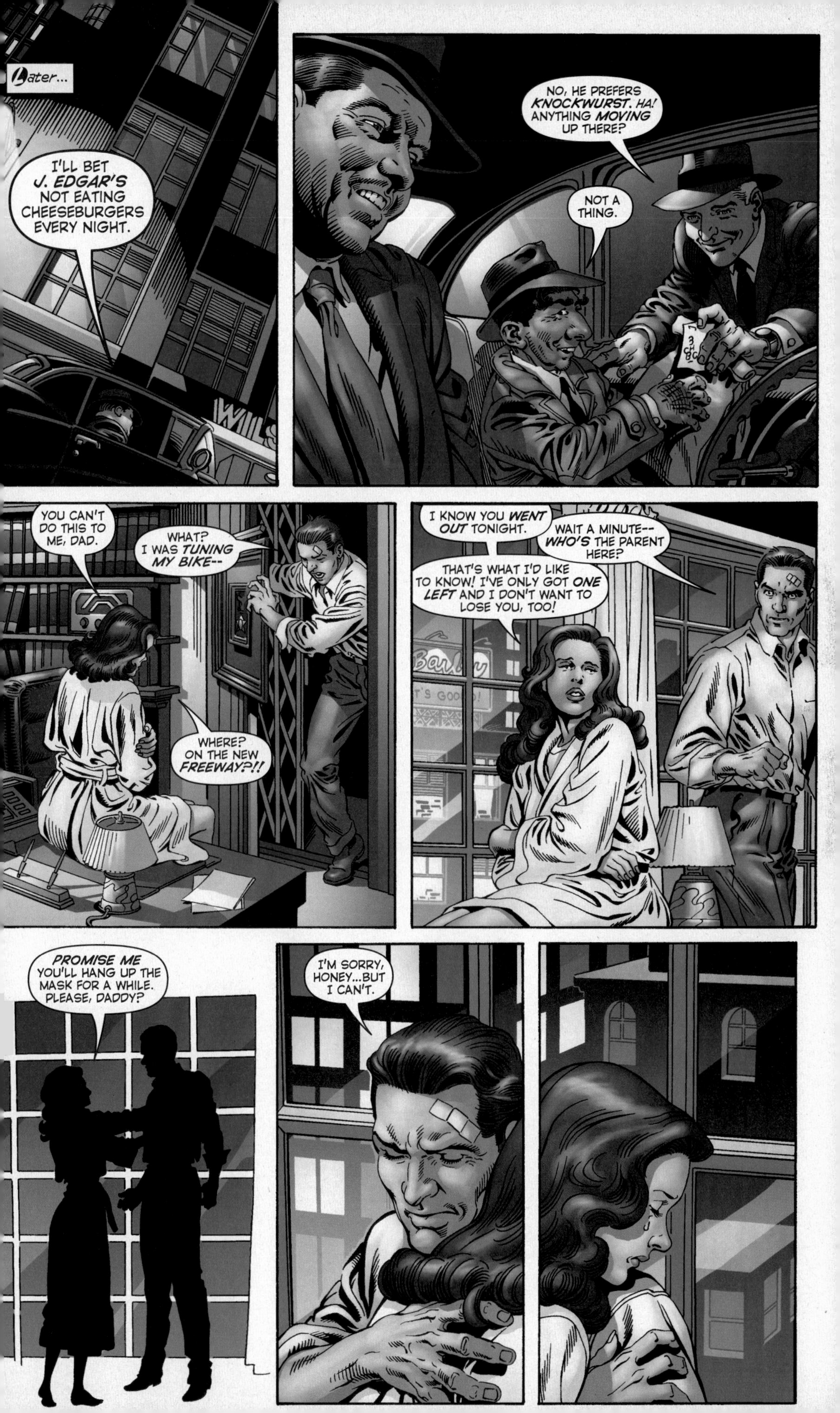
Later...
I'LL BET J. EDGAR'S NOT EATING CHEESEBURGERS EVERY NIGHT.
NO, HE PREFERS KNOCKWURST. HA! ANYTHING MOVING UP THERE?
NOT A THING.
YOU CAN'T DO THIS TO ME, DAD.
WHAT? I WAS TUNING MY BIKE--
WHERE? ON THE NEW FREEWAY?!!
I KNOW YOU WENT OUT TONIGHT.
WAIT A MINUTE-- WHO'S THE PARENT HERE?
THAT'S WHAT I'D LIKE TO KNOW! I'VE ONLY GOT ONE LEFT AND I DON'T WANT TO LOSE YOU, TOO!
PROMISE ME YOU'LL HANG UP THE MASK FOR A WHILE. PLEASE, DADDY?
I'M SORRY, HONEY...BUT I CAN'T.

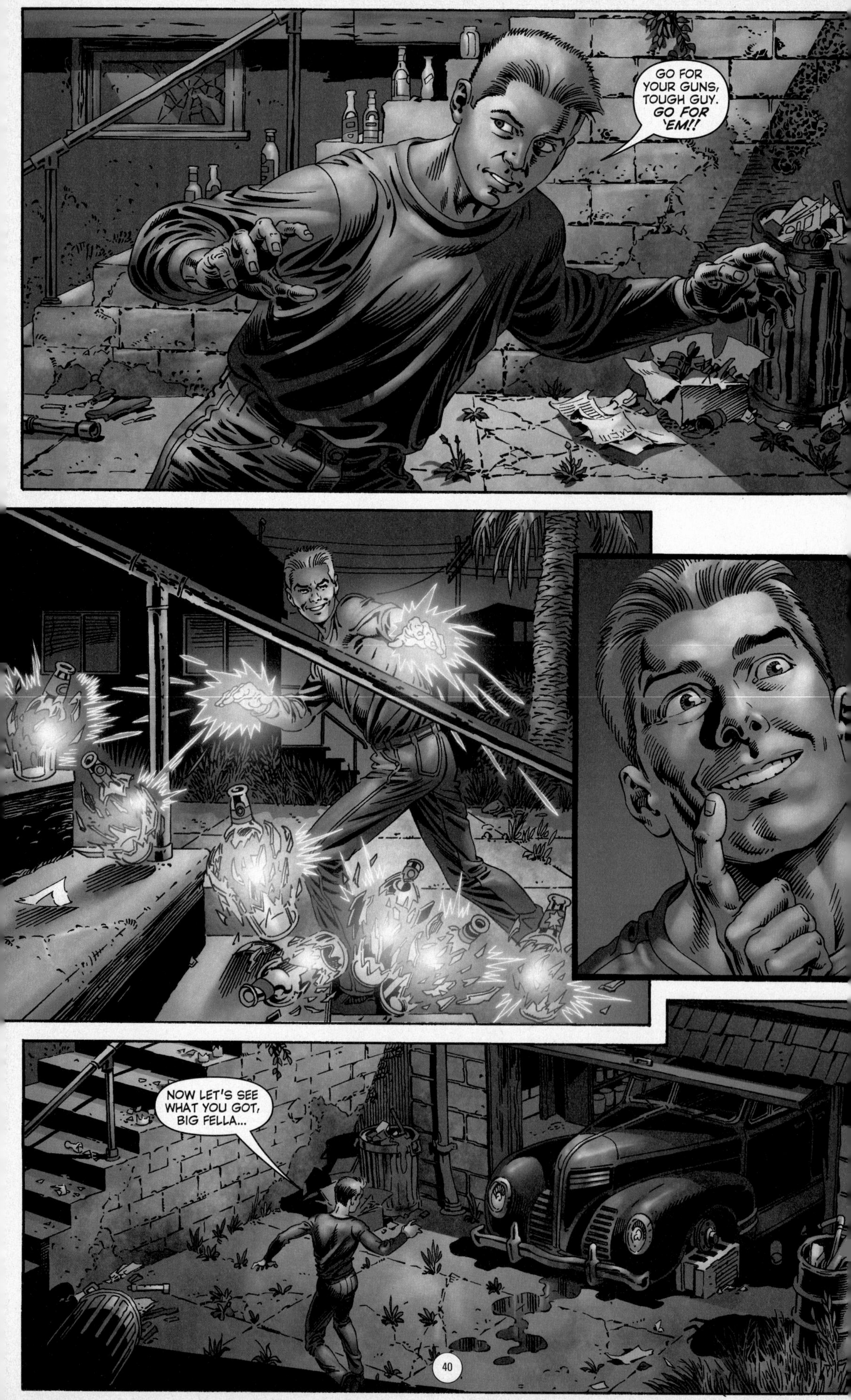
GO FOR YOUR GUNS, TOUGH GUY. GO FOR 'EM!!
NOW LET'S SEE WHAT YOU GOT, BIG FELLA...

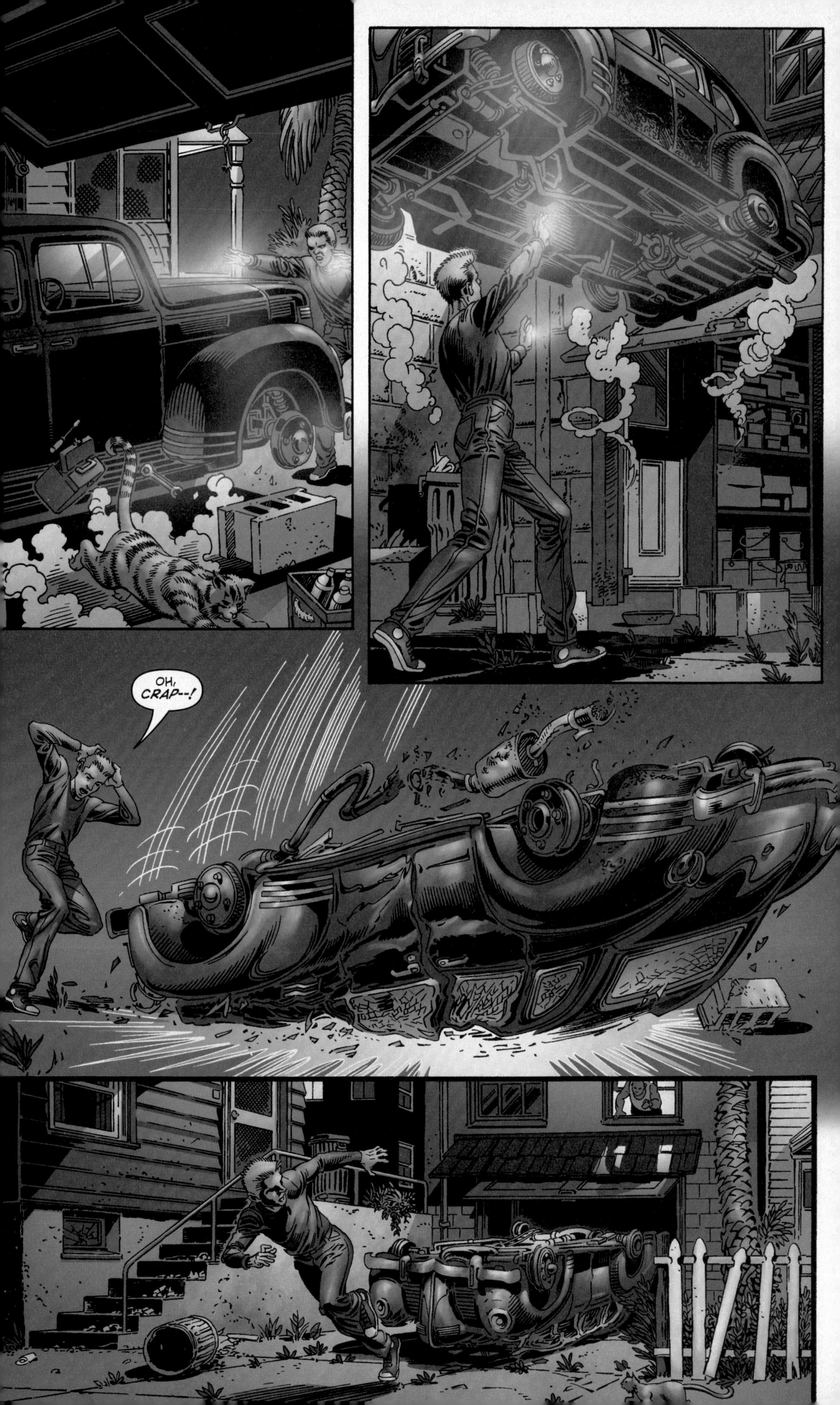
OH, CRAP--!

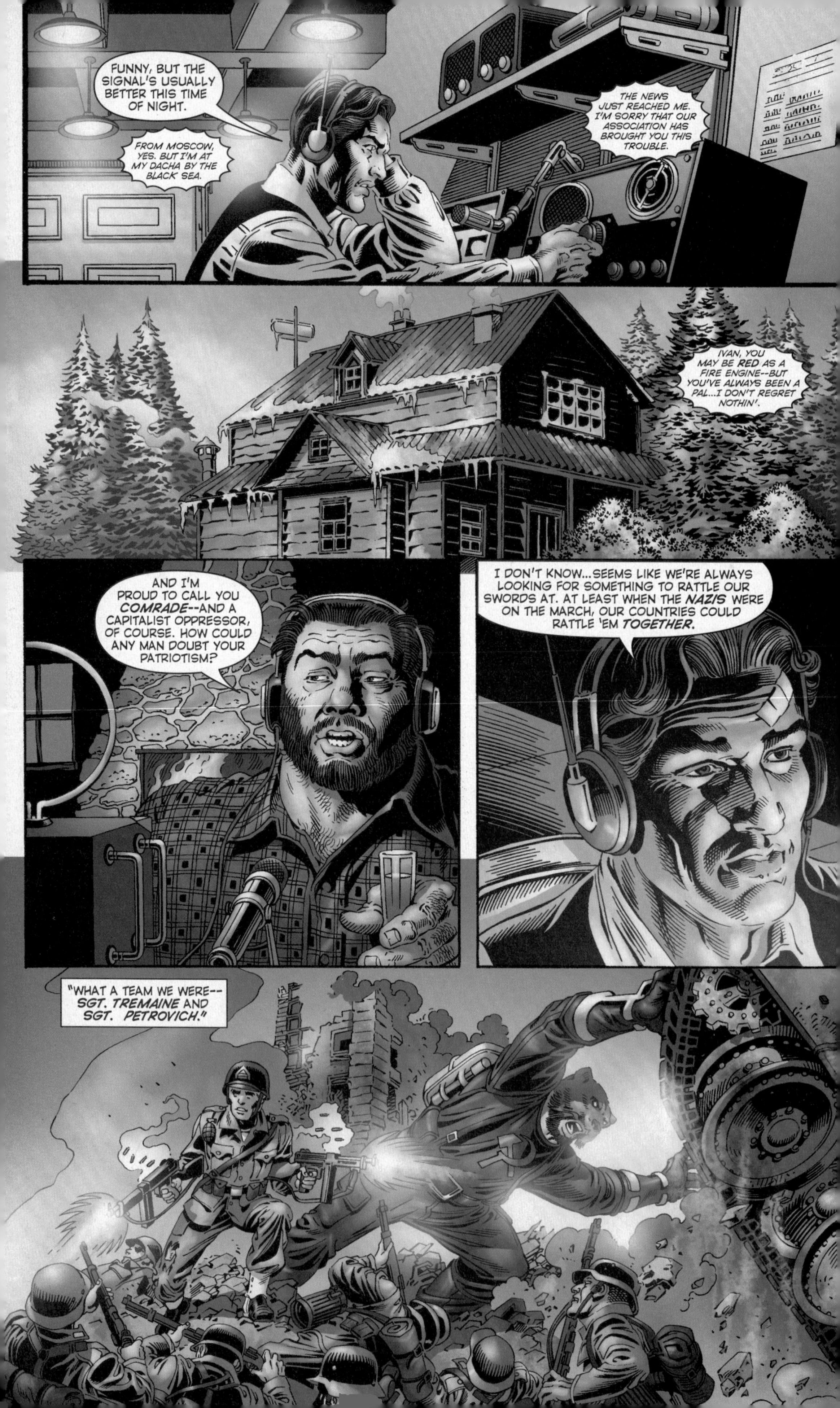

FUNNY, BUT THE SIGNAL'S USUALLY BETTER THIS TIME OF NIGHT.
FROM MOSCOW, YES. BUT I'M AT MY DACHA BY THE BLACK SEA.
THE NEWS JUST REACHED ME. I'M SORRY THAT OUR ASSOCIATION HAS BROUGHT YOU THIS TROUBLE.
IVAN, YOU MAY BE RED AS A FIRE ENGINE--BUT YOU'VE ALWAYS BEEN A PAL...I DON'T REGRET NOTHIN'.
AND I'M PROUD TO CALL YOU COMRADE--AND A CAPITALIST OPPRESSOR, OF COURSE. HOW COULD ANY MAN DOUBT YOUR PATRIOTISM?
I DON'T KNOW...SEEMS LIKE WE'RE ALWAYS LOOKING FOR SOMETHING TO RATTLE OUR SWORDS AT. AT LEAST WHEN THE NAZIS WERE ON THE MARCH, OUR COUNTRIES COULD RATTLE 'EM TOGETHER.
"WHAT A TEAM WE WERE-- SGT. TREMAINE AND SGT. PETROVICH."

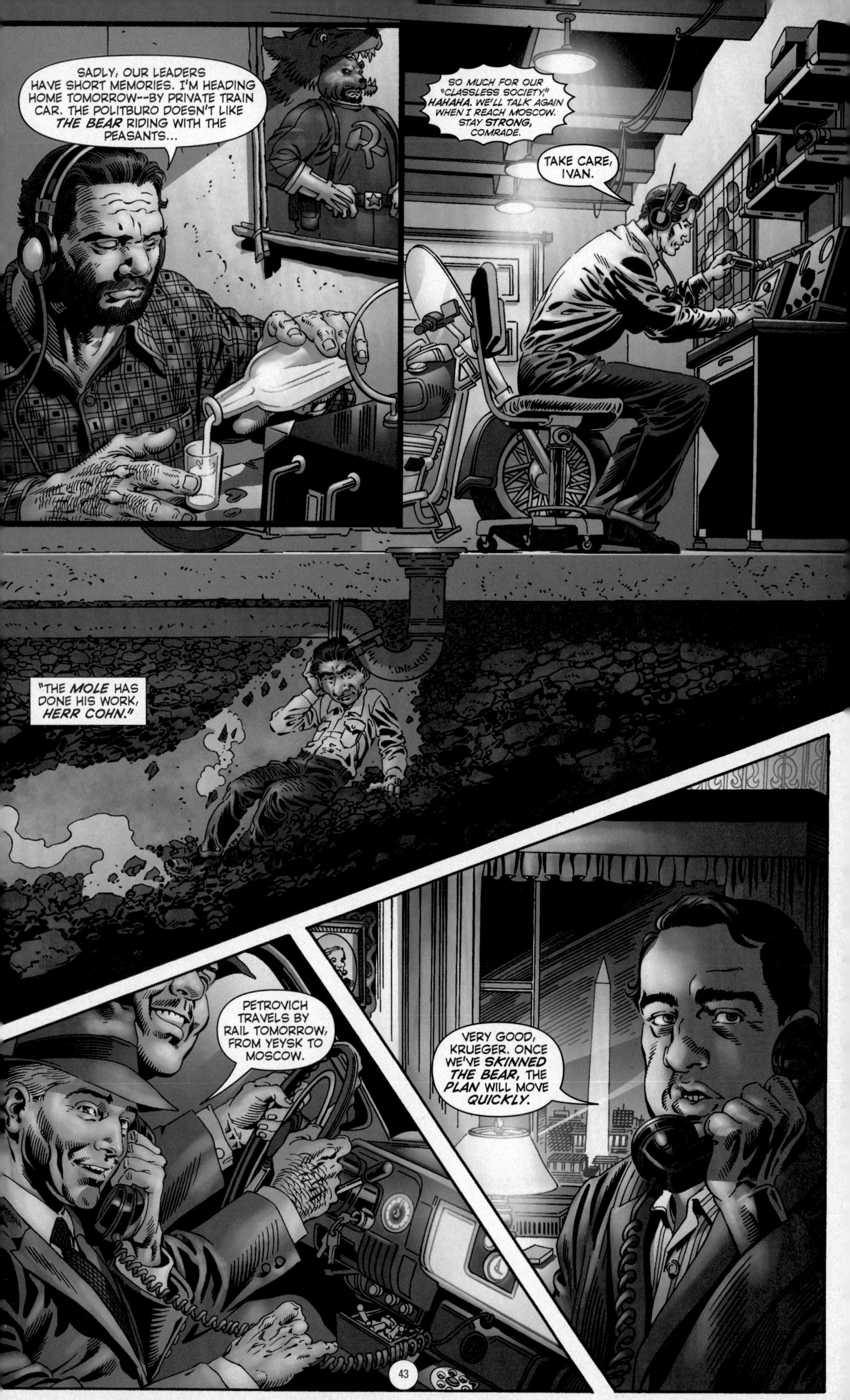
SADLY, OUR LEADERS HAVE SHORT MEMORIES. I'M HEADING HOME TOMORROW--BY PRIVATE TRAIN CAR. THE POLITBURO DOESN'T LIKE THE BEAR RIDING WITH THE PEASANTS...
SO MUCH FOR OUR "CLASSLESS SOCIETY," HAHAHA. WE'LL TALK AGAIN WHEN I REACH MOSCOW. STAY STRONG, COMRADE.
TAKE CARE, IVAN.
"THE MOLE HAS DONE HIS WORK, HERR COHN."
PETROVICH TRAVELS BY RAIL TOMORROW, FROM YEYSK TO MOSCOW.
VERY GOOD, KRUEGER. ONCE WE'VE SKINNED THE BEAR, THE PLAN WILL MOVE QUICKLY.

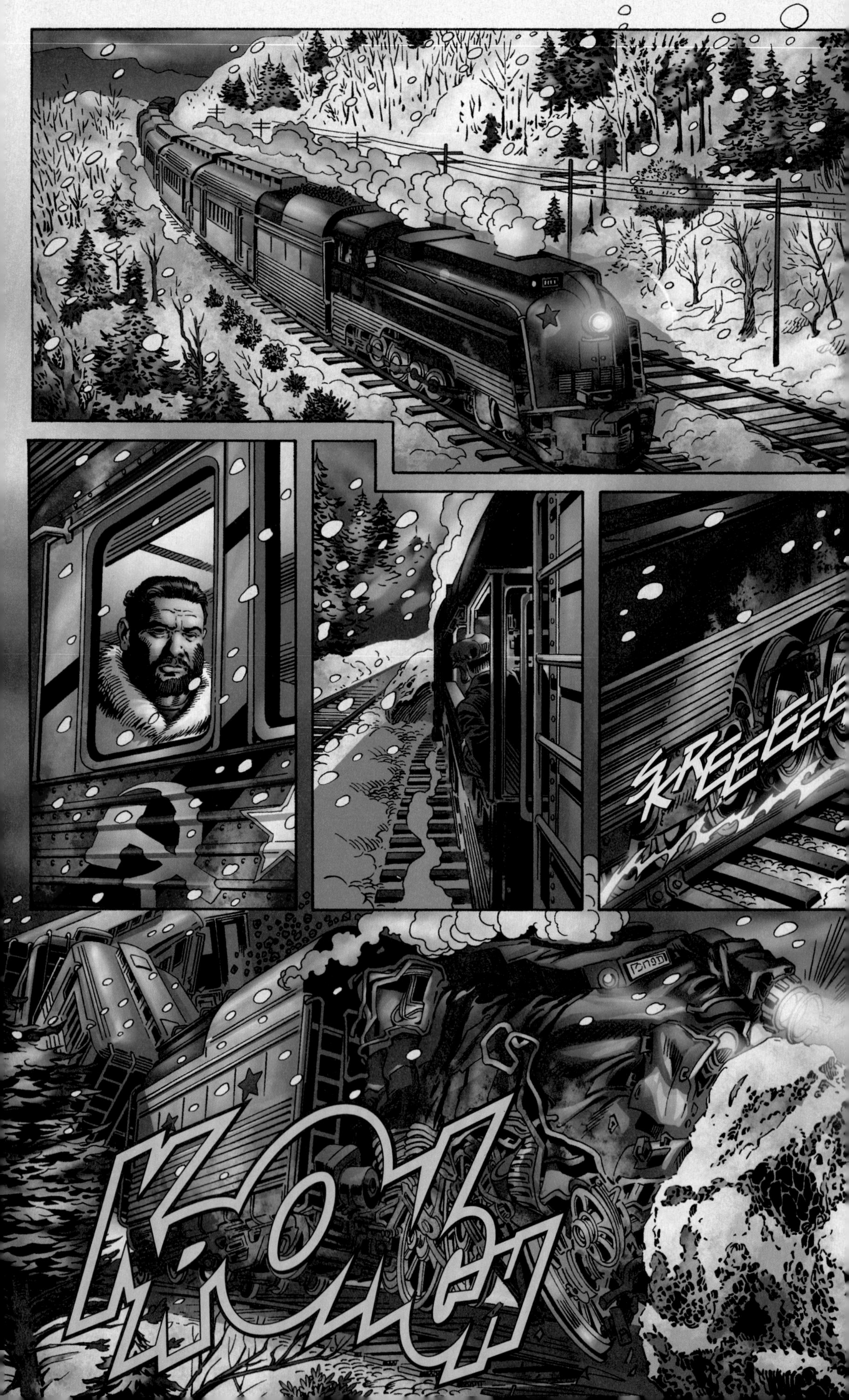
SKREEEEEEE
KRUNCH

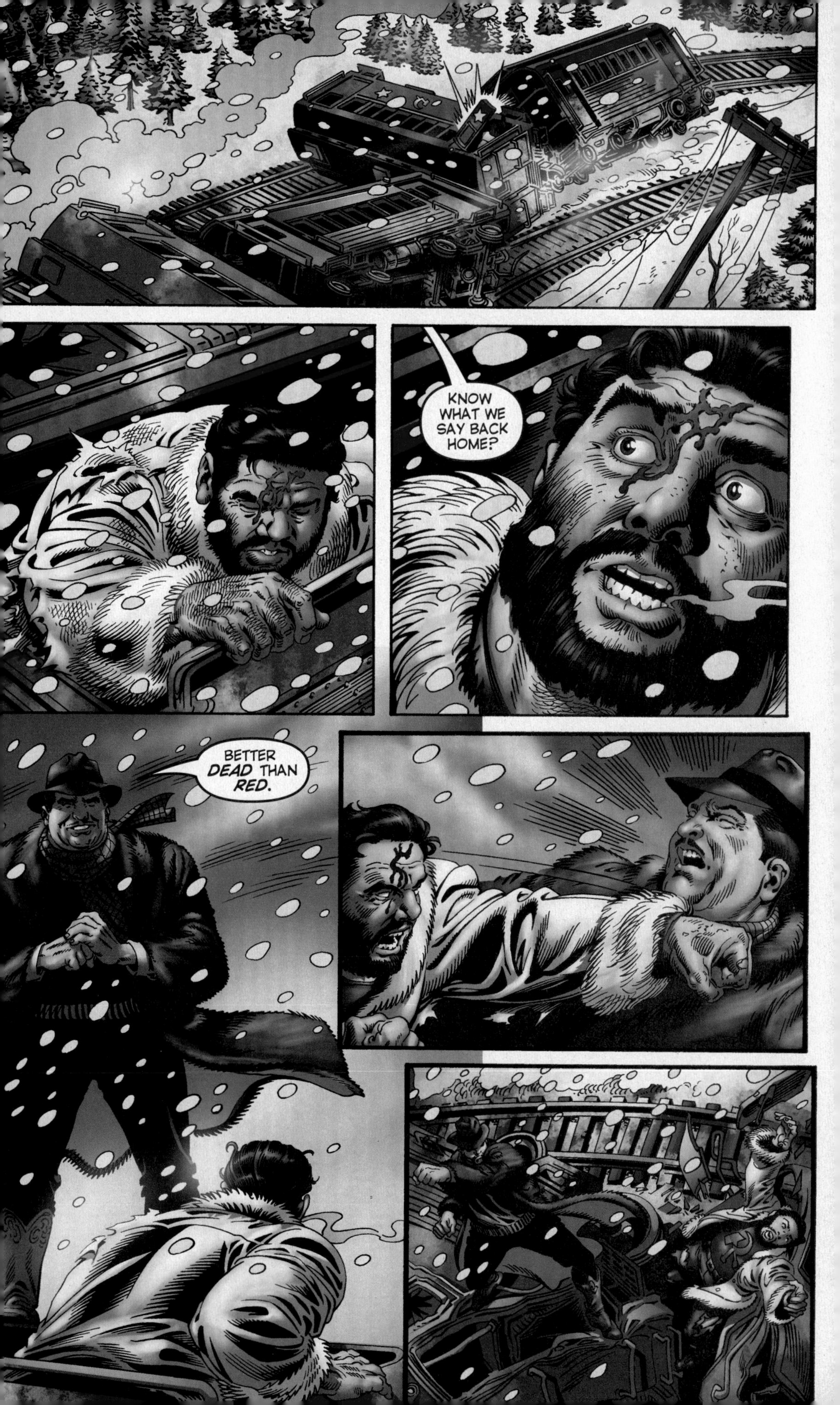
KNOW WHAT WE SAY BACK HOME?
BETTER DEAD THAN RED.

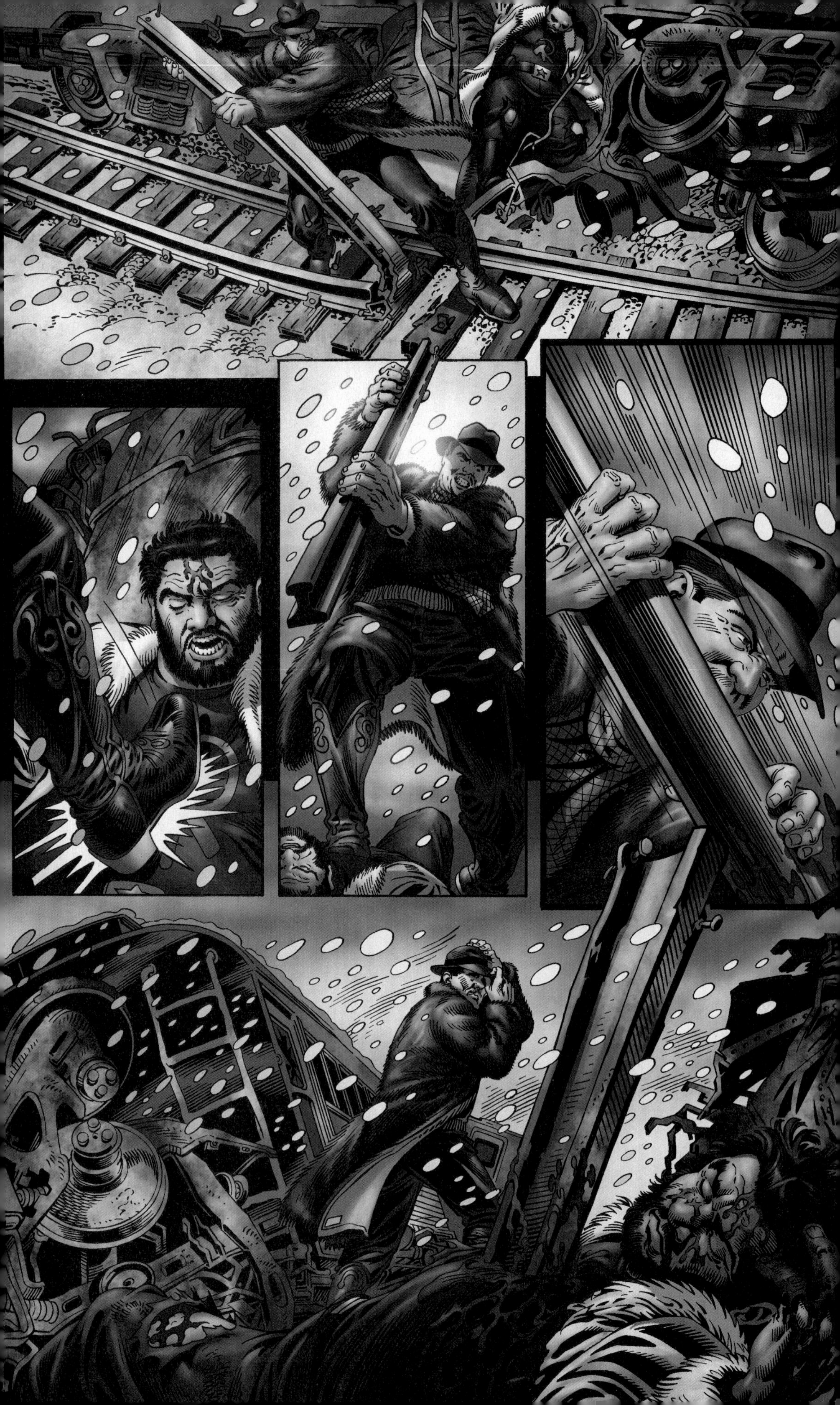

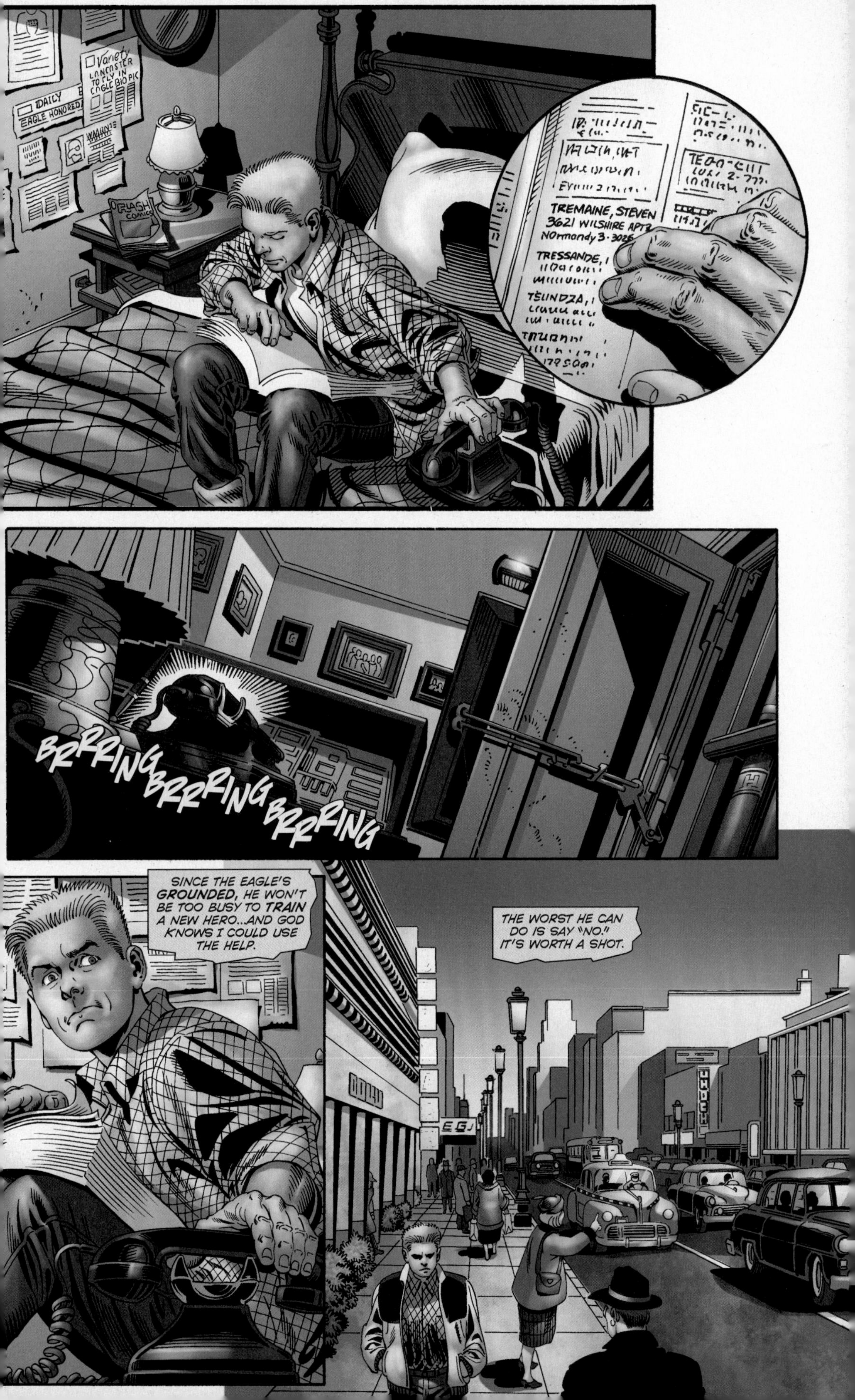

Variety
LANCASTER TO FLY IN EAGLE BIO PIC
DAILY
EAGLE HONORED
FLASH COMICS
TREMAINE, STEVEN
3621 WILSHIRE APT 2
NOrmandy 3-3026
TRESSANDE,
BRRRING BRRRING BRRRING
SINCE THE EAGLE'S GROUNDED, HE WON'T BE TOO BUSY TO TRAIN A NEW HERO...AND GOD KNOWS I COULD USE THE HELP.
THE WORST HE CAN DO IS SAY "NO." IT'S WORTH A SHOT.

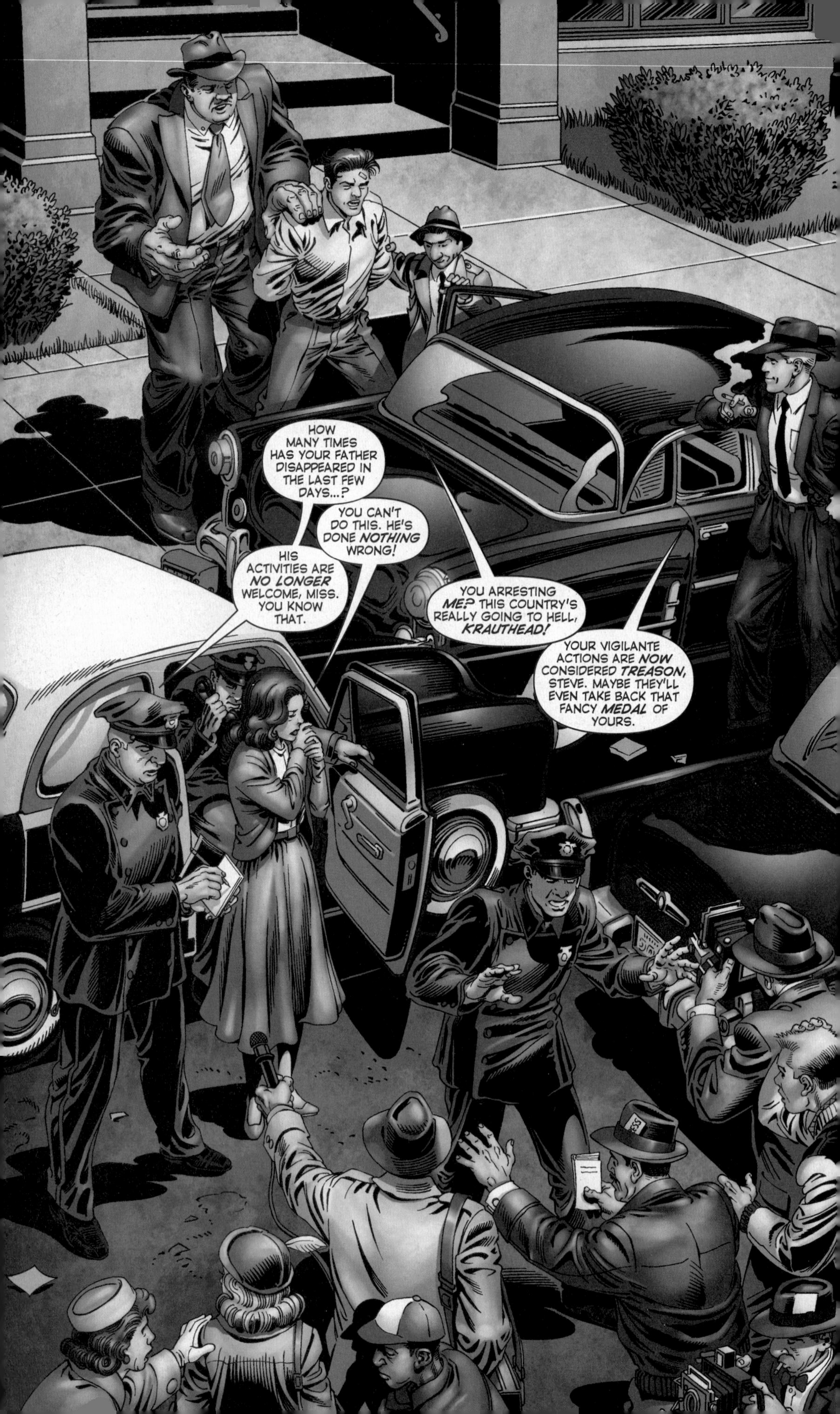
HOW MANY TIMES HAS YOUR FATHER DISAPPEARED IN THE LAST FEW DAYS...?
YOU CAN'T DO THIS. HE'S DONE *NOTHING* WRONG!
HIS ACTIVITIES ARE *NO LONGER* WELCOME, MISS. YOU KNOW THAT.
YOU ARRESTING *ME?* THIS COUNTRY'S REALLY GOING TO HELL, *KRAUTHEAD!*
YOUR VIGILANTE ACTIONS ARE *NOW* CONSIDERED *TREASON,* STEVE. MAYBE THEY'LL EVEN TAKE BACK THAT FANCY *MEDAL* OF YOURS.

CHAPTER 3

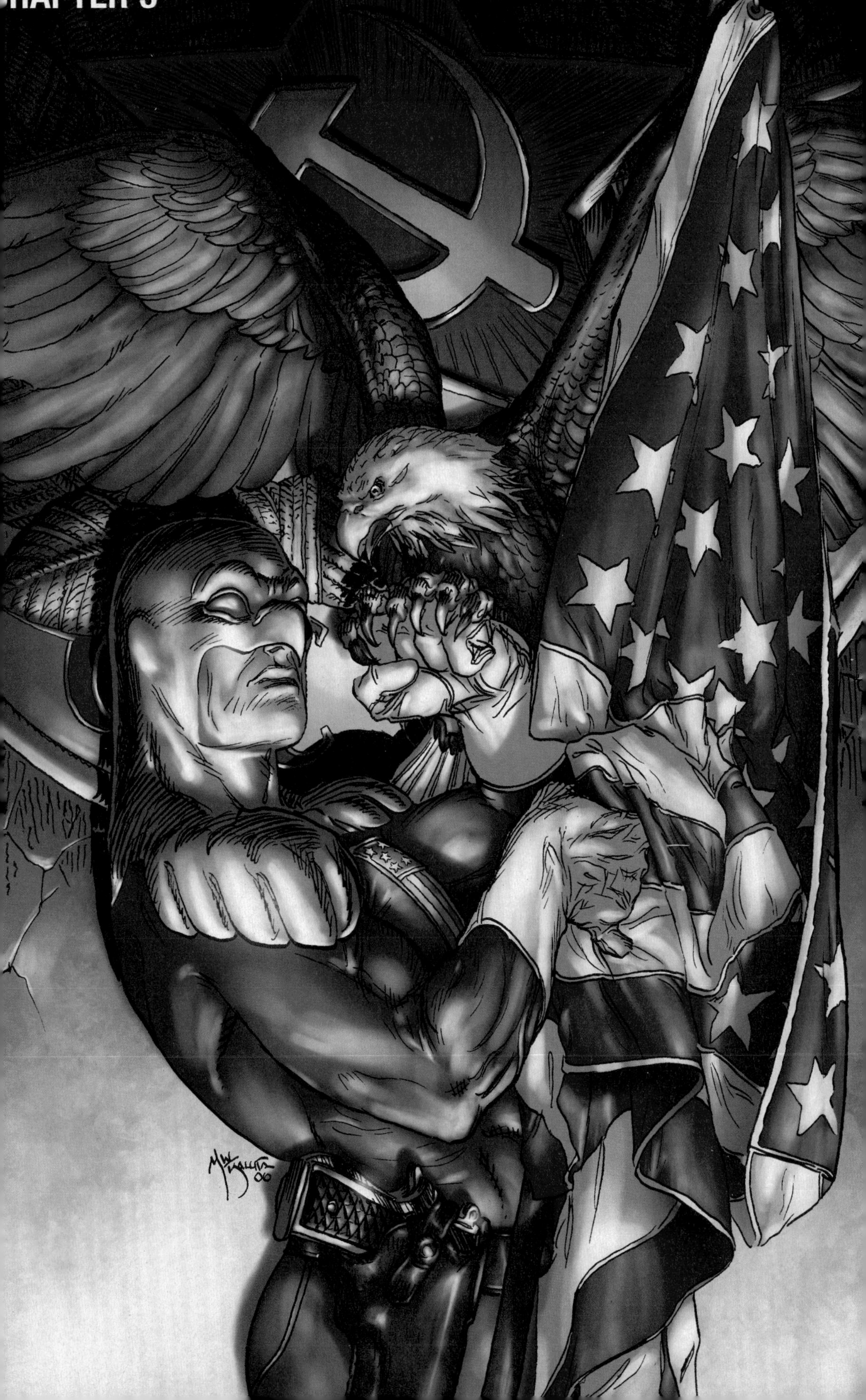

Red Menace

STEVE "EAGLE" TREMAINE ARRESTED

MAR 07

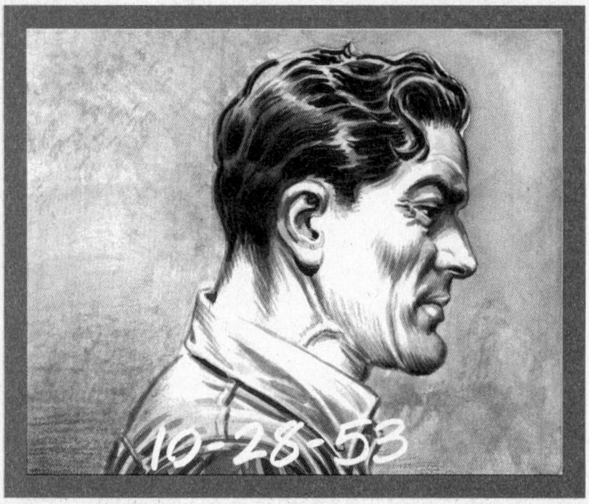
10-28-53

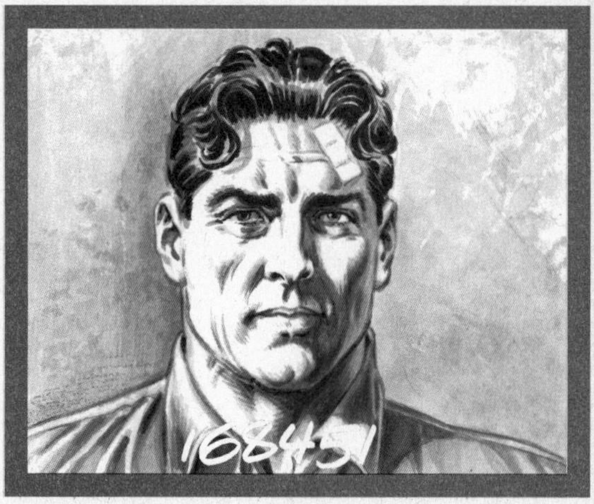
16845

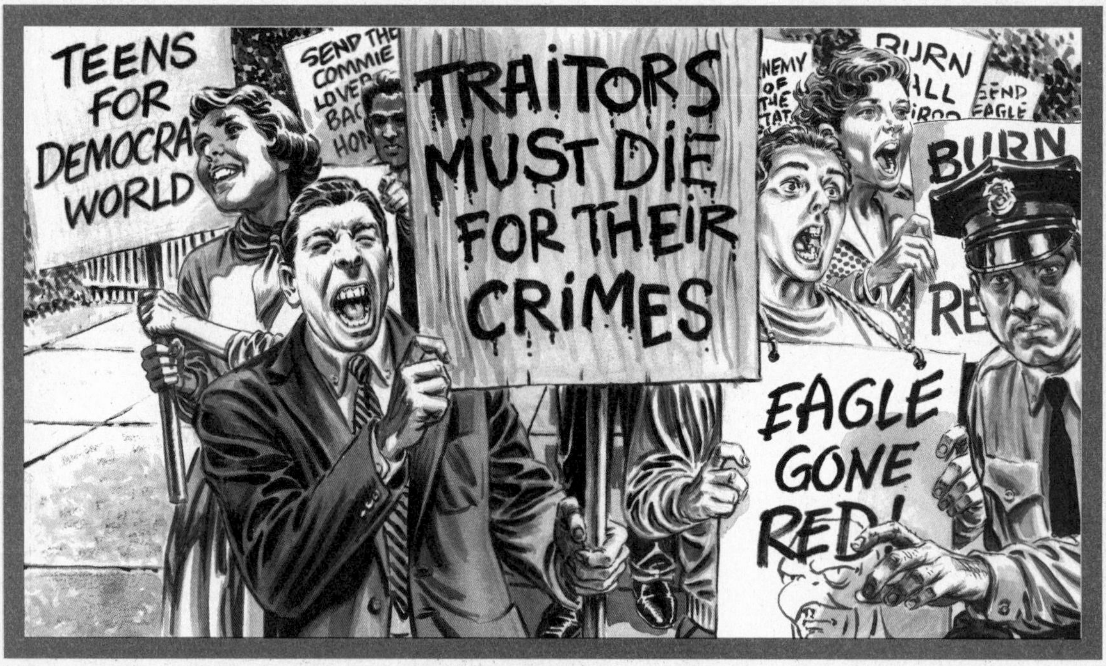
TEENS FOR DEMOCRA WORLD
SEND THE COMMIE LOVER BAC HOM
TRAITORS MUST DIE FOR THEIR CRIMES
NEMY OF THE TAT
BURN ALL
SEND EAGLE
BURN
RE
EAGLE GONE RED!

SCHOOLCHILDREN DENOUNCE THEIR FORMER HERO

Hung over and down and out Steve is coaxed into leaving his den and going on an outing to the horse races at Santa Anita with his daughter. They are now accompanied by Krueger, who watches Steve's every move as part of his house arrest. There is not much to watch as Steve is now the shell of

That night Steve sneaks out through his secret exit once more. But this time he leaves the Eagle suit behind, and takes his Whisper Bike to the nearest bar. Steve is recognized and attacked for being a commie. Even though Steve is drunk he puts up a hell of a fight,

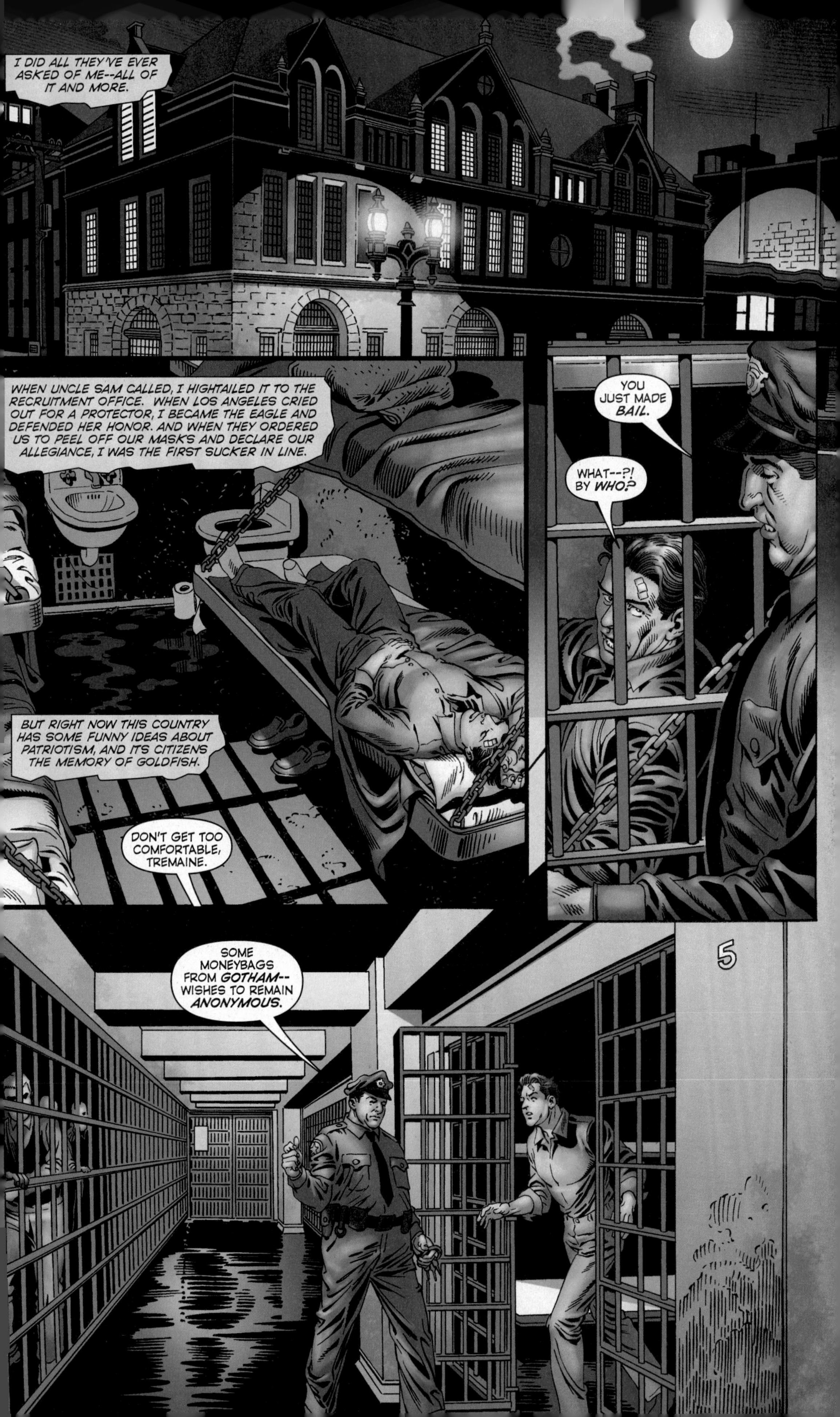
I DID ALL THEY'VE EVER ASKED OF ME--ALL OF IT AND MORE.
WHEN UNCLE SAM CALLED, I HIGHTAILED IT TO THE RECRUITMENT OFFICE. WHEN LOS ANGELES CRIED OUT FOR A PROTECTOR, I BECAME THE EAGLE AND DEFENDED HER HONOR. AND WHEN THEY ORDERED US TO PEEL OFF OUR MASKS AND DECLARE OUR ALLEGIANCE, I WAS THE FIRST SUCKER IN LINE.
BUT RIGHT NOW THIS COUNTRY HAS SOME FUNNY IDEAS ABOUT PATRIOTISM, AND ITS CITIZENS THE MEMORY OF GOLDFISH.
DON'T GET TOO COMFORTABLE, TREMAINE.
YOU JUST MADE BAIL.
WHAT--?! BY WHO?
SOME MONEYBAGS FROM GOTHAM-- WISHES TO REMAIN ANONYMOUS.
5

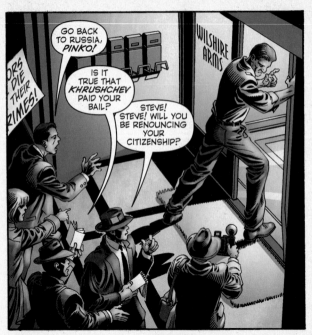

GO BACK TO RUSSIA, *PINKO!*

IS IT TRUE THAT *KHRUSHCHEV* PAID YOUR BAIL?

STEVE! STEVE! WILL YOU BE RENOUNCING YOUR CITIZENSHIP?

WILSHIRE ARMS

ORS DIE THEIR RIMES!

HELEN?

IT'S OKAY, SWEETIE. I CAN TAKE ANYTHING THOSE BASTARDS CAN DISH OUT.

NO, DAD. IT'S *IVAN.*

...ALSO KNOWN IN HIS HOME COUNTRY AS MASKED CRIME FIGHTER "THE BEAR," WAS FOUND DEAD AT THE SCENE. RUSSIAN AUTHORITIES ARE STILL INVESTIGATING THE CAUSE OF THE TRAIN DERAILMENT...

Philco

I... I'LL BE IN MY STUDY.

SORRY IT'S NOT VODKA, PARTNER.

SCOTCH WHISKY

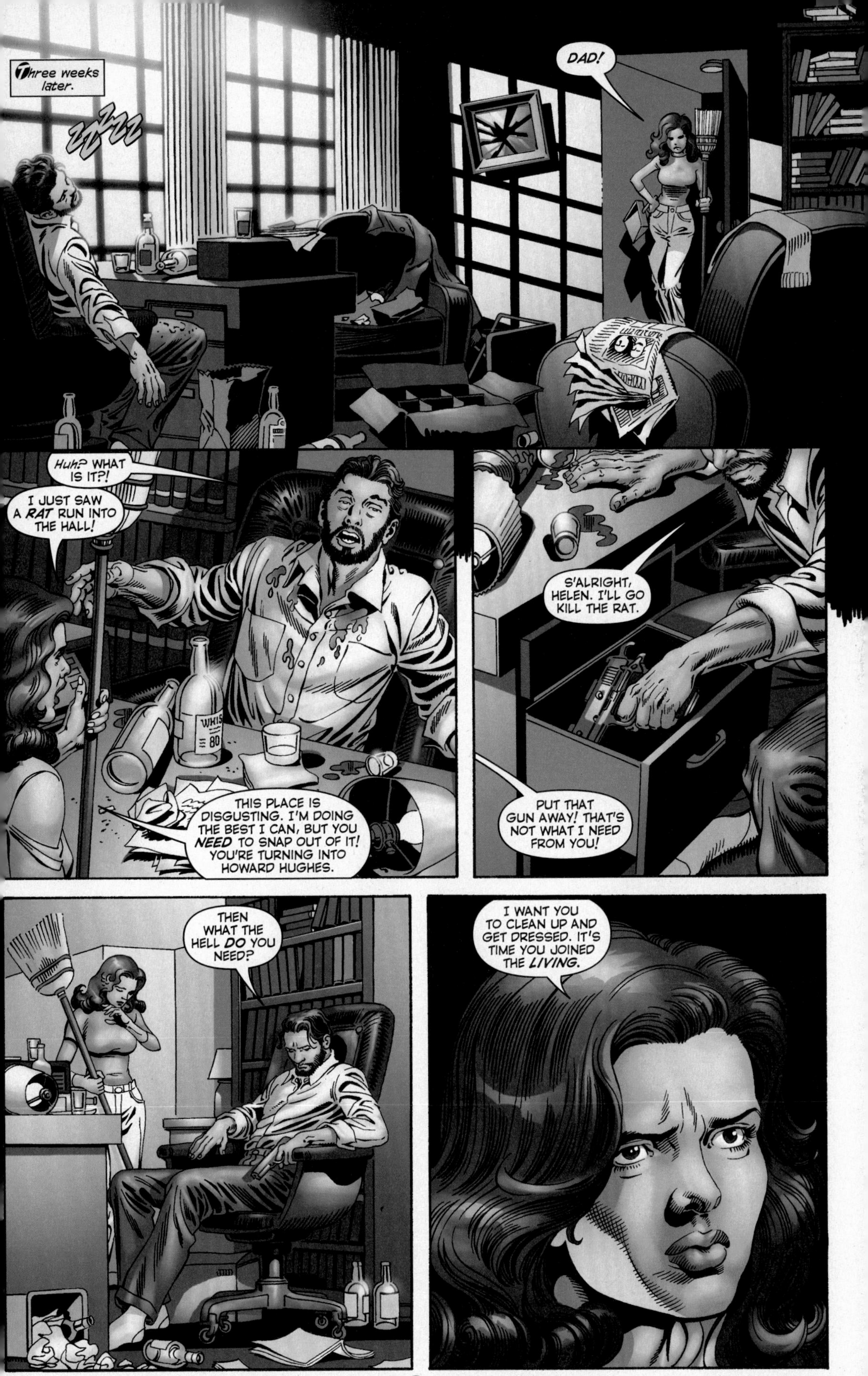
Three weeks later.
ZZZZZ
DAD!
Huh? WHAT IS IT?!
I JUST SAW A RAT RUN INTO THE HALL!
S'ALRIGHT, HELEN. I'LL GO KILL THE RAT.
THIS PLACE IS DISGUSTING. I'M DOING THE BEST I CAN, BUT YOU NEED TO SNAP OUT OF IT! YOU'RE TURNING INTO HOWARD HUGHES.
PUT THAT GUN AWAY! THAT'S NOT WHAT I NEED FROM YOU!
THEN WHAT THE HELL DO YOU NEED?
I WANT YOU TO CLEAN UP AND GET DRESSED. IT'S TIME YOU JOINED THE LIVING.

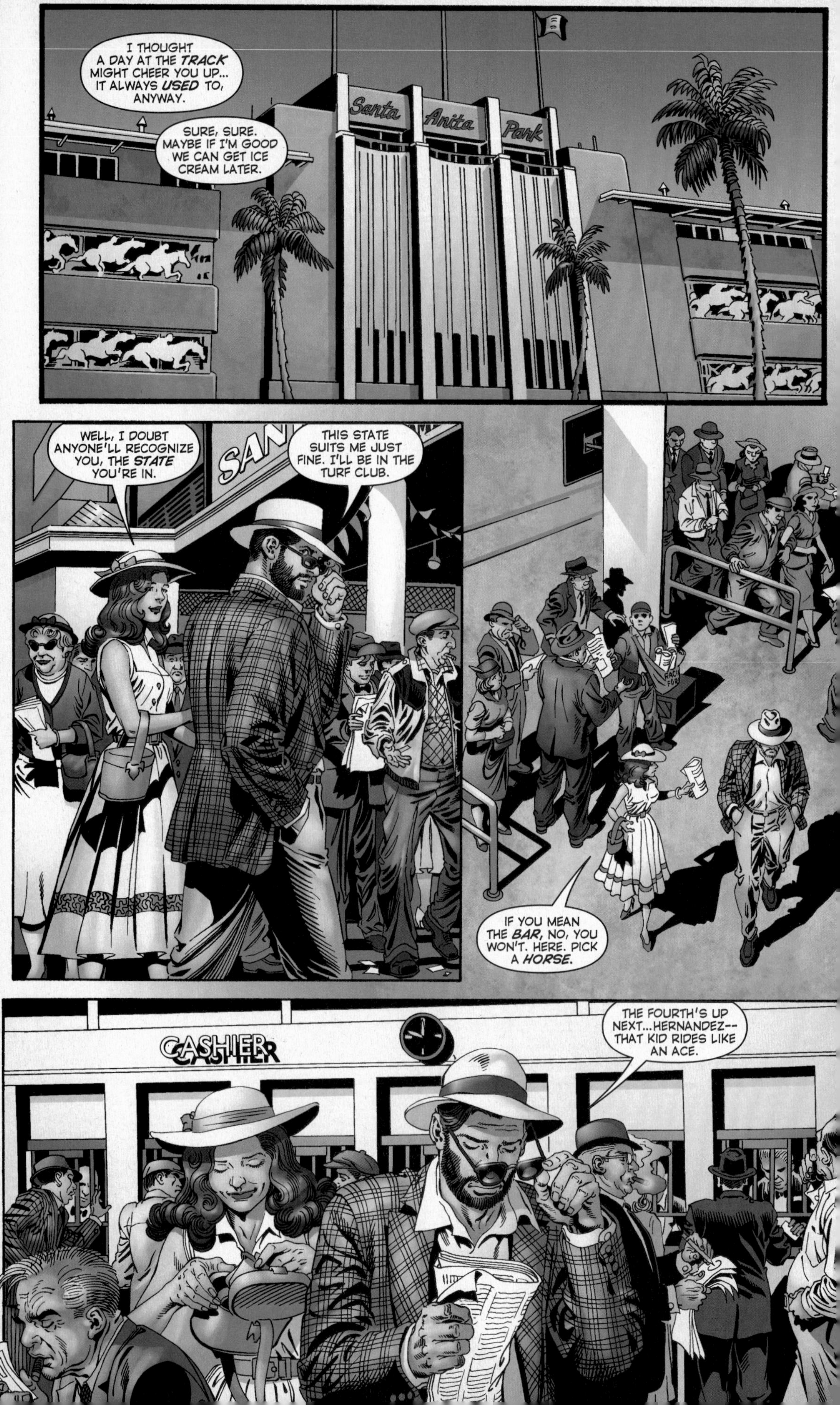

I THOUGHT A DAY AT THE TRACK MIGHT CHEER YOU UP... IT ALWAYS USED TO, ANYWAY.
SURE, SURE. MAYBE IF I'M GOOD WE CAN GET ICE CREAM LATER.
Santa Anita Park
WELL, I DOUBT ANYONE'LL RECOGNIZE YOU, THE STATE YOU'RE IN.
THIS STATE SUITS ME JUST FINE. I'LL BE IN THE TURF CLUB.
IF YOU MEAN THE BAR, NO, YOU WON'T. HERE. PICK A HORSE.
CASHIER
THE FOURTH'S UP NEXT...HERNANDEZ-- THAT KID RIDES LIKE AN ACE.

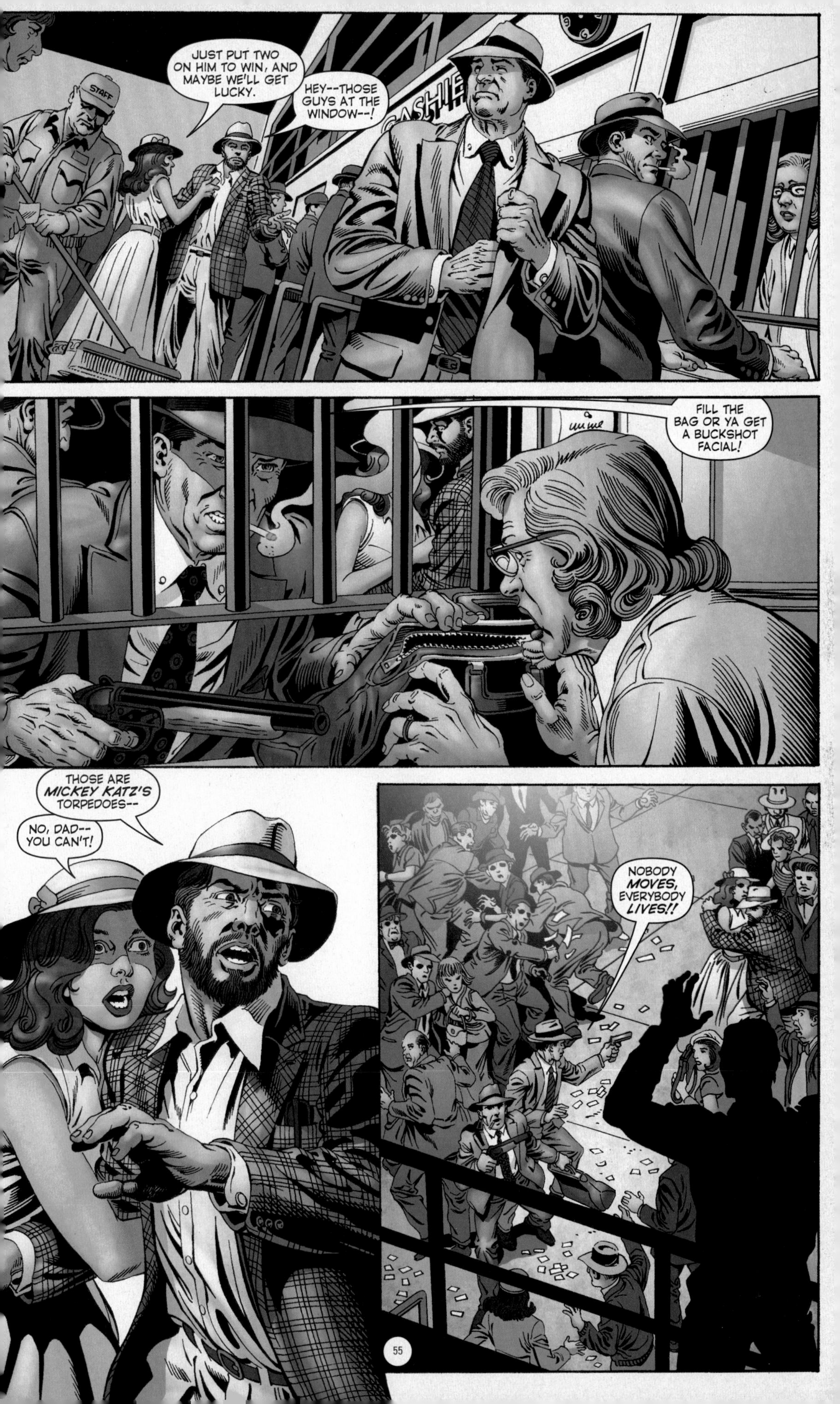

JUST PUT TWO ON HIM TO WIN, AND MAYBE WE'LL GET LUCKY.
HEY--THOSE GUYS AT THE WINDOW--!
STAFF
FILL THE BAG OR YA GET A BUCKSHOT FACIAL!
THOSE ARE *MICKEY KATZ'S* TORPEDOES--
NO, DAD-- YOU CAN'T!
NOBODY *MOVES*, EVERYBODY *LIVES!!*

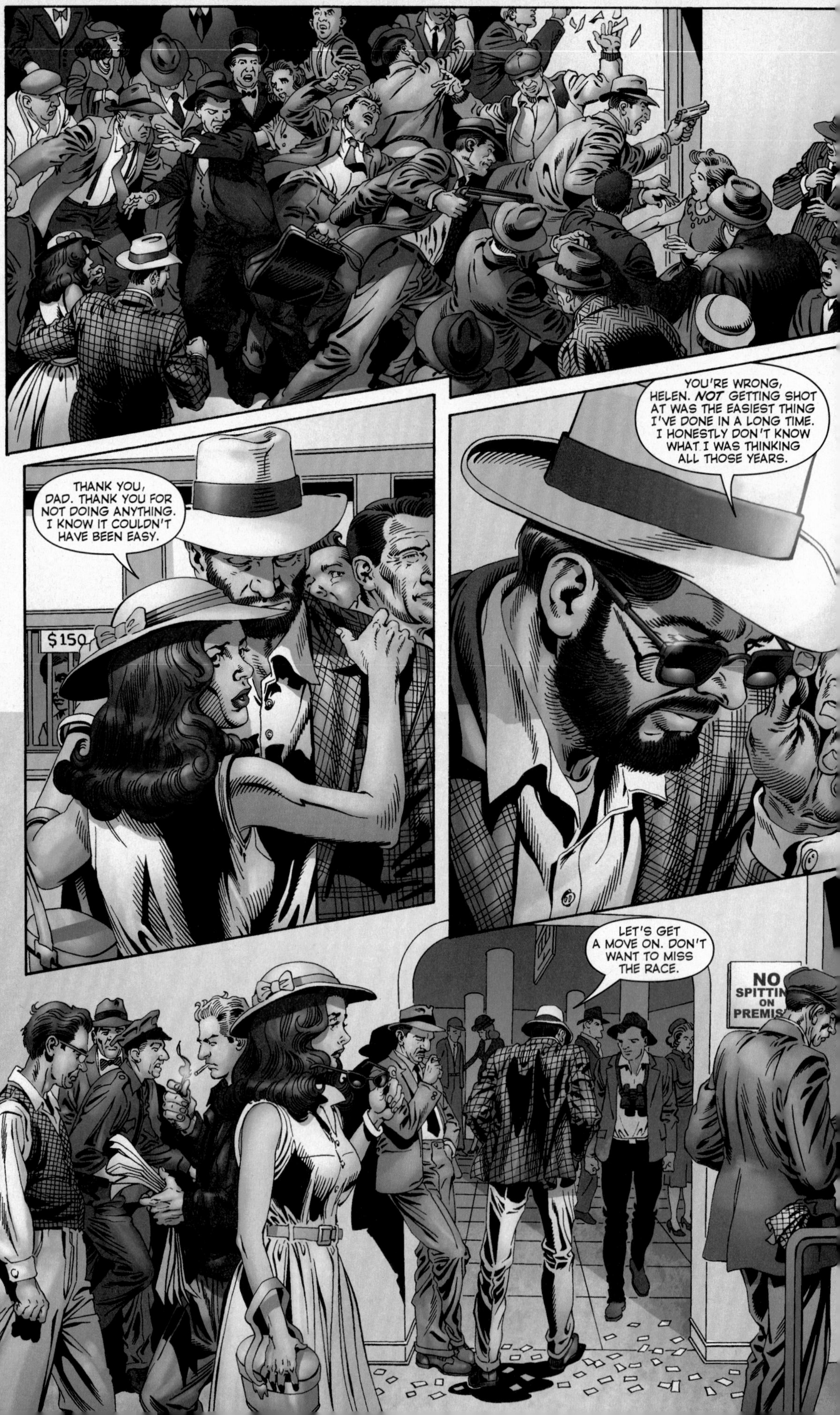
YOU'RE WRONG, HELEN. NOT GETTING SHOT AT WAS THE EASIEST THING I'VE DONE IN A LONG TIME. I HONESTLY DON'T KNOW WHAT I WAS THINKING ALL THOSE YEARS.
THANK YOU, DAD. THANK YOU FOR NOT DOING ANYTHING. I KNOW IT COULDN'T HAVE BEEN EASY.
$150
LET'S GET A MOVE ON. DON'T WANT TO MISS THE RACE.
NO SPITTIN ON PREMIS

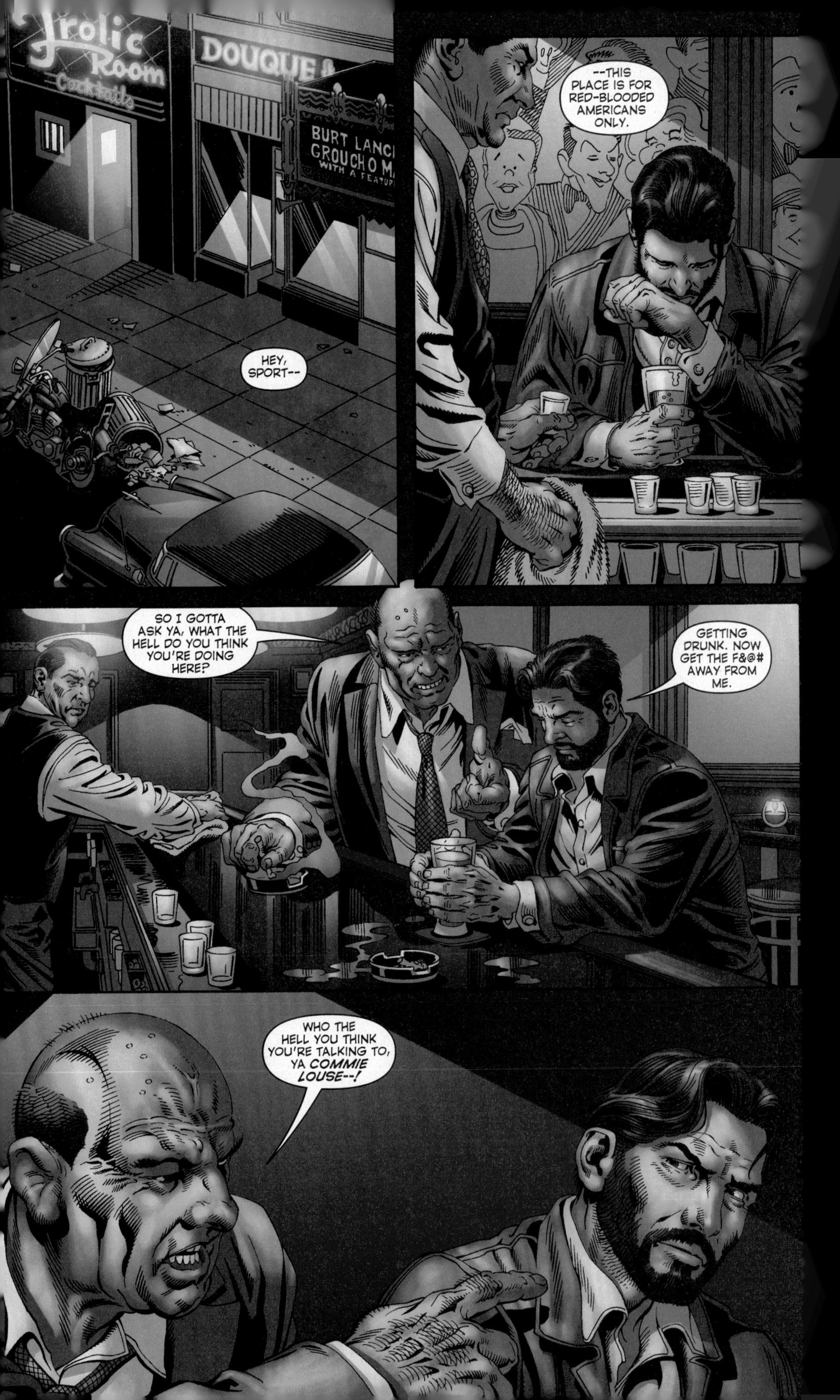
Frolic Room
Cocktails
DOUQUE
BURT LANC
GROUCHO M
WITH A FEATU
HEY, SPORT--
--THIS PLACE IS FOR RED-BLOODED AMERICANS ONLY.
SO I GOTTA ASK YA, WHAT THE HELL DO YOU THINK YOU'RE DOING HERE?
GETTING DRUNK. NOW GET THE F&@# AWAY FROM ME.
WHO THE HELL YOU THINK YOU'RE TALKING TO, YA *COMMIE LOUSE*--!

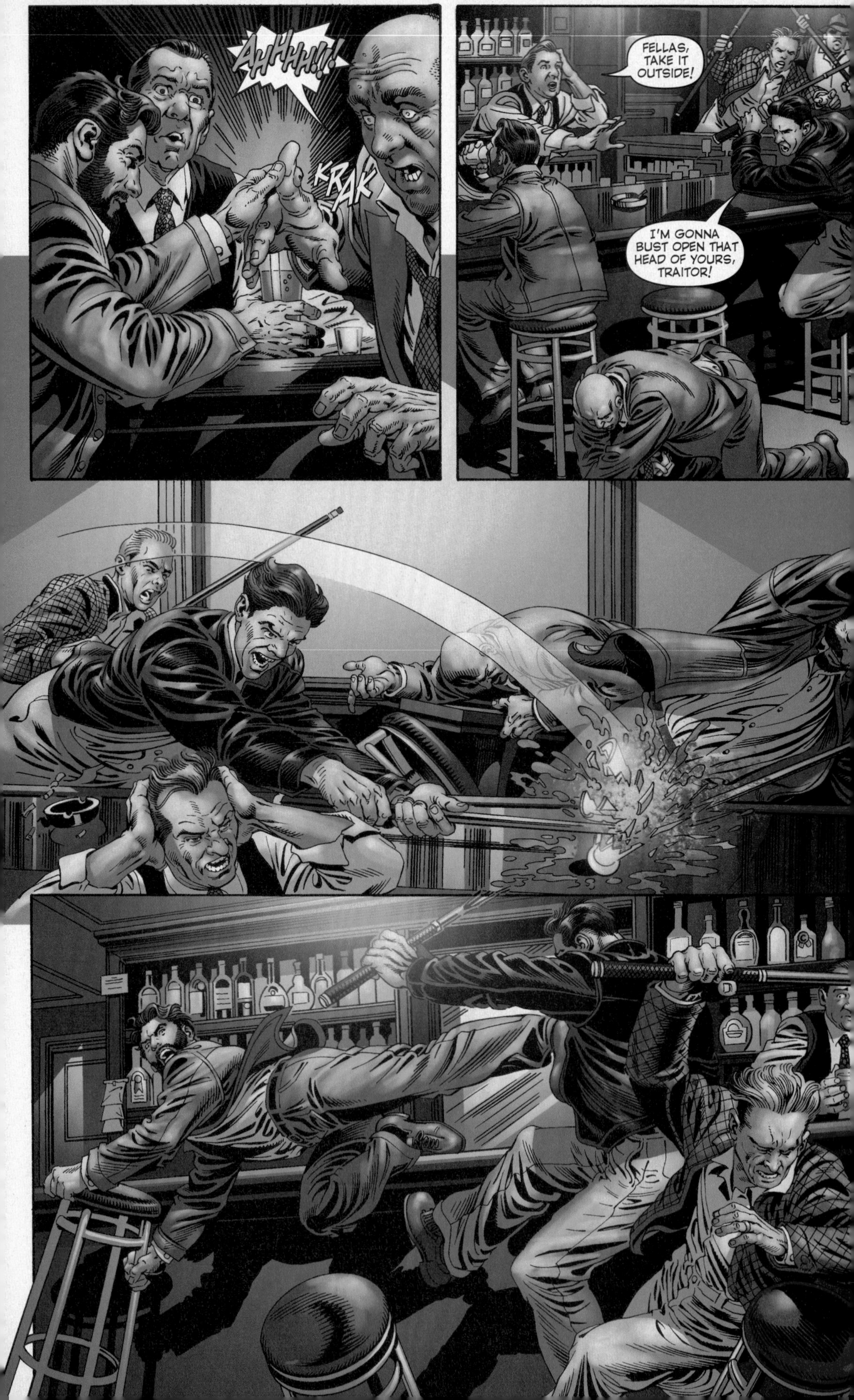
AHHHH!!!
KRAK
FELLAS, TAKE IT OUTSIDE!
I'M GONNA BUST OPEN THAT HEAD OF YOURS, TRAITOR!

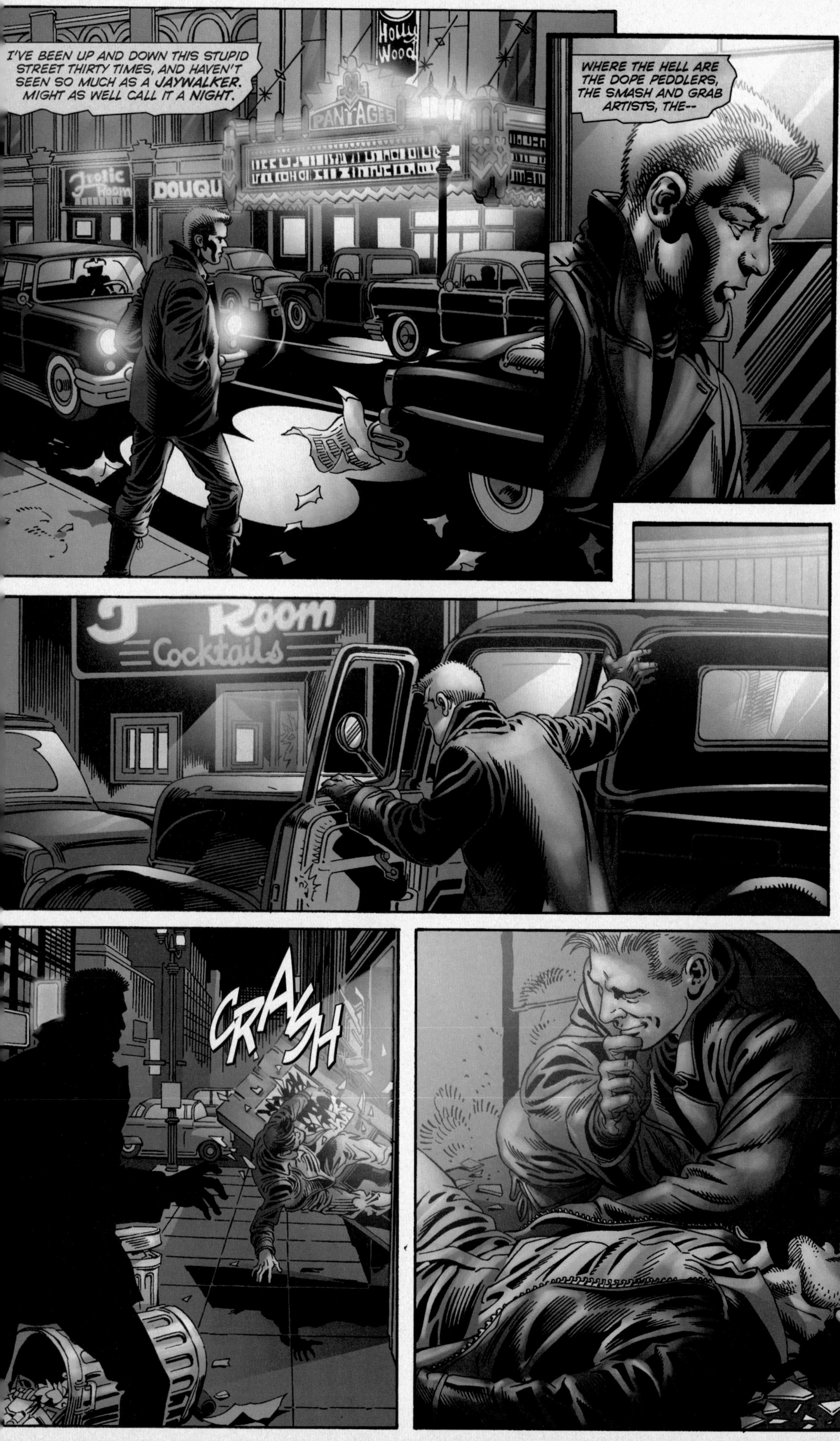
I'VE BEEN UP AND DOWN THIS STUPID STREET THIRTY TIMES, AND HAVEN'T SEEN SO MUCH AS A JAYWALKER. MIGHT AS WELL CALL IT A NIGHT.
Holly Wood
PANTAGES
Erotic Room
DOUQU
WHERE THE HELL ARE THE DOPE PEDDLERS, THE SMASH AND GRAB ARTISTS, THE--
Room
Cocktails
CRASH

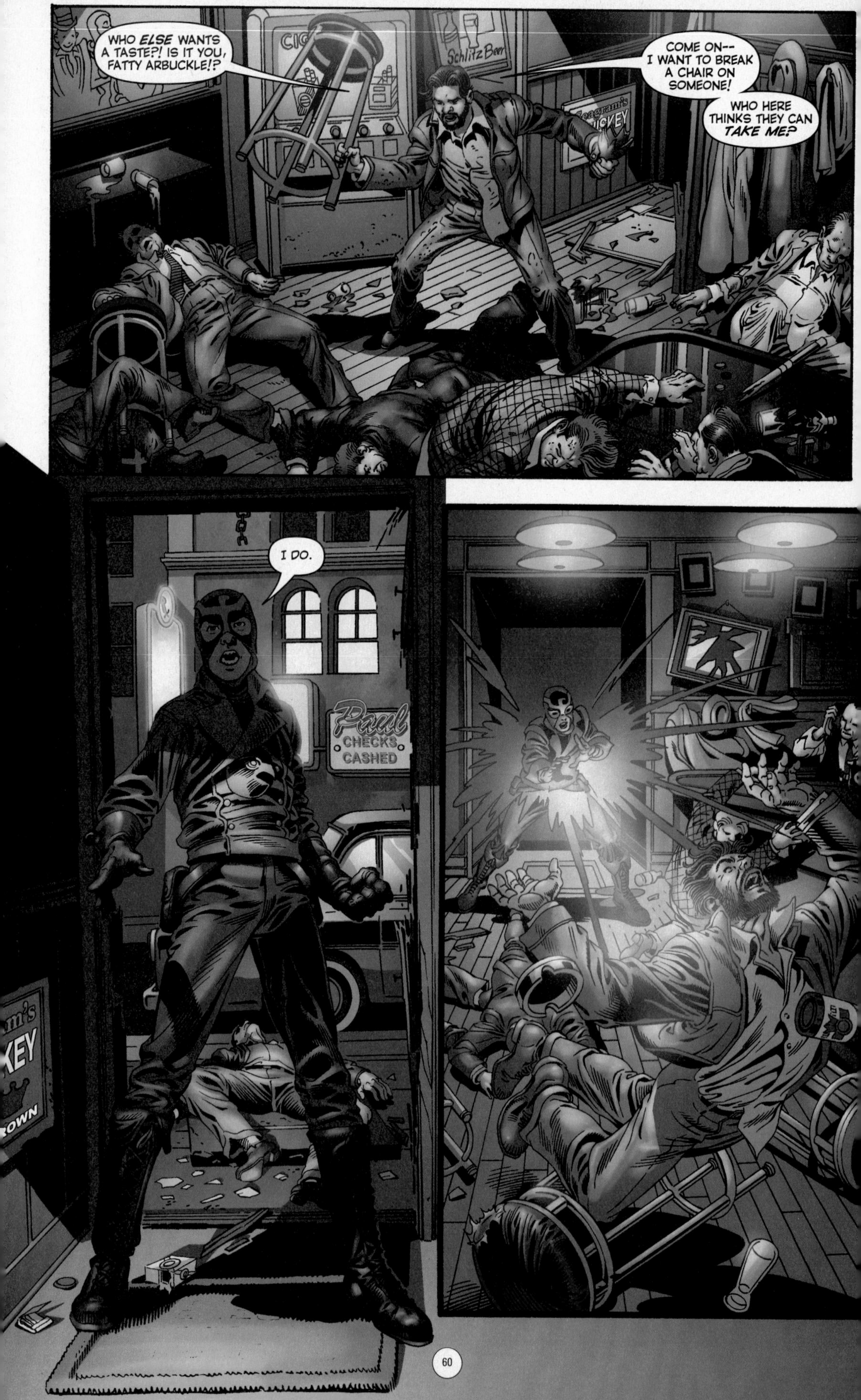
WHO ELSE WANTS A TASTE?! IS IT YOU, FATTY ARBUCKLE!?
COME ON-- I WANT TO BREAK A CHAIR ON SOMEONE!
WHO HERE THINKS THEY CAN TAKE ME?
I DO.
Paul CHECKS CASHED

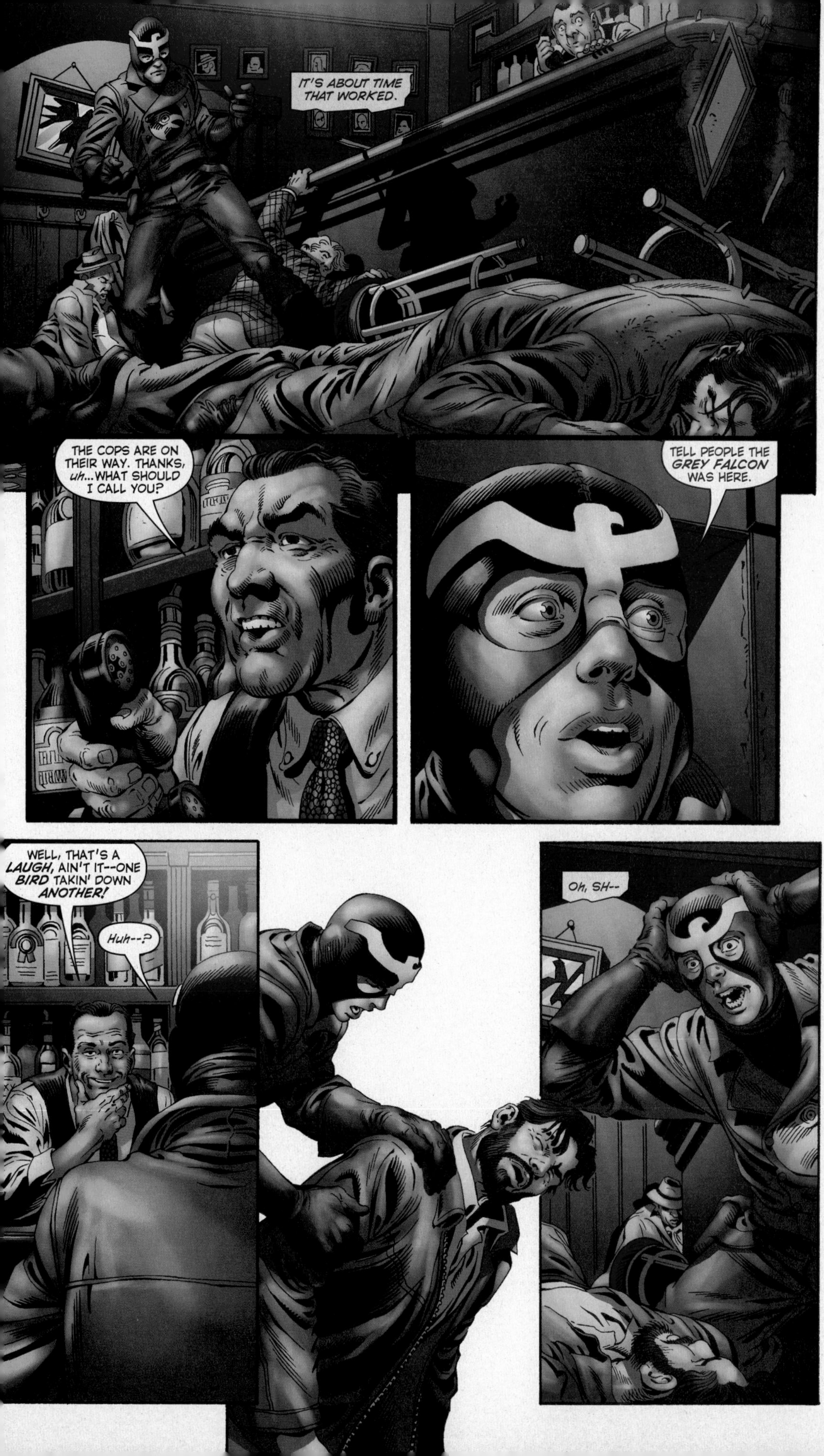
IT'S ABOUT TIME THAT WORKED.
THE COPS ARE ON THEIR WAY. THANKS, uh...WHAT SHOULD I CALL YOU?
TELL PEOPLE THE GREY FALCON WAS HERE.
WELL, THAT'S A LAUGH, AIN'T IT--ONE BIRD TAKIN' DOWN ANOTHER!
Huh--?
Oh, SH--

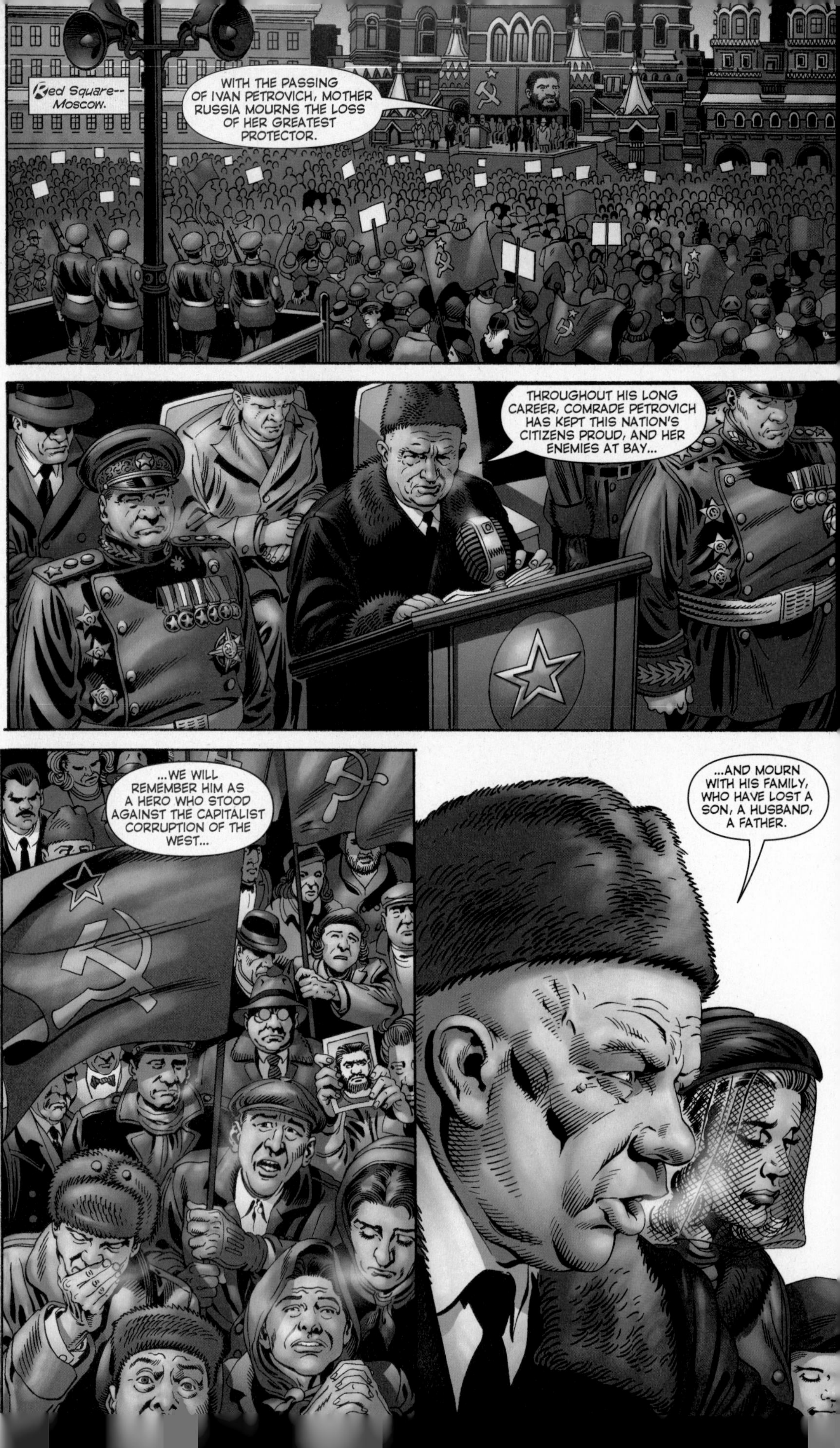
Red Square--Moscow.
WITH THE PASSING OF IVAN PETROVICH, MOTHER RUSSIA MOURNS THE LOSS OF HER GREATEST PROTECTOR.
THROUGHOUT HIS LONG CAREER, COMRADE PETROVICH HAS KEPT THIS NATION'S CITIZENS PROUD, AND HER ENEMIES AT BAY...
...WE WILL REMEMBER HIM AS A HERO WHO STOOD AGAINST THE CAPITALIST CORRUPTION OF THE WEST...
...AND MOURN WITH HIS FAMILY, WHO HAVE LOST A SON, A HUSBAND, A FATHER.

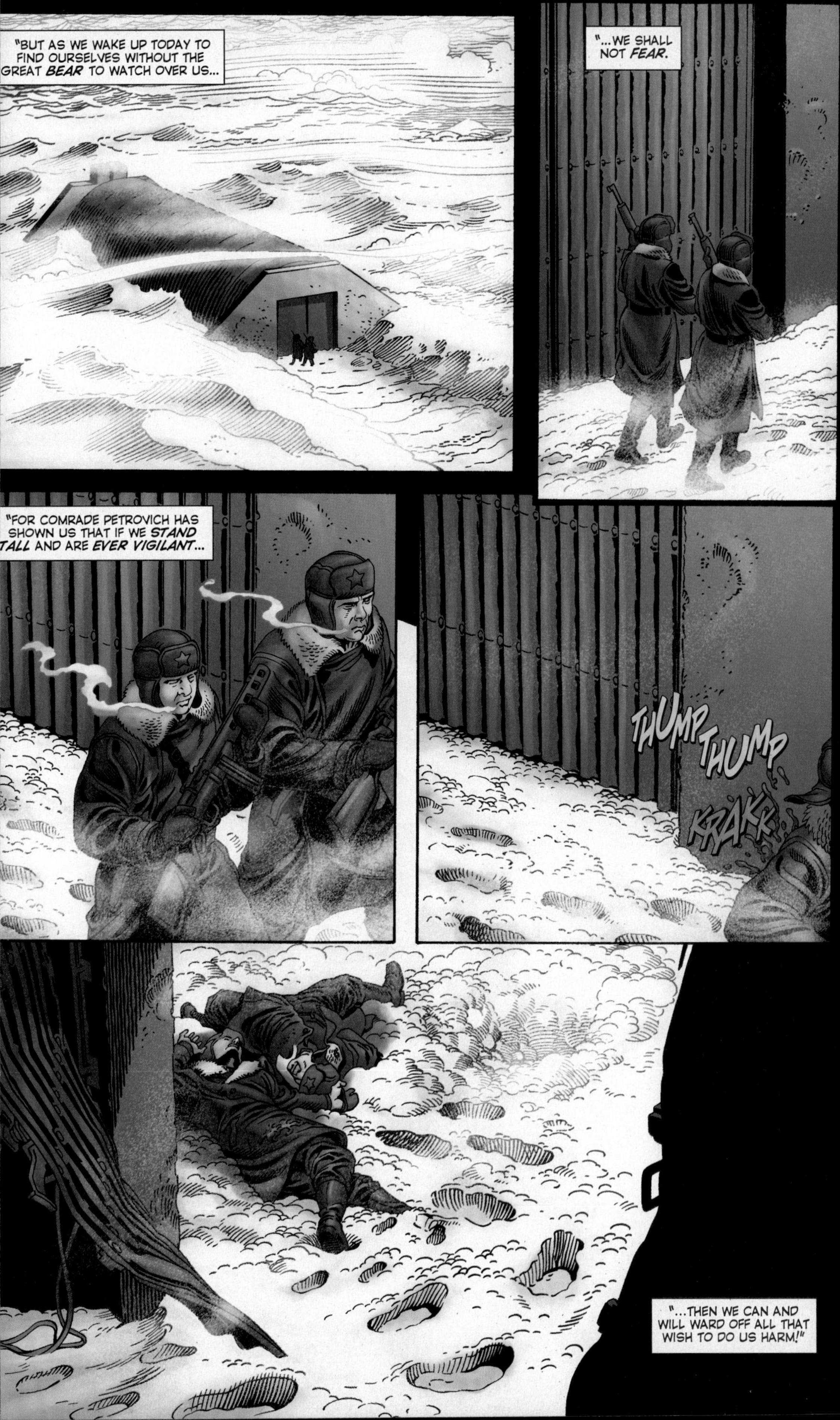
"BUT AS WE WAKE UP TODAY TO FIND OURSELVES WITHOUT THE GREAT BEAR TO WATCH OVER US...
"...WE SHALL NOT FEAR.
"FOR COMRADE PETROVICH HAS SHOWN US THAT IF WE STAND TALL AND ARE EVER VIGILANT...
THUMP THUMP
KRAKK
"...THEN WE CAN AND WILL WARD OFF ALL THAT WISH TO DO US HARM!"

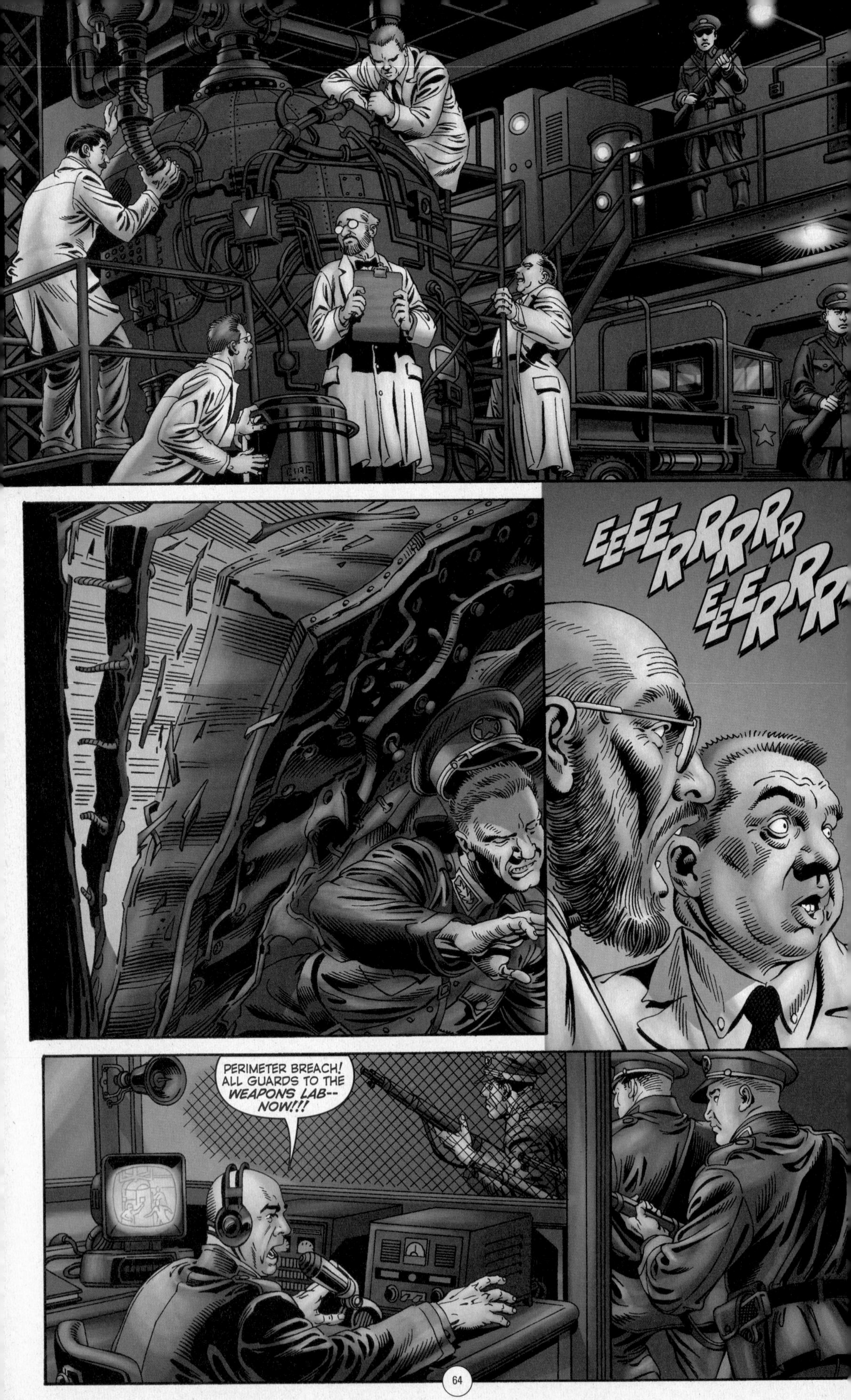
EEEERRRRR
EEERRR
PERIMETER BREACH! ALL GUARDS TO THE WEAPONS LAB-- NOW!!!

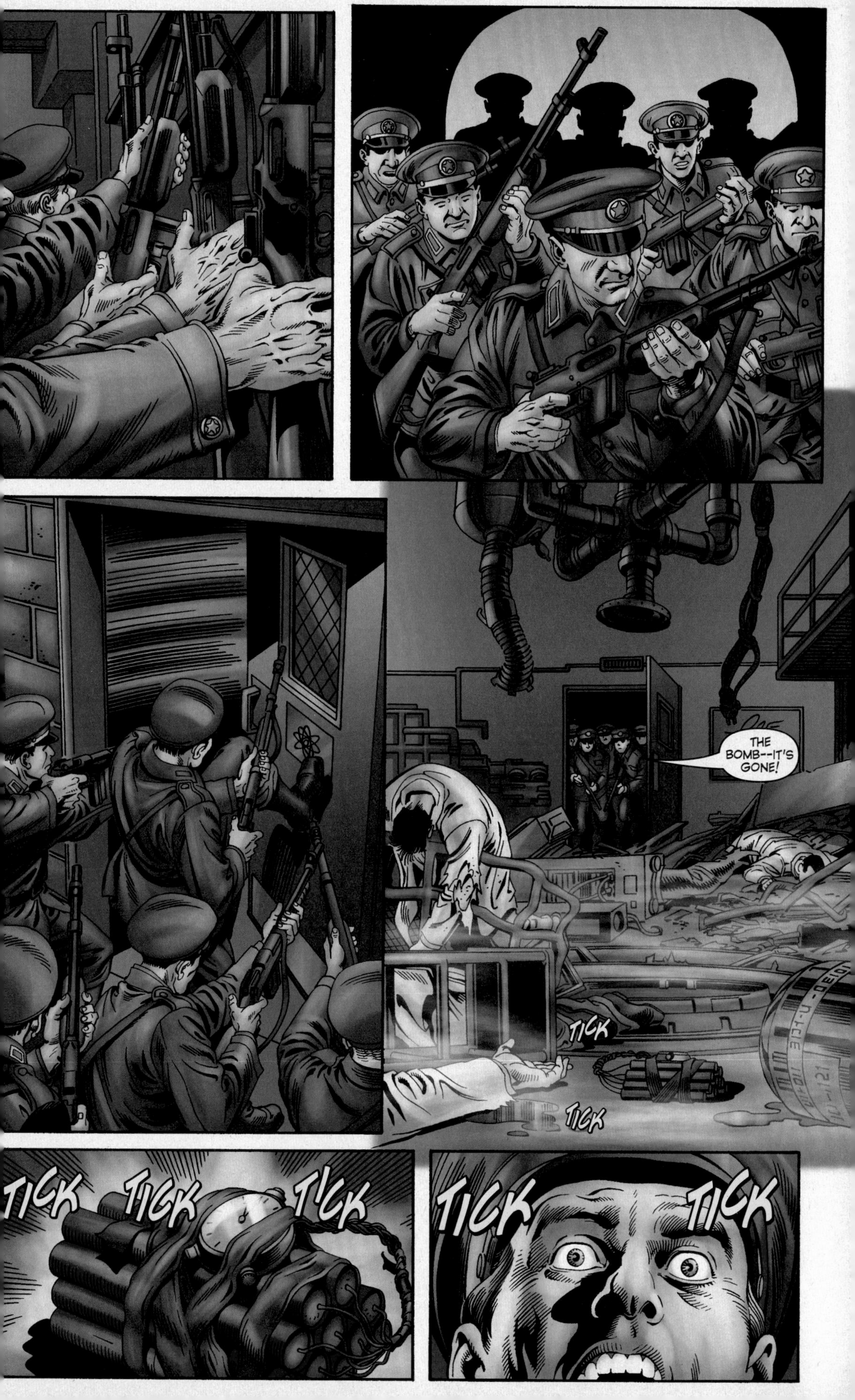
THE BOMB--IT'S GONE!
TICK
TICK
TICK TICK TICK
TICK TICK

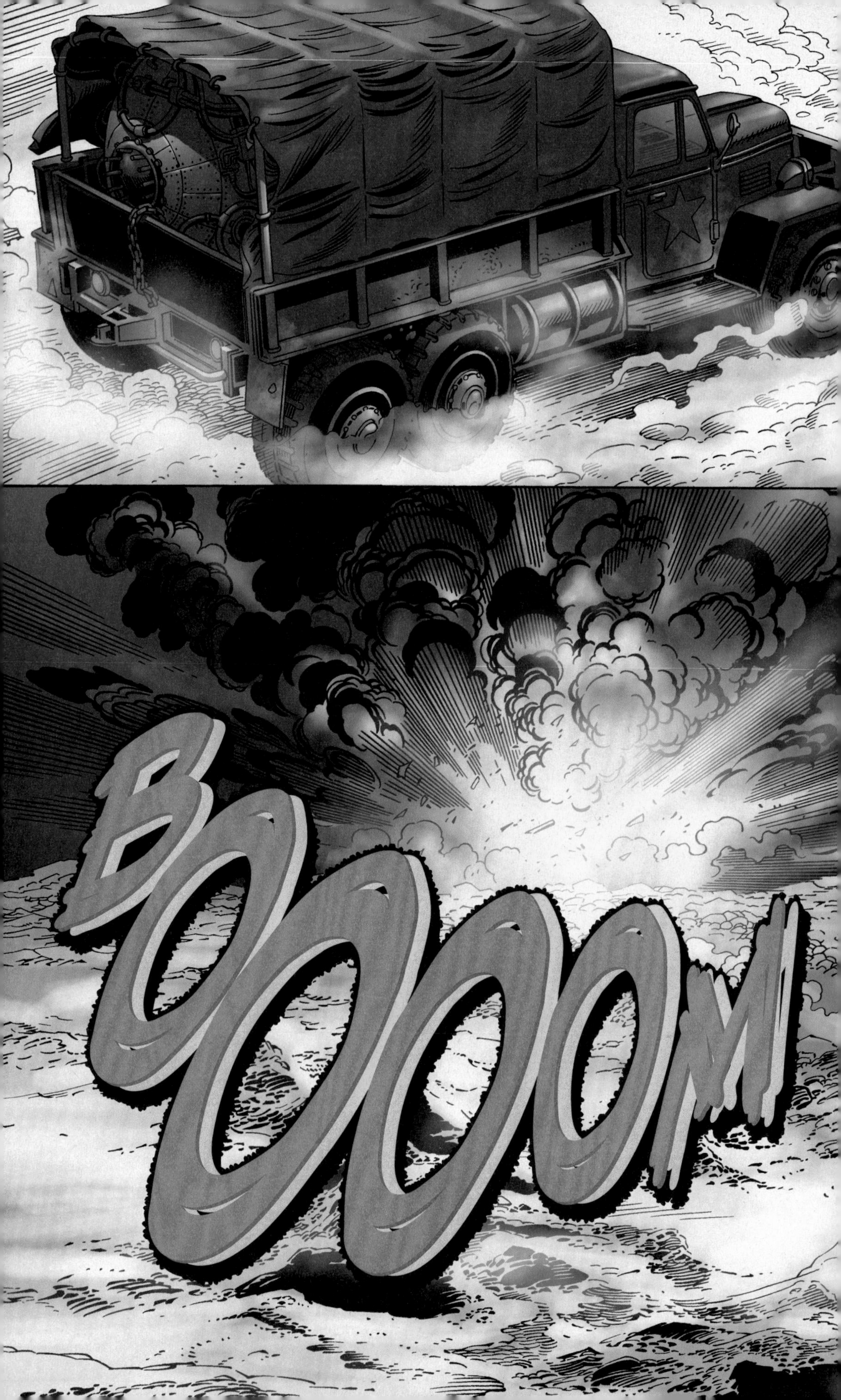
BOOOOOM!

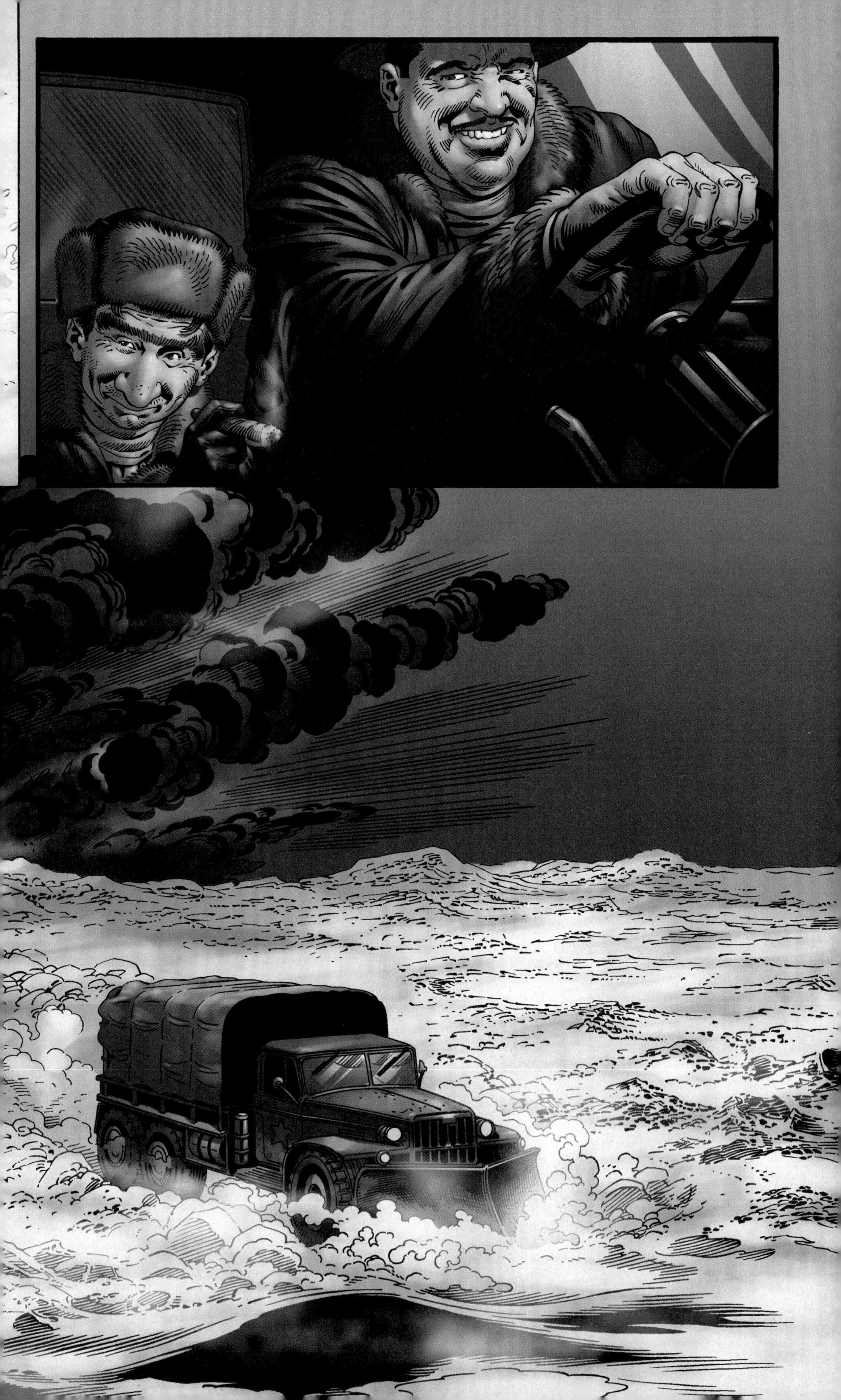

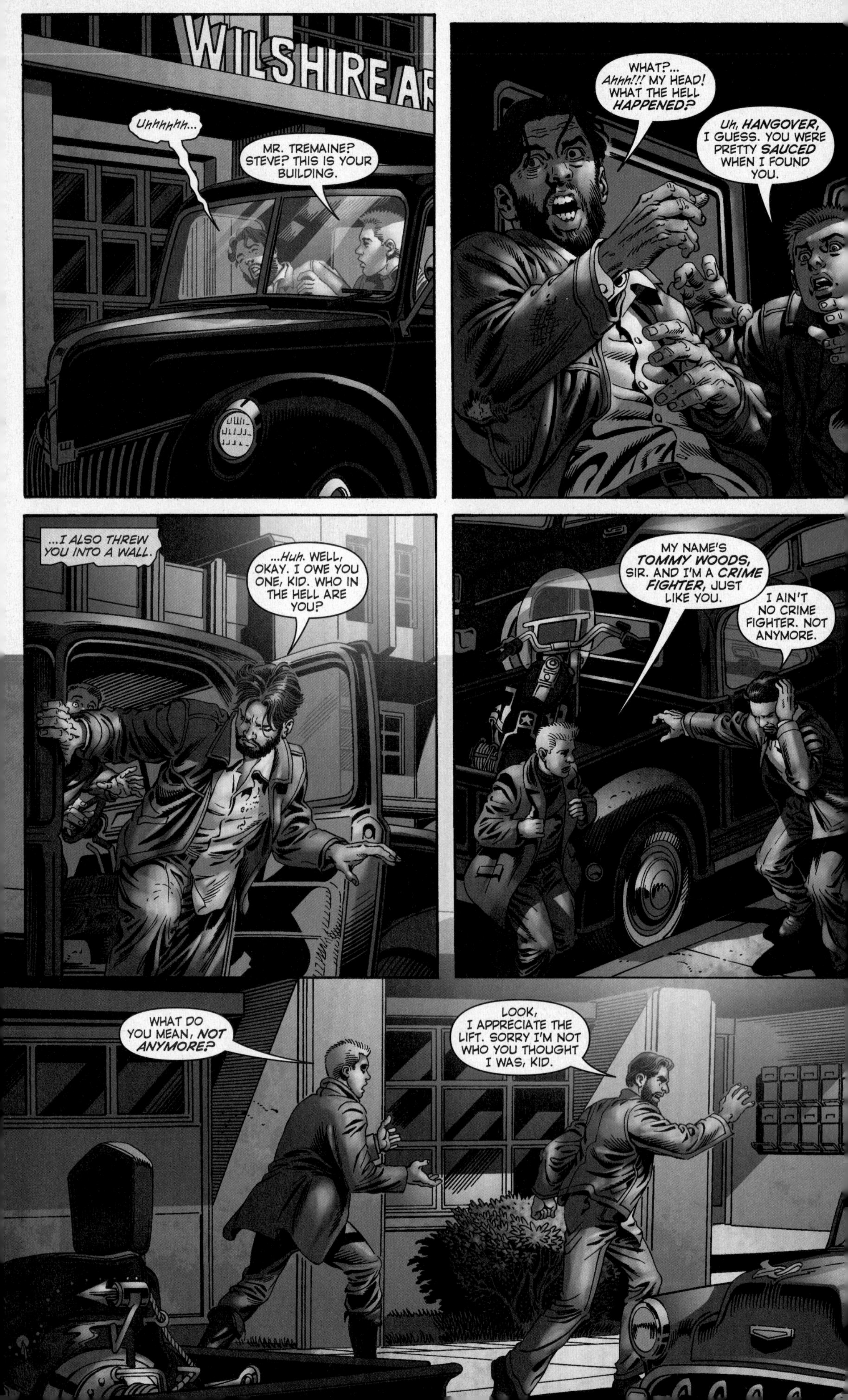
WILSHIRE AR
Unhhhhh...
MR. TREMAINE? STEVE? THIS IS YOUR BUILDING.
WHAT?... Ahhh!!! MY HEAD! WHAT THE HELL HAPPENED?
Uh, HANGOVER, I GUESS. YOU WERE PRETTY SAUCED WHEN I FOUND YOU.
...I ALSO THREW YOU INTO A WALL.
...Huh. WELL, OKAY. I OWE YOU ONE, KID. WHO IN THE HELL ARE YOU?
MY NAME'S TOMMY WOODS, SIR. AND I'M A CRIME FIGHTER, JUST LIKE YOU.
I AIN'T NO CRIME FIGHTER. NOT ANYMORE.
WHAT DO YOU MEAN, NOT ANYMORE?
LOOK, I APPRECIATE THE LIFT. SORRY I'M NOT WHO YOU THOUGHT I WAS, KID.

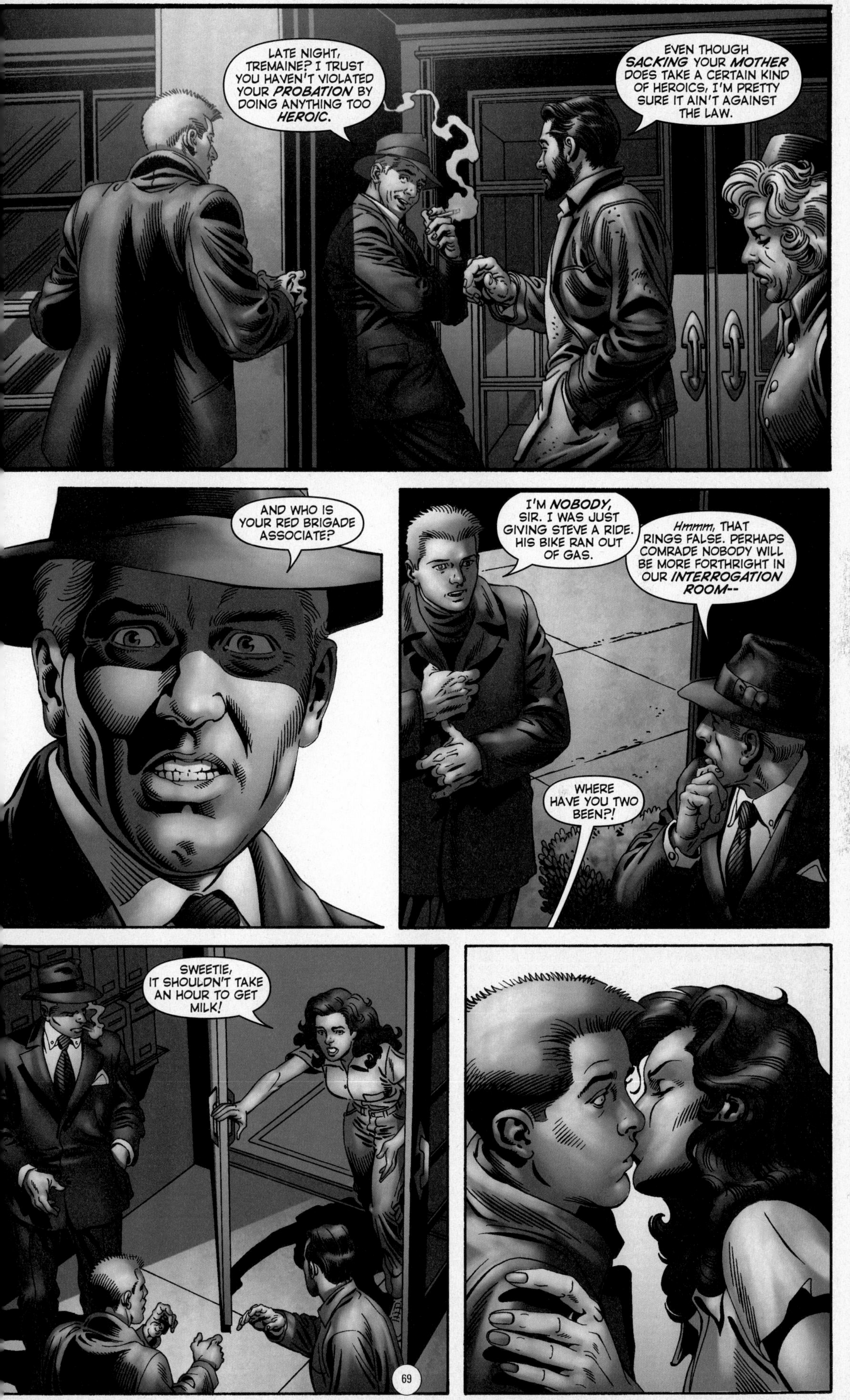
LATE NIGHT, TREMAINE? I TRUST YOU HAVEN'T VIOLATED YOUR *PROBATION* BY DOING ANYTHING TOO *HEROIC*.
EVEN THOUGH *SACKING* YOUR *MOTHER* DOES TAKE A CERTAIN KIND OF HEROICS, I'M PRETTY SURE IT AIN'T AGAINST THE LAW.
AND WHO IS YOUR RED BRIGADE ASSOCIATE?
I'M *NOBODY*, SIR. I WAS JUST GIVING STEVE A RIDE. HIS BIKE RAN OUT OF GAS.
Hmmm, THAT RINGS FALSE. PERHAPS COMRADE NOBODY WILL BE MORE FORTHRIGHT IN OUR *INTERROGATION ROOM--*
WHERE HAVE YOU TWO BEEN?!
SWEETIE, IT SHOULDN'T TAKE AN HOUR TO GET MILK!

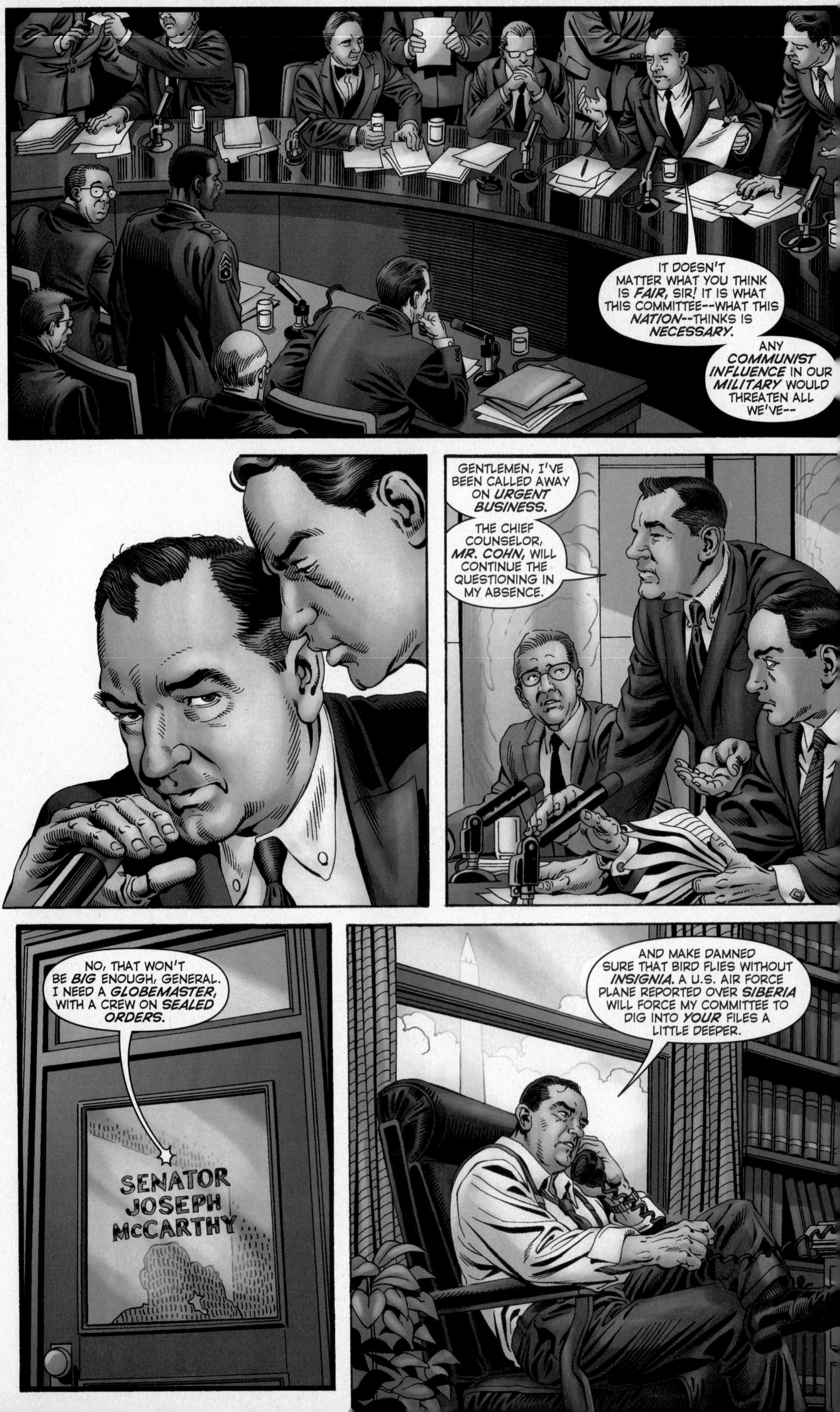
IT DOESN'T MATTER WHAT YOU THINK IS FAIR, SIR! IT IS WHAT THIS COMMITTEE--WHAT THIS NATION--THINKS IS NECESSARY.
ANY COMMUNIST INFLUENCE IN OUR MILITARY WOULD THREATEN ALL WE'VE--
GENTLEMEN, I'VE BEEN CALLED AWAY ON URGENT BUSINESS.
THE CHIEF COUNSELOR, MR. COHN, WILL CONTINUE THE QUESTIONING IN MY ABSENCE.
NO, THAT WON'T BE BIG ENOUGH, GENERAL. I NEED A GLOBEMASTER, WITH A CREW ON SEALED ORDERS.
SENATOR JOSEPH McCARTHY
AND MAKE DAMNED SURE THAT BIRD FLIES WITHOUT INSIGNIA. A U.S. AIR FORCE PLANE REPORTED OVER SIBERIA WILL FORCE MY COMMITTEE TO DIG INTO YOUR FILES A LITTLE DEEPER.

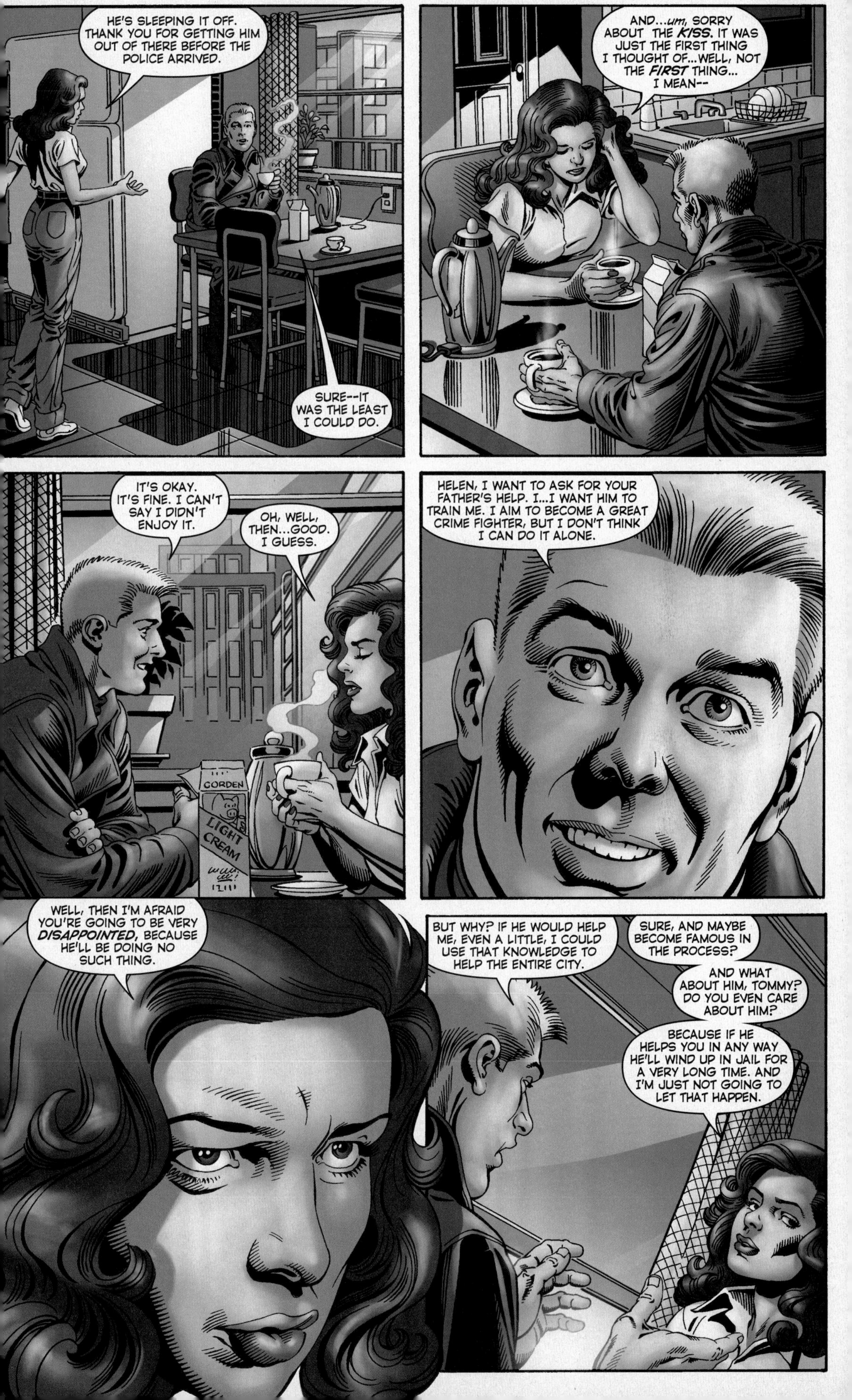
HE'S SLEEPING IT OFF. THANK YOU FOR GETTING HIM OUT OF THERE BEFORE THE POLICE ARRIVED.
SURE--IT WAS THE LEAST I COULD DO.
AND...um, SORRY ABOUT THE KISS. IT WAS JUST THE FIRST THING I THOUGHT OF...WELL, NOT THE FIRST THING... I MEAN--
IT'S OKAY. IT'S FINE. I CAN'T SAY I DIDN'T ENJOY IT.
OH, WELL, THEN...GOOD. I GUESS.
GORDEN
LIGHT CREAM
HELEN, I WANT TO ASK FOR YOUR FATHER'S HELP. I...I WANT HIM TO TRAIN ME. I AIM TO BECOME A GREAT CRIME FIGHTER, BUT I DON'T THINK I CAN DO IT ALONE.
WELL, THEN I'M AFRAID YOU'RE GOING TO BE VERY DISAPPOINTED, BECAUSE HE'LL BE DOING NO SUCH THING.
BUT WHY? IF HE WOULD HELP ME, EVEN A LITTLE, I COULD USE THAT KNOWLEDGE TO HELP THE ENTIRE CITY.
SURE, AND MAYBE BECOME FAMOUS IN THE PROCESS?
AND WHAT ABOUT HIM, TOMMY? DO YOU EVEN CARE ABOUT HIM?
BECAUSE IF HE HELPS YOU IN ANY WAY HE'LL WIND UP IN JAIL FOR A VERY LONG TIME. AND I'M JUST NOT GOING TO LET THAT HAPPEN.

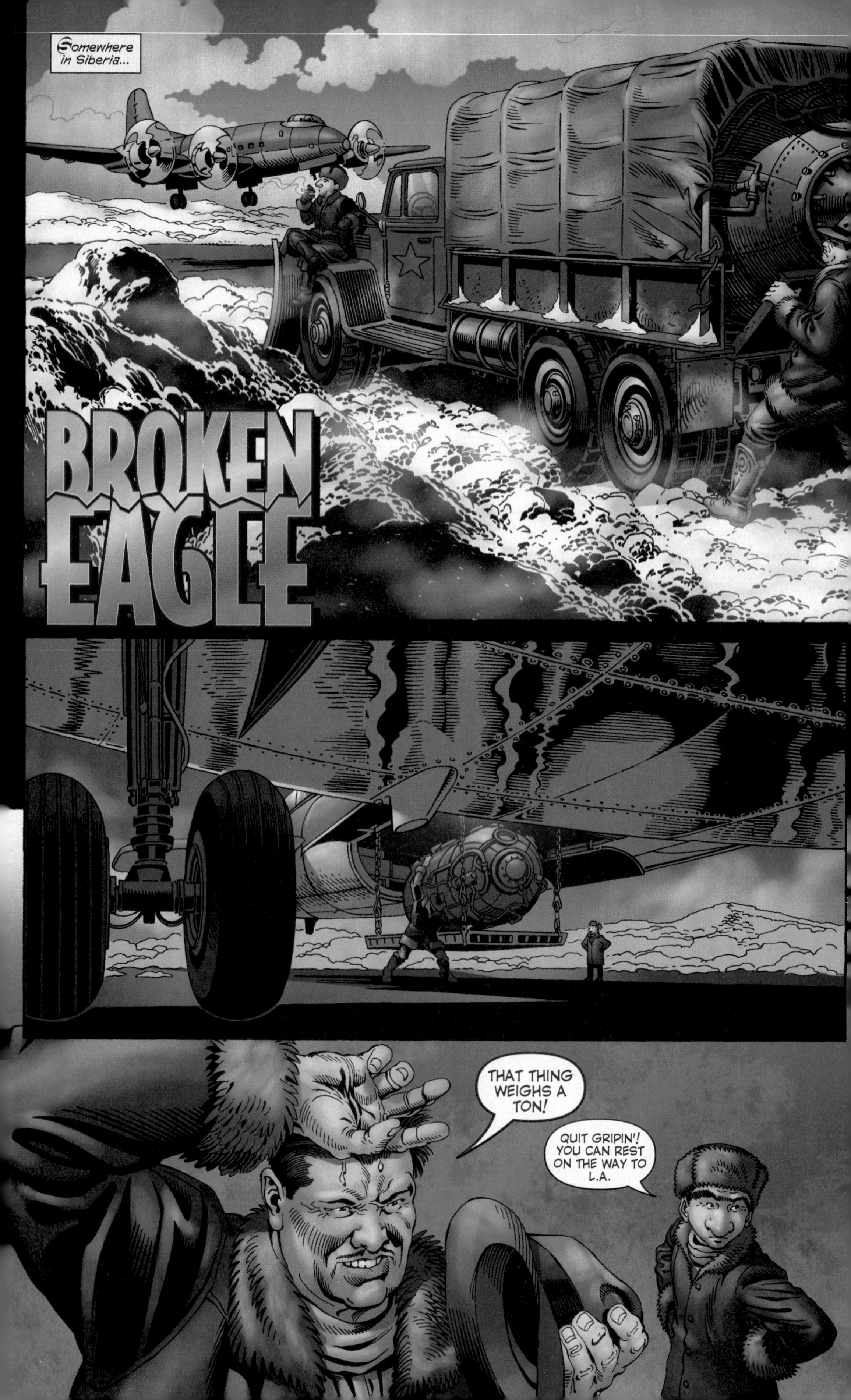
Somewhere in Siberia...
BROKEN EAGLE
THAT THING WEIGHS A TON!
QUIT GRIPIN'! YOU CAN REST ON THE WAY TO L.A.

HAPTER 4

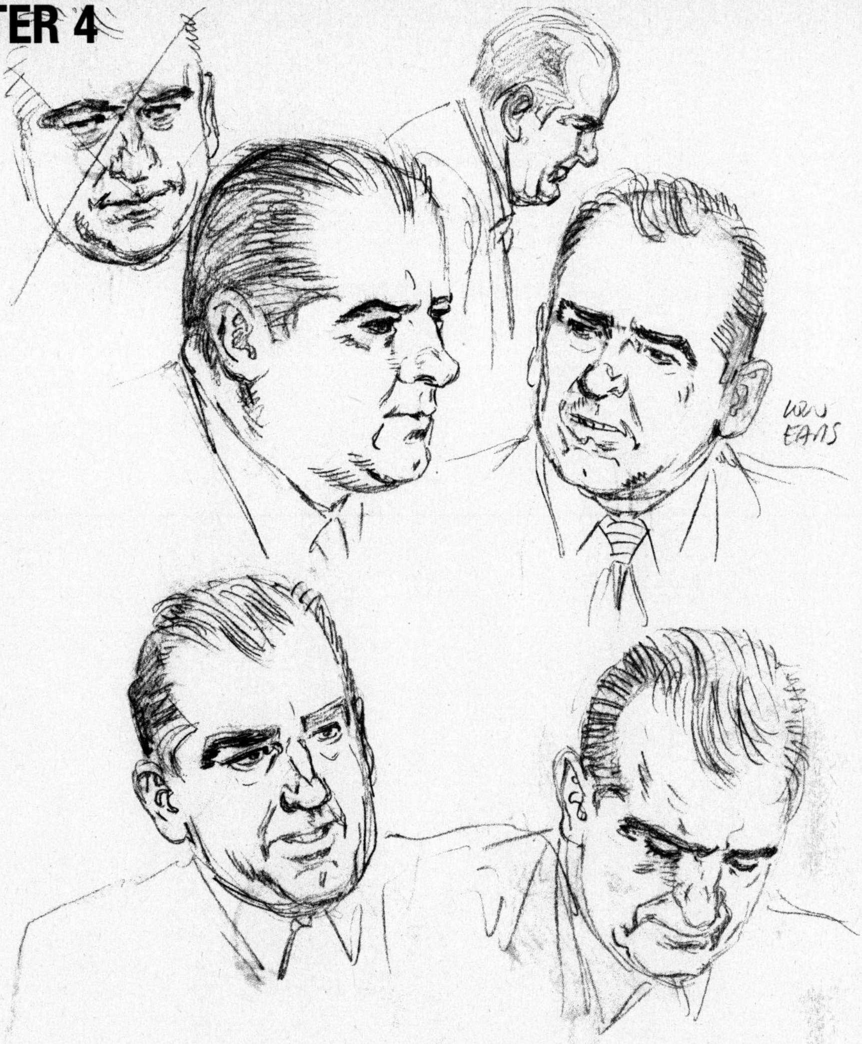

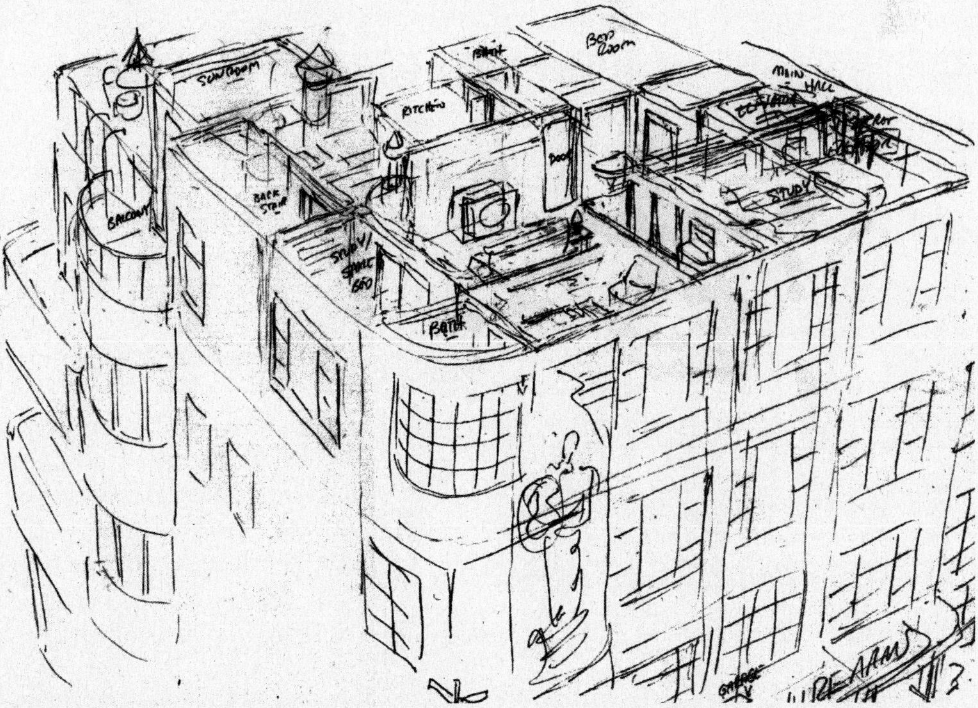
SUNROOM
BATH
BED ROOM
MAIN HALL
KITCHEN
DOOR
STUDY
BACK STAIR
BALCONY

Red Menace

NEW BIRD ON THE ROCK

APR 07

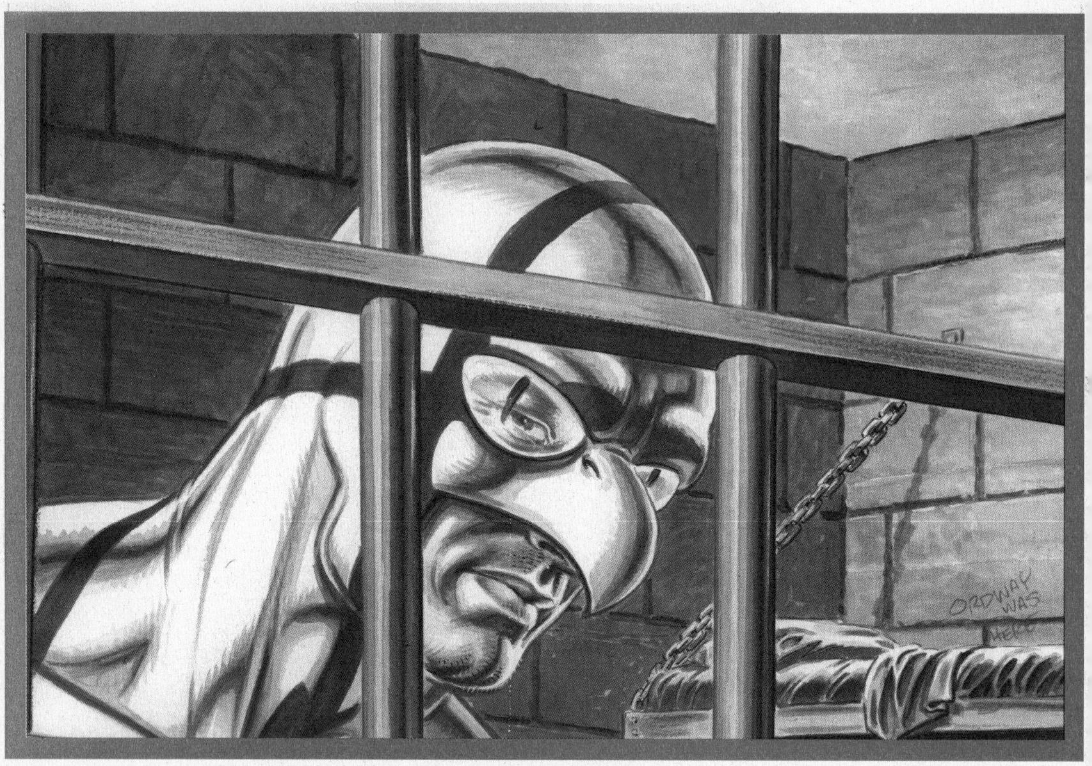
ORDWAY WAS HERE

HOOVER'S NEW FBI AGENTS PUT EAGLE INTO ALCATRAZ

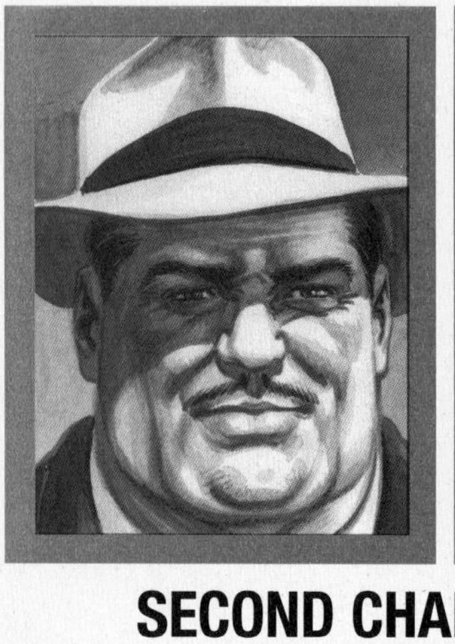

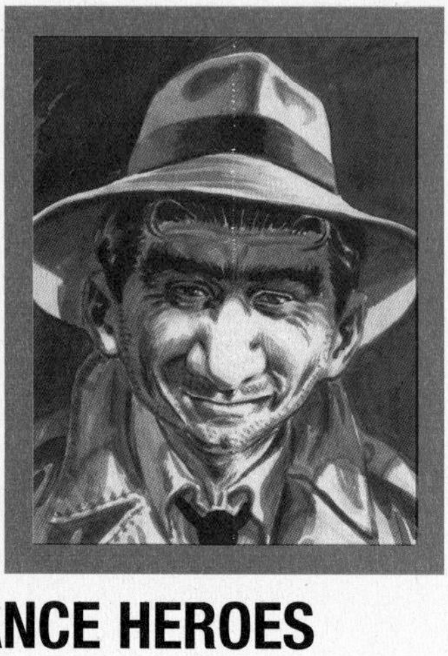

SECOND CHANCE HEROES

Drago's gang shoots up a Mick Coleman owned bookie joi Newsmen report on the escalation gang violence tearing up L.A. Repor Ed Murrow is even so bold as to blar the current situation in Los Angeles the loss of the Eagle to the "Red Scar

Tommy arrives and begs his way claiming to have a plan to capture fu tive Mickey Coleman and stop the ga war. He wants to show Steve plan…he's even drawn it up with blu prints. He knows that a big summit going down at the Ambassador Ho later that night. The Grey Falcon w make his mark. Steve tells the kid stay home and stay out of trouble…

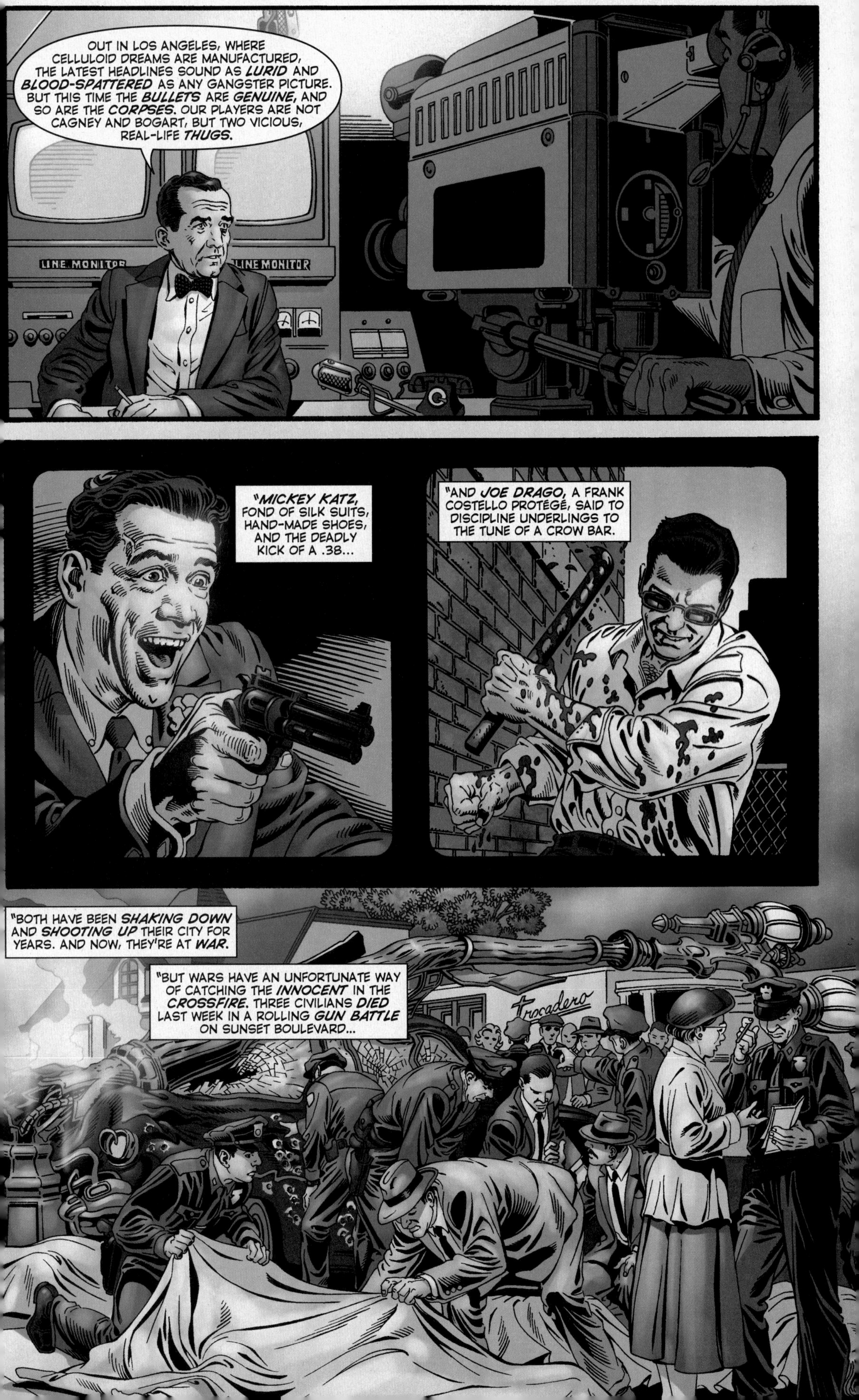
OUT IN LOS ANGELES, WHERE CELLULOID DREAMS ARE MANUFACTURED, THE LATEST HEADLINES SOUND AS LURID AND BLOOD-SPATTERED AS ANY GANGSTER PICTURE. BUT THIS TIME THE BULLETS ARE GENUINE, AND SO ARE THE CORPSES. OUR PLAYERS ARE NOT CAGNEY AND BOGART, BUT TWO VICIOUS, REAL-LIFE THUGS.
LINE MONITOR
LINE MONITOR
"MICKEY KATZ, FOND OF SILK SUITS, HAND-MADE SHOES, AND THE DEADLY KICK OF A .38...
"AND JOE DRAGO, A FRANK COSTELLO PROTÉGÉ, SAID TO DISCIPLINE UNDERLINGS TO THE TUNE OF A CROW BAR.
"BOTH HAVE BEEN SHAKING DOWN AND SHOOTING UP THEIR CITY FOR YEARS. AND NOW, THEY'RE AT WAR.
"BUT WARS HAVE AN UNFORTUNATE WAY OF CATCHING THE INNOCENT IN THE CROSSFIRE. THREE CIVILIANS DIED LAST WEEK IN A ROLLING GUN BATTLE ON SUNSET BOULEVARD...
Trocadero

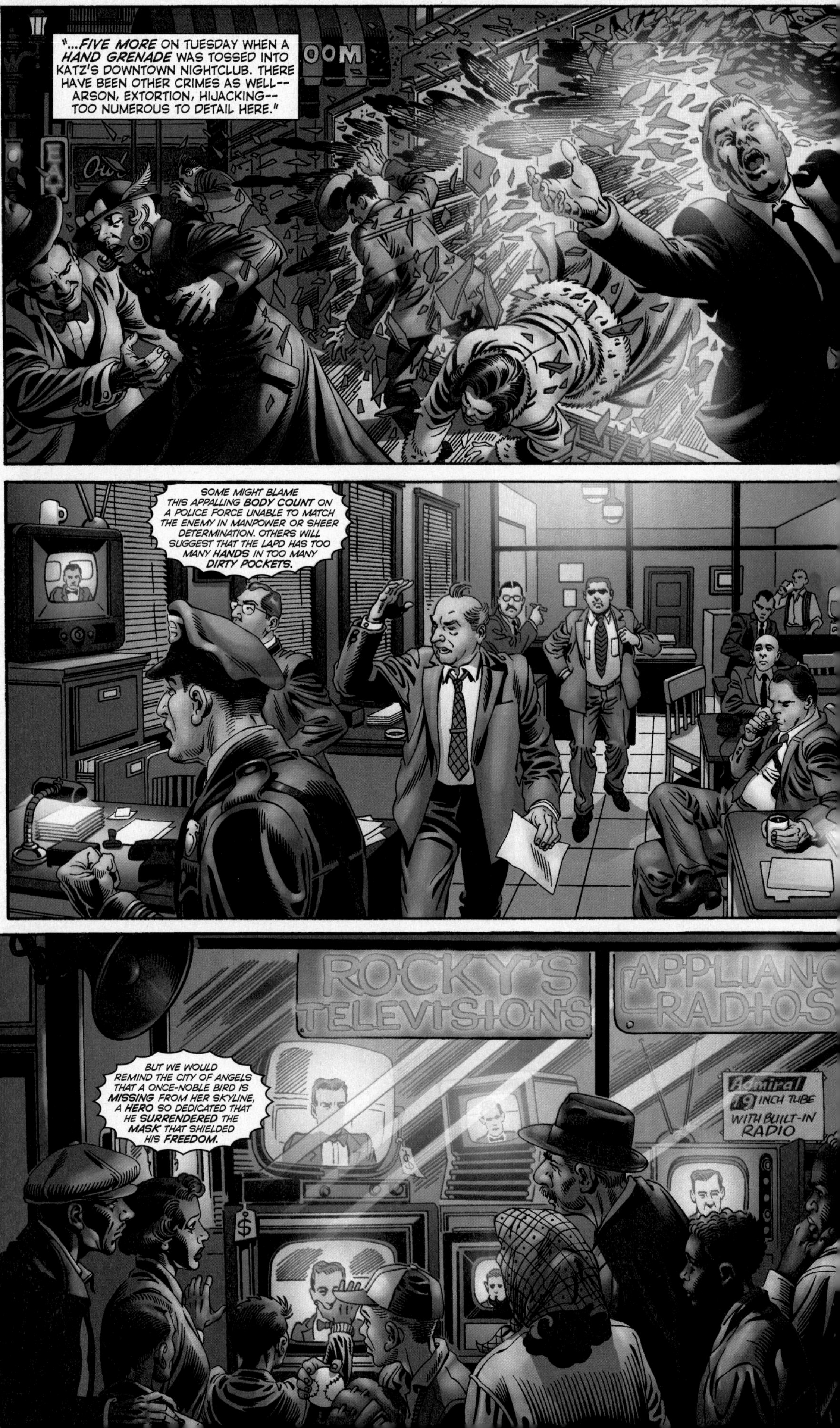
"...FIVE MORE ON TUESDAY WHEN A HAND GRENADE WAS TOSSED INTO KATZ'S DOWNTOWN NIGHTCLUB. THERE HAVE BEEN OTHER CRIMES AS WELL-- ARSON, EXTORTION, HIJACKING-- TOO NUMEROUS TO DETAIL HERE."
OOM
SOME MIGHT BLAME THIS APPALLING BODY COUNT ON A POLICE FORCE UNABLE TO MATCH THE ENEMY IN MANPOWER OR SHEER DETERMINATION. OTHERS WILL SUGGEST THAT THE LAPD HAS TOO MANY HANDS IN TOO MANY DIRTY POCKETS.
ROCKY'S
TELEVISIONS
APPLIANC
RADIOS
BUT WE WOULD REMIND THE CITY OF ANGELS THAT A ONCE-NOBLE BIRD IS MISSING FROM HER SKYLINE, A HERO SO DEDICATED THAT HE SURRENDERED THE MASK THAT SHIELDED HIS FREEDOM.
Admiral
19 INCH TUBE
WITH BUILT-IN
RADIO

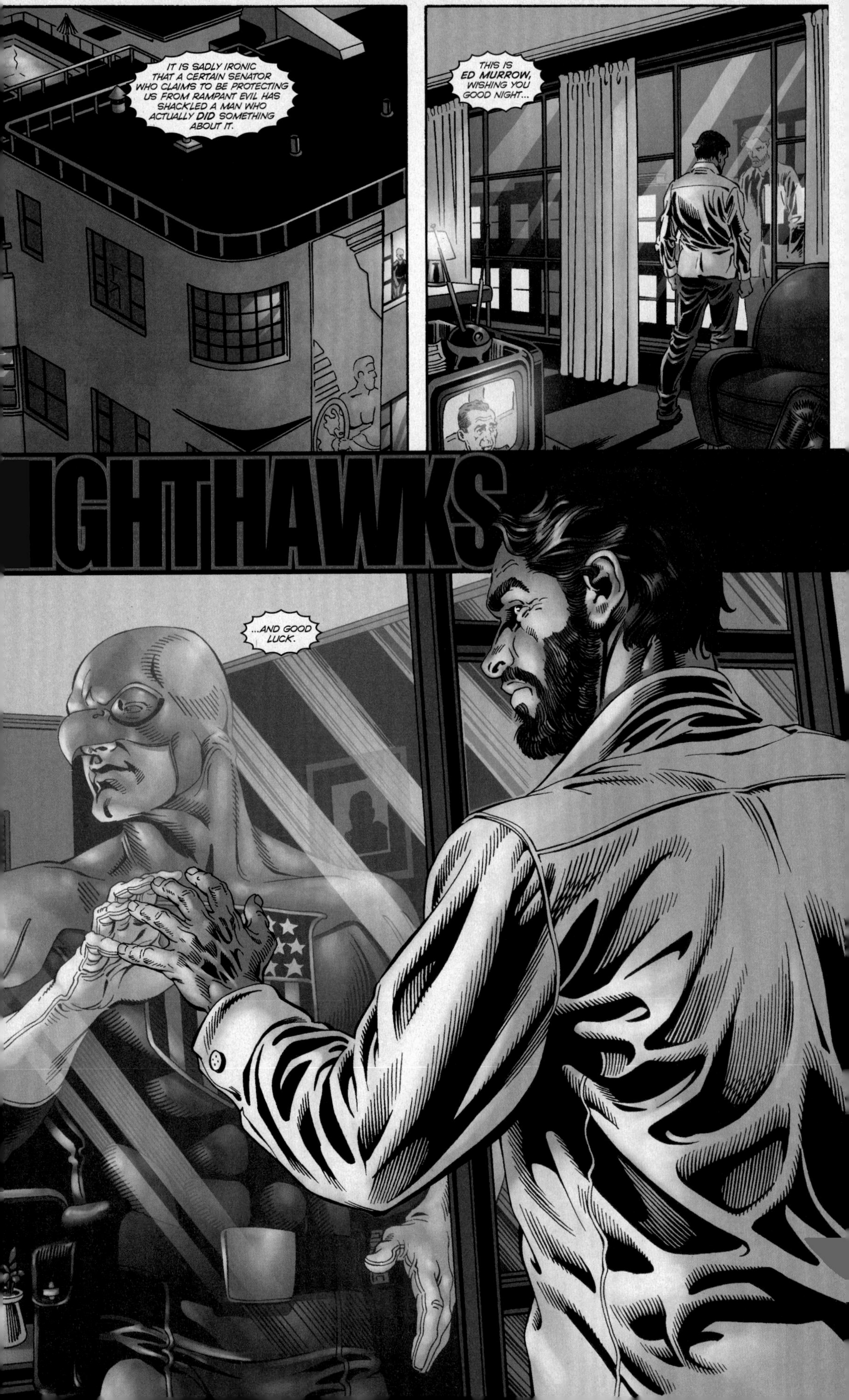
IT IS SADLY IRONIC THAT A CERTAIN SENATOR WHO CLAIMS TO BE PROTECTING US FROM RAMPANT EVIL HAS SHACKLED A MAN WHO ACTUALLY DID SOMETHING ABOUT IT.
THIS IS ED MURROW, WISHING YOU GOOD NIGHT...
IGHTHAWKS
...AND GOOD LUCK.

THUMP RATTLE

BROTHER...

...YOU PICKED THE WRONG NIGHT--

WAIT-- DON'T--!

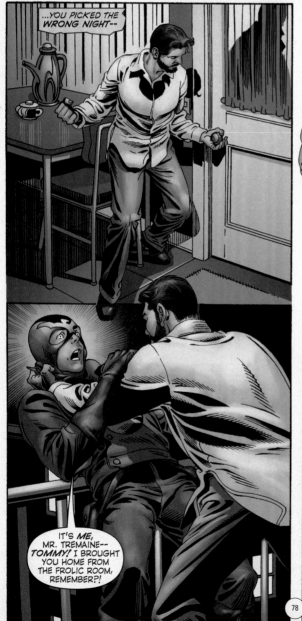

IT'S *ME*, MR. TREMAINE-- *TOMMY!* I BROUGHT YOU HOME FROM THE FROLIC ROOM, REMEMBER?!

YEAH, I REMEMBER. EVER HEAR OF A *FRONT DOOR?*

I FIGURED THE *FEDS* WOULD HAVE AN EYE ON YOU, SO I KEPT IT ON THE Q.T.

HELL OF A *CLIMB.*

WELL... I DIDN'T EXACTLY *CLIMB.*

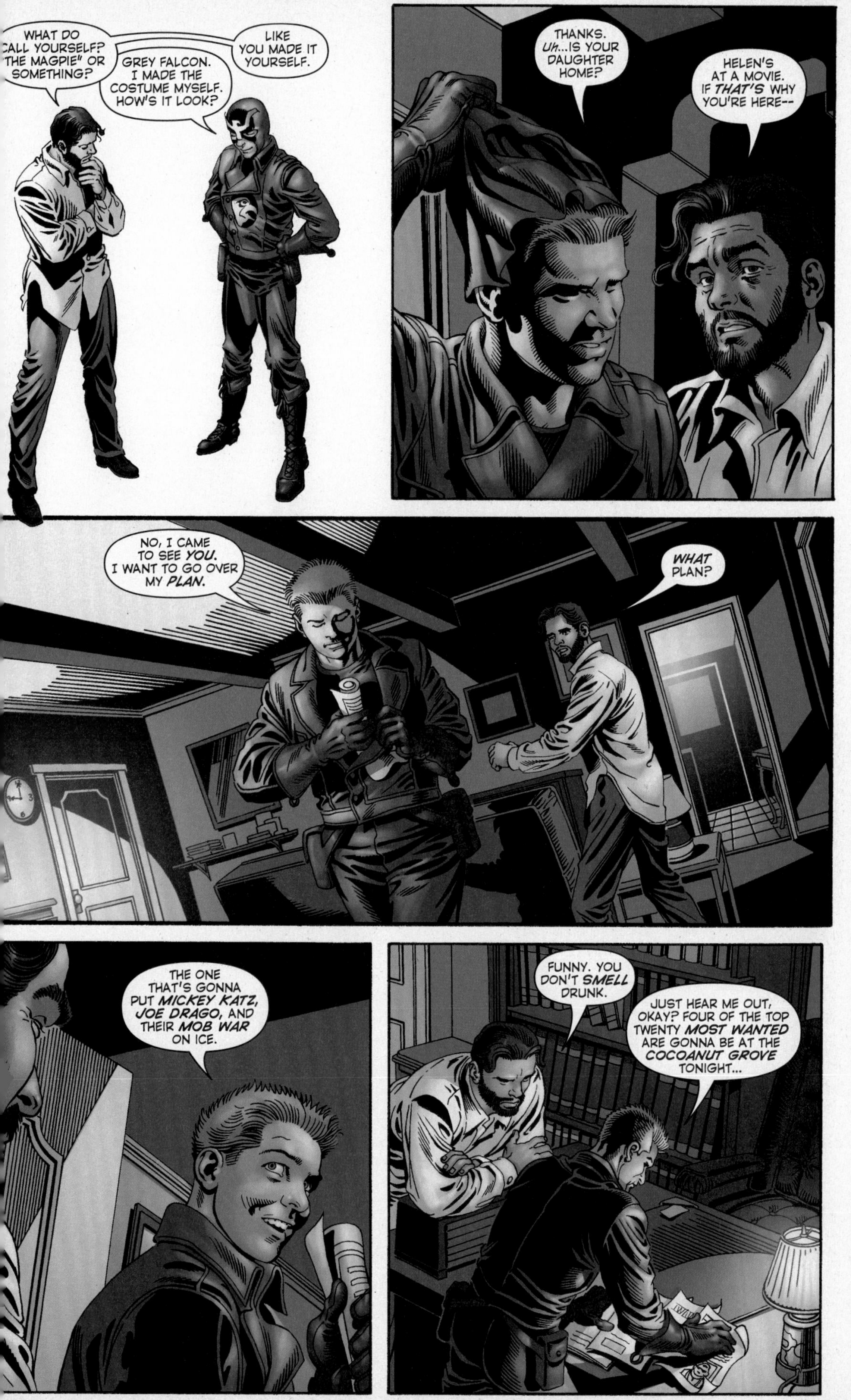
WHAT DO CALL YOURSELF? "THE MAGPIE" OR SOMETHING?
GREY FALCON. I MADE THE COSTUME MYSELF. HOW'S IT LOOK?
LIKE YOU MADE IT YOURSELF.
THANKS. Uh...IS YOUR DAUGHTER HOME?
HELEN'S AT A MOVIE. IF THAT'S WHY YOU'RE HERE--
NO, I CAME TO SEE YOU. I WANT TO GO OVER MY PLAN.
WHAT PLAN?
THE ONE THAT'S GONNA PUT MICKEY KATZ, JOE DRAGO, AND THEIR MOB WAR ON ICE.
FUNNY. YOU DON'T SMELL DRUNK.
JUST HEAR ME OUT, OKAY? FOUR OF THE TOP TWENTY MOST WANTED ARE GONNA BE AT THE COCOANUT GROVE TONIGHT...

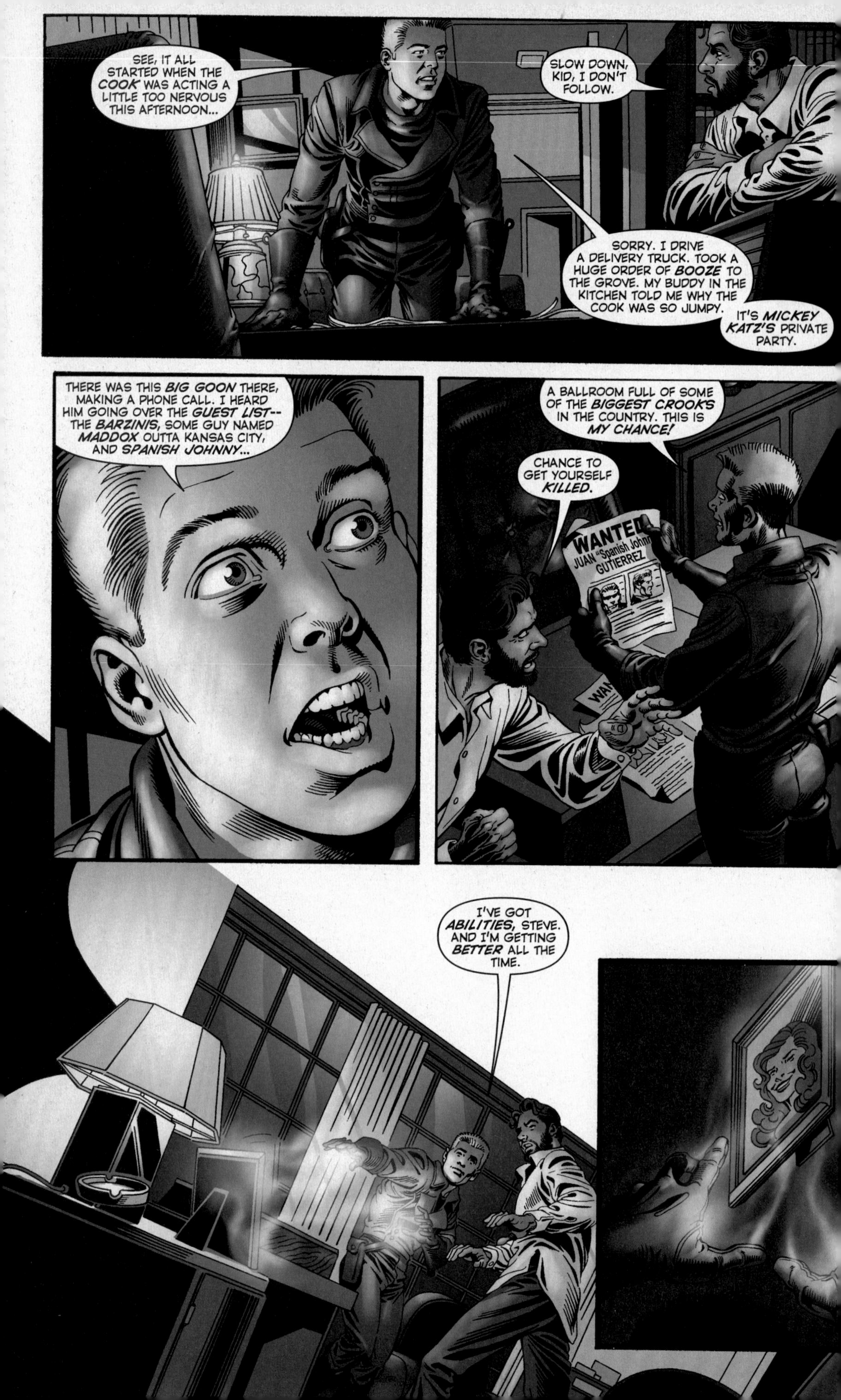
SEE, IT ALL STARTED WHEN THE COOK WAS ACTING A LITTLE TOO NERVOUS THIS AFTERNOON...
SLOW DOWN, KID, I DON'T FOLLOW.
SORRY. I DRIVE A DELIVERY TRUCK. TOOK A HUGE ORDER OF BOOZE TO THE GROVE. MY BUDDY IN THE KITCHEN TOLD ME WHY THE COOK WAS SO JUMPY.
IT'S MICKEY KATZ'S PRIVATE PARTY.
THERE WAS THIS BIG GOON THERE, MAKING A PHONE CALL. I HEARD HIM GOING OVER THE GUEST LIST-- THE BARZINIS, SOME GUY NAMED MADDOX OUTTA KANSAS CITY, AND SPANISH JOHNNY...
A BALLROOM FULL OF SOME OF THE BIGGEST CROOKS IN THE COUNTRY. THIS IS MY CHANCE!
CHANCE TO GET YOURSELF KILLED.
WANTED
JUAN "Spanish Johnn
GUTIERREZ
I'VE GOT ABILITIES, STEVE. AND I'M GETTING BETTER ALL THE TIME.

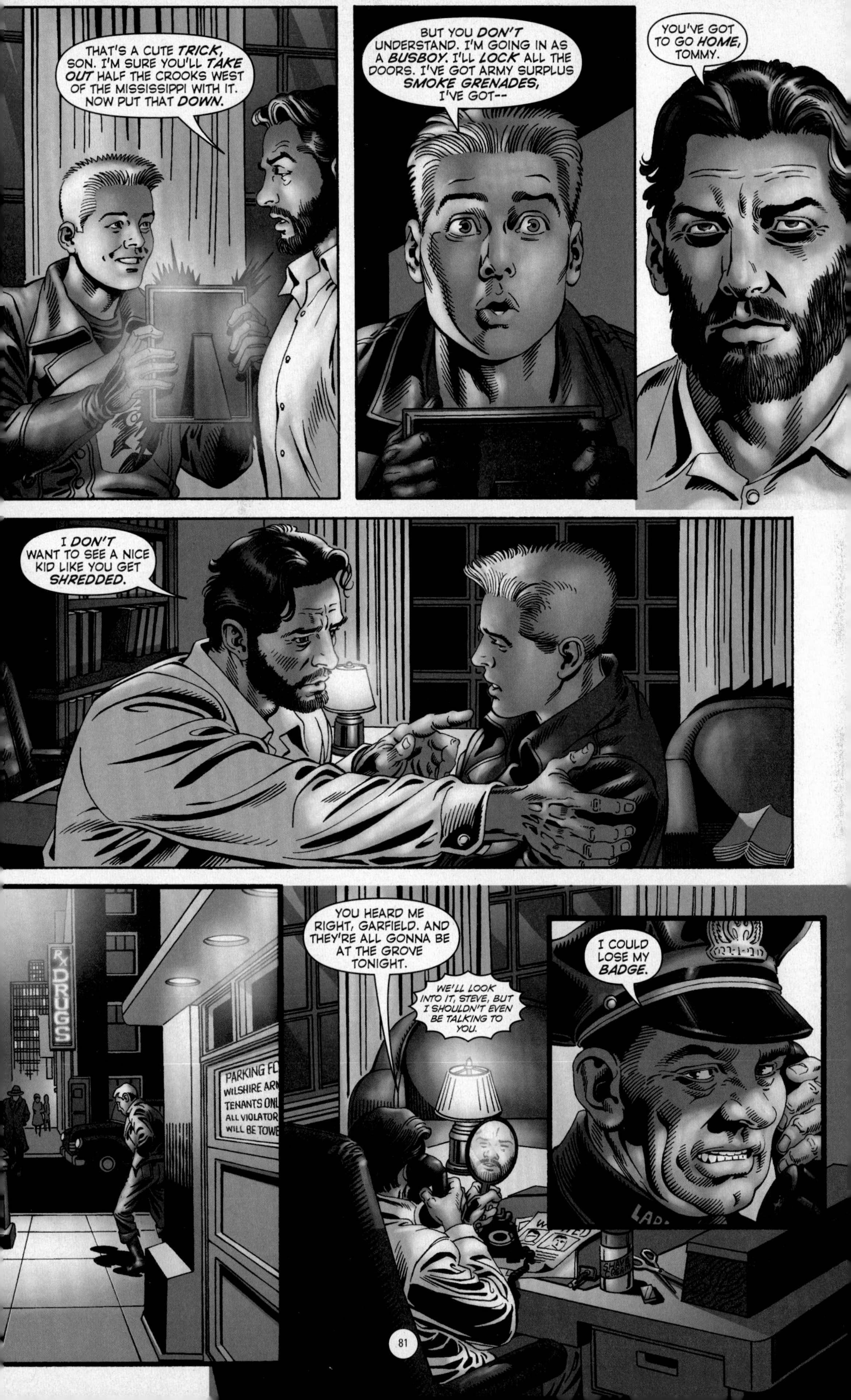

THAT'S A CUTE TRICK, SON. I'M SURE YOU'LL TAKE OUT HALF THE CROOKS WEST OF THE MISSISSIPPI WITH IT. NOW PUT THAT DOWN.
BUT YOU DON'T UNDERSTAND. I'M GOING IN AS A BUSBOY. I'LL LOCK ALL THE DOORS. I'VE GOT ARMY SURPLUS SMOKE GRENADES, I'VE GOT--
YOU'VE GOT TO GO HOME, TOMMY.
I DON'T WANT TO SEE A NICE KID LIKE YOU GET SHREDDED.
RX DRUGS
PARKING FO
WILSHIRE ARM
TENANTS ONL
ALL VIOLATOR
WILL BE TOWE
YOU HEARD ME RIGHT, GARFIELD. AND THEY'RE ALL GONNA BE AT THE GROVE TONIGHT.
WE'LL LOOK INTO IT, STEVE, BUT I SHOULDN'T EVEN BE TALKING TO YOU.
I COULD LOSE MY BADGE.

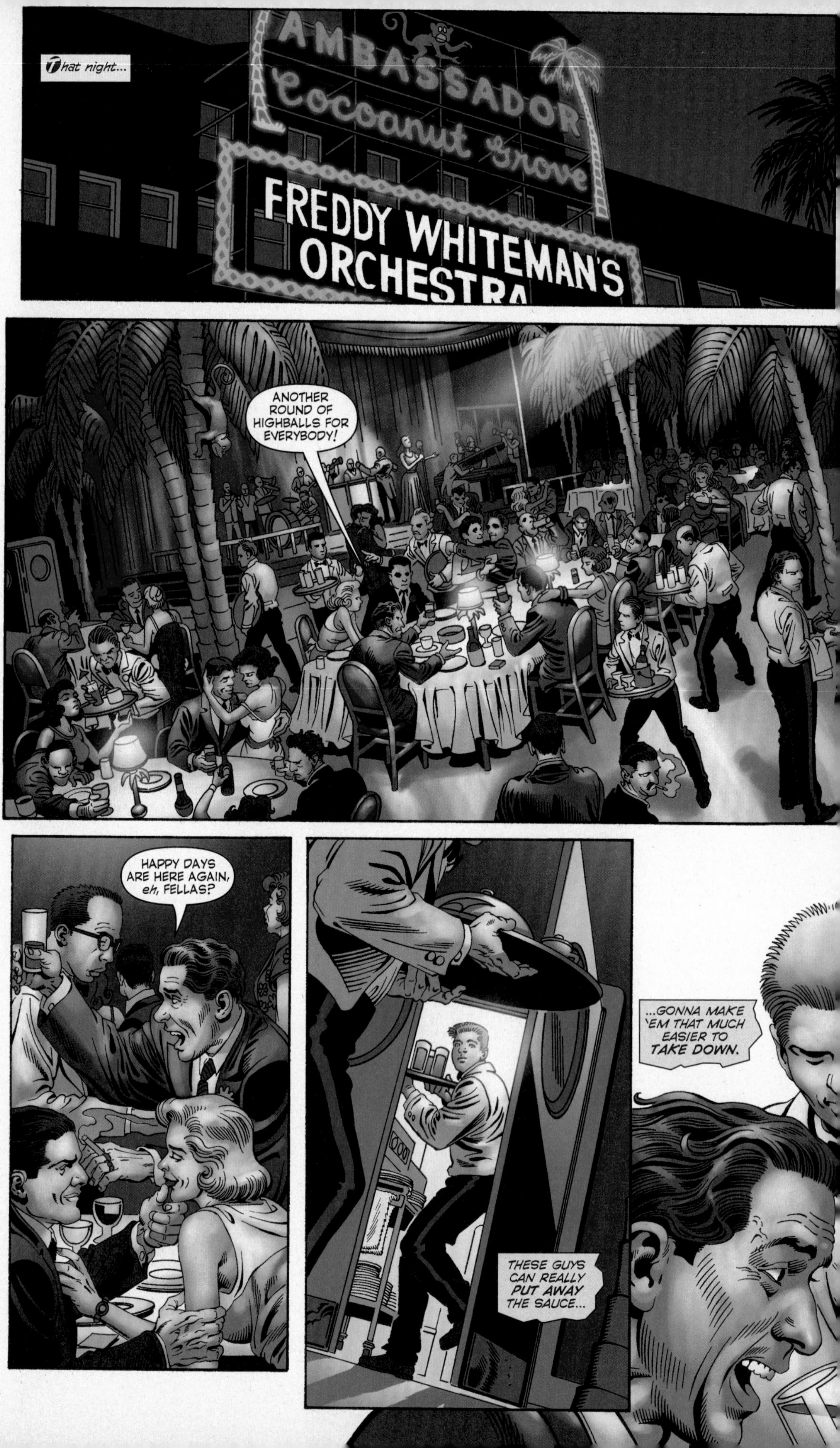
That night...
AMBASSADOR
Cocoanut Grove
FREDDY WHITEMAN'S
ORCHESTRA
ANOTHER ROUND OF HIGHBALLS FOR EVERYBODY!
HAPPY DAYS ARE HERE AGAIN, eh, FELLAS?
THESE GUYS CAN REALLY PUT AWAY THE SAUCE...
...GONNA MAKE 'EM THAT MUCH EASIER TO TAKE DOWN.

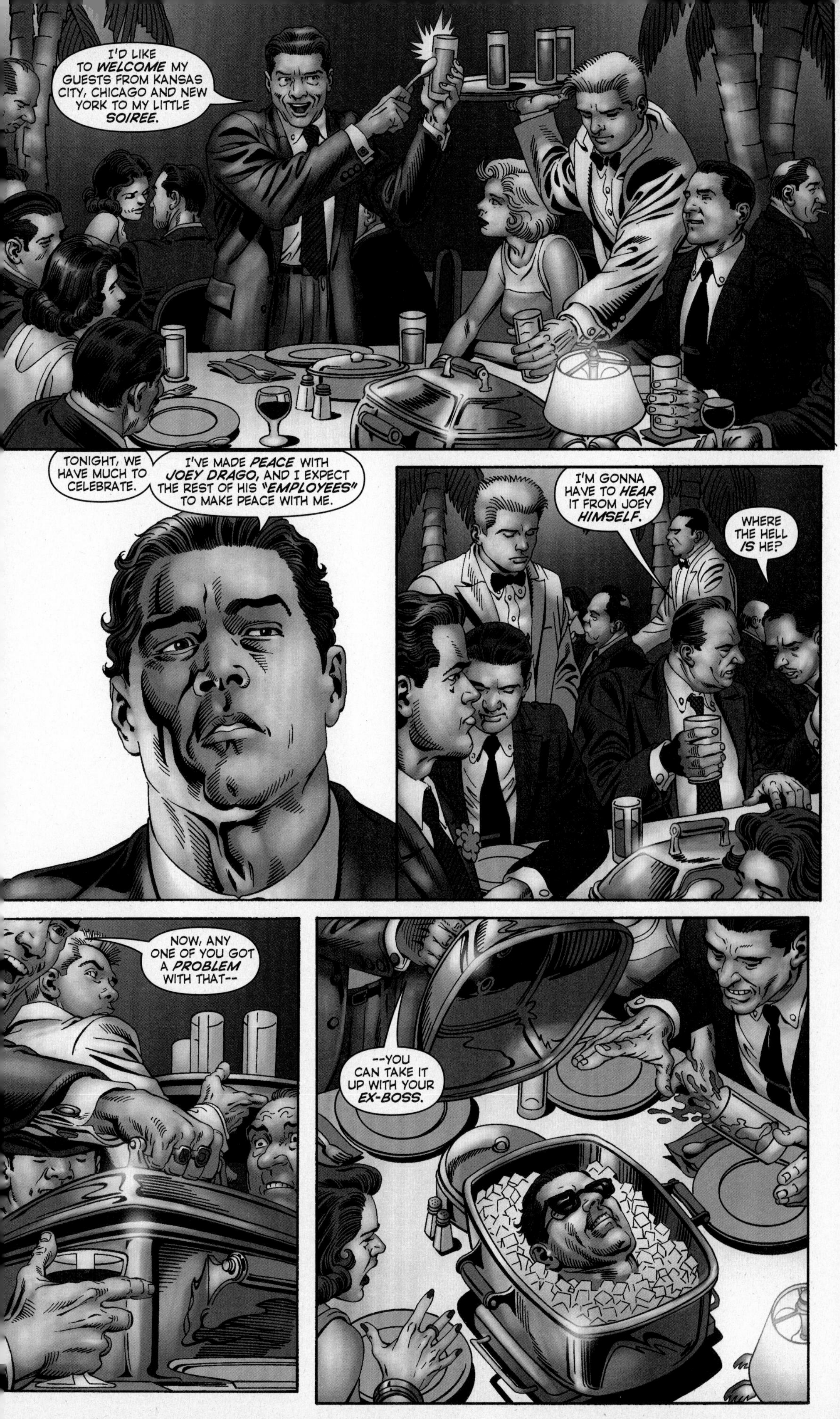
I'D LIKE TO WELCOME MY GUESTS FROM KANSAS CITY, CHICAGO AND NEW YORK TO MY LITTLE SOIREE.
TONIGHT, WE HAVE MUCH TO CELEBRATE.
I'VE MADE PEACE WITH JOEY DRAGO, AND I EXPECT THE REST OF HIS "EMPLOYEES" TO MAKE PEACE WITH ME.
I'M GONNA HAVE TO HEAR IT FROM JOEY HIMSELF.
WHERE THE HELL IS HE?
NOW, ANY ONE OF YOU GOT A PROBLEM WITH THAT--
--YOU CAN TAKE IT UP WITH YOUR EX-BOSS.

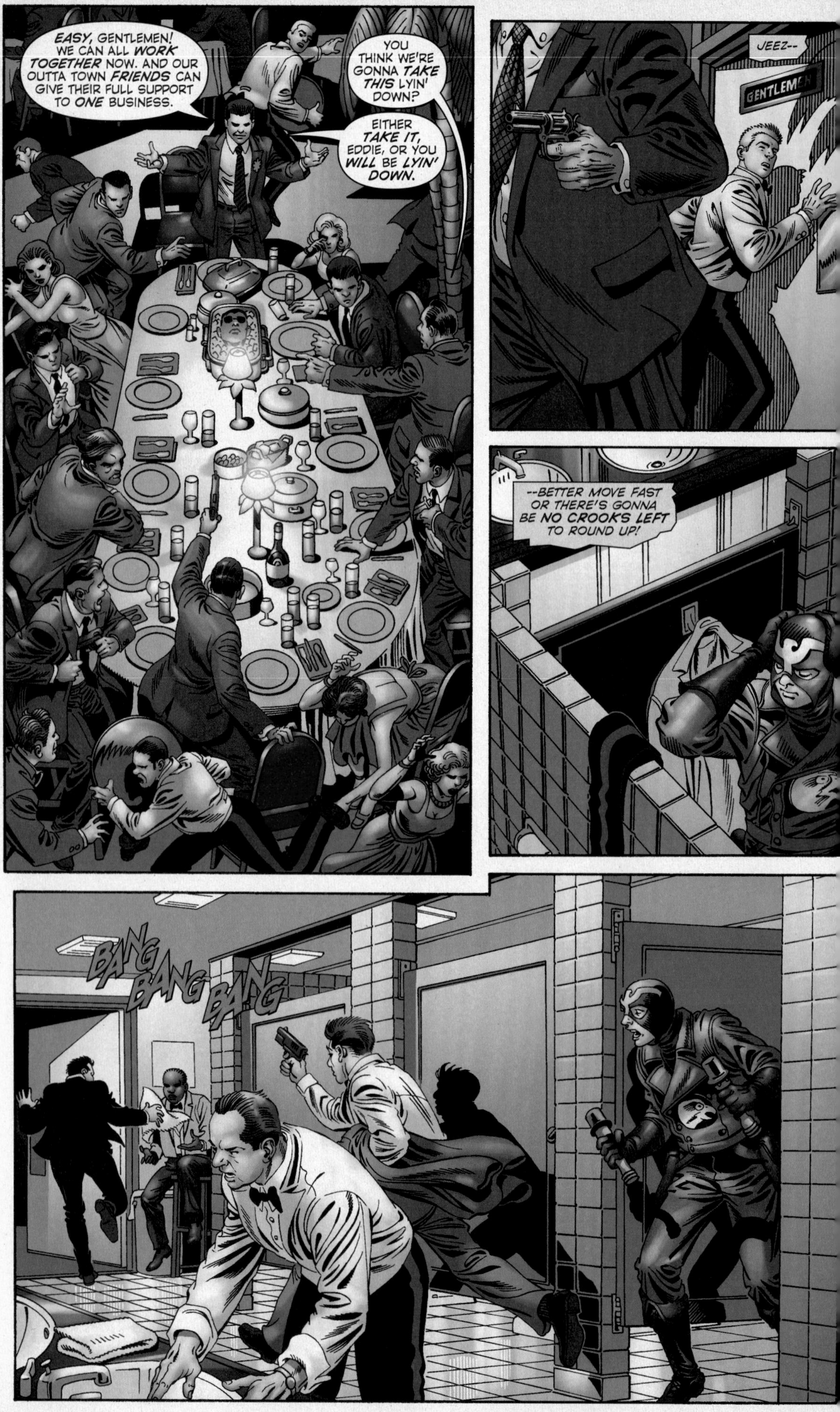
EASY, GENTLEMEN! WE CAN ALL WORK TOGETHER NOW. AND OUR OUTTA TOWN FRIENDS CAN GIVE THEIR FULL SUPPORT TO ONE BUSINESS.
YOU THINK WE'RE GONNA TAKE THIS LYIN' DOWN?
EITHER TAKE IT, EDDIE, OR YOU WILL BE LYIN' DOWN.
JEEZ--
GENTLEMEN
--BETTER MOVE FAST OR THERE'S GONNA BE NO CROOKS LEFT TO ROUND UP!
BANG
BANG
BANG

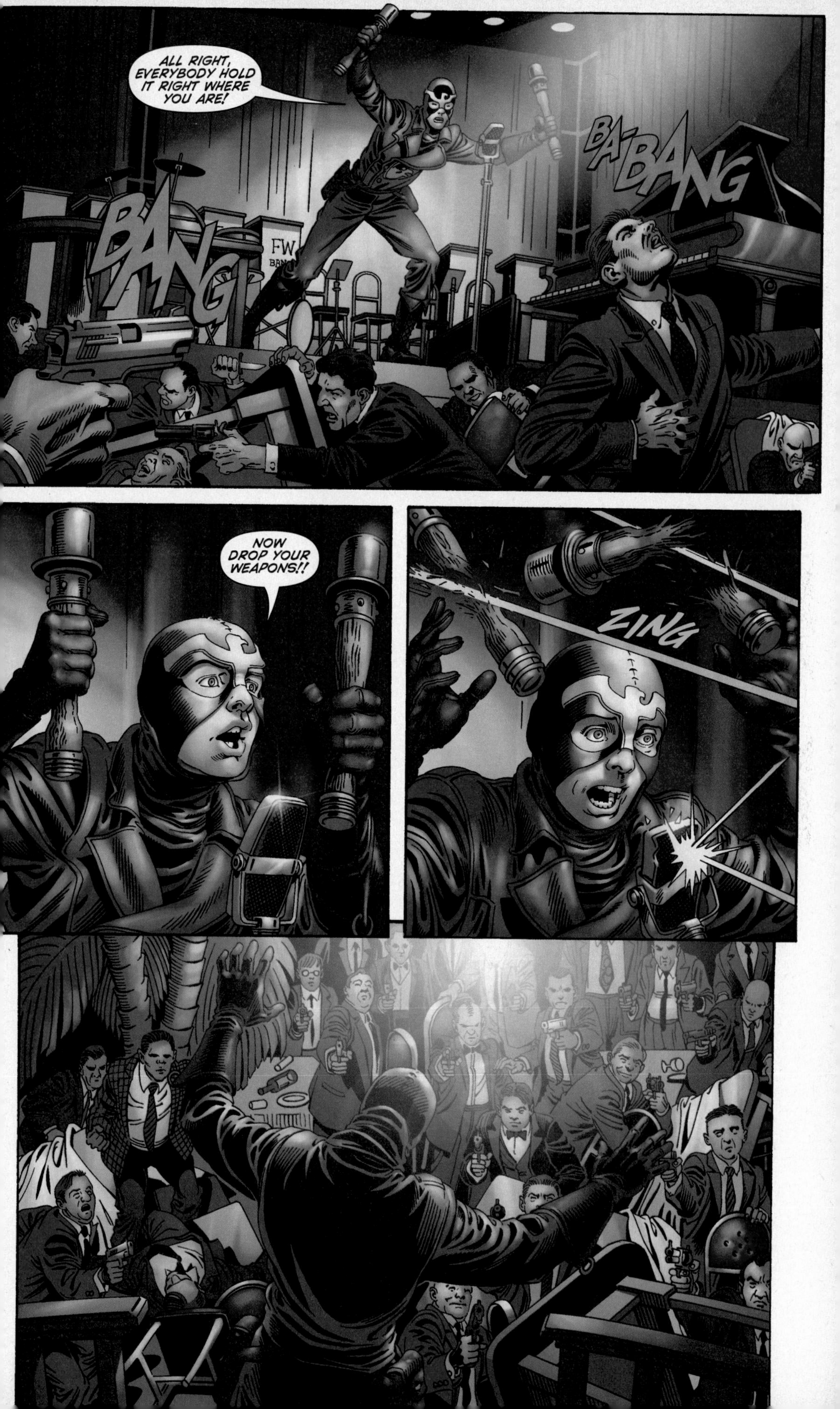
ALL RIGHT, EVERYBODY HOLD IT RIGHT WHERE YOU ARE!
BA-BANG
BANG
FW
NOW DROP YOUR WEAPONS!!
ZING

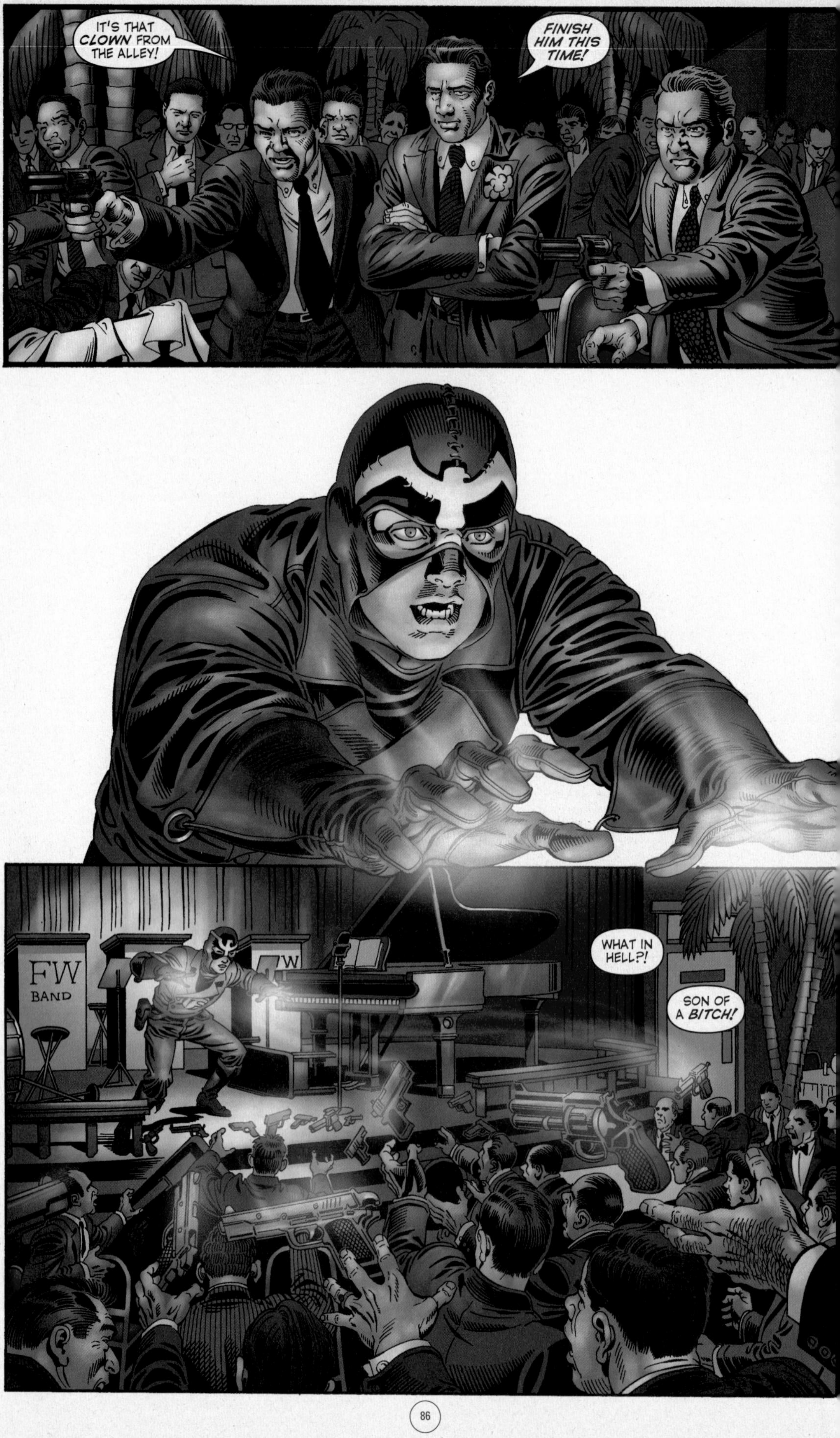
IT'S THAT CLOWN FROM THE ALLEY!
FINISH HIM THIS TIME!
FW BAND
WHAT IN HELL?!
SON OF A BITCH!

TIME TO **COOL DOWN**, FREAK SHOW.

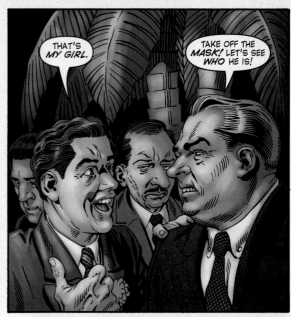

THAT'S **MY GIRL**.

TAKE OFF THE **MASK!** LET'S SEE WHO HE IS!

SO, **WHO IS** HE?

NEVER SEEN HIM BEFORE.

VROOOM

DOOR

VROOOM

SHOOT HIM!

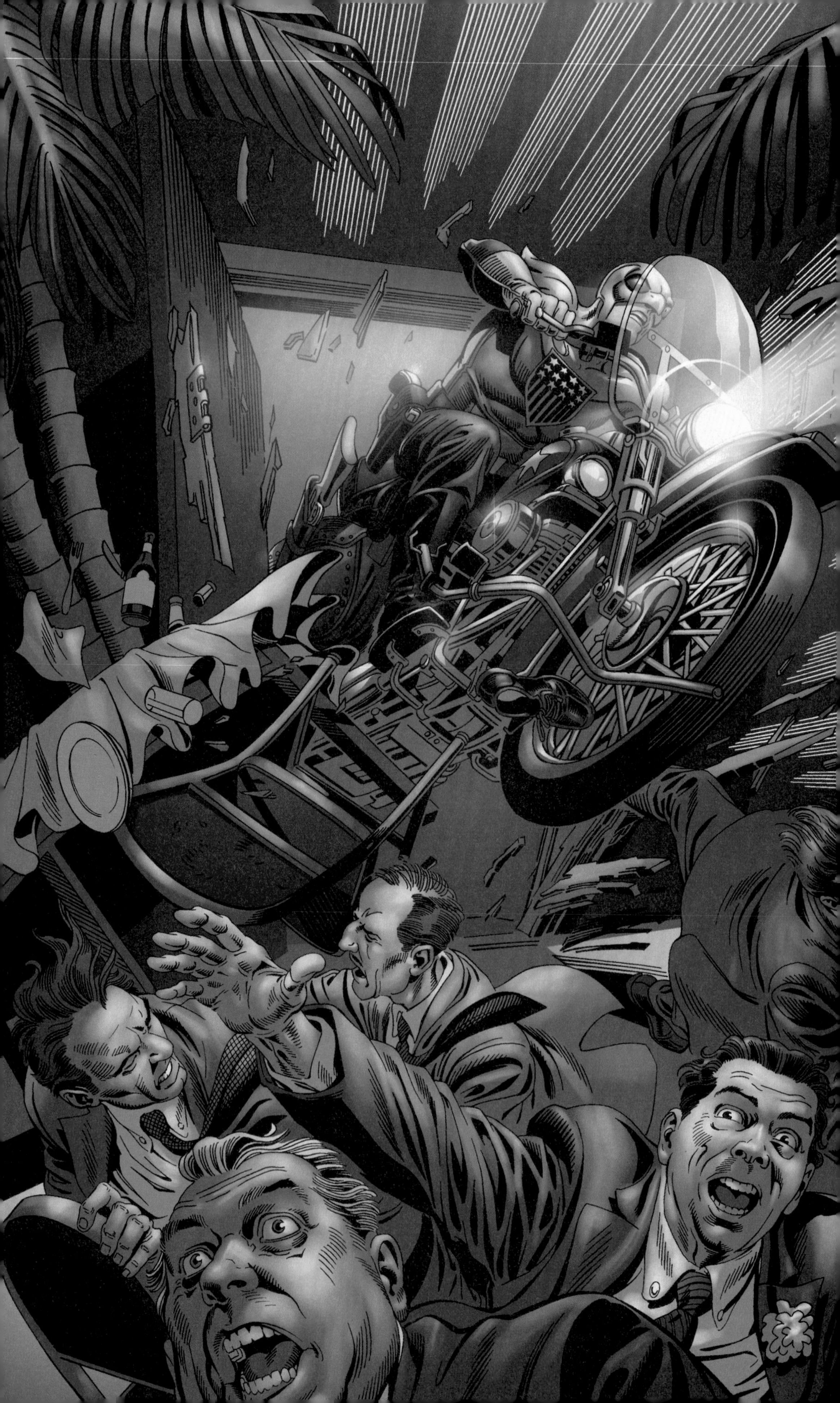

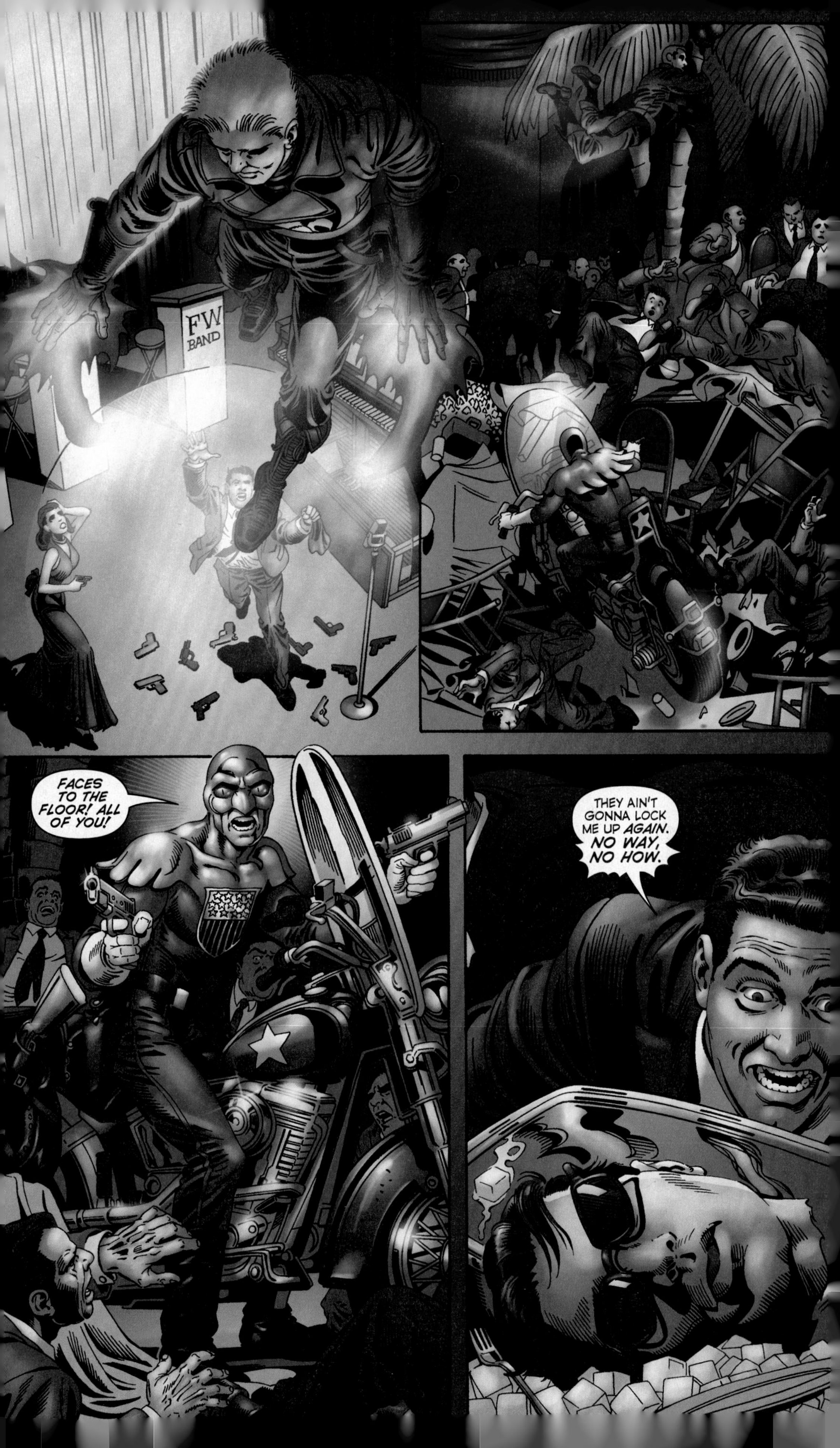
FW BAND
FACES TO THE FLOOR! ALL OF YOU!
THEY AIN'T GONNA LOCK ME UP AGAIN. NO WAY, NO HOW.

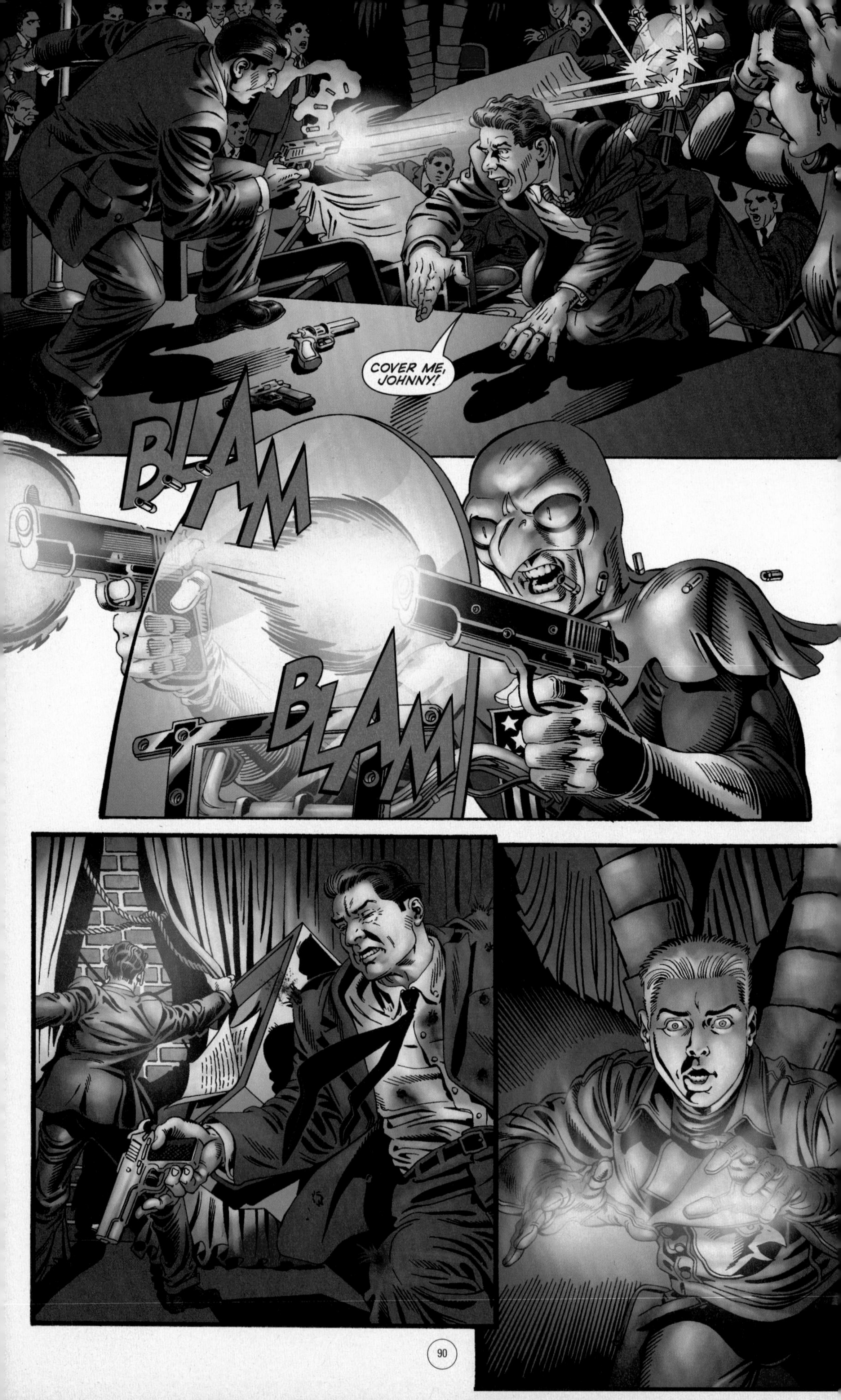
COVER ME, JOHNNY!
BLAM
BLAM

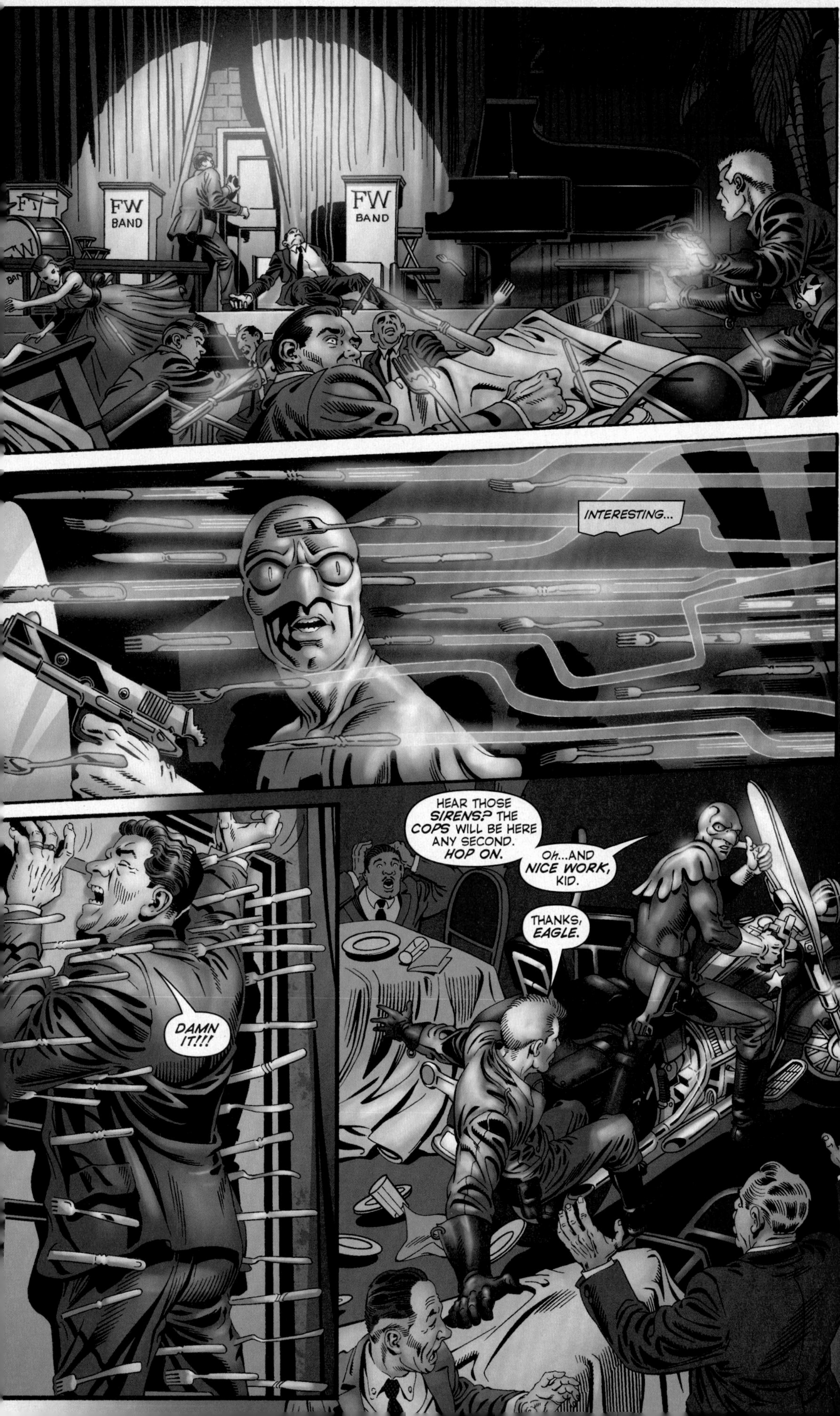
FW BAND
FW BAND
INTERESTING...
HEAR THOSE SIRENS? THE COPS WILL BE HERE ANY SECOND. HOP ON.
Oh...AND NICE WORK, KID.
THANKS, EAGLE.
DAMN IT!!!

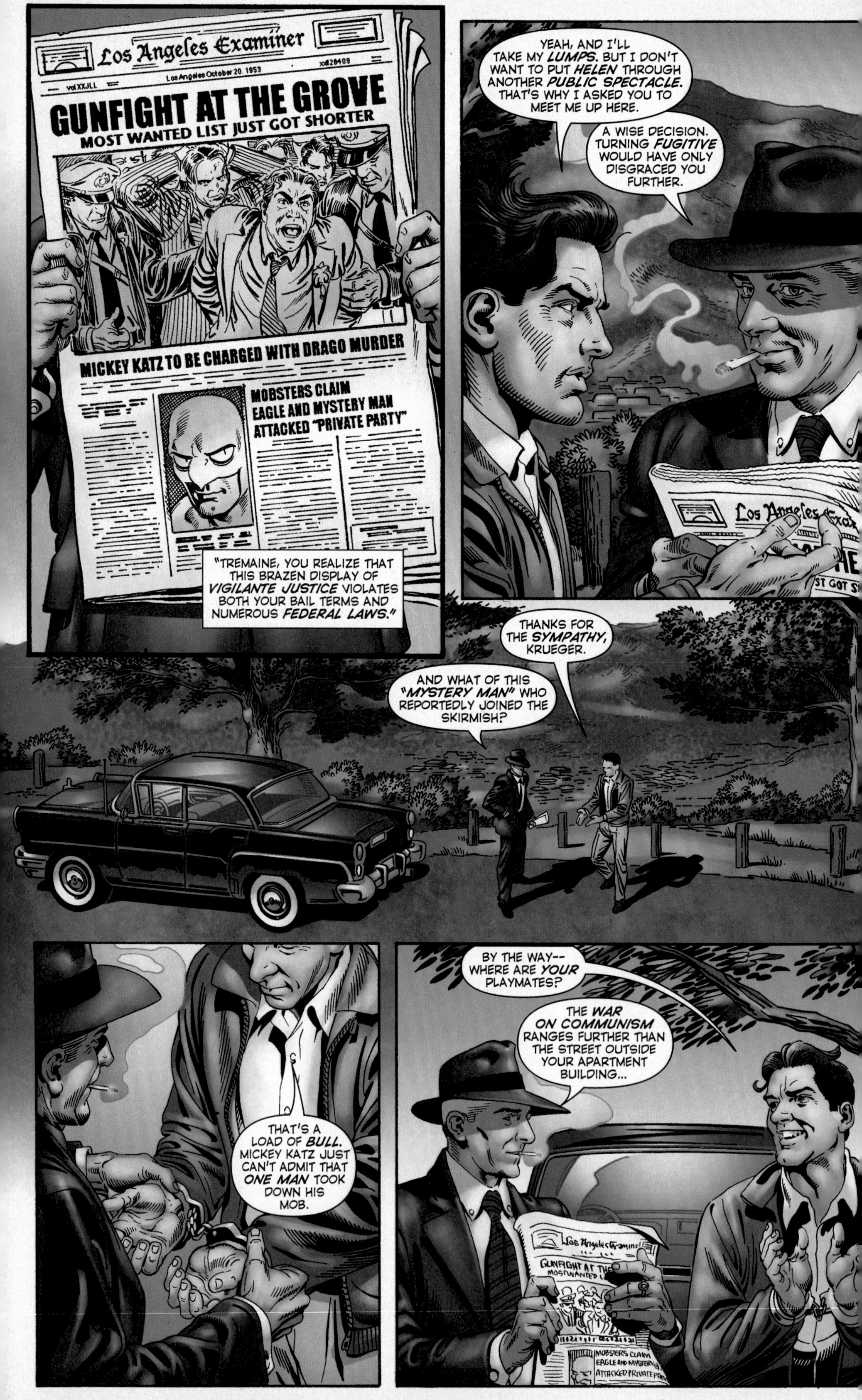
Los Angeles Examiner
GUNFIGHT AT THE GROVE
MOST WANTED LIST JUST GOT SHORTER
MICKEY KATZ TO BE CHARGED WITH DRAGO MURDER
MOBSTERS CLAIM EAGLE AND MYSTERY MAN ATTACKED "PRIVATE PARTY"
"TREMAINE, YOU REALIZE THAT THIS BRAZEN DISPLAY OF VIGILANTE JUSTICE VIOLATES BOTH YOUR BAIL TERMS AND NUMEROUS FEDERAL LAWS."
YEAH, AND I'LL TAKE MY LUMPS. BUT I DON'T WANT TO PUT HELEN THROUGH ANOTHER PUBLIC SPECTACLE. THAT'S WHY I ASKED YOU TO MEET ME UP HERE.
A WISE DECISION. TURNING FUGITIVE WOULD HAVE ONLY DISGRACED YOU FURTHER.
THANKS FOR THE SYMPATHY, KRUEGER.
AND WHAT OF THIS "MYSTERY MAN" WHO REPORTEDLY JOINED THE SKIRMISH?
THAT'S A LOAD OF BULL. MICKEY KATZ JUST CAN'T ADMIT THAT ONE MAN TOOK DOWN HIS MOB.
BY THE WAY-- WHERE ARE YOUR PLAYMATES?
THE WAR ON COMMUNISM RANGES FURTHER THAN THE STREET OUTSIDE YOUR APARTMENT BUILDING...

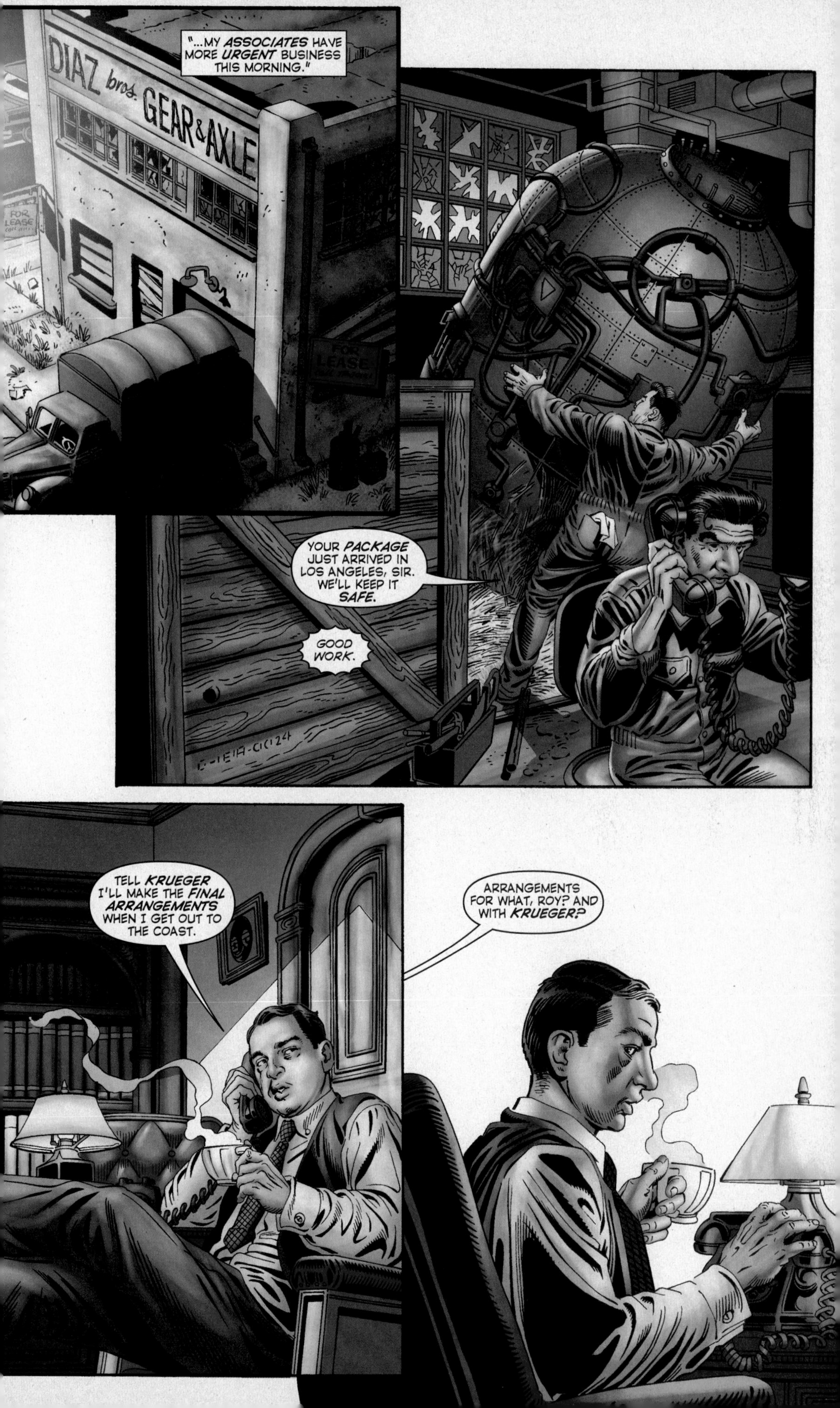
"...MY *ASSOCIATES* HAVE MORE *URGENT* BUSINESS THIS MORNING."
DIAZ bros. GEAR & AXLE
FOR LEASE
FOR LEASE
YOUR *PACKAGE* JUST ARRIVED IN LOS ANGELES, SIR. WE'LL KEEP IT *SAFE*.
GOOD WORK.
TELL *KRUEGER* I'LL MAKE THE *FINAL ARRANGEMENTS* WHEN I GET OUT TO THE COAST.
ARRANGEMENTS FOR WHAT, ROY? AND WITH *KRUEGER?*

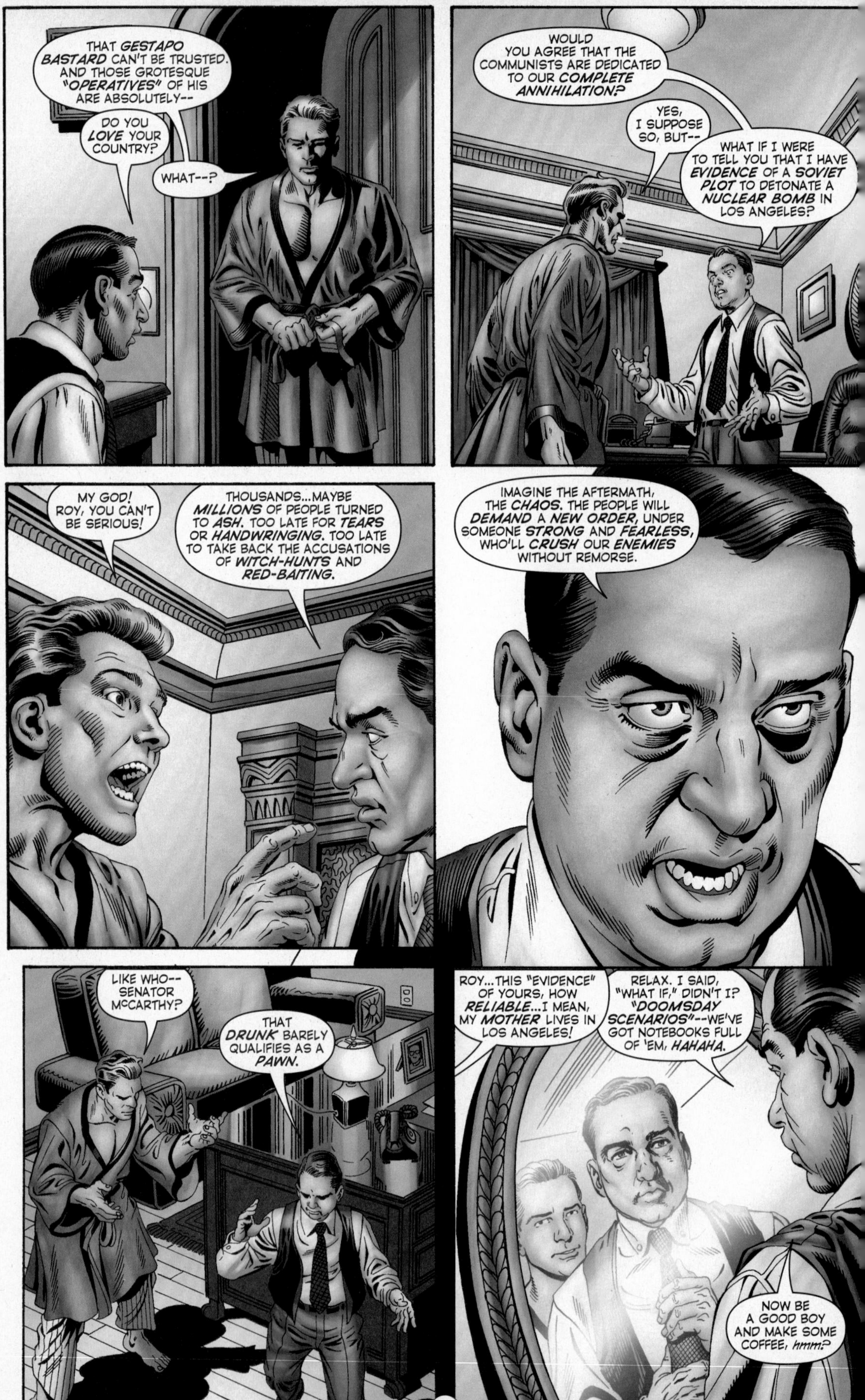
THAT *GESTAPO BASTARD* CAN'T BE TRUSTED. AND THOSE GROTESQUE *"OPERATIVES"* OF HIS ARE ABSOLUTELY--
DO YOU *LOVE* YOUR COUNTRY?
WHAT--?
WOULD YOU AGREE THAT THE COMMUNISTS ARE DEDICATED TO OUR *COMPLETE ANNIHILATION?*
YES, I SUPPOSE SO, BUT--
WHAT IF I WERE TO TELL YOU THAT I HAVE *EVIDENCE* OF A *SOVIET PLOT* TO DETONATE A *NUCLEAR BOMB* IN LOS ANGELES?
MY GOD! ROY, YOU CAN'T BE SERIOUS!
THOUSANDS...MAYBE *MILLIONS* OF PEOPLE TURNED TO *ASH*. TOO LATE FOR *TEARS* OR *HANDWRINGING*. TOO LATE TO TAKE BACK THE ACCUSATIONS OF *WITCH-HUNTS* AND *RED-BAITING*.
IMAGINE THE AFTERMATH, THE *CHAOS*. THE PEOPLE WILL *DEMAND* A *NEW ORDER*, UNDER SOMEONE *STRONG* AND *FEARLESS*, WHO'LL *CRUSH* OUR *ENEMIES* WITHOUT REMORSE.
LIKE WHO-- SENATOR McCARTHY?
THAT *DRUNK* BARELY QUALIFIES AS A *PAWN*.
ROY...THIS "EVIDENCE" OF YOURS, HOW *RELIABLE*...I MEAN, MY *MOTHER* LIVES IN LOS ANGELES!
RELAX. I SAID, "WHAT IF," DIDN'T I? *"DOOMSDAY SCENARIOS"*--WE'VE GOT NOTEBOOKS FULL OF 'EM, *HAHAHA*.
NOW BE A GOOD BOY AND MAKE SOME COFFEE, *hmm?*

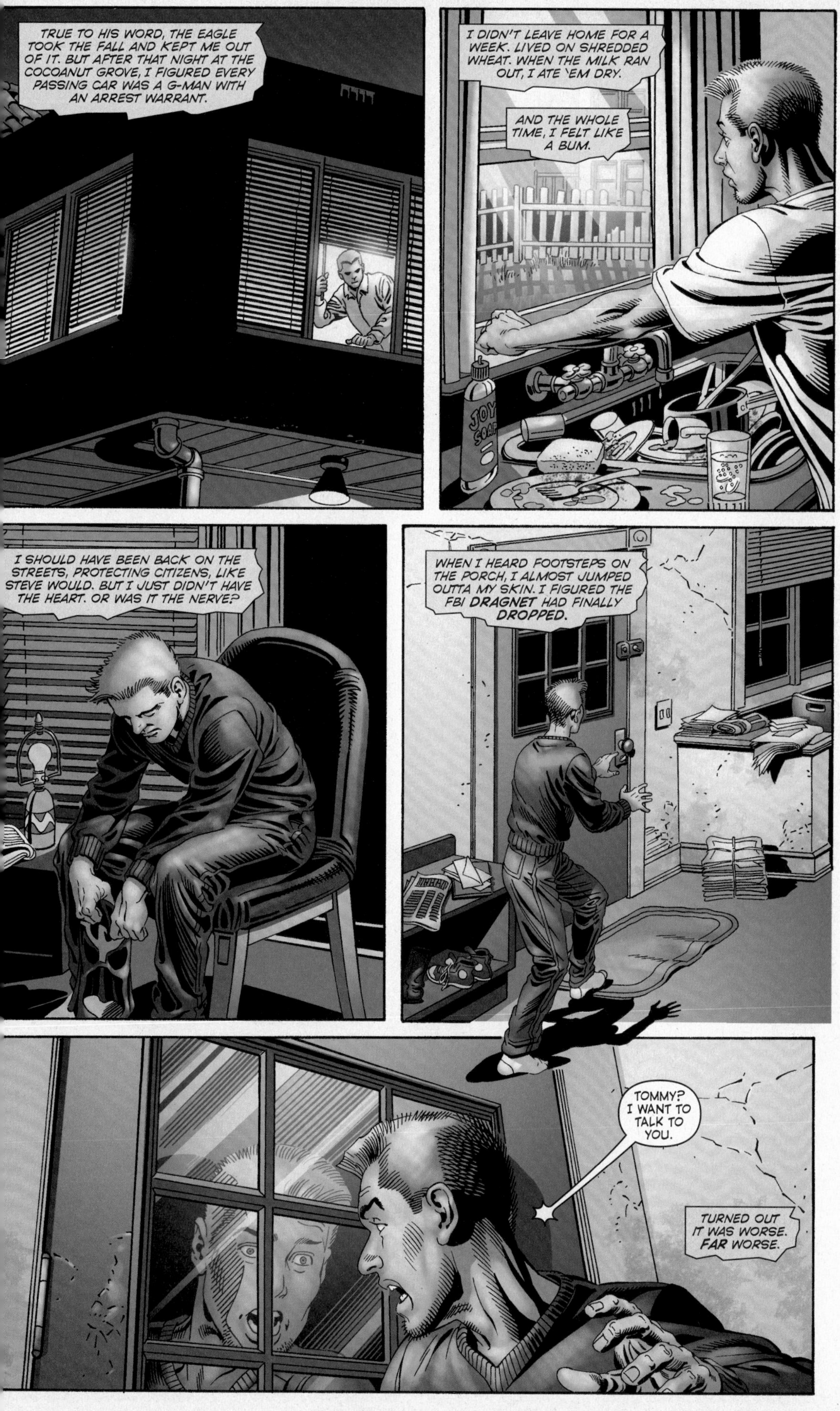
TRUE TO HIS WORD, THE EAGLE TOOK THE FALL AND KEPT ME OUT OF IT. BUT AFTER THAT NIGHT AT THE COCOANUT GROVE, I FIGURED EVERY PASSING CAR WAS A G-MAN WITH AN ARREST WARRANT.
I DIDN'T LEAVE HOME FOR A WEEK. LIVED ON SHREDDED WHEAT. WHEN THE MILK RAN OUT, I ATE 'EM DRY.
AND THE WHOLE TIME, I FELT LIKE A BUM.
JOY SOAP
I SHOULD HAVE BEEN BACK ON THE STREETS, PROTECTING CITIZENS, LIKE STEVE WOULD. BUT I JUST DIDN'T HAVE THE HEART. OR WAS IT THE NERVE?
WHEN I HEARD FOOTSTEPS ON THE PORCH, I ALMOST JUMPED OUTTA MY SKIN. I FIGURED THE FBI DRAGNET HAD FINALLY DROPPED.
TOMMY? I WANT TO TALK TO YOU.
TURNED OUT IT WAS WORSE. FAR WORSE.

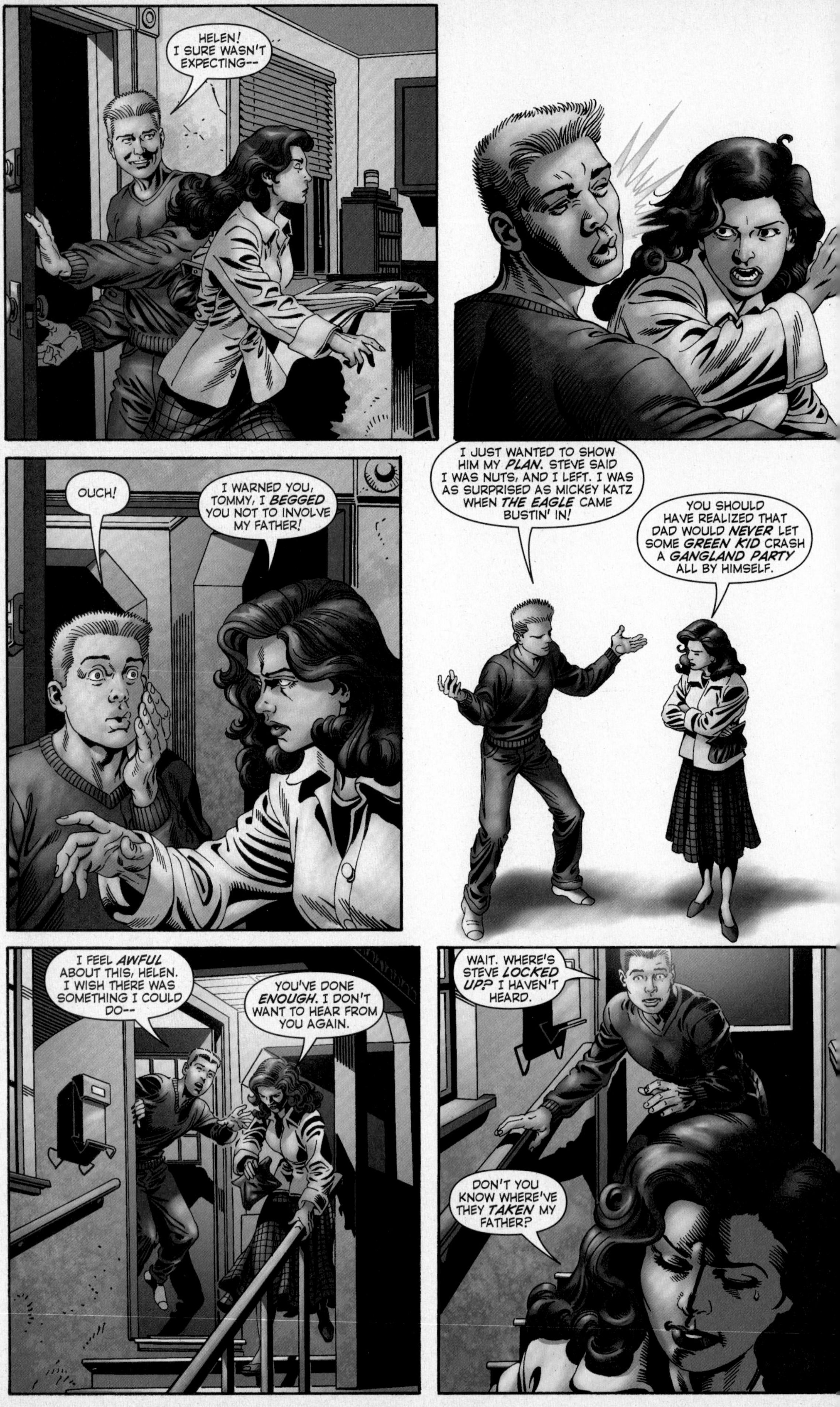
HELEN! I SURE WASN'T EXPECTING--
OUCH!
I WARNED YOU, TOMMY, I BEGGED YOU NOT TO INVOLVE MY FATHER!
I JUST WANTED TO SHOW HIM MY PLAN. STEVE SAID I WAS NUTS, AND I LEFT. I WAS AS SURPRISED AS MICKEY KATZ WHEN THE EAGLE CAME BUSTIN' IN!
YOU SHOULD HAVE REALIZED THAT DAD WOULD NEVER LET SOME GREEN KID CRASH A GANGLAND PARTY ALL BY HIMSELF.
I FEEL AWFUL ABOUT THIS, HELEN. I WISH THERE WAS SOMETHING I COULD DO--
YOU'VE DONE ENOUGH. I DON'T WANT TO HEAR FROM YOU AGAIN.
WAIT. WHERE'S STEVE LOCKED UP? I HAVEN'T HEARD.
DON'T YOU KNOW WHERE'VE THEY TAKEN MY FATHER?

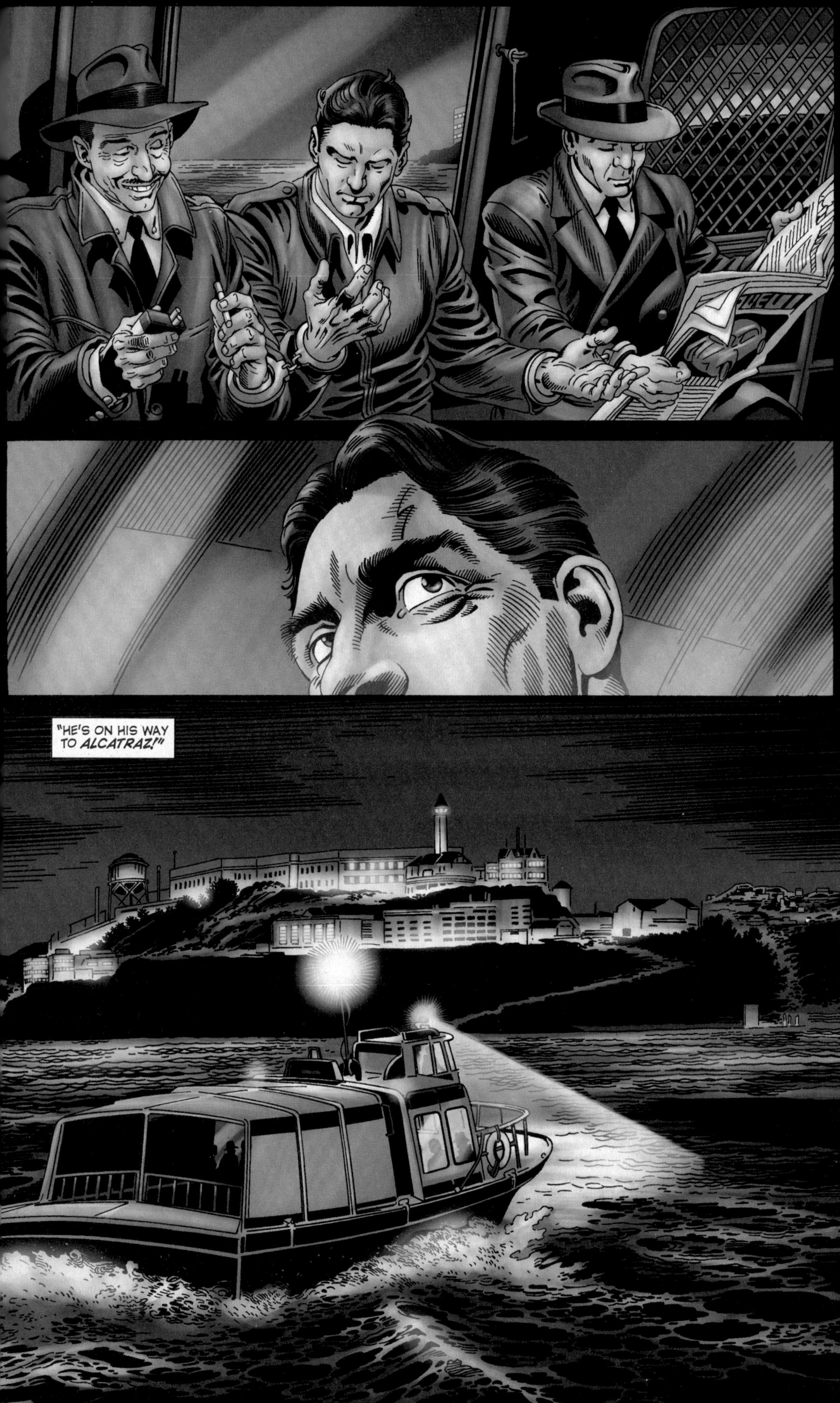
"HE'S ON HIS WAY
TO ALCATRAZ!"

CHAPTER 5

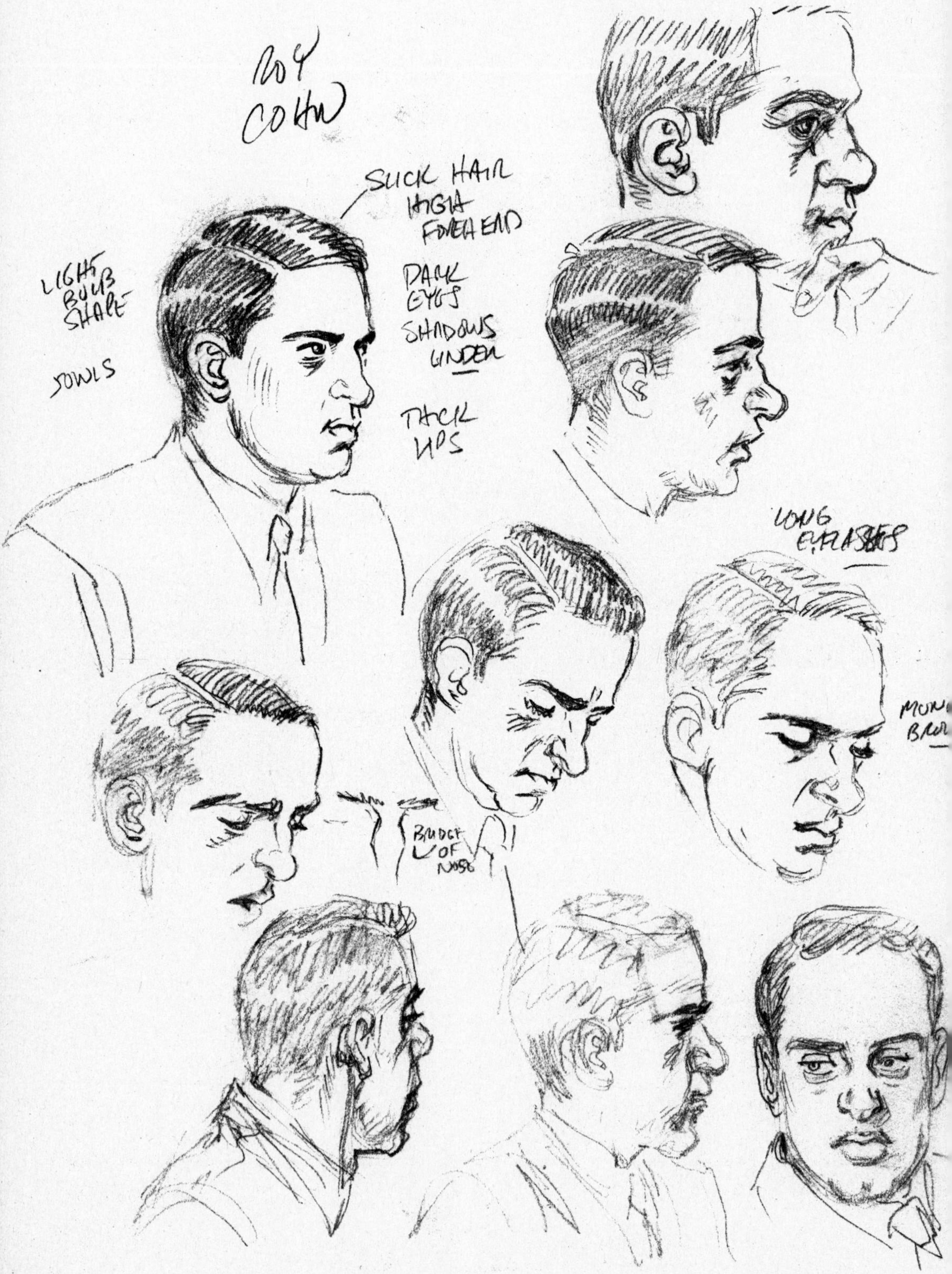

ROY COHN
SLICK HAIR HIGH FOREHEAD
LIGHT BULB SHAPE
JOWLS
DARK EYES SHADOWS UNDER
THICK LIPS
LONG EYELASHES
BRIDGE OF NOSE

Red Menace

BIRDS FLY THE COOP

The Eagle on The Rock: In the Alcatraz exercise yard, Steve's assaulted by another new inmate with a heavy grudge--Mickey Coleman. Steve

DAUGHTER OF EAGLE CRIES FOWL OVER COVERAGE OF DAD

Solitary cell: Steve discovers the prisoner in the adjoining cell is Robert Stroud...more famously known as the "Birdman of Alcatraz". Steve befriends the eccentric inmate, conversing through a crack in the wall, then via canaries from cell window to window.

Tommy and Helen. He's sure she'll never approve of this, but Tommy's got

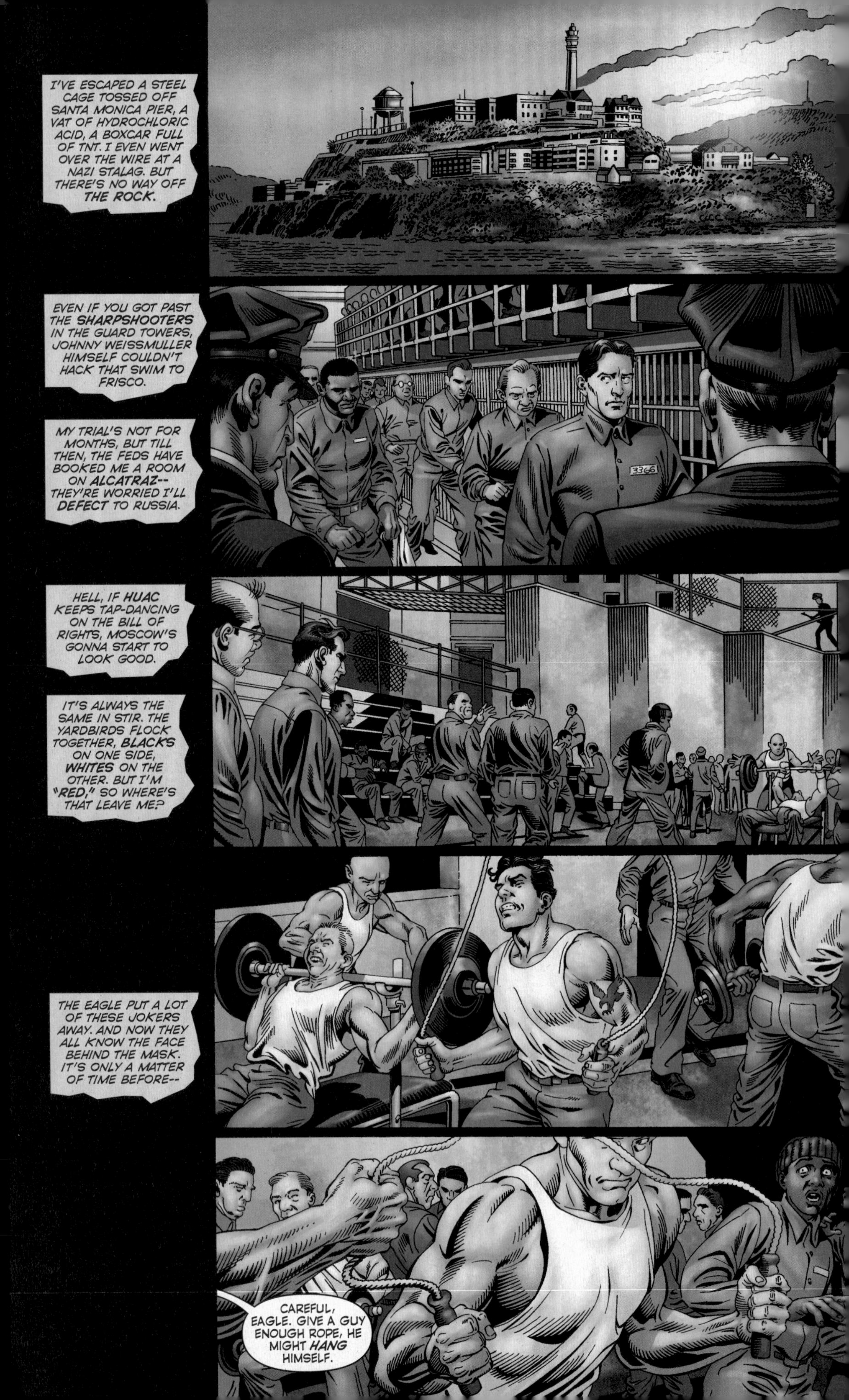

I'VE ESCAPED A STEEL CAGE TOSSED OFF SANTA MONICA PIER, A VAT OF HYDROCHLORIC ACID, A BOXCAR FULL OF TNT. I EVEN WENT OVER THE WIRE AT A NAZI STALAG. BUT THERE'S NO WAY OFF THE ROCK.
EVEN IF YOU GOT PAST THE SHARPSHOOTERS IN THE GUARD TOWERS, JOHNNY WEISSMULLER HIMSELF COULDN'T HACK THAT SWIM TO FRISCO.
MY TRIAL'S NOT FOR MONTHS, BUT TILL THEN, THE FEDS HAVE BOOKED ME A ROOM ON ALCATRAZ-- THEY'RE WORRIED I'LL DEFECT TO RUSSIA.
3366
HELL, IF HUAC KEEPS TAP-DANCING ON THE BILL OF RIGHTS, MOSCOW'S GONNA START TO LOOK GOOD.
IT'S ALWAYS THE SAME IN STIR. THE YARDBIRDS FLOCK TOGETHER, BLACKS ON ONE SIDE, WHITES ON THE OTHER. BUT I'M "RED," SO WHERE'S THAT LEAVE ME?
THE EAGLE PUT A LOT OF THESE JOKERS AWAY. AND NOW THEY ALL KNOW THE FACE BEHIND THE MASK. IT'S ONLY A MATTER OF TIME BEFORE--
CAREFUL, EAGLE. GIVE A GUY ENOUGH ROPE, HE MIGHT HANG HIMSELF.

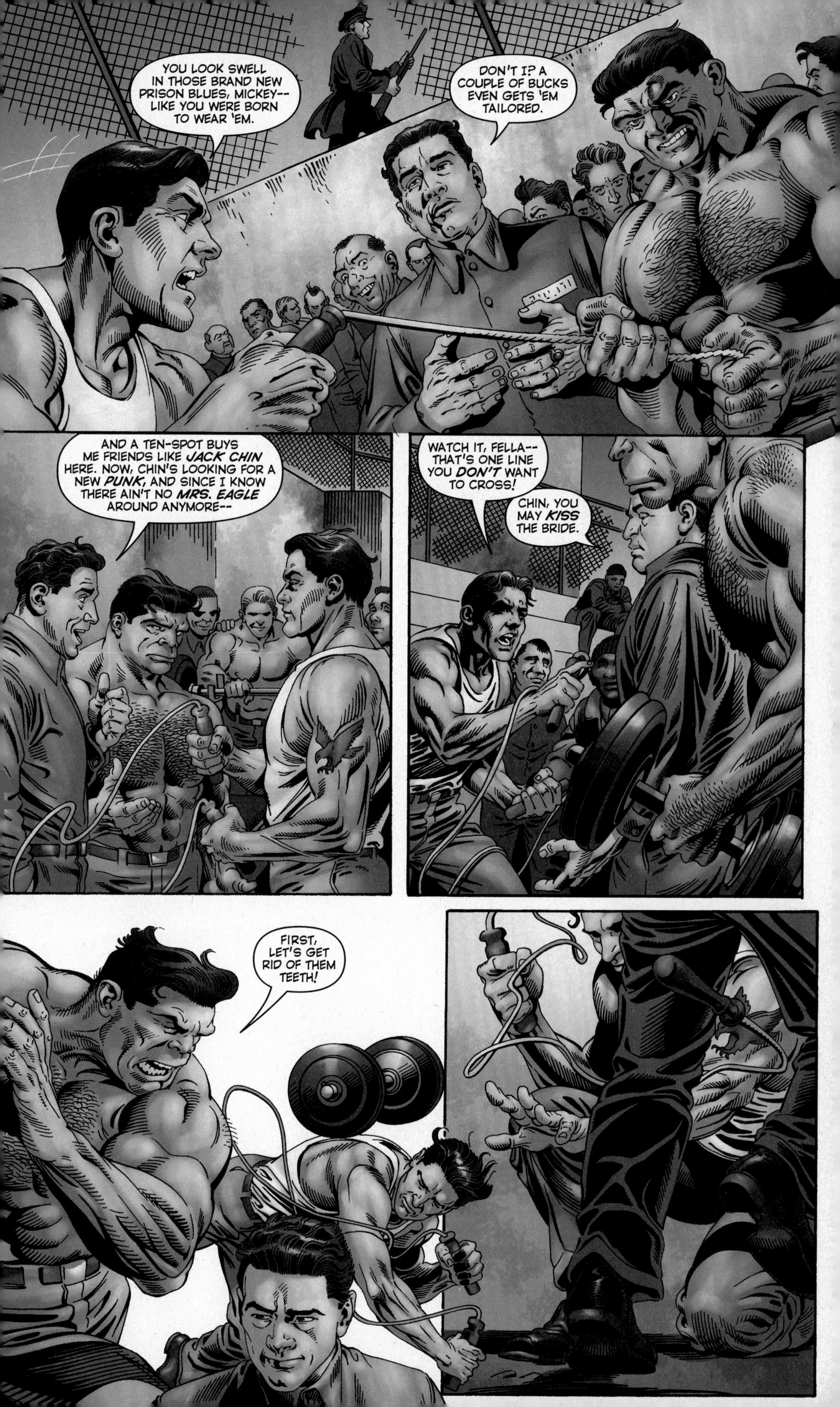

YOU LOOK SWELL IN THOSE BRAND NEW PRISON BLUES, MICKEY-- LIKE YOU WERE BORN TO WEAR 'EM.
DON'T I? A COUPLE OF BUCKS EVEN GETS 'EM TAILORED.
AND A TEN-SPOT BUYS ME FRIENDS LIKE JACK CHIN HERE. NOW, CHIN'S LOOKING FOR A NEW PUNK, AND SINCE I KNOW THERE AIN'T NO MRS. EAGLE AROUND ANYMORE--
WATCH IT, FELLA-- THAT'S ONE LINE YOU DON'T WANT TO CROSS!
CHIN, YOU MAY KISS THE BRIDE.
FIRST, LET'S GET RID OF THEM TEETH!

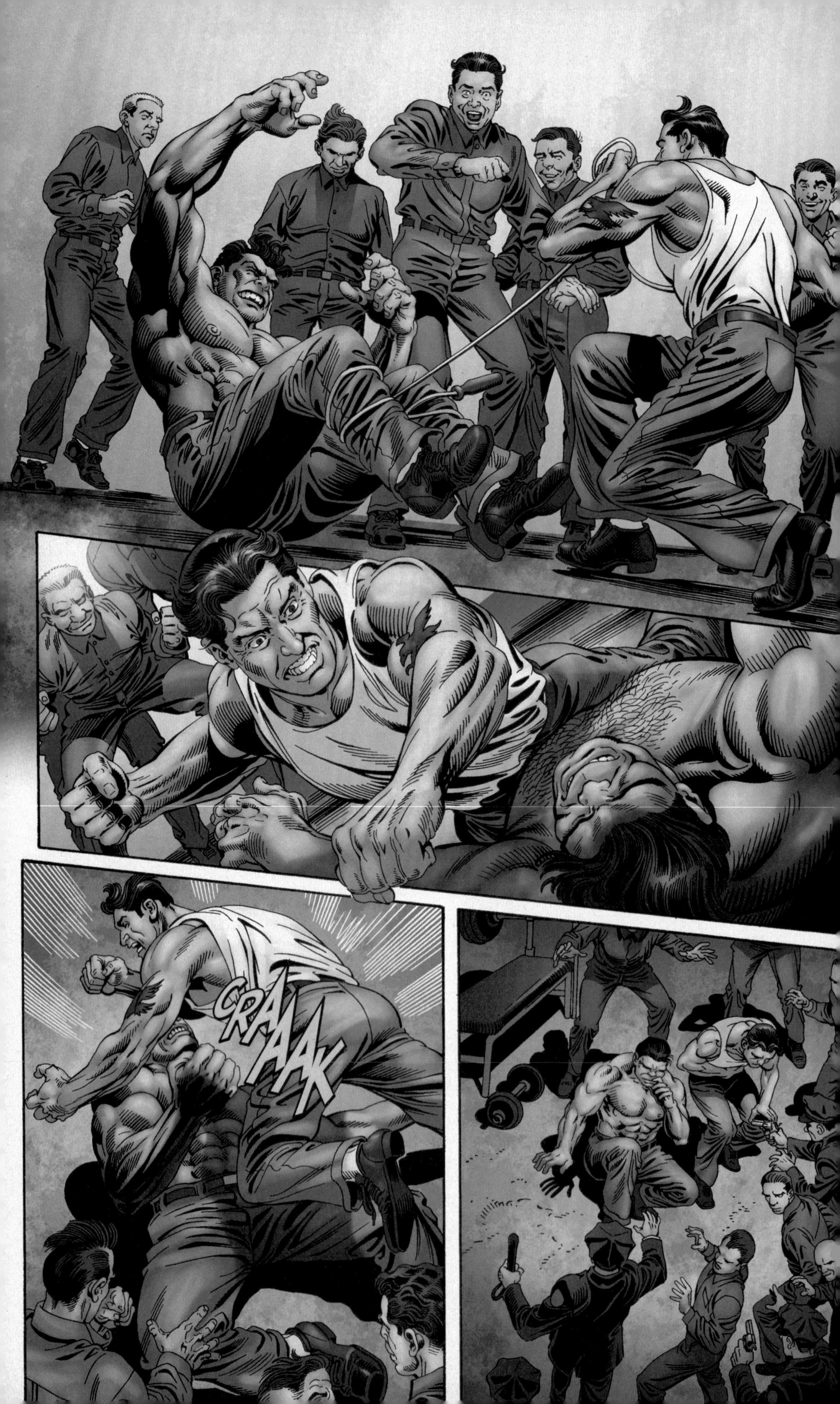
CRAAAK

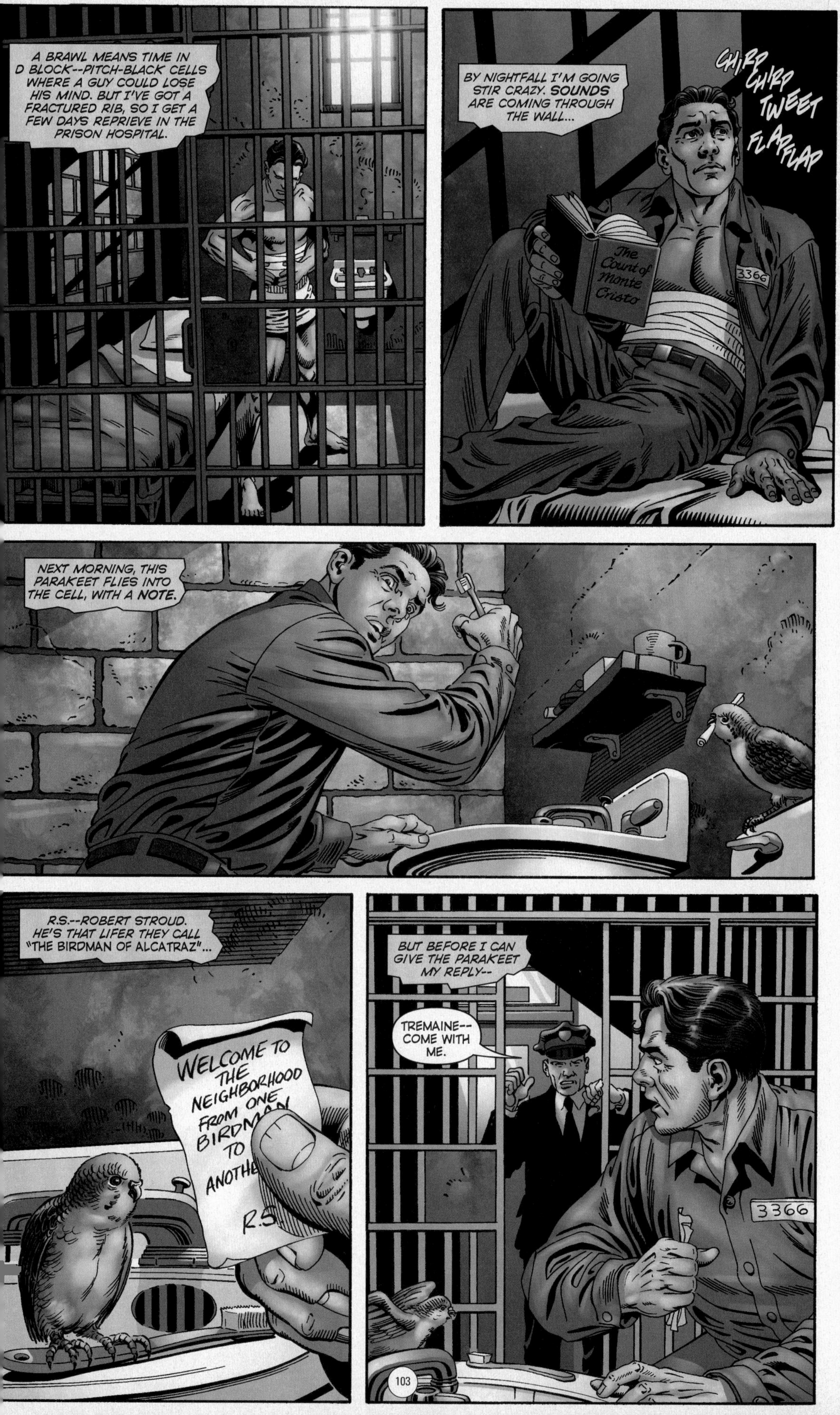
A BRAWL MEANS TIME IN D BLOCK--PITCH-BLACK CELLS WHERE A GUY COULD LOSE HIS MIND. BUT I'VE GOT A FRACTURED RIB, SO I GET A FEW DAYS REPRIEVE IN THE PRISON HOSPITAL.
BY NIGHTFALL I'M GOING STIR CRAZY. SOUNDS ARE COMING THROUGH THE WALL...
CHIRP CHIRP TWEET FLAPFLAP
The Count of Monte Cristo
3366
NEXT MORNING, THIS PARAKEET FLIES INTO THE CELL, WITH A NOTE.
R.S.--ROBERT STROUD. HE'S THAT LIFER THEY CALL "THE BIRDMAN OF ALCATRAZ"...
WELCOME TO THE NEIGHBORHOOD FROM ONE BIRDMAN TO ANOTHE
R.S.
BUT BEFORE I CAN GIVE THE PARAKEET MY REPLY--
TREMAINE-- COME WITH ME.
3366

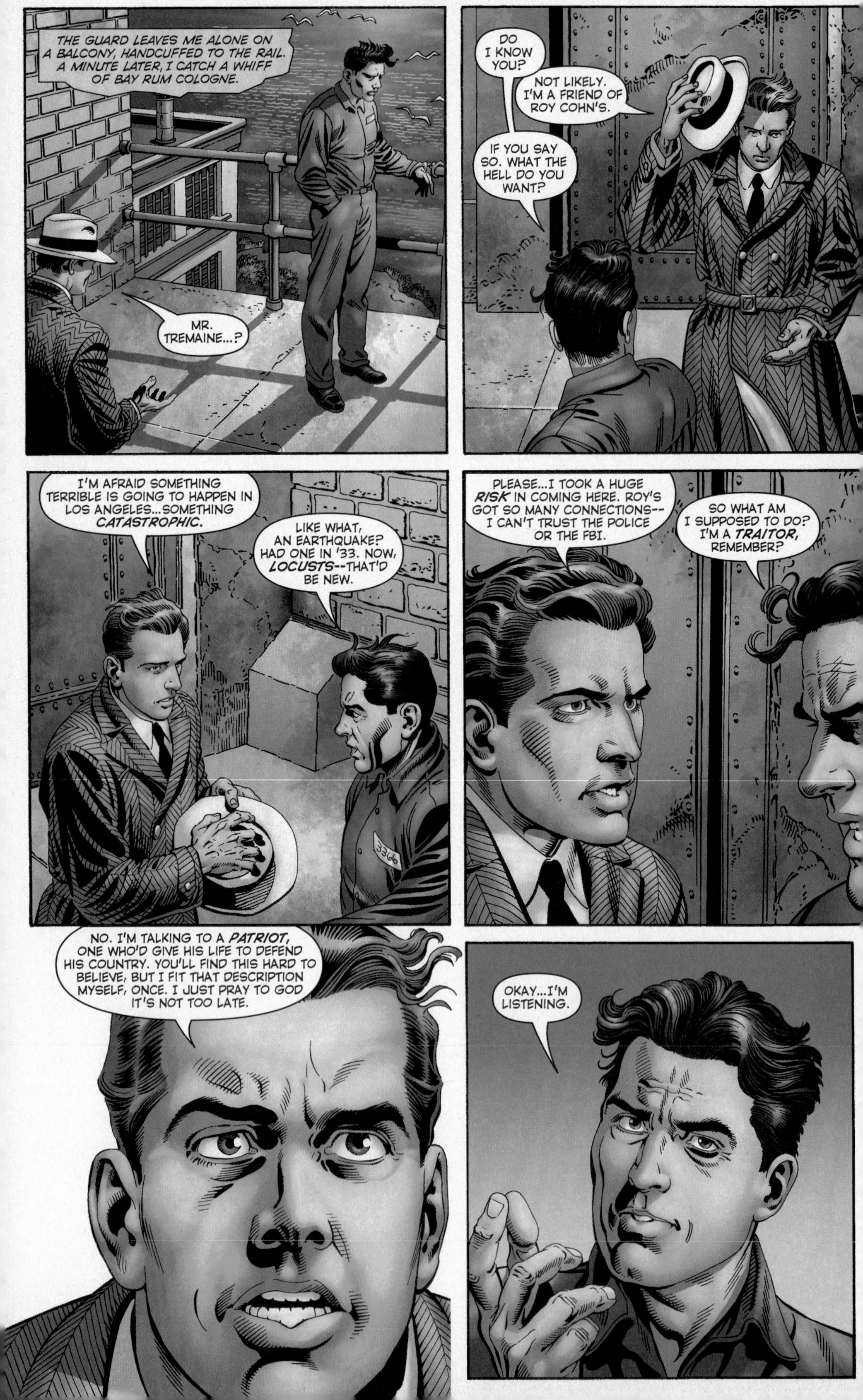
THE GUARD LEAVES ME ALONE ON A BALCONY, HANDCUFFED TO THE RAIL. A MINUTE LATER, I CATCH A WHIFF OF BAY RUM COLOGNE.
MR. TREMAINE...?
DO I KNOW YOU?
NOT LIKELY. I'M A FRIEND OF ROY COHN'S.
IF YOU SAY SO. WHAT THE HELL DO YOU WANT?
I'M AFRAID SOMETHING TERRIBLE IS GOING TO HAPPEN IN LOS ANGELES...SOMETHING CATASTROPHIC.
LIKE WHAT, AN EARTHQUAKE? HAD ONE IN '33. NOW, LOCUSTS--THAT'D BE NEW.
3366
PLEASE...I TOOK A HUGE RISK IN COMING HERE. ROY'S GOT SO MANY CONNECTIONS-- I CAN'T TRUST THE POLICE OR THE FBI.
SO WHAT AM I SUPPOSED TO DO? I'M A TRAITOR, REMEMBER?
NO. I'M TALKING TO A PATRIOT, ONE WHO'D GIVE HIS LIFE TO DEFEND HIS COUNTRY. YOU'LL FIND THIS HARD TO BELIEVE, BUT I FIT THAT DESCRIPTION MYSELF, ONCE. I JUST PRAY TO GOD IT'S NOT TOO LATE.
OKAY...I'M LISTENING.

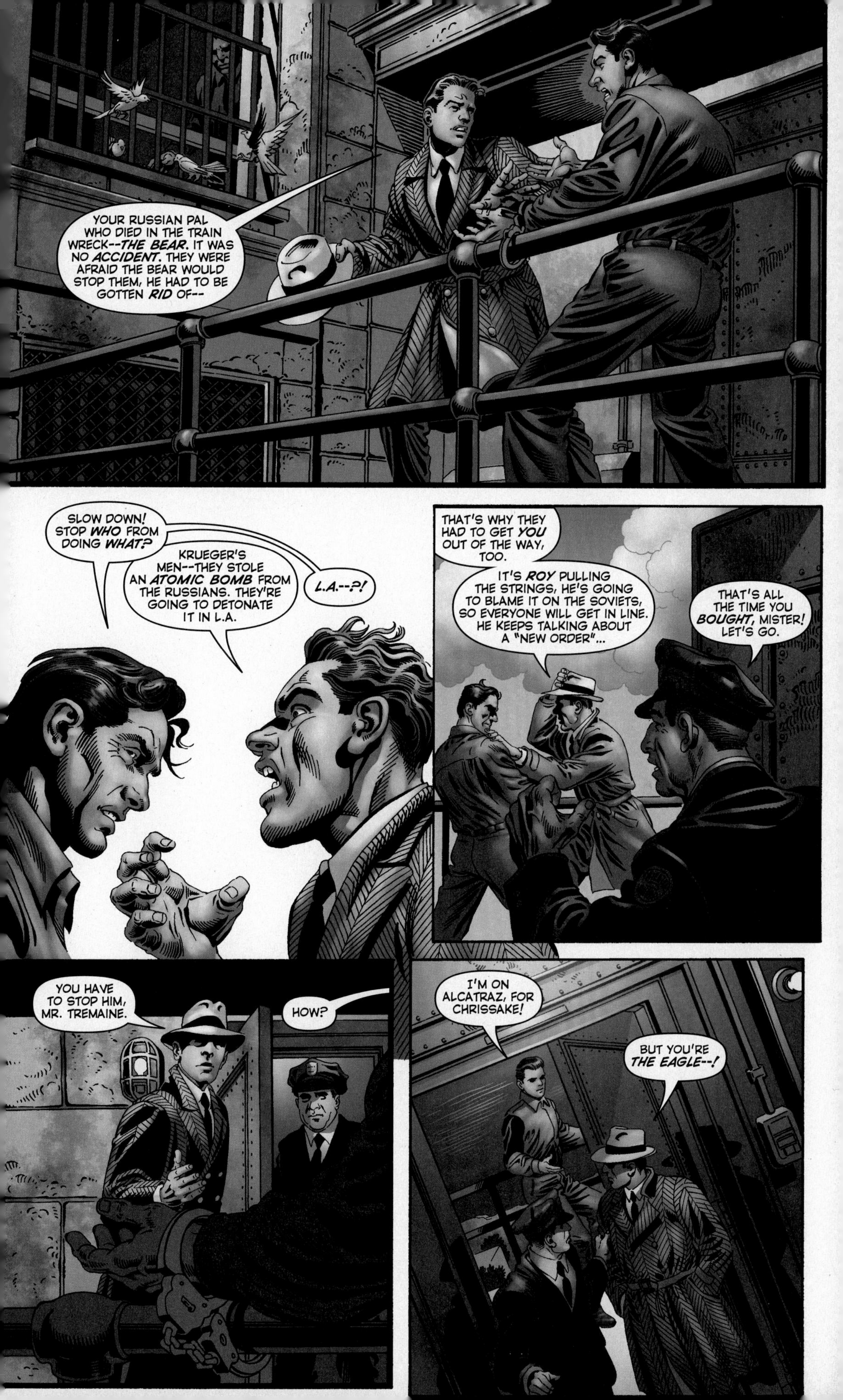

YOUR RUSSIAN PAL WHO DIED IN THE TRAIN WRECK--THE BEAR. IT WAS NO ACCIDENT. THEY WERE AFRAID THE BEAR WOULD STOP THEM, HE HAD TO BE GOTTEN RID OF--
SLOW DOWN! STOP WHO FROM DOING WHAT?
KRUEGER'S MEN--THEY STOLE AN ATOMIC BOMB FROM THE RUSSIANS. THEY'RE GOING TO DETONATE IT IN L.A.
L.A.--?!
THAT'S WHY THEY HAD TO GET YOU OUT OF THE WAY, TOO.
IT'S ROY PULLING THE STRINGS, HE'S GOING TO BLAME IT ON THE SOVIETS, SO EVERYONE WILL GET IN LINE. HE KEEPS TALKING ABOUT A "NEW ORDER"...
THAT'S ALL THE TIME YOU BOUGHT, MISTER! LET'S GO.
YOU HAVE TO STOP HIM, MR. TREMAINE.
HOW?
I'M ON ALCATRAZ, FOR CHRISSAKE!
BUT YOU'RE THE EAGLE--!

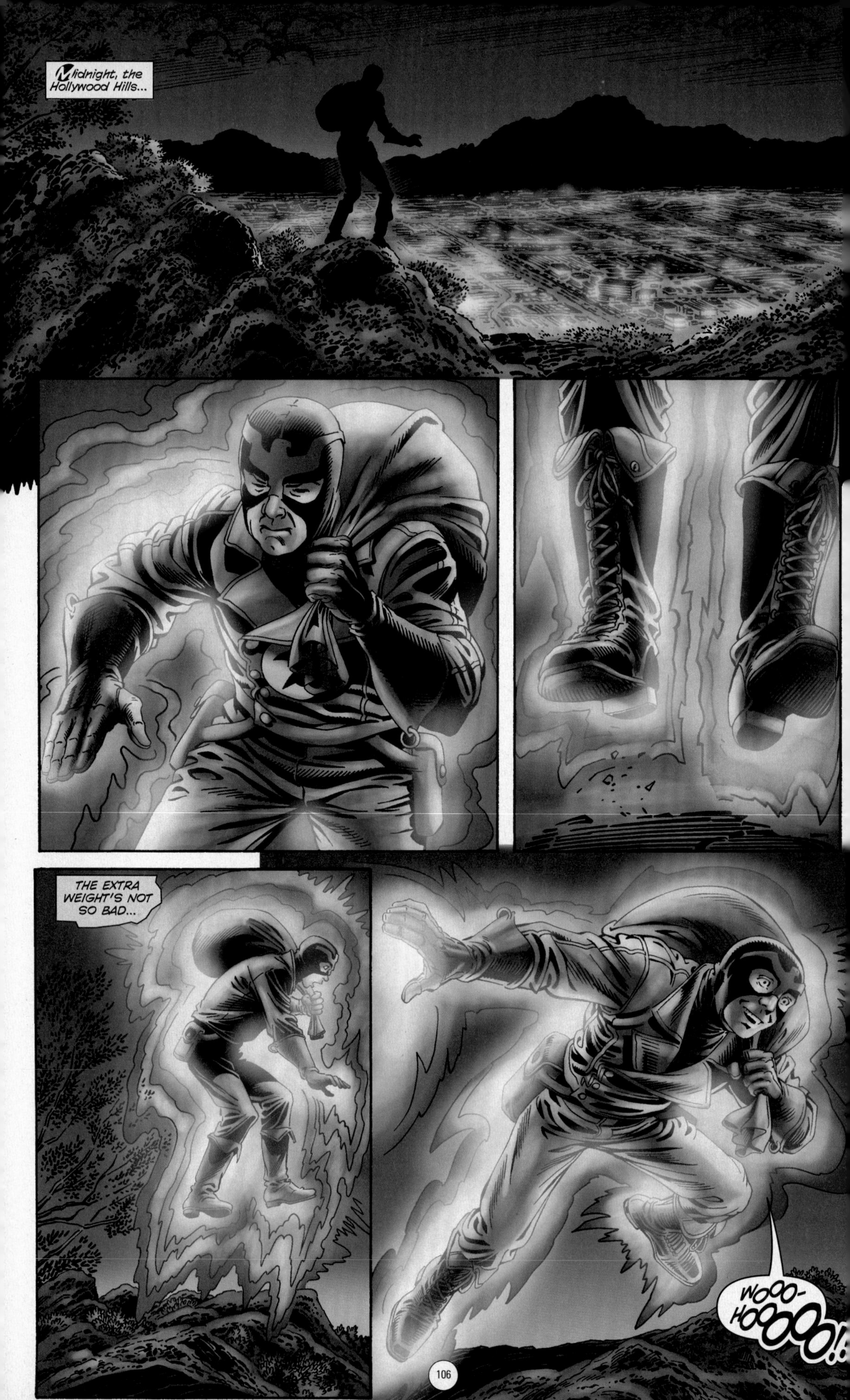

Midnight, the Hollywood Hills...
THE EXTRA WEIGHT'S NOT SO BAD...
WOOO-HOOOOO!!

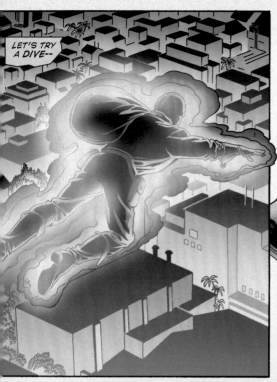

LET'S TRY A DIVE--

UH-OH!

GAAHHH!!

HEY YOU! GET DOWN FROM THERE!

SANTA CLAUS LANE
PARADE
NOVEMBER 25

...WORKING ON IT...

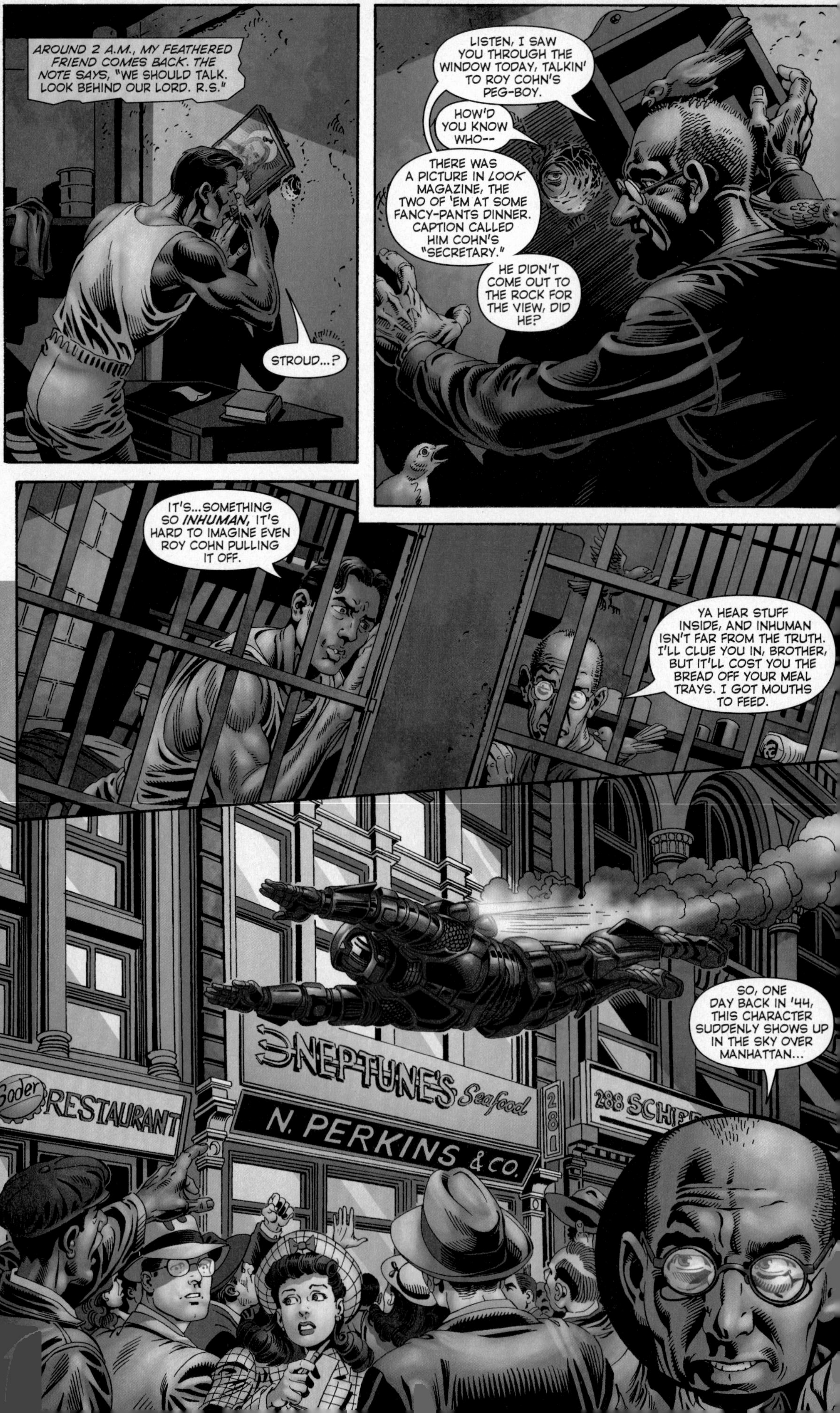

AROUND 2 A.M., MY FEATHERED FRIEND COMES BACK. THE NOTE SAYS, "WE SHOULD TALK. LOOK BEHIND OUR LORD. R.S."
STROUD...?
LISTEN, I SAW YOU THROUGH THE WINDOW TODAY, TALKIN' TO ROY COHN'S PEG-BOY.
HOW'D YOU KNOW WHO--
THERE WAS A PICTURE IN LOOK MAGAZINE, THE TWO OF 'EM AT SOME FANCY-PANTS DINNER. CAPTION CALLED HIM COHN'S "SECRETARY."
HE DIDN'T COME OUT TO THE ROCK FOR THE VIEW, DID HE?
IT'S...SOMETHING SO INHUMAN, IT'S HARD TO IMAGINE EVEN ROY COHN PULLING IT OFF.
YA HEAR STUFF INSIDE, AND INHUMAN ISN'T FAR FROM THE TRUTH. I'LL CLUE YOU IN, BROTHER, BUT IT'LL COST YOU THE BREAD OFF YOUR MEAL TRAYS. I GOT MOUTHS TO FEED.
NEPTUNE'S Seafood
Soder RESTAURANT
N. PERKINS & CO.
288 SCHIE
SO, ONE DAY BACK IN '44, THIS CHARACTER SUDDENLY SHOWS UP IN THE SKY OVER MANHATTAN...

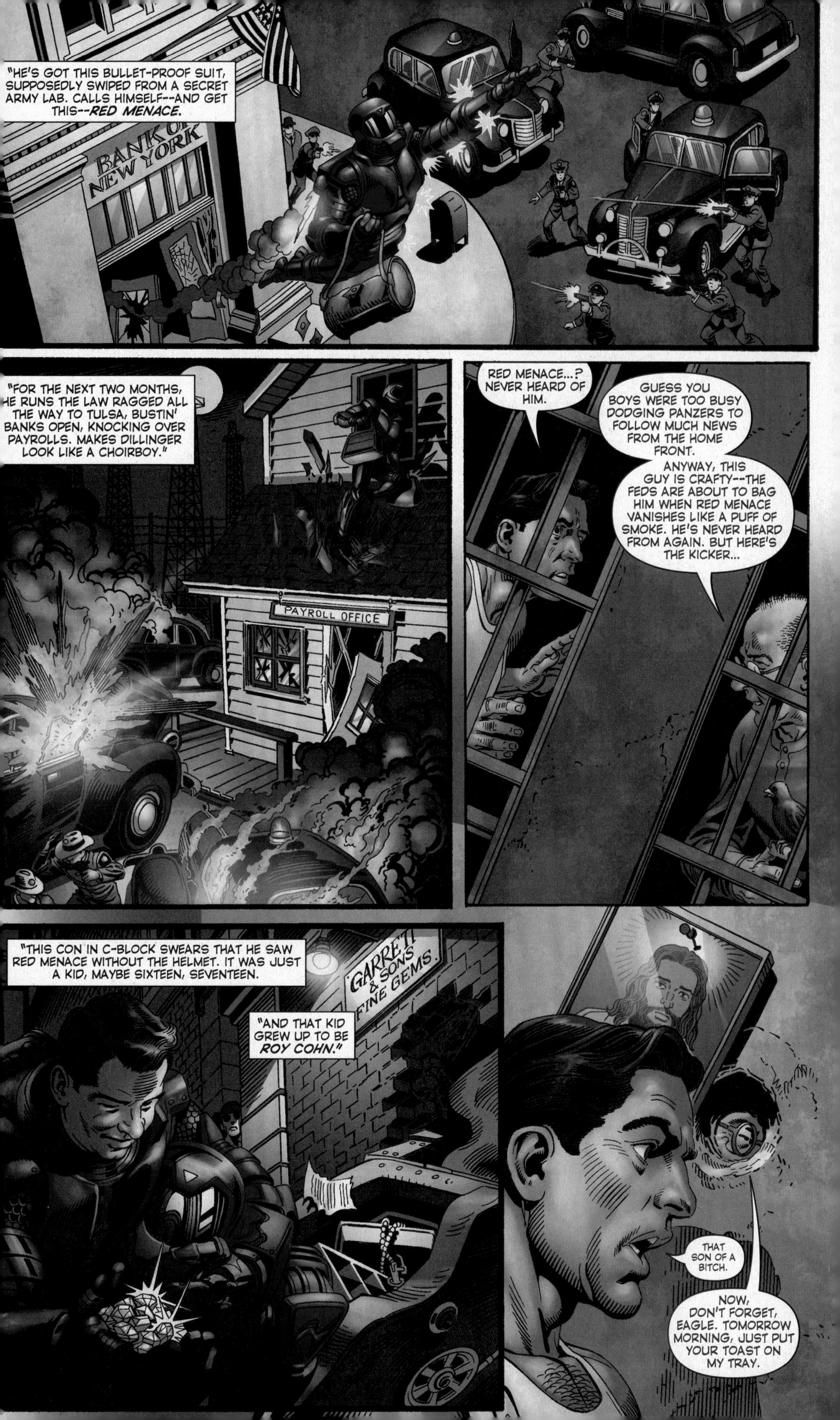
"HE'S GOT THIS BULLET-PROOF SUIT, SUPPOSEDLY SWIPED FROM A SECRET ARMY LAB. CALLS HIMSELF--AND GET THIS--*RED MENACE*.
BANK OF NEW YORK
"FOR THE NEXT TWO MONTHS, HE RUNS THE LAW RAGGED ALL THE WAY TO TULSA, BUSTIN' BANKS OPEN, KNOCKING OVER PAYROLLS. MAKES DILLINGER LOOK LIKE A CHOIRBOY."
PAYROLL OFFICE
RED MENACE...? NEVER HEARD OF HIM.
GUESS YOU BOYS WERE TOO BUSY DODGING PANZERS TO FOLLOW MUCH NEWS FROM THE HOME FRONT.
ANYWAY, THIS GUY IS CRAFTY--THE FEDS ARE ABOUT TO BAG HIM WHEN RED MENACE VANISHES LIKE A PUFF OF SMOKE. HE'S NEVER HEARD FROM AGAIN. BUT HERE'S THE KICKER...
"THIS CON IN C-BLOCK SWEARS THAT HE SAW RED MENACE WITHOUT THE HELMET. IT WAS JUST A KID, MAYBE SIXTEEN, SEVENTEEN.
GARRETT & SONS FINE GEMS
"AND THAT KID GREW UP TO BE *ROY COHN*."
THAT SON OF A BITCH.
NOW, DON'T FORGET, EAGLE. TOMORROW MORNING, JUST PUT YOUR TOAST ON MY TRAY.

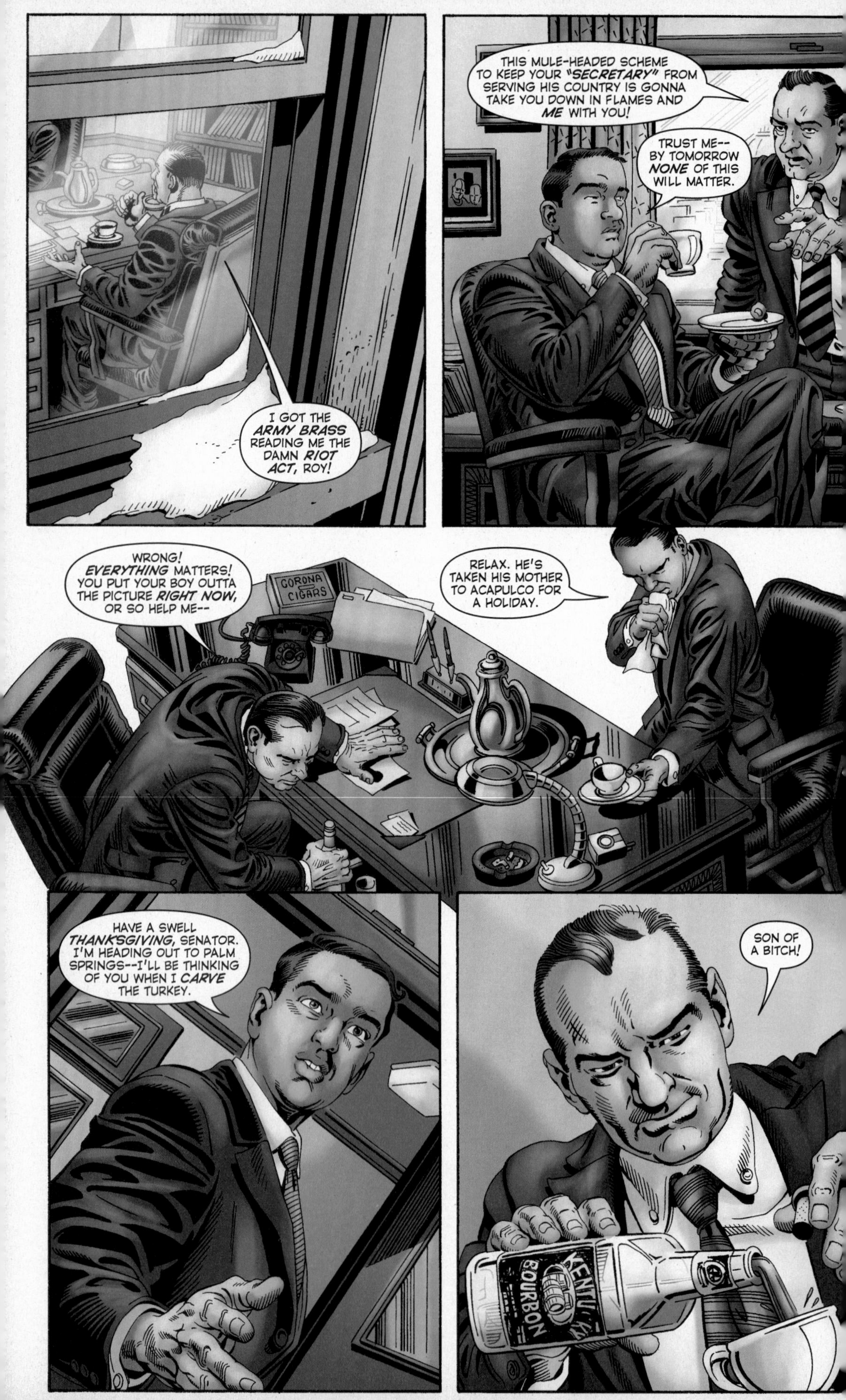

I GOT THE ARMY BRASS READING ME THE DAMN RIOT ACT, ROY!
THIS MULE-HEADED SCHEME TO KEEP YOUR "SECRETARY" FROM SERVING HIS COUNTRY IS GONNA TAKE YOU DOWN IN FLAMES AND ME WITH YOU!
TRUST ME-- BY TOMORROW NONE OF THIS WILL MATTER.
WRONG! EVERYTHING MATTERS! YOU PUT YOUR BOY OUTTA THE PICTURE RIGHT NOW, OR SO HELP ME--
CORONA CIGARS
RELAX. HE'S TAKEN HIS MOTHER TO ACAPULCO FOR A HOLIDAY.
HAVE A SWELL THANKSGIVING, SENATOR. I'M HEADING OUT TO PALM SPRINGS--I'LL BE THINKING OF YOU WHEN I CARVE THE TURKEY.
SON OF A BITCH!
KENTUCKY BOURBON

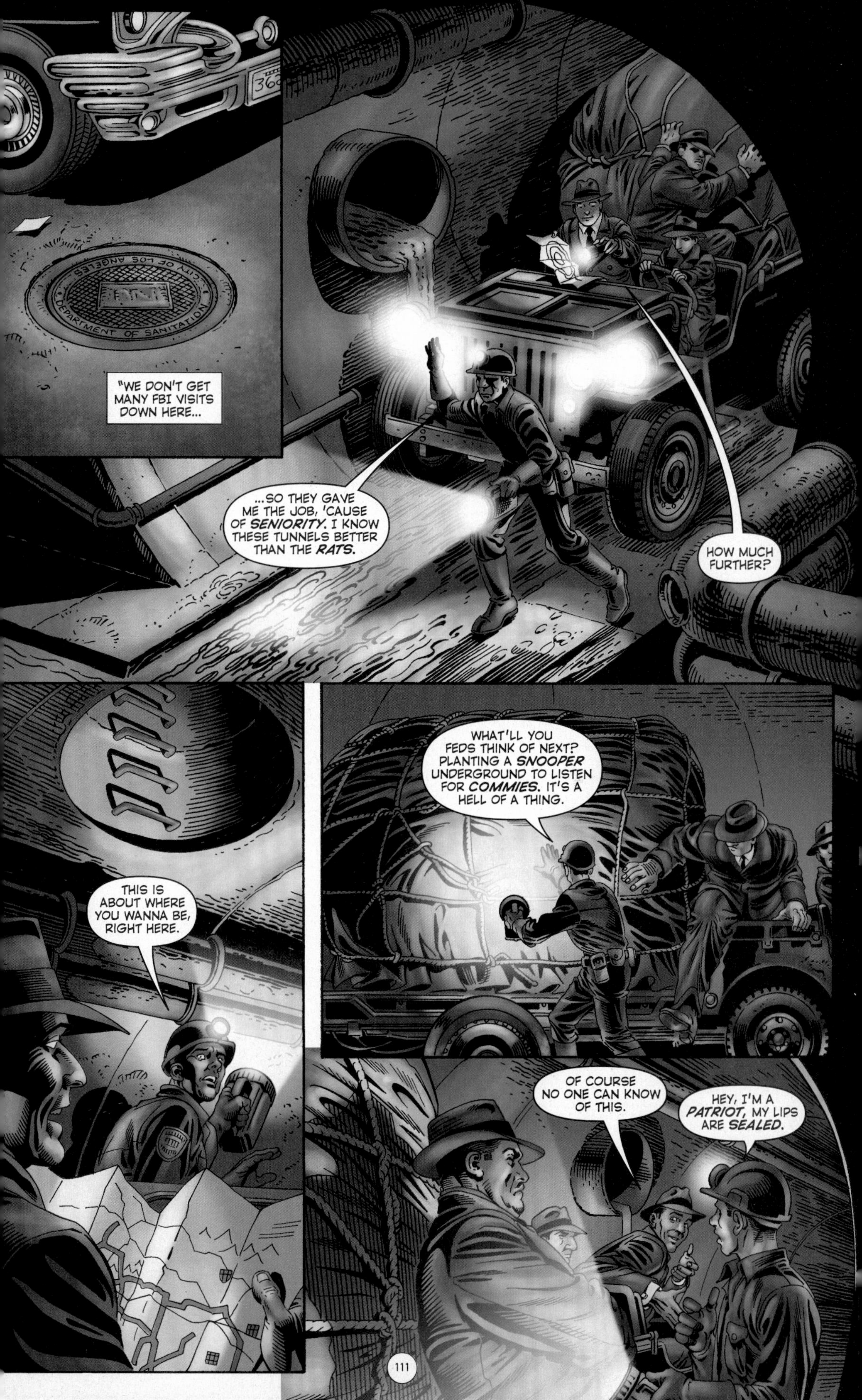
CITY OF LOS ANGELES
DEPARTMENT OF SANITATION
"WE DON'T GET MANY FBI VISITS DOWN HERE...
...SO THEY GAVE ME THE JOB, 'CAUSE OF SENIORITY. I KNOW THESE TUNNELS BETTER THAN THE RATS.
HOW MUCH FURTHER?
THIS IS ABOUT WHERE YOU WANNA BE, RIGHT HERE.
WHAT'LL YOU FEDS THINK OF NEXT? PLANTING A SNOOPER UNDERGROUND TO LISTEN FOR COMMIES. IT'S A HELL OF A THING.
OF COURSE NO ONE CAN KNOW OF THIS.
HEY, I'M A PATRIOT, MY LIPS ARE SEALED.

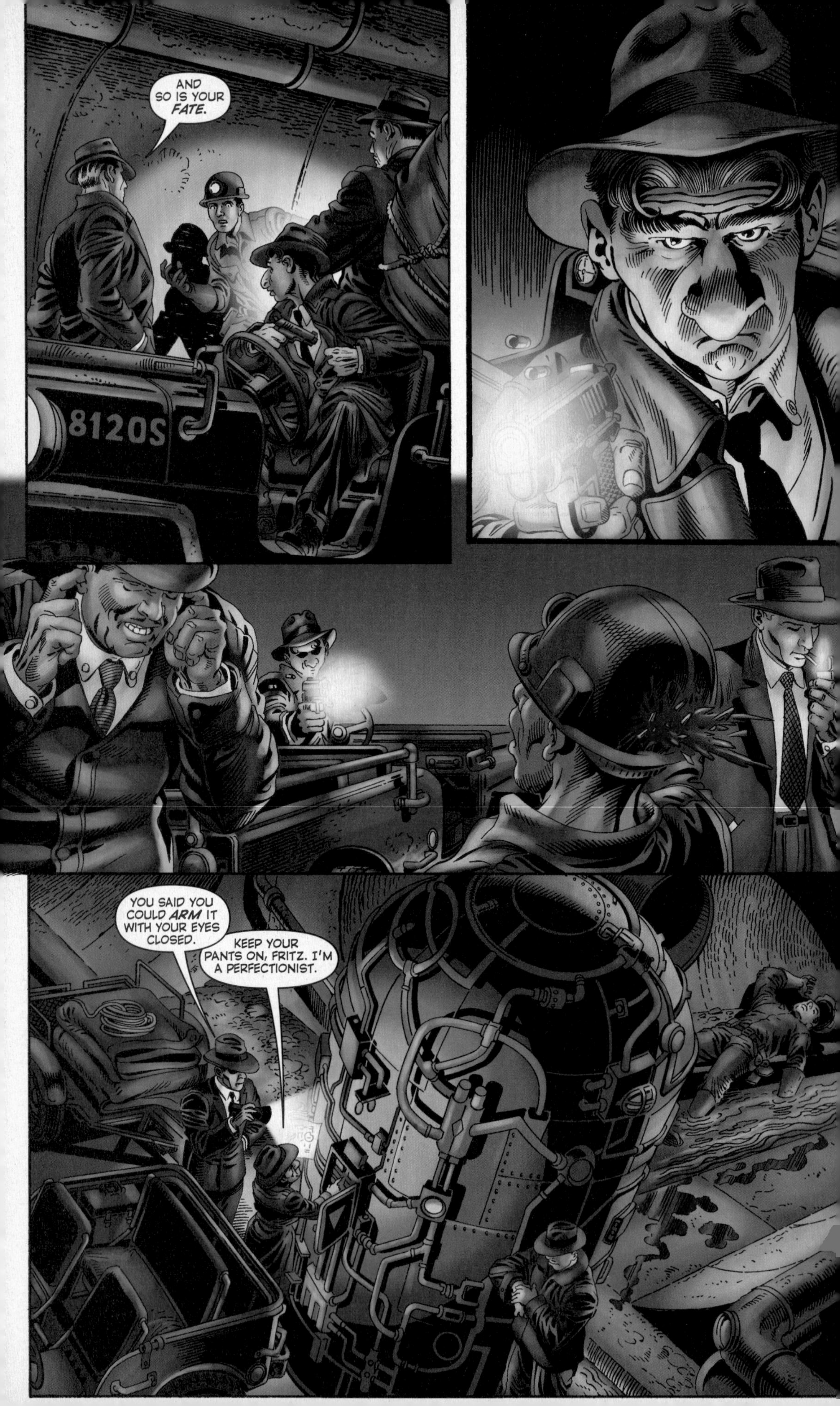
AND SO IS YOUR *FATE*.
8120S
YOU SAID YOU COULD *ARM* IT WITH YOUR EYES CLOSED.
KEEP YOUR PANTS ON, FRITZ. I'M A PERFECTIONIST.

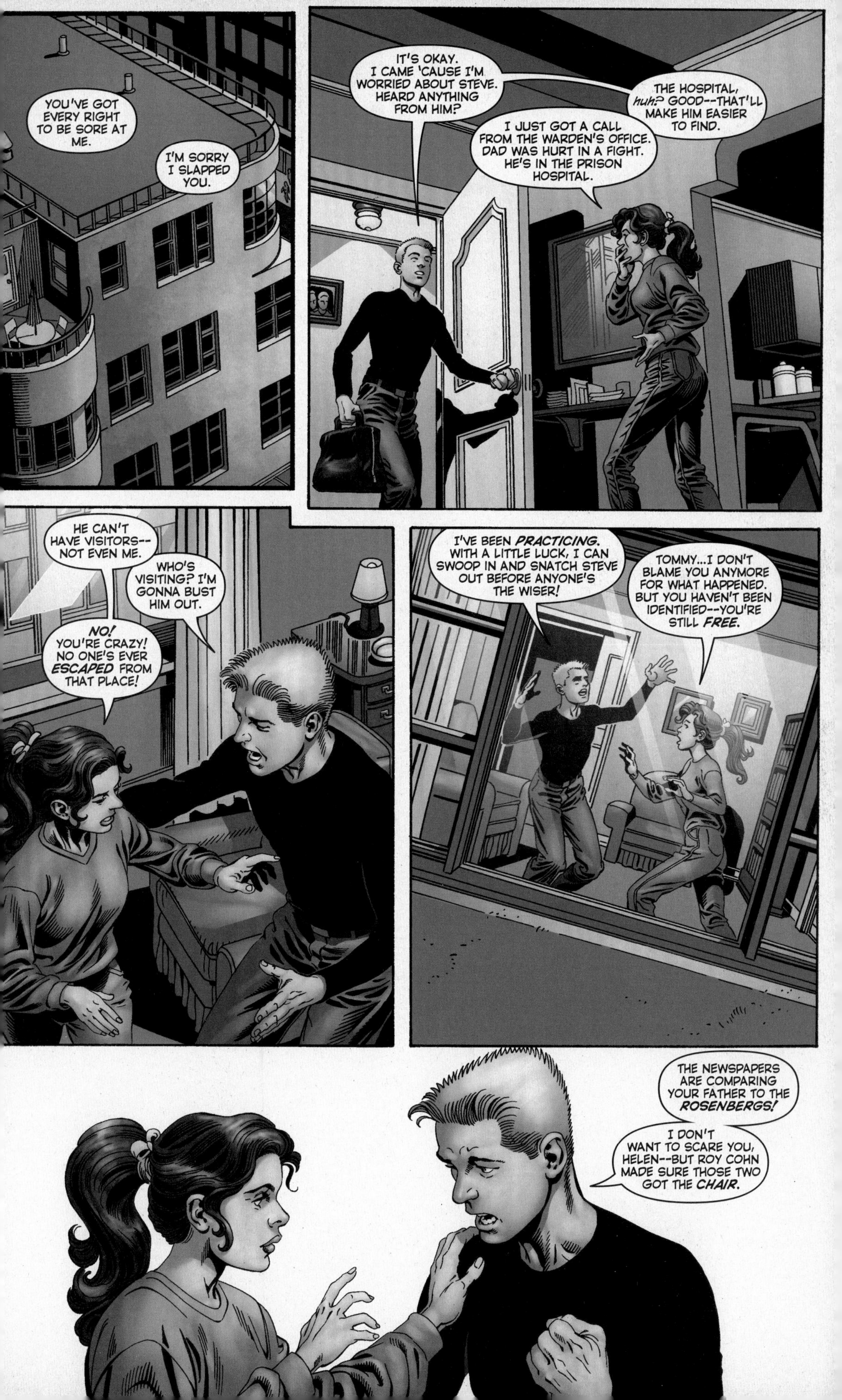

YOU'VE GOT EVERY RIGHT TO BE SORE AT ME.
I'M SORRY I SLAPPED YOU.
IT'S OKAY. I CAME 'CAUSE I'M WORRIED ABOUT STEVE. HEARD ANYTHING FROM HIM?
I JUST GOT A CALL FROM THE WARDEN'S OFFICE. DAD WAS HURT IN A FIGHT. HE'S IN THE PRISON HOSPITAL.
THE HOSPITAL, *huh?* GOOD--THAT'LL MAKE HIM EASIER TO FIND.
HE CAN'T HAVE VISITORS--NOT EVEN ME.
WHO'S VISITING? I'M GONNA BUST HIM OUT.
NO! YOU'RE CRAZY! NO ONE'S EVER ***ESCAPED*** FROM THAT PLACE!
I'VE BEEN ***PRACTICING.*** WITH A LITTLE LUCK, I CAN SWOOP IN AND SNATCH STEVE OUT BEFORE ANYONE'S THE WISER!
TOMMY...I DON'T BLAME YOU ANYMORE FOR WHAT HAPPENED. BUT YOU HAVEN'T BEEN IDENTIFIED--YOU'RE STILL ***FREE.***
THE NEWSPAPERS ARE COMPARING YOUR FATHER TO THE ***ROSENBERGS!***
I DON'T WANT TO SCARE YOU, HELEN--BUT ROY COHN MADE SURE THOSE TWO GOT THE ***CHAIR.***

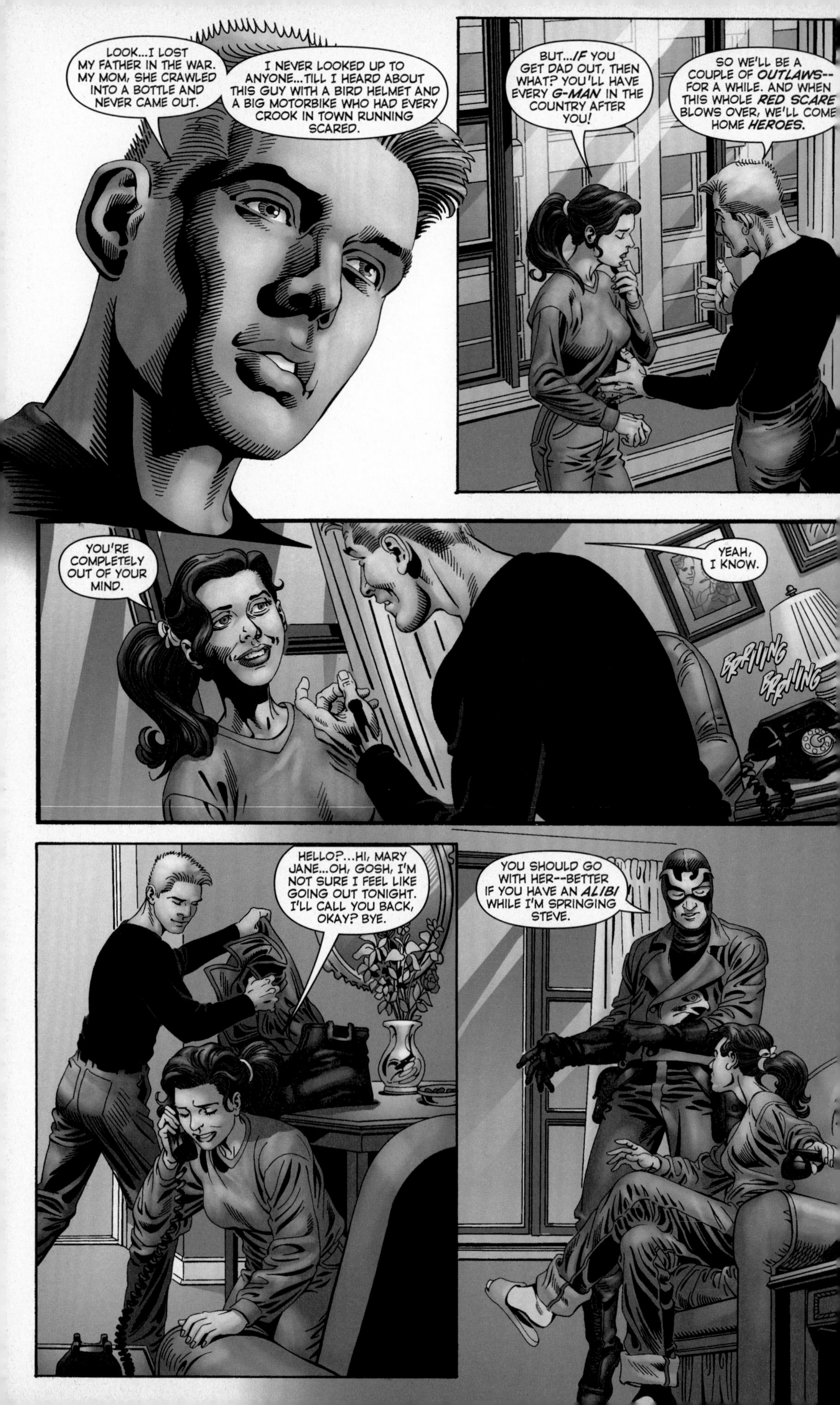
LOOK...I LOST MY FATHER IN THE WAR. MY MOM, SHE CRAWLED INTO A BOTTLE AND NEVER CAME OUT.
I NEVER LOOKED UP TO ANYONE...TILL I HEARD ABOUT THIS GUY WITH A BIRD HELMET AND A BIG MOTORBIKE WHO HAD EVERY CROOK IN TOWN RUNNING SCARED.
BUT...IF YOU GET DAD OUT, THEN WHAT? YOU'LL HAVE EVERY G-MAN IN THE COUNTRY AFTER YOU!
SO WE'LL BE A COUPLE OF OUTLAWS--FOR A WHILE. AND WHEN THIS WHOLE RED SCARE BLOWS OVER, WE'LL COME HOME HEROES.
YOU'RE COMPLETELY OUT OF YOUR MIND.
YEAH, I KNOW.
BRRIIING
BRRIIING
HELLO?...HI, MARY JANE...OH, GOSH, I'M NOT SURE I FEEL LIKE GOING OUT TONIGHT. I'LL CALL YOU BACK, OKAY? BYE.
YOU SHOULD GO WITH HER--BETTER IF YOU HAVE AN ALIBI WHILE I'M SPRINGING STEVE.

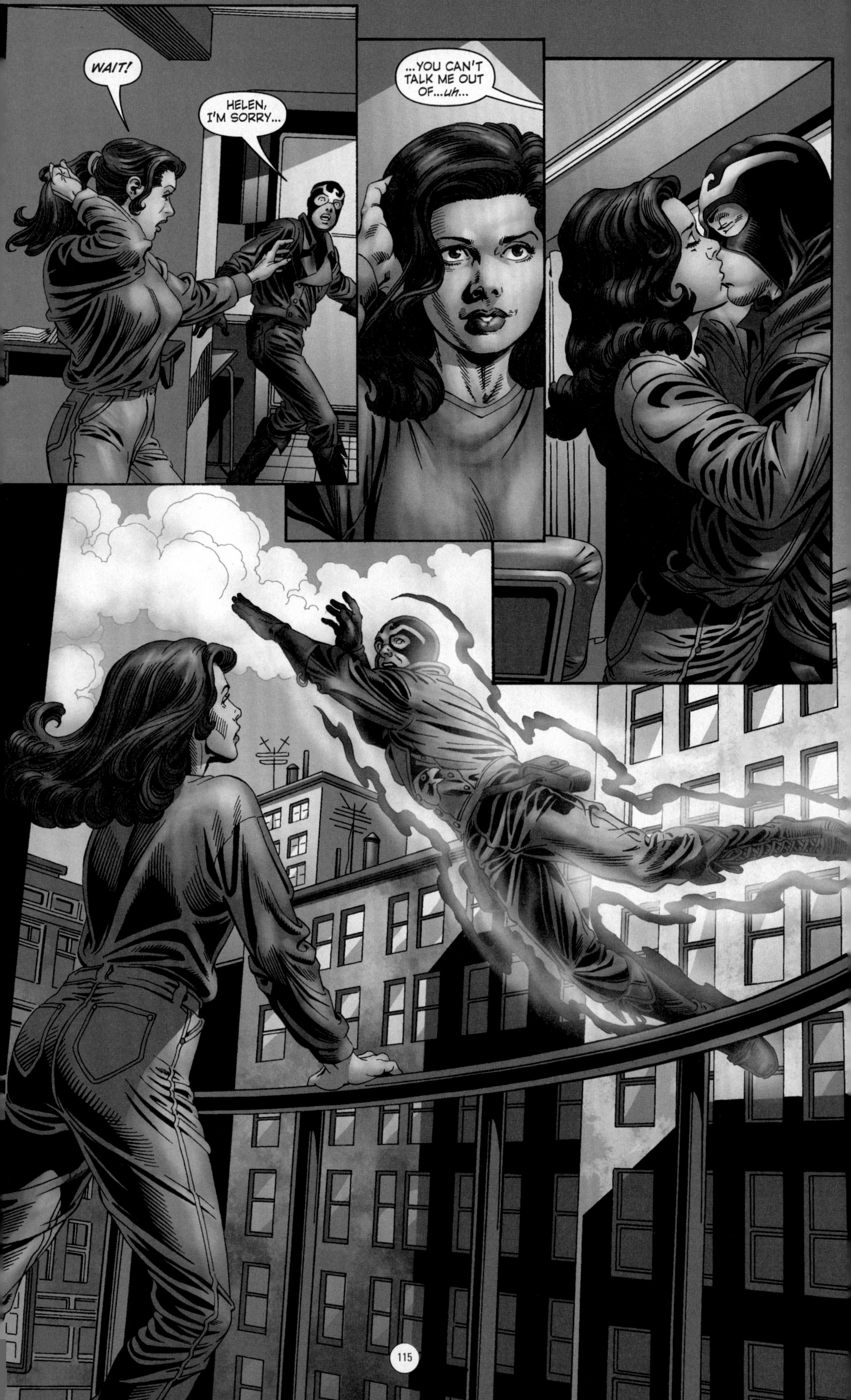
WAIT!
HELEN, I'M SORRY...
...YOU CAN'T TALK ME OUT OF...*uh*...

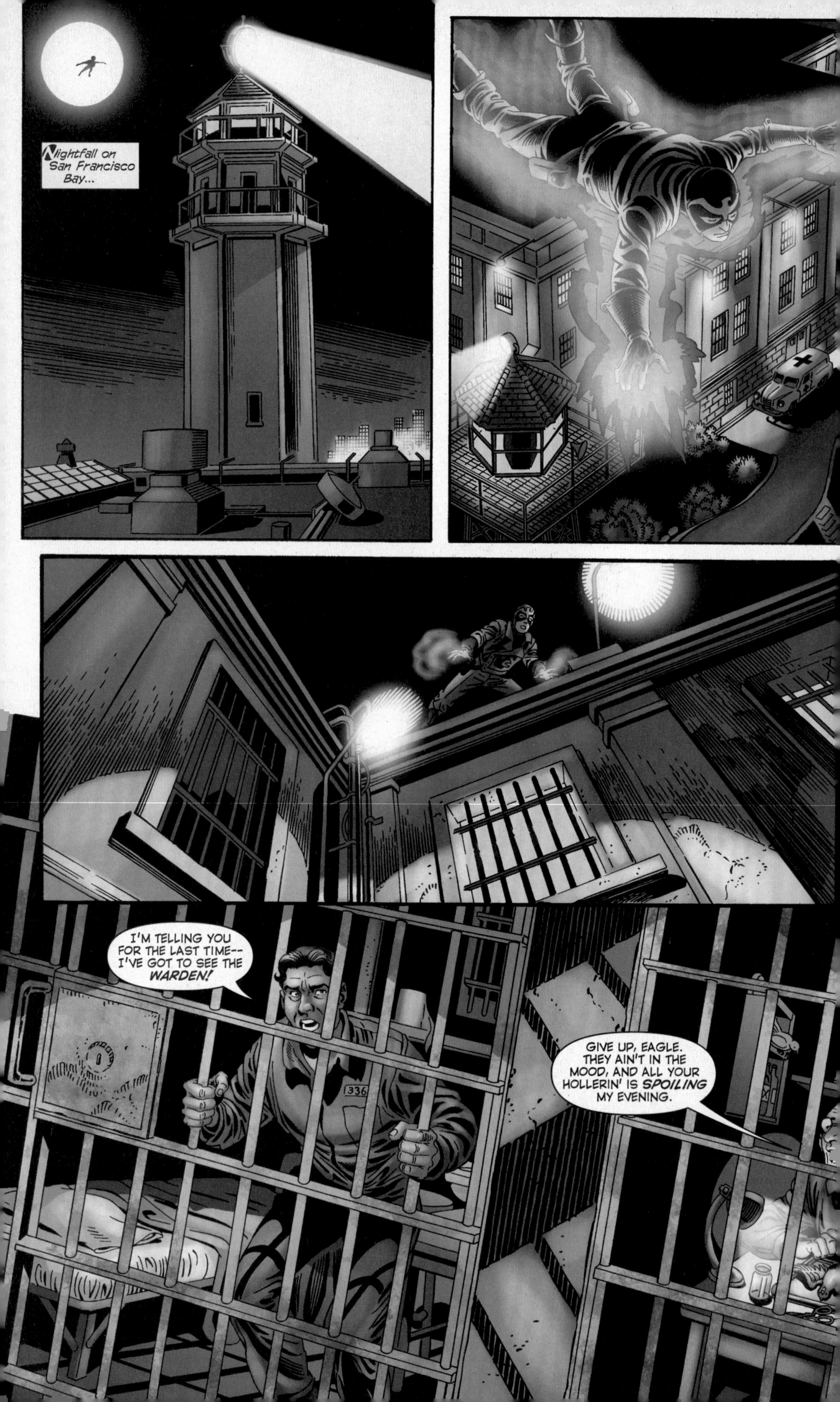
Nightfall on San Francisco Bay...
I'M TELLING YOU FOR THE LAST TIME-- I'VE GOT TO SEE THE WARDEN!
GIVE UP, EAGLE. THEY AIN'T IN THE MOOD, AND ALL YOUR HOLLERIN' IS SPOILING MY EVENING.

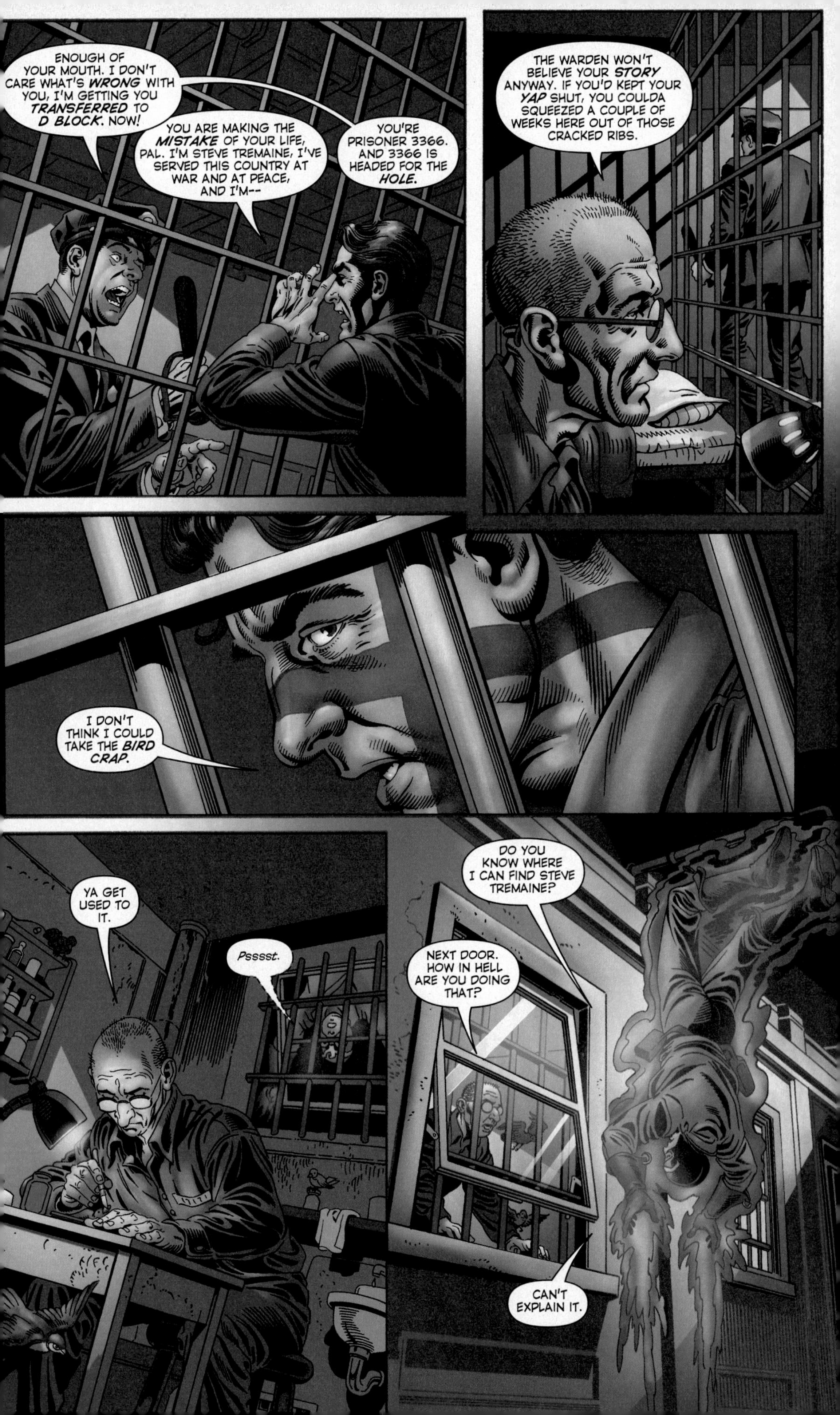
ENOUGH OF YOUR MOUTH. I DON'T CARE WHAT'S WRONG WITH YOU, I'M GETTING YOU TRANSFERRED TO D BLOCK. NOW!
YOU ARE MAKING THE MISTAKE OF YOUR LIFE, PAL. I'M STEVE TREMAINE, I'VE SERVED THIS COUNTRY AT WAR AND AT PEACE, AND I'M--
YOU'RE PRISONER 3366. AND 3366 IS HEADED FOR THE HOLE.
THE WARDEN WON'T BELIEVE YOUR STORY ANYWAY. IF YOU'D KEPT YOUR YAP SHUT, YOU COULDA SQUEEZED A COUPLE OF WEEKS HERE OUT OF THOSE CRACKED RIBS.
I DON'T THINK I COULD TAKE THE BIRD CRAP.
YA GET USED TO IT.
Psssst.
DO YOU KNOW WHERE I CAN FIND STEVE TREMAINE?
NEXT DOOR. HOW IN HELL ARE YOU DOING THAT?
CAN'T EXPLAIN IT.

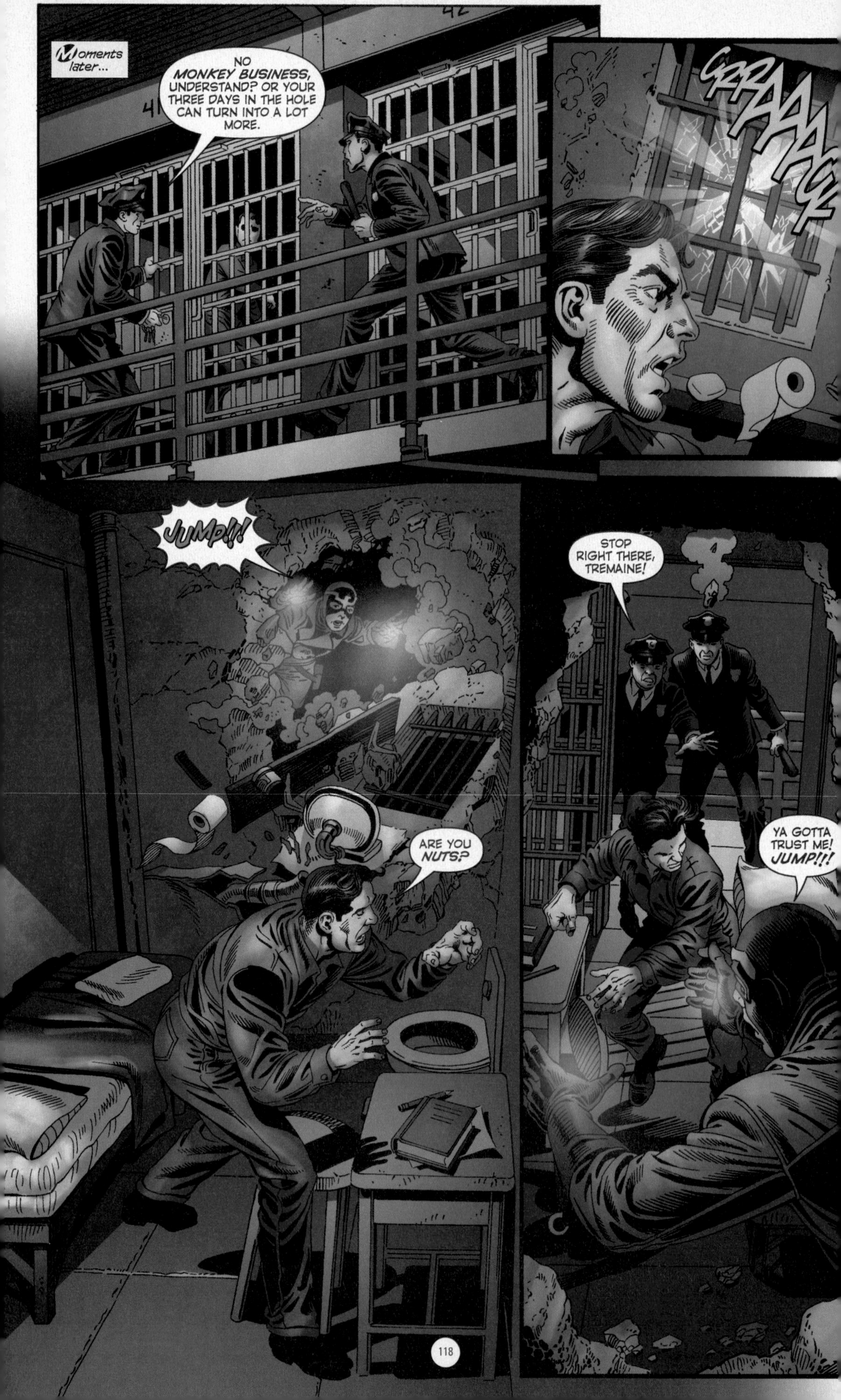
Moments later...
NO MONKEY BUSINESS, UNDERSTAND? OR YOUR THREE DAYS IN THE HOLE CAN TURN INTO A LOT MORE.
CRRAAAACK
JUMP!!!
ARE YOU NUTS?
STOP RIGHT THERE, TREMAINE!
YA GOTTA TRUST ME! JUMP!!!

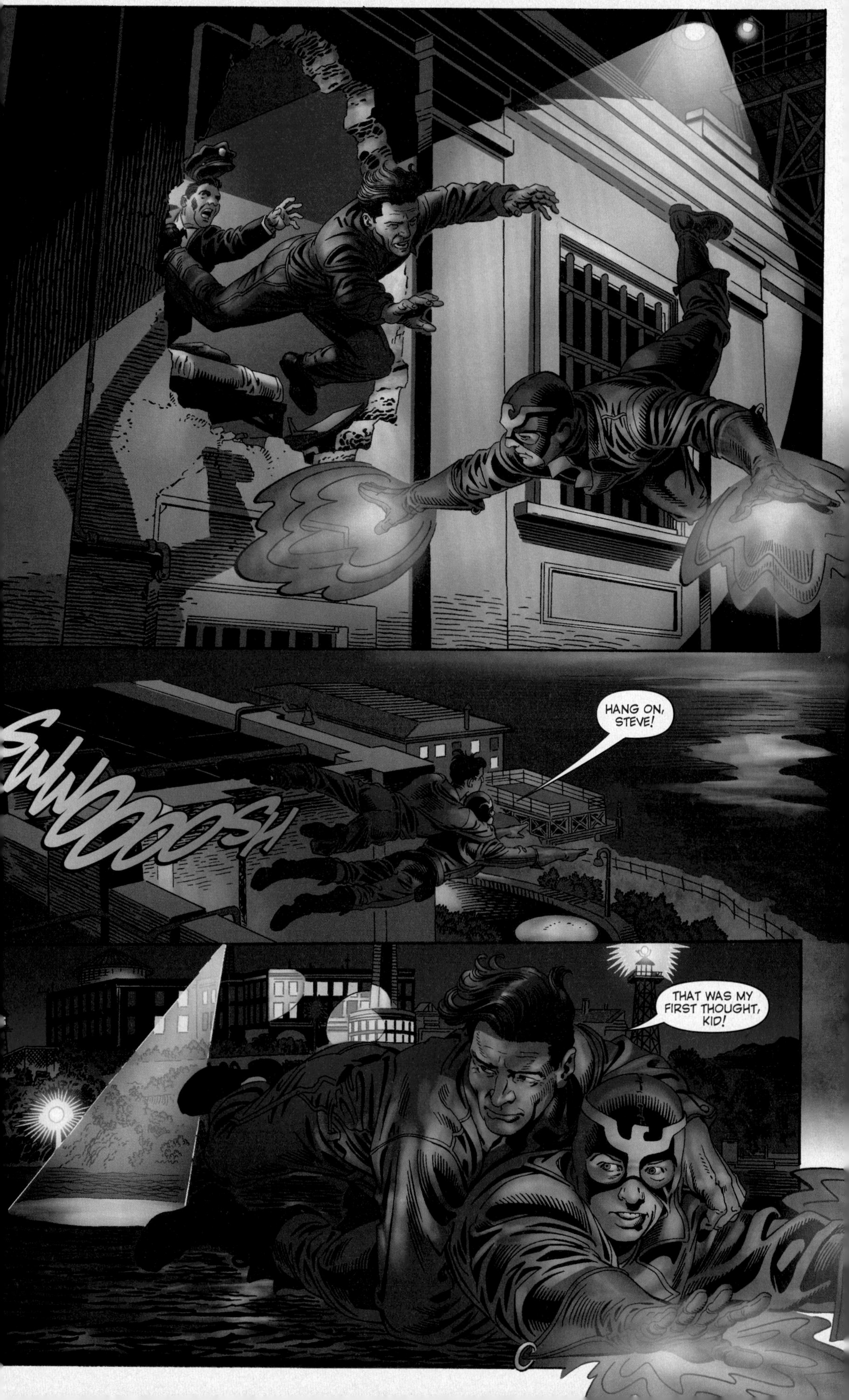
SWOOOOSH
HANG ON, STEVE!
THAT WAS MY FIRST THOUGHT, KID!

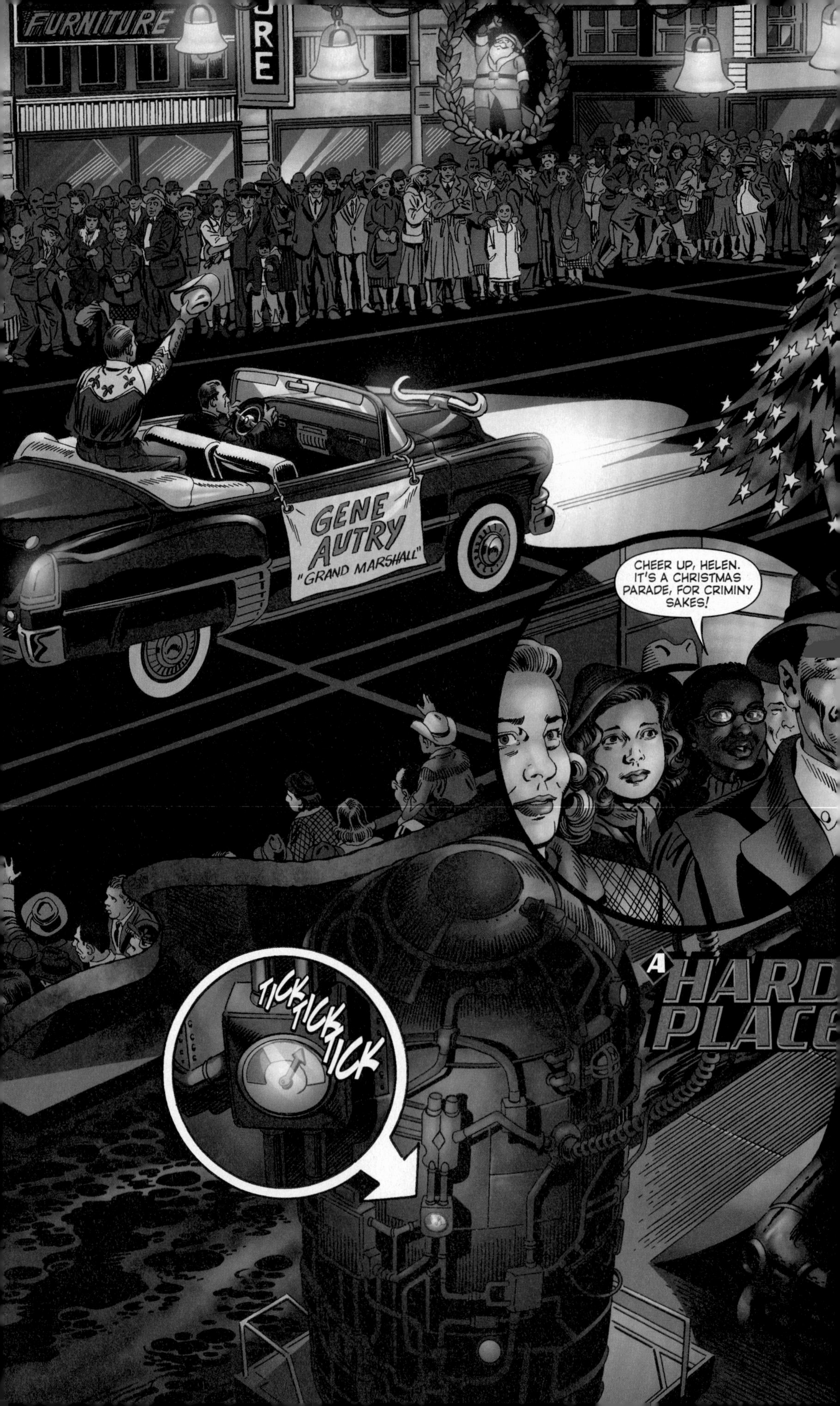
FURNITURE
GENE AUTRY "GRAND MARSHALL"
CHEER UP, HELEN. IT'S A CHRISTMAS PARADE, FOR CRIMINY SAKES!
TICK TICK TICK
A HARD PLACE

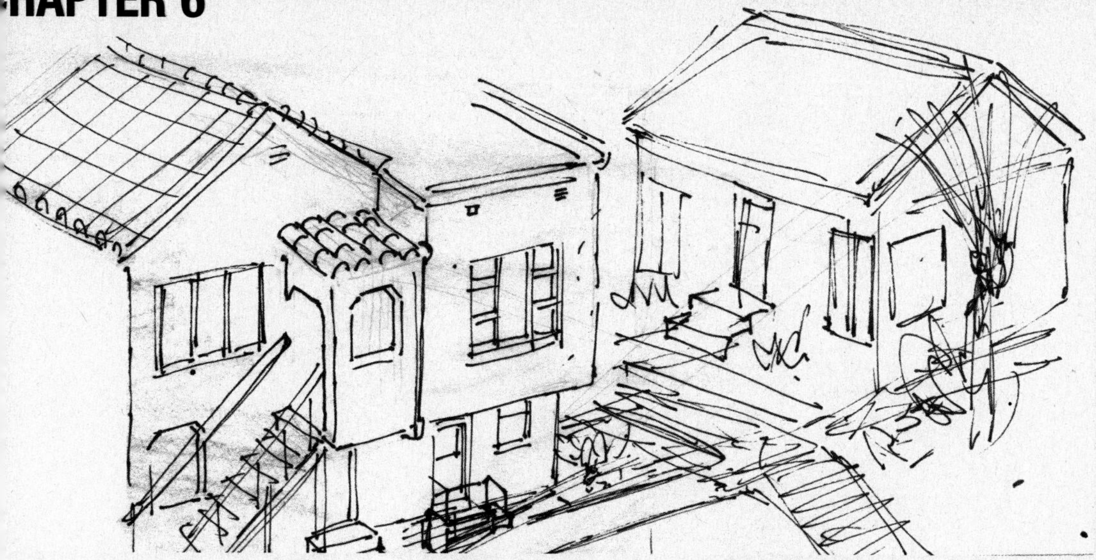

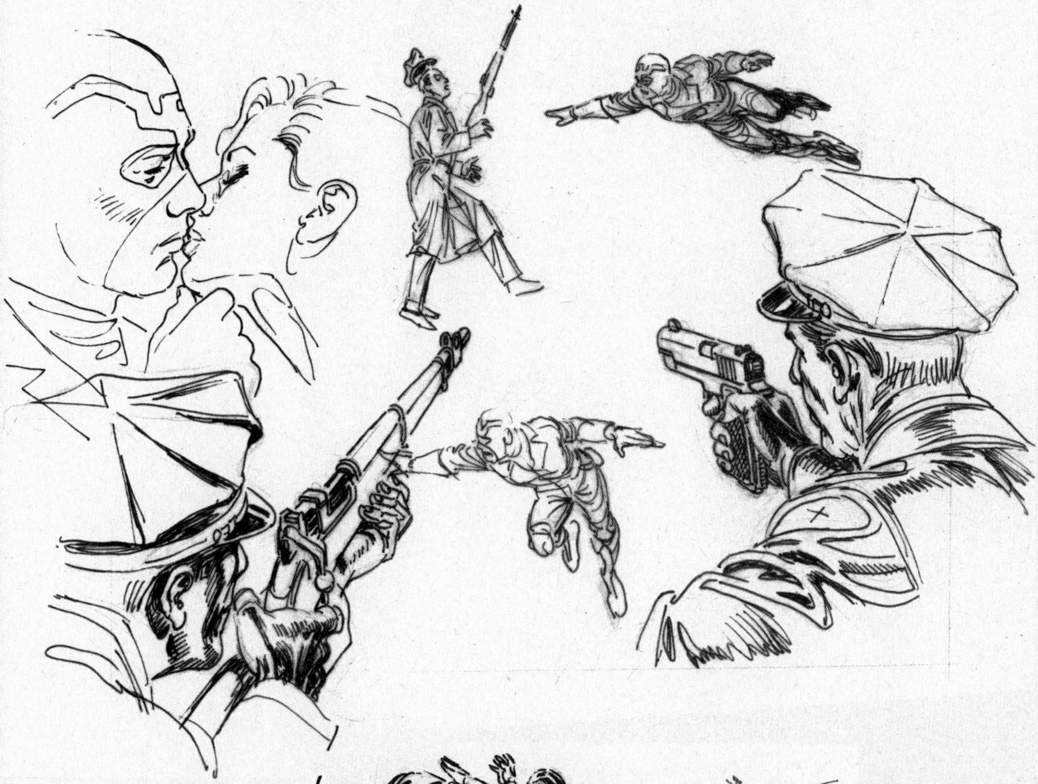

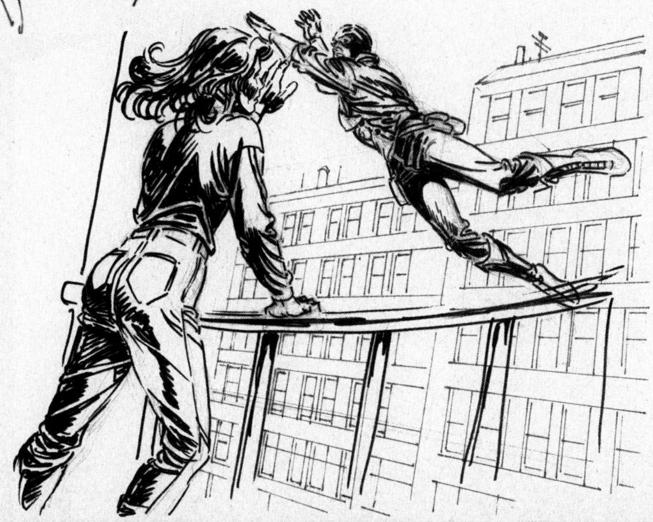

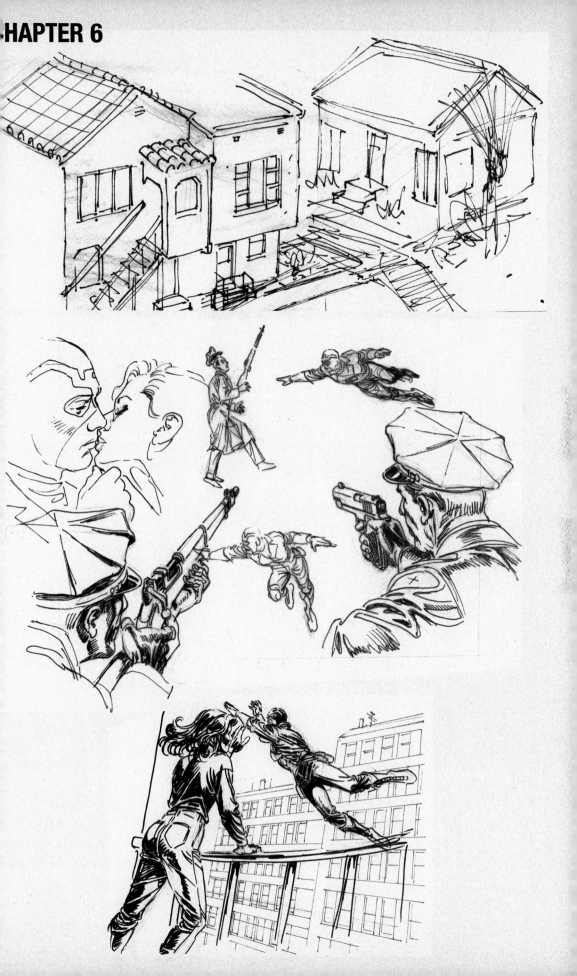

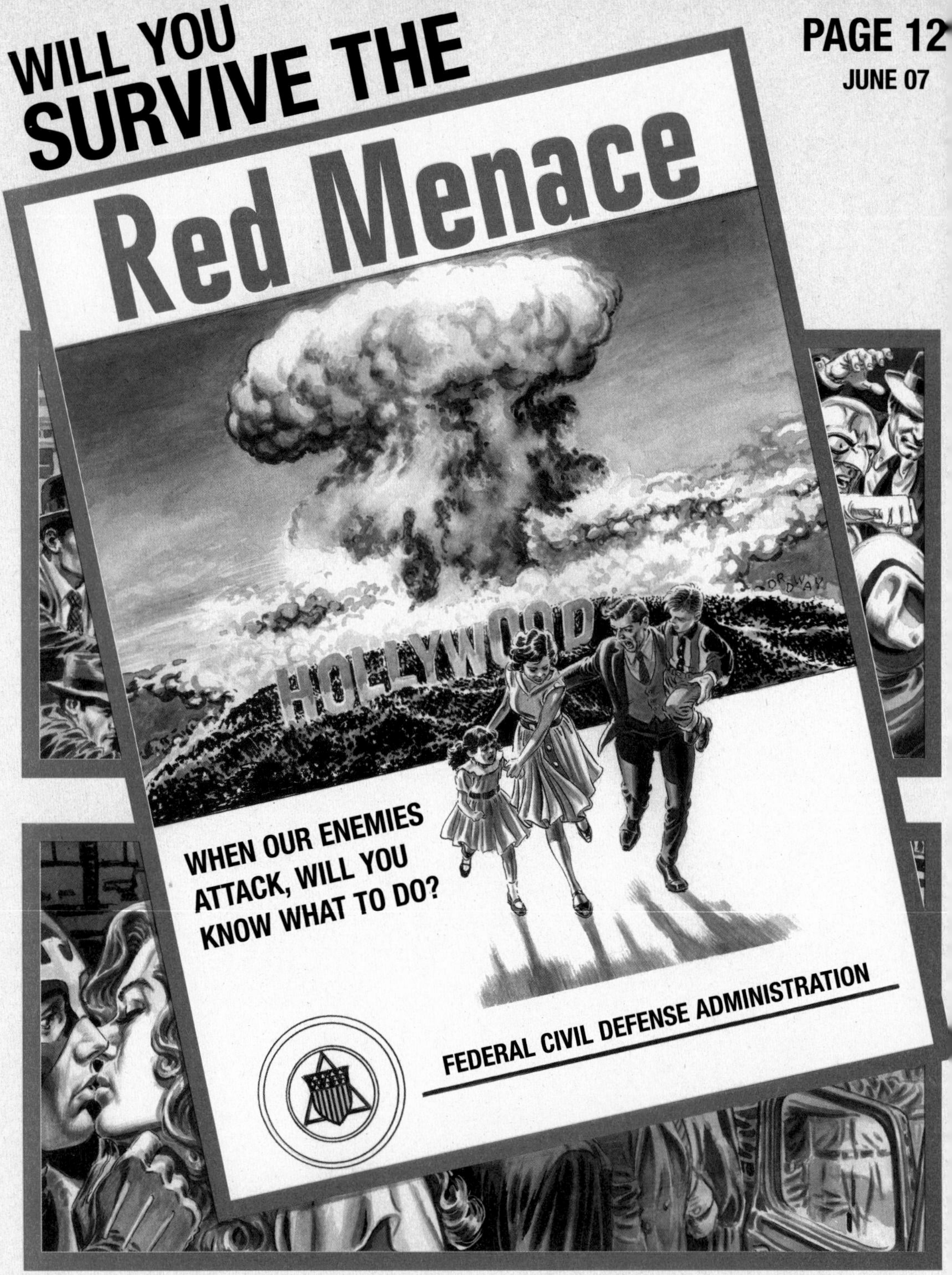
WILL YOU SURVIVE THE
Red Menace
HOLLYWOOD
ORDWAY
WHEN OUR ENEMIES ATTACK, WILL YOU KNOW WHAT TO DO?
FEDERAL CIVIL DEFENSE ADMINISTRATION

The country has begun to turn against McCarthy and Cohn. The Army investigation has lead to the famous, "Have you no decency, sir?" speech. Unconcerned that the public is turning against him, Roy Cohn and Schine arrive at a movie star pal's Palm Springs house to watch the The Eagle and the Grey Falcon are intercepted by the Red Menace and the rest of the Shadow Corps. Now, an epic battle of super heroes/villains ensues with the real "Red Menace" powered by his suit, which turns him into a flying weapons platform. The battle rages on and over

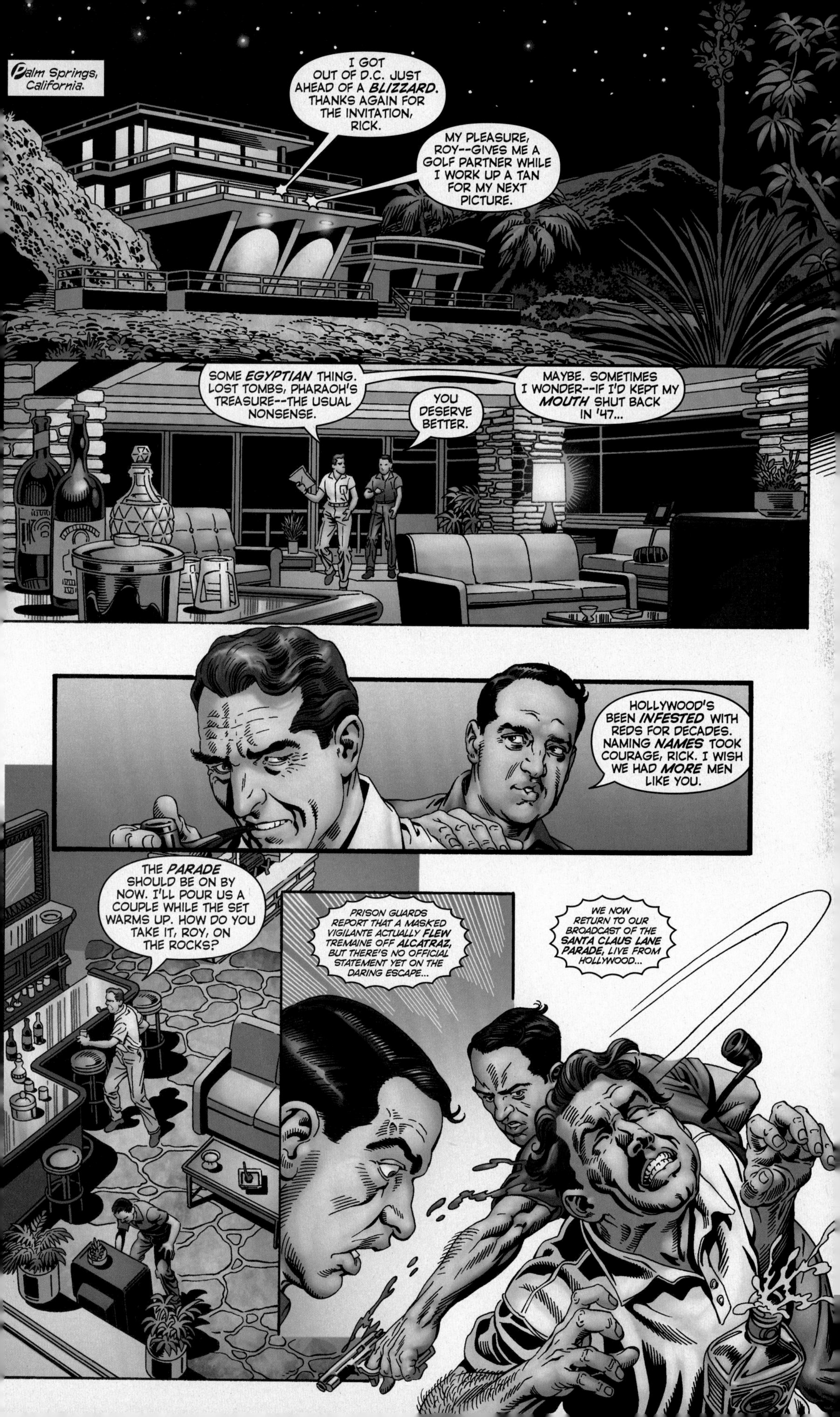
Palm Springs, California.
I GOT OUT OF D.C. JUST AHEAD OF A BLIZZARD. THANKS AGAIN FOR THE INVITATION, RICK.
MY PLEASURE, ROY--GIVES ME A GOLF PARTNER WHILE I WORK UP A TAN FOR MY NEXT PICTURE.
SOME EGYPTIAN THING. LOST TOMBS, PHARAOH'S TREASURE--THE USUAL NONSENSE.
YOU DESERVE BETTER.
MAYBE. SOMETIMES I WONDER--IF I'D KEPT MY MOUTH SHUT BACK IN '47...
HOLLYWOOD'S BEEN INFESTED WITH REDS FOR DECADES. NAMING NAMES TOOK COURAGE, RICK. I WISH WE HAD MORE MEN LIKE YOU.
THE PARADE SHOULD BE ON BY NOW. I'LL POUR US A COUPLE WHILE THE SET WARMS UP. HOW DO YOU TAKE IT, ROY, ON THE ROCKS?
PRISON GUARDS REPORT THAT A MASKED VIGILANTE ACTUALLY FLEW TREMAINE OFF ALCATRAZ, BUT THERE'S NO OFFICIAL STATEMENT YET ON THE DARING ESCAPE...
WE NOW RETURN TO OUR BROADCAST OF THE SANTA CLAUS LANE PARADE, LIVE FROM HOLLYWOOD...

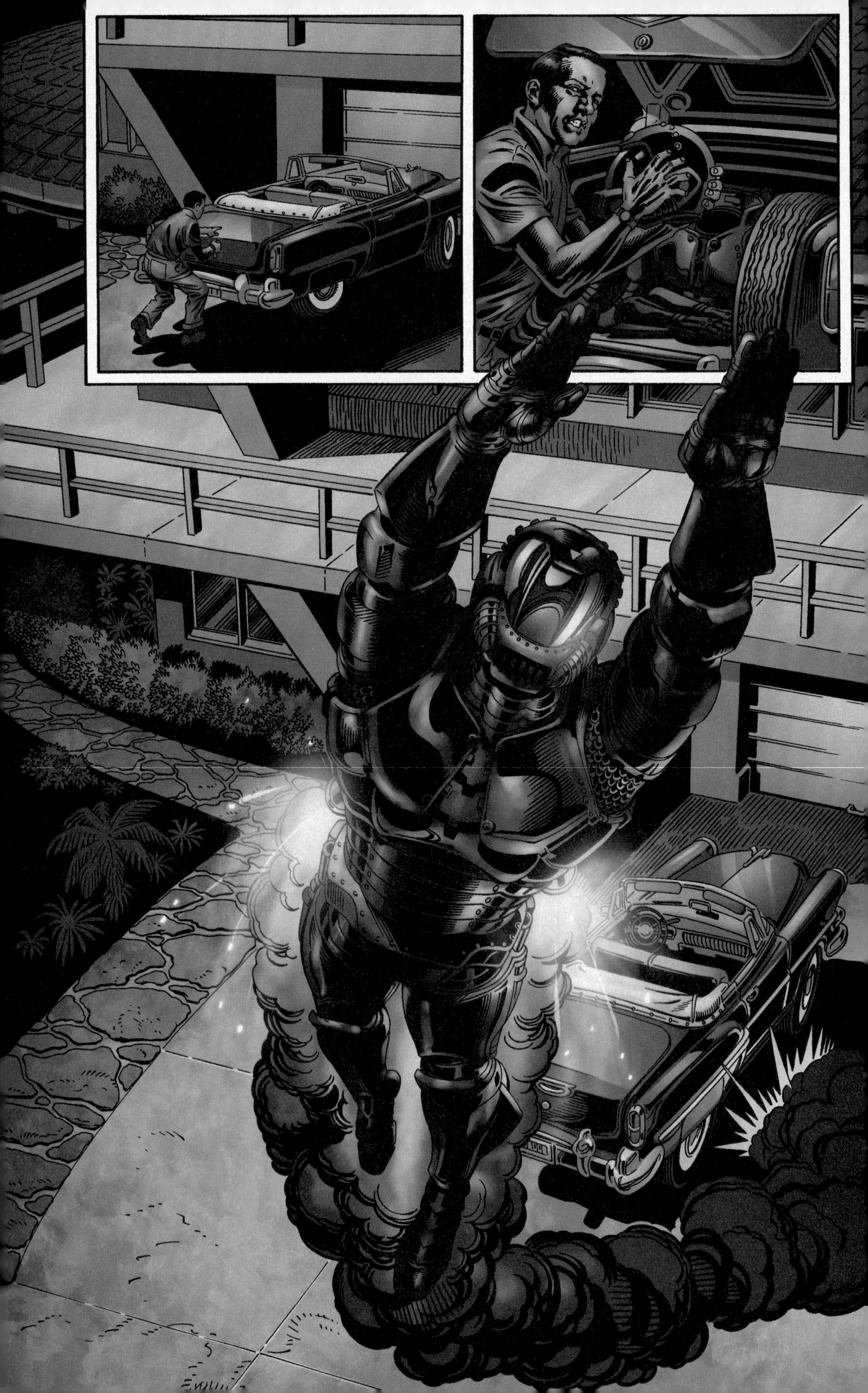

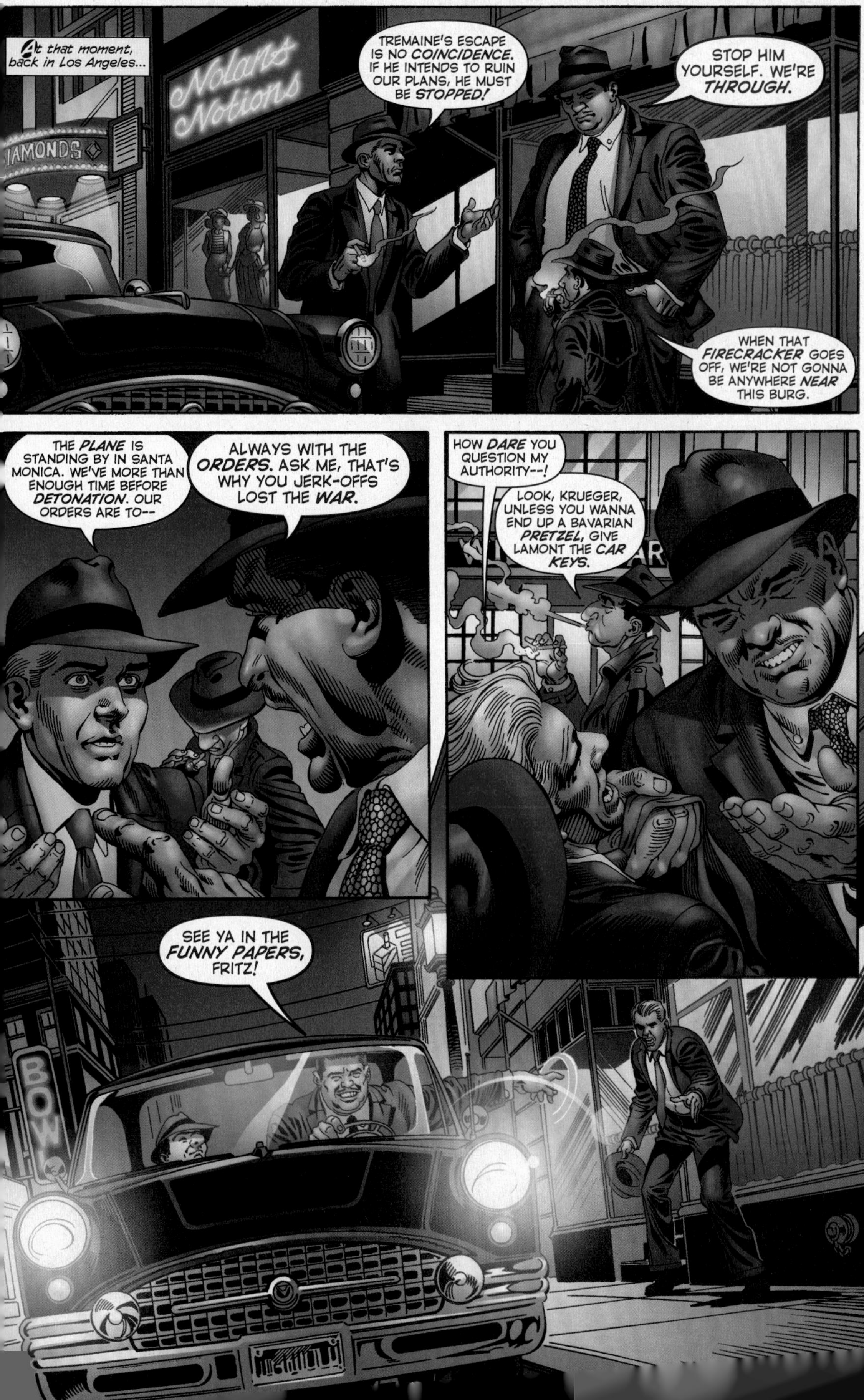
At that moment, back in Los Angeles...
Nolan's Notions
DIAMONDS
TREMAINE'S ESCAPE IS NO COINCIDENCE. IF HE INTENDS TO RUIN OUR PLANS, HE MUST BE STOPPED!
STOP HIM YOURSELF. WE'RE THROUGH.
WHEN THAT FIRECRACKER GOES OFF, WE'RE NOT GONNA BE ANYWHERE NEAR THIS BURG.
THE PLANE IS STANDING BY IN SANTA MONICA. WE'VE MORE THAN ENOUGH TIME BEFORE DETONATION. OUR ORDERS ARE TO--
ALWAYS WITH THE ORDERS. ASK ME, THAT'S WHY YOU JERK-OFFS LOST THE WAR.
HOW DARE YOU QUESTION MY AUTHORITY--!
LOOK, KRUEGER, UNLESS YOU WANNA END UP A BAVARIAN PRETZEL, GIVE LAMONT THE CAR KEYS.
SEE YA IN THE FUNNY PAPERS, FRITZ!
BOWL

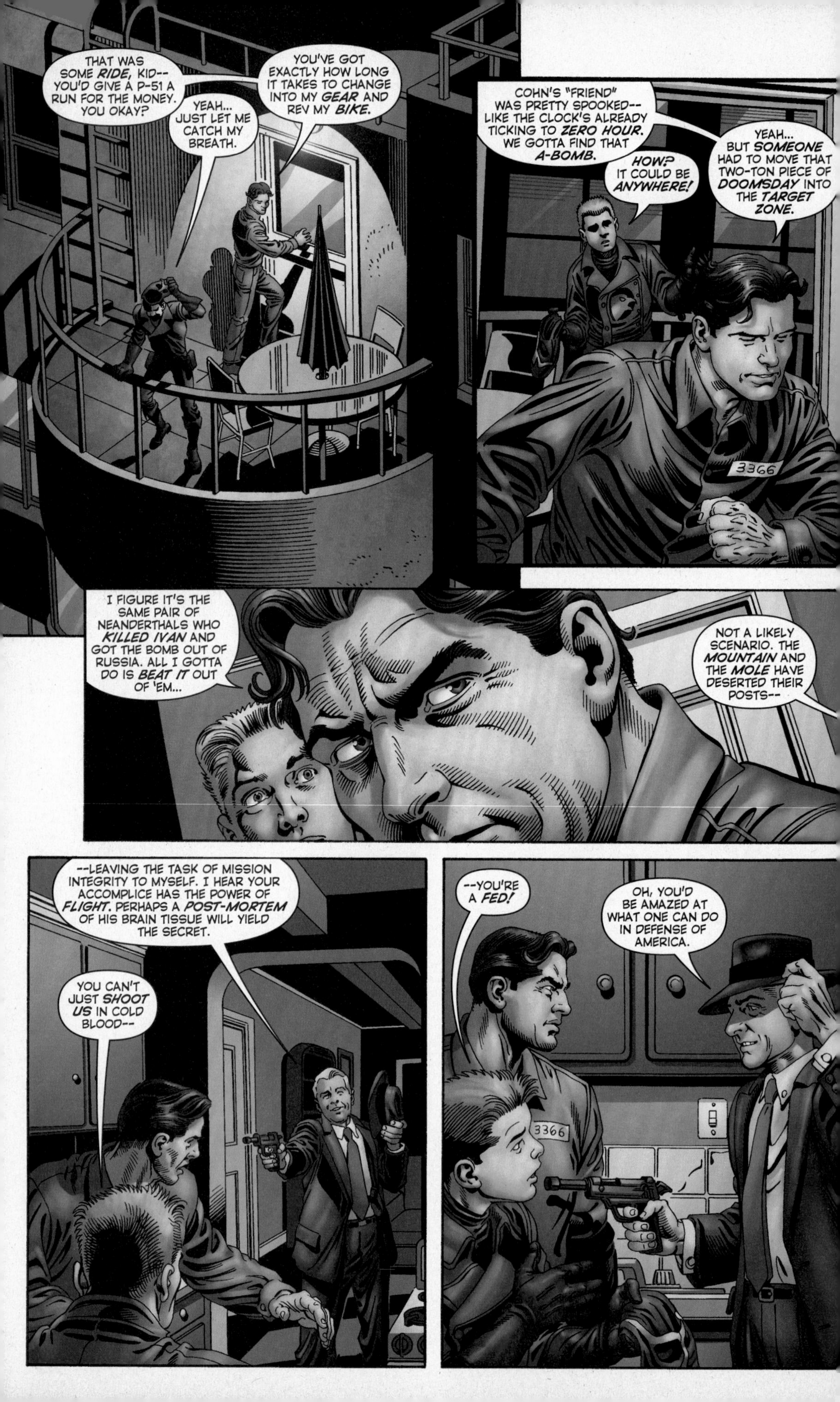
THAT WAS SOME RIDE, KID-- YOU'D GIVE A P-51 A RUN FOR THE MONEY. YOU OKAY?
YEAH... JUST LET ME CATCH MY BREATH.
YOU'VE GOT EXACTLY HOW LONG IT TAKES TO CHANGE INTO MY GEAR AND REV MY BIKE.
COHN'S "FRIEND" WAS PRETTY SPOOKED-- LIKE THE CLOCK'S ALREADY TICKING TO ZERO HOUR. WE GOTTA FIND THAT A-BOMB.
HOW? IT COULD BE ANYWHERE!
YEAH... BUT SOMEONE HAD TO MOVE THAT TWO-TON PIECE OF DOOMSDAY INTO THE TARGET ZONE.
3366
I FIGURE IT'S THE SAME PAIR OF NEANDERTHALS WHO KILLED IVAN AND GOT THE BOMB OUT OF RUSSIA. ALL I GOTTA DO IS BEAT IT OUT OF 'EM...
NOT A LIKELY SCENARIO. THE MOUNTAIN AND THE MOLE HAVE DESERTED THEIR POSTS--
--LEAVING THE TASK OF MISSION INTEGRITY TO MYSELF. I HEAR YOUR ACCOMPLICE HAS THE POWER OF FLIGHT. PERHAPS A POST-MORTEM OF HIS BRAIN TISSUE WILL YIELD THE SECRET.
YOU CAN'T JUST SHOOT US IN COLD BLOOD--
--YOU'RE A FED!
OH, YOU'D BE AMAZED AT WHAT ONE CAN DO IN DEFENSE OF AMERICA.
3366

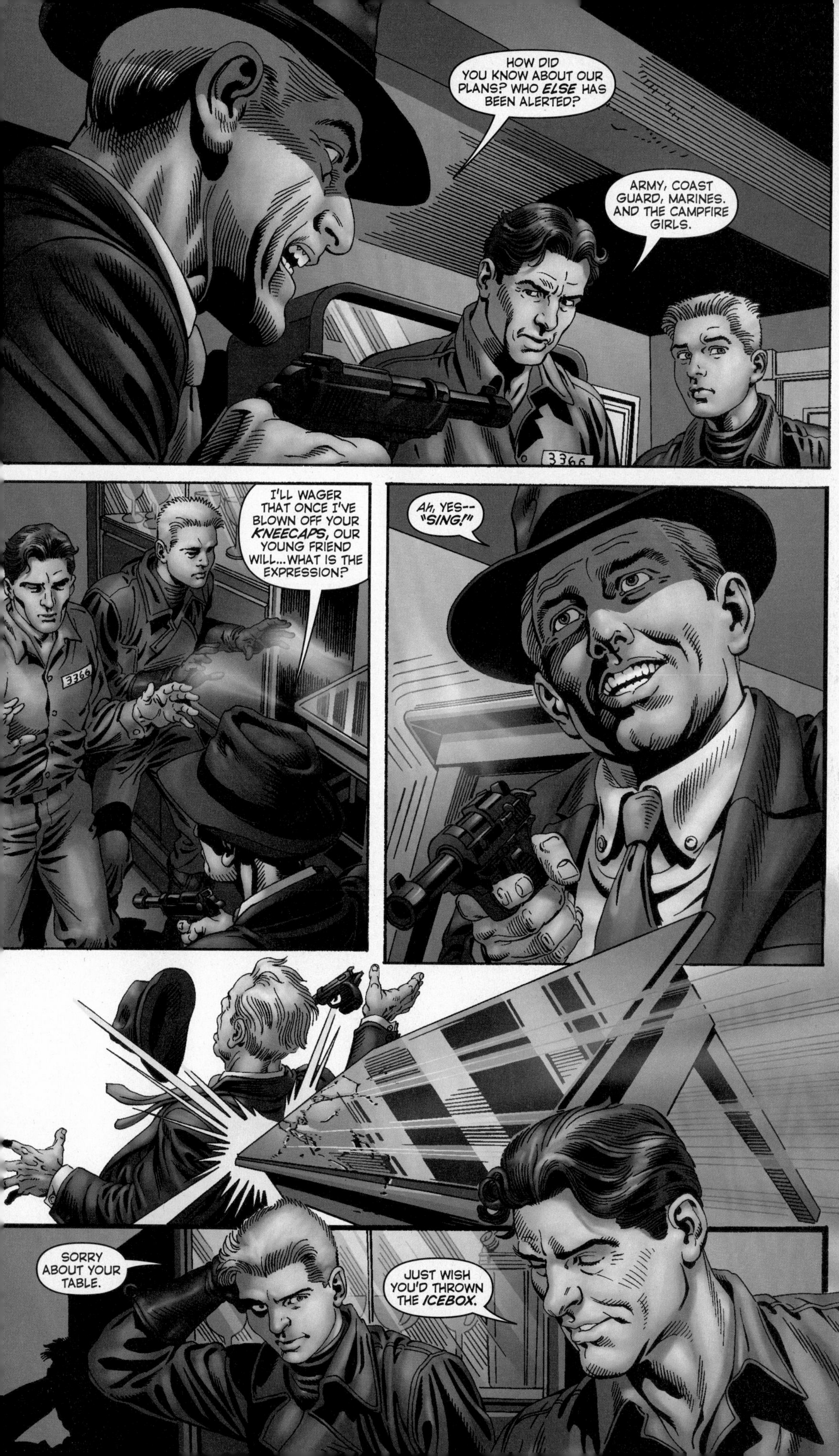
HOW DID YOU KNOW ABOUT OUR PLANS? WHO *ELSE* HAS BEEN ALERTED?
ARMY, COAST GUARD, MARINES. AND THE CAMPFIRE GIRLS.
3366
I'LL WAGER THAT ONCE I'VE BLOWN OFF YOUR *KNEECAPS*, OUR YOUNG FRIEND WILL...WHAT IS THE EXPRESSION?
3366
Ah, YES-- "SING!"
SORRY ABOUT YOUR TABLE.
JUST WISH YOU'D THROWN THE *ICEBOX*.

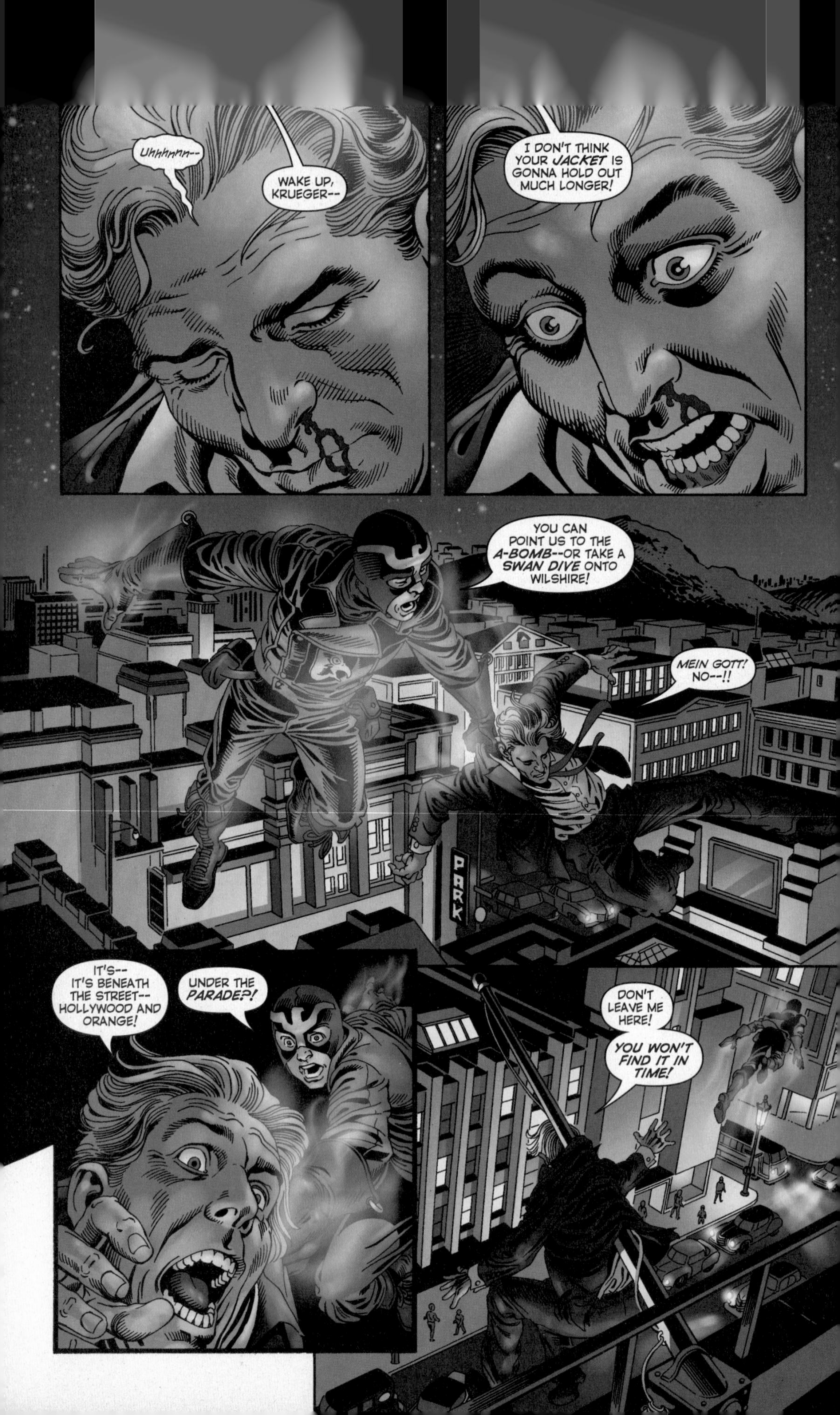
Uhhhnnn--
WAKE UP, KRUEGER--
I DON'T THINK YOUR JACKET IS GONNA HOLD OUT MUCH LONGER!
YOU CAN POINT US TO THE A-BOMB--OR TAKE A SWAN DIVE ONTO WILSHIRE!
MEIN GOTT! NO--!!
PARK
IT'S-- IT'S BENEATH THE STREET-- HOLLYWOOD AND ORANGE!
UNDER THE PARADE?!
DON'T LEAVE ME HERE!
YOU WON'T FIND IT IN TIME!

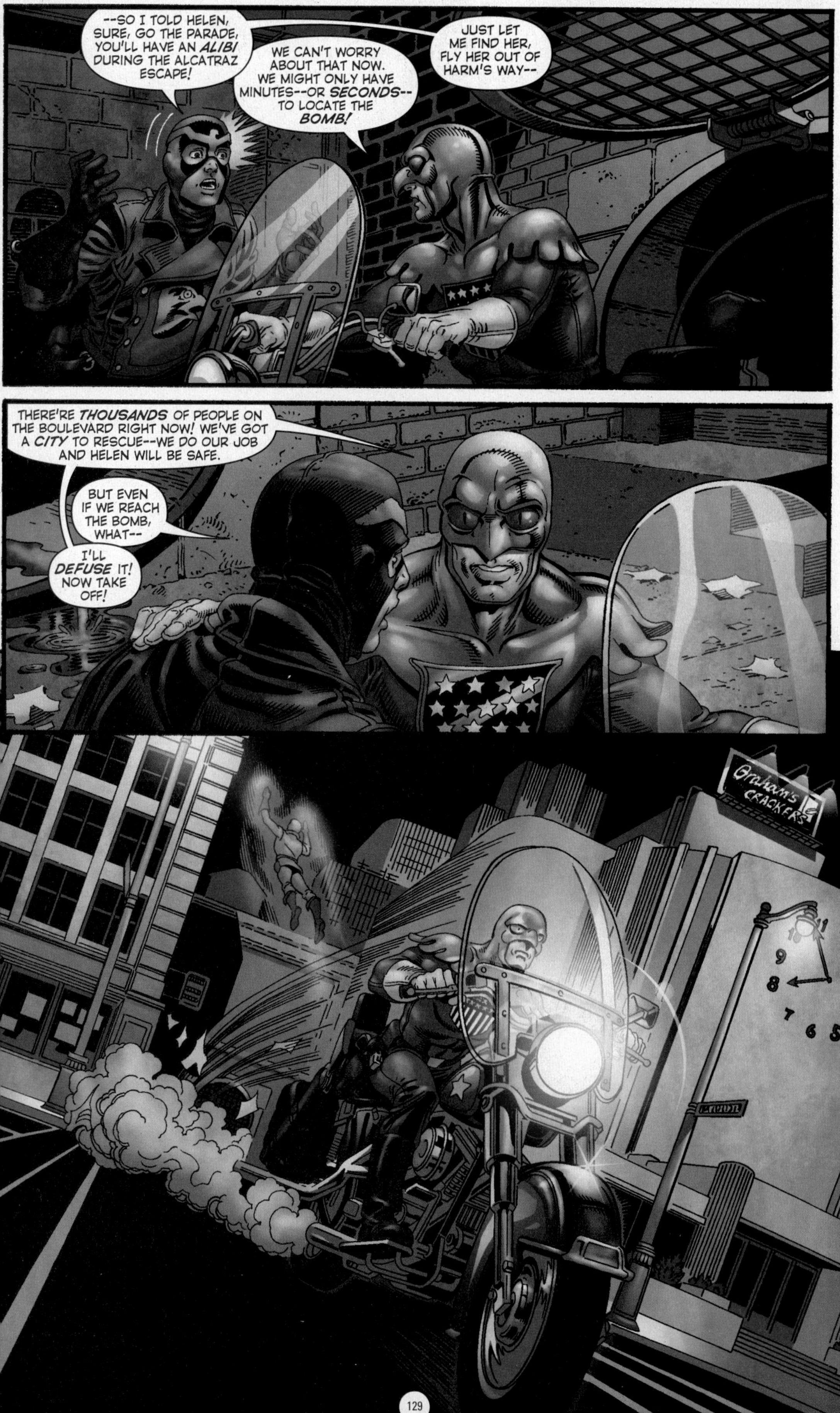
--SO I TOLD HELEN, SURE, GO THE PARADE, YOU'LL HAVE AN ALIBI DURING THE ALCATRAZ ESCAPE!
JUST LET ME FIND HER, FLY HER OUT OF HARM'S WAY--
WE CAN'T WORRY ABOUT THAT NOW. WE MIGHT ONLY HAVE MINUTES--OR SECONDS-- TO LOCATE THE BOMB!
THERE'RE THOUSANDS OF PEOPLE ON THE BOULEVARD RIGHT NOW! WE'VE GOT A CITY TO RESCUE--WE DO OUR JOB AND HELEN WILL BE SAFE.
BUT EVEN IF WE REACH THE BOMB, WHAT--
I'LL DEFUSE IT! NOW TAKE OFF!
Graham's CRACKERS

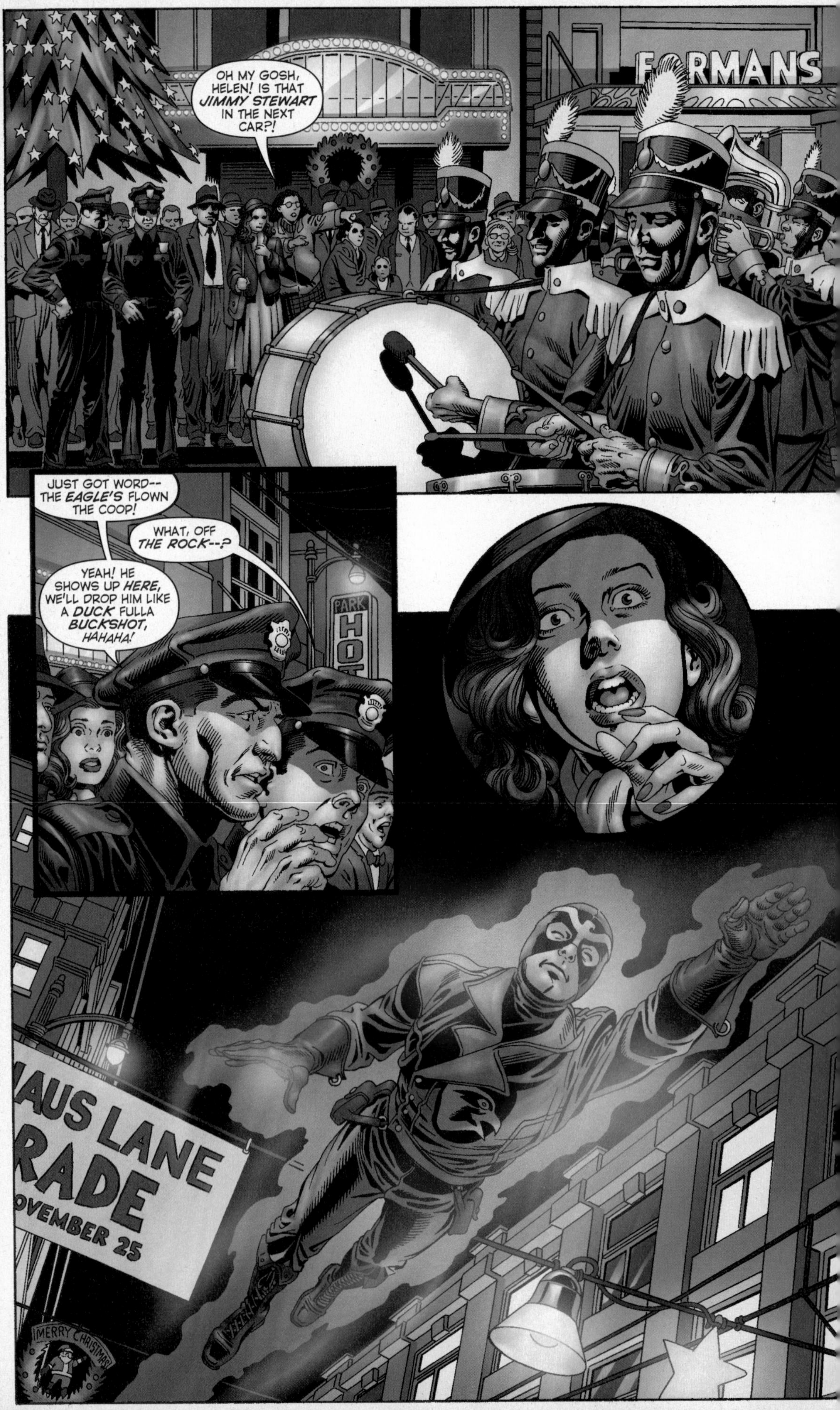
FORMANS
OH MY GOSH, HELEN! IS THAT JIMMY STEWART IN THE NEXT CAR?!
JUST GOT WORD-- THE EAGLE'S FLOWN THE COOP!
WHAT, OFF THE ROCK--?
YEAH! HE SHOWS UP HERE, WE'LL DROP HIM LIKE A DUCK FULLA BUCKSHOT, HAHAHA!
PARK
HOT
AUS LANE
RADE
OVEMBER 25
MERRY CHRISTMAS

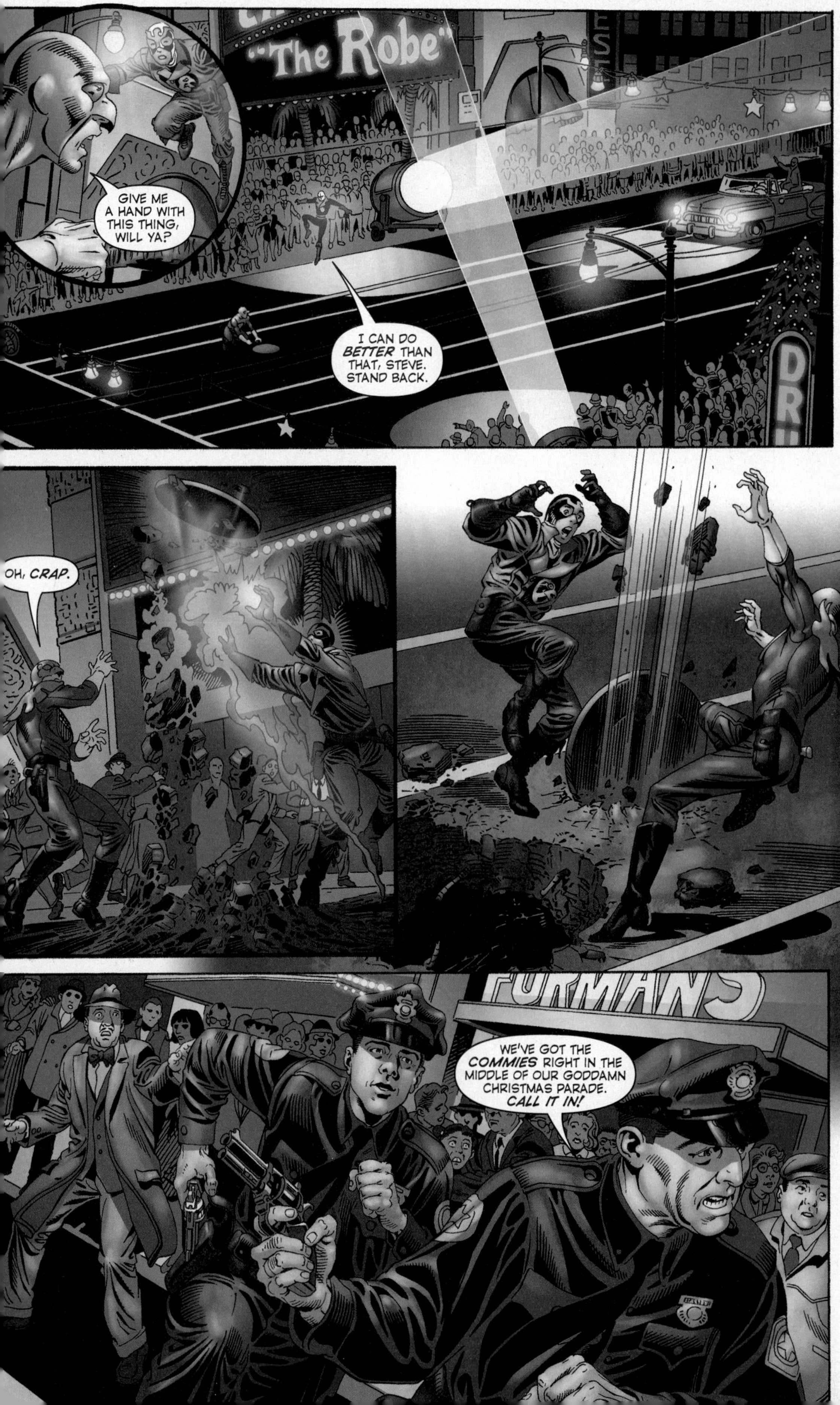
"The Robe"
GIVE ME A HAND WITH THIS THING, WILL YA?
I CAN DO *BETTER* THAN THAT, STEVE. STAND BACK.
OH, *CRAP*.
FURMANS
WE'VE GOT THE *COMMIES* RIGHT IN THE MIDDLE OF OUR GODDAMN CHRISTMAS PARADE. *CALL IT IN!*

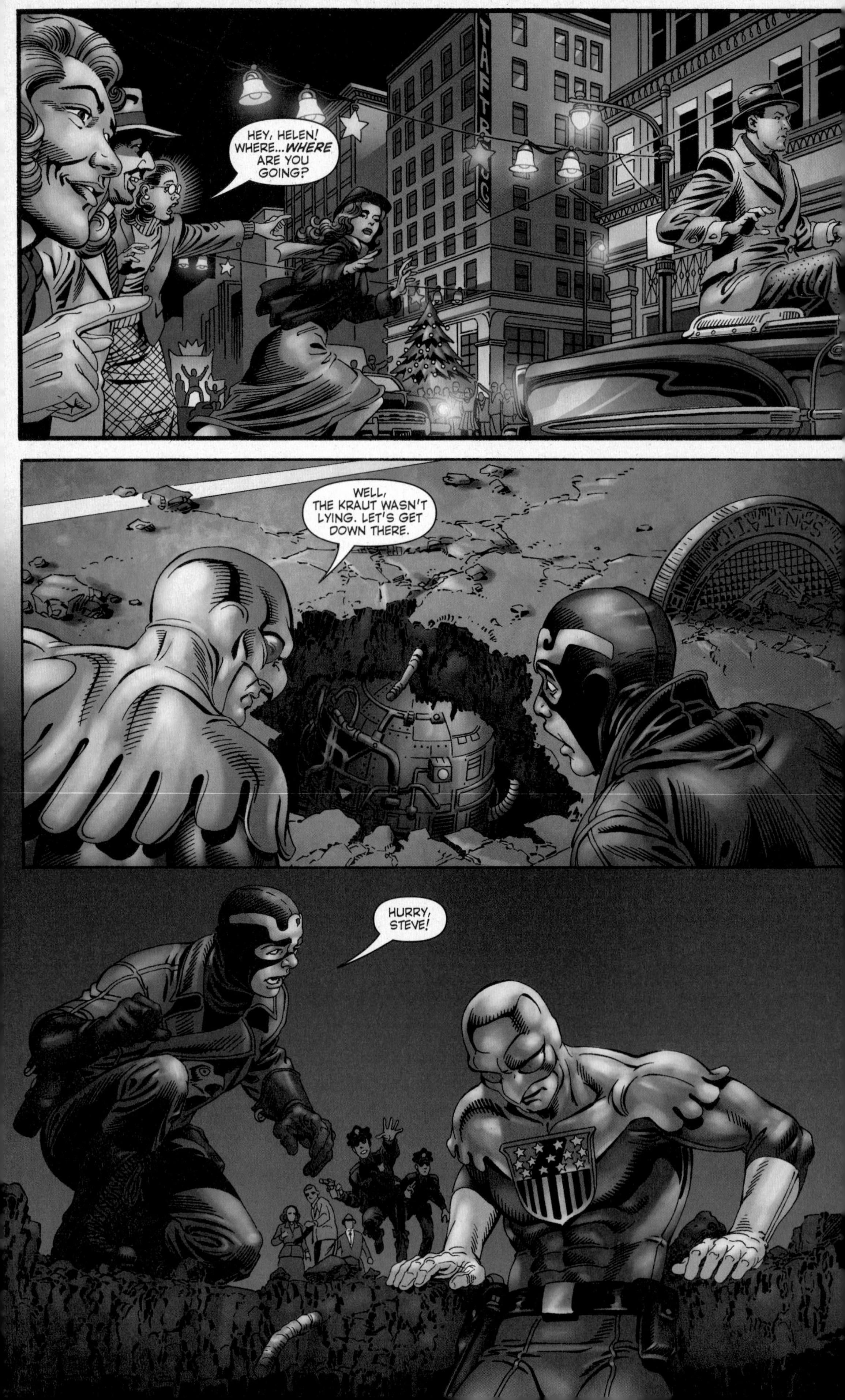
HEY, HELEN! WHERE...*WHERE* ARE YOU GOING?
WELL, THE KRAUT WASN'T LYING. LET'S GET DOWN THERE.
HURRY, STEVE!

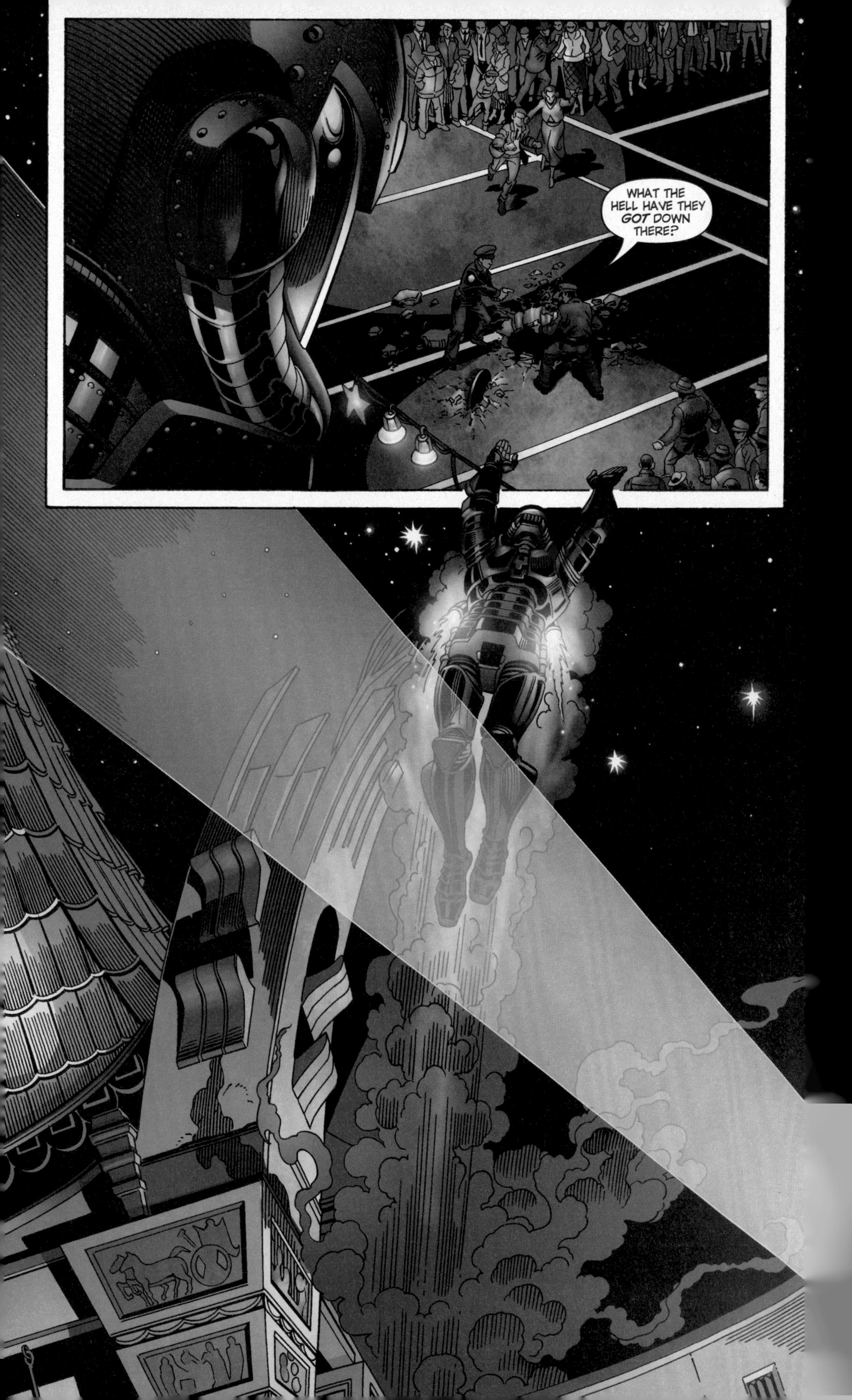
WHAT THE HELL HAVE THEY GOT DOWN THERE?

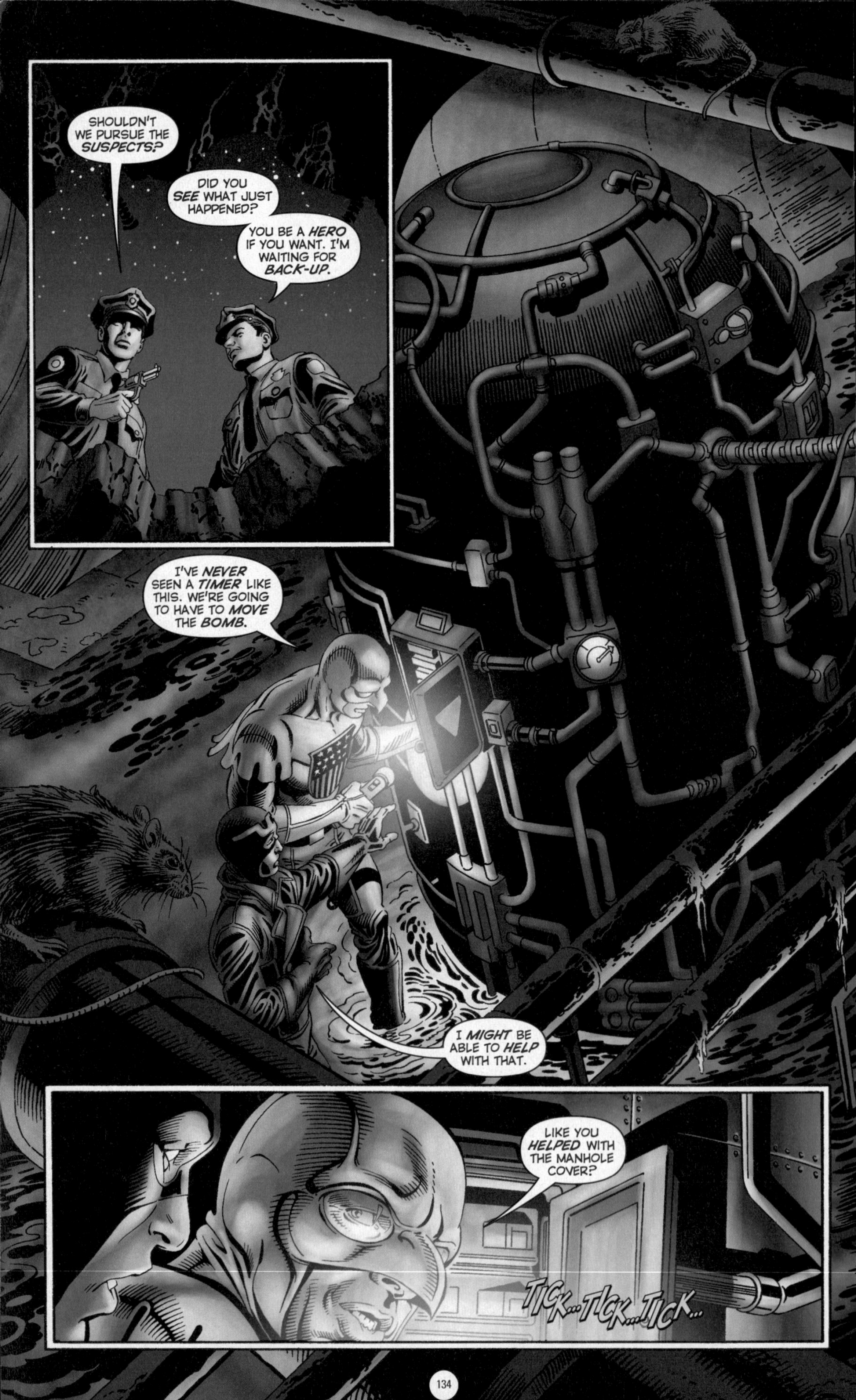
SHOULDN'T WE PURSUE THE SUSPECTS?
DID YOU SEE WHAT JUST HAPPENED?
YOU BE A HERO IF YOU WANT. I'M WAITING FOR BACK-UP.
I'VE NEVER SEEN A TIMER LIKE THIS. WE'RE GOING TO HAVE TO MOVE THE BOMB.
I MIGHT BE ABLE TO HELP WITH THAT.
LIKE YOU HELPED WITH THE MANHOLE COVER?
TICK...TICK...TICK...

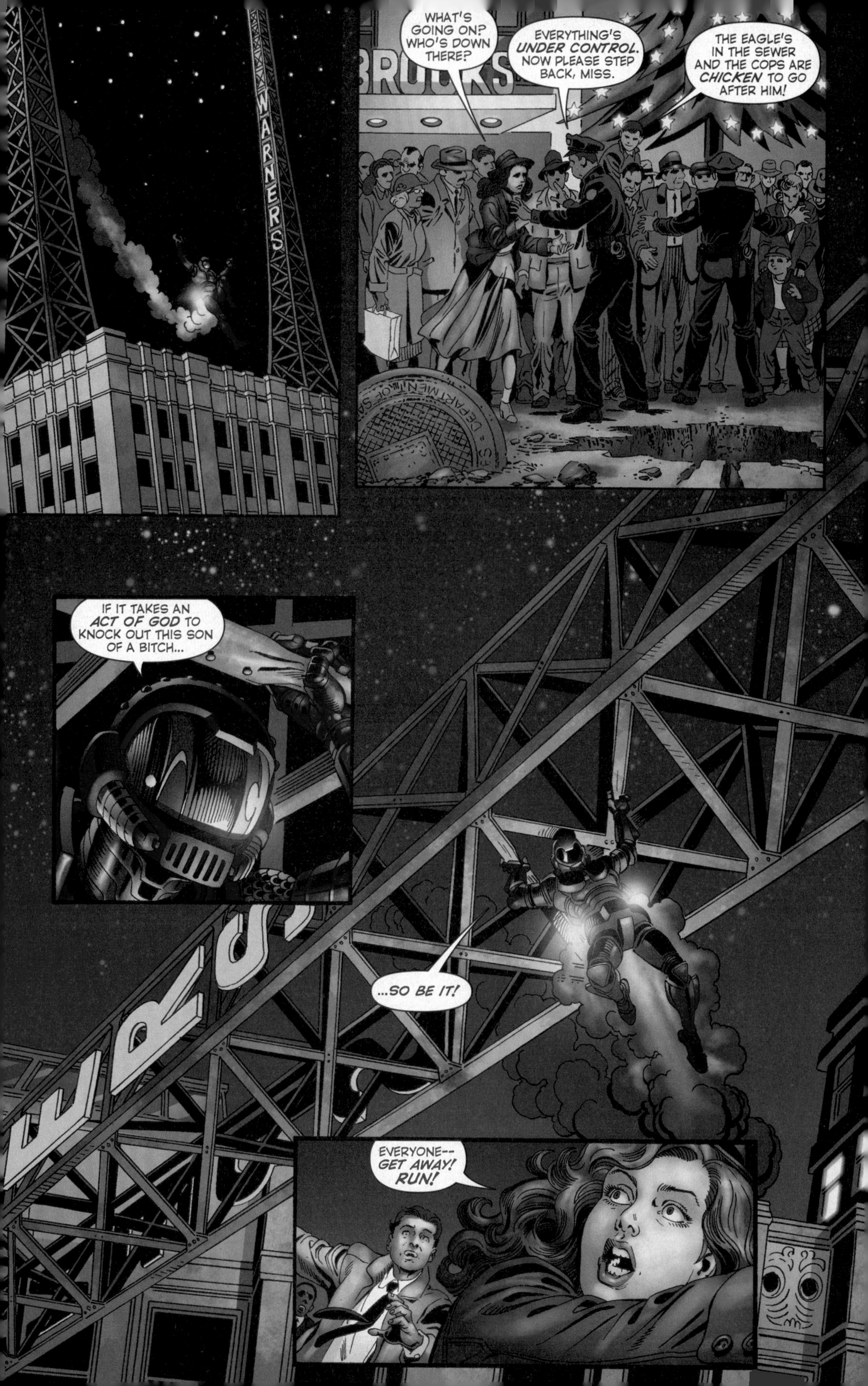
WARNERS
BROOKS
WHAT'S GOING ON? WHO'S DOWN THERE?
EVERYTHING'S UNDER CONTROL. NOW PLEASE STEP BACK, MISS.
THE EAGLE'S IN THE SEWER AND THE COPS ARE CHICKEN TO GO AFTER HIM!
IF IT TAKES AN ACT OF GOD TO KNOCK OUT THIS SON OF A BITCH...
...SO BE IT!
EVERYONE-- GET AWAY! RUN!

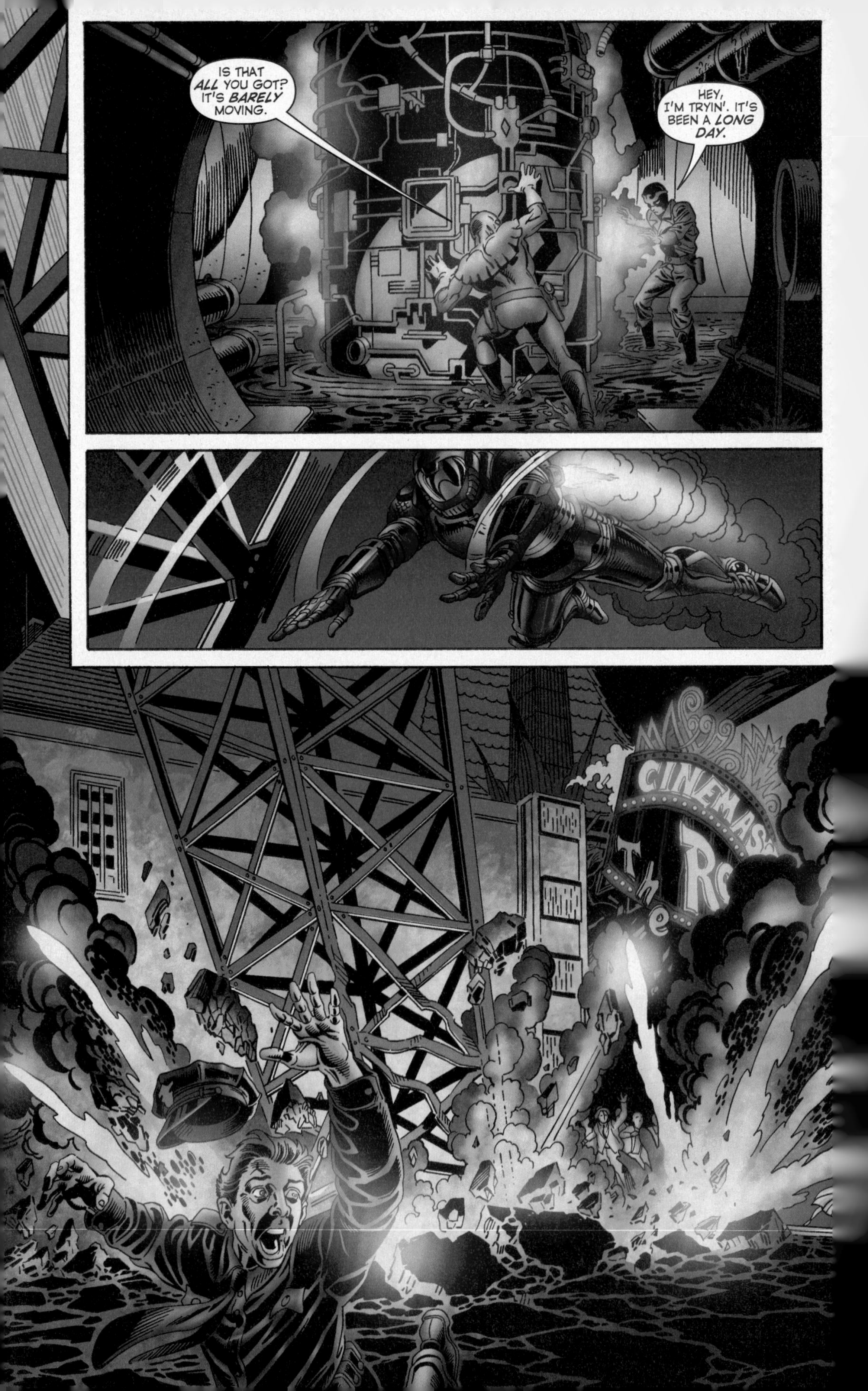
IS THAT ALL YOU GOT? IT'S BARELY MOVING.
HEY, I'M TRYIN'. IT'S BEEN A LONG DAY.
CINEMAS

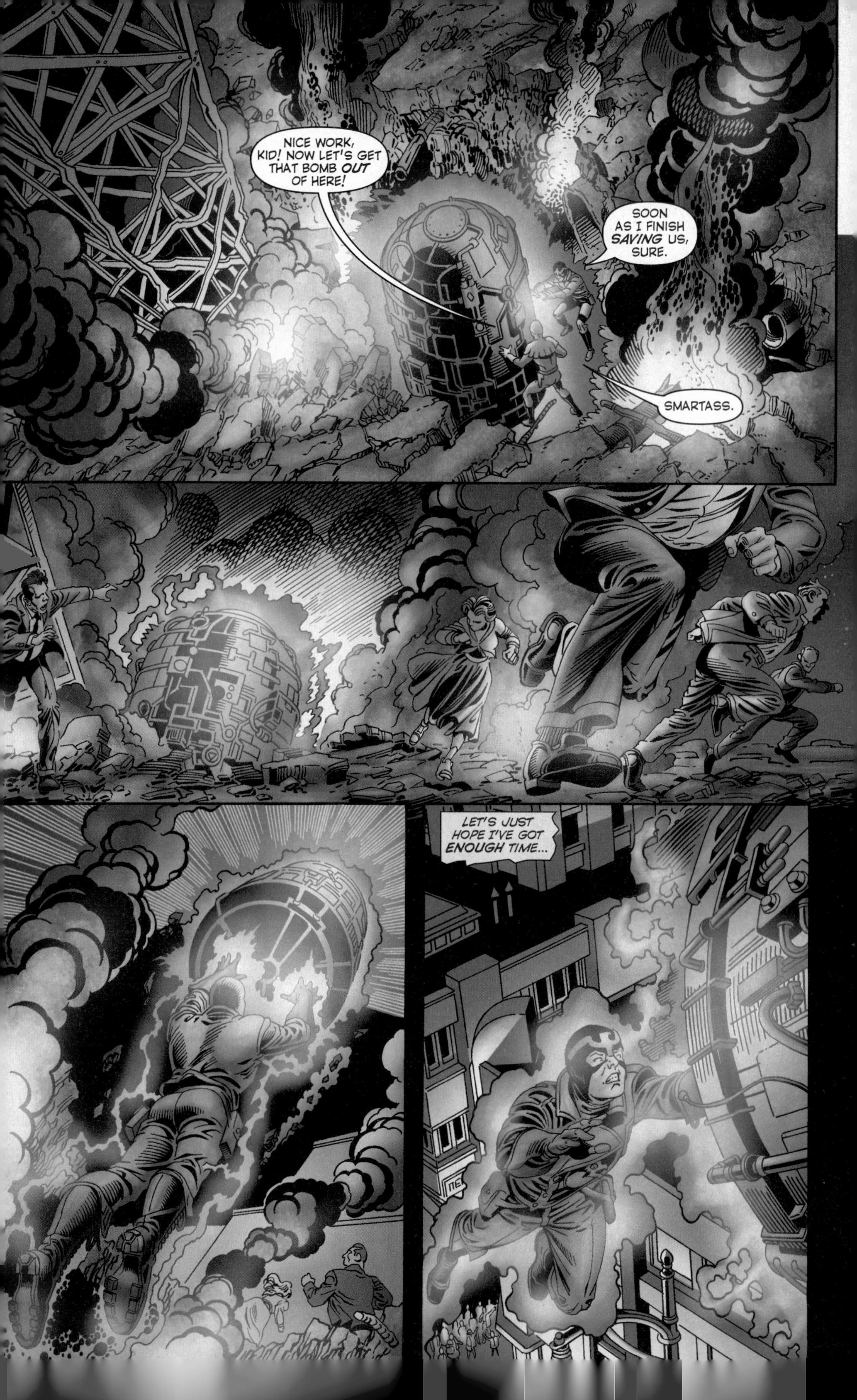
NICE WORK, KID! NOW LET'S GET THAT BOMB OUT OF HERE!
SOON AS I FINISH SAVING US, SURE.
SMARTASS.
LET'S JUST HOPE I'VE GOT ENOUGH TIME...

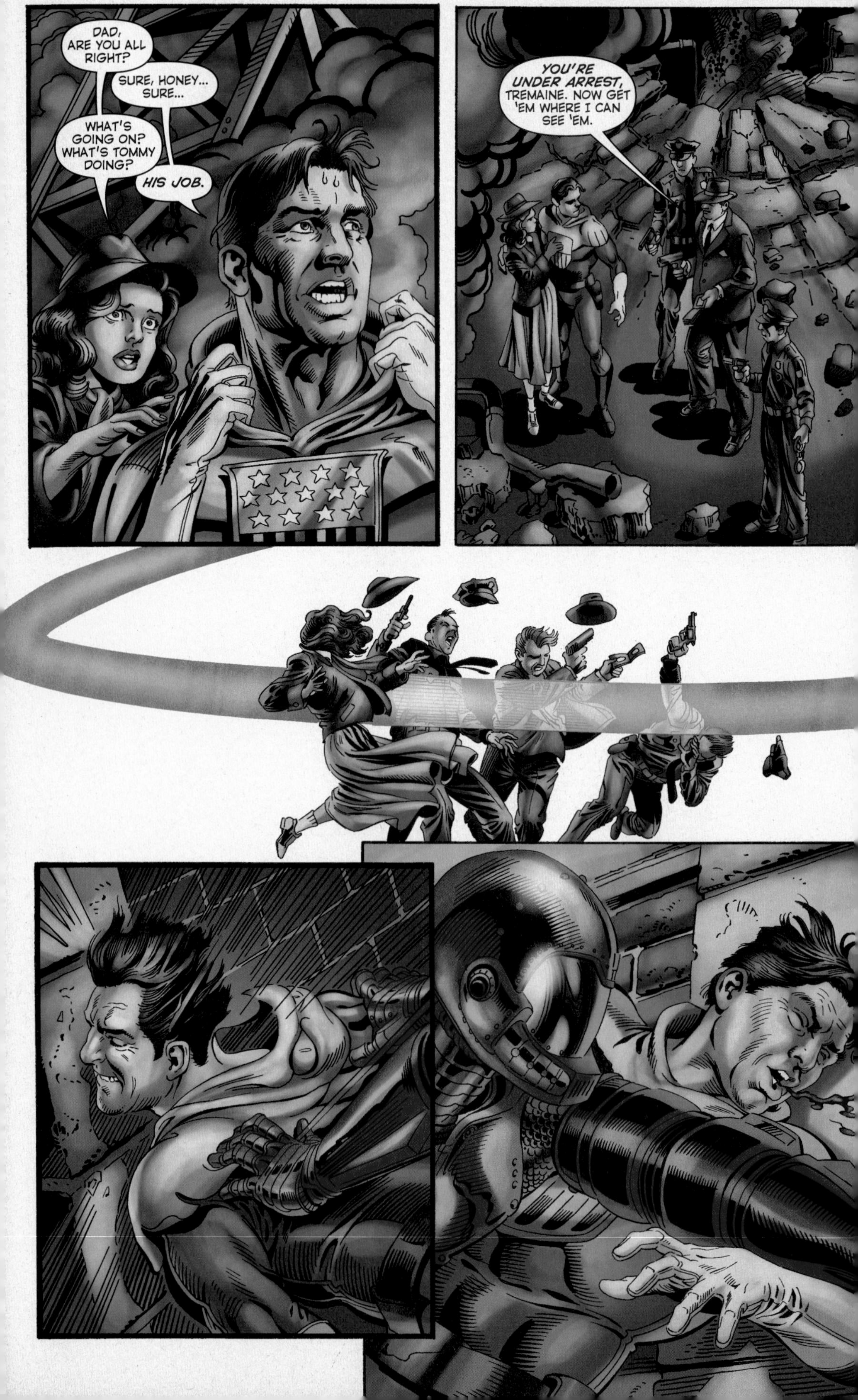
DAD, ARE YOU ALL RIGHT?
SURE, HONEY... SURE...
WHAT'S GOING ON? WHAT'S TOMMY DOING?
HIS JOB.
YOU'RE UNDER ARREST, TREMAINE. NOW GET 'EM WHERE I CAN SEE 'EM.

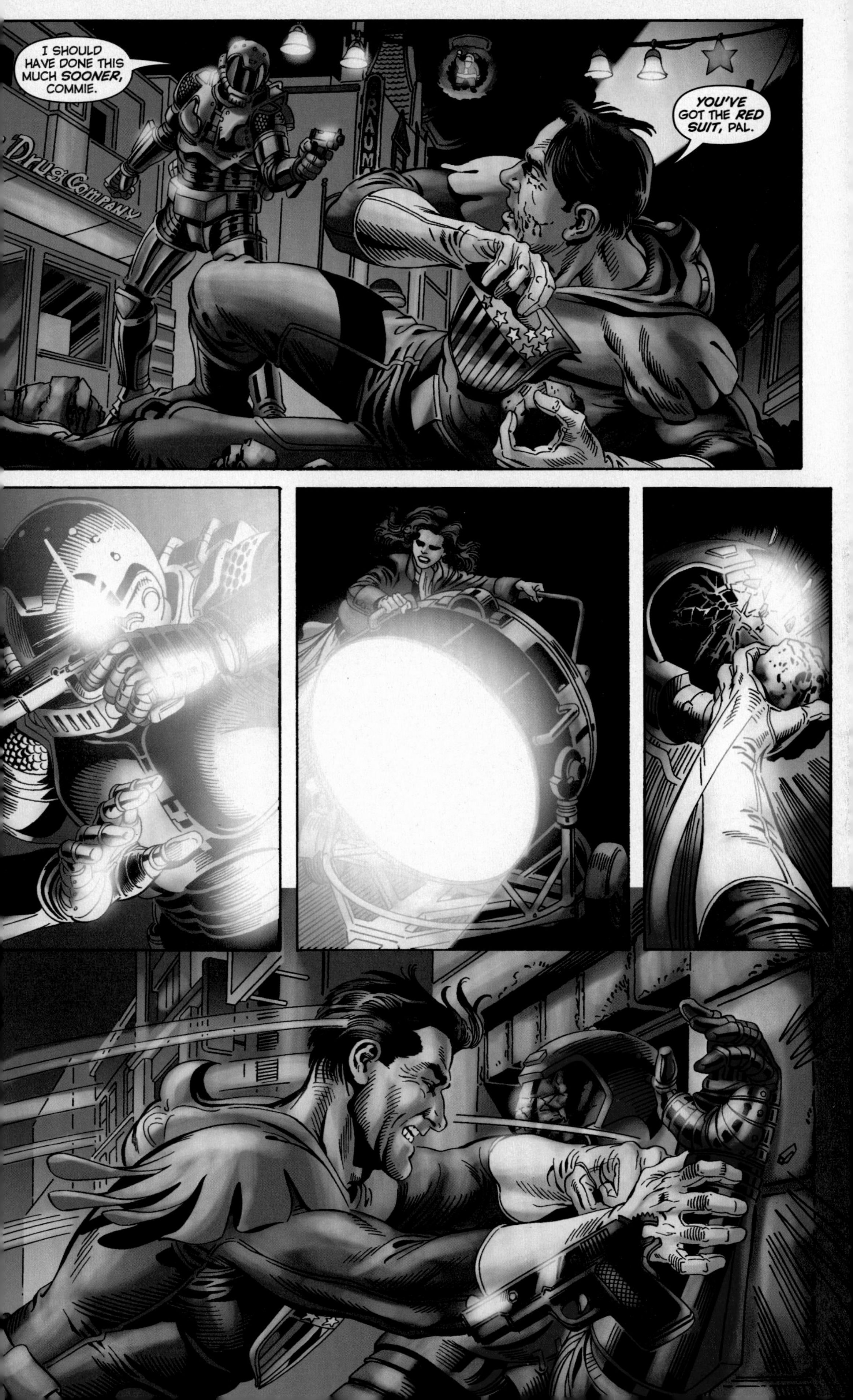
I SHOULD HAVE DONE THIS MUCH SOONER, COMMIE.
YOU'VE GOT THE RED SUIT, PAL.
Drug Company
GRAUM

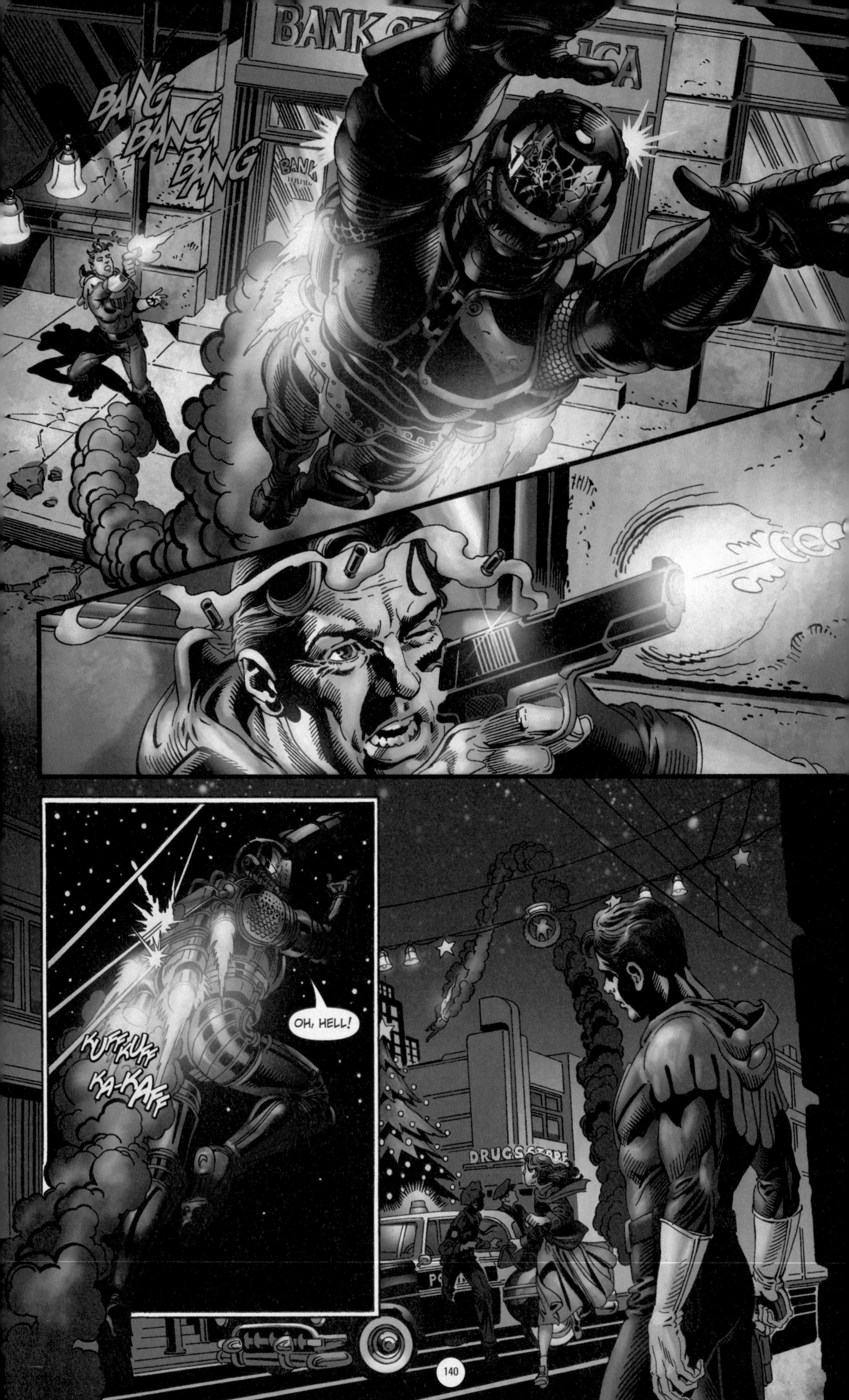
BANG
BANG
BANG
OH, HELL!
KUFF-KUFF
KA-KAFF
DRUGSTORE

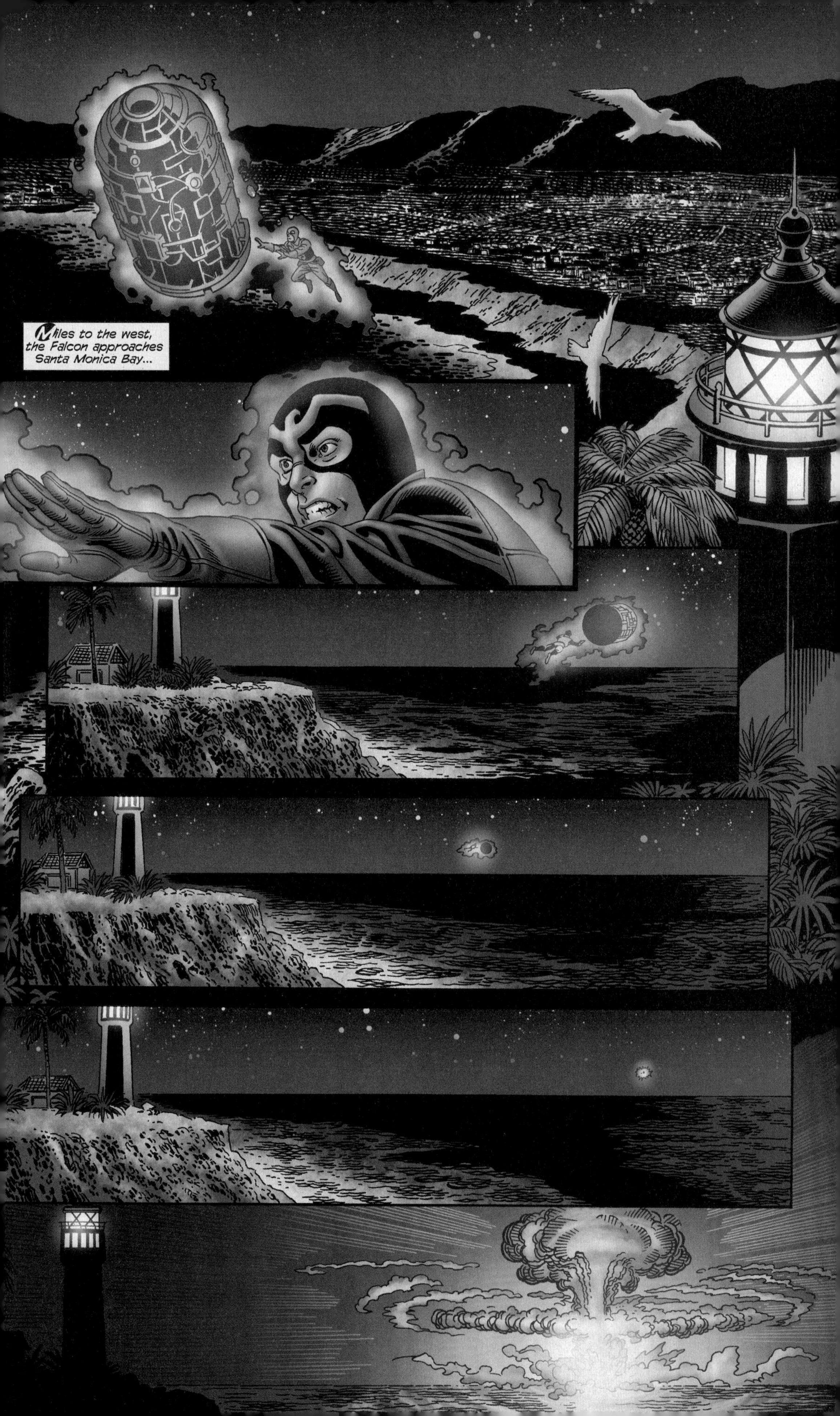
Miles to the west, the Falcon approaches Santa Monica Bay...

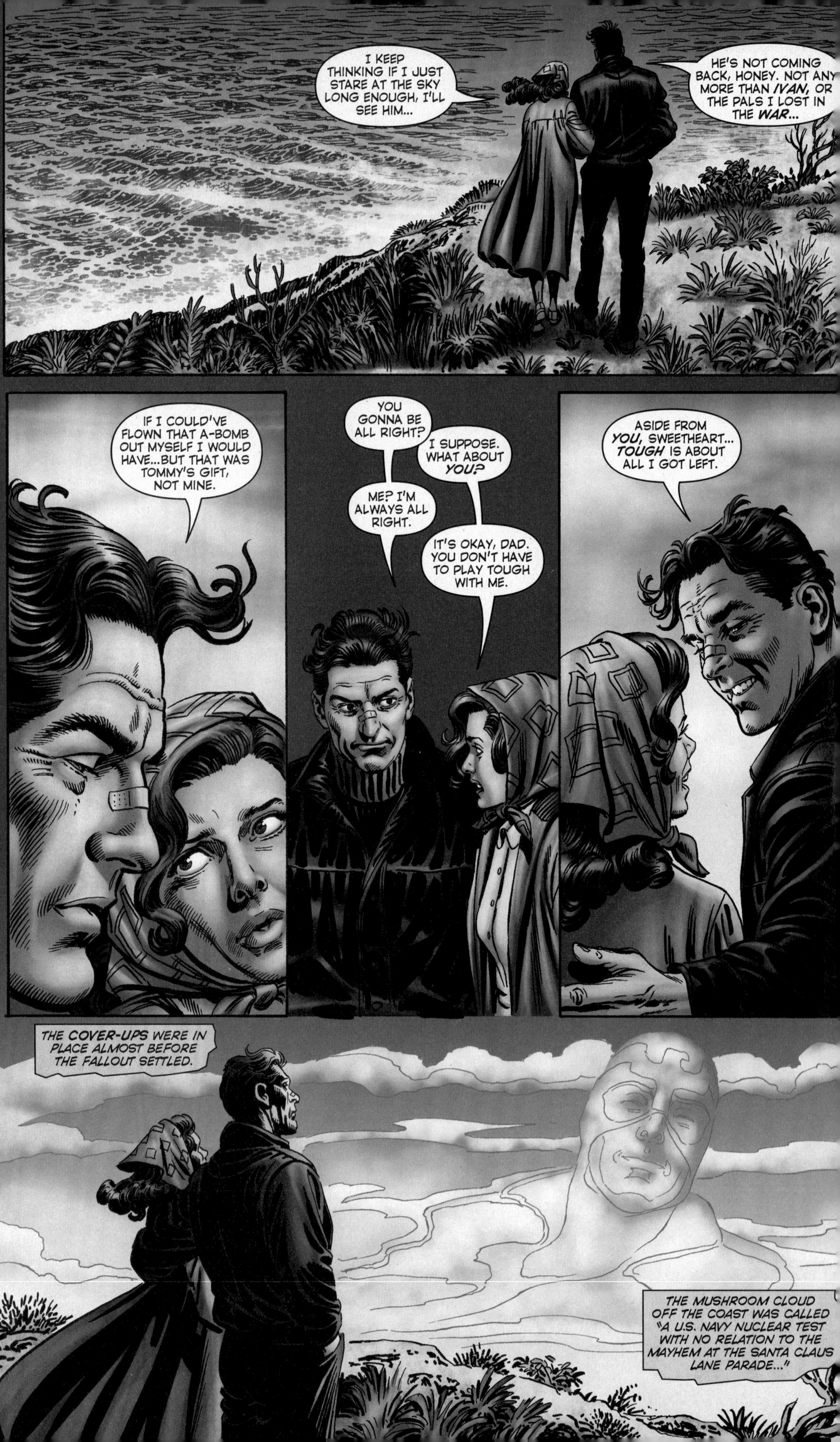
I KEEP THINKING IF I JUST STARE AT THE SKY LONG ENOUGH, I'LL SEE HIM...
HE'S NOT COMING BACK, HONEY. NOT ANY MORE THAN IVAN, OR THE PALS I LOST IN THE WAR...
IF I COULD'VE FLOWN THAT A-BOMB OUT MYSELF I WOULD HAVE...BUT THAT WAS TOMMY'S GIFT, NOT MINE.
YOU GONNA BE ALL RIGHT?
I SUPPOSE. WHAT ABOUT YOU?
ME? I'M ALWAYS ALL RIGHT.
IT'S OKAY, DAD. YOU DON'T HAVE TO PLAY TOUGH WITH ME.
ASIDE FROM YOU, SWEETHEART... TOUGH IS ABOUT ALL I GOT LEFT.
THE COVER-UPS WERE IN PLACE ALMOST BEFORE THE FALLOUT SETTLED.
THE MUSHROOM CLOUD OFF THE COAST WAS CALLED "A U.S. NAVY NUCLEAR TEST WITH NO RELATION TO THE MAYHEM AT THE SANTA CLAUS LANE PARADE..."

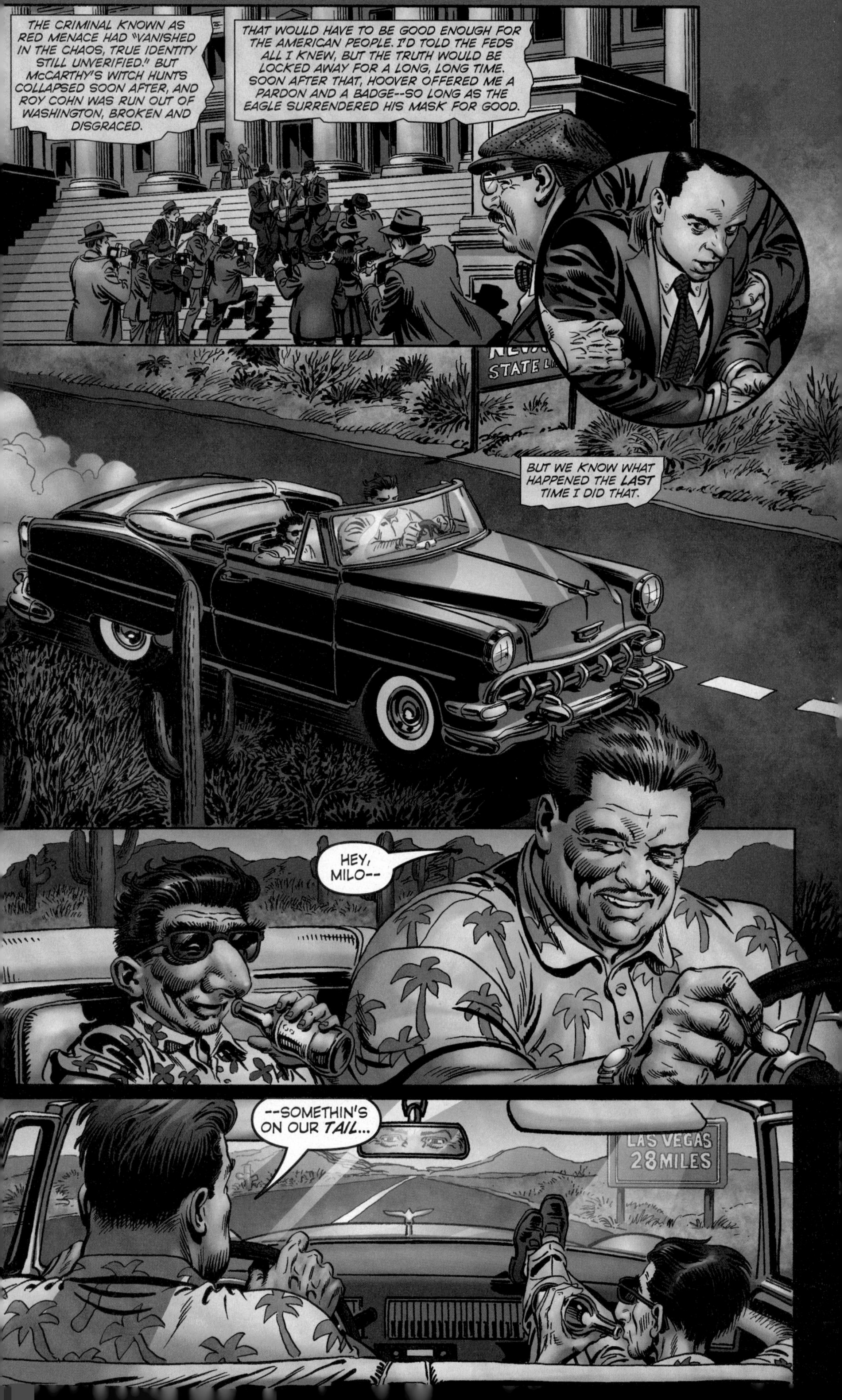
THE CRIMINAL KNOWN AS RED MENACE HAD "VANISHED IN THE CHAOS, TRUE IDENTITY STILL UNVERIFIED." BUT McCARTHY'S WITCH HUNTS COLLAPSED SOON AFTER, AND ROY COHN WAS RUN OUT OF WASHINGTON, BROKEN AND DISGRACED.
THAT WOULD HAVE TO BE GOOD ENOUGH FOR THE AMERICAN PEOPLE. I'D TOLD THE FEDS ALL I KNEW, BUT THE TRUTH WOULD BE LOCKED AWAY FOR A LONG, LONG TIME. SOON AFTER THAT, HOOVER OFFERED ME A PARDON AND A BADGE--SO LONG AS THE EAGLE SURRENDERED HIS MASK FOR GOOD.
BUT WE KNOW WHAT HAPPENED THE *LAST* TIME I DID THAT.
HEY, MILO--
--SOMETHIN'S ON OUR *TAIL*...
LAS VEGAS
28 MILES

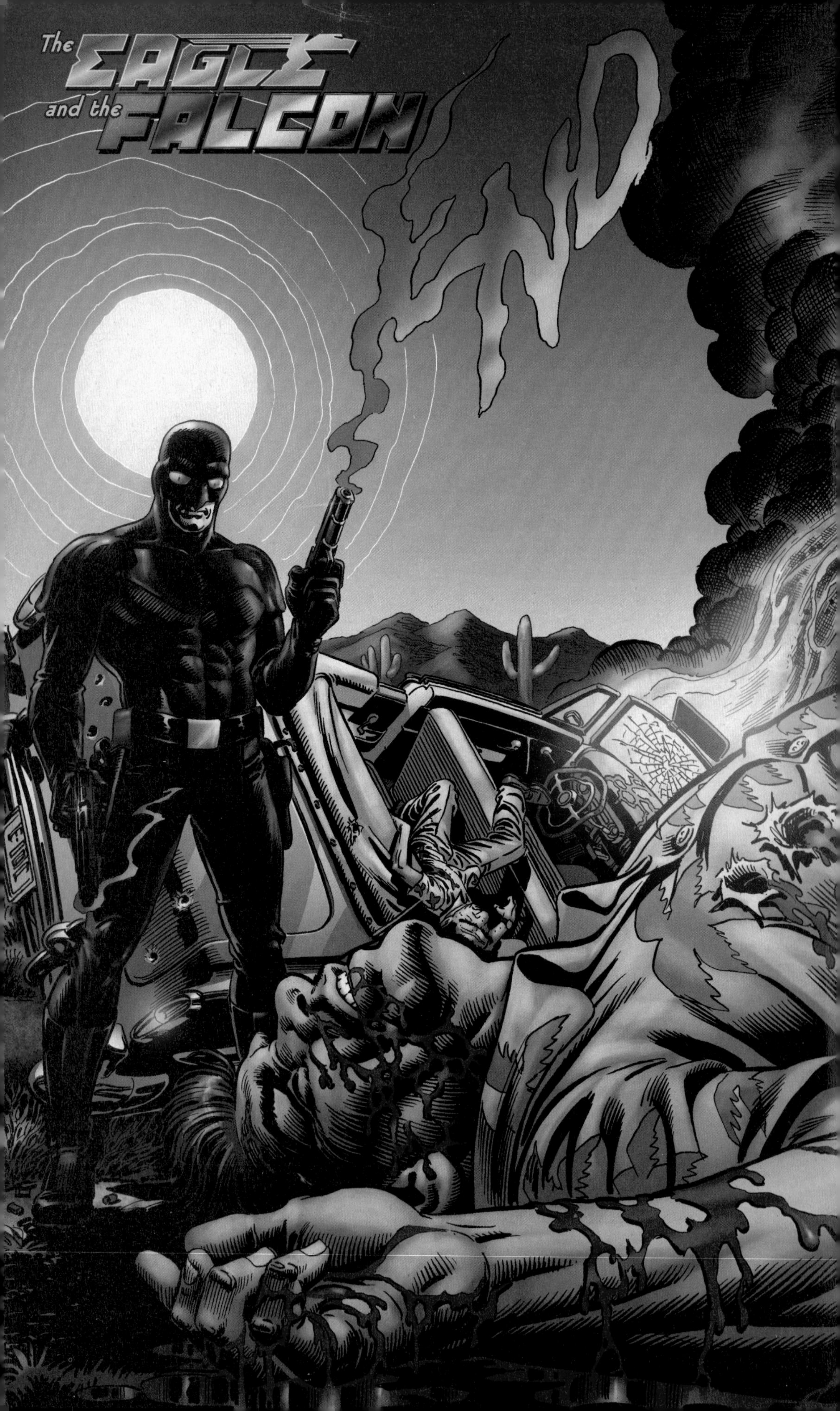
The EAGLE and the FALCON
END